SAS® Screen Control Language: Reference

Version 6
Second Edition

SAS Institute Inc.
SAS Campus Drive
Cary, NC 27513

The correct bibliographic citation for this manual is as follows: SAS Institute Inc., *SAS® Screen Control Language: Reference, Version 6, Second Edition*, Cary, NC: SAS Institute Inc., 1994. 648 pp.

SAS® Screen Control Language: Reference, Version 6, Second Edition

The SAS® System is an integrated system of software providing complete control over data access, management, analysis, and presentation. Base SAS software is the foundation of the SAS System. Products within the SAS System include SAS/ACCESS®, SAS/AF®, SAS/ASSIST®, SAS/CALC®, SAS/CONNECT®, SAS/CPE®, SAS/DMI®, SAS/EIS®, SAS/ENGLISH®, SAS/ETS®, SAS/FSP®, SAS/GRAPH®, SAS/IMAGE®, SAS/IML®, SAS/IMS-DL/I®, SAS/INSIGHT®, SAS/LAB®, SAS/NVISION®, SAS/OR®, SAS/PH-Clinical®, SAS/QC®, SAS/REPLAY-CICS®, SAS/SESSION®, SAS/SHARE®, SAS/STAT®, SAS/TOOLKIT®, SAS/TRADER®, SAS/TUTOR®, SAS/DB2™, SAS/GEO™, SAS/GIS™, SAS/PH-Kinetics™, SAS/SHARE*NET™, SAS/SPECTRAVIEW™, and SAS/SQL-DS™ software. Other SAS Institute products are SYSTEM 2000® Data Management Software, with basic SYSTEM 2000, CREATE™, Multi-User™, QueX™, Screen Writer™, and CICS interface software; InfoTap™ software; NeoVisuals® software; JMP®, JMP IN®, JMP Serve®, and JMP *Design*® software; SAS/RTERM® software; and the SAS/C® Compiler and the SAS/CX® Compiler; and Emulus® software. MultiVendor Architecture™ and MVA™ are trademarks of SAS Institute Inc. SAS Institute also offers SAS Consulting®, SAS Video Productions®, Ambassador Select®, and On-Site Ambassador™ services. *Authorline*®, Books by Users™, *Observations*®, *SAS Communications*®, *SAS Training*®, *SAS Views*®, the SASware Ballot®, and *JMPer Cable*® are published by SAS Institute Inc. The SAS Video Productions logo and the Books by Users SAS Institute's Author Service logo are registered trademarks and the Helplus logo is a trademark of SAS Institute Inc. All trademarks above are registered trademarks or trademarks of SAS Institute Inc. in the USA and other countries. ® indicates USA registration.

The Institute is a private company devoted to the support and further development of its software and related services.

DB2®, DB2/2™, and SQL/DS® are registered trademarks or trademarks of International Business Machines Corporation. ® indicates USA registration.

Other brand and product names are registered trademarks or trademarks of their respective companies.

Doc P18, 101394

Contents

Part 2 · SAS Screen Control Language Source-Level Debugger   153

Illustrations

Displays

Figures

Tables

Credits

Documentation

Design and Production	Design, Production, and Printing Services
Style Programming	Publications Technology Development
Technical Review	Stuart A. Austin, Charles C. Bass, Corey D. Benson, Patricia L. Berryman, David J. Biesack, Patti M. Brideson, Vicki Brocklebank, Adi Busch, Ann E. Carpenter, Yao Chen, Todd M. Dalness, Vincent C. DelGobbo, David A. Driggs, Marje Fecht, Annette T. Harris, Sue Her, Brian Johnson, Al Kulik, Lynn P. Leone, Michael A. Matthews, William J. Metcalf III, LaVon Missell, Ivy G. Parker, Yvonne Selby, Jean Chesser Service, Thomas E. Sherron, Jennifer L. Torrisi, Glen R. Walker, Harriet J. Watts, Kelley L. Wingo
Writing and Editing	John C. Barnum, Ann E. Carpenter, Ottis R. Cowper, Marilyn M. Hanson, Stephenie P. Joyner, Patricia Glasgow Moell, Julie McAlpine Platt, Patsy J. Poole, Josephine P. Pope, David A. Teal, John M. West

Software

Screen Control Language	Corey D. Benson, David J. Biesack, Patti M. Brideson, Yao Chen, Sue Her, Al Kulik, Glen R. Walker
Testing	Angela G. Allen, Rhonda D. Ayscue, Tara S. Brown, Larnell Lennon
Quality Assurance	Stuart A. Austin, Patricia L. Berryman, Todd M. Dalness, Vincent C. DelGobbo, William J. Metcalf III, Thomas E. Sherron, Jennifer L. Torrisi, Harriet J. Watts, Kelley L. Wingo
Technical Support	Charles C. Bass, Vicki Brocklebank, Ann E. Carpenter, David A. Driggs, Annette T. Harris, Brian Johnson, Lynn P. Leone, LaVon Missell, Ivy G. Parker, Yvonne Selby, Jean Chesser Service

x

Changes and Enhancements with Release 6.11

New Features in Release 6.11

The following functions and routines are new with Release 6.11. They are listed in Table 19.2, "SCL Elements by Category," and are described in Chapter 20, "Screen Control Language Dictionary."

SCL Element	Description
APPLY	Invokes a method whose arguments are passed from an SCL list
COMAMID	Returns the communications access methods for an operating system
DSID	Searches for a data set name and returns the data set identifier
FILEDIALOG	Opens a selection window listing files
FONTSEL	Opens the selector window for host or for portable fonts
KEYCOUNT	Returns the number of observations that meet the criteria specified by an index key
RGBDM	Returns the name supported by SAS Display Manager System (DM) for a color
STOP	Stops the execution of the current LINK stacks
SUPAPPLY	Invokes the inherited definition of a method and passes the method's arguments in an SCL list
TRACEBACK	Displays the traceback of the entire SCL execution stack
WAIT	Suspends execution of the next program statement
WORDTYPE	Identifies the type for a word on the command line

Access to Remote Library Services

SAS data sets and views have transparent access for Remote Library Services (RLS), which allows SCL applications read or write access to data sets, views, and catalogs across hardware platforms and SAS releases when you have SAS/SHARE or SAS/CONNECT installed at your location. SAS data sets have transparent RLS access for Release 6.10 and earlier. Catalog compatibility across platforms is architecture dependent. For more information, see Chapter 5, "Using SAS Data Sets," and *SAS/SHARE Software: Usage and Reference, Version 6, First Edition.*

Features Enhanced in Release 6.11

Reference Arrays

SCL supports reference arrays starting in Release 6.11. A reference array is a pointer to another defined array. Previously, when an array needed to be passed as a parameter to a METHOD or ENTRY statement, an array of equal size needed to be defined in both the calling and the called program. The array contents are passed from the caller to the callee, which maintains a local copy of the array. With reference arrays, it does not copy the array contents to the callee but instead shares the caller's array contents. For more information, see Chapter 2, "Using SCL Variables," and ARRAY in Chapter 20.

DMWINDOW

DMWINDOW supports SASCOLOR window elements in its color parameter.

DSNAME

With Release 6.11, DSNAME does not require a *dsid*. You can leave the *dsid* out in FSEDIT, FSBROWSE, and FSVIEW, and DSNAME gives information on the data set opened by the procedure. For more information, see DSNAME in Chapter 20.

ENTRY

ENTRY statement supports ARGLIST= and REST= new options.

EXECCMDI

EXECCMDI includes two new options for when the commands will be executed: EXEC executes commands in the command buffer immediately, and NOEXEC executes a non-global command when control returns to the application.

FIELD

FIELD function supports SASCOLOR window elements in its color parameter.

FILLIST

FILLIST You can specify file options in *type*. For example, to fill a list from an external print file and strip carriage control, use `'FILE(PRINT STRIPCC)'` for *type*. FILLIST also supports reading SAS/AF LIST entries.

FLDCOLOR

FLDCOLOR supports SASCOLOR window elements in its color parameter.

GETNITEMC
GETITEMN
GETNITEML

Support an additional parameter which reports the index in the list where the item was found.

GGLOBAL

GGLOBAL returns the value of HEIGHT for SYMBOL, PATTERN, LEGEND, or AXIS statement definitions.

HASATTR

HASATTR can check whether an identifier is a class or object identifier. For more information, see HASATTR in Chapter 20.

LEGEND

LEGEND supports SASCOLOR window elements in its color parameter.

METHOD

METHOD statement supports ARGLIST=, REST=, and /RESIDENT new options.

OBSINFO

OBSINFO includes an ALTER item, which reports whether the currently displayed observation can be edited. For details, see OBSINFO in Chapter 20.

PUTLEGEND

PUTLEGEND supports SASCOLOR window elements in its color parameter.

SAVELIST

You can specify file options in *type*. For example, to save a list to an external print file, stripping carriage control, use `'FILE(PRINT STRIPCC)'` for *type*. For more information, see SAVELIST in Chapter 20.

SETKEY

SETKEY includes a new *list-id* argument, which identifies the list that contains the values of the index key variables. The SCROLL/NOSCROLL options can be used to retrieve the observations randomly or sequentially. For details, see SETKEY in Chapter 20.

STRATTR

STRATTR supports SASCOLOR window elements in its color parameter.

WINFO

WINFO returns three new information items about a window. You can use PMENUSTATE to determine whether check marks or radio buttons display in the window's pull-down menus. XPIXCELL reports the width (in pixels) of the DM (display manager) font. YPIXCELL reports the height (in pixels) of the DM (display manager) font. For more information, see WINFO in Chapter 20.

SAS® Screen Control Language

CHAPTER *15*

**Managing Fields
and Windows**

CHAPTER *1* Screen Control Language

Introduction

SAS Screen Control Language (SCL) is a programming language that you use with SAS/AF and SAS/FSP software. SCL programs can combine information obtained from program statements with interactive input from users, providing two-way communication between applications and users.

You can also use many SCL functions in SAS/CALC software models and formulas. For more information, see *SAS/CALC Software: Usage and Reference, Version 6, First Edition*. SCL functions can also be used with Image Extensions to SAS/GRAPH software, which are described in SAS Technical Report P-263: *Image Extensions to SAS/GRAPH Software, Version 6, First Edition*.

SCL Elements

SCL has the same basic elements as the base SAS language:

☐ statements

☐ functions

☐ CALL routines

☐ operators

☐ macro capability

☐ variables.

Many of these elements are the same in SCL as in the base SAS language. In addition, SCL provides additional statements, functions, and routines that enable you to:

☐ control the flow of your applications

☐ manage all interactive elements of windows

☐ manipulate SAS data sets and external files

☐ create SCL routines that can be invoked from any SCL application

☐ create programs that can be called from other SAS/AF and SAS/FSP applications.

SCL Statements

SCL provides all of the program control statements of the base SAS language. However, many base SAS language statements that relate to the creation and manipulation of SAS data sets and external files are absent in SCL. In their place, SCL provides an extensive set of language elements for manipulating SAS data sets and external files. These elements are described in Chapter 5, "Using SAS Data Sets" and Chapter 6, "Using External Files."

SCL also provides additional categories of statements not found in the base SAS language. One group controls the behavior of aspects of application windows. The other group allows you to create routines that can be invoked from other SCL applications via the CALL METHOD routine.

Executable and Declarative Statements

As in the base SAS language, SCL statements are either executable or declarative.

Executable statements
   are compiled into intermediate code and result in some action when the SCL program is executed. (Some examples of executable statements are the CURSOR, IF-THEN/ELSE, and assignment statements.)

Declarative statements
   provide information to the SCL compiler but do not result in executable code. (Some examples of declarative statements are the ARRAY and LENGTH statements.) The SCL compiler will report error if you put declarative statements inside a DO group.

You can place declarative statements anywhere in your SCL program, but they typically appear at the beginning of the program before the first labeled section. You must place executable statements within one of the labeled sections of the SCL program.

In addition, you can include comment statements anywhere in your SCL programs. Comments provide information to the programmer but are ignored by the compiler and produce no executable code.

SCL Functions

SCL functions, like the functions in the base SAS language, are language elements that return a value based on one or more arguments supplied with the function name. Most of the special features of SCL are implemented as functions. In addition, SCL provides all of the functions of the base SAS language except for the DIF and LAG functions, which require a queue of previously processed observations that only the DATA step maintains.

Groups of SCL Functions

SCL functions can be divided into two broad groups according to the type of information the function returns. These groups are

□ functions that return a value representing the result of a manipulation of the argument values. For example, the SUBSTR function returns a substring of the string you supply as the first function argument.

□ functions that perform an action and return a value indicating the success or failure of that action. For these functions, the value that the function returns is called a *return code.* For example, the LIBNAME function returns the value 0 if it successfully assigns the specified libref to the specified SAS data library or directory. If the function cannot assign the libref, it returns a nonzero value that reports the failure of the operation. SYSMSG contains the text of the error message associated with the return code.

Note: Some functions use a return code value of 0 to indicate that the requested operation was successful, while other functions use a return code of 0 to indicate that the operation failed. Each function is described in Chapter 20, "SCL Dictionary."

Using Functions in Expressions

You can use functions almost any place in an SCL program statement where you can use variable names or literal values. For example, the following program fragment shows a way to perform an operation (in this case, the FETCH function) and take an action based on the value of the return code from the function:

```
rc=fetch(dsid);
    /* The return code -1 means the end of the file was reached.  */
if (rc=-1) then
    do;
        SCL statements to handle the end-of-file condition
    end;
```

To eliminate the variable for the return code, use the function directly in the IF statement's expression, as shown in this example.

```
if (fetch(dsid)=-1) then
    do;
        SCL statements to handle the end-of-file
        condition
    end;
```

In this case, the FETCH function is executed, and then the IF expression evaluates the return code to determine whether to perform the conditional action.

As long as you do not need the value of the function's return code for any other processing, the latter form is more efficient because it eliminates the unnecessary variable assignment.

SCL CALL Routines

Like functions, CALL routines perform actions based on the values of arguments supplied with the routine name. However, unlike functions, CALL routines do not return values. Many halt the program if the call is unsuccessful. Use CALL routines to implement features that do not require return codes.

SCL has a variety of CALL routines of its own and also supports all of the CALL routines of the base SAS language.

SCL Operators

SCL has no special operators beyond those provided in the base SAS language. The only restrictions on operators in SCL are for the minimum and maximum value operators. For these SAS operators, you must use the operator symbols (> < and < >, respectively) rather than the mnemonic equivalents (MIN and MAX, respectively).

SAS Macro Facility

You can use the SAS macro facility in SCL programs. That is, in your SCL programs you can use SAS macros and SAS macro variables defined elsewhere in your SAS session or in autocall libraries. For more information, see Chapter 7, "Using Program Modules."

The important thing to remember when using the macro facility with SCL is that macros and macro variables in SCL programs are resolved when you compile the SCL program, not when a user executes the application. You can use the SYMGET and SYMGETN functions to retrieve the value from a macro variable at execution time.

Comparisons with the SAS DATA Step

SCL supports the syntax of the SAS DATA step with the exceptions and additions noted in this chapter. Refer to *SAS Language: Reference, Version 6, First Edition* for details of the SAS language elements available in the DATA step.

SCL does not support the DATA step statements that relate specifically to creating SAS data sets, such as the DATA, SET, INFILE, and CARDS statements. However, SCL does provide special functions that can perform equivalent SAS data set manipulations. See Chapter 5 for details.

Statements

Table 19.1 "Statements by Category" in Chapter 19 "SCL Language Elements" lists the statements that are supported by SCL and where they are documented. In SCL, the ARRAY, DO, LENGTH, PUT, and SELECT statements execute differently from the DATA step. Because these statements are different in SCL, they have entries in Chapter 20, where the differences are documented in their entry.

The following list shows the DATA step statements that are valid in SCL programs and notes differences between a statement's support in SCL and in the DATA step.

ARRAY (Explicit)
> defines the elements of an explicit array. _NUMERIC_ , _CHARACTER_ and _ALL_ not supported. Implicit arrays are not allowed in SCL. See ARRAY in Chapter 20 for information about the enhanced features of this statement in SCL.

assignment
> assigns values to variables.

comment
> documents the purpose of the code.

CONTINUE
> See DO and CONTINUE in Chapter 20 for information on the differences in the behavior of this statement in SCL.

DO, iterative DO, DO-UNTIL, DO-WHILE
> SCL does not support the DO-list form of the DO statement, but it does support LEAVE and CONTINUE statements that extend the capabilities of DO-group processing. These statements are described in Chapter 20 in DO, CONTINUE, and LEAVE.

END
> marks the end of a DO group or SELECT group.

GOTO
:   jumps to a specified program label.

IF-THEN-ELSE
:   enables conditional execution of one or more statements

%INCLUDE

LEAVE
:   See DO and LEAVE in Chapter 20 for information on the differences in the behavior of this statement in SCL.

LENGTH
:   specifies the number of bytes allocated for storing variables. In SCL, the LENGTH statement can only set the lengths of nonwindow variables. See LENGTH in Chapter 20 for details on the differences in the behavior of this statement in SCL.

LINK
:   jumps to a specified program label but allows return to the following statement. SCL allows nesting of up to 25 LINK statements.

NULL

PUT
:   See PUT in Chapter 20 for details on the differences in the behavior of this statement in SCL.

RETURN
:   returns the control to the calling routine or application

RUN
:   treated as an alias for the RETURN statement.

SELECT-WHEN
:   enables conditional execution of one or several statements or groups of statements. See SELECT in Chapter 20 for details on the differences in the behavior of this statement in SCL.

STOP
:   treated as an alias for the RETURN statement.

SUM

Functions

SCL supports all DATA step functions except LAG*n* and DIF*n*. See Table 19.3, "SAS Functions," in Chapter 19 for a list of the DATA step functions that are supported by SCL. Refer to Chapter 11, "SAS Functions," in *SAS Language: Reference* for details on other DATA step functions that are supported by SCL.

Variables

Variables in SCL programs share most of the characteristics of variables in the DATA step. However, you should be aware of a few differences.

Numeric Variables

In SCL, all numeric variables have a length of 8. Even if you specify a different length for a numeric variable using a LENGTH statement, SCL still reserves 8 bytes for the variable when the program is compiled.

Character Variables

In SCL, the lengths of character variables are determined as follows:

□ For SAS/AF character-type window variables, the maximum length of a variable is equal to the length of the corresponding field in the application window. You cannot alter the maximum length of a window variable with a LENGTH statement.

For FSEDIT, the length of character window variables that correspond to variables in a data set is equal to the length specified in the data set.

□ For character-type nonwindow variables, the default maximum length is 200 characters. The maximum length of a nonwindow variable is not affected by the length of a string assigned to the variable in the SCL program.

For example, suppose your SCL program contains the following statement (and the window for the application does not include a field named NAME):

```
name='Smith';
```

As a result of this assignment statement, SCL creates a nonwindow variable named NAME with a maximum length of 200 characters. The length of the string in the assignment statement has no effect on the maximum length of the variable. In contrast, this same assignment in a DATA step would create a variable with a maximum length of only 5 characters.

You can use the LENGTH statement to specify a different maximum length for nonwindow character variables. This can significantly reduce memory requirements if your program uses many nonwindow variables. See LENGTH in Chapter 20 for details.

As in the DATA step, the LENGTH function in SCL returns the current trimmed length of the string (the position of the rightmost nonblank character in the variable value). However, SCL also provides the MLENGTH function, which returns the maximum length of a character variable and the LENGTH function with the NOTRIM option, which returns the untrimmed length of the string.

Expressions

SCL supports the standard DATA step expressions in an identical manner. The only exception is the IN operator, which has the following syntax:

i =variable IN (*list-of-values*)|*array-name*;

The following statements using the IN operator are equivalent:

```
array list{3}$ ('cat','bird','dog');
i='dog' in ('cat','bird','dog');
i='dog' in list;
```

In SCL, the IN operator returns 0 if no match is found or returns the index of the element if a match is found. In the example above, the IN operator returns the value 3. In the DATA step, the IN operator returns 0 if no match is found and 1 if a match is found. Therefore, these statements produce 1 because 'dog' is found. The DATA step does not support the form **i='dog' in list**. The IN operator is valid for both numeric and character lists as well as arrays. If a list used with the IN operator contains values with mixed data types, they are converted to the data type of the first value in the list when the program is compiled.

Combining Language Elements into Program Statements

This section describes the basic rules for constructing valid SCL program statements from the basic SCL language elements.

Rules for SCL Program Statements

The statements you use in your SCL programs must conform to the following rules:

□ You must end each SCL program statement with a semicolon.

□ You can place any number of SCL program statements on a single line as long as you separate the individual statements with semicolons. If you plan to use the SCL debugger, it is helpful to begin each statement on a separate line.

□ You can continue an SCL program statement from one line to the next as long as no keyword is split.

□ You can begin SCL program statements in any column.

□ You must separate words in SCL program statements with blanks or with special characters such as the equal sign (=) or other operators.

□ You must place arguments for SCL functions and CALL routines within parentheses.

□ If a function or CALL routine takes more than one argument, you must separate the arguments with commas.

□ Character arguments that are literal values must be enclosed in either single or double quotes (for example, 'Y' or 'N').

□ Numeric arguments do not require quotes.

Limits on Arguments for SCL Functions and CALL Routines

Some additional restrictions apply to the values you pass as arguments to SCL functions and CALL routines. Some SCL functions and CALL routines accept only variable names as arguments, but for most arguments you can specify either a literal value or the name of a variable that contains the desired value.

Note: For some functions, passing missing values for certain arguments causes the SCL program to stop executing and print an error message.

Refer to Chapter 20, "Screen Control Language Dictionary," for details on the restrictions on argument values.

CHAPTER *2* **Using SCL Variables**

Introduction

SCL variables have most of the same attributes as variables in the base SAS language:

☐ name

☐ type (character or numeric)

☐ length

Variables in the base SAS language also can have labels. SCL does not make use of variable labels.

Types of SCL Variables

SCL provides the following categories of variables:

Category	Characteristic	Usage
window	linked to a field in the window	passes values back and forth between the SCL program and the application's window
nonwindow	defined within an SCL program	holds temporary values that do not need to be displayed to users
system	provided by SCL	conveys information about the status of the application

As in the base SAS language, you can group variables into arrays to make it easier to apply the same process to all the variables in the group.

Window Variables

Most SCL applications provide a window for interacting with users. The areas of the window in which users can enter values and in which SCL programs can display values are called *fields*. Each field in an application's window has an associated variable in the application's SCL program.

When you use FRAME entries, you build windows that are graphical user interfaces (GUIs). GUIs are graphical-oriented user applications. Typically, they contain window elements such as bit-mapped and structured graphics, icons, pull-down and pop-up menus, command buttons, scroll bars, and sliders. Most also use a mouse device as a pointer device. With GUI-based applications, users typically navigate through the application by pointing and clicking on their selections with a mouse. With GUI-based applications, you can create applications with features like text and graphics on the same window. You can also create multiple extended tables for the same window or combine extended tables with graphics and other window elements.

The elements that make up windows built from FRAME entries are called widgets. A *widget* is a component of a graphical user interface that displays information or accepts user input. For more information on FRAME entry windows, see *SAS/AF Software: FRAME Entry Usage and Reference, Version 6, First Edition*.

SCL variables associated with fields and widgets are called *window variables*. Window variables are, therefore, the means by which users communicate with SCL programs and SCL programs communicate with users.

Determining Window Variable Attributes in SAS/AF Applications

When you build the window for a PROGRAM or FRAME entry, each field you define in the DISPLAY window is assigned a default type. You can use the PROGRAM entry's ATTR window or Text Entry Attributes window in the FRAME entry to modify the attributes of a field or text entry widget.

Name

By default, the window variable associated with each field in PROGRAM entries has the same name as the field. In FRAME entries, the variable associated with each object has the default name OBJ*n*, where *n* is the *n*th object of any class created in the window. You can give the window variable a different name by specifying that name in the **Alias** field in the ATTR window of the PROGRAM entry or the **Name** field of an object's attribute window in the FRAME entry.

Data Type

The data type for each window variable is determined by the value for the **Type** attribute. SAS/AF provides many special type values (ACTION, INPUT, VARLIST, and so on) for PROGRAM entry fields and text entry widgets in FRAME entries in the entry's window. However, the corresponding window variables are still either numeric or character. For more information on SAS/AF field types, refer to *SAS/AF Software: Usage and Reference* and Appendix 2, "Selectable Values for Text Object Attributes" in *SAS/AF Software: FRAME Entry Usage and Reference, Version 6, First Edition*.

Length

Lengths of window variables are determined as follows:

□ Numeric-type window variables always have a length of 8.

□ Character-type window variables have a maximum length that equals the width of the corresponding field in the application's window. For example, a field that occupies 20 columns in the window has an associated window variable with a maximum length of 20.

For both SAS/AF and SAS/FSP, you cannot alter the length of window variables (either character or numeric) with LENGTH statements in your SCL programs. If you specify a length for a window variable in a LENGTH statement, you get an error message when you compile the program.

Determining Window Variable Attributes in FSEDIT Applications

Fields in FSEDIT windows have the following characteristics:

□ Fields associated with variables in the SAS data set have the same name, type, length, format, and informat as the variables in the SAS data set. Either the length or the format determine the number of underscores to display for the field.

□ Computed fields have the name, type, format, and informat that you assign in the FSEDIT Names window when you define the fields.

Each field in an FSEDIT window has an associated window variable with the same name and type as the field.

Determining Window Variable Attributes in FSVIEW Applications

FSVIEW windows display columns of fields. Columns in FSVIEW windows have the following characteristics:

□ Columns associated with variables in the SAS data set have the same name, type, length, format, and informat as the variables in the SAS data set. (You can assign temporary names, formats, and informats, in the FSVIEW window.)

□ Computed columns have the name, type, format, and informat you assign when you define the formula for the column.

Each column in the FSVIEW window has an associated window variable with the same name, type, format, and informat as the column.

Nonwindow Variables

SCL programs can define and use variables that do not have associated fields in the window. These variables are called *nonwindow variables,* and they are used to hold values that do not need to be displayed to users. Also, for some SCL applications, there is no associated window and only nonwindow variables are used.

In FSEDIT applications, you can have nonwindow variables and unwanted variables. When you associate fields with window variables in the FSEDIT Identify window, you can exclude any SAS data set variables that you do not want displayed on the window by identifying the variables as unwanted. However, even unwanted variables can be referenced by your FSEDIT application's SCL program.

Determining Nonwindow Variable Attributes

Unless you define nonwindow variables explicitly with a LENGTH statement, the name and type of each nonwindow variable is determined by the first assignment statement in which the variable appears in the program. While window variable names are limited to no more than eight characters, nonwindow variable names can be up to 32 characters long. Because nonwindow variables are used only within the SCL program, they have no informat or format.

Determining Nonwindow Variable Lengths

The length of nonwindow variables is determined as follows:

□ Numeric-type nonwindow variables always have a length of 8.

□ Character-type nonwindow variables have a default maximum length of 200.

System Variables

SAS/AF and SAS/FSP automatically create a group of *system variables* for every SCL program you compile. The compiler automatically creates slots for the variables (except for _BLANK_) in the SCL data vector, which is described later in this chapter in "The SCL Data Vector." These variables, which are described in Table 2.1, communicate information between the program and the application so that their values are correct and you can use them in your program.

Table 2.1   *System Variables*

Variable	Type	Purpose
BLANK	character	reports whether a window variable contains a value, or sets a variable value to blank. (SAS/AF only)
CURROW	numeric	stores the number of the current row in an extended table (the value is correct only when the entry has an extended table)
MSG	character	the text displayed on the window's message line the next time the window is refreshed
STATUS	character	the status of program execution. You can check for the following values:

    C   the user issued the CANCEL command

    E   the user issued the END command.

In SCL programs for FRAME entries, you can check for the following additional values:

    ' '   a widget was modified or selected

    D   a widget was selected with a double click

    G   the GETROW section was called for the top row of an extended table

    K   a command other than an END or CANCEL, or their equivalents, was issued

    P   a pop-up menu event occurred.

You can also set the value of _STATUS_ to the following, using uppercase characters:

    R   to resume execution of the SCL program without exiting the application in SAS/AF or the current observation in FSEDIT. When you set the value of the _STATUS_ variable to **R** in SAS/AF, the procedure ignores the END or CANCEL command the user just issued. This value is useful only when set in the TERM section of your program because the specified action (not allowing an exit from the program or the current observation) occurs after the user has issued an END or CANCEL command in SAS/AF or attempted to leave an observation in FSEDIT.

    H   to terminate the current window without further input from the user. Control returns to the program or window that invoked the application. Note that the TERM section of the program is not executed in this case. In FSEDIT, if a user modified data set variable values in the current observation, the modified values are not written to the SAS data set.

Setting _STATUS_ does not imply an immediate return. The value of _STATUS_ is queried only after the SCL program returns control to the application.

There are dictionary entries in Chapter 20 for each of these variables.

System Instance Variables

System instance variables are a special category of system variables. They are provided automatically by SAS/AF, but the SCL compiler does not automatically create a space for them in the SCL data vector. These variables have the correct value if they are used, but do not occupy a space in the SCL data vector if they are not declared in an SCL program. These variables are described in Table 2.2.

To use a numeric special variable, you can simply reference it in your SCL program. To use _VALUE_, when it is used to report the value of a character widget, or _METHOD_ you have to declare it with a LENGTH statement. For example,

```
length _method_ $40;
length _value_ $80;
```

Use a length that is the maximum character length for the method or the widget's value, respectively.

The compiler may issue a warning that the variable is referenced but not assigned. You can safely ignore this warning. For example:

```
WARNING: [Line 4]  Variable _METHOD_ is uninitialized
```

Table 2.2 *Special Variables*

Variable	Type	Purpose
CFRAME	numeric	stores the identifier of the FRAME entry that is currently executing, when a widget is executing a method. Otherwise, it stores the identifier of the FRAME entry that is executing.
CURCOL	numeric	stores the value of the leftmost column in an extended table object in a FRAME entry. It is used to control horizontal scrolling.
EVENT	character	reports the type of event that occurred on a widget. It is only useful during a _SELECT_ method; at other times, it may not exist as an attribute or it will be blank. _EVENT_ can have one of the following values: ' ' modification or selection C command D double click P popmenu request S selection or single click.
FRAME	numeric	stores the identifier for the FRAME entry containing the widget, when the object is a FRAME entry widget; otherwise the identifier of the FRAME entry that is currently executing. You can use this variable to send methods to a FRAME entry from a widget's method. For example, a widget method can send a _REFRESH_ method to the FRAME entry, causing the FRAME entry to refresh its display.
METHOD	character	stores the name of the method that is currently executing.
SELF	numeric	stores the identifier of the object that is currently executing a method.
VALUE	character numeric	stores the value of a widget.

There are dictionary entries in Chapter 20 for each of these variables.

The SCL Data Vector

When base SAS software compiles a DATA step, it opens a temporary storage area called the *program data vector*. The program data vector holds the values of the variables defined in the DATA step.

Likewise, when SAS/AF or SAS/FSP software compiles an SCL program, it opens a storage area called the *SCL data vector* (SDV). The SDV holds the values of all window, nonwindow, and system variables used in the application.

For example, suppose an FSEDIT application has the window variables NAME, HEIGHT, AGE, and WEIGHT (from the SASUSER.CLASS data set) and the nonwindow variables HFACTOR and WFACTOR. When the program compiles, the SDV shown in Figure 2.1 is created.

Figure 2.1   *SCL Data Vector for a Typical Application*

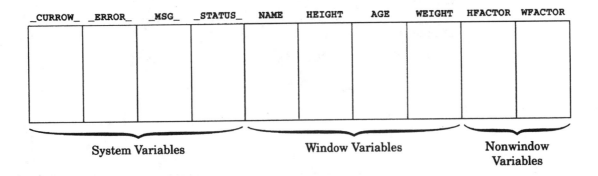

The system variables (_CURROW_, _ERROR_, _MSG_, AND _STATUS_) are created automatically. The window variables (NAME, AGE, HEIGHT, and WEIGHT) are created because they have associated fields in the window, even if the variables are not used in the SCL program. The nonwindow variables (HFACTOR and WFACTOR) are created as a result of explicit references in the SCL program.

Performing the Same Action for a Series of Variables

When you want to perform the same action for a series of SCL variables, you can often simplify your programs by defining temporary groups of variables called *arrays*. The differences between the ARRAY Statement Execution in SCL and the DATA step are described in Chapter 1, "Screen Control Language."

Grouping Variables into Arrays

Listing variables in an ARRAY statement provides a way to refer to variables that are elements of the array, for example,

```
array month{5} jan feb mar apr may;
```

In addition to the variable names, you also can use references of the form *array-name{position}*, where *position* is the index position of the variable's name in the list following the ARRAY statement. For example, if MAR is the third element of the array MONTH, you can use the array reference MONTH{3} to retrieve values from the variable MAR or to store values in MAR.

Repeating an Action for Variables in an Array

To perform the same action on a series of fields grouped into an array, you can use an iterative DO statement using the loop's index variable for the array subscript. The DO loop is especially convenient when arrays contain many elements.

For example, you could use a program like the following to sum the values and display the total in the SUM field:

```
array  month{5} jan feb mar apr may (1,2,3,4,5);

INIT:
return;

MAIN:
   sum=0;
   do i=1 to 5;
      sum+month{i};
   end;
return;
```

The DO loop in the MAIN section has the same effect as any one of the following statements:

```
sum=jan+feb+mar+apr+may;
sum=sum(of month{*});
sum=sum(of jan--may);
```

Grouping Variables with Sequential Names

If your application's program or window has a series of variables whose names end in sequential numbers (for example, SCORE1, SCORE2, SCORE3, and so forth), SCL provides a shorthand way of grouping these variables into an array.

For example, the following ARRAY statement groups the variables FACTOR1, FACTOR2, FACTOR3, and FACTOR4 into the array FACTOR:

```
array factor{4};
```

If the variables FACTOR1 through FACTOR4 do not already exist as window variables, SCL defines new nonwindow variables with those names.

Note: In releases prior to 6.10, you should not use leading zeros in names, like FACTOR01 or FACTOR02 because those SCL compilers cannot handle variable names with embedded zeros.

Conserving Memory by Using Temporary Arrays

If you want to use an array to hold values in your SCL program but do not need to refer to array elements by variable name, you can add the _TEMPORARY_ argument to your ARRAY statement:

```
array total{4} _temporary_;
```

When you use the _TEMPORARY_ argument, you must use subscripting to refer to the array elements. For the TOTAL array, you must use TOTAL{2} to refer to the second element. In this case, you cannot use the variable name TOTAL2 as an alternative reference for the array element TOTAL{2}.

Using the _TEMPORARY_ argument saves memory. By default, SCL allocates memory for both the name of the array and the names of the individual array elements. However, when you use the _TEMPORARY_ argument, SCL only allocates memory for the array name. For large arrays, this can result in significant memory savings.

Note: Do not use _TEMPORARY_ if you plan to fetch values from a SAS data set directly into the array elements with the SET function. Use the GETVARN and GETVARC functions when this value is specified. For details of these functions, see Chapter 20.

Initializing Array Elements

You can define initial values for the elements of an array by listing the initial values in parentheses following the list of variable names. By default, all elements in an array are initialized to missing values if the array elements did not previously exist. Commas are optional between variable values.

For example, the following array statement creates a two-dimensional array and sets element A1 to an initial value of 1 and element A2 to an initial value of 2:

```
array a{2} (1 2);
```

Assigning the Same Value to Multiple Elements

You can use repetition factors when initializing arrays. Repetition factors have the following form:

```
5 * (2 3 4)
```

where

- □ **5** is the repetition factor, the number of times the values in the following list of items are repeated.

- □ **(2 3 4)** is a list of initial values for the array elements. If the list consists of only a single item, you can omit the parentheses.

For example, the following statement uses repetition factors to initialize the values of the array A:

```
array a{20} (0,3*1,5*(2,3,4),0);
```

This example repeats the value 1 three times and the sequence 2, 3, 4 five times. The values assigned to the elements of the array A are:

```
0, 1, 1, 1, 2, 3, 4, 2, 3, 4, 2, 3, 4, 2, 3, 4, 2, 3, 4, 0
```

Initializing Multidimensional Arrays

To initialize a multidimensional array, list values for the first row of the array followed by values for the second row, and so on. For example, the following statement initializes a two-dimensional array named COUNT:

```
array count{2,3} (1 2 3 4 5 6);
```

Figure 2.2 shows the values of the elements of this array.

Figure 2.2
Elements of the COUNT Array

		column 1	column 2	column 3
			Columns	
	row 1	1	2	3
Rows	row 2	4	5	6

For more information on arrays, see ARRAY in Chapter 20.

CHAPTER 3

SCL Programs for SAS/AF® and SAS/FSP® Applications

Introduction

SCL programs in SAS/AF entries and FSEDIT SCREEN entries execute in at least three distinct phases:

□ an initialization or start-up phase

□ a main processing phase

□ a termination or cleanup phase.

During each of these phases, control of the entry can pass to the SCL program. Because SCL programs execute in phases, the programs are divided into labeled statement blocks. A different block of the SCL program executes during each phase. You use reserved labels to identify when each block of the SCL program executes.

Reserved labels are special statement labels that tell a SAS/AF or FSEDIT application when to execute the corresponding sections of the SCL program. Each label has an associated RETURN statement that marks the end of the labeled section. When the RETURN statement is encountered during program execution, control returns to the application window. FSVIEW does not use any reserved labels.

Using Labels to Control Program Execution

You control program execution in SAS/AF and SAS/FSP entries by grouping statements under the reserved labels. The labeled sections execute during the appropriate phases of execution. As you write SCL programs, think about how each statement or group of statements interacts with users and with other statements in the program so that you can correctly group the statements based on when they need to be processed.

SCL programs for FRAME entries and SCL entries that contain method block definitions do not require any reserved sections. SCL programs for PROGRAM and SCREEN entries must include at least one of the reserved labels, INIT, MAIN, or TERM. If a program in a PROGRAM or SCREEN entry does not include at least one of the reserved labels, control never passes to the program. If a program in one of these entries does not contain all three of these reserved labels, you get one or more warning messages when you compile the program. FSEINIT and FSETERM are FSEDIT labels that are optional in FSEDIT programs and are not allowed in SAS/AF programs. No warnings are issued if they are not used.

▶ *Caution: Do not place executable statements outside the labeled sections of your SCL programs.*

Executable statements outside a labeled section never execute because programs are invoked only at reserved labels. Declarative statements can appear anywhere in the program, even outside labeled sections.

How SCL Programs Execute in SAS/AF Applications

SAS/AF applications that employ SCL are built using FRAME, PROGRAM, and SCL entries. Widget classes, from which FRAME entry widgets are created, can use methods to perform actions. These methods are executed with SCL CALL routines, for example, CALL SEND.

You can use SCL programs in SAS/AF programs to perform tasks such as:

□ validating user input

□ calculating values for fields based on user input

□ providing messages and help to users

□ providing special user interface features such as menus, selection lists, and scrollable tables of information

□ reading from and writing to SAS data sets and external files

□ interfacing with other SAS System software as well as software from other vendors.

Figure 3.1 shows the general form of an SCL program for a SAS/AF application. This figure shows all of the reserved sections that can be used by SAS/AF applications to process the phases of program initialization, main processing, and termination.

Figure 3.1
SCL Program for a SAS/AF Entry

```
INIT:
      Statements to initialize the application
return;


MAIN:
      Statements to process user input
return;


TERM:
      Statements to terminate the application
return;
```

SCL programs for extended tables, which can be used in FRAME and PROGRAM entries, also can include the reserved labels PUTROW and GETROW, or PUT*n* or GET*n* by default in FRAME entries. These reserved labels are discussed in "Displaying Extended Tables" in Chapter 14, "Introduction to Application Interfaces."

Processing the INIT Section

Statements in the INIT section typically perform actions such as:

□ initializing variables

□ importing values through macro variables

□ displaying initial messages on the window's message line

□ opening SAS data sets and external files used by the entry.

When a user invokes an application with the AF command, all window variables for PROGRAM entries and text entry widgets for FRAME entries are set to the initial values assigned in the **Initial** attribute for the corresponding field. (The **Initial** attribute is specified in the ATTR window of PROGRAM entries and the

Text Entry Attribute window of FRAME entries.) Window variables for which no initial value is specified are assigned the special missing value _BLANK_.

If the AF command that invoked an application included the AUTORECALL option, the values that were saved from the last invocation of the application are read into the fields or widgets. These values override the initial values. *SAS/AF Software: Usage and Reference, Version 6, First Edition* contains information on the AUTORECALL option and also on saving values with the AUTOSAVE option and the SAVE command. For another technique for saving window values, see SAVESCREEN in Chapter 20, "SCL Dictionary."

By default, INIT executes only once, before the entry's window opens, for each invocation of a FRAME or PROGRAM entry. After the initialization steps are complete, the SCL statements in INIT execute until the section's RETURN statement is encountered.

Processing the MAIN Section

Statements in the MAIN section typically perform actions such as:

□ validating field values

□ calculating values for computed variables based on user input

□ invoking secondary windows

□ querying and executing commands issued by users

□ retrieving values from SAS data sets or from external files.

By default for entries without a window, MAIN executes immediately after INIT finishes.

By default for entries with a window, MAIN executes each time a user presses the ENTER or RETURN key (or any function key) after modifying one or more fields or text entry widgets, provided that the modified fields contain valid values. After a user modifies fields and presses ENTER, all modified fields are verified to contain values that satisfy their attribute specifications. (However, the **Required** attribute is not checked until a user attempts to end the entry.) In FRAME entries, MAIN also executes whenever a widget is activated by modifying it or selecting it.

If a FRAME entry program or a PROGRAM entry program with a CONTROL LABEL statement contains one or more labeled sections called window variable blocks, those sections start running sequentially for each field or widget, from upper left to lower right of the window. A window variable block is a special labeled section that runs automatically when window elements are modified and those elements have the same name as the label on the section in the program.

In a FRAME entry, the window variable sections execute for all widgets that have been modified or selected. If a text entry widget modification introduces an attribute error, the window variable section for that widget does not execute. However, window variable sections do execute for other widgets that were also modified.

In a PROGRAM entry, the window variable sections start executing for modified fields. If a field modification introduces an attribute error, the window variable section for that field does not execute. Execution stops without running the window variable sections for any remaining fields.

Handling Invalid Values

If an attribute error is detected, MAIN does not execute. Instead, fields or widgets containing invalid values are highlighted, using the error attributes specified, and an error message displays. You can allow users to correct an attribute error in the window. If the program contains CONTROL ERROR and CONTROL LABEL, you can include statements in the window variable section that make a correction, as shown in the following example:

```
INIT:
    control label error;
return;

FIELD:
    if error(field) then
        do;
            field=' ';
            erroroff field;
            _msg_='Value was invalid.  It has been reset.';

        end;
return;
```

Executing MAIN

After all field values are validated, the SCL statements in MAIN execute until the section's RETURN statement encountered. At that time, the new values of the window variables are displayed in the corresponding fields.

Forcing MAIN to Execute

Although the default behavior is for MAIN to execute only when all field or widget values are valid, you can force MAIN to execute even when some fields or widgets contain invalid values or when an application-specific command is issued. SCL provides CONTROL ENTER, CONTROL ERROR, CONTROL ALLCMDS, and CONTROL ALWAYS statements that cause the MAIN section to execute whenever a user presses ENTER or RETURN, even if no fields have been modified or modified fields do not contain valid values. If the entry's window contains descriptive text but no fields, MAIN cannot execute unless a CONTROL ENTER or CONTROL ALWAYS statement is in effect.

See Chapter 9, "Changing the Default Program Flow," for information on using the CONTROL ENTER and CONTROL ALWAYS statements.

Processing the TERM Section

Statements in the TERM section typically perform actions such as:

□ updating and closing SAS data sets and external files opened by the entry

□ exporting values through macro variables

□ submitting statements to the SAS System for execution.

For entries without a window, TERM executes immediately after MAIN finishes. For entries with a window, TERM executes when a user issues either an END or a CANCEL command.

When a user issues an END command and fields have been modified since the last execution of MAIN, MAIN executes again and then TERM executes. If any fields contain invalid values, MAIN processing highlights the errors and returns control to the application. In this case TERM does not execute.

If any fields or text entry widgets have the **Required** attribute, they are checked for the presence of a value. If any required fields are empty, TERM does not execute. Instead, the empty required fields are highlighted using the specified error attributes and an error message is displayed. The user must provide values for all required fields before the TERM section executes.

After all these conditions are satisfied, the SCL statements in TERM execute until the section's RETURN statement is encountered. After the TERM section executes, the window closes and the entry terminates. Control returns to the SAS System process that invoked the entry.

How SCL Programs Execute in FSEDIT Applications

SCL applications based on the FSEDIT or FSBROWSE procedure are built using SCREEN entries. You can create SCREEN entries that have no SCL program, but adding an SCL program gives your applications the power to perform all the functionality of SCL.

Note: Because FSEDIT applications generally can execute under the FSBROWSE procedure without modifications, the remainder of this chapter discusses only the FSEDIT procedure in most cases. Unless otherwise stated, any discussion of the FSEDIT procedure also applies to the FSBROWSE procedure. Use FSBROWSE if you want users to have read-only access to the initial data set.

SCL Programs in FSEDIT SCREEN Entries

You can use SCL programs in SCREEN entries to perform tasks such as:

□ calculating values for fields based on user input

□ validating user-entered values against

    □ values from other fields

    □ values stored in other variables in the SCL program

    □ values stored in secondary SAS data sets or external files

    □ updating secondary data sets and files

□ providing messages and help to users.

Figure 3.2 shows the general form of an SCL program in an FSEDIT SCREEN entry.

Figure 3.2
SCL Program for an FSEDIT
Application

```
FSEINIT:
     Statements to initialize the application
return;


INIT:
     Statements to prepare for each new observation
return;


MAIN:
     Statements to process user input
return;


TERM:
     Statements to prepare for saving the current observation
return;


FSETERM:
     Statements to terminate the application
return;
```

Processing the FSEINIT Section

Statements in the FSEINIT section typically perform actions such as:

□ initializing nonwindow variables

□ importing values through macro variables

□ opening other SAS data sets or external files used by the entry

□ specifying an initial message to be displayed on the window's message line when the first observation is displayed.

Because FSEINIT executes before the first observation is displayed, you cannot assign initial values to window variables in FSEINIT. If you specify initial messages by assigning values to the _MSG_ system variable in both FSEINIT and INIT, the message specified in FSEINIT is replaced by the message specified in INIT. By default, FSEDIT executes FSEINIT only once, when a user invokes the FSEDIT application.

Immediately after the FSEDIT session starts, the SCL statements in FSEINIT execute until the section's RETURN statement is encountered. The FSEINIT section is optional and no warning is produced at compile time if the section is omitted.

Processing the INIT Section

Statements in the INIT section typically perform actions such as:

□ manipulating values of SAS data set variables before they are displayed to users

□ initializing computed fields for the current observation

□ specifying an initial message to be displayed on the window's message line (once for each observation).

INIT executes before each observation is displayed as well as when observation 0 is displayed for empty SAS data sets. INIT executes even if the observation displayed is the same observation that was previously displayed, as when a user issues a BACKWARD command when the first observation in the SAS data set is displayed or a FORWARD command when the last observation is displayed. INIT also executes when the SAVE command is issued.

Before INIT executes, FSEDIT reads the current observation from the session's data set. Window variables that are associated with variables in the session's data set are initialized with values from the current observation. Thus, the variable values from the current observation are available for processing in INIT before they are displayed to users. Computed window variables, those that are not associated with SAS data set variables, are initialized to missing values.

If the current observation is a new one (added with an ADD command), there is no corresponding observation in the data set. In this situation, all window variables are set to the initial values assigned in the INITIAL attribute for the field in the FSEDIT Attribute window. Window variables are assigned missing values when no initial value is specified.

After these initialization steps, the SCL statements in the INIT section execute until the section's RETURN statement is encountered.

Processing the MAIN Section

Statements in the MAIN section typically perform actions such as:

□ validating field values

□ calculating values for computed variables based on user input

□ invoking secondary windows

□ querying and executing commands issued by users

□ retrieving values from other SAS data sets or from external files.

By default, MAIN executes each time a user presses the ENTER key (or any function key) after modifying one or more fields, provided that certain conditions are met.

After a user modifies fields and presses ENTER, the values in all modified fields are checked against the attributes specified in the FSEDIT Attributes or FSEDIT Names window. Fields associated with SAS data set variables have the same type and informat as the SAS data set variables they display. Computed fields have the type and informat you specify in the FSEDIT Names window when you create the custom FSEDIT window. You can specify values for the MIN and MAX attributes for all fields in the FSEDIT Attributes window when you build the SCREEN entry. The REQUIRED attribute is checked only for newly added observations and only when a user attempts to leave the current observation.

Handling Invalid Field Values

If an error is detected, MAIN does not execute. Instead, the fields containing invalid values are highlighted and an error message displays. All errors must be corrected before MAIN executes. By default, users can issue an OVERRIDE command to override the error condition and pass missing values to the window variables in place of the invalid values. To prevent this, you can change the OVERRIDE parameter by specifying **N** in the **Override on errors** field of the FSEDIT Parms window.

Executing the MAIN Section

After all field values are validated, the program's window variables are updated with the values from the corresponding fields and then the SCL statements in MAIN execute until the section's RETURN statement is encountered. After MAIN executes, the updated values of the window variables are displayed in the corresponding fields.

Forcing MAIN to Execute

Although the default behavior is for the MAIN section not to execute unless a field has been modified with a valid value, you can force MAIN to execute. SCL provides CONTROL ERROR, CONTROL ALWAYS, and CONTROL ALLCMDS statements that cause MAIN to execute whenever a user presses ENTER or RETURN, even if no fields have been modified or invalid values were entered.

Because the FSBROWSE procedure does not allow users to modify field values, the MAIN section of the SCL program in an FSBROWSE application cannot execute unless a CONTROL ENTER, CONTROL ALWAYS, or CONTROL ALLCMDS statement is in effect.

See Chapter 9 for information on using the CONTROL ENTER, CONTROL ALWAYS, and CONTROL ALLCMDS statements.

Processing the TERM Section

Statements in the TERM section typically perform actions such as:

□ manipulating SAS data set values before the observation is updated

□ updating additional SAS data sets.

The statements in TERM execute when a user attempts to leave the current observation, provided that one or more fields associated with data set variables have been changed in the current observation, or that the observation is new. Issuing any of the following commands causes the TERM section to execute, provided one or more fields have been changed in the current observation or the observation is new:

□ any command that moves to another observation (for example, the FORWARD or BACKWARD commands).

   TERM executes even if the command does not display a different observation (as when users issue a BACKWARD command when the first observation in the SAS data set is displayed or a FORWARD command when the last observation is displayed).

□ any command that searches for an observation containing a specified value (for example, the FIND, SEARCH, LOCATE, or WHERE commands).

   TERM executes even if the command fails to find an observation that matches the specified search criteria.

□ the ADD or DUP commands.

□ the SAVE command.

□ the END or CANCEL commands.

If a user has modified any fields since the last execution of MAIN, then MAIN executes again before TERM executes. If any fields contain invalid values, the MAIN section processing described previously highlights the errors and returns control to the application. In this case, TERM does not execute.

For new observations only (that is, for observations added with the ADD or DUP command or as a result of the ADD option in a PROC FSEDIT statement), variables with the REQUIRED attribute are checked for values. If any required fields are empty, TERM does not execute. Instead, the empty required fields are highlighted, using the error attributes specified in the FSEDIT Attributes window, and an error message displays. Users must provide values for all required fields before TERM executes.

By default, a user can issue an OVERRIDE command to override the error message and create a new observation with missing values for the required variables. To prevent this, you can change the OVERRIDE parameter by specifying **N** in the **Override on required** field in the FSEDIT Parms window.

Executing the TERM Section

After any preliminary processing is completed, the SCL statements in TERM execute until the section's RETURN statement is encountered. After TERM executes, the current observation in the session's data set is updated before a different observation is displayed or the FSEDIT session ends. By default, modified observations are not written immediately to the SAS data set when a user displays a different observation. Instead, modified observations are collected in memory until a user issues the SAVE command from the FSEDIT window or the AUTOSAVE value set for the FSEDIT session is reached.

The default value for the AUTOSAVE parameter is 25. You can specify a different value for a SCREEN entry by changing the value of **Autosave value** in the FSEDIT Parms window when you build the SCREEN entry. For example, if you change **Autosave value** to 1, the SAS data set is updated each time a user makes modifications and displays a different observation. This decreases the performance of your application by causing more disk access, but it reduces the chance that changes are lost in the event the application is interrupted before a user modifies the number of observations specified for the AUTOSAVE parameter.

Forcing the TERM Section to Execute

By default, TERM executes only if one or more fields associated with data set variables have been changed or if the observation is new. SCL provides the CONTROL TERM statement that causes TERM to execute whenever a user issues a command to leave the current observation, even if no fields have been modified. Because the FSBROWSE procedure does not allow users to modify field values, the TERM section of the SCL program in an FSBROWSE application cannot execute unless a CONTROL TERM statement is in effect.

See Chapter 9 for information on using the CONTROL TERM statement.

Processing the FSETERM Section

Statements in the FSETERM section typically perform actions such as:

□ closing other SAS data sets and external files opened by the entry

□ exporting values through macro variables.

Because no observation is displayed when FSETERM executes, changes to window variables are meaningless in this section. FSETERM executes when a user issues an END command. While you are building the SCREEN entry, FSETERM also is executed before the FSEDIT Program window is opened when you select option 3 from the FSEDIT Menu window and select to execute the FSETERM label. FSETERM is optional and does not produce a warning at compile time if the section is omitted.

If a user has changed any fields associated with data set variables for the current observation before issuing the END command, or if the observation is new, TERM executes before FSETERM. If a user has modified fields, but MAIN has not yet executed, MAIN executes before TERM and FSETERM.

After any preliminary processing is completed, the SCL statements in FSETERM execute until the section's RETURN statement is encountered.

After FSETERM executes, the FSEDIT window closes and the FSEDIT session terminates. Control returns to the process that invoked the entry.

How SCL Programs Execute in FSVIEW Applications

FSVIEW applications that employ SCL are built using FORMULA entries. In FSVIEW applications, you write individual *formulas* consisting of one or more lines of SCL code for each computed variable, rather than complete SCL programs as you do in FSEDIT or SAS/AF applications. The individual formulas are collected and executed when the table of observations is displayed in the FSVIEW window.

You can use SCL formulas in FORMULA entries to perform tasks such as:

□ calculating values for columns based on user input

□ checking user-entered values against

   □ values from other columns

   □ known values stored in tables in the SCL program

   □ known values stored in secondary SAS data sets or external files

□ providing messages and help to users.

Writing SCL Formulas for FORMULA Entries

Although FSVIEW provides only four lines for writing a formula, you can expand this by executing a CALL DISPLAY or CALL METHOD routine to a SAS/AF entry that contains an SCL program or by invoking a macro that contains more statements.

Note: You must be sure to issue the COMPILE command when you modify your macro.

Each formula in a FORMULA entry should be a self-contained block of SCL code. For example, if you open a SAS data set in a formula, you should close the data set within that same formula.

Note: The FSVIEW procedure does not support any of the reserved labels described for SAS/AF entries and FSEDIT SCREEN entries.

How the FSVIEW Procedure Executes Formulas

FSVIEW executes each formula in the following manner:

□ FSVIEW executes the SCL statement block for each formula for every observation displayed in the window when:

   □ the FSVIEW window opens

   □ a user scrolls the observations displayed in the window (for example, by issuing FORWARD and BACKWARD commands)

   □ a user issues the MODIFY command in the FSVIEW window

   □ a user makes an observation active while in record-level access

   □ a user adds a new observation.

   When a user changes an observation, only the SCL block for each formula for the changed observation executes.

□ Formulas for displayed variables execute from left to right in the order in which the corresponding columns appear in the FSVIEW window. That is, formulas for any ID columns execute first, followed by formulas for a the DROP command execute after the formulas for the shown variables in the order in which you dropped the variables.

   Note: The order in which the variables appear in the window (or in which the variables were dropped) determines execution order. The order in which you define the variables is not a factor.

   Formulas execute for each displayed row of variable values (that is, for each observation in the current FSVIEW window) in order from top to bottom in the window.

□ When users modify an observation, the FSVIEW procedure first checks whether values in the modified columns satisfy the type and informat of the corresponding variables. If not, the invalid values are highlighted, and no formulas are executed. If all modified values are valid, the SCL blocks for all formulas execute for the modified row only. The formulas for the row execute from left to right as described previously. If the modified row is the autoadd observation, the formula is not executed.

While formulas execute for each displayed row of variable values in the FSVIEW window, you can use SCL logic to perform tasks only when the FSVIEW procedure is invoked. To perform tasks only at initialization, you first need to issue a DEFINE command to define a new variable that is not in the data set. For example, on the command line in the FSVIEW window, type **define newvar**. The Define window opens, displaying the variable NEWVAR followed by an equal sign (=) and space for your SCL code.

A common task performed at initialization is associating help information with the FSVIEW window. If you have licensed SAS/AF software, you can develop custom HELP entries to be used within your FSVIEW application. To associate a HELP entry permanently with a formula, you must use SCL statements to execute the SETHELP command each time you invoke your FSVIEW session. These statements should be executed only once:

```
NEWVAR=newvar; if temp=. then do; temp=1;
call execcmdi('sethelp test.example.myhelp.help');end;
```

The variable NEWVAR is the new computed variable that is set to itself so more statements can follow. The variable TEMP serves as a flag to control when the statements in the formula are executed. The first time the formula executes, the value of TEMP is missing since it is an SCL variable that has not been referenced before and therefore has not been initialized. The missing value satisfies the IF condition and the statements in the DO block execute. The statement TEMP=1 ensures that the SETHELP command is executed only once by changing the value of TEMP so it no longer meets the IF condition.

After you have defined the computed variable, you can drop it from the display and its SCL statements still execute. To drop NEWVAR, issue the command **drop newvar** from the FSVIEW window.

Using Other Labels in SCL Programs

Although reserved labels serve a special purpose in SCL, you are free to use other labels in your programs. For example, you can use labels to designate modules to call with LINK statements or to branch to using a GOTO statement. Remember, however, that labels other than reserved labels and window variable labels are not automatically executed by default. In FSVIEW, you must define the labels in the formula currently being executed. You cannot reference a label in another formula.

There is more information on creating labeled sections in Chapter 7, "Using Program Modules."

Rules for Nonreserved Labels

Observe the following rules when adding nonreserved labels to your SCL programs:

□ The label must be a valid SAS name that is unique among the labels in the program.

□ The label must not duplicate one of the reserved labels FSEINIT, INIT, MAIN, TERM, FSETERM, PUTROW, or GETROW in an entry where they are reserved. For example, FSEINIT and FSETERM are not reserved labels in PROGRAM, FRAME, and SCL entries, and GETROW and PUTROW are not reserved labels in SCL and SCREEN entries.

□ The label must be followed by a colon (:). However, references to the label within the program must not include the colon.

For example, the following program shows how to call a labeled subroutine named RECALC from the MAIN section of an SCL program and how to use a label named ERROR as the target for a GOTO statement:

```
INIT:
   units='POUNDS';
   factor=0.10;
return;

MAIN:
   if weight=. then
      goto ERROR;
   if modified(units) then
      link RECALC;
   shipcost=weight*factor;
return;

ERROR:
   _msg_='Please specify a value for package weight.';
return;

RECALC:
   select(units);
      when('POUNDS') factor=0.10;
      when('KILOGRAMS') factor=0.22;
      otherwise;
   end;
return;

TERM:
return;
```

If the GOTO statement executes, the program jumps to the statement following the ERROR label. The statements following the ERROR label are treated as part of the MAIN section. The RETURN statement following the ERROR label ends the MAIN section.

If the LINK statement executes in the MAIN section, the program links to the RECALC section. The RETURN statement at the end of the RECALC section returns control to the program statement that follows the IF-THEN block containing the LINK statement.

Using Overlapping Sections in SCL Programs

It is not mandatory that each labeled section have its own separate RETURN statement. Once execution of statements at a reserved label begins, it continues until it encounters a RETURN statement, without regard for what other labels lie between.

For example, suppose you want to perform some of the same processing steps in both the INIT and MAIN sections, as shown in the following program fragment:

```
INIT:
    total=sum(var1,var2,var3,var4);
return;

MAIN:
    total=sum(var1,var2,var3,var4);
return;

TERM:
return;
```

You can avoid duplicating program statements by using the following construction:

```
INIT:

MAIN:
    total=sum(var1,var2,var3,var4);
return;

TERM:
return;
```

Because there is no RETURN statement at the end of INIT, the program executes the statements in MAIN as well without waiting for a user response. This means, however, that if the statements in MAIN depend on user input, they will produce unexpected results in the first execution of MAIN. In the example, if any of the variables being summed is a window variable, the program will produce unexpected results because the user will not be able to enter values before MAIN runs the first time.

34

CHAPTER *4* Defining SCL Lists for Creating Data Dynamically

Introduction

SCL supports data structures and functions for manipulating data in SCL lists. *SCL lists*, like arrays, are ordered collections of data. However, lists are more flexible than arrays in many ways.

Chapter 19, "SCL Language Elements," lists the SCL list functions and the tasks you can perform with them.

Example

This section shows you a program that creates an SCL list and the output it produces. The SCL list contains the variables in DICTIONARY.TABLES (a special read-only SQL table that stores information about all the SAS data sets and SAS data views that are allocated in the current SAS session). The variables in this view are the items of information about SAS data sets. The program produces an SCL list that is sorted in dataset order, name order, and length order.

To create the view listing the data sets, submit the following SQL procedure from the Program Editor:

```
        /*  Create the PROC SQL view DATSETS that contains information   */
        /*  about all the members of type DATA in the SAS data libraries */
        /*  that are associated with your SAS session.                   */
    proc sql noprint;
      create view datsets as
        select *
              from dictionary.tables
              where memtype = "DATA";
    quit;
```

The SCL program creates and displays an SCL list whose values come from the view DATSETS.

```
INIT:
    /* Open the view DATSETS for reading */
datasets = open('datsets', 'I');
if ( datasets > 0 ) then
  do;
        /* Make a list with NV items in it, one item per variable  */
        /* that is in the view DATSETS.                            */
    nv   = attrn(datasets, 'NVARS');
    vars = makelist(nv);

    do i = 1 to nv;
        /* Set item I in list VARS to the length of the variable. */
        /* The SETITEMN call is similar to an array assignment    */
        /*          array{i} = vLen;                              */
        /*                                                        */
      vLen  = varlen(datasets, i);
      rc = setitemn(vars, vLen, i);
        /* NAMEITEM gives item I the name of the Ith variable */
      vName = varname(datasets, i);
      x  = nameitem(vars, i, vName);
    end;
    rc = close(datasets);
        /* Print the variable names in the data set order, then   */
        /* sort by name and print, then sort by length and print  */
    rc = putlist(vars, 'Data set order:', 0);
    vars = sortlist(vars, 'NAME ASCENDING');
    rc = putlist(vars, 'Name order:', 0);
    vars = sortlist(vars,'value');
    rc = putlist(vars, 'Length order:', 0);
        /* Cleanup: delete the list we created */
    rc = dellist(vars);
  end;
else
  _msg_ = sysmsg();
return;
```

This program produces the output:

```
Data set order:(LIBNAME=8
                MEMNAME=8
                MEMTYPE=8
                MEMLABEL=40
                TYPEMEM=8
                CRDATE=8
                MODATE=8
                NOBS=8
                OBSLEN=8
                NVAR=8
                PROTECT=3
                COMPRESS=8
                REUSE=3
                BUFSIZE=8
                DELOBS=8
```

```
                                    INDXTYPE=9
                                    )[5]
                   Name order:(BUFSIZE=8
                               COMPRESS=8
                               CRDATE=8
                               DELOBS=8
                               INDXTYPE=9
                               LIBNAME=8
                               MEMLABEL=40
                               MEMNAME=8
                               MEMTYPE=8
                               MODATE=8
                               NOBS=8
                               NVAR=8
                               OBSLEN=8
                               PROTECT=3
                               REUSE=3
                               TYPEMEM=8
                               )[5]
                 Length order:(PROTECT=3
                               REUSE=3
                               BUFSIZE=8
                               COMPRESS=8
                               CRDATE=8
                               DELOBS=8
                               LIBNAME=8
                               MEMNAME=8
                               MEMTYPE=8
                               MODATE=8
                               NOBS=8
                               NVAR=8
                               OBSLEN=8
                               TYPEMEM=8
                               INDXTYPE=9
                               MEMLABEL=40
                               )[5]
```

Note: [5] is the list identifier assigned when this example was run and may be different each time the example is run.

Manipulating SCL Lists

You can create new lists and then insert numbers, character strings, and even other lists into them. You can replace or delete list items, and move them around by reversing, rotating, or sorting a list. You can also assign names to the items in a list and refer to items by their names rather than their index (position) in the list. Thus, you can use a list to implement data structures and access and assign values to list items by their names. Using this feature, you can add new fields to the list data structure or change the order of the list's items without modifying your SCL program.

   SCL lists are maintained entirely in memory. Keep this in mind as you develop your applications. If your data are more appropriately maintained in a SAS data set, you will probably want to design your application in that manner instead of trying to read the entire SAS data set into a list. However, if you know your data set will not contain a large number of observations and many variables, and you do not need to maintain data sharing, you may find it convenient to read the data set into a list. That is, you can use SCL lists for data that you would have liked to put into an array but might not have been able to because of the restrictions imposed by arrays.

Creating Data Dynamically

SCL lists are dynamic rather than static. That is, SCL programs create these lists at run time. This means list sizes are computed at run time rather than before the list is created. Further, a list's length can grow or shrink to accommodate the amount of data you want to maintain, unlike arrays, which have a fixed size.

SCL lists can contain items of mixed types, whereas SCL arrays are fixed in type. (Depending on its declaration, an array contains either numeric data or character data, but not both). One item in an SCL list can be a number and the next item can be a character string, while a third might be another list. Further, you have the freedom to replace a numeric value with a character value in a list, and vice versa. Although you can make lists that are of fixed type, you have the freedom to allow multiple types in the same list.

Identifying SCL Lists

You access lists with a list identifier, which is a unique number assigned to each list you create. This is similar to the SCL data set identifier with which you reference an open SAS data set. As with SCL data set identifiers, you do not know what number will be assigned to a list before your program executes. Therefore, you must store the list identifier in an SCL variable and then reference that variable in each operation you perform on the list. All the SCL functions that manipulate lists use a list identifier as an argument.

Note that assigning a list identifier to another variable does not copy the list. The two variables simply refer to the same list. In order to copy the contents of a list to an existing or new list, use the COPYLIST function.

Determining the Type of a List Item

In general, SCL list functions that process data values are suffixed with either N, C, or L to denote the item types of numeric, character, or list, respectively. You can use the ITEMTYPE function to determine the type of a list element and use a condition statement to determine which of the set of functions are used.

Creating New Lists

You create a new, empty list with the MAKELIST or MAKENLIST functions. You can then insert numbers, characters, or other lists into the list with the functions INSERTN, INSERTC, or INSERTL, respectively. You can also specify the default number of items in the initial list by supplying an argument to the MAKELIST function. For example, the following statement makes a list containing *n* items:

```
mylist=makelist(n);
```

Each of the *n* items will be initialized to a numeric missing value.

Note that *n* can be any nonnegative SCL numeric expression that is computed at run time, or it can be a simple nonnegative numeric constant such as 12, if you want to create a list with a known initial number of items. No matter how you create the list, you are free to expand or shrink it to contain as many items as you need, from 0 to as many items as your computer has memory to hold. You use the LISTLEN function to determine the length of a list.

Inserting and Replacing Items in Lists

You can insert and replace items in a list with the SETITEMN, SETNITEMN, SETITEMC, SETNITEMC, SETITEML, and SETNITEML functions. These functions can assign values to existing items or optionally add new items.

With arrays, you use

```
A{i}=x;
```

but with lists, you use

```
listid=setitemn(listid,x,i);
```

Use the INSERTC, INSERTL, or INSERTN function to add a new item to a list without replacing the existing items. See also "Assigning Names to List Items" later in this chapter.

Note: Character values stored SCL lists are limited to 200 characters per item.

Retrieving Values from Lists

You can retrieve the value of an item in the list with the GETITEMN, GETNITEMN, GETITEMC, GETNITEMC, GETITEML, or GETNITEML functions.

With arrays, you use

```
x=A{i};
```

but with SCL lists, you use

```
x=getitemn(listid,i);
```

See also "Assigning Names to List Items" later in this chapter.

Deleting Items from Lists

You can delete items from SCL lists by specifying the position, or index, of the item to delete, by clearing all of the values from a list, or by deleting the entire list. You can also pop items from lists, which allows you to create queues or stacks (see "Using Lists as Stacks and Queues" later in this chapter).

You can delete a list item with the DELITEM or DELNITEM function and specify the number or name of the item to delete. You can clear all the values from a list with the CLEARLIST function, which leaves the list with a length of 0. You can also delete an entire list with the DELLIST function. This function returns to the system the memory required to maintain the list and its items.

See also "Assigning Names to List Items" later in this chapter.

Referencing List Items by Index Number

List indexing is similar to array indexing. An index I specifies the position of an item in the list. The first item is at index I=1, and the last item is at index I=LISTLEN(mylistid), which is the length of the list. Thus, you can use DO loops to process all items in a list, as shown in the following example:

```
do i=1 to listlen(mylistid);
   t=itemtype(mylistid,i);
   put 'Item ' i ' is type ' t;
end;
```

Accessing Items Relative to the End of a List

It is also useful for you to be able to access items at or relative to the end of an SCL list. You can use negative indices to index an item from the end of the list. Counting from the end of a list, the last item is at index −1 and the first item is at position −*n*, where *n* is the length of the list. Thus, you do not need to subtract indices from *n* to access items relative to the end of the list. All of the SCL list functions recognize negative indices.

Indexing Errors

Indexing errors occur when you supply an invalid index to a list function, just as it is an error to use an invalid array index. Valid values for list indexes depend on the function. Some functions do not accept 0 as the index, while other functions do. Refer to the *index* or *start-index* arguments for the SCL list functions in Chapter 20, "Screen Control Language Dictionary."

Implementing Sublists and Nested Structures

SCL allows you to put one list of items inside another SCL list, thereby making a sublist of the outer list. For example, you can read the variables of a SAS data set observation into a list. You could then insert each observation into another list, and repeat this process for a range of observations in the data set. You then have a list of lists, where the "outer" list contains an element for each observation in the data set, and the "inner" sublists contain each observation. These lists are called *nested lists*.

To illustrate, consider the data set A created with the following DATA step program:

```
data a;
   input fname $ 1-12 lname $ 13-24 position $ 25-36 salary 38-42;
   cards;
   Walter      Bluerock    Developer   36000
   Jennifer    Godfrey     Manager     42000
   Kevin       Blake       Janitor     19000
   Ronald      Tweety      Publicist   29000
   ;
```

The SCL to read data set WORK.A into an SCL list is shown below. The outer list is the list in the variable DATASET. Each time through the loop, a new inner list is created. Its identifier is stored in the variable OBS, and OBS is inserted at the end of the DATASET list.

```
INIT:
```

```
dsid = open('a');
dataset = makelist();
rc = fetch(dsid);
nvars = attrn(dsid, 'NVARS');
do while (rc = 0);
   obs = makelist();
   do v = 1 to nvars;
      name = varname(dsid, v);
      type = vartype(dsid, v);
      if type = 'N' then
         rc = insertn(obs, getvarn(dsid, v), -1, name);
      else
         rc = insertc(obs, getvarc(dsid, v), -1, name);
   end;
   dataset = insertl(dataset, obs, -1);
   rc = fetch(dsid);
end;
rc = close(dsid);
call putlist(dataset, '', 2);
rc = dellist(dataset, 'recursive');
return;
```

This program produces the output:

```
(  (  FNAME='Walter'
      LNAME='Bluerock'
      POSITION='Developer'
      SALARY=36000
    )[7]      ❶
   (  FNAME='Jennifer'
      LNAME='Godfrey'
      POSITION='Manager'
      SALARY=42000
    )[9]   ❶
   (  FNAME='Kevin'
      LNAME='Blake'
      POSITION='Janitor'
      SALARY=19000
    )[11]   ❶
   (  FNAME='Ronald'
      LNAME='Tweety'
      POSITION='Publicist'
      SALARY=29000
    )[13]      ❶
  )[5]❶     ❷
```

❶ [5], [7], [9], [11], and [13] are the list identifiers assigned when this example was run. These values may be different each time the example is run.

❷ Listid 5 identifies the "outer" list. Each observation is an inner or nested list (listids 7, 9, 11, and 13).

Limitless Levels of Nesting

Nested lists are highly useful for creating collections of records or data structures. There is no limit to the amount of nesting or to the number of sublists that can be placed in a list, other than the amount of memory available to your SAS application. Further, you can create *recursive* list structures, where the list A can contain other lists that contain A either directly or indirectly. The list A can even contain itself as a list item.

Simulating Multi-dimensional Arrays with Nested Lists

You can declare multi-dimensional arrays in SCL, but all lists are one-dimensional. That is, to access an item in a list, you specify only one index. However, you can use nested lists to simulate multi-dimensional arrays. For example, to create a list structure that mimics a 2 by 3 array, you can use the following example:

```
array a[2,3] 8 _temporary_;
init:
   listid = makelist(2);
   lista = setiteml(listid, makelist(3), 1);
   listb = setiteml(listid, makelist(3), 2);
   call putlist(listid);
   do i = 1 to dim(a,1);
   do j = 1 to dim(a,2);
       a[i, j] = 10*i + j;
       put a[i,j]=;
       rc = setitemn(getiteml(listid,i), a[i,j], j);
     end;
   end;
   call putlist(listid);
return;
```

This output of this example is:

```
((. . . )[7] (. . . )[9] )[5]
A[ 1 , 1 ]=11
A[ 1 , 2 ]=12
A[ 1 , 3 ]=13
A[ 2 , 1 ]=21
A[ 2 , 2 ]=22
A[ 2 , 3 ]=23
((11 12 13 )[7] (21 22 23 )[9] )[5]
```

Note:　　[7], [9], and [5] are the list identifiers assigned when this example was run and may be different each time the example is run.

Assigning Names to List Items

SCL supports a feature called *named lists*, which allow you to assign a name to each item in a list, or only to some list items. The name can be any SCL character string, not just character strings that are valid SAS variable names, unless the list has the SASNAMES attribute.

Using the GETNITEMC, GETNITEMN, and GETNITEML functions, you can access these items by their name rather than by their position. This feature allows you to vary the contents of the list according to your application needs without having to keep track of where a particular item is in a list. You can also assign or replace values associated with a name with the SETNITEMC, SETNITEMN, or SETNITEML function. You can delete an item by its name with the DELNITEM function.

The names in a list do not have to be unique (unless the list has the NODUPNAMES attribute). Item names are converted to upper case, and trailing blanks are ignored when searching the list for a matching name. Thus, the names 'abc' and 'Abc' are converted to 'ABC'. If there are duplicate names, the functions find the first occurrence of the name (although you can specify any occurrence of the item you want). By inserting a new item at the beginning of the list, you can ''hide'' a previous value since a named search will find your new item first by default. When you want to restore the previous value, simply delete the new item from the list.

You can freely mix named items with unnamed items in a list. You can also use both kinds of indexing (by name or by index) in any list, regardless of how the list was created or whether all, some, or no items have names.

Indexing a Named Item by its Position

You can find the index of a named item in a list with the NAMEDITEM function. This allows you to access an item later by its index in the list, which is a faster search. However, searching by index is not safe if the index of the item might change between the time you find the index and the time you use the index.

The following statement replaces the value associated with the first occurrence of the item named **ACME** in the list NUMBERS with the value **(201) 555-2263**. These statements do not modify the list if the name **ACME** is not found:

```
i=nameditem(numbers,'Acme');
if i>0 then
    rc=setitemc(numbers,'(201) 555-2263',i);
```

Determining or Replacing an Item's Name

You can replace the name of an item with the NAMEITEM function. You can also use NAMEITEM when you want to find out the name of an item but you do not want to change the item's name.

Finding an Occurrence of a Name

In general, the functions that allow you to access a list item by its name operate on the first occurrence of the name by default. However, you can combine the optional arguments *occurrence* and *start-index* to refer to items other than the first occurrence. *Occurrence* allows you to specify the number of the occurrence of a named item that you want to find. For example, a value of three references the third occurrence, and a value of ten references the tenth occurrence. The following example demonstrates how to find the indexes of the first and third item named **SCL**.

```
    /* default occurrence is 1    */
first=nameditem(listid,'SCL');
    /* Find the third occurrence */
third=nameditem(listid,'SCL',3);
```

Specifying Where the Search for an Item Starts

The *start-index* argument specifies the position in the list to begin the search for a named item. The default is 1, which means the search begins at the first item in the list. If the value for *start-index* is negative, then the search starts at position ABS(*start-index*) from the end of the list and searches toward the front of the list. For example, a *start-index* of −1 references the list's last item, while a *start-index* of −2 references the list's second-to-last item. Thus, to change the value of the last occurrence of a list item named **X** to the value *y*, you can use a statement like the following:

```
listid=setnitemn(listid,y,'X',1,-1);
```

Using Shared Data Environments

A feature available with SCL lists is support for shared data environments. In earlier versions of SCL, if you wanted an entry to pass data to many other entries, you had to pass the data explicitly in each CALL DISPLAY statement or you had to put the values in macro variables. However, macro variables are limited in the amount of data they can contain (only scalar values) and to names that are valid SAS names. By placing data in a shared data environment, other programs and even other SAS applications can retrieve the data via a name. These names can be any valid SCL string, and the value associated with a name can be a numeric or character value or an entire list.

The two kinds of shared data environments are implemented with local SCL lists and global SCL lists.

Local Data Environment

Each SAS System application (such as an FSEDIT application, or a SAS/AF application started with the AF command) maintains its own application environment in a local environment list. You can store information that is local to the application, but which you want shared among all of an application's entries, in this local environment list. The function ENVLIST('L') returns the list identifier of the environment list for the current application. Other applications' lists are maintained in the memory of each application, and even though two lists in different applications may have the same list identifier, the lists are actually different. This is analogous to the same data set identifier being used by different SAS applications, although this identifier actually refers to different data sets opened at different times. For more details, see the ENVLIST function in Chapter 20, "SCL Dictionary."

Global Data Environment

There is also a global environment list that stores data that can be shared across all SAS applications started in the same SAS session. For example, one SAS application may place some data in the global environment list and then close. Another application may then open and read the data created by the first application. The global environment list is accessible via the list identifier returned by ENVLIST('G'). For more details, see the ENVLIST function in Chapter 20, "SCL Dictionary."

Using Lists as Stacks and Queues

You can create lists that function as stacks (first in, last out lists) or queues (first in, first out lists).

Using a List as a Stack

When you want to use a list as a stack, you use the INSERTC, INSERTN, or INSERTL function to insert an item into a list. The default insertion position for these functions is the beginning of the list, so you need only specify the list identifier and the data to be inserted.

To pop an item from a stack, use either the POPN, POPC, or POPL function. You can use the ITEMTYPE function to determine the type of the item at the top of the stack if your application does not know the type. If your application always puts the same data type onto your stack (for example, the stack is a stack of character strings and you only put items into the list with INSERTC), then you do not need to use ITEMTYPE to check the type of the item at the top of the stack before popping.

You can delete the top item in the stack with the DELITEM or DELNITEM functions if you do not want to keep the top value.

You can replace the top item with the SETITEMN, SETITEMC, or SETITEML function. You should not attempt to pop or delete an item unless you are sure the list contains at least one item.

You can use the LISTLEN function to return the length of the list before you use a function to pop or delete an item.

Using a List as a Queue

When you use a list as a queue, you also put items in the list with the INSERTN, INSERTC, or INSERTL function. However, you use an item index of −1 to insert the item at the end of the list.

To remove an item, you use the POPN, POPC, or POPL function with a negative index to pop items from the list. As with stacks, you should use the ITEMTYPE and LISTLEN functions to verify the item's type and the list's length before popping an item from the list.

For example,

```
INIT:
    listid=makelist();
    rc=insertc(listid,'1st',-1);
    rc=insertc(listid,'2nd',-1);
    rc=insertc(listid,'3rd',-1);
    rc=insertc(listid,'4th',-1);
    rc=insertc(listid,'5th',-1);
    put 'Test of first in, first out queue:';
    do i=1 to listlen(listid);
        cval=popc(listid);
        put i= cval=;
    end;
return;
```

This program produces the output:

```
Test of first in, first out queue:
I=1 CVAL=1st
```

```
I=2 CVAL=2nd
I=3 CVAL=3rd
I=4 CVAL=4th
I=5 CVAL=5th
```

Assigning List and Item Attributes

You can assign attributes to lists or to items in a list. Attributes are useful to control the use and modification of lists. For example, you can specify that a list is not available for update, which means that other programs called by your program (for example, via CALL DISPLAY) cannot change the data in the list or cannot add or delete items from the list. You can also assign attributes such as NOUPDATE and/or NODELETE to individual items in a list.

Since it is easy to change the type of any item in a list by simply replacing the value with a new value, it would be quite easy for one application to accidentally change a list in a way you did not intend. You can also specify that a list or items in a list have fixed type, so that another program cannot change a numeric value to a character value, etc. By assigning the proper attributes to the lists and items you create, you need not worry about other parts of the application corrupting your data, and you can avoid adding additional data validation statements to your programs.

Assigning list and item attributes is not required, but it can ease the process of application development because an attempt to violate an attribute, which indicates a bug in the application, causes the application to stop with a fatal error. Use the SETLATTR function to set the attributes of a list or item. The GETLATTR function returns a string describing the current attributes, and the HASATTR function returns 1 if the list or item has the specified attribute and 0 if it does not.

Using File Interfaces

Two SCL list functions allow you to store lists in SAS catalog entries or external files and to read lists from these files. The SAVELIST function stores a list, and the FILLIST function reads data from a catalog entry or external file and fills a list with the text from the file.

Saving Nested Lists to SCL Entries

When you save a list that contains sublists, both the list and its sublists are saved in the same SLIST entry. Thus, if the list data structures you create are highly recursive and have many cycles, you should be careful about saving your lists.

Suppose list A contains list B. When you save list A, you also save list B at the same time. Therefore, you do not need to save list B separately; list B is already stored in list A. In fact, if you store the lists in two separate SLIST entries and try to read them back, you do not get the same list structure you stored originally.

This example creates two lists, A and B, (with text values in them to identify their contents) and inserts list B into list A. It then saves them each to separate SLIST entries, A.SLIST and B.SLIST. Then, the program creates two more lists, APRIME and BPRIME, reads the two saved SLIST entries into those two lists, and then prints all the listids and list values.

```
INIT:
  a = makelist();
  a = insertc(a, 'This is list A');
  b = makelist();
  b = insertc(b, 'This string is in list B');
```

```
       a = insertl(a, b); /* insert B into A */

       rc=savelist('CATALOG','SASUSER.LISTS.A.SLIST', A);
       rc=savelist('CATALOG','SASUSER.LISTS.B.SLIST', B);

       other SCL statements...

       aPrime=makelist();
       bPrime=makelist();
       rc=fillist('CATALOG','SASUSER.LISTS.A.SLIST', aPrime);
       rc=fillist('CATALOG','SASUSER.LISTS.B.SLIST', bPrime);

       bInA = getiteml(aPrime);
       put a= b= aPrime= bPrime= bInA=;
       call putlist(a, 'List A:',0);
       call putlist(b, 'List B:',0);
       call putlist(aPrime, "List A':",0);
       call putlist(bPrime, "List B':",0);
   return;
```

Here is the output:

```
A=5 B=7 APRIME=9 BPRIME=11 BINA=13

List A:(('This string is in list B'
         )[7]
         'This is list A'
         )[5]
List B:('This string is in list B'
         )[7]
List A':(('This string is in list B'
          )[13]
          'This is list A'
          )[9]
List B':('This string is in list B'
          )[11]
```

Note here that the sublist B (13) read from A.SLIST is not the same as the sublist BPRIME (11) read from B.SLIST. That is, while A contains B, APRIME does not contain BPRIME.

Also note that the structures of list A and list APRIME are the same but the listids are different and do not match any of the listids read from B.SLIST.

Note: [5], [7], [9], [11], and [13] are the list identifiers assigned when this example was run and may be different each time the example is run.

Advantages

There is an advantage to the recursive nature of the SAVELIST function. For example, if list A contains sublists B and C, SAVELIST saves all three lists when you save A to an SLIST entry. Your application can take advantage of this if you have several unrelated lists that you want to save. By creating a new list and inserting the lists you want saved in the new list, you can save them all in one SLIST entry with one SAVELIST call, instead of saving each sublist in a separate SLIST entry with separate SAVELIST calls.

CHAPTER 5 Using SAS® Data Sets

Introduction

Whether you are designing menu-driven applications with SAS/AF software or a data entry and retrieval system with SAS/FSP software, you may want to write Screen Control Language (SCL) programs that can read or manipulate data stored in SAS data sets.

For example, when designing a menu-driven application, you may want to update one or more data sets based on user transactions from a single user interface. For a data entry and retrieval system, you may want to use a secondary data set to supplement the primary FSEDIT data set. You can use the secondary data set as a table lookup for sophisticated error checking and field validation. In addition, you may want to manipulate data sets to perform a task like the following:

□ display data set values in a window

□ create a new data set

□ copy, rename, sort, or delete a data set

□ index a SAS data set.

Many of the functions that perform data set operations return a SAS System return code, called *sysrc.* Chapter 18, "SAS System Return Codes" contains a list of return codes with a section for operations most commonly performed on data sets. You can check for these codes to write sophisticated error checking for your SCL programs.

The following sections describe the tasks your SCL programs can perform on SAS data sets with summary information about the SCL function or routine to use to perform that task. For details on those functions and routines, see the appropriate entry in Chapter 20, "SCL Dictionary".

Accessing SAS Data Sets

Before your applications can access the values in a SAS data set, you must establish a communication link between the SAS System, the data sets, and your application programs. You start this communication link by assigning librefs to the data libraries or directories in which the data sets are stored. You complete the communication link between the data sets and the SCL program by using the SCL OPEN function to open the data sets.

Some SCL call routines, such as CALL FSEDIT and CALL FSVIEW automatically open the data set they are editing. Therefore, the OPEN function is not needed to open the dataset specified on the CALL routine.

Assigning Librefs

You can assign librefs outside your SCL application when data sets are used by all of the application or by large parts of the application. To assign librefs outside the application, put the LIBNAME statement in the application's start-up file, often called an *autoexec file*. For more information on assigning librefs outside of your SCL program, see the SAS System documentation for your host operating system.

When data sets are not used by all or large parts of the application, you can also assign librefs from inside your SCL program by using the the LIBNAME function.

If you have SAS/SHARE or SAS/CONNECT installed at your location, you can also assign librefs using Remote Library Services. Remote Library Services (RLS) allows your SCL applications read or write access to data sets, views and catalogs across hardware platforms and SAS releases. SAS data sets and views have transparent RLS access for releases 6.11 and later. SAS data sets have transparent RLS access for releases 6.10 and earlier. Catalog compatibility across platforms is architecture dependent. For further information see *SAS/SHARE Software: Usage and Reference, Version 6, First Edition.*

Opening SAS Data Sets

Opening a SAS data set provides the gateway through which your application and data set can interact. This process does not actually access the information in the data set but makes it available for the program's use. The program accesses the information in the file by performing read operations on the data set.

The primary method of establishing a communication link between your application and the data sets it uses is with the OPEN function. However, there are some exceptions, for example, the FSEDIT and FSVIEW routines can open a data set and do not require the use of the OPEN function.

When you open a SAS data set, the following actions take place:

□ A temporary storage buffer called the data set data vector is automatically created for the data set. This storage area is used to store copies of the data set variable values found in the data set.

□ A unique numeric data set identifier is assigned to the data set. This identifier is used by other functions that manipulate data.

□ An access control level is assigned to the data set. This control level determines the level of access to the data set permitted to other users or applications that try to use the data set at the same time.

The OPEN function returns a unique, positive number, the *data set identifier*, which identifies the data set to the application. The data set identifier is used with other SCL functions that manipulate the data set. Because this number is unique for each currently open data set, it is useful in tracking multiple open data sets at the same time.

Note: If for some reason a data set cannot be opened, the OPEN function returns a value of 0 for the data set identifier. Therefore, to determine whether a data set has been opened successfully, test the value of the return code for the OPEN function in your SCL program. This technique ensures that you don't cause your program to halt by passing a 0 to another function that uses that data set identifier. You can use the SYSMSG() function to retrieve the message associated with the return code to determine why the data set could not be opened.

Number of Open Data Sets Allowed

In SCL your application can have a maximum of 999 data sets open simultaneously. However, your operating system may impose other limits. For further details, consult the SAS documentation for your operating system. You also can refer to the documentation provided by the vendor for your operating system.

Although SCL permits you to have a large number of data sets open simultaneously, be aware that memory is allocated for each data set from the time the data set is opened until it is closed. Therefore, try to minimize the number of data sets that are open at the same time and close them as soon as your program finishes with them for that session.

Data Set and SCL Data Vectors

When an SCL application opens a data set, the SAS System automatically opens a temporary storage area to hold the values of data set variables. This storage area, which is unique for each open data set, is called the *data set data vector* (DDV).

Initially, when you open a data set, its DDV is empty. However, to enable your application to work with the data set variables, you use SCL functions to copy the data set observations one at a time from the data set to the DDV. Once variable values for an observation are in the DDV, you can copy these values into the *SCL data vector* (SDV). From the SDV, your application can manipulate the variable values.

Before you can display or manipulate the values of data set variables, those variables must be linked to SCL variables through the DDV and the SDV. Special SCL functions and storage locations facilitate the transfer of values between SAS data sets and SCL variables. Figure 5.1 illustrates the SDV and the DDV created for an application that opens a SAS data set. This figure shows the paths taken by observations when they are read from the data set, displayed in the window, processed, and then returned to the data set.

Figure 5.1   *Path of Data in Data Set Read and Write Operations*

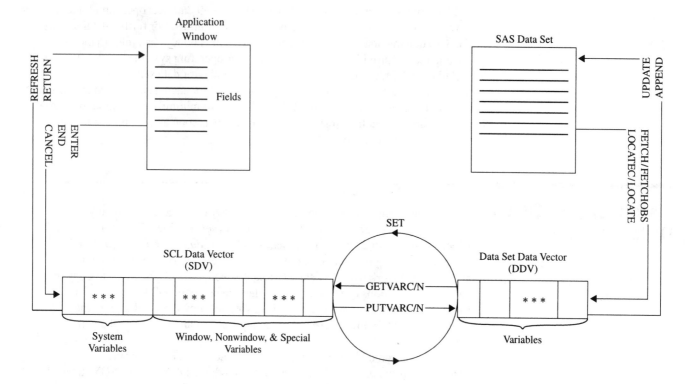

Two steps are required to transfer data from an open SAS data set to an SCL program:

1. The values of the variables for an observation in the open SAS data set are copied into the DDV.

2. The values of the variables in the DDV are copied to the SCL Data Vector (SDV). The SDV contains all the SCL variables (window variables, nonwindow variables, and system variables). The transfer of data from the DDV to the SDV can be either automatic (when SET is used) or under program control (when GETVARC or GETVARN are used).

Once the data are in the SDV, they can be manipulated using the normal SCL statements.

Two steps are also required to transfer data from an SCL program to an open SAS data set:

1. The values of the variables in the SDV are transferred to the DDV. The transfer of data from the SDV to the DDV can be either automatic (when SET is used) or under program control (when PUTVARC or PUTVARN are used).

2. The values in the DDV are written to the variables for an observation in the open SAS data.

Access Control Levels

When a data set is opened, the SAS System determines the control level for the data set. The *control level* is the extent to which access to the data set is restricted. For example, your application may be able to gain exclusive update access to the entire data set, or it may be able to gain exclusive update access to only the observation it is currently using. In either case, there are ramifications for any users or applications needing to access the data set at the same time. You can open the data set with one of the following control levels:

RECORD

The application gains exclusive update access only to the data set observation currently read (as with the FETCH and FETCHOBS functions). Therefore, with this control level, the same user can open the same data set multiple times (*multiple concurrent access*), or multiple users can open the same data set simultaneously for browsing or for editing if SAS/SHARE is used. However, to take advantage of RECORD-level locking for multiple users, you must use SAS/SHARE software, which permits concurrent access to data sets. For more information, refer to *SAS/SHARE Software: Usage and Reference, Version 6, First Edition.*

MEMBER

The application gains exclusive update access to the entire data set. No other user can open the data set while this control level is in effect and the same user cannot open the data set multiple times.

Specifying a Control Level

When you use the OPEN function to open a SAS data set in UPDATE mode, by default the data set is opened with RECORD-level control. However, in SCL you can use the CNTLLEV= data set option with the OPEN function to set the control level when you open a data set.

Reading SAS Data Sets

Many SCL programs may need to manipulate the variable values stored in SAS data sets. For example, you may want to

□ display data values in a window

□ use the values in arithmetic calculations

□ determine data values before taking certain actions.

Before you can manipulate the data, you must read them from the data set. After you manipulate the data, if the data values have changed, you can update the variable values in the data set. In addition to updating existing variable values, you also can add new data set observations or delete obsolete observations.

Once the data set is open (see "Opening SAS Data Sets" on page 50), you can access any of the variable values for all the observations in the data set. The first step in accessing the data involves reading, or copying, an observation from the data set to the DDV. To read an observation, you can use the FETCH function. By default, the FETCH function starts with the first observation in the data set and reads the next observation from the data set each time it executes.

Linking Data Set And SCL Variables

The next step in accessing the data is to link the data set variable values in the DDV with the SCL window and program variable values in the SDV. The function you use depends on whether the SCL variables and data set variables have the same name and type. If your application has some SCL variables that match data set variables and others that do not, you can use a combination of these techniques.

Variables with Matching Names

If your data set and SCL variables have the same names and types, you can link all of them automatically with a single SET routine statement. This is typically invoked immediately following the OPEN function.

Variables with Unmatched Names

When you have SCL variables that do not have the same names and types as data set variables, you must use a GETVARC or GETVARN statement for each unmatched variable to link them from the DDV to the SDV. Once the variables have been manipulated, use an individual PUTVARC or PUTVARN routine to link each one from the SDV back to the DDV.

If you use the SET routine and then also use the PUTVARC or PUTVARN routine for a data set variable that has a matching SCL variable, the CALL SET overrides the PUTVARC or PUTVARN.

To link one data set variable value in the DDV to the corresponding variable value in the SDV, you can use the GETVARC and GETVARN functions for character and numeric values, respectively. Both of these functions link only one variable at a time. Therefore, you must use the GETVARC or GETVARN function one time for each data set variable you want to link.

Note: The GETVARC and GETVARN functions establish only a temporary link between a data set variable and an SCL variable. When the statement executes, the variables are linked. After the statement executes, the link is terminated. This is different from the SET routine, which establishes a permanent link between any matching data set and SCL variables.

Determining a Variable's Data Set Position

Some functions, such as GETVARC, GETVARN, PUTVARC and PUTVARN, require a variable's data set position. If you do not know the position, you can use the VARNUM function to determine the position. Then, you can use the position repeatedly throughout your program.

The following SAS/AF example shows the VARNUM function used to determine the position of several variables. After the variable positions have been determined, the program links to a labeled section called GETVALUE to determine the variable values.

```
INIT:
   control enter;
   houses=open('sasuser.houses','u');
   if (houses=0) then _msg_=sysmsg();
   else
      do;
         rc=fetch(houses);
         vtype=varnum (houses,'style');
         vsize=varnum(houses,'sqfeet');
         vbedrms=varnum(houses,'bedrooms');
         vbathrms=varnum(houses,'baths');
         vaddress=varnum(houses,'street');
         vcost=varnum(houses,'price');
         link getvalue;
      end;
return;

MAIN:
   if (modified(cost)) then
      do;
             more SCL statements
         rc=update(houses);
         _msg_='Record has been updated.' ;
      end;
   else if (houses>0) then
      do;
         rc=fetch(houses);
         if (rc ne 0) then _msg_=sysmsg();
         link getvalue;
      end;
return;

TERM:
   if (houses>0) then rc=close(houses);
return;
GETVALUE:
   type=getvarc(houses,vtype);
   size=getvarn(houses,vsize);
   bedrms=getvarn(houses,vbedrms);
   bathrms=getvarn(houses,vbathrms);
   address=getvarc(houses,vaddress);
   cost=getvarn(houses,vcost);
return;
```

Using Table-Lookup Techniques

Table lookup, the process of looking up data in a data structure, has several useful
applications for data entry applications. For example, you may want to display
certain information in a window based on a value a user has entered. If this
information is stored in another data set, you can use table-lookup techniques to read
and display this information. In addition, you can use table lookup to perform field
validation by ensuring that a user-entered value is a valid value contained in a
specified data set.

Validating Field Values

In SAS/AF applications you can perform simple table-lookup validation without SCL. In this case, field values can be automatically compared against a list of values specified as the field's **List** attribute or in an associated LIST entry. However, with SCL you are not limited to comparing field values against static lists defined in the application. Instead, you can compare field values against variable values stored in a SAS data set. This technique provides more powerful table lookups for your SAS/AF applications in addition to a means of table lookup for your SAS/FSP applications.

To validate a field, you can use the LOCATEC, LOCATEN, or WHERE functions to search a secondary data set for a specific character or numeric value that has been entered by a user. For example, you might want to make sure that users enter names that exist in another data set.

Displaying Information from Data Sets in FSEDIT

In addition to using table-lookup techniques for field validation, in FSEDIT applications you also can use these techniques to display text from a secondary data set based on values that users enter in the fields. For example, when a user enters a valid name in the **Employee Name** field, you can look up the associated sales region and sales to date in the secondary data set and then display this information in the window.

In this case, you can use LOCATEC, LOCATEN, or WHERE along with FETCH to search the data set for the appropriate observation and read it into the DDV. After the values are in the DDV, you can use GETVARC or GETVARN to link the values to the SCL data vector (SDV). Once the data set and SCL variables are linked, the data are automatically displayed in the window.

Controlling Access to Data Set Observations

In many situations, you may want to read from a data set only observations that meet a set of specified conditions, or search criteria. For example, if you have a data set containing sales records, you may want to read just the subset of records for which the sales are greater than $300,000 but less than $600,000. To do this, you can use WHERE clause processing.

A *WHERE clause* is a set of conditions that observations must meet to be processed. In WHERE clause processing, you can use either permanent or temporary WHERE clauses.

Permanently Subsetting the Data

A *permanent WHERE clause* applies a set of search conditions that remain in effect until the data set is closed. You might use a permanent WHERE clause to improve the efficiency of your program by reading only a subset of the observations found in a SAS data set. You might also want to use a permanent WHERE clause in applications when you may want to limit the data set observations that are accessible, or visible, to users. For example, if you are working with a large data set, users may not need access to all the observations to use your application, or, for security reasons, you may want to restrict access to a set of observations meeting certain conditions.

SCL provides several features that enable you to subset a data set based on specified search conditions. To apply a permanent WHERE clause to a data set, you can use the WHERE= data set option with the OPEN function. For example, the following WHERE data set options selects only the records for which the sales are greater than $300,000 but less than $600,000:

```
/* Open the data set and enable users to access   */
/* a subset of the data set observations          */
salesid=open("sample.testdata(where=((sales > 300000)"||
           "and (sales < 600000)))",'i');
```

You can also use the WHERE= option with the FSEDIT or FSVIEW routines.

Enabling Users to Request Their Own Subset

In addition to restricting users' access to data set observations, you may want to enable users to subset the accessible records even further. In this case, you can apply a temporary WHERE clause with the WHERE function. A *temporary WHERE clause* applies a set of search conditions that can be modified or canceled by subsequent SCL statements. For example, suppose the data set is indexed on the variable SSN (social security number). You could apply a temporary WHERE clause like this:

```
rc=where(dsid, 'SSN='||ssn);
```

Searching with WHERE versus LOCATEC or LOCATEN

You can search efficiently with the WHERE function if you are working with a large data set that is indexed by the variable or variables you are searching for. It is also appropriate to use the WHERE function to locate observations meeting a set of search conditions when you are locating observations based on an expression involving several variables.

However, you can use LOCATEC or LOCATEN to find an observation when

□ the data set is small

□ you are searching for one observation meeting a single search condition (the observation containing a particular name)

□ you are looking for one observation meeting a single search condition in a large data set, if the data set is sorted by the variable you are searching for and you are using the more efficient binary search. See the following section for more information.

Searching Efficiently

By default, LOCATEC and LOCATEN search a SAS data set sequentially. However, a sequential search is not always the most efficient way to locate a particular observation, especially if your data set is sorted.

If a data set is already sorted by the variable you want to search for, you can specify a faster, more efficient binary search. For a binary search, use an additional optional argument with LOCATEC or LOCATEN to specify the order in which the data set is sorted (**A** for ascending order or **D** for descending order).

For example, assuming the SASUSER.CLASS data set is sorted in ascending order of NAME, you can use the following statement to perform a binary search:

```
dsid=open('sasuser.class');
vnum=varnum(dsid,'name');
sname='Gail';
val=locatec(dsid,vnum,sname,'a');
```

Undoing WHERE clauses

When you use WHERE clauses, they impose certain restrictions on other SCL functions that manipulate data. Therefore, in some cases, you may need to undo a WHERE clause in your SCL program before using other functions.

When you specify a WHERE clause, the WHERE conditions replace the conditions specified in the previous WHERE clause. However, you can augment a WHERE condition with the ALSO keyword. For example, the following WHERE clause adds the condition of "age greater than 15" to an existing WHERE clause.

```
rc=where(dsid,'also age > 15');
```

To undo the condition added by the ALSO keyword you could use the following statement:

```
rc=where(dsid,'undo');
```

To undo, or delete, a temporary WHERE clause, use the WHERE function and specify only the data set identifier argument. This process undoes all temporary WHERE clauses currently in effect.

Updating SAS Data Sets

When you read a data set observation, the data have to follow a path from the data set through the DDV to the SDV, where finally they can be manipulated. After the data are manipulated, they must follow the reverse path back to the data set. As you have already seen, if you use the SET routine to link the values from the DDV to the SDV, when you change these variable values they are automatically linked from the SDV back to the DDV and on to the data set. If you had not used the SET routine, the final step in the process would be to copy them from the DDV back to the data set by using the UPDATE function.

Appending Observations

When you need an SCL program to add new observations to a data set rather than to update the existing observations, you can use the APPEND function. If your SCL variables have the same name and type as the data set variables and you use the SET routine to link them, using the APPEND function is straightforward and the values are automatically written from the DDV to the data set.

Note: If the SET routine has not been called or if the APPEND function is used with the NOSET option, a blank observation is appended to the data set. This is a useful technique for appending observations when the SCL program or the window variables do not match the data set variables. For example, when the SET routine is not used, you would use a sequence of statements like those below to append a blank observation and then update it with values.

```
rc=append(dsid);
one or more PUTVARC or PUTVARN program statements
rc=update(dsid);
```

Deleting Observations

When you need an SCL program to delete observations from a data set, use the DELOBS function. When you use this function, the data set must be open in UPDATE mode.

The DELOBS function performs the following tasks:

□ marks the observation for deletion from the data set. However, the observation is still physically in the data set.

□ prevents any additional editing of the observation. Once an observation has been marked for deletion, it cannot be read.

Remaining Observations Not Renumbered

Although deleted observations are no longer accessible, all other observations retain their original physical observation numbers. Therefore, it is important to remember that an observation's physical number may not always coincide with its relative position in the data set. For example, the FETCHOBS function treats an observation value as a relative observation number. If observation 2 is marked for deletion and you use FETCHOBS to read the third observation, it reads the third *non-deleted* observation, in this case observation 4. However, you can use FETCHOBS with the ABS option to count deleted observations.

Non-deleted observations are not renumbered intentionally for the following reasons:

□ You can continue to use observation numbers as pointers. This is important when using the FSEDIT procedure or subsequent SAS statements that directly access observations by number, such as the POINT= option in a SAS language SET statement.

□ You can control observation renumbering if necessary.

Renumbering Observations

To renumber accessible data set observations, you must re-create the data set using one of the following techniques:

□ Read the remaining data set observations using the base SAS language SET statement (in a DATA step), and write these observations to a data set. (Use the SET statement available in base SAS software, not the SCL SET routine.) To avoid exiting from SCL, you can use a submit block.

```
dsid=open('sasuser.houses','u');
rc=fetch(dsid);  /* fetch first observation to DDV */
rc=delobs(dsid); /* delete first observation       */
rc=close(dsid);  /* close data set                 */
submit continue;
    data sasuser.houses;
        set sasuser.houses;
    run;
endsubmit;
return;
```

□ Copy the data set using either the COPY procedure or the COPY function in SCL. In this case, the input and output data sets must be different. The output data set is the only one renumbered.

□ Sort the data set using the SORT procedure or the SCL SORT function.

Note:　If the data set is already in sorted order, you must use the FORCE option.

Closing SAS Data Sets

After you have finished using a data set, you should close it with the CLOSE function at the appropriate point in your program. If a data set is still open when an application ends, the SAS System closes it automatically and displays a warning message.

In general, the position of the CLOSE function should complement the position of the OPEN function as listed in the following table.

If the OPEN function is in ...	Put the CLOSE function in ...
FSEINIT	FSETERM
INIT (in SAS/AF applications)	TERM (in SAS/AF applications)
MAIN	MAIN

Note: If you're designing a SAS/AF application in which more than one SCL program uses a specific data set, and the identifier for this data set can be passed to subsequent programs, close the data set in the TERM section of the last program that uses the data set.

Changing the Sequence of Reading Observations

When an application displays a subset of a SAS data set, you may want to let users display and scroll through all observations meeting the search conditions. To do this, you can use several SCL functions that enable you to reread observations. For example, when the program displays the first observation that meets the conditions, a user can mark it. Then they can continue to search the rest of the data set for any other observations meeting the search conditions, counting them along the way. After the last observation meeting the search criteria, the user can return to the first observation in the subset, the observation marked earlier. To implement this technique, you can use the sequence of steps shown in the following table:

Step	Use the Function ...	To ...
1	NOTE	mark an observation in the subset for later reading.
2	POINT	return to the observation you marked after you have located all observations meeting the search conditions.
3	DROPNOTE	delete the NOTE marker and free the memory used to store the note after you are finished using the noted observation.

Determining Attributes of Data Sets and Variables

For some applications, you need to determine characteristics of the data set or the data set variables you are working with in your SCL program. For instance, one approach is to determine the number of variables in the existing data set and then set up a program loop that executes one time for each variable. In the loop, you can query the attributes of each variable. To do this, you need to determine the following information:

□ the number of variables in the existing SAS data set

□ the name, type, length, format, informat, label, and position of each variable in the data set.

The following sections describe the SCL functions you can use to determine this. The functions also provide other information about SAS data sets and their variables. To use these functions, you must have opened the SAS data set and assigned a variable to contain its data set identifier value.

Querying Attributes of Data Sets

Data sets have a variety of numeric and character attributes associated with them. These attributes can provide some basic information to your SCL program. For example, to determine the number of variables in an existing SAS data set, use the NVARS argument to the ATTRN function. For a list of these attributes and how to retrieve them, refer to the ATTRC and ATTRN functions in Chapter 20.

Querying Attributes of Data Set Variables

Data set variables also have several attributes you may need to query for your program. The following table lists the attributes for data set variables that you can query and the SCL function to use.

To determine the ...	Use the function ...
unique values of a variable	VARLEVEL
variable name	VARNAME
variable number	VARNUM
variable type	VARTYPE
variable length	VARLEN
variable label	VARLABEL
variable format	VARFMT
variable informat	VARINFMT

Defining New Variables

After you have determined the name, type, length, label, format, and informat of each existing variable, you can add a new variable with these attributes to the variable list for a new data set. To do this, use the OPEN function with the `'N'` argument (for new mode) and then use the NEWVAR function.

▶ *Caution: Your program should check to see if the data set exists before opening it in New mode.*

The OPEN function used with *mode* `'N'` replaces an existing data set with the same name.

. . . .

Other Data Set Manipulations

There are other SCL functions that you can use to perform operations on SAS data sets. The tasks you can perform are listed in the following table, along with the function to use.

When you want to ...	Use the function ...
copy a data set	COPY* (use with a WHERE clause to create a new data set containing a subset of the observations in the original data set)
create a new data set	OPEN with *mode* NEW (data set must be closed and reopened in UPDATE mode if the program will update it). Use NEWVAR to create variables.
enable users to create a new data set interactively	NEW
enable users to create a new data set interactively from an external file	IMPORT
delete a data set	DELETE (the data set must be closed)
rename a data set	RENAME (the data set must be closed)
sort a data set	SORT (the data set must be opened in UPDATE mode).

* By default, if the target file already exists, the COPY function replaces that file without warning. To avoid unintentionally overwriting existing files, your program should check to see if the target file exists before executing the COPY function.

Manipulating Data Set Indexes

When you develop an application that creates a data set, you also may want to offer users the option of creating an index for that data set. An *index*, which provides fast access to observations, is an auxiliary data structure that specifies the location of observations based on the values of one or more variables, known as *key variables*. SAS data sets, both compressed and uncompressed, can be indexed by one or more variables to aid in the subsetting, grouping, or joining of observations. Data set indexes are particularly useful for optimizing WHERE-clause processing.

To create and manipulate data set indexes, you can use a set of SCL functions. However, SCL functions are just one means of building and querying data set indexes. Other means include:

□ the DATASETS procedure in base SAS software

□ the INDEX= option when creating a SAS dataset

□ the SQL procedure in base SAS software

□ the ACCESS window.

There are two types of indexes:

□ simple indexes

□ composite indexes.

A *simple index* is an index on a single variable, and a *composite index* is an index on more than one variable. A SAS data set can have multiple simple indexes, composite indexes, or a combination of these.

Creating Indexes

To create an index, use the ICREATE function after you have opened the data set in UTILITY mode.

Listing an Index's Variables

To list the variables in an index, use the IVARLIST function. This function returns the list of one or more variables indexed for the specified key in the SAS data set.

Determining Variables in Indexes

To find out if a specific variable is part of an index, you can use the ISINDEX function. The ISINDEX function returns the type of index for a variable in a SAS data set as follows:

BOTH   The variable is a member of both simple and composite indexes.

COMP   The variable is a member of a composite index.

REG   The variable is a member of a regular (simple) index.

blank   No index has been created for the specified variable.

Determining Index Options

To find the options and key variables for an index, you can use the IOPTION function. The IOPTION function returns a character string that consists of the options, separated by blanks, for the specified key and index variables.

Deleting Indexes

If you are finished with an index or you find that the index is not operating efficiently, you can delete it using the IDELETE function. Keep in mind that indexes are not always advantageous. Sometimes the costs outweigh the savings. For a detailed discussion of when to use indexes, refer to Chapter 6, "SAS Files," in *SAS Language: Reference, Version 6, First Edition.* To delete an index:

□ open the data set in UTILITY mode, (**v**)

□ specify the index to be deleted using the IDELETE function.

CHAPTER 6 Using External Files

Introduction

In addition to using Screen Control Language (SCL) to manipulate your SAS data sets, you also can use SCL to manipulate external files. *External files* are the files created and maintained on your host operating system (for example, files you have created with your system editor or files in which you have stored the output of SAS procedures).

When you use external files to store data or other information, you can use SCL functions to read files, update the contents of files, write information to new files, and perform utility operations on files. These functions enable you to create SCL programs for SAS/AF and SAS/FSP applications that

☐ read values from external files for field validation

☐ manipulate data values that your site maintains in external files

☐ write information in a form readable by applications created with the software of other vendors.

Your operating system maintains groups of external files in an aggregate storage location, which this book calls a *directory*. However, your operating system may identify these locations with different names (for example, partitioned data set, MACLIB, or subdirectory). If you need more details, refer to the SAS documentation for your operating system.

Using SCL, you can also perform operations easily on multiple files in the same directory. This process is simplified by the fact that you do not have to assign a fileref to each file before you open it. You can assign a fileref to the directory and then open as many of its files as your task requires.

Many of the functions that perform external file operations return a SAS System return code, called *sysrc*. Chapter 18, "SAS System Return Codes" contains a list of return codes with a section for operations most commonly performed on external files. You can check for these codes to write more sophisticated error checking for your SCL programs.

The following sections describe the tasks your SCL programs can perform on external files with summary information about the SCL function or routine to use to perform that task. For details on those functions and routines, see the appropriate entry in Chapter 20, "SCL Dictionary".

Accessing External Files

Before your applications can work with external files, you must establish a communication link between the SAS System, the file, and your SCL program. You start the communication link by assigning a fileref to the file, which links the file and the SAS System. You complete the communication link by using an SCL function to open the file, which links the file and the SCL program.

SCL also enables you to establish this communication link between the SAS System, a directory, and your SCL program. Then, your program can use any file in that directory without assigning it a fileref. This can make it easier for you to process multiple files in the same directory.

Assigning Filerefs

To establish the communication between the SAS System and the external file, you must assign that file a fileref. You can assign a fileref to an external file using the FILENAME function. If your application requires users to specify the name of the physical file, create a block of SCL code labeled with a window variable name to run only when a user enters a file name in that field. To use this technique for PROGRAM or SCREEN entries, your program needs a CONTROL LABEL statement so the label executes when the field is modified. CONTROL LABEL is the default in FRAME entries.

You can also put the FILENAME function in the MAIN section so that it executes after a user specifies the filename. In this case, add a statement to check that the field containing the filename has been modified so that the FILENAME statement does not run every time the MAIN section runs.

When your program can specify the name of the physical file without user input, put the function in the INIT section for SAS/AF applications or the FSEINIT sections of FSEDIT applications so that the function executes only once, before the window opens.

You can assign filerefs outside the application when files are used by all or large parts of your application. You assign filerefs to these files by using the FILENAME statement (in base SAS) in the application's start-up file, or autoexec file.

For more information on assigning filerefs, see the SAS documentation for your operating system.

Note: To just view an external file with SCL, you can use CALL FSLIST without establishing the communication link.

There are other SCL functions that you can use to manipulate filerefs. Use these functions to prevent your programs from terminating prematurely because of possible errors (for example, a fileref is already assigned or a physical file does not exist).

When you want to verify that ...	Use the function ...
a fileref has been assigned to a physical file for the current SAS session	FILEREF
the file associated with a specified fileref exists	FEXIST
the file associated with a physical name exists	FILEEXIST

Opening Files

To complete the communication link between your application and an external file, use the FOPEN function to open the file. Opening a file does not access the information in the file but simply makes the file available to the program. When you open an external file,

□ a unique identifier is assigned to the external file. This identifier is used by any other SCL functions that manipulate the file.

□ a temporary storage buffer is automatically created for the external file. This storage area is used to store copies of file records.

The FOPEN function returns the program's identification number for that file. This unique number is called the *file identifier*. You can use this identifier by storing it in an SCL variable and passing the variable name as an argument to all the SCL functions you use to manipulate that file or directory. This technique enables you to open and manipulate multiple files at the same time and clearly identify which file to manipulate.

When your application requires users to specify the name of the file before you open that file, you can create a labeled section to run only when a user enters a file name in the field associated with the label. When you use this technique for PROGRAM and SCREEN entries, your program needs a CONTROL LABEL statement so the label executes when the field is modified. In FRAME entries, however, CONTROL LABEL is the default. Alternatively, you can put the FOPEN statement in the MAIN section (with the appropriate check for the file being open) so that the statement executes after a user specifies the filename.

If your program can specify the name of the physical file without user input, open the file in the INIT section of SAS/AF applications or the FSEINIT section of FSEDIT applications so that the FOPEN statement executes only once, before the window opens or the FSEDIT session begins.

When you open a file, you specify an open mode. The mode determines the actions that can be performed on the file. With the FOPEN function, you can also specify the file's record length. If you specify a record length of 0, the existing record length is used. For details on the modes and record lengths and how to specify them, see FOPEN in Chapter 20.

Making an Open File Available to Other Programs

After you open an external file, its contents are available to all programs in your application. However, you must link the file with the programs by passing them the variable containing the file identifier. You can use one of the following techniques to communicate file identifier values to other programs in the application:

□ You can pass the file identifier as a parameter to other programs using the parameter-passing mechanism of the DISPLAY or METHOD routine with the ENTRY or METHOD statement. This method is preferred.

□ You can store the file identifier value using the SETPARMID routine and retrieve it using the GETPARMID function. This method limits you to passing only one file identifier at a time.

□ You can pass the file identifier value as a macro variable using the SYMPUTN routine and retrieve it using the SYMGETN function.

Number of Open Files Allowed

SCL allows a maximum of 999 external files to be open simultaneously in your application. However, your operating system may impose other limits. For further details, consult the SAS documentation for your operating system. You also can refer to the documentation provided by the vendor for your operating system.

Although SCL permits you to have a large number of files open simultaneously, you should be aware that memory is allocated for each file from the time the file is opened until it is closed. Therefore, you should try to minimize the number of files open at the same time and close files as soon as your program finishes its work with them.

File Data Buffers and SCL Data Vectors

The temporary storage buffer created for each file you open is called the *file data buffer* (FDB). If you open multiple files, a separate FDB is created for each file. The buffer is the length of the file's records, and it is empty until a record is read from the file. When you use a read function, a record is copied from the file into the FDB. When you use a write function, the contents of the FDB are moved to a record in the physical file and the file's FDB is cleared. Once a record is in the FDB, it remains there until the record is written back to the file, another record is read in, or the file is closed.

An SCL Data Vector (SDV) is also created when your SCL program starts executing. The SDV contains temporary storage areas for the program's SCL variables. Values of program variables are manipulated and stored in the SDV before they are written to or deleted from an external file. Figure 6.1 illustrates the SDV and the FDB created for an application that uses an external file. This figure shows the paths taken by file records when they are read from the file, displayed in the window, processed, and then returned to the file.

Figure 6.1 *Path of Data in File Read and Write Operations*

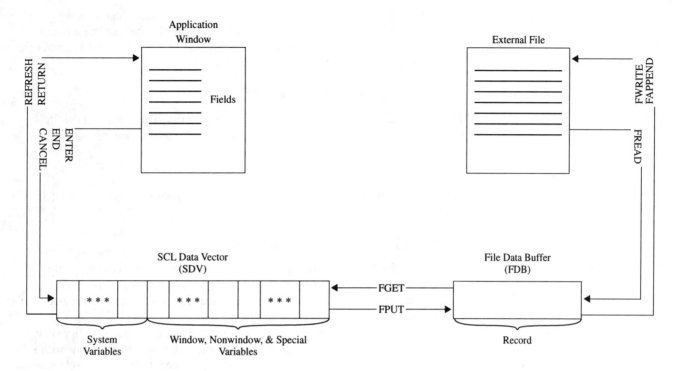

The steps required for reading an external file and returning values to it are described in the following sections.

Reading Values from External Files

Before an SCL program can use the information in an external file, it must read its records. For example, your application may need to use external file records to

□ display the values for users to browse or edit

□ modify existing values

□ add new values or records

□ delete values or records.

Reading values from external files is a two-step process. A value can be part of a record, or it may be an entire record. Unless there is a reason you must read each value separately, reading an entire record as a single value is the easier technique to use.

The following table describes the steps required to complete the process of reading values from an open file and the functions to use in each step.

Step	Action	Description	Function
1	read a record from the file	contents of the record are copied to the FDB	FREAD
2	read each value from the FDB to the SDV	contents of the FDB, interpreted as values, are copied to the SDV where they can be used by the application	FGET

Order of reading records

Many external files restrict you to reading records in sequential order from the first record to the last. However, when you are working with files that can be randomly accessed, you can use SCL functions to change that sequence and reread a record or start at the first record and reread the entire file.

Reading Records into the FDB

When the FREAD function reads the file records into the FDB, it starts at the file's first record and reads each record sequentially. Reading record values from the external file requires your SCL program to read

□ a record from the file into the FDB

□ the contents of the FDB into the SDV to make the values available to your SCL program.

Reading Record Values Into the SDV

When the FGET function reads values into the SDV, it makes the contents of the FDB available to the SCL program. You can control how this step in the read operation processes the contents of the FDB by reading the FDB contents as one single value or as a series of separate values.

If you can read the contents of the FDB as a single value, you can simplify your program and make it more flexible. To do this, you need to design a window with a single field to display the entire contents. Even if you need to read record values into separate window variables, you can read the FDB contents as a single value into a program variable in the SDV. Then, you can use SAS character functions (like SCAN or SUBSTR) to assign parts of that program variable to window variables. For example, the following program segment finds the length of the record and then reads the entire record as the single value into the window variable ROW.

```
length=finfo(fileid,'lrecl');
reclen=inputn(length,'best.');
rc=fget(fileid,row,reclen);
```

If ROW is a nonwindow variable instead of a window variable, values read from the FDB are in the SDV, but they do not display in the window until they are assigned to a window variable.

You determine whether the contents are treated as one value or as a series of values. There is a column pointer in the FDB that is set to 1 when the contents are read. By default, the FGET function copies the value from the current position of the column pointer to the next separator character. The default separator character is one blank. Therefore, the default action of the FGET function is to copy the value from the current position of the column pointer to the next blank. If you want to designate a different character to separate values in a record, you can use the FSEP function. After each FGET function, the column pointer is positioned one column past the character that was read last. When the FDB contains no more values, the FGET function returns a −1 to signal that it has reached the end of the FDB.

Reading Records as Separate Values

Reading the contents of the FDB as a series of separate values brings up a new set of issues for you to consider. Your applications may be less flexible because they must process a specified number of file values and display them in window variables of a specific size. Also, to read separate values, you need to know more about the external files your application will process. You need to know how many values are in a record, and it is helpful if you know the starting columns for the values or the characters that separate the values. Finally, you need to define separate window fields to display the values.

When you read the FDB contents as separate values, you can locate these values by positioning the FDB column pointer at the column where the value begins or by specifying the character that separates these values. By default, the separator character for file records is a blank.

Identifying a Value's Starting Column

When you know the numbers of the columns where the values start, you can use the FPOS function to move the read pointer to the column where the next value begins. When the FPOS and FGET functions are used together, the FPOS function sets the starting column for the FGET function, which reads the FDB contents up to the next separator character.

This example shows how to read separate values when you know the numbers of the columns where the values start. This program segment reads record values into the window variables NAME, HEIGHT, and WEIGHT by using the FPOS function to specify the position of the read pointer.

```
rc=fget(fileid,name);
rc=fpos(fileid,21);
rc=fget(fileid,height);
rc=fpos(fileid,28);
rc=fget(fileid,weight);
```

Modifying External Files

Your applications can enable users to modify the values in external files interactively. You can modify external files by updating existing records, adding new records, or deleting records. When you want to store record values in external files, you can use functions to update the FDB with the values stored in window variables or program variables. When you write the contents of the FDB to a file, you can update an existing record or append the record at the end of the file.

Writing Modified or New Records to the File

The following table shows the steps for returning values to a file that has been manipulated along with the functions required. You can use these functions only with files opened for writing.

Step	Action	Description	Function
1	write each value from a window or program variable	values are copied from the SDV to the FDB	FPUT
2	write the record values from the FDB to the external file	current values are in the external file, and the FDB is empty	FWRITE, FAPPEND

If users modify any values displayed from your external file, you need to write those changes back to the external file. To return values to the file, you use a two-step process that performs the reverse of the read operation so that you write each value from the SDV to the FDB and then you write each record from the FDB back to the file. When you write the records back to the file, you can choose to update an existing record or append the modified record as a new one at the end of the file.

Some operating systems do not allow you to append new records to external files. For example, you cannot append records to members of partitioned data sets under the MVS operating system. If you use one of those operating systems, you can effectively append records to files by maintaining blank records in the file, usually at the end of the file. Then, when you want to add a record, you can update an existing blank record.

After a value is written to the FDB with the FPUT function, the column pointer moves to the first column following that value.

To return modified records as updates to the file's records, use the FWRITE function to overwrite each record in the physical file with the contents of the FDB. After the FDB contents are written to the file, the FDB's column pointer is positioned in column 1, and the FDB is filled with blanks.

Closing Files

You should close an external file or directory when your application completes its work with it. To close a file, use the FCLOSE function. To close a directory, use the DCLOSE function.

Ordinarily, when you open a file or directory in INIT, you close it in TERM. When you open a file or directory in MAIN, you also close it in MAIN. In SAS/FSP applications, you usually open files in FSEINIT and close files in FSETERM so the files close after users complete work on their data sets.

Changing the Sequence of Reading Records

When you want to start reading a file from its beginning, you can move the read pointer to the first record in a file. Then, the next FGET or FPUT function manipulates the first record. To return the read pointer to the file's first record, use the FREWIND function.

In addition to the sequential reading of records, you can designate records for later reading or re-read a file's first record. Although SCL enables you to do this, some file types do not support this feature.

When a record is in the FDB, you can mark it so that the read pointer can read it later. For example, because there are no search functions for files, you may want to mark a found record so you can use it again. To designate a record for later reading, perform these steps.

Step	Use the function ...	To ...
1	FNOTE	mark the record currently in the FDB for later reading
2	FPOINT	return the read pointer to the marked record when you are ready to read it
3	FREAD	read the record marked by the read pointer
4	DROPNOTE	delete the note marker and free the memory allocated to store the note after you are finished using the marked record.

Other Manipulations for External Files

There are other SCL functions that enable you to determine the names and values of attributes your operating system maintains about external files. These functions are listed in the following sections and are described completely in the appropriate entry in Chapter 20.

Determining Attributes and Attribute Values

On your operating system, files and directories have several attributes that are assigned and maintained by your operating system's file management system (for example, the name and date modified attributes). These attributes can vary among operating systems. For more information on these attributes, refer to the SAS documentation for your operating system. The SCL functions that you can use to determine the attributes and attribute values for external files are listed in the following table.

When you want to determine the ...	Use the function ...
number of attributes maintained for your files by your operating system	FOPTNUM
name of an attribute maintained for the files on your operating system	FOPTNAME
value of an attribute maintained for the files on your operating system	FINFO

Determining Information About An FDB

You also can use SCL functions to find a file's record length and the position of the column pointer in the FDB. The functions you use are shown in the following table.

If you want to ...	Use the function ...
find the length of a record in the FDB	FRLEN
find the position of the column pointer in the FDB	FCOL

Reading and Modifying Files in the Same Directory

To assign a fileref to a directory, use the FILENAME function, just as you would to assign a fileref to a file. The term *directory* describes the aggregate grouping of files, or aggregate storage location, maintained by operating systems. On your operating system, however, these groupings may be called by a different name such as partitioned data set, MACLIB, directory, or subdirectory.

   Before you can perform operations on multiple files in a directory, you must open the directory, just as you open an external file. To open a directory, use the DOPEN function.

Determining the Number of Files in the Directory

When you want to find out the name of a file in a directory, you must know the number of files in the directory. To determine that number, use the DNUM function.

Note: In a program that displays the file names in an extended table, you use the value returned by the DNUM function to determine the number of rows to display in the extended table.

Finding the Names of Files

After you find the number of files in the directory, you can use the DREAD function to read their names. .note If you are using DREAD in a program that is not an extended table, put the function in a DO loop so that it processes from 1 to the value returned by the DNUM function, as follows:

```
dirid=dopen(fileref);
numfiles=dnum(dirid);
do i=1 to numfiles;
   name=dread(dirid,i);

   more SCL statements

end;
```

Manipulating Files in an Open Directory

When you open and close files in a directory you opened with the DOPEN function, you can manipulate any of the files without assigning a fileref to each file. To use this technique, you must

□ open the file

□ manipulate the file's records

□ close the file.

Opening Files in an Open Directory

When you are opening a file in a directory opened with the DOPEN function, you use the MOPEN function. This function returns a file identifier you can use with any function that uses a file identifier value returned by the FOPEN function. That means you can use any SCL file function on any file you have opened with the MOPEN function. You simply use the variable containing the value returned by the MOPEN function in place of the variable containing the value returned by the FOPEN function. For example, when you open files with the MOPEN function, you use the FCLOSE function to close the files.

▶ *Caution: Be careful to complete operations on all files before closing the directory.*

When you use the MOPEN function to open files, be sure your program completes its operations on all the directory's files before you use the DCLOSE function. When you use the DCLOSE function, SCL closes all the directory's files that were opened previously with the MOPEN function.

Closing Files in an Open Directory

When your program has finished its work with a file in an open directory, you must close that file. To close a file, use the FCLOSE function.

Changing All the Files in a Directory

When you use the directory and file functions, you can create applications that enable users to make a change in each file in a directory. For example, you might want to change a date or multiply all the salaries by the same percentage when everyone represented in the file receives the same percentage raise in pay.

To make the same change to all the files in a directory, you pass the directory name to the FILENAME function and then use the DOPEN function to open the directory. Then, take the following sequence of steps:

Step	Use the function ...	To ...
1	DNUM	return the number of files in the directory. Use the number as the end of a DO loop that processes each file.
2	DREAD	read the name of a file for each repetition of the loop
3	MOPEN	open the file
4	FREAD	read a record from the file
5	FPOS	move the FDB column pointer to the value's start column
6	FGET	copies data from the File Data Buffer (FDB) and assigns it to the specified character variable
7	FPOS	return the FDB column pointer to the value's start column after the change has been made
8	FPUT	write the modified value back to the FDB
9	FWRITE	write the modified record back to the external file
10	FCLOSE	close the file at the end of the processing loop

Closing the Directory

When your application has completed its work with the files in a directory, you should close the directory. To close a directory, use the DCLOSE function.

Other Manipulations for Directories

There are several SCL functions that enable you to find additional attribute information about directories. These functions are listed in the following table and are described in detail in Chapter 20.

If you want to find the ...	Use the function ...
number of directory attributes available for a file	DOPTNUM
name of a directory attribute for a file	DOPTNAME
value of a directory attribute for a file	DINFO

Introduction

In SCL, a *program module* is a program segment designed to be called within a program or from other programs. Modular programming refers to creating and managing program modules. If you have statements that are repeated in one or more programs, you can put the statements into a module and then call it when your program needs to perform the action defined in the module.

For example, if multiple programs in your application need to sort a numeric array, you can write a program module that performs the sort and then call the module from each program that needs to sort a numeric array.

Implementing program modules can help minimize the maintenance costs for an application, which is imperative since most applications are in a maintenance phase longer than they are in any other phase of the development cycle. You can significantly reduce your maintenance chores by keeping the implementation of a module simple yet allowing many programs to execute that implementation.

SCL supports modular programming by allowing you to use:

□ labeled sections

□ macro modules

□ SCL entry modules

□ method modules

Using Labeled Sections

When you have repeated statements in an SCL program, you can put one occurrence of the statements into a labeled section. A labeled section starts with any label that is not reserved and ends with a RETURN statement. Each time the statements in the labeled section are needed, you can call the module with a LINK statement or branch to it with a GOTO statement. Labeled sections are a good solution when you are working within one SCL program because they can help segment a program and divide it into smaller, simpler pieces. However, you can link to a labeled section only within the program where it is defined.

Window Variable Sections

SCL also provides a special type of labeled sections that automatically execute when fields are modified (for example, verify values entered in fields or widgets). To do this, use the name of the associated window variable as the statement label. For PROGRAM and SCREEN entries, you must specify CONTROL LABEL to initiate this type of processing. For FRAME entries, CONTROL LABEL is set by default. This type of labeled section, a window variable section, executes automatically when users take an action in the field or object. Your program can include labeled sections for any number of window variables. The sequence for executing window variable sections is determined by the physical position of the window element. Window variable sections execute sequentially for each window element, from left to right and top to bottom.

When a user modifies a field in a PROGRAM or SCREEN entry that contains a CONTROL LABEL statement and the modification introduces an attribute error, the window variable section for that field and any remaining fields do not execute.

To correct an attribute error, you can allow users to correct the error in the window, or you can include CONTROL ERROR and statements in the window variable section that make a correction, as shown in the following example.

```
INIT:
    control label error;
return;

FIELD:
    if error(field) then
        do;
            erroroff field;
            field=default-value-assigned-elsewhere;
            _msg_='Value was invalid.  It has been reset.';

        end;
return;
```

The program's MAIN section executes only after the window variable sections for all modified window variables have executed correctly. This feature reduces the overhead required each time MAIN executes because MAIN does not execute until all of window variable blocks execute without error.

To create a window variable section, perform the following steps:

□ Assign the name of a window variable as the label, and end the block with a RETURN statement.

□ Use a CONTROL LABEL statement in the INIT section in PROGRAM entries or the FSEINIT section in FSEDIT applications. This is not required for FRAME entries because CONTROL LABEL is on by default.

    Note: If CONTROL LABEL is specified, a window variable section must not contain a SUBMIT IMMEDIATE block.

If your program also uses CONTROL ERROR, CONTROL ALWAYS, or CONTROL ALLCMDS, MAIN executes after the window variable sections even if an error has been introduced. For more information on CONTROL, see the sections on forcing MAIN to execute in Chapter 3, "SCL Programs for SAS/AF and SAS/FSP Applications," Chapter 9, "Changing the Default Program Flow," and CONTROL in Chapter 20, "Screen Control Language Dictionary."

You can also use window variable sections in programs for extended tables. In these programs, the window variable block for each modified field executes before the PUTROW section executes for the row. Extended tables are described in Chapter 14, "Introduction to Application Interfaces."

Object Label Sections

SCL programs for FRAME entries can have a labeled section for each widget. These sections are called *object label* sections. When a user modifies or selects a widget in a FRAME entry, the labeled section for the widget executes. If a text entry widget modification introduces an attribute error, the window variable section for that widget does not execute. However, window variable sections do execute for other widgets that were modified and that did not introduce an attribute error. The MAIN section does not execute.

The program's MAIN section executes only after the window variable sections for all modified variables have executed correctly.

To create an object label section, assign the name of a widget as the label for the statement block and end the block with a RETURN statement.

To correct an attribute error, you can allow users to correct the error in the window, or you can include CONTROL ERROR, CONTROL ALWAYS, or CONTROL ALLCMDS, and statements in the object label section that make a correction, as shown in the following example.

```
INIT:
   control always;
return;


NAME:
  call notify('name','_in_error_',errflg);
  if errflg then
     do;
        call notifY('name','_erroroff_');
        name=' ';
        _msg_='Value was invalid.  It has been reset.';
     end;
  return;
```

If your program also uses CONTROL ERROR, CONTROL ALWAYS, or CONTROL ALLCMDS, MAIN executes after the object label sections even if an error has been introduced.

In programs for extended tables, the object label block for each modified field executes before the PUTROW section of PROGRAM entries or the PUT*n* section of a FRAME entry executes for the row.

Example

Suppose you have created a FRAME entry window containing the numeric text entry widgets AMOUNT, RATE, and PAYMENT. This example shows the object label sections that validate the value in these widgets. The MAIN section calculates payment. In this example, the CONTROL statement with the ERROR option is in the INIT section. (CONTROL LABEL is not needed because it is the default condition for FRAME entries.) If a user enters a value in **Rate**, the RATE section executes immediately. If **Rate** is not between 0 and 1, then the field is placed in error and a message indicates that you must correct the value. If a user enters a value in **Amount**, the AMOUNT section executes immediately. If **Amount** is not between 0 and 500, the field is placed in error and a message indicates that you must correct the value. The MAIN section executes following the labeled sections for any modified window variables and calculates **Payment**.

```
INIT:
  control error;
  amount=0;
```

```
       rate=.5;
    return;

    MAIN:
       payment=amount*rate;
    return;

    TERM:
    return;

    AMOUNT:
       if amount < 0 or amount > 500 then do;
         erroron amount;
         _msg_='Amount must be between $0 and $500.';
          stop;
       end;
       else erroroff amount;
    return;

    RATE:
       if rate<0 or rate>1 then do;
         erroron rate;
         _msg_='Rate ,ist be between 0 and 1.';
          stop;
       end;
       else erroroff rate;
    return;
```

Using Macro Modules

You can use the SAS macro facility to define macros and macro variables for your SCL program. You can then pass parameters between macros and the rest of your program. And, macros can be used by more than one program. However, macro modules can be more complicated to maintain than the original program segment because of the symbols and quoting required.

If a macro is used by more than one program, you must keep track of all the programs that use it so you can recompile all of them each time the macro is updated. Since SCL is compiled (rather than interpreted like the SAS language), each SCL program that calls a macro must be recompiled whenever that macro is updated to update the program with the new macro code.

Implementing modules as macros does not reduce the size of the compiled SCL code. Program statements generated by a macro are added to the compiled code as if those lines existed at that location in the program. An important point to remember when using the macro facility with SCL is that macros and macro variables in SCL programs are resolved when you compile the SCL program, not when a user executes the application. However, you can use the SYMGET function to retrieve the value from a macro variable at execution time.

For a list of SCL functions and routines to use with macros, see "Macros" under SCL Elements in Chapter 19, "SCL Language Elements."

Note: Macros and macro variables within submit blocks are not resolved when you compile the SCL program. Instead, they are passed with the rest of the submit block to the SAS System when the block is submitted. For more information on submit blocks, see Chapter 11, "Submitting SAS and SQL Statements."

Example

The SCL program with validation for amount and rate implemented as macros would be:

```
%macro valamnt(amount);
  if amount < 0 or amount > 500 then do;
    erroron amount;
    _msg_='Amount must be between $0 and $500.';
    stop;
  end;
  else erroroff amount;
%mend;
%macro rateamnt(rate);
  if rate<0 or rate>1 then do;
    erroron rate;
    _msg_='Rate must be between 0 and 1.';
    stop;
  end;
  else erroroff rate;
%mend;

INIT:
  control error;
  amount=0;
  rate=.5;
return;

MAIN:
  payment=amount*rate;
return;

TERM:
return;

AMOUNT:
  %valamnt(amount)
return;

RATE:
  %rateamnt(rate)
return;
```

Using SCL Entry Modules

SAS/AF provides SCL entries for storing a program module. SCL programs can access a module stored in an SCL entry, pass parameters to the module, and receive values from the module. Also, An SCL module can be used by any other SCL program. You call an SCL module with a CALL DISPLAY routine that passes it parameters and receives values returned by the SCL entry. The module's ENTRY statement receives parameters and returns values to the calling program.

If you were creating an SCL module for the previous example, you would store the labeled sections in separate SCL entries, for example AMOUNT.SCL and RATE.SCL. Then, you could call either of them with a CALL DISPLAY statement.

Note: When you are using SCL entries in FSEDIT applications, SAS/AF must be licensed on the machine on which you edit the SCL entry and compile it.

However, SAS/AF does not have to be licensed on machines that run the FSEDIT application.

Example

Store the following validation program for amount in SASUSER.VALIDATE.AMOUNT.SCL:

```
entry amount error 8;
INIT:
        /* The amount must be between 0 and 500.  */
    if (amount <0) or (amount>500) then error=1;
    else error=0;
return;
```

Store the following validation program for rate in SASUSER.VALIDATE.RATE.SCL:

```
entry rate error 8;
INIT:
        /* The rate must be between 0 and 1.  */
    if (rate <0) or (rate>1) then error=2;
    else error=0;
return;
```

The following SCL program computes payment:

```
INIT:
    control error;
    amount=0;
    rate=0.5;
return;

MAIN:
        /*  Call the SCL entry to validate the amount.  */
    call display('sasuser.validate.amount.scl',amount,error);
    if error=1 then
       do;
          erroron amount;
          _msg_='Amount must be between $0 and $500.';
          stop;
       end;
    else;
       erroroff amount;

        /*  Call the SCL entry to validate the rate.  */
    call display('sasuser.validate.rate.scl',rate,error);
    if error=2 then
       do;
          erroron rate;
          _msg_='Rate must be between 0 and 1.';
          stop;
       end;
    else;
       erroroff rate;
```

```
        /* Calculate payment.  */
    payment=amount*rate;
return;


TERM:
return;
```

Using Method Modules

SCL also provides method blocks for implementing program modules. These modules are called method blocks because they begin with a METHOD statement and end with an ENDMETHOD statement. This feature allows you to write a program module that performs an operation common to or shared by other applications and call it from any SAS/AF, FSEDIT, or FSVIEW application.

Method modules stored in an SCL entry can be called from any SAS/AF, FSEDIT, or FSVIEW application by using the CALL METHOD routine. This capability also allows you to pass parameters to the method. After the method module performs its operations, it can return modified values to the calling routine.

When you store method modules in SCL entries, you can use the METHOD statement to list parameters for communicating values passed from and returned to a calling METHOD routine. When you want to pass parameters between an SCL program and a method block, you use the same principles as when you are passing parameters between a CALL DISPLAY statement and an ENTRY statement. The parameter list and argument list must agree in the number of parameters passed and arguments passed and arguments received, their position in the lists and their data types, unless the REST= or ARGLIST= options are used in the METHOD statement. They do not have to agree in name. For more information, see the METHOD statement in Chapter 20, "Screen Control Language Dictionary."

Although a method module can be compiled and stored in SAS/AF PROGRAM entries and FSEDIT applications, a CALL METHOD routine cannot be used to invoke it. The method module is treated as a labeled section and can be called with a LINK or GOTO statement. Although parameters cannot be passed with a LINK or GOTO statement, you can reference global values. If you want to share a method module with other SCL programs, then store it in an SCL entry.

To create and use a method block, perform the following steps:

1. Write a labeled statement block followed by a METHOD statement and any parameters the method needs to use.

2. Write the SCL statements that perform the desired task.

3. End the block with an ENDMETHOD statement.

4. If the method module is stored in the PROGRAM entry or FSEDIT application, then you must use a LINK or GOTO statement to call it. Parameters cannot be passed in this manner, although you can reference global values.

5. Call the method module with a CALL METHOD routine if the module is an SCL entry. When you need to pass parameters to the method, you should use the CALL METHOD routine.

   If the method module is stored in the same SCL entry as that associated with a FRAME entry, then you must compile the SCL entry as a separate entity from the FRAME entry in addition to compiling the FRAME entry.

▶ *Caution: Some SCL entries will not compile independently of the associated FRAME entry.*

SCL entries containing window-specific statements such as PROTECT, CURSOR, and ERRORON will not compile independently and must be compiled in conjunction with the associated FRAME entry.

> **Note:** Method blocks stored in independent SCL entries must not contain any window-specific statement or function, such as FIELD, ERRORON, MODIFIED, etc.
>
> **Note:** To use METHOD blocks and the CALL METHOD routine, you must have SAS/AF licensed on the machine on which you edit and compile the application.

Example

The following example continues with the example shown earlier in the chapter and creates two method blocks for validating an amount and a rate. When the statement blocks are implemented as methods, you can store them in the same SCL entry and either can be called by its method name by programs that need the respective validation performed. For example, a program that needed to validate a rate could call the method with:

```
call method('sasuser.methods.validate.scl','rate',number,widgetid)
```

The following validation methods are stored in SASUSER.METHODS.VALIDATE.SCL:

```
AMOUNT:
   method amount 8 widgetid 8;
   if (amount < 0) or (amount > 500) then call send(widgetid,'_erroron_');
   else call send (widgetid,'_erroroff_');
   endmethod;
return;


RATE:
   method rate 8 widgetid 8;
   if (rate < 0) or (rate > 1) then call send(widgetid,'_erroron_');
   else call send (widgetid,'_erroroff_');
   endmethod;
return;
```

The calling program now uses CALL METHOD routines to call the validation methods. AMOUNT and RATE are object label sections that execute when a user enters a value into the associated text entry widget.

```
INIT:
   control error;
   amount=0;
   rate=0.5;
return;


AMOUNT:
   call notify('.','_get_current_widget_',widgetid);
   call method('sasuser.methods.validate.scl','amount',amount,widgetid);
return;


RATE:
   call notify('.','_get_current_widget_',widgetid);
   call method('sasuser.methods.validate.scl','rate',rate,widgetid);
return;
```

```
MAIN:
      /*  Calculate payment.  */
   payment=amount*rate;
return;

TERM:
return;
```

CHAPTER 8

Calling Other Entries from SCL Programs

Overview

Screen Control Language does not limit you to writing your entire application with only one window and one FRAME, PROGRAM, SCREEN, or FORMULA entry. An SCL program can call other SCL programs and open additional windows.

From an SCL program, you can call any of the following types of entries built with SAS/AF software:

□ CBT

□ FRAME

□ HELP

□ MENU

□ PROGRAM

□ SCL

An SCL program can also call:

□ FSEDIT or FSBROWSE sessions that employ SCREEN entries

□ FSVIEW sessions that employ FORMULA entries

The most versatile way to call SAS/AF entries from SCL programs is with the CALL DISPLAY or CALL GOTO routine, which can call any of the SAS/AF entry types. You can use these routines to call SAS/AF entries from FSEDIT programs as well as calling them from other SAS/AF entries. For more information on these routines, see DISPLAY and GOTO in Chapter 20, "Screen Control Language Dictionary."

Nesting Windows

Each time your SCL program calls an entry using the DISPLAY routine, the window for the current program becomes inactive and control passes to the called entry. The inactive window becomes active again when control returns to its SCL program. Users cannot modify fields or issue commands in an inactive window (except for the NEXT command to display the inactive windows). When a user issues an END or CANCEL command in the window for the called entry, control returns to the calling SCL program.

You can specify the entry name in any of the forms in the following table.

Form	Description
entry	specifies the name of a PROGRAM entry in the same catalog as the calling entry.

Form	Description
entry.type	specifies the name and type of an entry in the same catalog as the calling entry.
libref.catalog.entry	specifies the name of a PROGRAM entry in a SAS catalog that may be different from the calling entry.
libref.catalog.entry.type	specifies the name and type of an entry in a SAS catalog that may be different from the calling entry.

These are referred to as one-, two-, three-, and four-level names, respectively.

Calling Entries and Passing Parameters

When you call entries with the DISPLAY routine, you can pass values, called *parameters*, to the called programs. The parameters can be variable names, numeric or character literals, expressions, or arrays. When you use an array, the array must be defined in both the calling program and the called program. The calling program specifies only the array name in the CALL DISPLAY routine, and the called program specifies the array name in the ENTRY statement.

Using Passed Parameter Values

To use the parameters passed to it by the DISPLAY routine, the called program must explicitly define the names, types, and lengths of the parameters it expects to receive. You can use the ENTRY statement for this purpose.

The arguments for the ENTRY statement must match those in the DISPLAY routine in number and type, although you do not have to use the same variable names in both entries.

Values from the calling routine are assigned to the variables listed in the ENTRY statement according to the order of the parameters in the CALL DISPLAY and ENTRY statements, not according to their respective variable names.

▶ *Caution: Be careful to pass the correct number and type of parameters.*

When you pass an incorrect number of parameters or a parameter of the incorrect type (for example, character where numeric is expected), execution of the program halts. If this occurs, you should review the error messages in the SAS log (or in the MESSAGE window, if it is active) and make the appropriate corrections. See "Passing a Variable Number of Parameters" later in this section for a way to make some or all parameters optional.

. . . .

Returning Values to the Calling Entry

By default, the called entry also returns values to the calling program when the called entry ends. The variables specified in the ENTRY statement hold the current values for the parameters. These values are passed back to any of the CALL DISPLAY arguments that were specified as variable names. (You cannot return a parameter value to a literal value used as an argument to CALL DISPLAY.)

Preventing Entries from Returning Values

Sometimes you want a called program to receive values but not return values to its calling program. For example, you may want to ignore any changes users make to the passed values if users exit the called program with a CANCEL command. SCL provides the NOCHANGE routine to block called entries from returning values.

Passing a Variable Number of Parameters

By default, an error occurs if the numbers of parameters in the ENTRY and CALL DISPLAY statements do not match. However, a calling program can pass a variable number of parameters to the called program if you designate the OPTIONAL=, REST=, or ARGLIST= options on the ENTRY statement. This technique is particularly useful for entries called by several different entries, each with different requirements.

You identify optional arguments using the keyword OPTIONAL= in the ENTRY statement. The OPTIONAL= keyword and the list of optional parameters must follow any required parameters.

Calling SAS/FSP and SAS/AF Applications

You can call SAS/FSP applications from SAS/AF applications. You can also call SAS/AF applications from SAS/FSP applications. There are several ways you can call other applications.

Using SCL Routines

The preferred way to start SAS/FSP applications from within an SCL program is with the CALL FSEDIT, CALL FSVIEW, CALL FSLIST, or CALL LETTER routines. If you have a SAS/FSP application from which you want to call a SAS/AF application (for example, to display an extended table that serves as a custom selection list), the preferred technique is to use the CALL DISPLAY routine.

For more information on all of these routines, see Chapter 20.

Using Display Manager Commands

You can use the EXECCMDI routine to issue the global commands FSEDIT, FSBROWSE, FSVIEW, FSLIST, and FSLETTER. These Display Manager commands open FSEDIT, FSBROWSE, FSVIEW, FSLIST, and FSLETTER windows that are independent of your application. This means that the application's current window remains active, and users can switch between the active windows by issuing the NEXT command. For example, the following statement is an alternative way to open an FSVIEW window for browsing the data set SASUSER.HOUSES using the BRHOUSES.FORMULA entry in the SASUSER.HOUSES catalog:

```
call execcmdi('fsview sasuser.houses
    sasuser.houses.brhouses.formula');
```

For details on the syntax for the FSBROWSE, FSEDIT, FSVIEW, FSLIST, and FSLETTER commands, refer to *SAS/FSP Software: Usage and Reference Version 6, First Edition*.

Using Submit Blocks

If you want to open a SAS/FSP window with any of the special options available only in PROC statements, you can use submit blocks to submit these statements to the SAS System for execution. However, this method of opening FSBROWSE, FSEDIT, FSVIEW, FSLETTER, and FSLIST windows consumes more system resources than the other methods. As a consequence, you should use submit blocks only when you need to use a statement or procedure option not available with the SCL routines or the global commands.

For example, the following statements offer an alternative method of opening an FSVIEW window for browsing the data set SASUSER.HOUSES. The submit block includes a VAR statement to display only variables STYLE, STREET, and PRICE.

```
submit continue;
   proc fsview data=sasuser.houses;
      var style street price;
   run;
endsubmit;
```

For more information on using SAS/FSP in SAS/AF applications, see Chapter 14, "Introduction to Application Interfaces." Submit blocks and issuing host commands are discussed in greater detail in Chapter 11, "Submitting SAS and SQL Statements."

CHAPTER *9* # Changing the Default Program Flow

Introduction

Chapter 3, "SCL Programs for SAS/AF and SAS/FSP Applications," described the default flow of control in SCL programs. SCL provides the following features that enable you to modify the default flow of control:

□ the CONTROL statement

□ the _STATUS_ system variable.

Using the CONTROL Statement

You can use the CONTROL statement to

□ execute SCL programs when users have not modified any fields

□ execute SCL programs when fields contain invalid values

□ execute blocks of SCL statements when specific fields are modified

□ control execution of SCL programs at user interrupts.

CONTROL is an executable statement, so you must use it within one of the labeled sections of your SCL program. You typically place CONTROL statements in the INIT section of SAS/AF applications and in the FSEINIT section of FSEDIT applications because these sections are typically executed only once during the course of the application.

An option specified in a CONTROL statement remains in effect until the program terminates or until another CONTROL statement changes the option.

Using the _STATUS_ Variable

You can use the _STATUS_ system variable to

□ terminate execution of SCL programs from any point in the program.

□ force SCL programs to resume executing after users issue an END or CANCEL command in SAS/AF applications or attempt to leave the current observation in FSEDIT applications.

□ determine which command users issued to terminate the application.

Permitting Processing Without Field Modification

By default, the following portions of the SCL statements in an application execute only after users modify one or more fields in the window:

□ the MAIN section of the SCL program in a SAS/AF or FSEDIT application

□ the TERM section of the SCL program in an FSEDIT application when leaving the current observation

□ the SCL statements in the formulas of an FSVIEW application when the FSVIEW window is opened for editing with a MEMBER-level lock on the displayed SAS data set.

You can change the standard behavior of the application so that processing occurs even when users have not modified any fields.

Executing MAIN Without Field Modification: CONTROL ENTER

To pass control to the MAIN section of the SCL program whenever users press ENTER or a function key, use the following form of the CONTROL statement:

```
control enter;
```

The ENTER option causes the MAIN section to execute regardless of whether any fields have been modified (provided that no field contains an invalid value). ENTER is valid in SAS/AF, FSEDIT, FSBROWSE, and FSVIEW applications.

Using CONTROL ENTER in FSBROWSE Applications

In FSBROWSE applications, you must use the CONTROL ENTER statement to enable execution of the MAIN section of the SCL program. Because the FSBROWSE procedure does not permit field modification, the MAIN section of the SCL program in an FSBROWSE application never executes unless you use a CONTROL ENTER statement.

Using CONTROL ENTER in FSVIEW Applications

You can use the CONTROL ENTER statement in FSVIEW applications to execute the SCL statements in the formula for a particular observation when users press ENTER while the cursor is positioned on the observation.

The CONTROL ENTER statement is only meaningful when your application opens the displayed SAS data set with a MEMBER-level lock. When a RECORD-level lock is used, the SCL statements in the formula for the selected observation are always executed when users press ENTER while the cursor is on the observation.

Restoring the Default Behavior

To restore the default behavior, use a CONTROL statement with the NOENTER option, as follows:

```
control noenter;
```

When the NOENTER option is in effect, the MAIN section (or the formulas in an FSVIEW application) executes only if users modify one or more fields before pressing ENTER or a function key.

Executing TERM Without Field Modification: CONTROL TERM

To pass control to the TERM section of the SCL program in your FSEDIT or FSBROWSE application whenever users attempt to leave the current observation, use the following form of the CONTROL statement:

```
control term;
```

The TERM option causes the TERM section to execute regardless of whether any fields have been modified.

Note: The TERM option has no effect in SAS/AF or FSVIEW applications.

Using CONTROL TERM in FSBROWSE Applications

In FSBROWSE applications, you must use the CONTROL TERM statement to enable execution of the TERM section of the SCL program. Because the FSBROWSE procedure does not permit field modification, the TERM section of SCL programs in FSBROWSE applications never executes unless you use a CONTROL TERM statement.

Restoring the Default Behavior

If you need to restore the default behavior, use a CONTROL statement with the NOTERM option, as follows:

```
control noterm;
```

When the NOTERM option is in effect, the TERM section does not execute when a different observation is displayed unless users modify one or more fields in the current observation or the observation is new.

Permitting Processing When Fields Contain Invalid Values

By default, control does not pass to the MAIN section of the SCL program in a SAS/AF or FSEDIT application unless all field values are valid according to the informats and attributes specified for the fields. The MAIN section executes only after users correct all invalid field values.

Executing MAIN With Invalid Field Values: CONTROL ERROR

To pass control to the MAIN section of the SCL program even when the window contains fields with invalid values, use the following form of the CONTROL statement:

```
control error;
```

Note: The ERROR option has no effect in FSVIEW applications.

When the CONTROL ERROR statement is in effect, field attributes and informats no longer guarantee that window variables contain valid values.

▶ *Caution: When you use the CONTROL ERROR statement in your SCL program, you should check the validity of any window variable value before using it in a calculation.*

Restoring the Default Behavior

To restore the default behavior, use a CONTROL statement with the NOERROR
option, as follows:

```
control noerror;
```

When the NOERROR option is in effect, the MAIN section does not execute if any
window variables are invalid based on field attributes or informats.

Combining the ENTER and ERROR Options

To combine the effects of the ENTER and ERROR options, use the following form
of the CONTROL statement:

```
control always;
```

    Note: The CONTROL ALLCMDS statement, used to allow processing of
commands, also combines the effects of the ENTER and ERROR options.

Restoring the Default Behavior

To restore the default behavior, use a CONTROL statement with the NOALWAYS
option, as follows:

```
control noalways;
```

Executing SCL Statements When Individual Fields Are Modified

By default, only the MAIN section of the SCL program executes when field values
are changed in SAS/AF PROGRAM entries and FSEDIT applications. In FRAME
entries, a section of SCL code with a label that matches the name of the object also
executes whenever an object is modified. You can change the behavior of SAS/AF
PROGRAM entries and FSEDIT applications so that a section of SCL code with a
label that matches the field name executes whenever a field is changed.

Executing Labeled Sections: CONTROL LABEL

To execute individual labeled sections of SCL code in SAS/AF PROGRAM entries
and FSEDIT applications when users modify particular fields, you must

□ use a CONTROL statement of the following form:

```
control label;
```

    Note: CONTROL LABEL is the default in FRAME entries.

□ put the statements to execute when a field is modified in a block of code labeled
with the name of the field. For example, to display a message when a user
modifies a field called NAME, you can use the following labeled section of code:

```
INIT:
   control label;
   . . .
return;

NAME:
   _msg_="The NAME field has been modified.";
return;
```

When users modify a field while the CONTROL LABEL option is active, SCL

□ performs the usual field validation

□ executes any section of the SCL program labeled with the same name as the modified field

□ executes the MAIN section after executing the labeled section.

If more than one field is modified, the labeled sections are executed in the order in which the fields appear in the window, from left to right and top to bottom.

This feature enables you to treat labeled statement blocks as subroutines associated with selected fields. You can write additional field validation code without using code in the MAIN section to determine which fields the user has modified.

Restoring the Default Behavior

To restore the default behavior in SAS/AF PROGRAM entries or FSEDIT applications, use a CONTROL statement with the NOLABEL option, as follows:

```
control nolabel;
```

When the NOLABEL option is in effect, modifying a field does not cause execution of a labeled section of SCL code with the same name as the field.

Note: You can use a CONTROL NOLABEL statement to turn off the default behavior of executing labeled sections in FRAME entries.

Controlling Program Execution at User Interrupts

You can control program execution at user interrupts through an attention handler that you define. An *attention handler* is a labeled statement block that begins with a label you define and contains SCL statements that can alter the program's flow or execution status. This statement block ends with a RETURN statement.

For the attention-handler block to be honored, you specify the associated label name in a CONTROL BREAK statement that executes before the interrupt occurs, as follows:

```
control break label;
```

You can have more than one attention-handler block in a single SCL program, but only one of them is in effect at one time. Execution of a CONTROL BREAK statement replaces any attention handler block called with a CONTROL BREAK statement previously defined in the program.

When Interrupts Occur

When an interrupt occurs while SCL statements are executing (for example, when a user presses the ATTENTION key) and a CONTROL BREAK statement has been executed to put an attention-handler block into effect, the associated statement block is executed once the current statement finishes execution.

If an interrupt occurs and no CONTROL BREAK statement has been executed or when a previously defined attention-handler block has been disabled, no labeled section executes. A requester window opens and asks the user to choose whether program execution should resume (that is, ignore the interrupt) or the program should abort.

Restoring the Default Behavior

To restore the default behavior, issue a CONTROL statement with the NOBREAK option, as follows:

```
control nobreak;
```

You can also replace a CONTROL BREAK statement with a succeeding CONTROL BREAK statement that specifies a different program label.

Terminating SCL Programs

In SAS/AF and FSEDIT (and FSBROWSE) applications, you can close the current window and terminate the current entry from within an SCL program. To force the SCL program to stop executing, assign the value **H** to the _STATUS_ system variable, as follows:

```
_status_='H';
```

Note: Specify an uppercase value for the _STATUS_ system variable. Under some host operating systems, lowercase values for _STATUS_ are not recognized.

What Happens After the _STATUS_ System Variable is Set

Setting the _STATUS_ system variable to **H** does not immediately halt execution of the application. The value of the _STATUS_ variable is not checked until after the SCL program returns control following the next execution of a RETURN statement. Thus, any statements between the assignment statement and the next RETURN statement still execute.

After control returns to the task, the current entry terminates without further processing.

□ In SAS/AF applications, the TERM section of the entry's SCL program does not execute.

□ In FSEDIT applications, neither the TERM nor the FSETERM sections of the entry's SCL program execute. If users modified data set variable values in the current observation, the modified values are not written to the data set.

After the entry terminates, control returns to the program or window that invoked the entry.

Resuming Execution of the Application

Control passes to the TERM section of an SCL program

□ when users issue an END or CANCEL command in SAS/AF applications

□ When users issue an END command or attempt to scroll to a different observation in an FSEDIT application, provided at least one field has been changed or the observation is new.

You can force the SCL program to resume waiting for user input by assigning the value **R** to the _STATUS_ system variable, as follows:

```
_status_='R';
```

For SAS/AF applications, this has the effect of resuming execution of the SCL program without exiting from the application. For FSEDIT applications, this has the effect of keeping the current observation displayed.

Where To Set the Value of _STATUS_

Setting the _STATUS_ system variable to **R** is meaningful only in the TERM section of programs. If users have modified fields before issuing the END command, the MAIN section executes before the TERM section. However, setting the _STATUS_ system variable to **R** in the MAIN section of the program does not cause the program to resume executing.

    Note: Because, by default, the TERM section of FSEDIT applications is not executed unless fields have been modified or the observation is new, you may want to use a CONTROL TERM statement to ensure that the TERM section is always executed when using _STATUS_ in TERM to resume execution. Setting _STATUS_ to **R** in the FSETERM section does not resume execution of the program.

What Happens After _STATUS_ Is Set

Setting _STATUS_ to **R** does not immediately resume execution of the application. The value of the _STATUS_ system variable is not checked until after the SCL program returns control following the next execution of a RETURN statement. Thus, any statements in the TERM section between the assignment statement and the next RETURN statement still execute.

    Note: If you use _STATUS_ to resume your SAS/AF application or to redisplay the current observation in your FSEDIT application, your application should use the _MSG_ system variable to display a message to users explaining why they cannot leave the application or observation.

Determining the Command that Terminated the Entry

In some situations, you need to know whether users issued an END or a CANCEL command to terminate the current task. For example, you may want to perform certain processing in the TERM section only if users issue an END command, and to omit this processing if users issue a CANCEL command. Or you may want to prevent users from exiting from the task until they supply values in certain fields, unless they are cancelling the task.

    Whenever users issue an END or CANCEL command, SAS indicates which command was issued by setting the value of the _STATUS_ system variable to one of the following values:

When the value of _STATUS_ is . . .	Then the user issued . . .
C	a CANCEL command
E	an END command

You can test the value of the _STATUS_ system variable and use the test results to determine what actions to take for each of these commands.

    Note: In the FSEDIT procedure, the CANCEL command cancels changes to variables in the current observation. It does not terminate the task as it does in SAS/AF applications.

Testing the Value of the _STATUS_ System Variable

The _STATUS_ system variable is set after users issue an END or CANCEL command. The effects of these commands depend on the type of application.

In SAS/AF applications

both the CANCEL and END commands trigger execution of the TERM section of the SCL program, so the value of the _STATUS_ variable is typically tested in the TERM section of the program to determine which command caused the TERM section to execute.

In FSEDIT applications

the CANCEL command cancels any changes to variable values and re-reads the current observation, which triggers execution of the INIT section of the program. If field values were changed before the CANCEL command was issued, the TERM section is also executed before the INIT section. Thus, you typically test the _STATUS_ variable for a value of C in the TERM section to prevent updating secondary data sets when the changes were cancelled.

The END command executes the TERM section prior to the FSETERM section if fields have been modified or the observation is new. Thus, you typically test the _STATUS_ variable for a value of E in the TERM section to determine whether the TERM section is executing in response to an END command or an attempt to scroll to a different observation. You can use a CONTROL TERM statement to ensure that the TERM section is always executed, even if fields have not been modified.

CHAPTER *10* Using Macro Variables

Introduction

Macro variables, which are part of the macro facility in base SAS software, can be used in Screen Control Language (SCL) programs. Macro variables are independent of any particular SAS data set, application, or window. The values of macro variables are available to the entire SAS System for the duration of a particular SAS session.

In your SCL programs, you can:

□ store values in macro variables (for example, to pass information from the current SCL program to subsequent programs in the application, to subsequent applications, or to other parts of the SAS System).

□ retrieve values from macro variables (for example, to pass information to the current SCL program from programs that executed previously or from other parts of the SAS System, or to pass values from one observation to another in FSEDIT applications).

Examples of the types of information you frequently need to pass between entries in an application include:

□ names of SAS data sets to be opened

□ names of external files to be opened

□ data set identifiers of open SAS data sets

□ file identifiers of open external files

□ the current date (instead of using date functions repeatedly)

□ values to be repeated across observations in an FSEDIT session.

Storing Values in Macro Variables

To assign a literal value to a macro variable in an SCL program, you can use the standard macro variable assignment statement, %LET. For example, the following statement assigns the literal value **sales** (not the value of an SCL variable named SALES) to a macro variable named DSNAME:

```
%let dsname=sales;
```

This macro variable assignment is evaluated when you compile the SCL program, not when users execute the application. Thus, the %LET statement is useful for assigning literal values at compile time. For example, you can use macro variables defined in this manner to store a value or block of text you use repeatedly in the program. However, you must use a different approach if you want to store the value of an SCL variable in a macro variable while the SCL program executes (for example, to pass values between SCL programs).

Macro variables store only strings of text characters, so numeric values are stored as strings of text digits representing the values. To store values so that they can be retrieved properly, you must use the appropriate CALL routine, as described in the following table.

If you want to store . . .	Then use the routine . . .
a character value	SYMPUT
a numeric value	SYMPUTN

Note: Using the same name for a macro variable and an SCL variable does not cause a conflict. Macro variables are stored in the global symbol table, whereas SCL variables are stored in the SCL data vector (SDV). However, if your program uses submit blocks and you have both a macro variable and an SCL variable with the same name, a reference with a single ampersand substitutes the SCL variable. To force the macro variable to be substituted, reference it with two ampersands (&&). The following code demonstrates using the two ampersands:

```
dsname='sasuser.class';
call symput('dsname','sasuser.houses');
submit continue;
   options symbolgen;
   proc print data=&dsname;
   run;
   proc print data=&&dsname;
   run;
endsubmit;
```

This code is generated:

```
proc print data=sasuser.class;
run;
proc print data=sasuser.houses;
run;
```

Retrieving Values from Macro Variables

To retrieve the value of a macro variable within an SCL program, you can use a standard macro variable reference. For example, in the following statement the current text for the macro variable DSNAME is substituted for the macro variable reference when the program is compiled:

```
dsn="&dsname";
```

The important point to remember in this case is that the macro variable reference is resolved when you compile the SCL program, not when users execute the application. You must use a different approach if you want to retrieve the value of a macro variable while the program executes (for example, to pass values between SCL programs).

Macro variables store only strings of text characters, so numeric values are stored in macro variables as strings of text digits. The function you use to read the variable determines how the macro variable value is interpreted, as described in the following table.

If you want the macro variable contents interpreted as . . .	Then use the function . . .
a character value	SYMGET
a numeric value	SYMGETN

Using Automatic Macro Variables

In addition to macro variables that you define in your programs, the SAS System provides a number of predefined macro variables for every SAS session. These *automatic macro variables* supply information about the current SAS session and about the host operating system on which the SAS session is running. For example, you can use the automatic macro variable SYSDEVIC to obtain the name of the current graphics output device.

For a list of the available automatic macro variables, refer to Chapter 2, "Macro Variables," in the *SAS Guide to Macro Processing, Version 6, Second Edition*.

When you use automatic macro variables, remember to use the appropriate routines and functions to set and retrieve variable values. For example, consider the following two statements:

Using a macro variable reference:

```
jobid="&sysjobid";
```

Using an SCL function:

```
jobid=symget('sysjobid');
```

The first form, with the & (ampersand), is evaluated when the program is compiled. Thus, the variable JOBID is assigned an identifier value for the job or process that compiles the program. If you want the JOBID variable to contain a value for the job or process that is executing the application, you must use the second form, without the &. The SYMGET function extracts the macro variable value from the global symbol table at execution.

The values returned by SYSJOBID and other automatic macro variables depend on your host operating system. For more information on macro variables and the SAS macro facility, refer to the *SAS Guide to Macro Processing, Version 6, Second Edition*.

CHAPTER *11* # Submitting SAS® and SQL Statements and Issuing Host Commands

Introduction

Although Screen Control Language (SCL) provides a rich set of features, it does not provide functions and statements to accomplish directly all of the data access, management, presentation, and analysis tasks that the complete SAS System can perform, nor can it provide the equivalent for every command available under your host operating system. However, SCL does provide

□ the SUBMIT statement to generate SAS statements that are then submitted to the SAS System for processing, thus providing access to all other SAS System features.

□ the SYSTEM function to issue any host operating system command.

Submitting SAS and SQL Statements

You can submit statements to execute DATA steps and all the procedures in base SAS software, as well as procedures from any other product in the SAS System. You also can submit Structured Query Language (SQL) statements directly to the SAS System's SQL processor without submitting a PROC SQL statement. SQL statements enable you to query the contents of SAS files and to create and manipulate SAS data sets and SAS data views.

You can submit statements for processing on your local host or, if SAS/CONNECT software is installed at your site, on a remote host.

Note: In order to submit statements from within an FSEDIT application, you must have SAS/AF software installed at the site where you compile the SCL program in the SCREEN entry. However, users of your application do not need to have SAS/AF software installed in order to execute the application.

Submitting Statements versus Using SCL Features

You should submit statements when the task you want to perform is difficult or impossible using SCL features alone. Whenever equivalent SCL features are available, it is more efficient to use them than to submit SAS statements.

For example, the following two sets of statements produce the same result, opening an FSEDIT window to display the SAS data set WORK.DATA1 for editing:

SCL Feature:

```
call fsedit('work.data1');
```

Submitted Statements:

```
submit continue;
   proc fsedit data=work.data1;
   run;
endsubmit;
```

From within an application, fewer computer resources are required to execute the SCL CALL routine than to submit statements to the SAS System. Thus, the CALL routine is a better choice unless you need features of the procedure that the CALL routine doesn't provide—for example, PROC FSEDIT's VAR statement to select which variables that are displayed to the user.

Designating Submit Blocks

In your SCL programs, you designate the statements you want submitted to the SAS System for processing by placing the statements in submit blocks. A *submit block* begins with a SUBMIT statement, ends with an ENDSUBMIT statement, and consists of all the statements in between. The following statements illustrate these characteristics:

```
SUBMIT;       ❶
   proc print data=work.data1;
      var a b c;                   ❸
   run;
endsubmit;     ❷
```

❶ The SUBMIT statement starts the submit block.

❷ The ENDSUBMIT statement ends the submit block.

❸ These statements are submitted to the SAS System when the program executes.

Processing Submit Blocks

When the SAS/AF task or SAS/FSP procedure encounters a SUBMIT statement in an SCL program, it performs the following processing by default. This processing occurs at run time, when the SCL program executes, not when it is compiled.

Stage	Action
1	Copy all the statements between the SUBMIT statement and the next ENDSUBMIT statement into a special storage area called the *preview buffer*.

Stage	Action
	Note: The submitted statements are not checked for syntax or other errors when they are copied to the preview buffer. Errors in the submitted statements will not be detected until the statements are executed.
2	Scan the text in the preview buffer and make any requested substitutions. **Note:** Substitution is discussed in "Substituting Text in Submit Blocks" later in this chapter.
3	When the application ends, submit the contents of the preview buffer to the SAS System for execution. **Note:** Options are available to change when and where the contents of the preview buffer are submitted. See "Modifying the Behavior of Submit Blocks" later in this chapter for details.

Figure 11.1 illustrates how submit blocks are processed.

Note: Submit blocks are not processed when testing a SAS/AF application with the TESTAF command.

Figure 11.1
How Submit Blocks are Processed

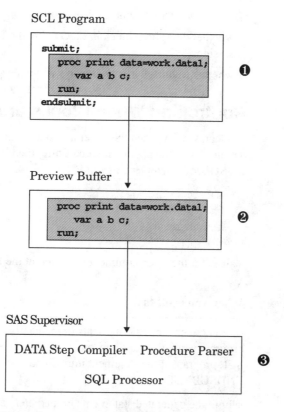

Note: If your application consists of more than one entry and you submit statements from a nested entry (that is, from an entry called by another entry in the application), then the submitted statements are not passed to the SAS System until the entire application ends. Simply ending the entry that contains the submit block does not process submitted statements.

How Submitted Statements are Formatted

By default, SCL reformats the submitted statements when it copies them to the preview buffer. All leading and trailing spaces in the submitted text are removed to conserve space. Semicolons in the submitted statements cause line breaks in the submitted text.

In some situations (for example, when the submitted statements include lines of raw data), you may want to prevent this formatting by SCL. You can do this using a CONTROL statement with the ASIS option. When you use a CONTROL ASIS statement, SCL honors the indention and spacing that appears in the submit block. CONTROL ASIS is more efficient because it reduces the time spent on formatting. Use a CONTROL NOASIS statement to restore the default behavior.

Modifying the Behavior of Submit Blocks

Figure 11.1 illustrates the default processing of submit blocks. You can add options to the SUBMIT statement to modify this default behavior. The SUBMIT statement has options that control

□ when the block is submitted

□ what happens after the block is submitted

□ where the block is sent for processing

□ whether the submit block is executed in the local SAS session or in a remote SAS session

□ whether a status window displays while the submit block is being processed.

Controlling When Blocks are Submitted

You can specify when the generated statements are submitted for execution and what action, if any, the application takes after the block is submitted. Add an argument to the SUBMIT statement, as follows:

```
submit when;
    SAS statements
endsubmit;
```

Values for the *when* argument are listed in the following table.

When you want to . . .	Then use . . .
submit the generated statements immediately, pause the SCL program while they execute, and then continue executing the SCL program at the statement immediately following ENDSUBMIT	CONTINUE
submit the generated statements immediately and then stop executing the current labeled section of the SCL program	IMMEDIATE
submit the generated statements immediately and then return to the primary window of the application	PRIMARY
submit the generated statements immediately and then terminate the application	TERMINATE

Note: CONTINUE is the only SUBMIT option that is valid in FSEDIT (and FSBROWSE) applications.

Submitting Immediately and Continuing the Program

When you specify SUBMIT CONTINUE, SCL takes the following actions:

Stage	Description
1	SCL immediately submits the current contents of the preview buffer and waits for the submitted statements to execute.
2	the SAS System processes the submitted statements and then returns control to the SCL program.
3	SCL continues to execute the program at the statement following the ENDSUBMIT statement.

> **Special Topic: Using SUBMIT CONTINUE in FSEDIT Applications**
>
> The behavior of a submit block with the CONTINUE option in an FSEDIT application depends on how the application was invoked.
>
> □ If you invoked the application with a PROC FSEDIT statement, then the statements in the submit block cannot be processed until the FSEDIT session ends, even though you specify SUBMIT CONTINUE. The statements cannot be executed as long as the FSEDIT procedure is executing.
>
> □ If you invoked the application with an FSEDIT command or with a CALL FSEDIT routine from another SCL program, then the statements in the submit block can execute immediately as long as no other procedure is currently executing.

Displaying a Status Window

SCL can display a temporary window to indicate that the application is waiting for a submit block to finish processing before continuing. The temporary window has the title Submit Block and displays the following message:

```
Processing statements in submit block.
```

When control returns to the application, this temporary window is closed.

Use the STATUS option with the SUBMIT CONTINUE statement to display the status window, as follows:

```
submit continue status;
```

Note: The status window is displayed by default when you use a SUBMIT CONTINUE statement in a PROGRAM entry that has no fields in its DISPLAY window.

Submitting Immediately and Passing Control

When you specify SUBMIT IMMEDIATE, SCL takes the following actions:

Stage	Description
1	control passes to the SAS/AF task (as if a RETURN statement had been executed). Any statements in the current labeled section of the SCL program following the ENDSUBMIT statement are not executed.
2	the SAS/AF task submits the current contents of the preview buffer and waits for the submitted statements to execute.
3	the SAS System processes the submitted statements and then returns control to the SAS/AF task. Any statements in the SCL program following the ENDSUBMIT statement are not executed.

▶ *Caution: Do not use the IMMEDIATE option in FRAME entry programs or in individually executed labeled sections.*

Programs in FRAME entries will not compile if they contain a SUBMIT IMMEDIATE statement.

SUBMIT IMMEDIATE blocks in labeled sections that are executed individually when a CONTROL LABEL statement is in effect can prevent the execution of other labeled sections.

Submitting Immediately and Returning to the Primary Window

When you specify SUBMIT PRIMARY, SCL takes the following actions:

Stage	Description
1	the current SCL program terminates. Any statements in the SCL program following the ENDSUBMIT statement are not executed.
2	the SAS/AF task immediately submits the current contents of the preview buffer and waits for the submitted statements to execute.
3	the SAS System processes the submitted statements. If the program containing the submit block was part of a larger application, control returns to the initial window of the application; otherwise, the application terminates.

The SUBMIT PRIMARY statement is useful if you want to close all the intermediate windows and return control to a primary window in the current execution stream. For more information on execution streams, see Chapter 31, "Managing Stacks and Streams" in *SAS Screen Control Language: Usage, Version 6, First Edition.*

Submitting Immediately and Ending the Application

When you specify SUBMIT TERMINATE, SCL takes the following actions:

Stage	Description
1	the current SCL program terminates. Any statements in the SCL program following the ENDSUBMIT statement are not executed, and control is not returned to any higher level if the current program is part of a larger application.

Stage	Description
2	the SAS/AF task submits the current contents of the preview buffer to the SAS System and then terminates.
3	the SAS System processes the submitted statements.

The SUBMIT TERMINATE statement is useful in situations where your application does not need to interact with users after the submitted statements are processed. However, you should specify the TERMINATE option only in special cases because re-invoking the application can be time-consuming.

Submitting Statements to the SQL Processor

In addition to submitting DATA and PROC steps, you also can route submitted statements directly to the SAS System's SQL processor without submitting a PROC SQL statement. Submitting SQL statements directly to the SQL processor is more efficient than submitting PROC SQL statements.

Structured Query Language (SQL) is a standardized, widely used language for retrieving and updating data in databases and relational tables. The SAS System's SQL processor enables you to

□ create tables and views

□ retrieve data stored in tables

□ retrieve data stored in SQL and SAS/ACCESS views

□ add or modify values in tables

□ add or modify values in SQL and SAS/ACCESS views.

For more information on SQL statements, refer to the *SAS Guide to the SQL Procedure: Usage and Reference, Version 6, First Edition.*

To send submitted statements to the SQL processor, use the following form of the SUBMIT statement:

```
submit continue sql;
   SQL statements
endsubmit;
```

Note: The SQL option is valid only when you specify CONTINUE for the first argument. PROC SQL and QUIT statements are not necessary.

Submitting Statements to a Remote Host

By default, statements are submitted for processing on the local host. If SAS/CONNECT software is available at your site, you can also submit statements for processing on a remote host. To send submitted statements to a remote host, use the following form of the SUBMIT statement:

```
submit options remote;
   SAS or SQL statements to execute on remote host
endsubmit;
```

In some situations, a user may want to switch between a remote host and the local host. The REMOTE command enables a user to force all submits to be sent to a remote host. The syntax of the REMOTE command is

REMOTE <ON|OFF>

If no option is specified, the command acts like a toggle. The REMOTE option on the SUBMIT block takes precedence over the REMOTE command. The AF application must have a display screen available in order to issue and recognize the REMOTE command.

Before SCL submits the generated code for execution, it checks to see if the user has issued the REMOTE ON command. If the user has, SCL checks to see if the remote link is still active. If it is active, SCL submits the code for execution; if it isn't active, SCL generates an error message and returns. The preview buffer is not cleared if the submit fails.

Substituting Text in Submit Blocks

In interactive applications, you often need to take different actions based on user input. SCL can substitute text in submit blocks based on the values of fields or SCL variables.

Rules for Substitution

SCL performs substitution in submit blocks according to the following rules:

□ When SCL encounters a name prefixed with an ampersand (&) in a submit block, it checks whether the name following the ampersand is the name of an SCL variable. (The SCL variable can be either a window or a nonwindow variable.) If so, SCL substitutes the value of the corresponding variable for the variable reference in the submit block.

For example, suppose a submit block contains the following statement:

```
proc print data=&dsname;
```

If the application includes a variable named DSNAME that contains the value **work.sample**, then the statement passed to the preview buffer will be as follows:

```
proc print data=work.sample;
```

□ If the name following the ampersand does not match any SCL variable, no substitution occurs. The name passes intact (including the ampersand) with the submitted statements. When the SAS System processes the statements, it attempts to resolve the name as a macro variable reference. SCL does not resolve macro variable references within submit blocks.

For example, suppose a submit block contains the following statement:

```
proc print data=&dsname;
```

If there is no SCL variable named DSNAME in the application, then the statement is passed unchanged to the preview buffer. The SAS System will attempt to resolve &DSNAME as a macro reference when the statements are processed.

▶ *Caution: Avoid using the same name for both an SCL variable and a macro variable that you want to use in submitted statements.*

SCL substitutes the value of the corresponding SCL variable for any name beginning with an ampersand. To guarantee that a name is passed as a macro variable reference in submitted statements, precede the name with two ampersands (for example, &&DSNAME).

Using Replacement Strings

If the SCL variable used in the substitution contains a null value, a blank is substituted in the submitted statements. This can cause problems if the substitution occurs in a statement that requires a value, so SCL allows you to define a replacement string for the variable. If the variable's value is not blank, the complete replacement string is substituted for the variable reference.

Use the REPLACE statement to define replacement strings, as follows:

```
replace variable 'replacement-string';
```

Note: The replacement string can include the variable's value, but that is not mandatory.

A REPLACE statement functions as an implicit IF-THEN statement that determines when to substitute the string in the submit block. Consider the following example:

```
replace dsname 'data=&dsname';
   . . .
submit;
   proc print &dsname;
   run;
endsubmit;
```

If DSNAME contains . . .	Then the submitted statements are . . .
'' (or _BLANK_)	proc print ; run;
work.sample	proc print data=work.sample; run;

Rules for the REPLACE Statement

The replacement string cannot exceed 200 characters because quoted character literals cannot exceed 200 characters. However, the generated text can exceed 200 characters.

REPLACE is a declarative statement, meaning that it is evaluated when the SCL program is compiled. You cannot generate different replacement strings based on conditions at execution time. For example, the following statements cause errors when you compile the program:

```
if (x) then
   replace y '&y';
else
   replace y '&z';
```

It is good programming practice to collect all REPLACE statements in one place in your SCL program, typically before the first executable statement.

Using the Replace Field Attribute

In SAS/AF applications, you also can define replacement strings for window variables using the Replace attribute in the BUILD procedure's ATTR window. The text specified in that field is substituted for the corresponding variable name when the variable name appears preceded with an ampersand in submitted statements. Refer to *SAS/AF Software: Usage and Reference, Version 6, First Edition* for details of the Replace attribute.

Note: REPLACE statements in the SCL program override the replacement string defined in the Replace attribute.

Issuing Commands to Host Operating Systems

You can issue commands to host operating systems from within your SCL programs. For example, you can issue commands to the operating system to

☐ perform system-specific data management or control tasks

☐ invoke non-SAS applications.

The commands that can be issued depend on the operating system under which your application runs. SCL places no restrictions on the commands you can issue to the operating system, nor does SCL check the command strings for validity before passing them to the operating system.

Use the SYSTEM function to issue commands to the operating system, as follows:

```
rc=system(command);
```

where *command* is the host command to be executed. Literal command strings should be enclosed in quotes. Whatever text you supply as the argument to the SYSTEM function passes to the operating system for execution.

CHAPTER *12* **Processing Commands Issued by Users**

Introduction

Users of your applications can issue SAS Display Manager System global commands, full-screen global commands, procedure-specific commands, and custom commands using the command line, function keys, or a menu bar. Your SCL program can intercept some of these commands and determine whether the command should execute.

You cannot intercept display manager global commands in SAS/AF and SAS/FSP applications because the SCL program is not executed when a display manager command is issued. However, in SAS/AF applications and FSEDIT applications, you can intercept procedure-specific and custom commands. In FRAME applications only, you can also intercept full-screen global commands. Procedure-specific commands for SAS/AF are described in *SAS/AF Software: Usage and Reference* and procedure-specific commands for SAS/FSP are described in *SAS/FSP Software: Usage and Reference*. Full-screen global commands are listed in "Using Full-Screen Global Commands". The following discussion refers to those commands that your application can intercept.

Enabling an Application to Intercept Commands

To intercept commands in your application, you must use a CONTROL statement with either the ENTER, ALWAYS, or ALLCMDS option specified. When one of these options is specified on the CONTROL statement, MAIN executes whenever you issue a command. This allows your SCL program to use the WORD function to query the command issued and intercept it if needed. When multiple commands are specified on the command line, separated by semicolons, MAIN is executed for each command specified on the command line. MAIN is executed only once unless multiple commands separated by semicolons are entered.

With CONTROL ALWAYS specified, custom commands entered on the command line that are not valid SAS commands are not flagged in error. With CONTROL ALLCMDS specified, these commands may be flagged in error. To prevent the error message, use NEXTCMD to clear the command from the command buffer. Make sure you do not execute NEXTCMD unconditionally or all commands will be removed from the command buffer before they execute and you will not be able to leave your application.

Refer to the discussion in this chapter on the CONTROL statement for specific benefits offered by each CONTROL statement option before you decide which is best for your application.

Reading Commands

To read the command issued, use the WORD function. WORD returns the first, second, or third word of the command issued. A word is the text from the current position up to the end of a leading number or the next blank or semicolon.

You can use a combination of the WORD function and the NEXTWORD routine to read multi-word commands. After using WORD to read the first word from the command line, use NEXTWORD to move the read pointer one word to the right. Then use WORD again to read the word. You can repeat this process until you have read the entire command.

Removing Commands from the Command Buffer

With CONTROL ALWAYS specified in FSEDIT applications or CONTROL ALLCMDS in SAS/AF applications, statements in MAIN execute when commands are placed in the command buffer. This happens:

□ after commands are entered on the command line

□ after the function key associated with a command is pressed

□ after a command is executed by the CALL EXECCMD routine in the SCL program.

A command is executed only if it is still in the command buffer after MAIN finishes executing. This allows you to conditionally prevent the execution of a command, for example DELETE or ADD in FSEDIT applications.

Commands can be removed unexpectedly from the command buffer by SCL statements that can clear the command buffer if they execute before the command is handled. The following list shows some SCL statements and functions that can remove a command from the command buffer if they execute before the command is handled.

```
CALL CBT
CALL DISPLAY
CALL FSEDIT
CALL FSLIST
CALL FSVIEW
CALL LETTER
CALL METHOD
CALL NEXTCMD
CALL NEXTWORD
CALL NOTIFY
CALL SEND
CATLIST
DATALISTC/DATALISTN
DIRLIST
LISTC/LISTN
REFRESH (FSEDIT only)
SHOWLIST
```

The command buffer is emptied when another window opens or another entry is called. These statements and functions can remove a command from the command buffer if they execute before the command is handled because they open another window or call another entry. In FSEDIT applications, REFRESH essentially redisplays the current FSEDIT window and thus empties the command buffer. CALL DISPLAY calls another entry and empties the command buffer even if the called entry does not have a display window.

Re-issuing a Command

SCL programs can capture a command and re-issue it after it has been removed from the command buffer. The special NOEXEC option on the CALL EXECCMDI routine allows the command that is captured to be executed when the window is redisplayed but tells SAS not to go through statements in the MAIN section again before executing the command. While the EXECCMDI routine is typically used to issue global commands, it can be used to execute a procedure-specific or custom command when the NOEXEC option is specified. With NOEXEC specified, the command is not executed immediately but when the window is redisplayed. You can only issue one command using the EXECCMDI routine with the NOEXEC option. For more information, refer to EXECCMDI in Chapter 20.

Example using EXECCMDI with NOEXEC

Suppose your FSEDIT application wants to intercept the DELETE command and display a small SAS/AF window that asks users to confirm their delete request. This confirmation window is called CONFIRM.FRAME. It has two pushbutton objects, YES and NO, and is controlled by the following program:

```
entry confirm $ 3;

YES:
   confirm='YES';
   _status_='H';
return;

NO:
   confirm='NO';
   _status_='H';
return;
```

The following FSEDIT SCL program opens CONFIRM.FRAME to confirm a delete request.

```
FSEINIT:
   control always;        ❶
   length confirm $ 3;
return;

INIT:
return;

MAIN:
   if word(1,'u') =: 'DEL' then    ❷
      do;
         call display('confirm.frame',confirm);
         if confirm='YES' then call execcmdi('delete','noexec');   ❸
      end;
return;

TERM:
return;
```

❶ CONTROL ALWAYS allows the MAIN section to execute when a user issues a command.

❷ When the DELETE command is issued, open the confirmation window.

❸ If the user confirms the delete request, reissue the DELETE command using CALL EXECCMDI with the NOEXEC option. The NOEXEC option allows the DELETE command to be handled without executing statements in the MAIN section again. If the user does not confirm the delete request, no further processing is necessary because the CALL DISPLAY routine has already removed the DELETE command from the command buffer.

Using Full-Screen Global Commands

The following commands are global in all SAS/AF and SAS/FSP windows. You can submit these full-screen global commands with EXECCMDI. In FRAME entry applications only, your SCL program can intercept these full-screen global commands if CONTROL ALLCMDS is specified.

Table 12.1
Full-Screen Global Commands

Window Position	WSIZE	WREGION
Window Management	DEBUG	SETWDATA
	RESOURCE	SETWNAME
	SETCR	SHOWTYPE
	SETHELP	SWAP
	SETPMENU	TYPE
Window Call	MSG	PREVIEW
Printing	FONT	PRTFILE
	FORMNAME	SPRINT
Miscellaneous	AFSYS	SHORTDUMP
	REMOTE	SYNC

CHAPTER *13* **Optimizing Application Performance**

Introduction

Like any programming language, Screen Control Language (SCL) provides a variety of different ways to accomplish most tasks. However, for any given problem some of the possible solutions are more efficient than others. That is, some programming techniques in SCL require fewer resources than others.

Factors Affecting Program Performance

A combination of the following factors determines the efficiency of an SCL programming technique:

□ computer resources, including the following:

   □ the amount of CPU time required for the computer to perform calculations

   □ the amount of time required to move information into storage from memory or into memory from storage on disk or tape

   □ the amount of memory space required to hold the data associated with the operation

   □ the amount of disk space required to hold the data associated with the operation

□ developer resources, including the amount of time required to develop, debug, and maintain applications.

Finding the most efficient programming techniques requires striking a balance among these factors.

Enhancing Program Performance

The following techniques describe ways you can make your programs more efficient.

Writing Efficient Code

SCL provides many different functions, statements, and routines. The following techniques provide ways to use selected language features more efficiently:

□ To save memory, use a LENGTH statement in your SCL programs to define character-type nonwindow variables. Character-type nonwindow variables are assigned a default length of 200 unless you specify a shorter length. You can use the DEFAULT= option in a LENGTH statement to change the default variable length.

□ When possible, limit the number of SCL variables your application references.

The following examples illustrate two ways to define a WHERE clause using the values of character window variables X and Y. The double quotes are used because the values are character.

Acceptable

```
tempvar1='x="';
tempvar2='" and y="';
tempvar3='"';
rc=where(dsid,tempvar1||x||tempvar2||y||tempvar3);
```

More efficient

```
rc=where(dsid,'x='||quote(x)||' and y='||quote(y));
```

Another way to eliminate unnecessary variables is to use functions directly in conditional expressions, as shown in the following examples:

Acceptable

```
rc=fetch(dsid);
if (rc=-1) then
    do;
        SCL statements to handle the end-of-file condition
    end;
```

More efficient

```
if (fetch(dsid)=-1) then
    do;
        SCL statements to handle the end-of-file condition
    end;
```

If you do not need the value of the function's return code for any other processing, the latter form is more efficient because it eliminates the unnecessary variable assignment.

□ Processing time is faster when you use an array as the argument to the IN operator instead of using a list of values. The following examples illustrate two ways to locate a particular value:

Acceptable

```
i=part in ('p001','p002','p003',...);
```

More efficient

```
array partno{100} $ _temporary_ ('p001','p002','p003',...);
i=part in partno;
```

□ Use the FIELD function to determine whether users modified any fields in a window. Using a list of field names as an argument to the FIELD function in this case is more efficient than using the MODIFIED function for each field. The following examples illustrate two ways to test whether users modified the PRINC, RATE, or TERM fields:

Acceptable

```
if modified(princ)
   or modified(rate)
   or modified(term) then
      payment=mort(princ,.,rate,term);
```

More efficient

```
if field('modified','princ rate term') then
   payment=mort(princ,.,rate,term);
```

□ If you want to display a selection list of values from SAS data set variables, using the DATALISTC or DATALISTN function is more efficient than building an extended table.

□ When you use the DISPLAY routine to invoke SAS/AF entries, use arguments to the DISPLAY routine and an ENTRY statement in the called entry to pass values between the entries. If you need to make values available to all entries in an application, not to simply one specific entry, then consider using the local environment list or global environment list rather than macro variables. SCL lists are more flexible than macro variables because they can represent entire structures of data instead of simple numbers or strings.

□ When building PROGRAM entries and text entry objects in FRAME entries, use the special SAS/AF field type attributes to decrease the number of SCL statements required to validate field values.

 For example, if you specify a field type of INPUT for a field in which users enter data set names, users can type a question mark (?) in the field to automatically display a selection list that shows the members of all SAS data libraries available for use.

□ Unless you need to modify attributes while the program is executing, define field and window attributes using the ATTR and GATTR windows in the BUILD procedure (for SAS/AF applications) or the FSEDIT Attributes and FSEDIT Parms windows (for FSEDIT applications) instead of using the attribute functions, routines, and statements in SCL programs.

□ When executing commands in an FSVIEW session, design your formulas so that the commands are issued only once rather than each time users scroll the observations in the FSVIEW window. For example, if you want to identify a custom HELP entry for the application, you can define a computed variable called HELPVBL with the following formula:

```
helpvbl=helpvbl; if temp=. then do;
         call execcmdi('sethelp perm.cat.my.help');
         temp=1; end;
```

Because the nonwindow variable TEMP contains a missing value only once, the first time the formula executes, the SETHELP command is issued only once. You can issue the DROP command to drop the column for HELPVBL from the display. Even without the variable displayed, the formula still executes.

Optimizing Data Set Operations

Use the following techniques to improve the efficiency of programs that open, read, and update SAS data sets:

□ Avoid opening and closing the same SAS data sets multiple times in an application. If you read from or write to the same SAS data set at several different points in an application, it is more efficient to open the data set once at the beginning of the application and close it when the application ends than to open and close the data set each time information is read from or written to it.

SAS data sets are typically opened in the FSEINIT section of FSEDIT applications and in the INIT section of SAS/AF applications, and closed in the FSETERM section of FSEDIT applications and in the TERM section of SAS/AF applications, because these sections are typically executed only once at the beginning and end of the application.

□ When you use the OPEN function, check whether the SAS data set was successfully opened. In many cases, you do not want to continue processing in the same manner if the data set was not opened.

□ If your program fetches a large amount of data from a SAS data set, use a FETCHOBS function in the INIT section to make subsequent fetch functions perform more quickly. The argument to the FETCHOBS function should be a value greater than the number of observations in the SAS data set so you attempt to fetch an observation beyond the end of the data set.

□ If your program reads a SAS data set with many variables but modifies a limited number of variable values, the PUTVARC and PUTVARN routines and the GETVARC and GETVARN functions are more efficient than the SET routine. With the CALL SET routine, all variables in the data set are read into the SCL data vector (SDV) every time an observation is fetched.

□ If you want to process only a subset of the observations in a SAS data set, it is more efficient to use the WHERE function or the WHERE= data set option with the OPEN function than to submit a DATA step to create a new data set containing only the desired subset.

□ You may be able to improve the efficiency of WHERE processing by indexing the data set. You can use the ICREATE function in SCL to build an index for a SAS data set. See *SAS Language: Reference* for more information about indexing data sets. WHERE clause processing can take advantage of indexing to locate observations more quickly.

□ Use the NOTE, POINT, and DROPNOTE functions to locate and quickly navigate among specific observations.

□ If you have limited disk space available, investigate using compressed data sets. Use the COMPRESS= data set option with the OPEN statement in SCL programs to create compressed data sets. See *SAS Language: Reference* for more information about compressed data sets, including a discussion of when using compression is appropriate.

Using Submit Blocks

Consider the following issues when designing submit blocks for your SCL applications:

□ Whenever possible, use SCL functions rather than submit blocks. For example, when you want to assign a fileref you should use the FILENAME function in SCL instead of a submit block to submit a FILENAME statement.

□ When using a submit block to submit Structured Query Language (SQL) statements, use the SQL argument in the SUBMIT statement rather than a submit block that submits the SQL procedure. The SUBMIT SQL statement invokes the SQL task, which is more efficient than invoking the SQL procedure by submitting a PROC SQL statement.

□ Use the EXECCMDI routine to issue global commands rather than a submit block with a DM statement.

Increasing Your Productivity

The following techniques offer ways you can make the best use of your development time when building applications:

□ While you are developing your application, use the SCL debugger when you need to examine variable values or watch the execution of your program one step at a time.

□ While you are developing your application, use the SYSMSG function to provide information about the return codes from various SCL functions. The SYSMSG function provides the error message produced by the SAS System. The following is an example of using SYSMSG to capture SAS System error messages:

```
dsid=open('sasuser.houses');
msg=sysmsg();
if dsid=0 then
    put "OPEN FAILED:" msg;
```

After you have debugged your program, you should remove the SYSMSG calls before creating the production version of your application so that users do not see messages they might not understand.

□ If you need to use the information in the return codes from SCL functions, it is more efficient to use the same variable repeatedly. While the development version of your application may use several variables to monitor the return codes from various SCL functions, consider modifying the source to check the same variable when creating the production version.

□ When you provide default or null character arguments to functions, the appropriate argument is ' ' (with a blank between the quotes), not '' (with no blank between the quotes). In SAS/AF applications, you can use the special value _BLANK_.

□ If you plan to use the SCL debugger during an FSEDIT session, use the PUT _ALL_ statement in the FSEINIT reserved label. This statement initializes all variables for the debugger. Remove the PUT statement when you complete the debugging process.

□ If you use the same catalog to contain all the entries that comprise your application, you only need to specify two-level names (*entry-name.entry-type*) instead of four-level names (*libref.catalog.entry-name.entry-type*) for most SCL functions. This also makes it easier to reuse the entries in other applications.
    Note: A few SCL functions do not accept two-level names. These exceptions are noted in Chapter 20, "Screen Control Language Dictionary."

□ To decrease the amount of disk space your production version requires, use the NOSOURCE option in the MERGE statement in the PROC BUILD statement when copying your application to the production library. It is important to save either an original catalog or the SCL program in a file because you cannot edit the SCL source when you specify the NOSOURCE option.

□ You may find it convenient to use the NOMSG option in the PROC BUILD statement so that the BUILD procedure writes all notes and warnings it generates during program compilation and testing to the SAS log rather than to the MESSAGE window. When you end the BUILD procedure, the NOMSG option ensures that compilation and execution information is still available in the SAS log.

□ If you use the LOG command to check the LOG window for messages, use the NEXT BUILD command to return to the SAS/AF development environment or the NEXT FSEDIT command to return to the FSEDIT window.

□ Review your source program. As you become more familiar with SCL, you may find that functions or methods of programming you originally overlooked can save either processing time or disk space.

Making Your Applications Easier to Maintain

The following techniques may save you time in the long term because they minimize questions from your users or save you maintenance time:

□ Use comments in your programs. Short notes make it easier to review your logic later.

□ If your terminal supports color, use different colors for the different elements of the SCL programs in your SAS/AF applications. For example, you could put comments in white, SCL statements in green, and submitted statements in blue.
   Note: This technique is not available in FSEDIT applications. The FSEDIT Program window allows only one color for program text.

□ Provide custom help for your users. In addition to using the general Help attribute to associate HELP or CBT entries with your applications, you can use the CALL CBT and CALL DISPLAY routines to display context-sensitive help information.
   You can also use legend windows to provide help information to users. Refer to Chapter 14, "Introduction to Application Interfaces," for more information on legend windows.

□ Always provide users with a means of exiting the program, (and, of course, the application).

□ You may find that action bars or selection lists provide an easier method of helping your users move through the application. With menus, users do not have to remember default key settings. This also is a good way to limit the choices users can make and thus the amount of programming you must do to prevent invalid selections.

□ To maximize control of program flow in SAS/AF PROGRAM and FRAME entries, you can turn off the window's command line by specifying **NONE** for the Banner attribute in the GATTR window. However, this also means that the window no longer provides a message line for displaying messages to users.
   You can define a field to hold the message text in lieu of the message line. For readers to view the message text, the field must be displayed, but you can specify a blank for the Pad attribute. This technique makes the field appear only when it contains a value. Also specify **YES** for the field's Protect attribute. Specify the CONTROL ALWAYS statement in the INIT section, and in the INIT and MAIN sections assign to the field the value you would have assigned to the _MSG_ system variable.

CHAPTER *14* **Introduction to Application Interfaces**

Introduction

This chapter describes application interface features that are largely or completely controlled or manipulated by SCL. Although fields are the basic interface between application users and the SCL program, this chapter focuses on other window elements that use SCL programs to receive user input and return values. These include:

□ built-in selection lists for displaying a list of valid values

□ extended tables for displaying data in tables

□ choice groups for providing mutually-exclusive choices in PROGRAM entries

□ block menus for providing menus displaying icons or blocks in PROGRAM entries

□ SAS/FSP windows for data management tasks

□ legend windows for providing user information

□ management of commands issued by users

SAS/AF FRAME entries provide an environment for building graphical user interface (GUI) applications that are object-oriented. Elements for FRAME entry windows consist of widgets, which are objects that are displayable. Basic user interface widgets that are comparable to PROGRAM entry fields and pushbuttons are text entry and pushbutton widgets. You can control many actions for widgets by specifying them as attributes or by using a method. Widgets perform actions via methods, which are executed using CALL routines in SCL. Each object type has a set of methods provided with SAS/AF software. For example, you can specify the array or SCL list containing the values to display in a list box as one of its attributes and track user selections and take actions using methods. *SAS/AF Software: FRAME Entry Usage and Reference, Version 6, First Edition* describes FRAME entry widgets and methods.

SAS/AF PROGRAM entries provide an environment for building windows consisting of fields and pushbuttons. The PROGRAM entry is described in *SAS/AF Software: Usage and Reference, Version 6, First Edition*. PROGRAM entry fields and features that contain fields are largely controlled by SCL programs.

SAS/FSP software allows you to create windowing interfaces between SAS data sets and users. SAS/AF applications can call FSEDIT applications and FSVIEW applications when users need to work with data sets, since features like scrolling are built into SAS/FSP software. Conversely, SAS/FSP applications can use SAS/AF windows to perform tasks like displaying enhanced help information or displaying a window for users to confirm a command (like DELETE) before it is executed. Creating SAS/FSP applications is described in *SAS/FSP Software: Usage and Reference, Version 6, First Edition.*

Basic Application Interface

For PROGRAM entries and FSEDIT applications, fields are the basic user-interface feature of application windows that use SCL programs. *Fields* are the areas of the window in which users enter information and in which your application displays information that changes in response to users' input or as a result of program calculations. When you design the windows for your applications, you also can add descriptive text such as titles, instructions, and field labels, but neither users nor the SCL program can change this text while the application is executing. CBT entries in SAS/AF also use fields to interact with users, but CBT entries are not discussed in this chapter because they do not use SCL programs.

Figure 14.1 shows a PROGRAM entry window with descriptive text and fields for data entry and display.

Figure 14.1
A Window with Fields and Descriptive Text

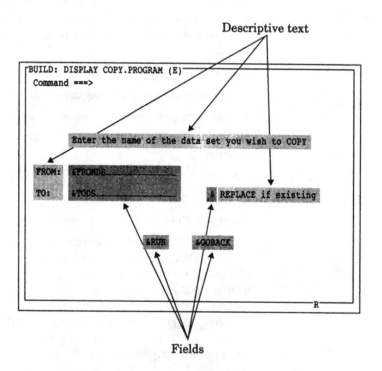

For FRAME entry applications, widgets display information to users and accept user input and they are the basic user interface feature of applications. For complete information on FRAME entry widgets, see *SAS/AF Software: FRAME Usage and Reference.* Display 14.1 shows a FRAME entry window containing a variety of widgets.

Display 14.1
Sample FRAME Entry

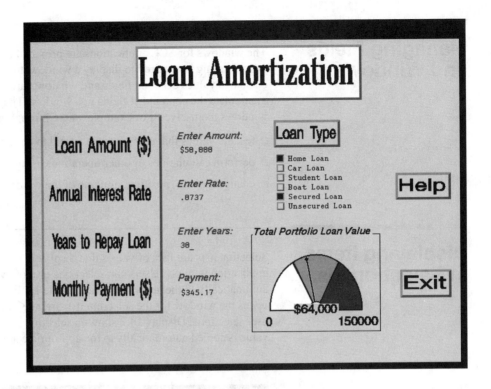

Loan Amortization, Loan Amount, Annual Interest Rate, Years to Repay Loan, Monthly Payment ($), and Loan Type are graphics text widgets. $50,000, .0737, 30, and $345.17 are text entry widgets with region titles. The items with square selection markers under Loan Type are checkboxes. The "dial" under Total Portfolio Loan Value is a critical success factor widget. Help and Exit are pushbutton widgets.

The widgets that you can select for a FRAME entry window are listed in the pop-up menu that opens when you choose the Make or Fill actions for creating a widget. Each type of widget used in the FRAME entry (called a class) can perform a set of actions, which are called methods. Methods are executed using a group of SCL routines (for example, CALL SEND or CALL NOTIFY), which are listed in Chapter 19, "SCL Language Elements" in the category "Object Oriented" and are described in Chapter 20, "Screen Control Language Dictionary."

Communicating Information Between Windows and SCL Programs

Each field in a PROGRAM entry window or widget in a FRAME entry window has a corresponding window variable in the application's SCL data vector. They are the connection between users and the SCL program that drives your application. The most basic way for SCL applications to receive input from users is for you to provide fields or widgets in the application's window in which users can enter or select values. These window variable values pass to corresponding variables in the SCL program. The most basic way for SCL applications to provide information to users is for an SCL program to store the desired information in variables whose values pass to the appropriate window variables for fields and widgets. SCL programs also communicate values between the data set or external file and the user interface and often manipulate these values.

Managing Fields and Windows

The windows for SCL applications are provided by the underlying software. No SCL programming is required to display a window, to define the fields in a window, or to exchange values between fields and window variables. However, SCL programs can manipulate the contents of fields in a window. They also can manipulate the windows themselves. For example, an SCL program can

□ test the values that users enter in a field to ensure those values are valid

□ perform calculations or other operations using the field values

□ change the size, position, or name of the window.

Displaying Items in Selection Lists

Selection lists are lists of values that display in a window that is separate from the application window. Users can select one or more values, which are copied automatically to the appropriate field in the application window. SCL automatically opens the window for the selection list, arranges and displays list items, and accepts user selections. Display 14.2 shows a selection list. When a user selects a value, the value is copied automatically to the appropriate area in the application window.

Display 14.2
Sample Selection List

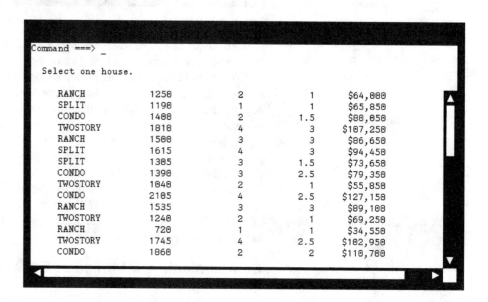

In PROGRAM entries, you can specify attributes in the ATTR and GATTR windows to display a selection list. However, SCL provides a set of features that allow you to create a selection list with a single SCL program statement.

For details on creating and using selection lists, see *SAS Screen Control Language: Usage, Version 6, First Edition.* For more information on list boxes, see *SAS/AF Software: FRAME Entry Usage and Reference.*

Creating Built-In Selection Lists

SCL provides a set of functions that automatically display a selection list window containing the type of items determined by the function. The following table shows the type of values displayed in the selection list and the SCL function that creates the list:

For a list containing ...	Use the function ...
entries in a SAS catalog	CATLIST
names of valid colors for a user's device	COLORLIST
values of one or more variables in a SAS data set	DATALISTC|DATALISTN
names of graphic hardware devices	DEVLIST
members of a SAS data library	DIRLIST
filerefs defined for a user's current SAS session	FILELIST
librefs defined for a user's current SAS session	LIBLIST
items listed in a HELP, LIST, or MENU entry	LISTC|LISTN *
up to 13 list items you specify in the function statement	SHOWLIST
names of variables in a SAS data set	VARLIST

* While you can execute the LISTC and LISTN functions from SAS/FSP applications, you must also have SAS/AF software to create the HELP, MENU, or LIST entries to be called.

For details on these functions, see the SCL dictionary in Chapter 20.

Controlling Window Location

You can control the location of a selection list window by allowing it to display in the default location or by specifying its size and location in the window. List windows displayed from the **List** attribute (instead of via SCL) cannot be resized. The WREGION function allows you to change the size and appearance of selection list windows. Use WREGION prior to invoking the selection list window to specify the size of that window. For example, the SAS/AF program that displays the selection list shown in Display 14.2 uses WREGION to open a window large enough for the entire data set to display.

```
INIT:
    houseid=open('sasuser.houses');
        /* Start the selection list window at column 20  */
        /* and make it 25 lines long.                    */
    call wregion(1,20,25,80,);
    choice=datalistc(houseid,'style sqfeet bedrooms baths price',
                'Select one house.');
return;
MAIN:
    statements to process user selections
return;
TERM:
    if houseid then houseid=close(houseid);
return;
```

Displaying Data in Extended Tables

SCL allows you to display information in multiple rows when you have designed only one row of fields in a PROGRAM entry or one row of widgets for an extended table widget in a FRAME entry. This feature is called an *extended table*, and the row is called a *logical row*. The SCL program defines the information displayed in the table. With additional SCL programming, you can enable users to select items from the table. Thus, you can use extended tables to create custom selection lists. Additional programming can also allow users to modify the table and return those values to a SAS data set or external file.

Users can issue commands to scroll forward and backward through the information in the table. SAS/AF software handles the task of scrolling the table, and no SCL programming is required for that.

PROGRAM entry windows can contain only one extended table. However, FRAME entry windows can contain multiple extended tables along with other widgets.

Display 14.3 shows an extended table.

Display 14.3
Sample Extended Table

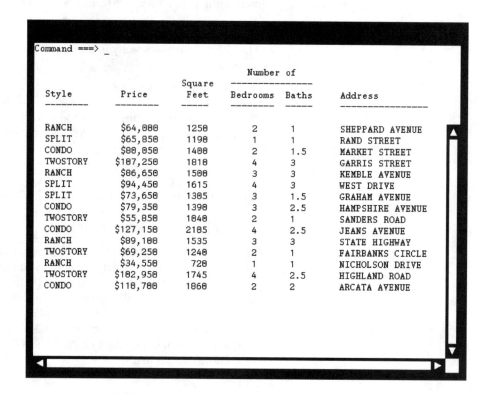

```
Command ===>  _

                                   Number of
                            Square  ----------------
   Style        Price        Feet  Bedrooms  Baths    Address
   --------     --------     -----  --------  -----    ----------------

   RANCH        $64,000      1250      2        1      SHEPPARD AVENUE
   SPLIT        $65,850      1190      1        1      RAND STREET
   CONDO        $80,050      1400      2        1.5    MARKET STREET
   TWOSTORY     $107,250     1810      4        3      GARRIS STREET
   RANCH        $86,650      1500      3        3      KEMBLE AVENUE
   SPLIT        $94,450      1615      4        3      WEST DRIVE
   SPLIT        $73,650      1305      3        1.5    GRAHAM AVENUE
   CONDO        $79,350      1390      3        2.5    HAMPSHIRE AVENUE
   TWOSTORY     $55,850      1040      2        1      SANDERS ROAD
   CONDO        $127,150     2105      4        2.5    JEANS AVENUE
   RANCH        $89,100      1535      3        3      STATE HIGHWAY
   TWOSTORY     $69,250      1240      2        1      FAIRBANKS CIRCLE
   RANCH        $34,550       720      1        1      NICHOLSON DRIVE
   TWOSTORY     $102,950     1745      4        2.5    HIGHLAND ROAD
   CONDO        $110,700     1860      2        2      ARCATA AVENUE
```

Using Extended Tables

The values you display in an extended table can come from a SAS data set, an SCL list, an array in the SCL program, or an external file. Whether the data display in a few rows or in a few thousand rows, on the DISPLAY window you create only the fields for one table row. Your SCL program processes these fields as an extended table of fields instead of as one row of fields.

Extended tables can be static or dynamic. Use a static table when you can specify the number of rows to display. Use a dynamic table when:

□ you do not know the size of the source of the table, for example the size of the data set or SCL list that displays in the table.

□ the number of data set observations can change because users can add or delete observations through the table

□ you want to display a subset of a SAS data set you have created with a WHERE clause.

For more information on creating windows for extended tables in PROGRAM entries, see *SAS/AF Software: Usage and Reference.* For more information on creating extended table widgets in FRAME entries and using extended table methods, see *SAS/AF Software: FRAME Entry Usage and Reference.* For details on the extended table functions and routines, see the table of SCL elements in Chapter 19, "SCL Language Elements" and the appropriate entries in Chapter 20.

The following table lists the SCL functions and routines you use to define and display an extended table and handle user selections or modifications.

Table 14.1
Defining and Displaying An Extended Table

To . . .	Use the . . .
define an extended table	SETROW routine in PROGRAM entries or the _SETROW_ method in FRAME entries
display table rows	GETROW section in PROGRAM entries GET*n** section in FRAME entries
identify the current table row	_CURROW_ system variable
modify or select table rows	PUTROW section in PROGRAM entries PUT*n** section in FRAME entries
remove a row's selected status	UNSELECT function in PROGRAM entries or the _UNSELECT_ method in FRAME entries
designate the end of a dynamic table	ENDTABLE routine in PROGRAM entries or the _ENDTABLE_ method in FRAME entries

* *n* is the number of the widget (in the order in which it was created, by default). This label should be the name that is assigned as the **Getrow** or **Putrow** label in the Extended Table Attributes window.

SAS Screen Control Language: Usage contains a detailed description of the steps for creating extended tables. It also describes how to use extended tables as custom selection lists, design tables in with a multi-line logical row, delete observations through extended tables, and display external files in extended tables.

Example Extended Table

This example shows the program for the extended table shown in Display 14.3.

```
INIT:
        /* Open the data set and associate like-named variables  */
        /* with window variables.  Define the extended table to   */
        /* have a row for each observation in the data set.       */
    dsid=open('sasuser.houses');
```

```
        call set(dsid);
        call setrow(attrn(dsid,'nobs'));
    return;
    MAIN:
    return;
    TERM:
          /*  Close the data set.  */
        if dsid then sysrc=close(dsid);
    return;
    GETROW:
          /* Display the observations in the table's rows.  */
        rc=fetchobs(dsid,_currow_);
    return;
    PUTROW:
          /* Get the modified observation back into the DDV.    */
          /* Then, update the data set with the values entered  */
          /* into the extended table.                           */
        rc=fetchobs(dsid,_currow_,'noset');
        rc=update(dsid);
    return;
```

Flow of Control in Extended Tables

This section summarizes the flow of control for an application that includes an extended table.

1. When the program is first invoked, INIT executes before the table is displayed.

2. If SETROW is called and the number of rows is greater than zero or the table is a dynamic table, the statements in GETROW execute repeatedly until either a full window or widget of rows is displayed or until the final row in the extended table is displayed. The final row occurs when either the maximum number of rows specified in SETROW is reached or, for a dynamic table, when ENDTABLE is called.

3. If a user issues a vertical scrolling command such as DOWN or BOTTOM, GETROW is called repeatedly until a full window of extended table values is displayed or until the final row in the table is displayed.

4. If a user modifies any variables in the non-scrollable area of a PROGRAM window and presses ENTER, or simply presses ENTER when CONTROL ENTER or CONTROL ALWAYS are specified, then the following occur:

   □ the statements in MAIN execute

   □ the statements in GETROW redisplay the extended table.

5. If a user presses ENTER after modifying any variables in the scrollable area (the table) of the display, the following occur:

   □ the statements in PUTROW execute for each modified row

   □ the statements in MAIN execute

   □ the statements in GETROW redisplay the extended table.

6. If a user leaves the application by issuing a global command such as OUTPUT, PGM, or NEXT (instead if END, CANCEL, or BYE) and then returns to the application, the statements in GETROW redisplay the extended table. These are the only statements that execute when the user returns.

7. If a user executes END, one of three things can happen:

□ If no fields were modified, then TERM executes.

□ If a field in the nonscrollable section has been modified or if CONTROL ENTER or CONTROL ALWAYS is specified, then the MAIN executes, followed by TERM.

□ If a field in the scrollable section has been modified, then the statements in PUTROW execute for each modified row and then MAIN executes, followed by TERM.

8. If a user executes the CANCEL command, no matter what other conditions are in effect, only TERM section executes.

Using SCL to Manipulate Choice Groups

Choice groups in PROGRAM entries display a set of stations that offer choices to users, who can select only one station. When a choice group contains multiple items, then the choices are mutually exclusive. Successive selections simply turn off the previous selection. For example, if a user makes a second selection, the second station is selected. and the previous station is turned off.

Radio box widgets in FRAME entries are analogous to choice groups, although you can control them by setting attributes instead of through the SCL program. Check boxes are similar widgets only users may select any number of check boxes when several of them are grouped together. For information on radio boxes and check boxes, see *SAS/AF Software: FRAME Entry Usage and Reference.*

Display 14.4 shows a window with a choice group called a linked action choice group, which pairs fields of type **ACTION** with choice group stations. When a user clicks on a project type, the text for the choice automatically displays in the **Project** field.

Display 14.4
Sample Choice Group

```
Command ===>

                        TRACK PROJECT HOURS


           Name:     Sam Jones

           Dept:     TWD

           Project:  Edit

                     _ Write     _ Review

                     * Edit      _ Projman


           Hours spent: 15___
```

Although you do not use SCL to create or use choice groups, you must use SCL to turn stations on or off and to determine which station a user selects. You also can use SCL to take actions based on selections. For information on creating choice groups in PROGRAM entries, see *SAS/AF Software: Usage and Reference.* For information on creating radio boxes, see *SAS/AF Software: FRAME Entry Usage and Reference.*

For your SCL program, the value of the choice group variable is the station currently selected. SAS/AF software automatically determines which station is selected and highlights selected stations on devices that allow it. You do not have to write statements into your SCL program to perform these tasks.

Controlling Actions for Stations

Your SCL program uses the value returned in the choice group variable (the choice group name or list box widget name) to control what happens when users make a selection. Your program can consist of one conditional statement that references the station's **List** attribute and displays the entry or executes the specified command. For example, if the **List** attribute for each station in the choice group CHOICE is the name of another entry in the application, this statement would allow a selected station to call another entry.

```
call display(choice);
```

Alternatively, your program can contain a conditional statement for each station, identifying it by the value of its **List** attribute. For example,

```
if choice='tennis' then call display(tennis.program);
if choice='end' then call execcmd('end');
```

You also can use a third technique of creating a SELECT statement that identifies each station by its sequential number in the group. For example,

```
select (isactive('choice'));
  when (1) call display('events.program');
  when (2) call display('tennis.program');
  when statements for remaining stations
  otherwise;
end;
```

Activating and Protecting Stations

You can write your program so that the default action is to either activate a station or protect it from selection. An activated station displays as highlighted and a protected station displays as grayed on devices that support these features. To activate a station, use the ACTIVATE function and specify the sequential number of the station in the choice group. In PROGRAM entries, you also use the ACTIVATE function to protect a station. To control a station's protected status in the FRAME entry, use the GRAY and UNGRAY functions.

Protecting means that users cannot tab to that station and pressing ENTER does not activate or select that station. When users try to select a protected station, no action takes place. To protect a station, you also use ACTIVATE but you supply the negative of the station's sequential number in the choice group.

SAS/AF Software: Usage and Reference provides a thorough description of creating and programming a choice group.

Creating Block or Icon Menus with SCL

You can implement menus that display choices as blocks or icons by using the BLOCK routine in SCL. In FRAME entries, you can also implement this kind of menu using block widgets or icon widgets. Block and icon widgets are described in *SAS/AF Software: FRAME Entry Usage and Reference*.

When you use the BLOCK function, SCL automatically opens the window for the menu, arranges and displays the blocks, and accepts user selections. For PROGRAM entries, the BLOCK function ignores all general attribute specifications. For details, see BLOCK in Chapter 20. For detailed instructions on creating and using block menus, see *SAS/AF Software: Usage and Reference*.

The BLOCK function controls the:

□ text displayed in the upper border of the menu

□ title box

□ color scheme

□ choice blocks containing menu selections. There can be up to 12 choice blocks or icons displayed in three rows of four blocks each.

Display 14.5 shows a block menu that displays icons.

Display 14.5
Sample Block Menu

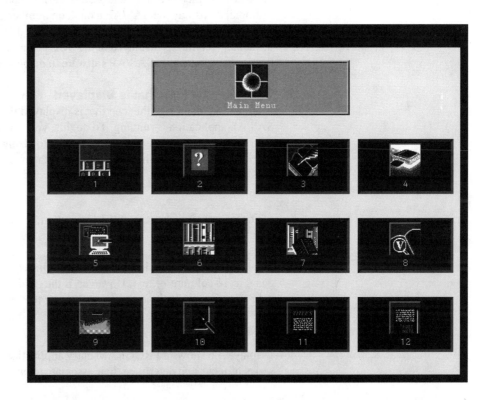

In FRAME entries, you implement a block menu by creating block or icon widgets. You assign the icon or block label text and icon numbers through the attribute window instead of using the BLOCK function.

Displaying Icons through SCL

An *icon* is a pictorial representation of an object or task that you can use to either replace or supplement text in your windows. If your display device and host operating system support icons, you can use icons in your SAS/AF applications to represent

□ pushbutton fields on SAS/AF PROGRAM entries

□ menu choices on block menus

□ windows.

Every icon has an identification number. Appendix A, "Icons" shows the icons that are provided with SAS software and the number associated with each one.

Note: See the SAS documentation for your operating system to find out if your system supports icons.

Using Icons For Pushbutton Fields

For PROGRAM entry fields that have the type PUSHBTNN or PUSHBTNC, you can display icons instead of push buttons. To display an icon for a push button field, you must identify the icon by entering its identification number between two backslash characters as the field's **List** attribute on the ATTR window. For example, to display the SAS/AF icon, icon number 17, enter \17\ as the field's **List** attribute. You can assign any number in this field and then specify the number for the actual icon that is displayed in the SCL program. Specifying an icon number as the **List** attribute tells SAS/AF software to display an icon instead of a push button.

Changing the Icon that is Displayed

You also can change the icon that is displayed for a push button while your SAS/AF application is running. To do this, you can use the SCL FIELD function with the new action, ICON *n*. For example, to change the icon displayed for the field to icon number 32, use the following SCL statement:

```
n=field('icon 32','icon');
```

For information about the FIELD function, refer to FIELD in Chapter 20.

Size of icons

The height of each icon is comparable to 6 lines of text, and the minimum width is equal to 10 columns of text. However, if the field which the icon represents is wider than 10 columns, the icon is displayed using the full width of the field.

Example

Display 14.6 shows a PROGRAM entry application that enables users to browse a series of icons and determine their associate identification numbers.

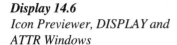

Display 14.6
Icon Previewer, DISPLAY and ATTR Windows

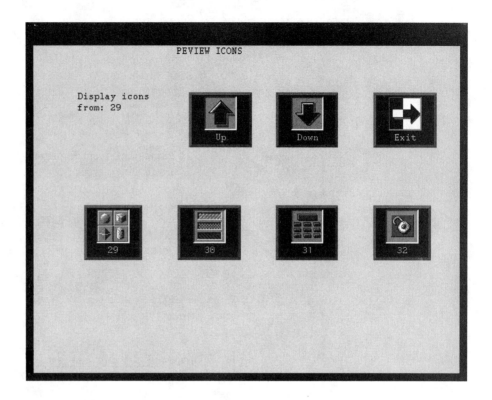

To create this window, edit ICON.PROGRAM. In the GATTR window, assign Banner=NONE. Create the fields described below, which will display as icons. Leave at least five blank lines below each field to account for the height of the icons. (Making each field 10 characters wide accounts for the width of the icons.) The field names and attributes are listed in the following table.

Name	Type	Width	Protect	Just	List	Initial
N	NUM	10	NONE	LEFT		
Up	PUSHBTNC	10	INITIAL	LEFT	\166\	Up
Down	PUSHBTNC	10	INITIAL	LEFT	\167\	Down
Exit	PUSHBTNC	10	INITIAL	LEFT	\111\	Exit
ICON1	PUSHBTNN	10	INITIAL	LEFT	\17\	
ICON2	PUSHBTNN	10	INITIAL	LEFT	\18\	
ICON3	PUSHBTNN	10	INITIAL	LEFT	\19\	
ICON4	PUSHBTNN	10	INITIAL	LEFT	\20\	

When you want a pushbutton field to display as an icon, you must put an icon number as the **List** attribute, even if this number is overridden in the program. That number as a **List** attribute signals the software to display an icon instead of a pushbutton. See Appendix A for the icons provided with SAS/AF software.

The following SCL program controls the icon previewer application. Enter it in the SOURCE window and then compile and test the application.

```
UP:   /* UP Pushbutton */
   if n=1014 then return;
   n+4;
```

```
                    link SHOW;
                 return;

                 DOWN:   /* DOWN Pushbutton */
                    if n=1 then return;
                    n=n-4;
                    link SHOW;
                 return;
                 N:         /* Change the icon displayed in the ICON fields  */
                            /* by falling through to SHOW section.           */
                 SHOW:
                    rc=field("ICON" || putn(n,"BEST."),"icon1");
                    rc=field("ICON" || putn(n+1,"BEST."),"icon2");
                    rc=field("ICON" || putn(n+2,"BEST."),"icon3");
                    rc=field("ICON" || putn(n+3,"BEST."),"icon4");
                 return;

                 EXIT:     /* EXIT Pushbutton */
                    call execcmd("Cancel");
                 return;

                 INIT:     /* Fall through to MAIN immediately after INIT  */
                    control label;
                    n=17;

                 MAIN:     /* Fall through to TERM immediately after MAIN  */
                    icon1=n;
                    icon2=n+1;
                    icon3=n+2;
                    icon4=n+3;

                 TERM:
                 return;
```

The reason that this program includes several overlapping sections is that the program is quite simple, and overlapping sections reduce the size of the compiled code.

When the SCL program executes, the icon displays the AF icon, number 17 and the number displays in the **Icon Number** field. The icon number is displayed in the icon itself, centered on the bottom line. When a user changes the icon number or selects the **Up** or **Down** icon to change the icon number, the program displays the corresponding icon. Selecting the **Exit** icon ends the preview application.

Using Icons on Block Menus

The BLOCK function has twelve parameters for specifying an icon to associate with each menu choice. For a detailed discussion of using icons with block menus, refer to BLOCK in Chapter 20.

Note: If your device or system cannot display icons, the default BLOCK menu appears.

Assigning Icons for Minimized Windows

The ICON function identifies the icon that is to represent a window when the window is minimized using either the native window manager or the ICON Display Manager command.

For more information about the ICON function, see ICON in Chapter 20.

Providing Information with a Legend Window

When you build an application, you may want to provide more information than you can display using techniques such as the _MSG_ system variable or selection lists. In these cases, you can use a legend window to provide the necessary help for users. A legend window is a display-only window that you can use as a dynamic help window in your applications.

In addition to supplementing selection list windows, a legend window provides a means of relating general information about the window or specific information about fields in the window. SCL provides functions and routines you can use to construct, display, and enhance a legend window to:

□ supplement selection lists

□ provide general window or field help

□ use legends with nested windows.

Display 14.7 shows a legend window that has been added to the icon previewer example.

Display 14.7
Sample Application with Legend Window

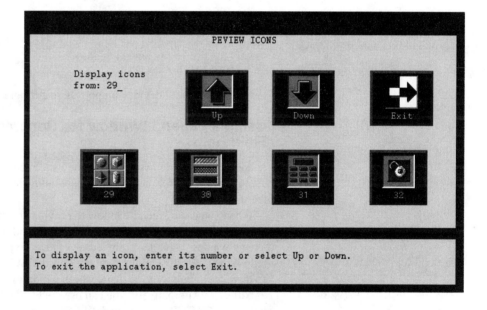

```
                          PEVIEW ICONS

  Display icons
  from: 29_


                          Up          Down          Exit


                29          30          31          32


To display an icon, enter its number or select Up or Down.
To exit the application, select Exit.
```

Using a Legend Window

When you provide a selection list as a part of your application, you can use an argument with a selection list function to display a brief line of instructions at the top of the selection list window. However, users may require additional information to effectively process the information in the selection list window. You can provide this information by using a legend window.

The following table shows the tasks required for adding a legend window to your application, as well as the function required. These functions allow you to specify a legend and enhance the appearance of the window.

To ...	Use the routine ...
display the text specified in the PUTLEGEND routine	LEGEND
add a title	LEGEND
change the background color	LEGEND
change the border color	LEGEND
change the border attribute (highlighting, blinking, underlining, or reverse video)	LEGEND
close a legend window	ENDLEGEND
save a legend window so you can redisplay it	PUSHLEGEND
restore a saved legend window	POPLEGEND
specify the text and control the color or display attribute of a line of text	PUTLEGEND for each line of legend text
specify the size of the legend window	WREGION

Note: Not all devices support these attributes.

Using a Legend Window for General Window or Field Help

In addition to supplementing selection lists, a legend window provides a means of communicating information about the window in general or about specific fields in the window.

When you use a legend window to provide general-window help or specific-field help, and the locations of the legend window and the current window overlap, the legend window is hidden from a user's view. To prevent this problem, use WDEF to reduce the size of the application window and WREGION to size the legend window so there is enough room to display both windows.

Note: Alternatively, you can use the FSEDIT Parms window or a SAS/AF window's GATTR window to define the shorter window. For more information about using this window, refer to Chapter 8, "Creating Data Entry Applications Using the FSEDIT Procedure," in *SAS/FSP Software: Usage and Reference.* The GATTR window is discussed in detail in Chapter 9, "Customizing Your Application Environment," in *SAS/AF Software: Usage and Reference.*

Once you have resized the current window, you can construct and display the legend window just as you did in the previous example application. In addition, you can program the legend window so that its information changes based on user input, or you can close the legend window when the information no longer applies.

Changing the Size and Location of a Legend Window

By default, a legend window provides four lines of text and is positioned at the top of the display, with each line the length of the maximum width of a zoomed window. However, the legend window can have as many rows and columns as a zoomed window will support. You can position the legend window in relation to the current window by issuing the WREGION routine to define the region for the legend window. To use WREGION, place it before the call to the LEGEND routine. If you specify the legend window's starting line as one less than the ending line of the application window, the top border of the legend window will start underneath the application window border and thus the border between the two windows will be smaller.

Note:　　By default, the next window displayed in the region defined by WREGION is sized to accommodate a command line. This is an important point to remember when calculating the size of your legend window. If you want the window to be sized assuming the legend does not have a command line, be sure to specify a null value for the command line option of WREGION.

For example, the sections of the program for the icon previewer that display the legend window are:

```
INIT:
    control label;
    n=17;
        /* Make application window shorter. */
    call wdef(1,1,20,80);
    link legend;
        /*  Define the legend window so its top border tucks  */
        /*  1 row under application window's bottom border.    */
    call wregion(19,1,7,80,'');
        /*  Display the legend in the legend window. */
    call legend();

    remainder of icon previewer program shown earlier

LEGEND:
    call putlegend(2,
        ' To display an icon, enter its number or select Up or Down.'
        'black');
    call putlegend(3,' To exit the application, select Exit.','black');
return;
```

Closing a Legend Window

In the previous examples, the legend window remains open even after the user has finished processing the instructions in the window. To close the legend window, you can use the ENDLEGEND routine. ENDLEGEND removes an open legend window from the display and clears the legend stack.

Refreshing a Legend Window

If you want to change the text that displays in a legend window once certain conditions are met, you can use the LEGEND routine to refresh the legend window. When the legend window is refreshed, the current text in the legend stack is displayed in the window.

When you refresh a legend window and you do not specify new arguments for a line that has been specified previously, that line is displayed based on the previous specifications. Therefore, in some cases you may need to use a PUTLEGEND routine to write a blank line to the legend window.

Using a Legend Window with Nested Windows

Managing legend windows can become more complicated when you start dealing with nested windows. Before calling another entry from the current SCL program, you must take steps to save the legend window, if there is one, so that it can be redisplayed once control returns to the calling entry. The processes of saving and restoring the legend window are called *pushing* and *popping*, respectively.

The following table shows the tasks to perform for pushing and popping legend text and the routines to use.

To...	Use the CALL Routine...
save the legend window for the calling program	PUSHLEGEND
restore the original legend window	POPLEGEND

Using SAS/FSP and SAS/CALC Windows in SAS/AF Applications

You can use SCL CALL routines to open SAS/FSP and SAS/CALC windows from your SAS/AF applications. SAS/FSP and SAS/CALC windows provide a ready-made interactive interface to a variety of data management tasks.

Using CALL Routines

The following table shows the tasks for which you can use the ready made front end application environment provided by SAS/FSP and SAS/CALC, as well as the CALL routine to use.

To allow users to ...	Use the CALL Routine ...
browse a SAS data set one observation at a time	FSEDIT with the BROWSE option
edit a SAS data set one observation at a time	FSEDIT
edit or browse a SAS data set displayed in a tabular format	FSVIEW
browse an external file	FSLIST
create, edit, or print a letter, memo, report, or other document	LETTER
create, edit, or print a spread sheet application	CALC

To use SAS/FSP windows, SAS/FSP must be licensed at your site. To use SAS/CALC windows, SAS/CALC must be licensed at your site.

Using Commands from SCL

In addition to using the CALL routines listed above, you can use one of the following commands in an EXECCMD or EXECCMDI routine: FSEDIT, FSBROWSE, FSLETTER, FSLIST, FSVIEW, and CALC.

Using Submit Blocks

To open a window with any of the special options available only in PROC statements (for example, PROC FSEDIT to open the FSEDIT window), you can use submit blocks to submit these statements to the SAS System for execution. However, this method of opening windows consumes more system resources than the other methods. As a consequence, you should use submit blocks only when you need to use a statement or procedure option not available with the SCL routines or the global commands. For more information on using SUBMIT blocks, see Chapter 11, "Submitting SAS and SQL Statements and Issuing Host Commands."

CHAPTER *15* Managing Fields and Windows

Introduction

Every interactive application you build with SAS/AF or SAS/FSP software communicates with its users through a window. SAS/AF or SAS/FSP displays the window and accepts input from users through fields in the window. Your Screen Control Language (SCL) programs can manipulate the window and the contents of its fields. You can use SCL to

□ process user input

□ validate user input

□ control fields and field values

□ change the appearance of windows.

For the discussion in this chapter, field is used to mean both fields in PROGRAM and SCREEN entries and text entry widgets in FRAME entries.

Processing User Input

The values a user enters in the fields of a window are not immediately available to your application. SAS/AF or SAS/FSP first verifies that the values a user entered in the fields match the type and informat for each field. Any field values that fail this test are displayed using the error color and highlighting style designated in the application.

By default, control does not pass to the application's SCL program until a user corrects all invalid values. The section "Providing Custom Error Handling" later in this chapter explains how you can change this default behavior.

Prompt Characters in SAS/AF Applications

SAS/AF applications also compare each field value against a prompt character before passing it to your SCL program for processing. A prompt character is a character a user can type as the first character in a field or text entry widget to open a window containing values that are valid for that field or widget. By default, the prompt character is a question mark (?). For example, if the first character of a field's value matches the prompt character specified for a PROGRAM entry, the following actions take place:

□ If you defined a **List** attribute of valid values for the field when you created the application, a selection list containing those values opens.

□ If you did not define a **List** attribute of valid values for the field, a dialog box opens explaining what type of values (character or numeric) are valid in the field.

The prompt character is not passed to the application.

If you want to prevent this processing and pass the prompt character to your SCL programs, turn on the NOPROMPT option in the ATTR window for any fields to which you want to pass the prompt character. For text entry widgets, select **Noprompt** in the Text Entry Attributes window.

Validating User Input

Field attributes provide an additional level of automatic field validation. Field attributes can specify the following criteria that the field values must satisfy to be accepted as valid:

□ SAS/AF applications compare each field value against criteria specified in the field's **List** attribute or in a LIST entry associated with the field. These criteria can include lists of discrete valid values, ranges of valid values, or both.

□ FSEDIT applications test whether each field value is greater than the value specified for the field's MAX attribute or less than the value specified for the field's MIN attribute.

□ FSVIEW applications do not support field attributes.

Your programs can perform *table-lookup validation* by comparing the field value against a list of possible correct values. One SCL feature that is useful for this purpose is the LOOKUPC function, which returns the position of a given character string in a list of strings (or 0 if the search string is not found).

Performing More Advanced Validation

If you only need to test field values against a static list of values, you can use the error-checking features provided by SAS/AF software. For example, you could specify the value **Y N** as the **List** attribute for a field in which a user should enter only one of those letters to have the SAS/AF task automatically perform this field validation. However, your SCL program can perform more sophisticated error checking once the updated field values are passed to the SCL program in your application.

With SCL, you are not limited to comparing field values against static lists defined in the application. For example, you can perform table lookup using values in SAS data sets. For more information on table lookup, see Chapter 5, "Using SAS Data Sets".

Validating One Field Against Another

In many applications, relationships exist among the information in the various fields. You can perform *cross-field validation* by comparing the value in one field against the value in another field.

For example, the following program segment checks that when a user calculates an interest rate, the value entered for the PAYMENT multiplied by the value entered for the number of payments (NP) must be greater than (or at least equal to) the amount borrowed (PRINC). Otherwise, the interest would be less than 0 percent.

```
INIT:
return;
MAIN:
   if payment*np ge princ then
      do;
         /* Process valid parameter value combinations. */
      end;
   else
```

```
          do;
             /* Process invalid parameter value combinations. */
          end;
   return;
   TERM:
   return;
```

Handling Invalid Field Values

When the SAS System determines that a field value does not satisfy the attributes for that field, it takes the following actions:

□ The field value is displayed in the error color and error highlighting style specified in the application.

□ The cursor is positioned in the field. If more than one field contains an invalid value, the cursor is placed in the upper-leftmost field that contains an invalid value.

□ A message is displayed on the window's message line describing why the value is invalid.

□ An audible alarm is sounded (if the user's output device supports audible alarms).

If you want your application to respond to invalid field values the same way that the SAS System responds to field values that do not match their attributes, you must take the following steps:

□ Use the ERRORON statement or the ERRORON argument for the FIELD function to turn on error highlighting for the field containing the invalid value.
    Note: The FSVIEW procedure in SAS/FSP software does not support the ERRORON statement or the ERRORON argument for the FIELD function.

□ Assign the appropriate error message to the _MSG_ system variable.

□ Use the ALARM statement to sound the audible alarm (a short beep).

Turning on Error Highlighting

When you turn on error highlighting for a field, the field is displayed in a special color and highlighting style in the following ways:

□ In FSEDIT applications, you specify the error color for each field in the ECOLOR frame of the FSEDIT Attributes window, and you specify the highlighting style in the EATTR frame of the FSEDIT Attributes window.

□ In SAS/AF applications, you specify the error color for each PROGRAM entry field in the **Error color** field of the ATTR window, and you specify the error highlighting style in the **Error attr** field.
    In a FRAME entry, you specify these attributes for a Text Entry widget in the Validation window in the Error Style **Color** and **Attr** fields.

□ The FSVIEW procedure uses a default error color and highlighting style that you cannot customize.

Note: There is one important difference between what happens when your program highlights fields and what happens when the SAS System highlights fields. If the SAS/AF task or SAS/FSP procedure determines that the field value is invalid according to its attributes or informat, then by default it does not pass control to your SCL program until the error is corrected. This is not the case when you highlight fields with the ERRORON statement or the FIELD function. Control and field values still pass to the SCL program.

You can use either the ERRORON statement or the FIELD function with the

ERRORON option to turn on error highlighting for one or more fields. In FRAME entries, you can also use the _ERRORON_ method to turn error highlighting on. Once you turn on error highlighting for a field, a user must issue the CANCEL command in SAS/AF to exit the application without correcting the error.

Note: You also can use the ERRORON statement to turn on error highlighting in this situation because the ERRORON statement accepts a list of field names as an argument. The advantage of the FIELD function over the ERRORON statement is in situations where the names of the fields to be highlighted are stored in a variable or in an array rather than in a literal list.

Turning off Error Highlighting

In SAS/AF, once you turn on error highlighting for a field, it remains in effect until you turn it off. Even if a user corrects the field value, it remains highlighted unless you restore the field to its original status. In FSEDIT, the field remains in error until the user enters a new value in the field or your program turns the error highlighting off. If the new value still meets your error condition, the field remains in error.

You can use either the ERROROFF statement or the FIELD function with the ERROROFF option to turn off error highlighting for any or all fields. In FRAME entries, you can also use the _ERROROFF_ method to turn error highlighting off.

Note: You also can use the ERROROFF statement to turn off error highlighting in this situation because the ERROROFF statement accepts a list of field names as an argument. The advantage of the FIELD function over the ERROROFF statement is in situations where the names of the fields to be restored are stored in a variable or in an array rather than in a literal list.

Displaying Messages to Users

You can use the system variable _MSG_ to display text on the window's message line. The text that is in the _MSG_ system variable when control returns to the application is displayed on the window's message line. For example,

```
_msg_='The name you specified is not valid.  Please enter a new name.';
```

Sounding an Alarm

You can use the ALARM statement to sound a short beep to warn a user that an error has occurred (if the user's output devices support audio output).

Providing Custom Error Handling

The SAS/AF task (or SAS/FSP application) by default does not pass control to the SCL program when any fields contain values that do not satisfy associated field attributes. However, you can use the CONTROL statement in SCL to override this default behavior so that your application provides custom error handling. When you use a CONTROL statement with the ERROR option, control passes to the SCL program even when some field values are flagged as invalid.

Note: CONTROL is an executable statement. In SAS/AF applications, you typically use the CONTROL ERROR statement in the INIT section of the SCL program. In FSEDIT applications, you typically use the CONTROL ERROR statement in the FSEINIT section.

▶ *Caution: Use extra validity checking with CONTROL ERROR*

If you use the CONTROL ERROR statement in an SCL program, you need to check the validity of any window variable value before using the value in a calculation. When CONTROL ERROR is in effect, field attributes no longer guarantee that window variables contain values in the range specified in the attributes.

Determining Which Fields Contain Invalid Values

You can use the ERROR function to determine which fields contain invalid values.

As an alternative to the ERROR function, you can use the FIELD function with the ERROR option. The FIELD function is useful when dealing with multiple variables because you can use a list of field names as an argument.

Avoiding Unnecessary Processing

Many programs perform more processing than necessary. For example, the LOOKUPC function may be called during each execution of the MAIN section, even if a user has not changed the value in a field. Remember that a user only has to modify one field before pressing the ENTER key to cause the MAIN section to execute.

In most applications, you want to process only those fields that a user has modified since the last execution of the SCL program.

Determining When a Field Is Modified

You can use the MODIFIED function to determine whether a user has modified the value in a particular field. A field is flagged as modified when a user types anything in it, even the same characters that are already in the field. This function returns a 1 (TRUE) if the specified field has been modified or a 0 (FALSE) if it has not.

Note: The modified status of modified fields is lost whenever control returns to the application, regardless of whether the modified fields have been processed in the SCL program. To ensure that all modified fields are processed, test the modified status of all significant fields before returning control to the application.

Determining When Any of a Group of Fields Is Modified

When you want to test multiple fields at once, use the FIELD function with the MODIFIED option. The FIELD function provides similar functionality to the MODIFIED statement, but it accepts lists of variable names and arrays as arguments, whereas the MODIFIED function accepts only a single variable name as an argument.

Controlling Fields and Field Values

SCL provides a number of other statements, functions, and CALL routines you can use to control fields in the window. Your applications can

□ manipulate field values

□ modify a field's protection status

□ save the current field values (in SAS/AF applications only).

The following sections describe and illustrate the SCL features you use to accomplish these tasks.

Manipulating Field Values

If the values a user enters in a window's fields satisfy the SAS System's validation tests, they pass into window variables. You can then manipulate these window variable values in your application's SCL program. Chapter 1, "Screen Control Language," describes the categories of language elements that you can use to manipulate window variables.

Using Field Values in Expressions

You can use window variables in all types of calculations. For example, the following program statement multiplies the contents of the PAYMENT field by the contents of the NP field to calculate a value for the TOTAL field.

```
total=payment*np;
```

You also can use conditional statements like IF-THEN/ELSE and SELECT-WHEN in your SCL programs to choose among various actions based on field values.

Using Field Values as Function Arguments

You can use any of the functions and CALL routines from the base SAS language (except LAG and DIF) to manipulate window variable values. For example,

```
wintitle='Application Main Menu';
call wname=(wintitle);
```

Further, SCL provides special functions, CALL routines, and statements of its own for processing field values in window variables. For tables of these functions and routines listed by functionality, see Chapter 19, "SCL Language Elements".

Changing a Field's Protection Status

When you build an application, you can designate fields to protect. Users cannot change the value of a protected field, and the TAB key does not move the cursor to a protected field. In FRAME entries, you can also protect most widgets by graying them.

You can designate fields to protect in the following ways:

□ In SAS/AF applications, select **YES** for the Protect attribute in the ATTR window for a PROGRAM entry field or the Protection attribute in the Text Entry Attributes window for a text entry widget in a FRAME entry.

□ In FSEDIT applications, enter a **P** in the corresponding fields in the PROTECTED screen of the FSEDIT Attributes window.

□ In FSVIEW applications, issue the PROTECT ON command to designate protected columns.

Your SCL programs can change the value displayed in a protected field by changing the value of the corresponding window variable.

You can use the PROTECT statement to turn on protection for one or more fields and the UNPROTECT statement to turn off protection for one or more fields. You also can use the FIELD function with the PROTECT and UNPROTECT options to achieve the same results. In FRAME entries, you can also use the _GRAY_ and _UNGRAY_ methods to change the protection status for most widgets. You can also determine if a field is protected with the FIELD function's PROTECTED option. In FRAME entries, use the _IS_GRAY_ method.

Note: In FSVIEW applications, computed variables with formulas always are protected. You cannot use either the FIELD function with the UNPROTECT option or the UNPROTECT statement to turn off protection for these columns. For data set variables, use the PROTECT OFF command.

Saving Field Values

You can take a snapshot of the current values in all fields of a SAS/AF PROGRAM entry's window. Users can recall the stored values to the fields using the RECALL command in the window. Users also can initialize fields with the stored values by adding the AUTORECALL=YES option to the AF command when starting the application. A typical use for this feature is to save the current field values when the application is halted so that the values can be restored when the user resumes using the application.

To capture the current field values, use the SAVESCREEN routine. This routine stores values in the user's SASUSER.PROFILE catalogs in an entry named *entry-name*.AFPGM, where *entry-name* is the name of the PROGRAM or FRAME entry being executed. You can also the AUTOSAVE=YES option on the AF command to save these values when a user exits from a PROGRAM entry in the application system. Using SAVESCREEN or the AUTOSAVE option is equivalent to a user issuing a SAVE command on the command line of the window.

Changing the Appearance of Windows

When you build your application, you have the opportunity to customize various characteristics of the window. For example, you can specify the size of the window, the position of the window within the display, and the colors of various window elements. However, you also can modify the original window characteristics from within the application.

SCL provides functions and routines that you can use to change

□ the size or position of the window

□ the title of the window

□ the PMENU entry associated with the window

□ the size of the next window opened by the application.

You also can use the EXECCMD routine to issue commands local to the task and the EXECCMDI routine to issue global SAS Display Manager System commands to change some other window characteristics that you cannot modify with specific SCL functions (for example, the color of various window areas). EXECCMD and EXECCMDI handle commands differently, as described in the following table.

Routine	How the routine issues commands
EXECCMD	collects the commands, continues executing the current phase of the SCL program until it either completes that phase or encounters a statement that opens another window, and then issues the commands
EXECCMDI	immediately issues the global command and then finishes executing the current phase of the SCL program

The following sections describe how to determine the current setting of various window characteristics and how to change those characteristics from within the application.

Querying Window Characteristics

Before you change a window characteristic, you often need to know the current settings for that characteristic. Use the WINFO function in your SCL program to obtain information about the current characteristics of your window. For a list of all the information that WINFO can report, see Chapter 20.

Changing the Size or Position of Windows

You can specify the default size and position of your window when you build your application. You can specify the window's size and position attributes the following ways:

□ in the entry's General Attributes window, for SAS/AF applications or using the SETWSZ command after manually changing the window size. SETWSZ stores the current window size with the entry. The next time you invoke the application, the window will display in the size specified in the last SETWSZ command.

□ in the FSEDIT Parms window, for FSEDIT applications (or in the FSBROWSE Parms window for FSBROWSE applications).

□ using the SETWSZ command, for FSVIEW applications, after manually changing the window size. SETWSZ stores the current window size with the formula. The next time you invoke FSVIEW with that formula, the window will display in the size based on the information stored with the formula.

To change the size or position of the window from within an application, use the WDEF routine or the WDEF command. For more information on this display manager global command, see *SAS Language: Reference*.

Controlling the Size and Position of the Next Window Opened

To control how much of your current window is overlaid by other windows opened by the application, use the WREGION routine to specify the size and position of the next window displayed by the application.

You cannot use the WREGION routine to set the size of FSEDIT or FSBROWSE windows opened from within your application. The FSEDIT and FSBROWSE procedures ignore the window size specified with the WREGION routine. Instead use WDEF in the FSEINIT section of FSEDIT programs, issue the WDEF command from the FSEDIT session, or save size information in the FSEDIT Parms window.

Changing the Title of a Window

Every window can have a title displayed in the upper window border. In SAS/FSP applications, the default window title is always the procedure name followed by the name of the SAS data set displayed in the window. In SAS/AF applications, you can assign a name in the General Attributes window of the FRAME or PROGRAM entry when you create the application.

In both SAS/AF and SAS/FSP applications, you can change the current window name using the WNAME routine in SCL. You can also use the SETWNAME and SETWDATA commands for this purpose. Use SETWNAME <*name-text*> to specify the window name displayed at the left side of the window's title bar or centered in the title bar (depending on the windowing interface). Use SETWDATA <*data-text*> to specify the window data displayed at the right side of the title bar or centered in the title bar following the window title (depending on the windowing interface).

Hiding Data Set Names in SAS/FSP Applications

You can use the WNAME routine to hide the name of the data set being displayed in an FSEDIT, FSBROWSE, or FSVIEW application. For example, you can use the following statement in the FSEINIT section of the application's SCL program to blank the default window title:

```
call wname(' ');
```

Changing the Color of Window Areas

To change window colors and display attributes dynamically through SCL, use the EXECCMD or EXECCMDI routine to issue the display manager global COLOR command. This command does not have an argument for altering the color of an individual field in the window. To change field color dynamically, use either the FIELD function with the COLOR option dynamically, the FLDATTR function, or the FLDCOLOR function. You can also change the color of window areas in the FSEDIT Parms window associated with a modified screen or the BUILD Parms or DISPLAY Edparms entry for SAS/AF. For details on using the COLOR command, see *SAS Language: Reference, Version 6, First Edition.*

You can use the COLOR command in SAS language to specify the color of a window's:

□ background

□ border

□ command line

□ background and border color for pull-down menus

□ message line

□ line numbers

□ scroll bar

□ text

You can also change the color and highlighting of areas of the LOG and OUTPUT windows using the DMWINDOW function in SCL. The DMWINDOW function is described in Chapter 20.

SAS® Screen Control Language Source-Level Debugger

CHAPTER *16* # Using the SAS® Screen Control Language Source-Level Debugger

Overview

The Screen Control Language debugger is a powerful interactive utility that can monitor the execution of SCL programs. The debugger enables you to locate logical errors while a program is executing. You enter debugger commands on the debugger command line. The debugger displays the source program, specifying which line is executing. The results are displayed in the Message window.

The debugger can:

☐ suspend execution at selected statements and programs. This is called *setting breakpoints*. Breakpoints can be set based on the evaluation of an expression.

☐ monitor the values of selected variables. When the variable is set to some specified value, the debugger stops the program execution at the statement where this occurred. This is called *setting watch variables*.

☐ set or query the values of SCL variables.

☐ display the attributes of variables.

☐ bypass a group of statements.

☐ continue execution of a halted program.

☐ single step, including stepping over called functions.

☐ display the execution stacks of active programs.

☐ display the values of the arguments passed into a program entry (values of variables in the ENTRY statement).

☐ print each statement as it executes.

☐ create and use SAS macros containing debugger commands.

☐ execute commands conditionally.

☐ retrieve previous commands.

☐ receive help on individual commands.

Establishing the Debugging Environment

To use the debugger, you must compile your programs with the compile-time option DEBUG ON. This option directs the SCL compiler to collect information used for debugging, which results in a larger code size. Therefore, it is recommended you always recompile your programs with the DEBUG OFF option before installing your application in production mode.

You can set the DEBUG option for an application two ways:

□ from inside the procedures. You can issue the DEBUG ON command from the BUILD, FSEDIT, and FSVIEW windows to turn on the DEBUG option. Once the DEBUG option is turned on through the DEBUG command, it is active in all currently running tasks.

□ from the procedure statement. You can set the DEBUG option by invoking the FSEDIT procedure, as shown:

```
proc fsedit data=dataset screen=screen debug; run;
```

Note: If you turn on the DEBUG option from a procedure statement, the option is not active in all currently running tasks.

You can set the DEBUG ON options using the command line, pmenu, or function key within the FSEDIT and FSVIEW procedures

In the BUILD procedure, using the DEBUG option in the COMPILE statement compiles all the programs with the DEBUG option. For example, the following statements compile all the programs in the catalog with the DEBUG option turned on:

```
proc build c=sasuser.myproj;
   compile debug;
```

You must specify ENTRYTYPE=SCL or ENTRYTYPE=FRAME in the PROC BUILD statement to compile FRAME or SCL entries. By default, the COMPILE statement only compiles PROGRAM entries.

The SCL Debugger allows you to test and debug a specific SCL program or label in an SCL program. When execution suspends at the first executable statement in a label, you may need to set the ENTRY or METHOD argument to allow the program to continue execution.

Issuing the QUIT command in the debugger window or ending the procedure session terminates the debugger session. Issuing the DEBUG OFF command or ending the SAS session turns off the DEBUG option.

Invoking the Debugger

After the program has been correctly compiled with the DEBUG option, you can invoke the debugger using an option in an AF or AFAPPL command or a procedure statement, or you can invoke it while you are working on an application.

Invoking the Debugger for SAS/AF Applications

There are four ways to invoke the debugger for a SAS/AF application:

□ Use the DEBUG=YES option with the AF command that you use to execute a SAS/AF application that has been compiled with DEBUG ON, as in this example:

```
af c=libref.catalog.entry.type debug=yes
```

□ Use the DEBUG option in conjunction with the TESTAF option in a PROC

BUILD statement, as in this example:

```
proc build c=libref.catalog.entry.type testaf debug;
```

□ Set the DEBUG option on by using the DEBUG ON command, compile the program, issue the SAVE command, and then issue the TESTAF or AF command in the BUILD window.

□ Set the DEBUG option on and compile the program. Then invoke TESTAF by entering **T** in the entry's selection field in the catalog directory.

Invoking the Debugger for FSEDIT and FSVIEW Applications

To invoke the debugger with the procedure statement, you can use the DEBUG option, as shown here:

```
proc fsedit data=SAS-data-set screen=screen-entry debug; run;
```

or

```
proc fsview data=SAS-data-set formula=formula-entry debug; run;
```

To invoke the debugger when you are working on an application, issue the command DEBUG ON from the SOURCE window. When you end the window, the program compiles.

Using the SOURCE Window and the MESSAGE Window

When a debugging session is initiated, it displays two windows: the debugger SOURCE window at the top and the debugger MESSAGE window at the bottom.

The debugger SOURCE window displays the text of the current SCL program. The debugger MESSAGE window echoes the commands you enter from the debugger command prompt DEBUG>, which is at the bottom of the window.

Both the SOURCE and MESSAGE windows have a command line or pmenu at the top. You can enter SAS Display Manager and SAS/AF or SAS/FSP global commands from here. You can even enter a debugger command from the command line of the MESSAGE window, instead of from the DEBUG> prompt, by preceding the debugger command with the word SCL.

Terminating the Debugger

While in a debugging session, you can enter the debugger QUIT command to terminate the debugger and end out of the current stream. If the current stream is nested, the last window in the previous stream will be activated; otherwise, control returns to the point at which the application was started.

Entering Debugger Commands

You can enter debugger commands three ways:

□ from the debugger command prompt DEBUG>.

□ from the command line at the top of the MESSAGE window. However, each debugger command entered from the command line has to be preceded with the word SCL, as in this example that sets a breakpoint at line 10:

```
scl b 10
```

□ from the action bar if the PMENU facility is active.

When a debugger command is entered, the SCL debugger gives the following responses:

□ echoes the command line in the MESSAGE window.

□ checks the syntax of the command and the parameters just entered.

The debugger reports the error messages for any syntax errors and the position of the errors. In addition, the original command you just entered on the command line is displayed in the MESSAGE window. You can issue the ? command to recall text, fix the error and press the ENTER key to re-execute the command.

□ prints the results in the MESSAGE window if there are no syntax or semantic errors.

There are two ways to retrieve the commands previously entered without retyping them. One way to retrieve commands is using the ? command. The ? command enables you to retrieve up to the last five commands. The other way to retrieve commands previously entered is using a function key defined as the AGAIN command. Position the cursor on a line in the MESSAGE window and press the key defined as the AGAIN command. The text on that line is displayed on the debugger prompt line. You can re-edit that line and re-execute the command or commands.

Debugger Commands by Functional Category

The following sections provide a brief introduction to the commands available in the SCL debugger. The commands are grouped according to their functionality. For more complete details about these commands, see Chapter 17, "SCL Debugger Command Dictionary."

Controlling Program Execution

While you are in a debugger session, you can use the following commands to monitor the flow of the program and even change the way the program executes:

GO   continues program execution until a specified statement or until the next breakpoint (if any).

JUMP   restarts program execution at any specific executable statement. This command causes the interpreter to bypass execution of any intermediate statement.

STEP   steps through the program statement by statement. By default, the ENTER key is set to STEP.

Manipulating Debugging Requests

The following group of debugger commands enables you to set breakpoints, tracepoints, and watched variables to suspend or trace the execution so that you can further manipulate the program variables. Whenever a debugging request is set, it remains in effect until you delete it using the DELETE command.

BREAK   sets a breakpoint at a particular executable program statement. For the current program, an exclamation mark replaces the line number of the corresponding program line in the debugger SOURCE window to visibly indicate the line at which the breakpoint is established. When a breakpoint is encountered, the execution of the program is suspended and the cursor is placed on the DEBUG prompt line in the MESSAGE window.

When using the BREAK command, you can specify program locations using either line numbers or labels. You can set breakpoints only on lines that contain executable statements. The debugger warns you if you try to do otherwise (for example, on a comment line).

DELETE
: removes breakpoints, tracepoints, or watched variables currently set by the BREAK, TRACE, and WATCH commands.

LIST
: displays all the breakpoints, tracepoints, and watched variables that are set by the BREAK, TRACE, and WATCH commands.

TRACE
: sets a tracepoint. When a tracepoint is encountered, the debugger prints the information in the MESSAGE window and continues processing.

WATCH
: sets a watched variable. If the value of the watched variable is modified by the program, the debugger suspends execution at the statement where the change occurred and prints the old and the new values of the variable in the MESSAGE window. This command is especially useful in large programs to detect when the value of a particular variable is being modified.

Manipulating SCL Variables from the Debugger

When program execution is suspended, the debugger allows you to examine the values and attributes of variables. If the value of a variable would result in a logic error, you can then modify it so that you can continue the debugging session. Use these commands to manipulate SCL variables from the debugger:

ARGS
: displays the values of arguments that are passed into the current program through the ENTRY statement.

CALCULATE
: acts as an online calculator. It evaluates standard debugger expressions and displays the result. This is useful when you try to set the value of a variable to the result of an expression.

DESCRIBE
: displays the attributes of a variable. The attributes described for a variable include NAME (the name of the variable), TYPE (NUM for numeric, CHAR for character, and NUM ARRAY, CHAR ARRAY, and ARRAY ELMT for array elements), LENGTH (size of the variable), and CLASS (WINDOW for window variables, NONWINDOW for nonwindow variables, and SYSTEM for system variables).

EXAMINE
: displays the values of variables.

PARM
: displays the values of parameters that you are passing if the next executable statement contains a function call.

PUTLIST
: displays the contents of an SCL list.

SET
: changes the value of a variable in the SCL program. This enables you to continue the debugging session instead of having to stop, modify the source, and recompile the program. You can also assign new values to variables in other active entries.

Controlling the Windows

The following commands manipulate the debugger windows:

ENVIRONMENT   enables you to set a developer environment by redisplaying the source of any program in the execution stack. When a developer environment is set, the debugger generates messages showing you what the current program environment and the developer environment are. You can then scroll through the source program, set debugging requests, and operate on the variables.

HELP   displays the information on debugger commands.

QUIT   terminates a debugger session.

SWAP   switches control between the SOURCE and MESSAGE windows.

TRACEBACK   displays the execution stack.

Tailoring the Debugger

The debugger allows you to tailor your debugging sessions to your own needs using the following commands or clauses:

ENTER   enables you to assign one or more frequently used commands to the ENTER key. The default for ENTER is STEP, which steps through the program statement by statement.

IF   enables you to conditionally execute other commands.

Using the SAS Macro Interface

The SAS macro facility is a versatile tool used to communicate between SAS procedures and DATA steps. The SCL debugger has a complete interface with the SAS macro facility. You can define a macro to replace a frequently-used debugger command list, as in this example:

```
DEBUG> %macro mymacro;e var1 var2 var3;%mend mymacro;
```

After the macro MYMACRO is defined, you can invoke the macro as follows:

```
DEBUG> %mymacro
```

The macro MYMACRO is expanded to

```
e var1 var2 var3
```

17 **SCL Debugger Command Dictionary**

Overview

This chapter provides descriptions of all the commands that can be used with the Screen Control Language debugger. The commands are listed in alphabetical order. Chapter 16, "Using the SAS Screen Control Language Source-Level Debugger," discusses these commands in functional groupings.

Terminology

This section explains the special terms used in this chapter and in Chapter 16.

breakpoint
> a location for program suspension. A breakpoint established through the BREAK command is permanent until you remove it with the DELETE command.

executable statement
> an SCL statement that performs an action at run time. All SCL statements are executable except for the following:

> □ ARRAY, ENTRY, LENGTH, and REPLACE

> □ comments

> □ statements inside SUBMIT blocks.

execution stack
> a stack that keeps run-time information of SCL programs being executed with the current program at the top of the stack. When a program is being executed, the SCL compiler loads all its information onto the execution stack, for example

```
TEST3.PROGRAM
TEST2.PROGRAM
TEST1.PROGRAM
```

> In this example, TEST1 called TEST2 with the DISPLAY function, which in turn called TEST3. TEST3 is the program that is currently executing.

expression
> any valid debugger expression. Debugger expressions are the same as SCL expressions except that function calls and the IN operator are not supported. An expression can be simple or compound. A compound expression uses AND or OR (for example, x+y, a>b & b<c, str1=str2).

loaded program
> an SCL program that still resides in the execution stack.

temporary breakpoint

a breakpoint that is removed as soon as the execution is suspended. A temporary breakpoint is ignored if another permanent breakpoint is encountered before the execution reaches it.

tracepoint

a location for tracing the execution of your program without stopping its execution. A tracepoint established through the TRACE command is permanent until you remove it with the DELETE command.

variable

the name of a window variable, a nonwindow variable, an array element, an array index reference, an entire array, or a system variable.

watched variable

a variable that the debugger monitors during the program execution. If the value of a watched variable is modified, the debugger suspends the execution and displays information. The debugger monitors a watched variable continuously until it is removed by the DELETE command.

Common Arguments

The following terms identify common arguments in this chapter's dictionary entries.

AFTER *count*

Enables conditional execution of BREAK, TRACE, and WATCH commands by specifying how many times the marked statement or variable must be encountered before the command is executed.

The syntax of the AFTER *count* argument is

AFTER *count*

where *count* is a positive integer.

For example, the following command sets a breakpoint at line 14 that is honored only before every fourth execution of the statement:

```
b 14 after 3
```

DO *list*

One or more debugger commands enclosed by a DO and an END statement.

The syntax of the DO *list* argument is

DO; *command-list*; END;

where *command-list* argument is a list of debugger commands separated by semicolons.

The following examples show typical DO lists:

□ Set a breakpoint at the first executable statement of the INIT label of program TEST; examine the value of variable A; and reset the value of the SCL variable, TOP:

```
b test\init do; e a; set top=0; end;
```

□ Set a breakpoint at line 4 and examine the values of variables X and Y.

```
b 4 do; e x; e y;end;
```

location

Specifies the place in an SCL program where the program execution is suspended or restarted. Most of the suspension and execution commands in the debugger take *location* as an argument. Valid locations include the following:

ALL   all places at which the specified debugging request is encountered (all tracepoints, all breakpoints, or all watches).

ENTRY   a reserved name that refers to the first executable statement in all program entries in the application.

entry-name\   the name of a catalog entry that contains an SCL program. A backslash must follow the entry name. After the entry name, you can also specify a line number or a label (for example, TEST2\250 or TEST1\TERM). If a SAS/AF entry is called from a SAS/AF entry or FSEDIT screen that resides in a different catalog, *entry-name* must be a four-level name. However, if a SAS/AF entry is called from a SAS/AF entry or FSEDIT screen that resides in the same catalog, *entry-name* may be a two-level name. If you provide a one-level entry name, an entry type of PROGRAM is assumed.

label   the name of a reserved or user-defined SCL label.

linenum   the number of a program line. The specified line must contain at least one executable SCL statement.

RETURN   the next RETURN statement.

WHEN *clause*

Enables conditional execution of commands by specifying criteria that must be met in order for the command to be executed.

The syntax of the WHEN *clause* argument is

WHEN *expression* ⟨DO *list*⟩

where *expression* is a debugger expression to evaluate.

The WHEN *clause* argument can be optionally followed by a DO list, as in the following example:

```
b 4 when (x<y & y>z) do; e x; e y;end;
```

When X<Y and Y>Z are both true, the debugger sets a breakpoint at line 4 and also examines the values of variables X and Y.

Organization

Each dictionary entry in this chapter contains the following information:

Name   names the command.

Synopsis   provides a short description highlighting the command's main use.

Abbreviation provides abbreviations of the debugger command, if the command name can be abbreviated.

See Also   tells where to look for information on related commands and related topics.

Syntax	presents the syntax for the command in standard form.
	If the command takes arguments, these are also presented in a standard form, along with descriptions of the values that can be supplied.
Details	provides a detailed explanation of the command.
Example	presents one or more brief examples that demonstrate the syntax and usage of the command.
Notes	provides additional information useful to developers.

Alphabetical List of Debugger Commands

This chapter contains descriptions of the following SCL debugger commands:

ARGS	JUMP
BREAK	LIST
CALCULATE	PARM
DELETE	PUTLIST
DESCRIBE	QUIT
ENTER	SET
ENVIRONMENT	STEP
EXAMINE	SWAP
GO	TRACE
HELP	TRACEBACK
IF	WATCH

ARGS

Displays the values of arguments given in the current program's ENTRY statement

See Also:
DESCRIBE
EXAMINE
PARM
PUTLIST

ARGS

Details

The ARGS command displays the values of the arguments received from a calling program and declared in the current program's ENTRY statement. This command is valid only when the current program contains an ENTRY statement. If you use this command when you are debugging an entry that does not contain an ENTRY statement, an error message is displayed. For more information about the ENTRY statement, see Chapter 20, "Screen Control Language Dictionary."

Example

Suppose that the program being examined begins with the following statement:

```
entry d e f 8;
```

The output of the ARGS command for the above statement is:

```
args
Arguments passed to ENTRY:
1 D = 10
2 E = 4
3 F = 6
```

BREAK

Suspends program execution at an executable statement

Abbreviation: B

See Also:
DELETE
LIST
TRACE
WATCH

BREAK *<location <AFTER count> <WHEN clause | DO list>>*

Argument	Description
location	Specifies where to set a breakpoint (the current line, by default):
	ALL sets a breakpoint at every SCL executable program statement.
	ENTRY sets a breakpoint at the first executable statement in all of the application's SOURCE entries.
	entry-name names a catalog entry with an SCL program.
	label sets a breakpoint at the first executable statement in a source section *label*. This label can be a system label or a user-defined label.
	line-num sets a breakpoint at source line *line-num*.
AFTER *count*	The breakpoint is honored after the statement has been executed the specified number of times by the program.
WHEN *clause*	Standard debugger WHEN clause as described in "Common Arguments" on page 162.
DO *list*	Standard debugger DO list as described in "Common Arguments" on page 162.

Details

The BREAK command sets a breakpoint at a specified statement. A breakpoint is an executable SCL program statement at which the debugger suspends program execution. When an SCL program detects a breakpoint, it:

□ suspends program execution

□ checks any count that you specified with the AFTER command and resumes program execution if the specified number of breakpoint activations has not been reached

□ evaluates the condition specified in the debugger expressions of a WHEN clause and resumes execution if the condition evaluated is FALSE

□ displays the entry name and line number at which execution is suspended

□ executes any command that is present in a DO list in the BREAK command

□ returns control to the developer.

If a breakpoint is set at a source line that contains more than one statement, the breakpoint applies to each statement on the source line. If a breakpoint is set at a line that contains SAS macro expansion, the debugger breaks at each statement generated by the macro expansion.

Examples

□ Set a breakpoint at line 5 in the current program:

```
DEBUG> b 5
```

The output to the MESSAGE window is:

```
b 5
Stop at line  9 in SASUSER.SCL.TEST2.PROGRAM
Set breakpoint at line 5 in SASUSER.SCL.TEST2.PROGRAM
```

□ Set a breakpoint in each executable statement:

```
DEBUG> b _all_
```

□ Set a breakpoint in each executable line and print all the values:

```
DEBUG> b _all_ do; E _all_; end;
```

□ Set a breakpoint at the first executable statement in each program:

```
DEBUG> b entry
```

□ Set a breakpoint at the first executable statement in the MAIN section:

```
DEBUG> b main
```

□ Set a breakpoint at the first executable statement in the entry TEST1.PROGRAM:

```
DEBUG> b test1\
```

□ Set a breakpoint at line 45 in the entry TEST1.PROGRAM:

```
DEBUG> b test1\45
```

□ Set a breakpoint at the MAIN label in the entry TEST1.PROGRAM:

```
DEBUG> b test1\main
```

□ Set a breakpoint at line 45 before the fourth execution of line 45:

```
DEBUG> b 45 after 3
```

□ Set a breakpoint at line 45 in the entry TEST1.PROGRAM only when both the divisor and the dividend are 0:

```
DEBUG> b test1\45 when (divisor=0 AND dividend=0)
```

□ Set a breakpoint at line 45 only when both the divisor and dividend are 0 before the fourth execution of line 45:

```
DEBUG> b 45 after 3 when (divisor=0 AND dividend=0)
```

□ Set a breakpoint at line 45 of the program and examine the values of variables NAME and AGE:

```
DEBUG> b 45 do; E name age; end;
```

CALCULATE

**Evaluates a debugger
expression and displays the
result**

Abbreviation: CALC

CALCULATE *expression*

Argument	Description
expression	Any standard debugger expression

Details

The CALCULATE command is an online calculator that evaluates standard
debugger expressions for the debugger.

Examples

□ Add 1.1, 1.2, 3.4 and multiply the result by 0.5:

```
DEBUG> calc (1.1+1.2+3.4)*0.5
```

The output to the MESSAGE window is:

```
calc (1.1+1.2+3.4)*0.5
2.85
```

□ Calculate the values of the variable SALE minus the variable DOWNPAY and
then multiply the result by the value of the variable RATE. Divide that value by
12 and add 50:

```
DEBUG> calc (((sale-downpay)*rate)/12)+50
```

DELETE

**Deletes breakpoints,
tracepoints, or watched
variables**

Abbreviation: D

See Also:
BREAK
LIST
TRACE
WATCH

DELETE *debug-request* *<location >*

Argument	Description
debug-request	SCL debugger commands to be deleted:
	BREAK Deletes breakpoints.
	TRACE Deletes tracepoints.
	WATCH Deletes watched variables.
location	Specifies where a debugging request is to be deleted.
	If the value of *debug-request* is BREAK or TRACE, *location* can be:
	ALL deletes from all programs that are in the active task of an application's execution stack.
	ENTRY specifies that all debugging requests are deleted from the first executable statement in all program entries.
	entry-name deletes from the first executable statement of the specified program label.
	label deletes from the the first executable statement of the specified program entry.
	line-num deletes from the statement in *line-num*.
	If the value of *debug-request* is WATCH, *location* can be:
	ALL specifies that the watch status is deleted for all watched variables.
	<entry-name \> variable specifies the name of a particular watched variable for which the watch status is deleted.

Details

The DELETE command enables you to delete any breakpoint, tracepoint, or watched variable in one or more programs that you specify.

Examples

□ Delete all breakpoints from the entry TEST1.PROGRAM:

```
DEBUG> d b test1\
```

The output to the MESSAGE window is:

```
d b test1
Stop at line  5 in SASUSER.SCL.TEST2.PROGRAM
Delete all the breakpoints in SASUSER.SCL.TEST1.PROGRAM
```

□ Delete all breakpoints from the first executable statement of all entries:

```
                        DEBUG> d b entry
```

□ Delete the tracepoint at line 35 in the program currently executing:

```
    DEBUG> d t 35
```

□ Delete the tracepoint set at the first executable statement of the MAIN section of the program currently executing:

```
    DEBUG> d t main
```

□ Delete the watch status from all variables in all the programs of the application's execution stack:

```
    DEBUG> d w _all_
```

□ Delete the watch status from the variable ABC in the program currently executing:

```
    DEBUG> d w abc
```

□ Delete the watch status from the variable XYZ in the entry TEST3.PROGRAM:

```
    DEBUG> d w test3\xyz
```

DESCRIBE

Displays the attributes of a variable

Abbreviation: DES

See Also:
ARGS
EXAMINE
PARM
PUTLIST

DESCRIBE *arg-list* | _ALL_

Argument	Description
arg-list	One or more arguments specified in the form *<entry-name\ >variable*, where
	entry-name names a catalog entry containing an SCL program.
	variable identifies a standard SCL variable. The program where the specified variable is defined must already be lo 'ed in the execution stack.
ALL	All variables defined in all programs in the current execution stack.

Details

The DESCRIBE command displays the attributes of one or more specified variables. The attributes reported are the name, data type, length, and class.

Name   names the variable whose attributes are to be displayed.

Type   indicates the data type of the variable:

NUM	numeric
CHAR	character
NUM ARRAY	numeric array
CHAR ARRAY	character array
ARRAY ELMT	array element

Length   indicates the length of the variable. All numeric variables have a length of 8 bytes.

Class   indicates the class of the variable.

SYSTEM   specifies a system variable. System variables are _MSG_, _CURROW_, _ERROR_ and _STATUS_.

WINDOW   specifies a window variable.

NONWINDOW   specifies a nonwindow variable.

Examples

□ Display the name, data type, length and class of variable A:

```
DEBUG> des a
```

The output to the MESSAGE window is:

```
des a
Name     Type       Length Class
======== ========== ====== =========
A        NUM           8    NONWINDOW
```

□ Display the name, data type, length, and class of all elements in the array ARR:

```
DEBUG> des arr
```

□ Display the attributes of array element ARR{i+j}:

```
DEBUG> des arr{i+j}
```

□ Display the attributes of variable A in the entry TEST1.PROGRAM:

```
DEBUG> des test1\a
```

□ Display the attributes of all elements of array BRR in the entry TEST2.SCL:

```
DEBUG> des test2.scl\brr
```

ENTER

Assigns one or more debugger commands to the ENTER key

See Also:
STEP

ENTER *<command-list>*

Argument	Description
command-list	One or more debugger commands separated by semicolons.

Details

The ENTER command assigns one or more debugger commands to the ENTER key. Each debugger command assignment replaces an existing debugger command assignment. To clear the key setting, enter the command without any options. By default, the ENTER key is set to the STEP command.

Example

The following example illustrates the use of the ENTER command:

□ Assign the commands EXAMINE and DESCRIBE, both for the variable ABC, to the ENTER key:

```
DEBUG> enter e abc; des abc
```

ENVIRONMENT

Displays the developer debugging environment

Abbreviation: ENV

See Also:
SWAP

ENVIRONMENT *<<entry-name\><line-num>* | RUN>

Argument	Description
entry-name	The name of a program in the execution stack.
line-num	The number of the program line to be displayed in reverse-video.
RUN	Specifies that the debugger return to executing the program at the active program in the application's execution stack.

Details

The ENVIRONMENT command enables you to display and modify the source, or set a developer environment, for any program in the execution stack while another program is active. When a developer environment is set, the debugger generates messages showing both the current program environment and the developer environment. In the developer environment, you can scroll through the source program, set debugging requests, and operate on the variables. For example, while PROGRAM2 is active, the ENVIRONMENT command can be used to display the source code for PROGRAM1, reset the values of several variables in PROGRAM1, and then return to PROGRAM2.

By default, the ENVIRONMENT command without options issued from the current executing program sets the current program environment as the developer environment. If the ENVIRONMENT command without an argument is issued from a program other than the current program, it resets the developer environment to the program line with the CALL DISPLAY statement that displays one of the loaded programs.

Setting a developer environment does not change the way a program executes. To return control to the active program, do one of the following:

□ Issue the ENV RUN command to reset the environment to the active program.

□ Use the GO, STEP or JUMP commands to leave the developer environment and resume execution.

Example

Assume that an execution stack looks like this:

TEST3.PROGRAM	line 37
TEST2.PROGRAM	line 24
TEST1.PROGRAM	line 10

The following examples illustrate valid ENVIRONMENT commands and describe their effect on the preceding execution stack:

□ Display the source of TEST1.PROGRAM with line 10 in reverse video:

```
DEBUG> env test1.program\10
```

The output to the MESSAGE window is:

```
env test1
Stop at line 37 in SASUSER.SCL.TEST3.PROGRAM
Developer environment at line 10 in SASUSER.SCL.TEST1.PROGRAM
```

□ Display the source of TEST2.PROGRAM with line 45 in reverse video:

```
DEBUG> env test2\45
```

□ Return to the current program environment (TEST3.PROGRAM at line 37):

```
DEBUG> env run
```

□ Attempt to return to the program TEST4.PROGRAM:

```
DEBUG> env test4\
```

Because TEST4.PROGRAM is not in the SCL execution stack, the SOURCE window still displays TEST3.PROGRAM. The output to the MESSAGE window is:

```
Program TEST4 is not active
```

EXAMINE

Displays the value of one or more variables

Abbreviations: EX, E

See Also:
ARGS
DESCRIBE
PARM
PUTLIST

EXAMINE *arg-list* | _ALL_

Argument	Description
arg-list	One or more arguments specified in the form *<entry-name\>variable*, where
	entry-name names a catalog entry containing an SCL program entry.
	variable identifies a standard SCL variable. The entry program where *variable* is defined must already be loaded in the execution stack.
ALL	All variables defined in all programs in the current execution stack.

Details

The EXAMINE command displays the value of one or more specified variables.

Examples

□ Display the values of variables N and STR:

```
DEBUG> e n str
```

The output to the MESSAGE window is:

```
e n str
N = 10
STR = 'abcdef'
```

□ Display variable A in the entry TEST1.PROGRAM, variable B in the current program, and variable C in the entry TEST2.PROGRAM:

```
DEBUG> e test1\a b test2\c
```

□ Display the elements i, j, and k of the array CRR:

```
DEBUG> e crr{i, j, k}
```

□ Display the elements i+1, j*2, k-3 of the array CRR:

```
DEBUG> e crr{i+1, j*2, k-3}
```

GO

Starts or resumes execution of the active program

Abbreviation: G

See Also:
JUMP
STEP

GO <*entry-name* | *line-num* | *label-name* | RETURN>

Argument	Description
entry-name	The name of a catalog entry containing an SCL program.
line-num	The number of a program line at which execution is to be suspended.
label-name	Specifies that execution is to be suspended at the first executable statement in a program section *label*. This label can be a system label or a user-defined label.
RETURN	Specifies that program execution suspends at the next RETURN statement.

Details

The GO command starts or resumes execution of the active program. By default, program statements execute continuously. However, you can specify one of the optional arguments to establish a temporary breakpoint that stops the program at the corresponding statement.

A temporary breakpoint established through the GO command is ignored if a breakpoint previously set is encountered before the temporary breakpoint. That is, the program execution suspends at the breakpoint previously set by the BREAK command rather than at the temporary breakpoint.

The GO command specified with a program label starts or resumes program execution and suspends execution at the first executable statement in the specified section. Both user-defined and system-defined labels can be specified with the GO command.

Examples

□ Resume executing the program and execute its statements continuously:

```
DEBUG> g
```

□ Resume program execution and then suspend execution at the next RETURN statement:

```
DEBUG> g return
```

□ Resume program execution and then suspend execution at the statement in line 104:

```
DEBUG> g 104
```

□ Resume program execution and then suspend execution at the first statement of the MAIN section:

```
DEBUG> go main
```

□ Resume program execution and then suspend execution at the statement in line 15 in program TEST2:

```
DEBUG> go test2\15
```

HELP

Displays information about debugger commands

HELP *<command>*

Argument	Description
command	Any debugger command.

Details

The HELP command displays information describing the syntax and usage of debugger commands.

By default, a directory of the debugger commands is displayed. You can then select any command to receive information about that command. If you only need information for a specific command, specify the command name right after the HELP command.

You can also issue the HELP command from the command line of the debugger MESSAGE window.

Examples

□ Displays a directory of the debugger commands:

```
DEBUG> help
```

□ Displays the syntax and usage information for the BREAK command:

```
DEBUG> help b
```

IF

Evaluates an expression and conditionally executes one or more debugger commands

IF *expression* THEN *clause*; <ELSE *clause*>

Argument	Description
expression	An expression to be evaluated before performing one or more commands.
clause	A single debugger command or a standard debugger DO list.

Details

The IF command immediately evaluates an expression and conditionally executes one or more debugger commands.

The IF command must contain a THEN clause with one or more commands to execute if the expression is true. It can also contain an ELSE clause with one or more commands to execute if the expression is false. The ELSE clause must be separated from the THEN clause with a semicolon, and the ELSE clause cannot be entered separately.

Examples

□ Examine the value of the variable X if X is greater than 0:

```
DEBUG> if x>0 then e x
```

□ Examine the value of the variable X if X is greater than 0, or the value of the variable Y if X is less than or equal to 0:

```
DEBUG> if (x>0) then e x; else e y
```

□ Execute the following actions if the value of variable X is less than variable Y and Y is less than variable Z:

   □ delete all breakpoints in all program entries

   □ set a breakpoint in the entry TEST2.PROGRAM at the first executable statement

   □ resume program execution.

```
DEBUG> if ((x<y) & (y<z)) then do; d b _all_; b test2\;g;end;
```

□ Execute the following actions if the value of the variable X is 1:

   □ examine the value of variable A

   □ set a breakpoint at line 5 of the program currently executing.

   Execute these actions if the value of X is not 1:

   □ examine the value of variable B

   □ set a breakpoint at line 15 of the program currently executing

```
DEBUG> if x=1 then do; e a; b 5; end; else do; e b; b 15; end;
```

□ Set a breakpoint at line 15 of the program. Whenever the execution suspends at line 15, if the value of the variable DIVISOR is greater than 3, execute the STEP command; otherwise, examine the value of the variable DIVIDEND.

```
DEBUG> b 15 do; if divisor>3 then st; else e dividend; end;
```

JUMP

Restarts execution of a suspended program

Abbreviation: J

See Also:
GO
STEP

JUMP *line-num*

Argument	Description
line-num	The number of a program line at which to restart the suspended program.

Details

The JUMP command restarts program execution at the executable statement in the specified line. It is different from the GO command because none of the statements between the suspended statement and the specified line are executed. With this capability, the JUMP command enables you to skip execution of some code that causes incorrect results or program failure.

The JUMP command can restart only the current source entry. The values of all variables are the same as the values at the original suspending point.

Although the JUMP command can jump to any statement in the current source, if the target statement resides in a different section of code, the first RETURN statement encountered in the section containing the target statement is treated as the RETURN statement from the section where the JUMP command was executed.

For example, suppose you were in the TERM section and you issued a JUMP command to jump to a statement in the MAIN section. When the program resumes execution, the first RETURN statement it encounters in the MAIN section terminates the program (as the RETURN statement does in the TERM section) instead of redisplaying the screen.

Note: If you use the JUMP command to jump to a statement that is inside a DO loop, you may get an illogical result.

Example

The following example illustrates the use of the JUMP command:

```
DEBUG> j 5
```

The output to the MESSAGE window is:

```
Stop at line 5 in SASUSER.SCL.TEST2.PROGRAM
```

LIST

Displays a list of all program breakpoints, tracepoints, or watched variables

Abbreviation: L

See Also:
BREAK
DELETE
TRACE
WATCH

LIST <<BREAK | TRACE | WATCH | _ALL_> <*entry-name*\ | _ALL_>>

Argument	Description
ALL	Specifies that the list contain all breakpoints, tracepoints and watched variables. LIST _ALL_ performs the same function as LIST.
BREAK	Specifies that the list contain only breakpoints.
TRACE	Specifies that the list contain only tracepoints.
WATCH	Specifies that the list contain only watched variables.
entry-name\	Specifies the name of a catalog entry containing an SCL program. A backslash must follow the entry name.
ALL	Specifies that the debugging requests currently set for all entries are to be displayed.

Details

The LIST command displays a list of all debugging requests that have been set for an application. These requests include breakpoints, tracepoints, and watched variables. By default, the list contains all of the debugging requests for the current entry.

Examples

□ List all the breakpoints, tracepoints, and watched variables for the current program:

```
DEBUG> l _all_
```

The output to the MESSAGE window is:

```
l _all_
Stop at line  5 in SASUSER.SCL.TEST2.PROGRAM
List all the breakpoints in program SASUSER.SCL.TEST2.PROGRAM
Breakpoint has been set at line 4
Breakpoint has been set at line 8
Breakpoint has been set at line 10
List all tracepoints in program SASUSER.SCL.TEST2.PROGRAM
No tracepoint has been set in program SASUSER.SCL.TEST2.PROGRAM
No variables have been watched in program SASUSER.SCL.TEST2.PROGRAM
```

□ List all the breakpoints, tracepoints, and watched variables for all active programs in the execution stack:

```
DEBUG> l _all_ _all_
```

□ List all of the breakpoints in the current entry:

```
DEBUG> l b
```

□ List all the breakpoints in all active programs in the execution stack:

```
DEBUG> l b _all_
```

□ List all the breakpoints, tracepoints, and watched variables in the entry TEST1.PROGRAM:

```
DEBUG> l _all_ test1\
```

□ List all the watched variables in the entry TEST3.PROGRAM:

```
DEBUG> l w test3\
```

PARM

Displays the values of variables being passed as parameters to any SCL function or routine

See Also:
ARGS
DESCRIBE
EXAMINE

PARM

Details

The PARM command displays the values of variables passed as parameters to an SCL function or routine. This command is valid only when the next executable statement contains a function call. The debugger warns you otherwise.

If a nested function call is encountered, that is, the parameters passed to a function or routine are themselves function calls, the PARM command displays the parameter list only for the nested function. You have to keep using the PARM command to display the parameter list for other function calls. For example, assume the next executable statement is as follows:

```
str1=substr(upcase(string), min(x,y), max(x,y));
```

A PARM command first displays the parameter STRING passed to the function UPCASE. A second PARM command displays the parameter list X, Y passed to the function MIN. Subsequent PARM commands would display the parameter lists passed to the function MAX and then to SUBSTR.

Example

A PARM command issued at the following statement

```
call display ('test2', x, y);
```

generates the output:

```
parm
Arguments passed to DISPLAY:
  1 (Character Literal)='test2'
Parameters passed to DISPLAY ENTRY:
  1 X=0
  2 Y=4
```

Notes

Once the values of arguments for a function or routine have been displayed, you cannot repeat the PARM command for the same function unless you are re-executing it.

PUTLIST

Displays the contents of an SCL list

See Also:
ARGS
DESCRIBE
EXAMINE
PARM
PUTLIST (SCL dictionary)

PUTLIST *<arg-list | n>*

Argument	Description
arg-list	One or more SCL list identifiers returned by the MAKELIST or COPYLIST function. Use the form *<entry-name\ > variable*, where:
	entry-name names a program entry where a succeeding variable is defined.
	variable identifies a standard SCL variable.
n	one or more numeric literals that represent the list to be printed.

Details

The PUTLIST command displays the contents of an SCL list in the DEBUGGER MESSAGE window. The list starts with left parenthesis '(' to mark its beginning, followed by the list of items separated by blanks. Each named item is preceded by its name and an equal sign (=), but nothing is printed before items that do not have names. The PUTLIST function ends the list with a right parenthesis ')', followed by the list's identifier number within square brackets.

If a list appears more than once in the list being printed, the PUTLIST command displays just (. . .) *listid* for the second and subsequent occurrences of the list. You should scan the output of the PUTLIST command for another occurrence of *listid* to view the full contents of the list. This prevents infinite loops if a list contains itself as a sublist.

Examples

Print the contents of List A, which contains the numbers 17 and 328 and the character string 'Any string.'

```
DEBUG > putlist a


( 17
  328
  'Any string'
)  7
```

Print the lists identified by numbers 7 and 5.

```
DEBUG> putlist 7 5


( STYLE=8
  SQFEET=8
  BEDROOMS=8
  BATHS=8
  STREET=16
  PRICE=8
)  7
( NAME=8
  SEX=1
  AGE=8
```

```
              HEIGHT=8
              WEIGHT=8
            )  5
```

QUIT

Terminates a debugger session

Abbreviation: Q

QUIT

Details

The QUIT command terminates a debugger session and returns control to the point at which the debugger was invoked. You can use this command on the debugger command line at any time during program execution.

SET

Assigns new values to a specified variable

Abbreviation: S

SET <*entry-name*>*variable expression*

Argument	Description
entry-name	the name of a catalog entry containing an SCL program entry.
variable	a standard SCL variable. The entry program where *variable* is defined must already be loaded in the execution stack.
expression	any standard debugger expression.

Details

The SET command assigns a value or the result of a debugger expression to the specified variable. When you detect an error during program execution, you can use this command to assign new values to variables. This enables you to continue the debugging session instead of having to stop, modify a variable value, and recompile the program. You can also assign new values to variables in other active entries.

Examples

□ Set variable A to the value of 3:

```
DEBUG> s a=3
```

The output to the MESSAGE window is:

```
Stop at line 5 in SASUSER.SCL.TEST2.PROGRAM
A = 3
```

□ Set variable A in program PROG1 to the value of the result of the expression a+c*3:

```
DEBUG> s prog1\a=a+c*3
```

□ Assign to the variable B the value 12345 concatenated with the previous value of B:

```
DEBUG> s b='12345'||b
```

□ Set array element ARR{1}to the value of the result of the expression a+3:

```
DEBUG> s arr{1}=a+3
```

□ Set array element CRR{1,2,3}to the value of the result of the expression crr{1,1,2}+crr{1,1,3}

```
DEBUG> s crr{1,2,3}=crr{1,1,2}+crr{1,1,3}
```

□ Set the values of a whole array:

```
DEBUG> s crr={'a', 'b', 'c', 'd'}
```

STEP

Executes statements one at a time in the active program

Abbreviation: ST

See Also:
ENTER
GO
JUMP

STEP <OVER|O>

Argument	Description
OVER	Specifies that if the next executable statement is a CALL DISPLAY, FSEDIT, or FSVIEW statement, the whole reference counts as a statement. By default, the STEP command suspends the program execution at the first executable statement of the called program if that program was compiled with DEBUG ON.

Details

The STEP command executes one statement in the active program, starting with the suspended statement. When you issue a STEP command, the command:

□ executes the next statement

□ displays the entry name and line number

□ returns control to the developer and displays the DEBUG> prompt.

By default, the STEP command suspends the execution at the first executable statement in the called program if the current statement is a CALL DISPLAY or CALL FSEDIT statement. The OVER option forces the debugger to count the call of the DISPLAY, FSEDIT, or FSVIEW routine as a statement, and program execution stops at the statement after the CALL statement. However, if the called program contains a display, execution is not suspended until you leave the display window.

When the STEP command is used to execute a SELECT statement, it jumps directly to the appropriate WHEN or OTHERWISE clause without stepping through any intervening WHEN statements.

Example

Suppose you are using the STEP command to execute your program, which is stopped at line 15. If VAL contains 99, the STEP command goes to line 116 immediately.

```
line #
  15   select (val);
  16      when (1)
  17            call display('a1');
  18      when (2)
```

```
 19         call display('a2');
   ...............
113     when (98)
114         call display('a98');
115     when (99)
116         call display('a99');
117     when (100)
118         call display('a100');
119     otherwise
120         call display('other');
121   end;
```

SWAP

Switches control between the SOURCE window and the MESSAGE window

See Also:
ENVIRONMENT

SWAP

Details

The SWAP command enables you to switch control between the MESSAGE window and the SOURCE window when the debugger is running. When a debugging session is initiated, the control defaults to the MESSAGE window until you issue a command. While the program is still being executed, the SWAP command enables you to switch control between the SOURCE and MESSAGE window so that you can scroll and view the text of the program and also continue monitoring the program execution.

TRACE

Sets a tracepoint for tracing the execution of the corresponding statement

Abbreviation: T

See Also:
BREAK
DELETE
LIST
WATCH

TRACE *<location* <AFTER *count><*WHEN *clause* | DO *list>>*

Argument	Description
location	Specifies where to set a tracepoint (at the current line, by default).
	ALL set a tracepoint at every SCL executable program statement.
	ENTRY set a tracepoint at the first executable statement in every one of the application's program entries.
	entry-name set a tracepoint in an SCL program.
	label set a tracepoint at the first executable statement in an SCL reserved label or a user-defined label.
	line-num set a tracepoint at program line number *line-num.*
AFTER *count*	A count maintained along with the tracepoint. When the count value equals the integer given with the AFTER option, program execution is suspended.
WHEN *clause*	Standard debugger WHEN clause as described in "Common Arguments" on page 162.
DO *list*	Standard debugger DO list as described in "Common Arguments" on page 162.

Details

The TRACE command sets a tracepoint at a specified statement and traces the execution of that statement.

A tracepoint differs from a breakpoint because a tracepoint resumes program execution after temporary suspension. Also, a tracepoint has a higher priority than a breakpoint. If a statement has been specified both as a tracepoint and a breakpoint, the debugger first prints the trace message and then suspends program execution. Each time the tracepoint statement is encountered, the debugger does the following:

□ suspends program execution

□ checks any count that you specified with the AFTER command and resumes program execution if the specified number of tracepoint activations has not been reached

□ evaluates any conditions you specified a WHEN-clause and resumes execution if the condition evaluated is false

□ displays the entry name and line number at which execution is suspended

□ executes any command that is present in a DO list argument

□ resumes program execution.

Examples

□ Trace the statement at line 45:

```
DEBUG> t 45
```

□ Trace each executable statement:

```
DEBUG> t _all_
```

□ Trace each executable statement and print all the values:

```
DEBUG> t _all_ do; e _all_; end
```

□ Trace the first executable statement in each program:

```
DEBUG> t entry
```

□ Trace the first executable statement in the program's MAIN section:

```
DEBUG> t MAIN
```

□ Trace the statement at line 45 after each third execution:

```
DEBUG> t 45 after 3
```

□ Trace the statement at line 45 when the values of the variables DIVISOR and DIVIDEND are both 0:

```
DEBUG> t 45 when (divisor=0 and dividend=0)
```

□ Trace the statement at line 5 in the entry TEST1.

```
DEBUG t test1\5
```

TRACEBACK

Displays the traceback of the entire SCL execution stack

Abbreviation: TB

TRACEBACK

Details

The TRACEBACK command displays the entire execution stack. The entire execution stack consists of the current program being executed and all programs that were called to display the current program.

Example

Assume that a debugging execution stack looks like this when SUB2.PROGRAM is executing:

SUB2.PROGRAM	line 49
SUB1.PROGRAM	line 16
MAIN.PROGRAM	line 8

The output of the TRACEBACK command is:

```
In routine SASUSER.SCL.SUB2.PROGRAM  line 49
Called from SASUSER.SCL.SUB1.PROGRAM  line 16
Called from SASUSER.SCL.MAIN.PROGRAM  line 8
```

WATCH

Suspends program execution when the value of a specified variable has been modified

Abbreviation: W

See Also:
BREAK
DELETE
LIST
TRACE

WATCH <*entry-name\\>variable* <AFTER *count* > <WHEN *clause* | DO *list* >

Argument	Description
entry-name	The name of a catalog entry containing an SCL program.
variable	A standard SCL variable. A variable is called a watched entry parameter if it is defined as both a watched variable and an ENTRY statement parameter. A program is not suspended when the value of a watched entry parameter is changed by a called program. However, execution of the program does suspend when a changed value for a watched entry parameter is copied back to the calling program.
AFTER *count*	A count maintained along with the watched variable. When the count value equals the integer given with the AFTER option, program execution is suspended. Therefore, for an AFTER specification of 3, the program halts when the value of the watched variable is changed for the third time.
WHEN *clause*	Standard debugger WHEN clause as described in "Common Arguments" on page 162.
DO *list*	Standard debugger DO list as described in "Common Arguments" on page 162.

Details

The WATCH command specifies a variable to monitor and suspends program execution when its value is modified. Each time the variable is modified, the debugger does the following:

□ suspends program execution

□ checks for any AFTER count and resumes program execution if the specified number of changes has not been reached

□ evaluates the WHEN condition and resumes execution if the WHEN condition is false

□ displays the entry name and line number at which execution has been suspended

□ displays the variable's old value

□ displays the variable's new value

□ executes any commands in a DO list in the WATCH command

□ returns control to the developer and displays the DEBUG> prompt.

You can only watch variables in the currently loaded program.

Examples

□ Monitor the variable DIVISOR in TEST2 for value changes:

```
DEBUG> w divisor
```

The output to the MESSAGE window is:

```
Stop at line 6 in SASUSER.SCL.TEST2.PROGRAM
Watch variable DIVISOR has been modified
Old value=1
New value=99
```

□ Monitor all the elements in the array ARR for value changes:

```
DEBUG> w arr
```

□ Monitor the variable DIVISOR in TEST1.PROGRAM for value changes:

```
DEBUG> w test1\divisor
```

□ Monitor the variable a{1} for value changes and suspend program execution after its value has been altered three times:

```
DEBUG> w a{1} after 3
```

□ Monitor a{1} for value changes and suspend program execution when neither X nor Y is 0:

```
DEBUG> w a{1} when (x^=0 and y^=0)
```

□ Monitor FIELD1 for value changes and suspend program execution after the third change in the value of FIELD1 and when the variables DIVIDEND and DIVISOR both equal 0:

```
DEBUG> w field1 after 3 when (dividend=0 and divisor=0)
```

SAS® Screen Control Language Elements

CHAPTER *18* SAS® System Return Codes

Introduction

Many of the SCL functions that interface to external databases and file systems return special values called *SAS system return codes*. These return codes report the success or failure of the function and report error and warning conditions. Application developers can use SAS system return codes to write applications with sophisticated error checking.

This chapter discusses how your application can query and use the SAS system return codes that SCL generates. It also describes a special Institute-supplied autocall macro that is provided to facilitate the handling of these codes.

Using SAS System Return Codes

The value of a SAS system return code can be interpreted as:

Return code	Meaning
0	The operation was completed successfully.
>0	An error condition was detected during the operation.
<0	The operation was completed, but a warning was generated.

Not all SCL functions that return completion code values return SAS system return codes. Some functions return a completion code values that reports the success or failure of the requested operation (usually 1 for success or 0 for failure).

These values are referred to in this book simply as return codes because they do not have the special property of SAS system return codes described in the preceding table.

Obtaining a SAS System Return Code

Some functions, notably OPEN, DOPEN, FOPEN, and MOPEN, return values other than SAS system return codes. For these functions, use the SYSRC function to obtain the SAS system return code for the operation. The SAS System retains the value of the return code for the most recent warning or error condition, and the SYSRC function reads the stored value.

The following example assigns the SAS system return code to the variable ERRNUM if the OPEN operation fails:

```
dsid=open('prices','I');
if dsid=0 then errnum=sysrc();
put "Open failed" errnum;
```

Note: If you call the SYSRC function after executing a function that returns SAS system return codes, the value returned by the SYSRC function will be the same as the value returned by the original function.

Obtaining the Message for a SAS System Return Code

In many cases, it is sufficient to know the value of a SAS system return code to determine the success or failure of the operation. However, in some cases warning messages can be useful for informing users of special situations that may need to be corrected.

You can use the SYSMSG function to return the text of error messages produced by the most recent SCL warning or error.

For example, the following statements illustrate how to display the SAS System message for the error condition produced when the FETCH function returns a nonzero return code:

```
rc=fetch(dsid);
if rc then _msg_=sysmsg();
```

The message string returned by SYSMSG() is reset to blank after each call to SYSMSG() until the next error or warning condition occurs.

Testing for a Specific Error or Warning Condition

When an SCL function returns a nonzero SAS system return code, you can use the %SYSRC macro to determine whether the code indicates one of a defined set of error and warning conditions. The %SYSRC macro is provided in the autocall library supplied by SAS Institute.

Note: To use autocall macros, the MAUTOSOURCE system option must be in effect and the SASAUTOS= system option must point to the Institute-supplied autocall macro library. Refer to Chapter 20, "SAS Macro Facility," in *SAS Language: Reference, Version 6, First Edition* for details of the autocall facility.

To test whether a given return code is one of the documented conditions, pass a mnemonic name for the condition to the %SYSRC macro. The syntax is

rc =%SYSRC(*mnemonic*);

Table 18.1 later in this chapter lists the mnemonic for each defined error condition. The syntax of the mnemonics contains:

□ an underscore (_) for the first character.

□ S for the second character.

□ E (for error conditions) or W (for warning conditions) for the third character.

□ a shortened version of the name of the error for the remaining characters.

For example, _SWEOF is the mnemonic for the end-of-file warning condition.

Note: The return code for an end-of-file condition is a warning (_SWEOF). The value of the return code is − 1. This is a special return code that is explicitly documented in this book.

Mnemonics are assigned to only those error or warning conditions considered relevant to an application developer. In some cases, SCL returns values that do not have a corresponding mnemonic. In these cases, the value indicates a warning condition if negative and an error condition if positive.

For example, the following statements can be used to test whether the record requested by the FETCH function was successfully locked to your application:

```
rc=fetch(dsid);
if (rc) then
    do;
        if (rc=%sysrc(_swnoupd)) then
            _msg_='Another user has locked the requested observation';
        else
            _msg_=sysmsg();   /* fetch failed for some other reason */
    end;
```

Mnemonics for SAS System Return Codes

Table 18.1 and Table 18.2 list the mnemonics for SAS System return codes. Table 18.1 is sorted alphabetically by the mnemonic name. Table 18.2 is sorted by the number. Both tables provide the number returned by the return code and a description of the condition that produces the condition. The codes are organized by general categories of operations that can produce the conditions.

Table 18.1
Mnemonics for Warning and Error Conditions (sorted alphabetically by Mnemonic)

Mnemonic	Number	Description
Library Assign/Deassign Messages		
_SEDUPLB	70004	The libref refers to the same physical library as another libref.
_SEIBASN	70006	The specified libref is not assigned.
_SEINUSE	70025	The library or member is not available for use.
_SEINVLB	70002	The library is not in a valid format for the access method.
_SEINVLN	20014	The libref is not valid.
_SELBACC	70029	The action requested cannot be performed because you do not have the required access level on the library.
_SELBUSE	70025	The library is still in use.
_SELGASN	70006	The specified libref is not assigned.
_SENOASN	20004	The libref is not assigned.
_SENOLNM	20031	The libref is not available for use.
_SESEQLB	630032	The library is in sequential (tape) format.
_SWDUPLB	− 70004	The libref refers to the same physical file as another libref.
_SWNOLIB	− 70008	The library does not exist.
Fileref Messages		
_SELOGNM	20002	The fileref is assigned to an invalid file.
_SWLNASN	− 20004	The fileref is not assigned.

Mnemonic	Number	Description
SAS Data Set Messages		
_SEBAUTH	70045	The data set has passwords.
_SEBDIND	630009	The index name is not a valid SAS name.
_SEDSMOD	70018	The data set is not open in the correct mode for the specified operation.
_SEDTLEN	20012	The data length is invalid.
_SEINDCF	630008	The new name conflicts with an index name.
_SEINVMD	20015	The open mode is invalid.
_SEINVPN	20017	The physical name is invalid.
_SEMBACC	70030	You do not have the level of access required to open the data set in the requested mode.
_SENOLCK	630053	A record-level lock is not available.
_SENOMAC	660025	Member-level access to the data set is denied.
_SENOSAS	70037	The file is not a SAS data set.
_SEVARCF	630019	The new name conflicts with an existing variable name.
_SWBOF	− 570001	You tried to read the previous observation when you are on the first observation.
_SWNOWHR	− 630004	The record no longer satisfies the WHERE clause.
_SWSEQ	− 630032	The task requires reading observations in a random order, but the engine you are using allows only sequential access.
_SWWAUG	− 580016	The WHERE clause has been augmented.
_SWWCLR	− 580017	The WHERE clause has been cleared.
_SWWREP	− 580015	The WHERE clause has been replaced.
SAS File Open and Update Messages		
_SEBDSNM	630087	The file name is not a valid SAS name.
_SEDLREC	630049	The record has been deleted from the file.
_SEFOPEN	20036	The file is currently open.
_SEINVON	70022	The option name is invalid.
_SEINVOV	70023	The option value is invalid.
_SEINVPS	20018	The value of the File Data Buffer pointer is invalid.
_SELOCK	70031	The file is locked by another user.
_SENOACC	20029	You do not have the level of access required to open the file in the requested mode.
_SENOALL	630100	_ALL_ is not allowed as part of a file name in this release.

Mnemonic	Number	Description
_SENOCHN	630058	The record was not changed because it would cause a duplicate value for an index that does not allow duplicates.
_SENODEL	10011	Records cannot be deleted from this file.
_SENODLT	20030	The file could not be deleted.
_SENOERT	20035	The file is not open for writing.
_SENOOAC	70030	You are not authorized for the requested open mode.
_SENOOPN	20037	The file or directory is not open.
_SENOPF	20006	The physical file does not exist.
_SENORD	20032	The file is not opened for reading.
_SENORDX	630066	The file is not radix addressable.
_SENOTRD	570002	No record has been read from the file yet.
_SENOUPD	630006	The file cannot be opened for update because the engine is read-only.
_SENOWRT	70040	You do not have write access to the member.
_SEOBJLK	20025	The file or directory is in exclusive use by another user.
_SERECRD	630052	No records have been read from the input file.
_SWACMEM	− 630032	Access to the directory will be provided one member at a time
_SWEOF	− 1	End of file.
_SWNOFLE	− 20006	The file does not exist.
_SWNOPF	− 70008	The file or directory does not exist.
_SWNOREP	− 630002	The file was not replaced because of the NOREPLACE option.
_SWNOTFL	− 20002	The item pointed to exists but is not a file.
_SWNOUPD	− 630054	This record cannot be updated at this time.

Library/Member/Entry Messages

Mnemonic	Number	Description
_SEBDMT	70015	The member type specification is invalid.
_SEDLT	70033	The member was not deleted.
_SELKUSR	630097	The library or library member locked by another user.
_SEMLEN	70028	The member name is too long for this system.
_SENOLKH	630099	The library or library member is not currently locked.
_SENOMEM	70009	The member does not exist.
_SWKNXL	− 670212	You have locked a library, member, or entry, that does not exist yet.

Mnemonic	Number	Description
_SWLKUSR	− 630097	The library or library member is locked by another user.
_SWLKYOU	− 630098	You have already locked the library or library member.
_SWNOLKH	− 630099	The library or library member is not currently locked.

Miscellaneous Operations

Mnemonic	Number	Description
_SEDEVOF	10008	The device is offline or unavailable.
_SEDSKFL	70039	The disk or tape is full.
_SEINVDV	20011	The device type is invalid.
_SENORNG	20034	There is no write ring in the tape opened for write access.
_SOK	0	The function was successful.
_SWINVCC	− 20001	The carriage control character is invalid.
_SWNODSK	− 20005	The device is not a disk.
_SWPAUAC	− 630104	Pause in I/O, process accumulated data up to this point.
_SWPAUSL	− 630105	Pause in I/O, slide data window forward and process accumulated data up to this point.
_SWPAUU1	− 630106	Pause in I/O, extra user control point 1.
_SWPAUU2	− 630107	Pause in I/O, extra user control point 2.

Table 18.2
Mnemonics for Warning and Error Conditions (sorted by Number)

Number	Mnemonic	Description
− 1	_SWEOF	End of file.
− 20001	_SWINVCC	The carriage control character is invalid.
− 20002	_SWNOTFL	The item pointed to exists but is not a file.
− 20004	_SWLNASN	The fileref is not assigned.
− 20005	_SWNODSK	The device is not a disk.
− 20006	_SWNOFLE	The file does not exist.
− 70004	_SWDUPLB	The libref refers to the same physical file as another libref.
− 70008	_SWNOPF	The file or directory does not exist.
− 70008	_SWNOLIB	The library does not exist.
− 570001	_SWBOF	You tried to read the previous observation when you are on the first observation.
− 580015	_SWWREP	The WHERE clause has been replaced.

Number	Mnemonic	Description
− 580016	_SWWAUG	The WHERE clause has been augmented.
− 580017	_SWWCLR	The WHERE clause has been cleared.
− 630002	_SWNOREP	The file was not replaced because of the NOREPLACE option.
− 630004	_SWNOWHR	The record no longer satisfies the WHERE clause.
− 630032	_SWSEQ	The task requires reading observations in a random order, but the engine you are using allows only sequential access.
− 630032	_SWACMEM	Access to the directory will be provided one member at a time
− 630054	_SWNOUPD	This record cannot be updated at this time.
− 630097	_SWLKUSR	The library or library member is locked by another user.
− 630098	_SWLKYOU	You have already locked the library or library member.
− 630099	_SWNOLKH	The library or library member is not currently locked.
− 630104	_SWPAUAC	Pause in I/O, process accumulated data up to this point.
− 630105	_SWPAUSL	Pause in I/O, slide data window forward and process accumulated data up to this point.
− 630106	_SWPAUU1	Pause in I/O, extra user control point 1.
− 630107	_SWPAUU2	Pause in I/O, extra user control point 2.
− 670212	_SWKNXL	You have locked a library, member, or entry, that does not exist yet.
0	_SOK	The function was successful.
10008	_SEDEVOF	The device is offline or unavailable.
10011	_SENODEL	Records cannot be deleted from this file.
20002	_SELOGNM	The fileref is assigned to an invalid file.
20004	_SENOASN	The libref is not assigned.
20006	_SENOPF	The physical file does not exist.
20011	_SEINVDV	The device type is invalid.
20012	_SEDTLEN	The data length is invalid.
20014	_SEINVLN	The libref is not valid.
20015	_SEINVMD	The open mode is invalid.
20017	_SEINVPN	The physical name is invalid.
20018	_SEINVPS	The value of the File Data Buffer pointer is invalid.
20025	_SEOBJLK	The file or directory is in exclusive use by another user.
20029	_SENOACC	You do not have the level of access required to open the file in the requested mode.
20030	_SENODLT	The file could not be deleted.

Number	Mnemonic	Description
20031	_SENOLNM	The libref is not available for use.
20032	_SENORD	The file is not opened for reading.
20034	_SENORNG	There is no write ring in the tape opened for write access.
20035	_SENOERT	The file is not open for writing.
20036	_SEFOPEN	The file is currently open.
20037	_SENOOPN	The file or directory is not open.
70002	_SEINVLB	The library is not in a valid format for the access method.
70004	_SEDUPLB	The libref refers to the same physical library as another libref.
70006	_SEIBASN	The specified libref is not assigned.
70006	_SELGASN	The specified libref is not assigned.
70009	_SENOMEM	The member does not exist.
70015	_SEBDMT	The member type specification is invalid.
70018	_SEDSMOD	The data set is not open in the correct mode for the specified operation.
70022	_SEINVON	The option name is invalid.
70023	_SEINVOV	The option value is invalid.
70025	_SEINUSE	The library or member is not available for use.
70025	_SELBUSE	The library is still in use.
70028	_SEMLEN	The member name is too long for this system.
70029	_SELBACC	The action requested cannot be performed because you do not have the required access level on the library.
70030	_SEMBACC	You do not have the level of access required to open the data set in the requested mode.
70030	_SENOOAC	You are not authorized for the requested open mode.
70031	_SELOCK	The file is locked by another user.
70033	_SEDLT	The member was not deleted.
70037	_SENOSAS	The file is not a SAS data set.
70039	_SEDSKFL	The disk or tape is full.
70040	_SENOWRT	You do not have write access to the member.
70045	_SEBAUTH	The data set has passwords.
570002	_SENOTRD	No record has been read from the file yet.
630006	_SENOUPD	The file cannot be opened for update because the engine is read-only.
630008	_SEINDCF	The new name conflicts with an index name.
630009	_SEBDIND	The index name is not a valid SAS name.
630019	_SEVARCF	The new name conflicts with an existing variable name.

Number	Mnemonic	Description
630032	_SESEQLB	The library is in sequential (tape) format.
630049	_SEDLREC	The record has been deleted from the file.
630052	_SERECRD	No records have been read from the input file.
630053	_SENOLCK	A record-level lock is not available.
630058	_SENOCHN	The record was not changed because it would cause a duplicate value for an index that does not allow duplicates.
630066	_SENORDX	The file is not radix addressable.
630087	_SEBDSNM	The file name is not a valid SAS name.
630097	_SELKUSR	The library or library member locked by another user.
630099	_SENOLKH	The library or library member is not currently locked.
630100	_SENOALL	_ALL_ is not allowed as part of a file name in this release.
660025	_SENOMAC	Member-level access to the data set is denied.

Overview

This chapter lists the statements, functions, and CALL routines that can be used in Screen Control Language programs. Many elements of SAS language are valid in SCL programs and are listed in this chapter. For more information on them, see *SAS Language: Reference, Version 6, First Edition.* The language elements that are valid in SCL are shown in tables with features grouped by functionality. These tables present:

☐ statements that are valid in SCL

☐ elements specific to SCL

☐ SAS language functions

☐ elements of the DATA Step Graphics Interface in SAS/GRAPH software.

Statements in SCL

Table 19.1 lists DATA step statements and SCL statements that are valid in SCL and where they are documented.

Table 19.1
Statements by Category

Statement	Described in
Assignment Statements	
Assignment statement	*SAS Language: Reference*
SUM statement	*SAS Language: Reference*
Control Flow Statements	
CONTINUE	Chapter 20
CONTROL	Chapter 20
DO/END	Chapter 20
DO iterative	*SAS Language: Reference*
DO WHILE	*SAS Language: Reference*
DO UNTIL	*SAS Language: Reference*

Statement	Described in
IF/THEN/ELSE	*SAS Language: Reference*
GOTO	*SAS Language: Reference*
LEAVE	Chapter 20
LINK	*SAS Language: Reference*
RETURN	*SAS Language: Reference*
RUN	Chapter 20
SELECT/WHEN	Chapter 20
STOP	Chapter 20

Declarative Statements

Statement	Described in
ARRAY	Chapter 20
LENGTH	Chapter 20
REPLACE	Chapter 20
METHOD	Chapter 20

Field Statements

Statement	Described in
CURSOR	Chapter 20
ERRORON/ERRORROFF	Chapter 20
HOME	Chapter 20
PROTECT/UNPROTECT	Chapter 20

Modular Programming Statements

Statement	Described in
ENTRY	Chapter 20
METHOD	Chapter 20
ENDMETHOD	Chapter 20

SAS Macro statements

All SAS macro statements are supported. For more information, see *SAS Guide to Macro Processing, Version 6, Second Edition.*

SUBMIT Statements

Statement	Described in
REPLACE	Chapter 20
SUBMIT/ENDSUBMIT	Chapter 20

Miscellaneous

Statement	Described in
ALARM	Chapter 20
CALL	*SAS Language: Reference*
Comment statements	*SAS Language: Reference*
NULL	*SAS Language: Reference*

Statement	Described in
PUT	Chapter 20
REFRESH	Chapter 20

SCL Elements

Table 19.2 summarizes the SCL functions, routines, and statements provided in Screen Control Language. The elements are grouped by functional category. Refer to Chapter 20, "Screen Control Language Dictionary," for complete descriptions of the SCL functions, routines, and statements. Names denoted by a star (*) are features that are available with Release 6.11.

Table 19.2   *SCL Elements by Category*

Category	Description
Catalog	
CATALOG	opens a directory window that lists entries for a SAS catalog
CATLIST	displays a selection list window that lists entries in a SAS catalog and returns user selections
CEXIST	verifies the existence of a SAS catalog or SAS catalog entry
COPY	copies a SAS data set, view, catalog, or catalog entry
RENAME	renames a SAS data set, view, catalog, or catalog entry
SEARCH	creates or manipulates the current catalog search path
* SEARCHPATH	reports the complete pathname of a SAS catalog entry
Character	
CENTER	returns a centered character string
LEFT	returns a left-aligned character string
LENGTH	returns the length of a trimmed character string
MLENGTH	returns the maximum length of a character string
RIGHT	returns a right-aligned character value
Choice Group	
ACTIVATE	activates or grays a specified station in a choice group, check box, or radio box
GRAY	grays a single station of a choice group, an entire choice group, a radio box, or a check box
ISACTIVE	returns the number of the active box or check box or the active station in a choice group
ISGRAY	reports whether a choice group, check box, or radio box is grayed
UNGRAY	ungrays a single station in a choice group, an entire choice group, a check box, or a radio box

Category	Description
Command	
EXECCMD	executes one or more commands when control returns to the application
EXECCMDI	executes one or more global commands before processing the next statement, or when NOEXEC is specified, executes one nonglobal command when control returns to the application
LASTCMD	returns the text of the last command issued from the application window
LOOKUPC	searches for a string among a list of valid tokens
NEXTCMD	discards the current command on the command line
NEXTWORD	deletes the current word and advances to the next word in the current command
SYSTEM	issues a host system command
WORD	returns a word from the command on the command line
* WORDTYPE	identifies the type for a word on the command line
Cursor	
CURFLD	returns the name of the field or FRAME entry on which the cursor is currently positioned
CURSOR	positions the cursor in a specified field or FRAME entry
CURWORD	returns the word that the cursor is positioned on
SETCR	controls the cursor's response to the carriage return key
Data File	
APPEND	appends a new observation to a SAS data set
ATTRC	returns the value of a character attribute for a SAS data set
ATTRN	returns the value of a numeric attribute for the specified SAS data set
CLOSE	closes a SAS data set
CONTENTS	Displays the contents of a SAS data set
COPY	copies a SAS data set, view, catalog, or catalog entry
CUROBS	returns the observation number of the current observation
DATALISTC	displays a selection list window containing values of selected variables from observations in a SAS data set and returns user selections
DATALISTN	displays a selection list window containing values of specified variables from observations in a SAS data set
DELETE	deletes a SAS data set, catalog, catalog entry, view, or access descriptor
DELOBS	deletes an observation from a SAS data set
DROPNOTE	deletes a note marker from a SAS data set or an external file
* DSID	Searches for a data set name and returns the data set identifier
DSNAME	returns the data set name associated with a data set identifier
EXIST	verifies the existence of a SAS data library member
FETCH	reads the next nondeleted observation from a SAS data set into the Data Set Data Vector (DDV)

Category	Description
FETCHOBS	reads a specified observation from a SAS data set into the Data Set Data Vector (DDV)
GETVARC	assigns the value of a SAS data set variable to a character SCL variable
GETVARN	assigns the value of a SAS data set variable to a numeric SCL variable
ICREATE	creates an index for a SAS data set
IDELETE	deletes an index from a SAS data set
IMPORT	Creates a SAS data set from an external file
IOPTION	returns options for index and key variables
ISINDEX	returns the type of index for a SAS data set variable
IVARLIST	returns the variable names for an index key
* KEYCOUNT	Returns the number of observations that meet the criteria specified by an index key
LIBLIST	displays a selection list window of libref names and returns the user's selection
LIBNAME	assigns or deassigns a libref for a SAS data library
LIBREF	verifies that a libref has been assigned
LOCK	locks or unlocks a SAS file or SAS catalog entry
LOCATEC	searches a SAS data set for an observation that contains a specified character value
LOCATEN	searches a SAS data set for an observation that contains a specified numeric value
NEW	defines a new SAS data set interactively
NEWVAR	adds a variable to a new SAS data set
NOTE	returns an observation ID for the current observation of a SAS data set
OBSINFO	returns information on the current observation in an FSEDIT application
OPEN	opens a SAS data file
POINT	locates an observation identified by the NOTE function
PUTVARC	writes a character value to the Data Set Data Vector (DDV) for a SAS data set
PUTVARN	writes a numeric value to the Data Set Data Vector (DDV) for a SAS data set
RENAME	renames a SAS data set, view, catalog, or catalog entry
REWIND	positions the data set pointer to the beginning of a SAS data set
SET	links SAS data set variables to SCL variables of the same name and data type
SETKEY	defines an index key for retrieving observations from a SAS data set
SORT	sorts a SAS data set by one or more variables
UNLOCK	releases a lock on the current observation
UPDATE	writes values from the Data Set Data Vector (DDV) to the current observation in a SAS data set
VARLIST	displays a selection list window of the variables in a SAS data set and returns user's selections
WHERE	applies a WHERE clause to a SAS data set

Category	Description
Directory	
DCLOSE	closes a directory
DINFO	returns information about a directory
DNUM	returns the number of members in a directory
DOPEN	opens a directory
DOPTNAME	returns directory attribute information
DOPTNUM	returns the number of information items available for a directory
DREAD	returns the name of a directory member
MOPEN	opens a directory member file
Extended Table	
CURTOP	returns the number of the row currently displayed at the top of an extended table
ENDTABLE	establishes the maximum number of rows for a dynamic extended table
ISSEL	returns the selection number for a specified row of a selection list
NSELECT	returns the number of rows that have been selected in a selection list
SELECT	selects a specified row of a selection list
SELECTED	returns the number of the row that corresponds to a user's choice in a selection list
SETROW	defines extended tables, dynamic tables, and selection lists
TOPROW	scrolls a row to the top of an extended table
UNSELECT	unselects a specified row of a selection list
External File	
FAPPEND	appends a record to the end of an external file
FCLOSE	closes an external file, directory,or directory member
FCOL	returns the current column position in the File Data Buffer (FDB)
FDELETE	deletes an external file
FEXIST	verifies the existence of an external file associated with a fileref
FGET	reads data from the File Data Buffer (FDB)
* FILEDIALOG	opens a selection window listing files
FILEEXIST	verifies the existence of an external file by its physical name
FILENAME	assigns or deassigns a fileref for an external file, directory, or output device
FILEREF	verifies that a fileref has been assigned for the current SAS session
FINFO	returns a file information item
FNOTE	identifies the last record that was read
FOPEN	opens an external file
FOPTNAME	returns the name of an item of information about a file
FOPTNUM	returns the number of information items available about an external file

Category	Description
FPOINT	positions the read pointer on the next record to be read
FPOS	sets the position of the column pointer in the File Data Buffer
FPUT	moves data to the File Data Buffer (FDB) of an external file starting at the FDB's current column position
FREAD	reads a record from an external file into the File Data Buffer (FDB)
FREWIND	positions the file pointer to the start of the file
FRLEN	returns the size of the last record read, or, if the file is opened for output, returns the current record size
FSEP	sets the token delimiters for the FGET function
FWRITE	writes a record to an external file
IMPORT	creates a SAS data set from an external file
PATHNAME	returns the physical name of a SAS data library or an external file

Field or Widget

Category	Description
CLRFLD	clears the value from up to ten character variables whose values match the specified value
CURFLD	returns the name of the field or FRAME entry on which the cursor is currently positioned
CURSOR	positions the cursor in a specified field or FRAME entry
DISPLAYED	reports whether a field or FRAME entry is currently visible
ERROR	reports whether a field or FRAME entry contains an invalid value
ERROROFF	clears the error flag on one or more fields or FRAME entries flagged with the ERRORON statement
ERRORON	sets the error flag for one or more fields or FRAME entries
FIELD	performs an action on or reports the state of fields or FRAME entries
FLDATTR	changes the color and display attribute of a field, text object entry, or text label object to those stored in an attribute string
FLDCOLOR	changes the color and display attribute of a field, text entry object, or text label object to those stored in an attribute string
MODIFIED	reports whether a field or FRAME entry has been modified
PROTECT	assigns protection to a field or FRAME entry
SETFLD	assigns a value to up to ten blank variables
STRATTR	defines a color and highlighting attribute string
UNPROTECT	removes protection from a field or FRAME entry

Formatting

Category	Description
FORMAT	verifies that the specified format is valid
INFORMAT	verifies that the specified informat is valid
INPUTC	reads a character string using a character informat

Category	Description
INPUTN	reads a character string using a numeric format
PUTC	returns the formatted value of a character value using the specified character format
PUTN	returns the formatted value of a numeric value using the specified numeric format

Keys

EVENT	Reports whether a user has pressed a function or ENTER key or mouse button
FKEYNAME	returns the name of the specified function key
GETFKEY	returns the command assigned to a function key
LASTKEY	returns the number of the last function key pressed from the window
NUMFKEYS	returns the number of function keys available for the device
SETFKEY	assigns a command to a function key

Legend

ENDLEGEND	closes the LEGEND window
LEGEND	displays a LEGEND window or refreshes the current LEGEND window
POPLEGEND	restores to the LEGEND window the last contents saved with the PUSHLEGEND routine
PUSHLEGEND	saves the contents of the LEGEND window
PUTLEGEND	specifies the contents of one line in the LEGEND window

List

CLEARLIST	clears the items from an SCL list without deleting the list and optionally clears all sublist items
COPYLIST	copies or merges the contents of an SCL list into an existing list or a new list
CURLIST	designates or reports the current SCL list
DELITEM	deletes an item from an SCL list and optionally deletes all of its sublists
DELLIST	deletes a list and optionally deletes all of its sublists
DELNITEM	deletes a named item from an SCL list
DESCRIBE	fills an SCL list with items of descriptive information about a SAS data set, view, or catalog entry
ENVLIST	returns the list identifier of an SCL environment list
FILLIST	fills an SCL list with text and data
GETITEMC	returns a character value that is identified by its position in an SCL list
GETITEML	returns a sublist identifier that is identified by its position in an SCL list
GETITEMN	returns a numeric value that is identified by its position in an SCL list
GETLATTR	returns the attributes of an SCL list or an item in the list
GETNITEMC	returns a character value identified by its name in an SCL list
GETNITEML	returns a list identifier value identified by its name in an SCL list
GETNITEMN	returns the value of a numeric list item identified by its name in an SCL list

Category	Description
HASATTR	reports whether an SCL list or list item has a specified attribute
INSERTC	inserts a character value into an SCL list
INSERTL	inserts a list identifier into an SCL list
INSERTN	inserts a numeric value into an SCL list
ITEMTYPE	reports the type of an item in an SCL list
LISTLEN	reports the length of an SCL list
LVARLEVEL	fills an SCL list with the unique values of a variable from a SAS data set
MAKELIST	creates an SCL list
MAKENLIST	creates an SCL list with named items
NAMEDITEM	returns the index of a named item in a list
NAMEITEM	returns and optionally replaces the name of an item in an SCL list
POPC	removes and returns a character value from an SCL list
POPL	removes and returns a list identifier from an SCL list
POPMENU	displays a pop-up menu containing character items in an SCL list
POPN	removes and returns a numeric value from an SCL list
PUTLIST	displays the contents of an SCL list in the MESSAGE or LOG window
REVLIST	reverses the order of the items in an SCL list
ROTLIST	rotates the items in an SCL list
SAVELIST	stores SCL list items in a SAS catalog entry or an external file
SEARCHC	searches for a character value in an SCL list and returns its position number
SEARCHL	searches for a list identifier in an SCL list and returns its position number
SEARCHN	searches for a numeric value in an SCL list and returns its position number
SETITEMC	stores a character value at an indexed position in an SCL list
SETITEML	stores a list identifier at an indexed position in an SCL list
SETITEMN	stores a numeric value at an indexed position in an SCL list
SETLATTR	sets the attributes of an SCL list or an item in a list
SETNITEMC	assigns a character value to a named item in an SCL list
SETNITEML	assigns a list identifier to a named item in an SCL list
SETNITEMN	assigns a numeric value to a named item in an SCL list
SORTLIST	sorts the items in an SCL list by value or by name

Macro

SYMGET	returns the character value stored in a macro variable
SYMGETN	returns the numeric value stored in a macro variable
SYMPUT	stores a character value in a SAS macro variable
SYMPUTN	stores a numeric value in a SAS macro variable

Category	Description
Message	
STDMSG	displays the text of the SAS System message generated by an unknown command
SYSMSG	returns the text of SCL error messages or warning messages
SYSRC	returns a system error number or the exit status of the most recently called entry
Modular Programming	
CBT	runs a CBT entry
DISPLAY	runs an entry created with SAS/AF software
ENDMETHOD	ends a METHOD statement block
ENTRY	receives parameters from CALL DISPLAY
GETPARMID	returns the numeric value stored by the SETPARMID routine
GOTO	branches immediately to another entry
METHOD (routine)	executes a method block defined in an SCL entry
METHOD (statement)	begins a statement block that can be called by the METHOD routine
NOCHANGE	causes the called program to return the same values for the variables it received as parameters in an ENTRY statement
SETPARMID	makes the value of an SCL numeric variable available between SCL programs
Object Oriented	
* APPLY	Invokes a method whose arguments are passed from an SCL list
INSTANCE	Creates an instance of a class and returns its identifier
LOADCLASS	Loads a class for later instantiation and returns its identifier number
LOADRES	Loads a RESOURCE entry
NOTIFY	Sends a method to a widget that is identified by its name
SEND	Sends a method to an object that is identified by its number
* SUPAPPLY	Invokes the inherited definition of a method and passes the method's arguments in an SCL list
SUPER	Invokes the inherited definition of a method
SAS System Options	
* COMAMID	Returns the communications access methods for an operating system
GETFOOT	returns the text assigned to a FOOTNOTE statement
GETTITLE	returns the text assigned to a TITLE statement
GGLOBAL	returns the text of a SYMBOL, PATTERN, LEGEND, or AXIS statement definition
GGLOBALE	deletes an internal table of SYMBOL, PATTERN, LEGEND, or AXIS definitions
GGLOBALN	returns the number of SYMBOL, PATTERN, LEGEND, or AXIS statements that are currently defined
OPTGETC	returns the current setting of a SAS System option having a character value
OPTGETN	returns the current setting of a SAS System option having a numeric or binary value

Category	Description
OPTSETC	assigns a value to a SAS System option with a character setting
OPTSETN	assigns a value to a SAS System option with a numeric or binary setting
SETFOOT	sets a FOOTNOTE statement
SETTITLE	sets a TITLE statement
SYSTEM	issues a host system command

Interfaces to SAS Software

BUILD	invokes the BUILD window in SAS/AF software (SAS/AF software required)
CALC	invokes the CALC window in SAS/CALC software (SAS/CALC software required)
* COMAMID	returns the communications access methods for an operating system
FSEDIT	displays a SAS data set by observation (SAS/FSP software required)
FSLIST	displays an external file for browsing (SAS/FSP software required)
FSVIEW	displays a SAS data set as a table of observations (SAS/FSP software required)
LETTER	displays the FSLETTER window or sends a letter created with the FSLETTER procedure (SAS/FSP software required)
RLINK	reports whether a link exists between the current SAS session and a remote SAS session (SAS/CONNECT software required)
RSESSION	returns the name, description, and SAS System version of a remote session (SAS/CONNECT software required)
RSTITLE	defines a description for an existing connection to a remote session (SAS/CONNECT software required)
SASTASK	determines whether a SAS procedure is running
SUBMIT	submits statements to the SAS System for execution

Selection List

CATLIST	displays a selection list window that lists entries in a SAS catalog and returns user selections
COLORLIST	displays a selection list of the names of a device's valid colors and returns user selections
DATALISTC	displays a selection list window containing values of selected variables from observations in a SAS data set and returns user selections
DATALISTN	displays a selection list window containing values of specified variables from observations in a SAS data set
DEVLIST	displays a selection list of graphic hardware devices and returns user selections
DIRLIST	opens a selection list window of members of a SAS data library and returns a user's selections
* FILEDIALOG	opens a selection window listing files
FILELIST	displays a selection list window showing the currently assigned filerefs and returns user selections
* FONTSEL	opens the selector window for host or for portable fonts

Category	Description
LIBLIST	displays a selection list window of libref names and returns the user's selection
LISTC	displays a selection list window that lists character values and returns the user's selection
LISTN	displays a selection list window containing numeric values and returns user selections
SHOWLIST	displays a selection list window containing up to 12 items and returns user selections
VARLIST	displays a selection list window of the variables in a SAS data set and returns the user's selections

Submit Block

ENDSUBMIT	ends statements to be submitted to the SAS System for execution
PREVIEW	manipulates an application's preview buffer
REPLACE	substitutes a replacement string for a reference to an SCL variable in the SUBMIT block
SASTASK	determines whether a SAS procedure is running
SUBMIT	submits statements to the SAS System for execution

System Variables

BLANK	Special missing value for SAS/AF applications
CURROW	Contains the number of the current row for an extended table
ERROR	defined but not used by SCL
MSG	contains the text to display on the window's message line the next time the window is refreshed
STATUS	contains the status of program execution or overrides the normal flow of control

System Instance Variables

CFRAME	contains the identifier of the FRAME entry that is currently executing
CURCOL	contains the value of the leftmost column in an extended table object in a FRAME entry
FRAME	contains the identifier of the FRAME entry that contains the widget, or the identifier of the FRAME entry if the FRAME entry is being used as a method
METHOD	contains the name of the method that is currently executing
SELF	contains the identifier of the object for the currently executing method, or the identifier of the FRAME entry if the FRAME entry is not running as a method
VALUE	contains the value of a FRAME entry object

Utility

ACCESS	opens the ACCESS window, which lists members of a SAS data library
ASORT	performs a sort on an array
CONTENTS	Displays the contents of a SAS data set
CONTROL	controls execution of labeled program sections and formatting of SUBMIT blocks

Category	Description
FILENAME	assigns or deassigns a fileref for an external file, directory, or output device
FILEREF	verifies that a fileref has been assigned for the current SAS session
IMPORT	Creates a SAS data set from an external file
LIBNAME	assigns or deassigns a libref for a SAS data library
LIBREF	verifies that a libref has been assigned
PATHNAME	returns the physical name of a SAS data library or an external file
* RGBDM	returns the name supported by SAS Display Manager System (DM) for a color
SASNAME	verifies that a name is a valid SAS name
* TRACEBACK	Displays the traceback of the entire SCL execution stack
* WAIT	Suspends execution of the next program statement

Variable

Category	Description
MODVAR	changes the name, label, format, or informat of a variable in a SAS data set
VARFMT	returns the format assigned to a SAS data set variable
VARINFMT	returns the informat assigned to a SAS data set variable
VARLABEL	returns the label assigned to a SAS data set variable
VARLEN	returns the length of a SAS data set variable
VARLEVEL	reports the unique values of a SAS data set variable
VARNAME	returns the name of a SAS data set variable
VARNUM	returns the number of a SAS data set variable
VARSTAT	calculates simple statistics for SAS data set variables
VARTYPE	returns the data type of a SAS data set variable

Window

Category	Description
ALARM	sounds the device's alarm
BLOCK	displays a menu containing up to 12 choice blocks and returns the number of the user's choice
DMWINDOW	sets the color and highlighting for lines in the display manager OUTPUT and LOG windows
ENDBLOCK	closes the window created by the BLOCK function
HOME	positions the cursor on a window's command area
ICON	associates an icon with the window
PMENU	changes the PMENU for an application
REFRESH	redisplays a window using current field or widget values
* RGBDM	returns the name supported by display manager (DM) for a color
SAVESCREEN	saves the values of data entry fields without exiting from the window
SCREENNAME	returns the name of the current window
WDEF	resizes the active window

Category	Description
WINFO	returns information about the current window
WNAME	specifies a name for the active window
WOUTPUT	manipulates the display manager OUTPUT window
WREGION	defines the boundaries for the next window that displays

* Features available with Release 6.11.

SAS Language Elements

The following sections list the SAS functions and CALL routines that can be used in Screen Control Language programs. These language elements are described in detail in *SAS Language: Reference, Version 6, First Edition* .

SAS Functions

Table 19.3 summarizes the SAS language functions that are most frequently used in Screen Control Language programs. The functions are grouped by category. Refer to Chapter 11, "SAS Functions," in *SAS Language: Reference* for detailed descriptions of these functions.

Table 19.3   *SAS Functions by Category*

Category	Description
Arithmetic	
ABS	returns the absolute value
DIM	returns the current dimension of an array
HBOUND	returns the upper bound of an array
LBOUND	returns the lower bound of an array
MOD	calculates the remainder
SIGN	returns the sign of the argument or 0
SQRT	calculates the square root
Character	
BYTE	returns one character from the collating sequence
COLLATE	generates a string of characters in the collating sequence
COMPRESS	removes blanks or specified characters from a character variable
INDEX	searches for a pattern of characters
INDEXC	finds the first occurrence of any one of a set of characters
RANK	returns the position of a character in the collating sequence
REPEAT	repeats characters
REVERSE	reverses characters; however, because SCL variables have varying lengths, the REVERSE function does not change an argument's trailing blanks into leading blanks for the result as it does in base SAS software

Category	Description
SCAN	scans for words
SUBSTR	extracts a substring
TRANSLATE	changes characters
TRIM	removes trailing blanks
UPCASE	converts to uppercase
VERIFY	validates a character value

Date and Time

DATE	returns today's date as a SAS date value
DATEJUL	converts a Julian date to a SAS date value
DATEPART	extracts the date part of a SAS datetime value or literal
DATETIME	returns the current date and time of day
DAY	returns the day of the month from a SAS date value
DHMS	returns a SAS datetime value from date, hour, minute, and second
HMS	returns a SAS time value from hour, minute, and second
HOUR	returns the hour from a SAS datetime or time value or literal
INTCK	returns the number of time intervals
INTNX	advances a date, time, or datetime value by a given interval
JULDATE	returns the Julian date from a SAS date value or literal
MDY	returns a SAS date value from month, day, and year
MINUTE	returns the minute from a SAS time or datetime value or literal
MONTH	returns the month from a SAS date value or literal
QTR	returns the quarter from a SAS date value or literal
SECOND	returns the second from a SAS time or datetime value or literal
TIME	returns the current time of day
TIMEPART	extracts the time part of a SAS datetime value or literal
TODAY	returns the current date as a SAS date value
WEEKDAY	returns the day of the week from a SAS date value or literal
YEAR	returns the year from a SAS date value
YYQ	returns a SAS date value from the year and quarter

Financial

COMPOUND	computes compounded value
DACCDB	calculates accumulated declining balance depreciation
DACCDBSL	calculates accumulated declining balance converting to straight-line depreciation
DACCSL	calculates accumulated straight-line depreciation
DACCSYD	calculates accumulated sum-of-years-digits depreciation

Category	Description
DACCTAB	calculates accumulated depreciation from a table
DEPDB	calculates declining balance depreciation
DEPDBSL	calculates declining balance converting to straight-line depreciation
DEPSL	calculates straight-line depreciation
DEPSYD	calculates sum-of-years-digits depreciation
DEPTAB	calculates depreciation from a table
INTRR	calculates internal rate of return as a fraction
IRR	calculates internal rate of return as a percentage
MORT	calculates mortgage loan calculations
NETPV	calculates net present value as a fraction
NPV	calculates net present value as a percentage
SAVING	calculates future value of periodic saving

Mathematical

Category	Description
DIGAMMA	computes the derivative of the log of the GAMMA function
ERF	calculates the error function
ERFC	returns the complement of the ERF function
EXP	raises e (2.71828) to a specified power
GAMMA	produces the complete gamma function
LGAMMA	calculates the natural logarithm of the gamma function of a value
LOG	calculates the natural logarithm (base e)
LOG2	calculates the logarithm to the base 2
LOG10	calculates the common logarithm
TRIGAMMA	computes the second derivative of the log of the GAMMA function

Probability

Category	Description
POISSON	calculates the Poisson probability distribution
PROBBETA	calculates the beta probability distribution
PROBBNML	calculates the binomial probability distribution
PROBCHI	calculates the chi-squared probability distribution
PROBF	calculates the F probability distribution
PROBGAM	calculates the gamma probability distribution
PROBHYPR	calculates the hypergeometric probability distribution
PROBIT	calculates the inverse normal distribution
PROBNEGB	calculates the negative binomial probability distribution
PROBNORM	calculates the standard normal probability distribution
PROBT	calculates a student's t distribution

Category	Description
Quantile	
BETAINV	returns a quantile from the beta distribution
CINV	returns a quantile from the chi-squared distribution
FINV	returns a quantile from the F distribution
GAMINV	returns a quantile from the inverse gamma distribution
TINV	returns a quantile from a Student's t distribution
Random Number	
NORMAL	generates a normally distributed pseudo-random variate
RANBIN	generates an observation from a binomial distribution
RANCAU	generates an observation from a Cauchy distribution
RANEXP	generates an observation from an exponential distribution
RANGAM	generates an observation from a gamma distribution
RANNOR	generates an observation from a normal distribution
RANPOI	generates an observation from a Poisson distribution
RANTBL	generates an observation from a tabled probability mass function
RANTRI	generates an observation from a triangular distribution
RANUNI	generates an observation from a uniform distribution
UNIFORM	generates a pseudo-random variate uniformly distributed on the interval (0,1)
Sample Statistic	
CSS	calculates the corrected sum of squares
CV	calculates the coefficient of variation
KURTOSIS	calculates the kurtosis
MAX	returns the largest value
MEAN	computes the arithmetic mean (average)
MIN	returns the smallest value
N	returns the number of nonmissing arguments
NMISS	returns the number of missing arguments
ORDINAL	returns the largest value in part of a list
RANGE	calculates the range
SKEWNESS	calculates the skewness
STD	calculates the standard deviation
STDERR	calculates the standard error of the mean
SUM	calculates the sum of the arguments
USS	calculates the uncorrected sum of squares
VAR	calculates the variance

Category	Description
State and ZIP Code	
FIPNAME	converts FIPS codes to state names (all uppercase)
FIPNAMEL	converts FIPS codes to state names in uppercase and lowercase
FIPSTATE	converts FIPS state codes to two-character postal codes
STFIPS	converts state postal codes to FIPS state codes
STNAME	converts state postal codes to state names (all uppercase)
STNAMEL	converts state postal codes to state names (uppercase and lowercase)
ZIPFIPS	converts ZIP codes to FIPS state codes
ZIPNAME	converts ZIP codes to state names (all uppercase)
ZIPNAMEL	converts ZIP codes to state names (uppercase and lowercase)
ZIPSTATE	converts ZIP codes to two-letter state codes
Trigonometric and Hyperbolic	
ARCOS	calculates the arc cosine
ARSIN	calculates the arc sine
ATAN	calculates the arc tangent
COS	calculates the cosine
COSH	calculates the hyperbolic cosine
SIN	calculates the sine
SINH	calculates the hyperbolic sine
TAN	calculates the tangent
TANH	calculates the hyperbolic tangent
Truncation	
CEIL	returns the smallest integer greater than or equal to the argument
FLOOR	returns the largest integer less than or equal to the argument
FUZZ	returns the integer if the argument is within 1E-12
INT	returns the integer value (truncates)
ROUND	rounds a value to the nearest round-off unit
TRUNC	truncates a numeric value to a specified length

SAS CALL Routines

Table 19.4 summarizes the SAS language CALL routines that can be used in Screen Control Language programs. Refer to Chapter 12, "SAS CALL Routines," in *SAS Language: Reference* for detailed descriptions of these routines.

Table 19.4
SAS CALL Routines

Routine	Description
RANBIN	generates an observation from a binomial distribution
RANCAU	generates an observation from a Cauchy distribution
RANEXP	generates an observation from an exponential distribution
RANGAM	generates an observation from a gamma distribution
RANNOR	generates an observation from a normal distribution
RANPOI	generates an observation from a Poisson distribution
RANTBL	generates an observation from a tabled probability mass function
RANTRI	generates an observation from a triangular distribution
RANUNI	generates an observation from a uniform distribution
SOUND	generates a sound

SAS/GRAPH Software Elements

With SAS/GRAPH software, you can use the functions and routines provided in the DATA Step Graphics Interface (DSGI) to create graphics output from Screen Control Language programs. Refer to Chapter 20, "The DATA Step Graphics Interface," in *SAS/GRAPH Software: Reference, Version 6, First Edition, Volume 1* for a description of the DATA Step Graphics Interface. Refer to Chapter 21, "DATA Step Graphics Interface Dictionary," in *SAS/GRAPH Software: Reference, Volume 1* for descriptions of individual DSGI functions and CALL routines.

If SAS/GRAPH software is installed at your site and you are using Release 6.10 or later, your SAS/AF and SAS/FSP applications can display images. Applications can have images displayed on the same window as the rest of the data or in a separate window. In some cases, you may be able to add images to existing applications by making only a few changes.

The images can be stored in a variety of standard industry formats such as TIFF, GIF, Targa, and PCX formats, or they can be stored in SAS catalogs. Images are controlled by SCL functions and routines provided by the Image Extensions to SAS/GRAPH software, which are documented in *SAS Technical Report P-263: Image Extensions to SAS/GRAPH Software, Version 6.*

CHAPTER *20* Screen Control Language Dictionary

Overview

This chapter provides summary descriptions of the functions, statements, and call routines that compose Screen Control Language. Chapter 19, "SCL Language Elements" lists these language elements in functional groupings.

Many statements and almost all of the functions of the SAS DATA step are also valid in SCL programs. DATA step statements that are valid in SCL are listed in Table 19.1, "Statements by Category" along with SCL statements. DATA step functions are listed in Table 19.3, "SAS Functions by Category." Refer to Chapter 1, "Screen Control Language," for information on the exceptions. Refer to Chapter 11, "SAS Functions," in *SAS Language: Reference, Version 6, First Edition* for information on these functions.

Terminology

This section describes the terminology used in dictionary entries.

Data Set Data Vector (DDV)
: a data buffer associated with an open SAS data set. Each open SAS data set has its own DDV. See Chapter 5, "Using SAS Data Sets" for more information on the DDV.

field
: the area of a PROGRAM or SCREEN entry window in which the contents of a window variable are displayed. A field is comparable to a text entry widget in a FRAME entry window.

File Data Buffer (FDB)
: a data buffer associated with an open external file. Each open external file has its own FDB. See Chapter 6, "Using External Files" for more information on the FDB.

nonwindow variable
: an SCL variable that is defined in the SCL program, but which has no corresponding field in a window.

result list
: an SCL list designated by the CURLIST function as the list where other SCL selection list function store their results.

SCL Data Vector (SDV)
: a data buffer used to store the current value of all SCL variables for the current program. See Chapter 5, "Using SAS Data Sets" for more information on the SDV.

SCL variable
> any variable that can be used in an SCL program.

system variable
> a reserved variable defined in SCL whose value is automatically stored in the SDV (_BLANK_, _CURROW_, _ERROR_,_ MSG_, and _STATUS_). System variables are discussed in Chapter 2, "Using SCL Variables."

system instance variable
> a reserved variable defined in SCL whose value SCL automatically stores in the SDV if the variable is referenced in the program (_CFRAME_, _CURCOL_, _FRAME_, _METHOD_, _SELF_, and _VALUE_).

window variable
> an SCL variable that is associated with a field or widget in the application window.

Common Arguments

The following terms identify common arguments in the SCL dictionary entries:

attribute
> a display attribute from the following list:

NONE	HIREV
BLINKING	REVERSE
HIGHLIGHT	UNDERLINE

> **Note:** Not all devices support all of these display attributes.

catalog-name
> the name of a SAS catalog. The catalog name must follow standard SAS naming conventions. The usual form is

> *<libref.>catalog-name*

> **Note:** On some operating systems, the catalog name is limited to seven characters.

class-id
> a number assigned to a class when it is loaded in a FRAME entry. This number identifies the class to the SAS System.

color
> a color from the following list:

BLACK	GRAY	PINK
BLUE	GREEN	RED
BROWN	MAGENTA	WHITE
CYAN	ORANGE	YELLOW

> **Note:** Not all devices support all of these colors.

■ **Release 6.10** . . . . Any SCL function that accepts a color argument can use a SASCOLOR window element instead of a color from the preceding list. You can view the list of SASCOLOR window elements by issuing the SASCOLOR command from any window. For more information on the SASCOLOR command, see *SAS Software: Changes and Enhancements, Release 6.10*. For example, you can specify the default foreground color for VAR1 by using:

```
rc = field('color foreground','var1');
```

. . . . ■

data-set-id

the data set identifier value returned by the OPEN function. SCL can open multiple SAS data sets simultaneously. Each open SAS data set is identified to the SAS System and the SCL program by a unique numeric data set identifier. This *data-set-id* value is used to identify the desired data set in functions that manipulate SAS data sets. It is legal to assign the *data-set-id* value to another variable or pass it as a parameter to another program.

data-set-name

the name of a SAS data set. The value must follow standard SAS naming conventions. The syntax of *data-set-name* is

<libref .>data-set-name<(data-set-options)>

where *data-set-options* are any valid SAS data set options. Refer to Chapter 15, "SAS Data Set Options," in *SAS Language: Reference* for details. For information on data set options that are host-specific, see the SAS documentation for your operating system.

entry

the name of an entry in a SAS catalog. A two-level name is assumed to be *libref.catalog.* A three-level name is assumed to be *libref.catalog.entry.*PROGRAM. A four-level name is *libref.catalog.entry.type.*

file-id

the file identifier value returned by the FOPEN function. SCL can open multiple external files simultaneously. Each open file is identified to the SAS System and the SCL program by a unique numeric file identifier value. This *file-id* value is used to manipulate the files. The *file-id* value can be assigned to another variable or passed as a parameter to another program.

index

The position number of an item in an SCL list.

list-id

A unique number assigned to an SCL list when it is created. This number identifies the list to the SAS system. An invalid list identifier is a value that does not correspond to an existing SCL list.

member

The name of a member in a SAS data library.

occurrence

The number of the occurrence of an item in an SCL list.

object-id A number assigned to an object when it is created. This number identifies the object to the SAS System.

index

The position number of an item in an SCL list.

start-index

The position in an SCL list to begin searching for a value.

sysrc

Return codes that report the success or failure of functions that interface to external databases and files. These codes can contain error and warning conditions. Application developers can use SAS system return codes to write applications with sophisticated error checking. For a list of the codes returned for operations most commonly performed, see Chapter 18, "SAS System Return Codes."

type
The type of SAS data library member, for example, DATA, VIEW, or CATALOG.

Organization

Each dictionary entry in this chapter contains the following information:

Name — names the function, routine, or statement.

Synopsis — provides short description highlighting the element's main use.

See Also — lists related functions, routines, and statements.

Syntax — presents syntax in standard form. Arguments enclosed in angle brackets (<>) are optional and can be omitted.

The elements are described in a table with three columns in the order in which they are appear in the syntax. The first column lists the element name. The second column contains either N for numeric or C for character. The third column describes the return value or argument.

Details — provides a more detailed explanation of the element.

If the element opens a window, this section also includes a brief description of any special commands that are valid in the window.

Examples — presents one or more brief examples that demonstrate the syntax and usage of the element.

Release captions — describe features that are available with the release noted in the caption.

Caution captions — describe information on avoiding conditions that can cause problems, like a program halt.

Host captions — describe information that may differ among operating systems.

Dictionary Entries

ACCESS

Opens the ACCESS window, which lists members of a SAS data library

See Also:
CONTENTS

CALL ACCESS(*<libref<,type<,pmenu<,title>>>>*);

Where...	Is type...	And represents...
libref	C	A libref for a SAS data library or _ALL_ for all librefs currently defined in the SAS session.
type	C	The type of SAS data library member to display:

    ALL to display all SAS data library member types.

    'DATA' to display SAS data files.

    'CATALOG' to display SAS catalogs.

    'VIEW' to display SAS views.

    'ACCESS' to display access descriptors created using SAS/ACCESS software.

pmenu	C	A PMENU entry designed with the PMENU procedure, which contains a custom menu bar for the ACCESS window. Specify a null string (*' '*) for this argument to use the default action bar.

    Note: The menu bar (custom or default) is not displayed unless the PMENU facility is activated for the window.

title	C	The title assigned to the window (Access, by default).

Details

The ACCESS window enables users to

□ list, rename, and delete members of a SAS data library. Members of a SAS data library can be SAS data files, SAS views, SAS catalogs, and SAS access descriptors created using SAS/ACCESS software.

□ change variable names, informats, formats, and labels in SAS data sets.

□ create and sort variables

□ create, review, and delete indexes

□ view data set observations

□ rename, delete, and copy entries within a catalog or between catalogs.

By default, the window lists all of the SAS data libraries available to the user and for each library lists all of its members. The default name for the window is Access.

The commands a user can issue in the ACCESS window and in ACCESS window selection fields are listed in the following tables.

Note: Users can enter a question mark (?) in the first space of the selection field to display a list of all of the valid selection commands explained above.

Table 20.1 *ACCESS Window Commands*

Command	Description
COPY *source* <*destination*>	Copies members of one SAS data library to another library. If *destination* is not specified, the name and type of *source* is used. When *type* is **_ALL_**, a one-level destination name is always assumed to be the name of a SAS data library. Either *source* or *destination* can be in one of the following forms:

	member	to specify WORK.*member*.DATA, if all libraries and all member types are displayed. If a default library is assigned with the LIBRARY command, then that library is used. If a default member type is assigned with the MEMTYPE command, then that member type is listed.
	libref.member	to specify *libref.member*.DATA, if all member types are displayed. If a default member type is assigned with the MEMTYPE command, then that member type is listed.
	libref.member.type	to specify *libref.member.type*.

Use the wildcard _ALL_ to copy all member names or member types that match. For example, to copy all SAS data sets from the SAS data library SALES to the library CURRENT, use the command **copy sales._all_.data current**. Notice that the second argument (CURRENT) is only a one-level name. When copying with wildcards, a one-level second argument is always assumed to be a SAS data library.

This command can be used only if SAS/ACCESS software is licensed at the user's site.

Command	Description
CREATE *libref.name*.ACCESS	creates a master descriptor file for SAS/ACCESS software. This command can be used only if SAS/ACCESS software is licensed at the user's site.
EXTRACT *libref.name1*.VIEW *libref.name2*.DATA	creates a data set from a view by extracting data accessed from the view of an external database into a SAS data set. This command can be used only if SAS/ACCESS software is licensed at the user's site.
LABEL	displays the labels for SAS data sets. By default, the labels are not displayed. This command works as a toggle.
LIBRARY <*libref* | _ALL_>	changes the displayed SAS data library. Use _ALL_ to display all SAS data libraries. If no argument is given, a message displays showing the current library.
MEMTYPE <*type* | _ALL_>	changes the member type to display. Use _ALL_ to display all member types within a SAS data library. If no argument is given, a message displays showing member type.
REPLACE *source destination*	replaces members of one SAS data library with members of another library. Uses the same syntax as the COPY command.
RESET	resets the SAS data library and member type back to _ALL_. This command also displays any new members created from another SAS session.
SORT <*index1*> <*index2*> <*index3*>	sorts the display. *Index* can be:

	LIBNAME	sorts the display by libref names.
	NAME	sorts the display by member names.
	MEMTYPE	sorts the display by member types.

You can specify up to three indexes. Sorting is done on *index1* first. Then, within *index1*, sorting is done on *index2*, and within *index2*, sorting is done on *index3*.

Command	Description
	When the window is first displayed, it is sorted by libref, then by member name, and then by member type. For example, to sort the display by member names and then within those member names to sort by member types, issue the command **sort name memtype**.
	To restore the original order, issue the command **sort libname type name**.

Table 20.2   *ACCESS Window Selection Field Commands*

Command	Description
B	displays a SAS data library member for browsing. This command is valid for types DATA, CATALOG, and VIEW.
	For member types DATA and VIEW, this command opens an FSBROWSE window to display the SAS data set or view contents. See *SAS/FSP Software: Usage and Reference* for details of the commands that can be used in an FSBROWSE window.
	Note: This command is valid only if SAS/FSP software is licensed at the user's site.
	For member type CATALOG, this command opens a Catalog Directory window to display the contents of the specified catalog. See the description of the CATALOG function later in this chapter for details of the commands that can be used in a Catalog Directory window.
BD	displays a descriptor member for browsing. This is valid for types ACCESS and VIEW.
BL	opens an FSVIEW window to display the contents of a SAS data set for browsing in a tabular format. This command is valid for types DATA and VIEW. See *SAS/FSP Software: Usage and Reference* for details of the commands that can be used in an FSVIEW window.
	Note: This command is valid only if SAS/FSP software is licensed at the user's site.
C	displays the contents of a member. This command is valid for types DATA, VIEW, and CATALOG.
	For member types DATA and VIEW, this command opens a Contents window to display the descriptor portion of the SAS data set or view. See the description of the CONTENTS function later in this chapter for details of the commands that can be used in a Contents window.
	For member type CATALOG, this command opens a Catalog Directory window to display the contents of the specified catalog. See the description of the CATALOG function later in this chapter for details of the commands that can be used in a Catalog Directory window.
CV	creates a view descriptor file from an access descriptor file. This command is valid only for member type ACCESS. Refer to the SAS/ACCESS documentation for the particular database management system for more information on creating view descriptors from access descriptors.
	This command can be used only if SAS/ACCESS software is licensed at the user's site.
D	deletes a SAS data library member. This command is valid for all member types.
E	displays a SAS data library member for editing. This command is valid for types DATA, CATALOG, and VIEW.
	For member types DATA and VIEW, this command opens an FSEDIT window to display the SAS data set or view contents. (SAS data views created using the SQL procedure cannot be opened for editing.) See *SAS/FSP Software: Usage and Reference* for details of the commands that can be used in an FSEDIT window.
	Note: This command is valid only if SAS/FSP software is licensed at the user's site.

Command	Description
	For member type CATALOG, this command opens a Catalog Directory window to display the contents of the specified catalog. See the description of the CATALOG function later in this chapter for details of the commands that can be used in a Catalog Directory window.
ED	displays a descriptor member for editing. This is valid for types ACCESS, and in some cases, VIEW.
EL	opens an FSVIEW window to display the contents of a SAS data set for editing in a tabular format. This command is valid for types DATA and VIEW. (SAS data views created using the SQL procedure cannot be opened for editing.) See *SAS/FSP Software: Usage and Reference* for details of the commands that can be used in an FSVIEW window. **Note:** This command is valid only if SAS/FSP software is licensed at the user's site.
PW	can be placed by a SAS/ACCESS view descriptor, SAS ACCESS access descriptor, PROC SQL view, DATA step view, or SAS data file. It enables you to assign ALTER, WRITE, READ, or PW passwords to the data set. Note that you cannot assign, change, or remove any password without knowing the password for the highest level of protection that currently exists on the file.
R	renames a SAS data library member. This command is valid for all member types. If labels have been turned on, this command also enables you to change the member's label.
V	verifies a delete request (D command). This command is valid for all member types.

Examples

List all libraries and all types, and use the default PMENU and window title:

```
call access();
```

List only the SAS data sets in MYLIB:

```
call access('mylib','data');
```

ACTIVATE

Activates or grays a specified station in a choice group, check box, or radio box

SAS/AF software only

See Also:
GRAY
ISACTIVE
ISGRAY
UNGRAY

rc=**ACTIVATE**(*var-name,station<,row>*);

Where...	Is type...	And represents...
rc	N	Whether the operation was successful: 0 if successful $\neq 0$ if not successful.
var-name	C	The choice group or FRAME entry widget to be activated.
station	N	The station to be activated or grayed: > 0 for the number of the station to be activated, < 0 for the number of the station designated by the absolute value of the argument to be grayed instead of activated. A grayed station cannot be selected. 0 if no station is to be activated.
row	N	The number of the row when the choice group is in the scrollable section of an extended table. The *row* parameter is valid for PROGRAM entries but not for FRAME entries. Specify *row* only when you want to activate a station from outside the extended table's GETROW or PUTROW section. Do not specify *row* if you want to activate a station from GETROW or PUTROW.

Details

ACTIVATE assigns the active station's value to the choice group variable. FRAME entry widgets can also use the _ACTIVATE_ method.

Because choice groups can be defined only in SAS/AF software, you cannot use ACTIVATE in FSEDIT or FSVIEW programs.

In some applications, especially in extended tables with choice groups in the table section of the application window, it is convenient to be able to query and set the active stations of choice groups. ACTIVATE enables an SCL program to set the active station under program control.

The *station* value is the number of the field within the choice group. For example, if your application has three fields named A, B, and C, and they all belong to the same choice group, you can make the B field active by passing 2 for the *station* value (B is the second field).

For linked action fields in choice groups, the ACTION-type pair is considered one station. Linked action fields have the following form:

```
    &  &A_____      &  &B_____      &  &C_____
```

To make the linked action pair for B active, pass 2 for the value of *station*, not 4.

Examples

Activate the second station in the choice group HOBBY:

```
rc=activate('hobby',2);
```

Make the third station in the fourth row of an extended table the active station in the choice group LIST:

```
if (activate('list',3,4)) then
   do;
      SCL statements to handle the error condition
   end;
```

ALARM

Sounds the device's alarm

See Also:
CURSOR
FIELD

ALARM;

Details

The ALARM statement sounds the bell when the statement executes. This statement works for devices that support sounds.

APPEND

Appends a new observation to a SAS data set

See Also:
OPEN
PUTVARC
PUTVARN
SET
UPDATE

sysrc=**APPEND**(*data-set-id*<,'NOSET'>);

Where...	Is type...	And represents...
sysrc	N	Whether the operation was successful: 0 if successful $\neq$ 0 if an error or warning condition occurred.
data-set-id	N	The data set identifier returned by the OPEN function.
NOSET	C	The instruction to append an observation to the SAS data set with all variable values set to missing even if the SET routine has been called.

Details

APPEND adds an observation to a SAS data set using the current values in the Data Set Data Vector (DDV) unless the NOSET argument is specified or SET has not been called. Otherwise, missing values are written to the new observation.

Example

Add an observation to the SAS data set WORK.DATAONE, which has two variables, FNAME and SSN. Because SET is called, the values **ROBERT** and **999-99-9999** are written to the new observation.

```
dsid=open('work.dataone','u');
call set(dsid);
fname='ROBERT';
```

```
ssn='999-99-9999';
if (append(dsid)) then
   do;
      _msg_=sysmsg();
   end;
```

APPLY

Invokes a method whose arguments are passed from an SCL list

Release 6.11 Feature

See Also:
NOTIFY
SEND
SUPAPPLY
SUPER

CALL APPLY(*object-id,method-name,arg-list-id*);

Where...	Is type...	And represents...
object-id	N	The object whose method is being invoked.
method-name	C	The method to invoke.
arg-list-id	N	The identifier of list containing the arguments required by the method. An invalid *arg-list-id* produces an error condition.

Details

CALL APPLY provides the functionality of CALL SEND except that you can build a dynamic parameter list at run time instead of coding a fixed parameter list.

For example, instead of using the following statement to invoke a method you have defined and named METHOD

```
call send(object,'method',10,'abc','xyz',x);
```

you can use

```
args = makelist(4);
args = setitemn(args,10,1);
args = setitemc(args,'abc',2);
args = setitemc(args,'xyz',3);
args = setitemn(args,x,4;
call apply(object,'method',args);
```

More useful is the ability to combine APPLY with the ARGLIST= and REST= keywords in order to write methods that accept variable argument lists:

```
length _method_ $40;
m: method arglist=args;

call apply(otherObject,_method_, args);
```

This calls the method with the same arguments to the otherObject.

For example, an object receiving a method could rebroadcast the method to all objects on its _RECEIVERS_ list:

```
m: method arglist=args;
   _receivers_ = getniteml(_self_, '_receivers_', 1, 1, 0);
   if _receivers_ then
      do r = listlen(_receivers_) to 1 by -1;
         call apply(getiteml(_receivers_, r), _method_, args);
```

```
        end;
    endmethod;
```

ARRAY

Defines elements of an explicit array

SAS Statement with limitations in SCL

See also:
ENTRY
METHOD

ARRAY *array-name*<{*n*}><$> <*length*> <*elements*> <(*initial-values*)>;

Where...	Is type...	And represents...
array-name	C	The name of the array, which cannot be the same as the name of a window variable. However window variables can be elements of an array.
n	N	The dimension of the array, or an asterisk (*) to indicate the dimension is determined from the number of array elements or initial values. Multidimensional arrays are allowed. If an asterisk is specified without any array elements or initial values, the array is a reference array. The dimension of this array will be determined at execution time based on the corresponding array in the calling program.
length	N	The maximum length of elements in the array. For character arrays, the maximum length cannot exceed 200. The default length is 8 characters. *length* is ignored for numeric arrays.
elements	C	The variables (either window or nonwindow) that make up the array or **_TEMPORARY_** to create a list of temporary data elements.
initial-values	C	Values to initialize some or all of the array elements. Separate these values with commas or blanks. By default, all the elements in an array are initialized to missing.

Details

If you have arrays that you reference only with subscripting, then you can save memory by using the _TEMPORARY_ keyword. The SCL compiler has to allocate memory for the the array name and the names of the array elements. However, if this keyword is used, the compiler only allocates memory for the array name. For large arrays, this could result in significant memory savings.

   Note: Do not use **_TEMPORARY_** for *elements* if you plan to fetch values from a SAS data set directly into an array using the SET routine. Use GETVARN and GETVARC when this keyword is specified.

■ **Release 6.11** . . . .

Reference Array

A reference array is a pointer to another defined array. Previously, when an array needed to be passed as a parameter to a METHOD or ENTRY statement, an array of equal size needed to be defined in both the calling and the called program. This technique used twice the amount of memory that was actually required. With reference arrays, only one array needs to be defined with the actual size. The array in the called program uses the actual memory of the array in the calling program.

   By using reference arrays, you can create general array functions because the array dimension is determined by the calling program. That is, you do not need to hardcode the array dimension in your SCL program that contains the ENTRY or METHOD statement. Refer to the example later in this section for an illustration of this concept.

Using multidimesional reference arrays is allowed when the dimensions match. For example, if a two dimensional array is passed in, the reference array must also be two dimensional.

Reference arrays can currently only be used as parameters in a METHOD or ENTRY statement. Once a reference array has been created by a call to another program, it can be used in any way that a regular array can be used.

. . . . ■

Differences from DATA Step in ARRAY Statement Execution

The ARRAY statement in SCL is very similar to the ARRAY statement in the DATA step and is used to define single or multidimensional arrays. The ARRAY statement in SCL differs from the DATA step ARRAY statement in the following ways:

□ SCL does not support implicitly subscripted arrays.

□ SCL does not support the _NUMERIC_, _CHAR_, or _ALL_ keywords.

□ SCL allows a repetition factor for initialization of arrays.

□ SCL allows arrays to be used with the IN operator.

□ SCL supports reference arrays (starting in Release 6.11).

For details on the ARRAY statement in SAS language, see *SAS Language: Reference*.

Examples

The following examples illustrate functionality that is unique to the ARRAY statement in SCL.

Using Repetition Factors for Array Initialization.
The following statement:

```
array a{20}(0,3*1 ,5*(2,3,4));
```

Initializes the values of the elements of array A to:

```
0, 1, 1, 1, 2, 3, 4, 2, 3, 4, 2, 3, 4, 2, 3, 4, 2, 3, 4, .
```

Note that 1 is repeated three times and the pattern 2,3,4 is repeated five times. The last element of the array is a missing value because the array was defined as having 20 elements, but only 19 initial values were specified.

Using an Array with the IN Operator
The following code segment:

```
array a 8 (2 4 6 8 10);

INIT:
  b=6;
  if b in a then put 'B is in array A';
  c=b in a;
  put c=;
```

```
                    return;
```

Produces the output:

```
    B is in array A
    C=3
```

■ **Release 6.11** . . . . **Using a Reference Array with a METHOD Statement** Assume that an entry SORT.SCL contains the method definition shown below. The method illustrates using a reference array to define a generic sort routine. The routine is termed generic because NSORT does not need to know the size of the array being passed, since the reference array NARRAY takes on the definition of the array specified in the CALL METHOD routine.

```
    array narray(*);

    nsort: method narray 8;
      size = dim( narray );
      do i = 1 to size - 1;
        do j = i + 1 to size;
          if narray( i ) > narray( j ) then
            do;
              ntemp = narray( i );
              narray( i ) = narray( j );
              narray( j ) = ntemp;
            end;
        end;
      end;
    endmethod;
```

A sample calling program that executes the NSORT method is shown below.

```
    array numarray(100);

    MAIN:
      do i=1 to dim(numarray);
        numarray(i)=dim(numarray)-i+1;
      end;
      call method('sort.scl', 'nsort', numarray);
      return;
```

. . . . ■

ASORT

Performs a sort on an array

rc=**ASORT**(*array*<*,order*><*,elements*>);

Where...	Is type...	And represents...

rc	N	Whether the operation was successful:
		   0 if successful
		   $\neq 0$ if not successful

array	C	An SCL array declared in an ARRAY statement.

order	C	The order for the sort:
		   'A' ascending order (Default)
		
		   'D' descending order

elements	N	The number of elements to sort.

Details

By default, the array is sorted in ascending order. You can use the optional *order* argument to specify either ascending or descending order.

By default, the entire array is sorted. You can use the optional *elements* argument to restrict sorting to the specified number of elements (starting from the beginning of the array).

If the value of the *elements* argument is greater than the total number of array elements, the program halts execution and sends an error message to the log.

Examples

Sort the array ARR in ascending order:

```
if (asort(arr)) then _msg_=sysmsg();
else _msg_='Sort was successful';
```

Sort the first ten items of array ARR in descending order:

```
if (asort(arr,'d',10)) then _msg_=sysmsg();
else _msg_='Sort was successful';
```

ATTRC

Returns the value of a character attribute for a SAS data set

attr-value=**ATTRC**(*data-set-id,attr-name*);

See Also:
ATTRN
DESCRIBE
OPEN

Where...	Is type...	And represents...
attr-value	C	The value of the character attribute.
data-set-id	N	The data set identifier returned by the OPEN function. If the value of the *data-set-id* argument is invalid, the program halts execution and returns control to the application.
attr-name	C	The attribute name, listed in Table 20.3. If *attr-name* is invalid, a missing value is returned for *attr-value*.

Table 20.3 *Options for the ATTRC Function*

Option	Description
'CHARSET'	Returns a string indicating the character set of the machine that created the data set. It returns one of the following values or an empty string if the data set is not sorted:
	ASCII ASCII character set
	EBCDIC EBCDIC character set
	HASCII extended ASCII character set
	ANSI OS/2 ANSI standard ASCII character set
	OEM OS/2 OEM code format
'ENGINE'	The name of the engine used to access the data set
'LABEL'	The label assigned to the data set
'LIB'	The libref of the SAS data library in which the data set resides
'MEM'	The SAS data library member name
'MODE'	The mode in which the SAS data set was opened such as:
	I INPUT mode, allows random access if the engine supports it; otherwise, defaults to IN mode
	IN INPUT mode, reads sequentially and allows revisiting observations
	IS INPUT mode, reads sequentially but does not allow revisiting observations
	N NEW mode (to create a new data set)
	U UPDATE mode, allows random access if the engine supports it; otherwise, defaults to UN mode
	UN UPDATE mode, reads sequentially and allows revisiting observations
	US UPDATE mode, reads sequentially but does not allow revisiting observations
	V UTILITY mode, allows modification of variable attributes and indexes associated with the data set.

Option	Description
'MTYPE'	SAS data library member type.
'SORTEDBY'	Returns an empty string if the data set is not sorted. Otherwise returns the names of the BY variables in the standard BY statement format.
'SORTLVL'	Returns an empty string if the data set is not sorted. Otherwise returns:

	WEAK	Sort order of data set is not validated. The distinguishing character of a WEAK assertion is that it was established by a dataset option. The system cannot validate its correctness. The most common way to set it is by the SORTEDBY data set option.
	STRONG	Sort order of the data set is validated. That is, the order of its observations may be depended upon. The most common way to set a "STRONG" assertion is through PROC SORT or the OUT= option on the CONTENTS procedure.

Option	Description
'SORTSEQ'	Returns an empty string if the data set is sorted on the native machine or if the sort collating sequence is the default for the operating system. Otherwise returns the name of the alternate collating sequence used to sort the file.
'TYPE'	SAS data set type.

Example

Ensure that the SAS data set has been opened in UPDATE mode. If the data set is not opened in UPDATE mode, an error message is displayed on the message line.

```
mode=attrc(dsid,'MODE');
if (mode ne 'U') then
    _msg_='Data set has not been opened in UPDATE mode.';
```

If the value of the *attr-name* argument is invalid, a missing value is returned for *attr-value*.

ATTRN

Returns the value of a numeric attribute for the specified SAS data set

See Also:
ATTRC
OPEN

attr-value=**ATTRN**(*data-set-id*,*attr-name*);

Where...	Is type...	And represents...
attr-value	N	The value of the numeric attribute.
data-set-id	N	The identifier assigned when the data set was opened. If *data-set-id* is invalid, the program halts execution.
attr-name	C	The numeric attribute, listed in Table 20.4.
		If the value of *attr-name* is invalid, a missing value is returned for *attr-value*.

Table 20.4   *Options for the ATTRN Function*

Attribute	Description
'ALTERPW'	whether a password is required to alter the data set
	1 the data set is alter protected
	0 the data set is not alter protected
'ANOBS'	whether the engine knows the number of observations:
	1 the engine knows the correct number of observations
	0 the engine does not know the correct number of observations
'ANY'	whether the data set has observations:
	−1 the data set has no observations or variables
	0 the data set has no observations
	1 the data set has observations and variables
'ARAND'	whether the engine supports random access:
	1 the engine supports random access
	0 the engine does not support random access
'ARWU'	whether the engine can manipulate files:
	1 the engine is not read-only. It can create or update SAS files.
	0 the engine is read-only.
'CRDTE'	data set creation date. The value returned is the internal SAS DATETIME value for the creation date. Use the DATETIME format to display this value.
'INDEX'	whether the data set supports indexing:
	1 indexing is supported
	0 indexing is not supported
'ISINDEX'	whether the data set is indexed:
	1 at least one index exists for the data set
	0 the data set is not indexed

Attribute	Description
`'ISSUBSET'`	whether the data set is a subset: 1 at least one WHERE clause is active 0 no WHERE clause is active
`'LRECL'`	logical record length
`'MODTE'`	last date and time the data set was modified. Use the DATETIME format to display this value.
`'NDEL'`	number of deleted observations in the data set
`'NLOBS'`	number of logical observations (those not marked for deletion). An active WHERE clause does not affect this number.
`'NOBS'`	number of physical observations (includes those marked for deletion). An active WHERE clause does not affect this number.
`'NVARS'`	number of variables in the data set
`'PW'`	whether a password is required to access the data set 1 the data set is protected 0 the data set is not protected
`'RADIX'`	data set radix addressability: 1 access by observation number is allowed 0 access by observation number is not allowed **Note:** A data set on a tape engine is index addressable although it cannot be accessed by observation number.
`'READPW'`	whether a password is required to read the data set: 1 the data set is read protected 0 the data set is not read protected
`'TAPE'`	data set tape file status: 1 the data set is a sequential tape file 0 the data set is not a sequential tape file
`'WHSTMT'`	active WHERE clauses: 0 no WHERE clause is active 1 a permanent WHERE clause is active 2 a temporary WHERE clause is active 3 both permanent and temporary WHERE clauses are active
`'WRITEPW'`	whether a password is required to write to the data set: 1 the data set is write protected 0 the data set is not write protected.

Example

Check whether a WHERE clause is currently active for a data set:

```
iswhere=attrn(dsid,'whstmt');
if (iswhere) then
    _msg_='A WHERE clause is currently active.';
```

BLANK

Special missing value for SAS/AF applications

Character System Variable

SAS/AF Only

See Also:
CLRFLD
SETFLD

Details

BLANK is a System Variable that is created for every SCL program you compile. The compiler creates a space for _BLANK_ in the SCL data vector.

In SAS/AF applications, you can compare the value of window variables against the value _BLANK_ to test whether a value has been entered in a field in the window. The test is valid for both numeric and character variables. You can also use _BLANK_ in assignment statements to reset a window variable to a blank, as though the user had not entered a value in the field. You cannot reset the value of the _BLANK_ variable itself.

In comparison operations, _BLANK_ is considered the smallest missing value.

Example

The following code fragment prints a message if X is modified and is blank.

```
if modified(x) and x eq _blank_ then
    _msg_ = 'Please enter a value';
```

BLOCK

Displays a menu containing up to 12 choice blocks and returns the number of the user's choice

See Also:
ENDBLOCK

choice=**BLOCK** (*window-name,title,color,text-1 ,. . .,text-12 <,icon-1,. . .,icon-12>*);

Where...	Is type...	And represents...
choice	N	Or returns the number (1-12) of the block selected by the user, or:
		− 99 if a user requested help for the SAS System
		− 1 to − 12 if a user requested help for the block
		0 if a user issued the END, CANCEL, or BYE command
		99 if an unknown command is issued (see WORD)
window-name	C	The window's title (up to 80 characters).
title	C	The title (up to 60 characters) for the menu's title box.
color	N	The combination of colors to be used for the blocks: 0 to 31. Some devices do not support changing the background color. If you have specified that icons be used with BLOCK, the color combination specified may not take effect. Icons display as host specific widgets and therefore the color of the icon may be controlled by the host operating system.
		Note: Under Windows or OS/2, use the Color Pallette to alter icon colors. Under X windows, set X resources to control icon colors.
text-1 ,. . ., text-12	C	Up to 14 characters of text for each block or icon to display. The blocks or icons are displayed in groups of four. Blocks for the first four *text* values are displayed on the first row, blocks for the second four *text* values are displayed on the middle row, and blocks for the last four *text* values are displayed on the last row. Twelve values are required, but you can use null values for block positions that you do not want displayed.
icon-1 ,. . ., icon-12	N	Numbers for icons to be displayed in place of the blocks. If no values for icons are provided, or if the host system does not support icons, standard rectangular blocks are used. If you specify a number for which no icon is defined, icon number 1010 (the default SAS icon) is displayed. If at least one icon number is specified, and the total number of icons is less than the total number of text labels, the default SAS icon is displayed for text labels without an associated icon number.

Details

The number of text values that you specify determines the number of blocks of icons displayed on the menu.

To display an icon menu, you must specify at least one icon position, although you can display the default SAS icon by specifying 0 for positions for which a value for *text* is supplied. For more information on using icons with the BLOCK function, see Chapter 14, "Introduction to Application Interfaces."

Because BLOCK does not generate a physical display window, window options such as KEYS are not recognized. The BLOCK function windows recognize only DMKEYS settings. To alter DMKEYS settings for a BLOCK menu, you can use GETFKEY and SETFKEY in a program that runs before the BLOCK menu opens. This program must have a display screen associated with it.

This function attempts to display the blocks in the best manner depending upon the characteristics of the user's display device. The function displays up to three rows of four blocks. Blocks are displayed in the order in which the *text* arguments appear in the function. Only the nonblank choices are displayed, and the blocks in each row are centered in the row.

When the function is called, it queries the current value of *choice*. If the value of *choice* corresponds to a valid selection number, the cursor is positioned on the correct block. Otherwise, the cursor is positioned in the upper-left corner of the window.

To make a selection from the block menu, the user must move the cursor to the appropriate block and press ENTER or click the mouse. BLOCK returns the index of the selection.

If the user presses the HELP key on one of the selections, then the negative of the selection is returned. If the user presses the HELP key while the cursor is not on one of the blocks, the value −99 is returned.

If the user issues the END or CANCEL command via a function key, the value 0 is returned.

Use ENDBLOCK to close the menu window opened by BLOCK.

The color combinations that can be specified with the *color* argument are as follows:

Color	Background	Border	Text	Icon	Shadow
0	black	white	white	white	white
1	black	gray	cyan	gray	blue
2	black	gray	cyan	gray	blue
3	black	cyan	cyan	gray	cyan
4	black	gray	white	cyan	gray
5	black	cyan	yellow	cyan	blue
6	black	gray	white	blue	gray
7	black	gray	yellow	blue	gray
8	black	gray	white	red	gray
9	black	gray	white	pink	gray
10	black	gray	white	yellow	gray
11	black	gray	white	red	blue
12	blue	gray	cyan	gray	black

Color	Background	Border	Text	Icon	Shadow
13	blue	gray	yellow	gray	black
14	blue	gray	white	gray	black
15	blue	gray	white	magenta	black
16	blue	gray	white	red	black
17	blue	gray	white	cyan	black
18	blue	yellow	white	yellow	black
19	blue	gray	white	magenta	gray
20	blue	gray	white	red	gray
21	gray	blue	black	blue	black
22	gray	red	black	red	black
23	gray	magenta	black	magenta	black
24	gray	blue	black	cyan	blue
25	gray	cyan	black	cyan	black
26	red	gray	white	gray	black
27	red	gray	black	gray	black
28	pink	gray	white	gray	black
29	pink	gray	black	gray	black
30	yellow	gray	black	gray	black
31	brown	gray	gray	gray	black
32*	background	border	foreground	secondary background	black
33*	secondary background	secondary border	foreground	background	black

* SASCOLOR window element names. See *color* in "Common Arguments" on page 222 for more information.

Example

Create a menu with five choices represented by icons. The first row contains two icons, **Outline** and **Index**. The second row contains two icons, **Compare Files** and **Calendar**. The third row contains a single icon, **End**.

Because the CHOICE variable is assigned the value 5 before BLOCK is called, the cursor is positioned on the Compare Files icon when the window opens. When a user makes a selection, the SELECT statement either exits the DO loop or calls another PROGRAM entry. When control returns from the called program, the menu is displayed again.

```
INIT:
choice=5;

LOOP:
    do while(choice ne 0);
        choice=block('Writers Toolbox','Main Menu',6,'Outline','Index',
```

```
                                    '','','Compare Files','Calendar','','','End','','','',
                               1,2,0,0,3,4,0,0,111,0,0,0);
                          select(choice);
                             when(1) call display('outl.program');
                             when(2) call display('index.program');
                             when(5) call display('compare.program');
                             when(6) call display('calend.program');
                             when(9) leave LOOP;
                             otherwise
                                do;
                                   if (choice<0) then
                                      call display('help.program',choice);
                                end;
                          end;
                       end;
                       call endblock();
                    return;
```

BUILD

Invokes the BUILD window in SAS/AF software

See Also:
CALL CBT
CALL DISPLAY

CALL BUILD(*entry*<,*open-mode*<,*resource*<,*pmenu*>>>);

Where...	Is type...	And represents...
entry	C	An entry in a SAS catalog.
		A one-level name is assumed to be WORK.*catalog*. A two-level name is assumed to be *libref.catalog*. A three-level name is assumed to be *libref.catalog.entry*.PROGRAM. A four-level name is *libref.catalog.entry.type*.
open-mode	C	The mode in which to open the catalog:
		'EDIT' | **'E'** open the catalog entry for editing. (Default)
		'BROWSE' | **'B'** open the catalog entry for browsing.
		'COMPILE' | **'C'** <**NOMSG**> compile the FRAME, PROGRAM, or SCL entry specified in *entry*.
resource	C	The RESOURCE entry if *entry* is a FRAME. A one- or three-level name can be specified. A one-level name assumes the RESOURCE entry is in the current, SASUSER.PROFILE, or SASHELP.FSP catalog.
pmenu	C	The PMENU for the BUILD DISPLAY window to use. The default is the normal BUILD pmenu. A one- or two- or three-level name can be specified. A one-level name assumes the PMENU entry is in the current, SASUSER.PROFILE, or SASHELP.FSP catalog. For PROGRAM and FRAME entries, you can specify a secondary PMENU entry for the SOURCE window. Separate the secondary PMENU from the main PMENU with a space.

Details

You can use the BUILD routine to open catalog entries from within an application. You can also compile the source code for PROGRAM or FRAME or SCL entries without displaying the contents of the entries. You can also use BUILD to view SAS/CALC, SAS/FSP, SAS/GRAPH, or SAS/AF entries.

The NOMSG option for COMPILE mode does not suppress any compiler error or warning messages. However, this option prevents NOTE messages from being sent to the SAS log or to the MESSAGE window when the source code is compiled. For example, with NOMSG you do not see the following:

```
NOTE: Compiling entry-name.
```

```
NOTE: Code generated for entry-name. Code size=nnnn.
```

Note: SAS/AF software must be licensed at your user's site to use the BUILD routine except for invoking LOG, SOURCE, and OUTPUT entries.

Examples

Open a PROGRAM entry named NAME in the catalog MYLIB.MYCAT in edit mode:

```
call build('mylib.mycat.name');
```

Compile the source code for the entry A.FRAME in the WORK.TEST catalog without opening a DISPLAY window for the entry and without displaying any NOTES:

```
call build('work.test.a.frame','compile nomsg');
```

Edit a FRAME using a particular RESOURCE and PMENU:

```
call build('lib.cat.name.frame','e','work.a.build.resource',
                                     'work.a.build.pmenu');
```

Edit a PROGRAM entry using a custom PMENU for both the DISPLAY and SOURCE windows. The DISPLAY window uses MYPMENU1.PMENU, and the SOURCE window uses MYPMENU2.PMENU.

```
call build('work.a.a.program','e','','mypmenu1 mypmenu2');
```

CALC

Invokes the CALC window in SAS/CALC software

SAS/CALC software required

CALL CALC(*entry* <*,open-mode*>);

Where...	Is type...	And represents...
entry	C	The name of a catalog entry. A one-level name is assumed to be a catalog name in the WORK library. A two-level name is assumed to be *libref.catalog.* A three-level name is assumed to be *libref.catalog.entry.*CALC. A four-level name is *libref.catalog.entry.type.*
open-mode	C	The mode in which to open the catalog:

    'EDIT'   open a spreadsheet for editing. A dialog window is first opened in which users enter various spreadsheet parameters. (Default)

    'OPEN'   similar to EDIT mode, except the dialog window is not opened if the spreadsheet already exists.

Details

The CALC routine opens any catalog entry from within an SCL program. By default, the SAS/CALC spreadsheet opens.

Note: SAS/CALC software must be licensed at your users' site to use the CALC routine.

Example

Open a CALC window for editing a spreadsheet named EXPENSE.CALC in the catalog WORK.SHEETS:

```
call calc('work.sheets.expense.calc','edit');
```

CATALOG

Opens a directory window that lists entries for a SAS catalog

See Also:
ACCESS
BUILD
CATLIST

*sysrc=***CATALOG**(*catalog-name*<,*show-type*><,*mode*>);

Where...	Is type...	And represents...
sysrc	N	Whether the operation was successful: 0 if successful ≠ 0 if an error or warning condition occurred
catalog-name	C	An existing SAS catalog. If you specify a catalog that does not exist and *mode* of E, this function creates an empty catalog, opens its directory window, and returns 0 in *sysrc.*
show-type	C	The type of SAS catalog entries to be displayed in the Catalog Directory. Any catalog entry type can be specified.
mode	C	Whether catalog entries can be selected for editing: **'B'** open the catalog for browsing only; entries cannot be selected for editing. **'E'** open the catalog entries for editing. (Default)

Details

By default, the Catalog Directory window opens for editing and all of the entries in the specified catalog are displayed.

Catalog Directory Commands

Users can issue the following commands in the Catalog Directory window via the command line or command menu bar. They can also use the selection fields beside the entries to execute actions on an entry. The selection field commands are listed in the SF column. Users can also type a question mark on the selection field to get a list of all available commands.

Note: If the CATALOG function call does not include *show-type* to define a default catalog entry type, then *entry* for the following commands must be specified as *entry-name.entry-type.* If *entry* does not include a type specification, then the default type is used.

Command	SF	Description
BROWSE *entry*	B	opens the specified LOG, OUTPUT, or SOURCE entry for browsing or replays the graph in a GRSEG entry or an IMAGE entry.
DELETE *entry*	D	marks an entry for deletion and prompts you to verify the command before the entry is actually deleted.
EDIT *entry*	E	opens the specified LOG, OUTPUT, and SOURCE for editing or replays the graph in a GRSEG entry.
PRINT *entry* <FORM=*form-type*><FILE=*destination*><APPEND|REPLACE>	P	prints the specified LOG, OUTPUT, and SOURCE or replays the graph in a GRSEG entry.

Command	SF	Description
		FORM= specifies a form entry to provide printer and formatting information. If this argument is omitted, the current default form is used.
		FILE= sends the output to an external file rather than to a printer. *Destination* can be either a currently defined fileref or a physical filename enclosed in quotes and in the form required by the host operating system. If *destination* already exists, it is replaced unless APPEND is specified.
RENAME *entry new-name*	R	changes the name of an entry.
RUN *entry*	X|G	edits a LOG or OUTPUT entry. X also executes a SOURCE entry. G also replays the graph stored in a GRSEG entry.
SHOWTYPE *type*		limits the display to the specified type. To display all types, use SHOWTYPE ALL. If *type* is omitted, SHOWTYPE displays the current type.

Example

Open a Catalog Directory window to display just the SOURCE entries from the catalog MYLIB.TEST for browsing only. If an error occurs, an appropriate error message is displayed.

```
if (catalog('mylib.test','source','b')) then
    do;
        _msg_=sysmsg();
        return;
    end;
```

CATLIST

Displays a selection list window that lists entries in a SAS catalog and returns user selections

See Also:
DIRLIST
FILELIST
LIBLIST

selections=**CATLIST**(*catalog-name,type,num-sel,prefix<,message<,autoclose>>*);

Where...	Is type...	And represents...
selections	C	One or more user selections from the list. Multiple selections are separated by blanks.
catalog-name	C	An existing SAS catalog in the form of *libref.catalog*, or `'*'` to allow a user to interactively select a libref, catalog, and entry. Help is available for this window by selecting **Extended Help** from the **Help** item in the menu bar.
type	C	The type of entry to be listed. Use `'ALL'` or `''` to display all entry types.
num-sel	N	The maximum number of items a user can select. To display the list for information only (no selections allowed), specify **0**. To specify an unlimited number of selections, use a value larger than the number of available selections such as 9999.
prefix	C	Whether selected entries are prefixed by the catalog name: `'Y'` to return selected names in the form of *libref.catalog.entry.type.* `'N'` or `''` to return selected names in the form of *entry.type.*
message	C	Text for a message displayed above the selection list. The default message tells users to make up to the number of selections specified in *num-sel*.
autoclose	C	Whether the selection list window closes automatically after a user makes a selection when only one choice is allowed: `'Y'` for the window to close automatically. (Default) `'N'` for the window to close only when the user explicitly closes it. **Note:** This option is ignored when *num-sel* is not 1.

Details

You can provide a default or initial selected value in the list by providing a value for the *selections* variable prior to calling CATLIST. If *selections* contains valid values when the function is invoked, those names are automatically designated as selected when the selection list is displayed.

If a user closes the selection list window without making a selection, CATLIST returns a blank value unless there was an initial value for the *selections* variable before CATLIST was called.

Selections from the window can be returned in the current result list, if one is available. The current result list is a special SCL list that is automatically filled with the values selected from a selection list. To create a current result list, use the

MAKELIST function to create it and the CURLIST function to designate it as the current result list. The current result list must exist before you call the CATLIST function.

When CATLIST is invoked, the current result list is cleared. After CATLIST is invoked, the result list contains the following named items:

Element	Type	Description
TAG	C	Identifies the list as one created by CATLIST
COUNT	N	Number of elements selected. If users make no selections, or if they issue a CANCEL command in the list window, COUNT is 0.
NAME	C	Name of each catalog entry selected. If the *prefix* argument is **Y**, the prefix is appended to the beginning of each name. There is one NAME element for each selection made. The value of NAME is in uppercase.
DESC	C	Description of each catalog entry selected. There is one DESC element for each selection made. The value of DESC is in the case entered originally.
DATE	C	Date each selected catalog entry was last modified. There is one DATE element for each selection made.

Example

Display a selection list containing all the entries for the catalog MYLIB.TEST. Users can make up to five selections. Use GETNITEMC to retrieve the selected values from the current result list.

```
listid=makelist();
rc=curlist(listid);
list=catlist('mylib.test','all',5,'y');
n=getnitemn(listid,'COUNT');
do i=1 to n;
   name=getnitemc(listid,'NAME',i);
   desc=getnitemc(listid,'DESC',i);
   date=getnitemc(listid,'DATE',i);
   put name= desc= date=;
end;
```

CBT

Runs a CBT entry

See Also:
DISPLAY
GOTO

CALL CBT(*entry*<,*frame*><,*frame-name*>);

Where...	Is type...	And represents...
entry	C	The name of the CBT entry. *entry* to specify a CBT entry in the current catalog.
		entry.type to specify an entry in the current catalog.
		libref.catalog.entry to specify a CBT entry in a different catalog.
		libref.cat-name.entry.type to specify an entry in a different catalog.
frame	N	The number of the CBT frame to be displayed initially.
frame-name	C	The name of the frame. If this option is specified then the *frame* value is ignored.

Details

The CBT routine calls a CBT entry from within another application. You can optionally specify the frame name or number at which the CBT entry is opened. For information on CBT entries, see *SAS/AF Software: Usage and Reference.*

You can use CBT entries to link detailed instructional information with an application so the information is readily available.

These restrictions apply when a CBT entry is called from within an SCL program:

□ The SAVE command is not recognized.

□ =X returns the user to the calling program.

□ QCANCEL returns the user to the calling program.

□ QEND returns the user to the calling program.

Examples

Display the second frame of the entry EXAMPLE.CBT:

```
call cbt('example',2);
```

Display the frame named ABC of the entry EXAMPLE.CBT:

```
call cbt('example',1,'abc');
```

Suppose an application requires that the user be familiar with certain terminology that is unique to an installation. You can design and build a CBT course (in this example, TERMINAL.CBT) that teaches the appropriate information. The following example runs the CBT entry if a user issues the command TEACH. Then, it returns control to the SCL statement following the call to TERMINAL.CBT when the user exits the CBT course:

```
control always;
if (upcase(word(1))='TEACH') then
   do;
      call nextcmd();
```

```
                    call cbt('terminal');
                end;
```

CENTER

Returns a centered character string

See Also:
LEFT
RIGHT

centered-string=**CENTER**(*string<,length>*);

Where...	Is type...	And represents...
centered-string	C	The centered character string. If the destination variable, *centered-string*, already exists, then specifying a length in the CENTER function changes the length of *centered-string* to the specified length.
string	C	The character string to be centered.
length	N	The length in which the character string is to be centered. The default is the maximum length of *centered-string*.

Details

The default length is the maximum length of *centered-string*. The string is centered by padding with spaces. To left- or right-justify a character string, use LEFT and RIGHT. For CENTER to work properly when *centered-string* is a window variable, set the justification attribute (**JUST**) for *centered-string* to **'NONE'**.

CEXIST

Verifies the existence of a SAS catalog or SAS catalog entry

See Also:
EXIST

rc=**CEXIST**(*entry* < ,'U'>);

Where...	Is type...	And represents...
rc	N	Whether the operation was successful: 1 if the SAS catalog or catalog entry exists 0 if the SAS catalog or catalog entry does not exist.
entry	C	A SAS catalog, or the name of an entry in a catalog. If the *entry* value is a one- or two-level name, then it is assumed to be the name of a catalog. Use a three- or four-level name to test for the existence of an entry within a catalog.
'U'	C	To test for whether the catalog can be opened for updating.

Example

Test whether the catalog LIB.CAT1 exists and can be opened for update. If the catalog does not exist, a message is displayed on the message line.

```
if (cexist('lib.cat1','u')) then
    _msg_='The catalog LIB.CAT1 exists and can be opened for update.';
else _msg_=sysmsg();
```

Verify the existence of the entry X.PROGRAM in LIB.CAT1:

```
if (cexist('lib.cat1.x.program')) then
    _msg_='Entry X.PROGRAM exists';
else _msg_=sysmsg();
```

CFRAME

Contains the identifier of the FRAME entry that is currently executing

Numeric System Instance Variable

See Also:
FRAME

Details

CFRAME is a System Instance Variable. It is provided automatically by the FRAME entry in SAS/AF, but the SCL compiler does not automatically create a space for it in the SCL data vector. Because of this, you get a warning when you compile your FRAME or SCL entry if you have a reference to _CFRAME_. See _FRAME_ for more details on how to prevent the warning.

CFRAME only has a valid value when the FRAME entry's SCL code is running or when a FRAME entry or FRAME entry object method is running.

Example

Suppose the entry FIRST.FRAME contains an icon. The icon's _SELECT_ method is defined to run the SAS/AF FRAME entry SECOND.FRAME, which contains the program:

```
INIT:
      /* send a method to the current FRAME */
   call send(_CFRAME_, '_set_msg_', 'Running the _SELECT_ method');
return;


TERM:
      /* send a method to the FRAME that contains the icon */
   call send(_FRAME_, '_set_msg_', '_SELECT_ has finished.');
return;
```

When FIRST.FRAME displays and a user selects the icon, SECOND.FRAME displays with the message 'Running the _SELECT_ method'. After the user ends from SECOND.FRAME, FIRST.FRAME displays the message '_SELECT_ has finished.' This is accomplished by sending the _SET_MSG_ method to _CFRAME_ (the FRAME entry that's currently running) in the INIT section and sending _SET_MSG_ to _FRAME_ (the FRAME entry that contains the icon) in the TERM section.

CLEARLIST

Clears the items from an SCL list without deleting the list and optionally clears all sublist items

See Also:
COPYLIST
DELITEM
DELNITEM
MAKELIST
MAKENLIST
POPC
POPL
POPN

▶ *Caution:* *Before you clear a list recursively, make sure it is not needed by other parts of the SCL program.*

rc=**CLEARLIST**(*list-id*<,*recursively*>);

Where...	Is type...	And represents...

rc	N	Whether the operation is successful:
		  0 if successful
		  $\neq 0$ if not successful

list-id	N	The identifier of the list containing the items to clear. An invalid *list-id* produces an error condition.

recursively	C	Whether to recursively clear all the list's sublists and all sublists of its sublists.
		  'N' Sublists are not cleared. (Default)
		  'Y' All sublists are cleared.

Details

CLEARLIST clears all the items from the SCL list identified by *list-id*. The list is not deleted, but its length is reduced to 0. If *recursively* is **'Y'**, all the list's sublists, including sublists of sublists, are also cleared, and so on.

Be careful when clearing lists recursively because you have the potential to clear lists that are needed by other parts of the SCL program. The *recursively* option clears all of a list's sublists, even if they are referenced in other SCL lists or by other SCL variables.

. . . .

An error condition results if:

□ the list has the NOUPDATE or FIXEDLENGTH attribute.

□ any item in the list (or its sublists, if *recursively* is **'Y'**) has the NODELETE attribute.

□ *recursively* is **'Y'**, and any sublist has the NOUPDATE or FIXEDLENGTH attribute.

□ *list-id* is an object or class identifier.

If an error condition does result, no further items or sublists are cleared.

Example

Clear all sublists from an existing list identified by MYLIST without deleting items that are not sublists:

```
     /* Copy the list.  */
  cp=copylist(mylist);

     /* Clear the entire list, including sublists  */
     /* that also appear in CP.                    */
  rc=clearlist(mylist,'Y');


     /* Copy the old list data.  */
```

```
                    /* Sublists have been cleared.  */
                 mylist=copylist(cp,'N',mylist);

                    /* Delete the copied list. */
                 rc=dellist(cp);
```

CLOSE

Closes a SAS data set

See Also:
OPEN

sysrc=**CLOSE**(*data-set-id*);

Where...	Is type...	And represents...
sysrc	N	Whether the operation was successful: 0 if successful $\neq 0$ if not successful.
data-set-id	N	The identifier assigned when the data set was opened. If *data-set-id* is invalid, the program halts execution.

Details

Close all SAS data sets as soon as they are no longer needed by the application.

You do not need to open and close a SAS data set in each program of an application. If an application contains several programs that use the same data set, the first program can open the data set and use the parameter passing mechanism described in Chapter 8, "Calling Other Entries from SCL Programs" to make the data set identifier value available to other programs. However, always close an open data set when it is no longer needed in an application.

Example

Use OPEN to open a SAS data set. If the data set successfully opens, indicated by a positive value for the variable PAYID, use CLOSE to close the data set PAYROLL.

```
payid=open('payroll','u');
   SCL statements
if (payid>0) then payid=close(payid);
```

CLRFLD

Clears the value from up to ten character variables whose values match the specified value

See Also:
SETFLD

CALL CLRFLD(*pattern,variable-1<, . . . ,variable-10>*);

Where...	Is type...	And represents...
pattern	C	The character string to match.
variable-1,. . ., variable-10	C	Up to ten character variables. If the value of a specified variable exactly matches *pattern*, the variable is blanked.

Details

Variables that do not match exactly the *pattern* argument are not changed. No error occurs if there are no matches.

Example

Clear any variable in the group SYM1 through SYM5 whose value is **PATTERN**:

```
call clrfld('pattern',sym1,sym2,sym3,sym4,sym5);
```

COLORLIST

Displays a selection list of the names of a device's valid colors and returns user selections

See Also:
CURLIST
DEVLIST

selections=**COLORLIST**(*color-set,num-sel<,message<,autoclose>>*);

Where...	Is type...	And represents...
selections	C	One or more user selections from the list. Multiple selections are separated by blanks.
color-set	C	The set of colors displayed in the selection list:
		device If a SAS/GRAPH device is specified, the selection list includes only the colors that are valid for the specified device, and an **All . . .** choice to display all possible colors. *device* can be the name of a monitor, plotter, printer, or camera. This name can be up to eight characters long and must be specified within quotes. If the device entry is not found, the list contains all possible colors without regard to whether the device supports them.
		' ' Displays a list of all available colors. This list contains every available color without regard to whether the device supports them.
		? Opens the Color Selector window in which a user can design a color. Only one color can be defined, so *num-sel* is ignored. For additional information, use the window's online help.
num-sel	N	The maximum number of items a user can select from the list. To display the list for information purposes only (no selections allowed), specify **0**. To specify an unlimited number of selections, use a value larger than the number of available selections such as 9999.

Where...	Is type...	And represents...
message	C	Text for a message displayed above the selection list. The default message tells users to make up to the number of selections specified in *num-sel*.
autoclose	C	Whether the selection list window closes automatically after a user makes a selection when only one choice is allowed:

      'Y'   for the window to close automatically. (Default)

      'N'   for the window to close only when the user explicitly closes it.

      This option is ignored when *num-sel* is 1.

Details

By default, the message above the selection list asks the user to make *num-sel* selections and the selection list window closes when the user makes a choice and presses ENTER if the selection list allows only one choice.

You can provide a default or initial selected value in the list by providing a value for the *selections* variable prior to calling COLORLIST. If *selections* contains valid values when the function is invoked, those names are automatically designated as selected when the selection list is displayed.

If a user closes the selection list window without making a selection, COLORLIST returns a blank value unless there was an initial value for the *selections* variable before COLORLIST was called.

Selections from the window can be placed in the current result, if one is available. The current result list is a special SCL list that is automatically filled with the values selected from a selection list. To create a current result list, use the MAKELIST function to create it and the CURLIST function to designate it as the current result list. The current result list must exist before you call the COLORLIST function.

You can use COLORLIST to allow a user to interactively design the RGB components for a color. If a user designs a color that is not supported on that device, the closest color that is supported is used.

When COLORLIST is invoked, the current result list is cleared. After COLORLIST is invoked, the result list contains one element for each color name selected. The selections can be retrieved using GETITEMC.

Examples

Display a list of devices of type MONITOR available in the catalog SASHELP.DEVICES and allow users to select a device. Users can choose up to four colors from the selection list. If no device is chosen, display a list of all possible colors.

```
usrdev=devlist('sashelp.devices','monitor','Select a device. ');
device=substr(usrdev,41,8);
devcolor=colorlist(device,4);
```

Use a current result list to process multiple selections.

```
listid=makelist();
rc=curlist(listid);
selection=devlist('sashelp.devices','monitor','Select a device.');
device=substr(selection,41,8);
devcolor=colorlist(device,4);
```

```
n=listlen(listid);
do i=1 to n;
   color=getitemc(listid,i);
   put color=;
end;
```

Display a color selection dialog window:

```
color=colorlist('?',1,'Design a color for the bars');
```

COMAMID

Returns the communications access methods for an operating system

Release 6.11 Feature

comamids=**COMAMID**(*options*);

Where...	Is type...	And represents...
comamids	C	The communications access methods (comamids) for your operating system or for SAS/SHARE or SAS/CONNECT, if they are requested. Multiple values are separated by blanks.
options	C	A request for comamid values that are supported for your operating system by SAS/SHARE or SAS/CONNECT: **'S'** for comamid values supported by SAS/SHARE **'C'** for comamid values supported by SAS/CONNECT

Details

COMAMID provides a list of communication access method values for a user's operating system. If no value is provided for *options*, all comamid values for the operating system are returned.

If you want to display the list to application users, you can do that using other SCL features. For example, you can display the values in a list box by specifying that the source of list box values is the variable you used as the return value for COMAMID.

Note: COMAMID verifies communication access method values so that if the module to support a value is not installed, that value is not returned in the string of comamid values.

Example

Find out the comamids that are valid for the operating system.

```
INIT:
   comamids=COMAMID();
   put comamids=;
return;
```

This example produces the following output on an HP Unix system:

```
COMAMIDS= TCP TELNET
```

Find out the comamids that are supported by SAS/SHARE:

```
INIT:
   comamids=COMAMID('S');
```

```
        put 'Comamids for SAS/SHARE are 'comamids=;
   return;
```

This example produces the following output on an HP Unix system:

```
Comamids for SAS/SHARE are  COMAMIDS=TCP
```

CONTENTS

Displays the contents of a SAS data set

See Also:
ACCESS

*sysrc=***CONTENTS**(*data-set-name<,mode>*);

Where...	Is type...	And represents...
sysrc	N	The success of the operation: 　0　CONTENTS window was displayed for the specified SAS data set 　≠ 0　An error or warning condition occurred during the operation.
data-set-name	C	Name of the SAS data set. (SAS data set options are not allowed in this argument.)
mode	C	Whether the information in the CONTENTS window can be modified: **'B'**　Displays the CONTENTS window for browsing only. **'E'**　Allows modification of information in the CONTENTS window. (Default) If member-level locking is not available, the CONTENTS window is displayed in BROWSE mode instead. **NOTE:**　Any value beginning with a character other than **'B'** or **'b'** also selects EDIT mode.

Details

The CONTENTS function enables the user to view and change the variable names, formats, informats, and labels. If the CONTENTS window is opened for editing, the user can type over variable names, formats, informats, and labels to change the current values.

By default, the CONTENTS window is open for editing. If the specified data set is currently open, you must specify BROWSE for the *mode* argument.

CONTENTS Window Commands

Users can issue the following commands in the CONTENTS window:

INDEX CREATE
opens the Index Create window in which indexes can be created for the displayed SAS data set. (Refer to Chapter 6 in *SAS Language: Reference* for more information on data set indexes.) This command is valid only if the CONTENTS window is opened for editing.
Users can issue the following commands in the Index Create window:

END   closes the Index Create window.

REVIEW   opens the Index Review window to display the indexes already defined for this SAS data set. Existing indexes can also be deleted in this window.

RUN   creates an index after all required information has been specified.

INDEX REVIEW

opens the Index Review window in which the user can view the indexes currently defined for the SAS data set.

If the CONTENTS window is opened for editing, the user can use the DELETE command (or the D action field command) in the Index Review window to delete any of the listed indexes.

SORT <NAME|ORDER>

sorts the variables in the CONTENTS window display. By default, variables are listed in the order they are defined in the data set. SORT NAME sorts the display by variable names in descending alphabetical order. SORT ORDER (or SORT alone) restores the original order.

This command affects only the CONTENTS window display. The actual order of the variables in the data set is not affected.

Example

Display the variables for the data set MYLIB.HOUSES:

```
if (contents('mylib.houses')) then
   do;
      _msg_=sysmsg();
         SCL statements to handle case where contents cannot be displayed
   end;
```

CONTINUE

Stops processing the current DO loop and resumes with the next iteration of that DO loop

SAS Statement with limitations in SCL

See also:
DO iterative
LEAVE

CONTINUE;

Details

The CONTINUE statement is provided in SCL to control the execution of DO loops. When you need to force the statements in a DO loop to stop executing, you can use the CONTINUE statement to stop executing successive statements in a DO loop and to move back up and re-execute the DO loop starting with the header statement.

When you use DO WHILE and DO UNTIL statements, use caution to prevent the CONTINUE statement from forcing the program into an infinite loop. For example, the following statements produce an infinite loop because the value of the variable I never exceeds 2. When I has the value of 2, the IF statement always causes a branch around the next two SCL statements.

```
       /* This example causes an infinite loop */
INIT:
i=1;
do while (i<1000);
    if mod(i,2)=0 then
       continue;
    sum+i;
    i+1;
end;
return;
```

For details on the CONTINUE statement in SAS language, see SAS Technical Report P-222 *Changes and Enhancements to Base SAS Software.*

Example

Count the number of females in the SAS data set WORK.PERSONEL and display their average age. WORK.PERSONEL contains the variable SEX, which contains the values 'F' for female and 'M' for male and the variable AGE, which contains numeric values for age. The display window contains 2 numeric fields: AVGAGE and FEMALES. If the value of SEX is not F (female), the CONTINUE statement skips the other statements and returns to the DO WHILE statement to read the next observation. The results are displayed in the application window, although the records are not displayed.

```
INIT:
    females=0;
    total=0;
    persnlid=open('personel');
    call set(persnlid);
       /* Process observations until all the observations are read. */
    do while (fetch(persnlid) ne -1);
          /* Skip males when processing. */
       if sex ne 'F' then
          continue;
       females+1;
       total+age;
    end;
          /* Display the results in the fields FEMALES and AVGAGE. */
       avgage=total/females;
```

```
        return;

    MAIN:
        /* other SCL statements   */
    return;

    TERM:
        rc=close(persnlid);
    return;
```

CONTROL

Controls execution of labeled program sections and formatting of SUBMIT blocks

See also:
WORD
Chapter 3

CONTROL *options*;

Where...	Is type...	And represents...
options	C	The type of control for program statements, described in Table 20.5. One or more options are allowed.

Details

The CONTROL statement controls execution of labeled program sections and also controls the formatting of code in a SUBMIT block. A CONTROL statement option remains in effect until another CONTROL statement option overrides it. Multiple CONTROL statement options may be in effect at the same time.

Table 20.5 *Options for the CONTROL Statement*

Options	Description
ALLCMDS|NOALLCMDS	In SAS/AF applications, NOALLCMDS is in effect by default. Any global or procedure-specific commands users issue execute immediately without executing the SCL program. An SCL program cannot intercept any procedure-specific commands issued in the application. Use ALLCMDS to have SCL intercept any procedure-specific or custom command issued in the application. Use NEXTCMD to ignore invalid commands. Use NOALLCMDS to restore the default behavior.
	ALLCMDS combines the effects of ENTER and ERROR. It specifies that statements in the MAIN section execute even if a user issues commands not recognized by the procedure.
	In SAS/AF applications, ALLCMDS provides the same functionality as ALWAYS, which enables you to intercept custom commands. However, ALLCMDS also allows your SCL program to intercept any procedure-specific commands. In FRAME entries only, ALLCMDS allows your SCL program to intercept full-screen global commands. See "Using Full-Screen Global Commands" in Chapter 12 for a listing of these full-screen global commands.
	In FSEDIT applications, ALLCMDS and ALWAYS have the same functionality, and both allow your SCL program to intercept any procedure-specific or custom commands.
	With ALLCMDS specified, both SAS/AF and FSEDIT execute statements in the MAIN section before handling a command issued with the EXECCMD routine. This behavior could introduce an infinite loop. Either execute the EXECCMD routine conditionally or specify the command using EXECCMDI with the NOEXEC parameter.

Options	Description
	FSVIEW applications ignore this option.
ALWAYS|NOALWAYS	In SAS/AF applications or FSEDIT applications, NOALWAYS is in effect by default. Statements in the MAIN section execute only when a user modifies a window variable with a valid value and presses ENTER or a function key. Use ALWAYS to have statements in the MAIN section execute even if a user issues commands not recognized by the procedure. ALWAYS combines the effects of ENTER and ERROR.
	ALWAYS can be used if your application supports custom commands. With ALWAYS specified, FSEDIT executes statements in the MAIN section before handling a command issued with the EXECCMD routine. This behavior could introduce an infinite loop. Either execute the EXECCMD routine conditionally or specify the command using EXECCMDI with the NOEXEC parameter.
	FSVIEW applications ignore this option.
ASIS|NOASIS	NOASIS is in effect by default. SCL formats SUBMIT block code to eliminate unnecessary spaces and line breaks. Use ASIS to allow the SUBMIT block to be submitted without formatting. You must use this option when the position of your SAS code is important (for example, if you are using a submit block to submit a CARDS statement with a datastep). ASIS is more efficient because it reduces the time spent on formatting.
BREAK *label*|NOBREAK	NOBREAK is in effect by default. No labeled section is called if an interrupt occurs while the SCL statements are executing. A requestor window opens and asks the user whether program execution should resume (that is, ignore the interrupt) or the program should abort. If a user chooses to abort execution, no more statements are executed for the current program and control returns to the calling program. Use BREAK to specify a labeled section to which control passes if an interrupt or break condition occurs while the SCL statements are executing. *label* is the program label of the section to execute once the current statement finishes execution. This labeled section can include SCL statements to report status and handle the interrupt. Use the _STATUS_ system variable to control execution such as `'H'` to halt and `'R'` to resume.
	A program can contain any number of CONTROL BREAK statements. For example, there can be one in each of the INIT, MAIN, and TERM sections or any other labeled section. When a CONTROL BREAK statement executes, any previous CONTROL BREAK statement is overwritten so that only one is in effect at a time.
	Use NOBREAK to restore the default behavior. NOBREAK clears the current CONTROL BREAK specification.
	FSVIEW applications ignore this option.
ENTER|NOENTER	NOENTER is in effect by default. Statements in the MAIN section execute only when a user enters a valid value in a window variable and presses ENTER or any function key. Thus, pressing ENTER or a function key alone is not sufficient to execute statements in MAIN if a window variable has not been modified. Use the ENTER option so MAIN executes when a user presses ENTER or a function key recognized by the procedure and window variable modification is not required.
	In FSVIEW applications, this option is honored only if the cursor is on a valid observation when ENTER or a function key is pressed.
ERROR|NOERROR	NOERROR is in effect by default. Statements in MAIN do not execute if any field contains a value that causes an attribute error. This default action also means that some statements in MAIN do not execute if there are multiple fields in error and a user has not modified all of these fields. Use ERROR so that statements in MAIN execute even if the window contains fields that are in error.

Options	Description
	With FSEDIT, if you use ERROROFF to remove the error status from a continued portion of the field, you must also use a CONTROL ERROR statement in the program. If a user does not type in the continued portion of the field and the program does not have a CONTROL ERROR statement, the error flag is not removed from the continued portion of the field and the default error message may display, saying that a data value is not valid.
LABEL|NOLABEL	NOLABEL is in effect by default for PROGRAM entries and FSEDIT applications. MAIN executes after any window variable is modified. Use LABEL so that sections labeled with a window variable name (called a window variable section) execute before MAIN executes. For FRAME entries, CONTROL LABEL is the default.
	Statements in a window variable section execute after the associated window variable is modified, but only if the value does not introduce an error. That is, the value must satisfy any attributes defined for the window variable.
	Statements in MAIN do not execute until statements in all the window variable sections for modified fields execute successfully. The sequence for executing window variable sections is determined by the physical position of the field in the window from left to right and top to bottom.
	If a field modification introduces an attribute error, the associated window variable section does not execute. However, other window variable sections for modified window variables do execute. To correct an attribute error, you can allow users to correct the error in the window, or you can include SCL statements that make a correction in the labeled section for other fields.
	If ERROR, ALWAYS, or ALLCMDS is also specified, MAIN executes after the window variable labeled sections even if an error was introduced.
	If the window contains an extended table, the window variable section for each modified window variable executes for a row before PUTROW executes. MAIN executes after PUTROW executes.
	Note: If CONTROL LABEL is specified, a window variable section must not contain a SUBMIT IMMEDIATE block.
TERM|NOTERM	NOTERM is in effect by default. This option is valid only for FSEDIT applications. The default action for FSEDIT is that statements in the TERM section do not execute when a user scrolls off the current observation unless the user changed one or more data set variables so that the current observation needs to be updated in the data set or the observation is new. Use the TERM option to force execution of the statements in the TERM section even if a user does not modify any data set variables in the current observation.

Example 1

Use the ASIS option:

```
control asis;
submit;
   data a;
      input x y z;
      cards;
      10 20 30
      40 50 60
   run;
endsubmit;
```

With the CONTROL ASIS statement in place, the SUBMIT block executes without errors. If you remove the CONTROL ASIS statement, SCL formats the code within the block as follows when it is submitted for processing:

```
data a;
input x y z;
cards;
10 20 30 40 50 60 run;
```

When formatted in this manner, the final statement contains a syntax error and the code cannot execute properly.

Example 2

Define a break handler section labeled STOPINIT. When a user interrupts while SCL statements in INIT are executing, the STOPINIT label executes. If the loop index I is less than 350, execution of the program halts and control returns to the calling program. Otherwise, execution resumes. After the first loop is finished, reset so there is no break handler. If a user interrupts during the second loop, the SCL Break requestor window displays and the statements in STOPINIT do not execute. The user can either abort or resume. Follow the same steps to define a new break handler section labeled STOPTERM in the TERM section.

```
INIT:
     /* define break label STOPINIT                            */
  control break stopinit;

     /* loop 500 times to allow interrupt checking with control break */
     /* if user interrupts, statements in label STOPINIT execute     */
  do i=1 to 500;
    put i=;
  end;

     /* reset so there is no break handler                      */
  control nobreak;

     /* loop 500 times to allow interrupt checking w/o control break */
  do i = 1 to 500;
    if (int(i/25) eq (i/25)) then put i=;
  end;
return;

MAIN:
return;

TERM:
     /* Define the new break label STOPTERM.  */
  control break stopterm;

     /* Loop 500 times to allow interrupt checking with control   */
     /* break.  If user interrupts, statements in label STOPTERM */
     /* execute.                                                 */
  do j=1 to 500;
    put j=;
  end;
```

```
          /* Reset so there is no break handler.  */
      control nobreak;

          /* Loop 500 times to allow interrupt checking w/o control  */
          /* break.                                                   */
      do j = 1 to 500;
        if (int(j/25) eq (j/25)) then put j=;
      end;
  return;


STOPINIT:
          /* HALT if loop counter is less than 350, otherwise RESUME.  */
          /* Report the current status.                                */
      put i=;
      if (i < 350) then
        _status_ = 'H';
      else
        _status_ = 'R';
  return;


STOPTERM:
          /* HALT if loop counter is less than 350, otherwise RESUME.  */
          /* Report the current status.                                */
      put j=;
      if (j < 350) then
        _status_ = 'H';
      else
        _status_ = 'R';
  return;
```

COPY

Copies a SAS data set, view, catalog, or catalog entry

See Also:
DELETE
RENAME

sysrc=**COPY**(*old-name,new-name*<,*type*>);

Where...	Is type...	And represents...

sysrc	N	Whether the operation was successful:
		  0 if successful
		
		  $\neq$ 0 if not successful

old-name	C	The SAS file or catalog entry to copy. This can be a one-, two-, or four-level name and can include data set options.
new-name	C	The new name for the SAS file or catalog entry. This must be a three- or four-level name if *type* is **'CATALOG'**. If a catalog entry is being copied, the function sets the entry type of the new entry to that of the old entry. You can also specify data set options.
type	C	The type of SAS file or catalog entry to be copied: **'ACCESS'** member is an access descriptor created using SAS/ACCESS software. **'CATALOG'** member is a SAS catalog or a catalog entry. **'DATA'** member is a SAS data file. (Default) **'VIEW'** member is a SAS data view.

Details

To copy a catalog entry, specify the complete four-level name of the entry for *old-name*, a three-level name for *new-name*, and **'CATALOG'** for *type*.

You can use the WHERE= data set option to copy only those observations that meet your WHERE subset to the new data set.

If the SAS data set being copied is indexed, all indexes are rebuilt for the new SAS data set.

new-name is ignored when you use COPY to copy GRSEG catalog entries created using SAS/GRAPH software. A copied GRSEG entry will have either the same name as the original entry or, if an entry with that name already exists in the target catalog, a unique name generated by the SAS System.

▶ *Caution: This function can overwrite existing files.*

If a data set or catalog with the specified new name already exists, COPY overwrites the existing data set or catalog without warning.

. . . .

Example

Copy SAS data set DATA1 to DATA2 and copy WORK.TEMP.A.PROGRAM to SASUSER.PROFILE.B.PROGRAM:

```
if (copy('data1','data2')) then
  do;
    _msg_=sysmsg();
    SCL statements to handle the error condition
  end;
rc=copy('work.temp.a.program','sasuser.profile.b.program', 'catalog')
```

```
if (rc) then
    do;
        _msg_=sysmsg();
        SCL statements to handle the error condition
    end;
```

COPYLIST

Copies or merges the contents of an SCL list into an existing list or a new list

See Also:
DELLIST
GETLATTR
HASATTR
MAKELIST
MAKENLIST
PUTLIST
SETLATTR

new-list-id=**COPYLIST**(*list-id<,options><,target-list-id>*);

Where...	Is type...	And represents...
new-list-id	N	The identifier of the new list to contain a copy of the contents of *list-id*, if *target-list-id* is not supplied, or *target-list-id* if a target list is supplied.
list-id	N	The identifier of the list to copy or merge into the target list. An invalid *list-id* produces an error condition.
options	C	Whether list values are merged and how sublists are copied or merged. You can use one or more of the following values, separated by spaces. Later keywords override previous keywords.

'NONRECURSIVELY' | 'NO' | 'N'
copies or merges only sublist identifiers as values for sublist items. (Default)

'MERGE' | 'M'
merges the contents of the source *list-id* into the *target-list-id*, replacing like-named existing items items in the target list. You may combine this option with the recursive option. An error occurs if *target-list-id* is not supplied or is not a valid list identifier.

'RECURSIVELY' | 'YES' | 'Y'
copies or merges all items of sublists and of sublists of sublists, and so on.

target-list-id	N	The identifier of the list into which the source list is copied or merged. If supplied, *target-list-id* is also returned. Otherwise, a new list is created and returned. New sublists are created with the same environment (local or global) as the target list.

An error condition results if the target list has attributes that prevent copying data into it such as NOUPDATE and FIXEDLENGTH.

Details

The copy operation appends items from the source list to the end of the target list, while the merge operation copies them into the target list, replacing existing named items.

If *target-list-id* is omitted, the function creates a new list in the same environment ('L' or 'G') as the list being copied and makes the new list the *target-list-id*. (For a description of list environments, see ENVLIST.) If *target-list-id* is supplied, its identifier is returned in *new-list-id*.

When a list is copied recursively, the items in all sublists are also copied rather than just the sublist identifiers. However, even this duplication is avoided if it would result in an infinite recursion. When copying a list recursively, SCL does not perform an infinite recursive copy. For example, if a list contains itself, COPYLIST detects the circular structure and recreates the structure in the copy.

Merging occurs by item names. All items in the source list (and its sublists, if merging recursively) must have names. For each item, the name is used to find a matching name in the target list, as with NAMEDITEM(target, name). If the same name appears multiple times in the source list, each item is merged independently. That is, the last occurrence of the name will overwrite previous merged values and will *not* match with subsequent items in the target list. Thus, you should strive to keep item names unique in the source list to avoid wasted processing. If the corresponding item is not found in the target list, a new item is created.

In the merge operation, a list or sublist is only merged once, even if it appears multiple times. Also, a warning is printed for items that do not have names.

If an item in the source list has the NOWRITE attribute, the corresponding item in the target list is *deleted*, unless it has NODELETE, in which case it is not merged. If a scalar item replaces a sublist item in a merge, the replaced list is not deleted because it may be used elsewhere. The SCL program must explicitly delete the old list.

All attributes of the list and its contents are preserved when a list is copied. The password is not copied so that you can modify the copy without knowing the password of the original list. The copy has no password. (See SETLATTR for a discussion of passwords of lists.)

COPYLIST ignores any invalid options and uses its defaults instead.

Example Copying a Single List

```
      /* make B a local named list with 2 items named x, y */
b=makenlist('L','x','y');
b=setnitemc(b,'ABC','x');
b=setnitemc(b,'XYZ','y');

      /* make A a local named list with 3 items named A, B, and C */
a=makenlist('L','A','B','C');
a=setnitemn(a,3.5,'A');
a=setniteml(a,b,'B');
a=setnitemn(a,9.75,'C');

call putlist(a,'A=',2);
NREC=copylist(a,'N');             /* nonrecursive copy */
call putlist(NREC,'NREC=',2);
REC=copylist(a,'Y');              /* recursive copy */
call putlist(REC,'REC=',2);
```

This program produces the following output:

```
A=(   A=3.5
      B=(  x='ABC'
           y='XYZ'
         )[ 3]
      C=9.75
    )[ 5]
NREC=(  A=3.5
        B=(  x='ABC'
             y='XYZ'
           )[ 3]
        C=9.75
      )[ 7]
REC=(  A=3.5
       B=(  x='ABC'
            y='XYZ'
          )[ 11]
       C=9.75
     )[ 9]
```

The sublist named B in the outer list NREC is the same list as the sublist named B in the outer list named A, from which NREC was copied non-recursively. Both lists named B have the same list identifier (3), which means they are in fact the same list. However, the sublist named B in the outer list REC, which was copied recursively from list A, is a different list, although it has the same contents as the list named B from A. The sublist in the outer list REC has a list identifier of 11, not 3, which shows it is a different list.

Note: [5], [7], and [9] are the list identifiers assigned when this example was run and may be different each time the example is run.

Example Appending a List to Itself

Append the list MYLIST to itself. Both NEWLIST and MYLIST contain the list identifier for the copy of MYLIST.

```
mylist=makelist();
mylist=insertn(mylist,1,-1);
mylist=insertn(mylist,2,-1);
mylist=insertn(mylist,3,-1);
newlist = copylist(mylist,'N',mylist);
```

NEWLIST contains the values 1, 2, 3, 1, 2, 3.

Example Merging One List Into Another List

```
INIT:
   a = makenlist('L','A','B','C','D','E','F');
   do i = 1 to listlen(a);
      a = setitemc(a, nameitem(a,i),i);
   end;
   c = insertc(makelist(),'?',-1,'NOT');
   a = insertl(a, c,-1,'WHY');
   b = makenlist('L','A','E','I','O','U');
   do i = 1 to listlen(b);
      b = setitemn(b, rank(nameitem(b,i)),i);
   end;
   b = insertl(b, insertn(makelist(),0,-1,'NOT'),-1,'WHY');
```

```
                 call putlist(a,'A before merge:');
                 call putlist(b,'B before merge:');
                 b = copylist(a,'yes merge',b);
                 call putlist(b,'B after merge :');
             return;
```

The result is:

```
A before merge:(A='A' B='B' C='C' D='D' E='E' F='F' WHY=(NOT='?' )[7] )[5]
B before merge:(A=65 E=69 I=73 O=79 U=85 WHY=(NOT=0 )[11] )[9]
B after  merge :(A='A' E='E' I=73 O=79 U=85 WHY=(NOT='?' )[11] B='B' C='C'
D='D' F='F' )[9]
```

The result list B contains items from A where the names intersect and original items from B for items not found in A. Because the sublist WHY was found in both, a recursive merge replaced 0 from the sublist of B with '?' from the sublist of A.

Note: 7, 5, 11, and 9 are the list identifiers assigned when this example was run and may be different each time the example is run.

Example Copying Multiple Instances of a List

Copy a list, which contains a copy of itself, non-recursively and recursively. The outer list R1 contains two items, named SELF and R1, which are actually the same list as R1. When a non-recursive copy, R2, is made, the copy has items named SELF and R1 which are still the list R1. Only when R1 is copied recursively as R3 does the copy contain itself instead of R1.

```
          /*  Create the list L, fill it, and print R1.   */
      r1=makenlist('l','a','SELF','r1', 'x');
      r1=setniteml(r1,r1,'SELF'));
      r1=setniteml(r1,r1,'r1'));
      r1=setnitemn(r1,1,'a'));
      r1=setnitemn(r1,99,'x'));
      call putlist(r1,'R1=',2));
          /*  Copy R1 nonrecursively into R2 and print R2.  */
      r2=copylist(r1,'n');
      call putlist(r2,'R2=',2);
          /*  Copy R1 recursively into R3 and print R3.  */
      r3=copylist(r1,'y');
      call putlist(r3,'R3=',2);
```

The list R2, which was created with a nonrecursive copy operation, contains the list R1. Note that the structure of the list R3 is identical to that of R1: it contains two copies of itself, at items named SELF and R1, because these items are lists whose list identifier is the same as the list R3.
This program yields the output:

```
R1=(  a=1
      SELF=(...)[13]
      R1=(...)[13]
      x=99
    )[13]
R2=(  a=1
      SELF=(  a=1
              SELF=(...)[13]
              R1=(...)[13]
```

```
                           x=99
                        ) [13]
                R1=( . . . ) [13]
                x=99
            ) [15]
     R3=(   a=1
            SELF=( . . . ) [17]
            R1=( . . . ) [17]
            x=99
         ) [17]
```

Note: 13, 15, and 17 are the list identifiers assigned when this example was run and may be different each time the example is run.

Example Merging Nonrecursively and Recursively

Merge the contents of the list identified in SOURCEID into the list identified in TARGETID. The second call does a recursive merge.

```
targetid=copylist(sourceid,"MERGE",targetid);
targetid=copylist(sourceid,"MERGE YES",targetid);
```

CURCOL

Contains the value of the leftmost column in an extended table object in a FRAME entry

Numeric System Instance

Variable

SAS/AF only

See Also:
CURROW

Details

CURROW is a System Instance Variable. It is provided automatically by the FRAME entry in SAS/AF. For SCL entries, the SCL compiler does not automatically create a space for _CURROW_ in the SCL data vector. Because of this, you get a warning when you compile your SCL entry if you have a reference to _CURROW_. See _FRAME_ for more details on how to prevent the warning.

CURCOL is updated when the getrow or putrow section of an extended table is executing or when the _GETROW_ or _PUTROW_ method of an extended table object is executing. Therefore, _CURCOL_ must only be referenced within these sections.

CURCOL is only available in SAS/AF FRAME entries.

Example

Suppose you have a text entry object, TEXT, in an extended table object. TEXT is assigned a value in the getrow section based on a substring of a longer string. When the extended table is scrolled left and right, the value of _CURCOL_ is updated and is used as the *position* argument to the SUBSTR function.

```
GET1:
   text = substr( longstring, _curcol_ );
return;
```

For more information on horizontal scrolling extended table objects, see *SAS/AF Software: FRAME Entry Usage and Reference.*

CURFLD

Returns the name of the field or FRAME entry object on which the cursor is currently positioned

See also:
CONTROL
CURSOR
CURWORD

wvar-name =**CURFLD**();

Where...	Is type...	And represents...
wvar-name	C	The field or FRAME entry object in the window on which the cursor is currently positioned.

Details

The CURFLD function returns the name of the field or FRAME entry object on which the cursor is located. If the cursor is not positioned on a window variable, a null string is returned. CURFLD is usually used in conjunction with a CONTROL statement that includes the ENTER, ALWAYS, or ALLCMDS option.

You can use CONTROL LABEL to achieve the same result more efficiently.

FRAME entries can also use the _GET_CURRENT_NAME_ method.

Example

Use CURFLD to control the behavior of a PROGRAM entry application:

```
INIT:
   control enter;
return;

MAIN:
   select( curfld() );
      when('PHONE') call display('phone.help');
      when('EMPLOYEE') call display('employee.program');
      otherwise;
   end;
return;
```

Note that this example can be implemented without CURFLD if the program uses window variable sections and CONTROL LABEL.

```
INIT:
   control label;
return;
PHONE:
   call display('phone.help');
return;
EMPLOYEE:
   call display('employee.program');
return;
```

CURLIST

Designates or reports the current result SCL list

See Also:
CATLIST
COLORLIST
COPYLIST
DATALISTC
DATALISTN
DELLIST
DEVLIST
DIRLIST
FILELIST
LIBLIST
LISTC
LISTN
LVARLEVEL
MAKELIST
MAKENLIST
PUTLIST
VARLIST

list-id =**CURLIST**(*<new-list-id>*);

Where...	Is type...	And represents...
list-id	N	The identifier of the list to receive the values returned by the next SCL selection list function that is invoked. **> 0** The list identifier of the SCL list previously defined as current with the CURLIST function. **0** No list is defined as the current list.
new-list-id	N	The identifier of the list to be designated as the current list. An invalid *new-list-id* produces an error condition.

Details

When a value is provided for *new-list-id*, CURLIST designates the SCL list identified by *new-list-id* as the current result list. *new-list-id* must be the list identifier returned by the MAKELIST, MAKENLIST, or COPYLIST function that created this list. If you omit *new-list-id*, this function returns the identifier of the SCL list already designated as the current result list by CURLIST. If no argument is passed to CURLIST and no current result list has been specified, CURLIST returns 0.

The current result list is filled automatically with the values selected when the next SCL selection list function executes.

The functions that can fill the current result list are the SCL selection list functions CATLIST, COLORLIST, DATALISTC, DATALISTN, DEVLIST, DIRLIST, FILELIST, LIBLIST, LISTC, LISTN, LVARLEVEL, and VARLIST. For example, CATLIST is an SCL selection list function that opens a selection list window displaying the names of catalog entries. The value returned by CATLIST is a character string containing each catalog name users select separated by blanks. Because SCL character variables are limited to 200 characters, the SCL selection list functions cannot return more entries than will fit in 200 characters. Selection list functions like CATLIST can also automatically fill the current result list, as specified by CURLIST, with a character item for each selection users make. The length of that list is unbounded.

When one of the selection list functions is invoked, the values users select replace the entire contents of the current result list. To preserve the contents of the current result list, use COPYLIST to copy the list before calling another selection list function.

Example

Set up a selection list, invoke a selection list function, and access the selections:

```
clist=makelist();
oldcurlist=curlist(clist);
    /* Allow user to choose up to 16 graphs.  */
graphs=catlist('SASUSER.DEMO','GRSEG',16,'Y');
n=getnitemn(clist,'COUNT');
do g=1 to n;
     graphName=getnitemc(clist,'name',g);
   put 'Selection #' g ' is ' graphName;
end;
   /* Delete temporary curlist and restore previous curlist. */
rc=dellist(clist);
oldcurlist=curlist(oldcurlist);
```

CUROBS

Returns the observation number of the current observation

obs-number=**CUROBS**(*data-set-id*);

Where...	Is type...	And represents...
obs-number	N	The current observation number.
data-set-id	N	The data set identifier assigned when the data set was opened. If *data-set-id* is invalid, the program halts execution.

▶ *Caution: This function should only be used with an uncompressed SAS data set accessed using a native library engine.*

Details

If the engine being used does not support observation numbers, the function returns a missing value.

In FSEDIT and FSVIEW applications, the *data-set-id* argument is optional. If the argument is not specified, CUROBS returns the value for the SAS data set displayed by the procedure. With a SAS data view, the function returns the relative observation number.

Example

Use FETCHOBS to fetch the tenth observation in the data set MYDATA. The value of *obs-number* returned by CUROBS is 10.

```
dsid=open('mydata','i');
rc=fetchobs(dsid,10);
obsnum=curobs(dsid);
```

In an FSEDIT SCL program, get the number of the observation currently displayed:

```
obsnum=curobs();
```

CURROW

Contains the number of the current row for an extended table

Numeric System Variable

SAS/AF Only

See Also:
CURCOL
SETROW

Details

CURROW is a System Variable that is created for every SCL program you compile. The compiler creates a space for _CURROW_ in the SCL data vector.

CURROW is updated when the getrow or putrow section of an extended table is executing or when the _GETROW_ or _PUTROW_ method of an extended table object is executing. Therefore, _CURROW_ must only be referenced within these sections.

CURROW is available in SAS/AF PROGRAM entries as well as FRAME entries. See Chapter 14 "Introduction to Application Interfaces" or *SAS Screen Control Language: Usage.* for more details on extended tables.

Example

The following getrow section of a FRAME entry fetches an observation from a previously opened data set using _CURROW_ as the observation number.

```
GET1:
    if fetchobs( dsid, _currow_ ) ne 0 then
        call notify( 'table', '_endtable_' )
return;
```

CURSOR

Positions the cursor in a specified field or FRAME entry object

See Also:
CURFLD
CURWORD
DISPLAYED
ERROR
ERROROFF
ERRORON
FIELD
HOME
MODIFIED
PROTECT
UNPROTECT

CURSOR *wvar-name*;

Where...	Is type...	And represents...
wvar-name	C	The field or FRAME entry object in the window to position the cursor on.

Details

The CURSOR statement does not move the cursor immediately while the SCL program is executing. Rather, it dictates where the cursor will be positioned after the window is updated when SCL returns control to the procedure. If multiple cursor statements execute, the cursor is positioned on the variable specified in the last CURSOR statement. In SAS/AF applications, a REFRESH statement also positions the cursor based on the last cursor statement.

The field of FRAME entry object cannot be an element of an array. To report this information for an array element, use FIELD instead.

FRAME entry objects can also use the _CURSOR_ method.

Example

Move the cursor to ADDRESS if NAME is filled in:

```
if modified (name) and name ne '' then
    cursor address;
```

CURTOP

Returns the number of the row currently displayed at the top of an extended table

SAS/AF software only

See Also:
ENDTABLE
SETROW
TOPROW

row=**CURTOP**();

Where...	Is type...	And represents...
row	N	The row of the extended table currently displayed at the top.

Details

CURTOP can only be used on extended tables in PROGRAM entries. Because extended tables can only be defined in SAS/AF software, this function cannot be used in FSEDIT or FSVIEW programs.

Example

Store the number of the table's top row in the variable TOPROW:

```
toprow=curtop();
```

CURWORD

Returns the word that the cursor is positioned on

See Also:
CONTROL
CURFLD
CURSOR
LOOKUPC

word=**CURWORD**();

Where...	Is type...	And represents...
word	C	The text of the word.

Details

CURWORD returns the word on which the cursor was located when the user last pressed ENTER. The character string retrieved begins with the first character of the word on which the cursor was positioned and extends to the first space after the word. CURWORD is usually used in conjunction with a CONTROL statement that includes the ENTER, ALWAYS, or ALLCMDS option.

Because CURWORD can determine the word on which a user has positioned the cursor, buttons with words can be programmed to select actions.

If CURWORD is used on a window variable that has been modified, justification is performed on the field before CURWORD executes.

Example

Suppose a PROGRAM entry DISPLAY window contains buttons with the words PROJECT1 and PROJECT2. The entry's program determines the action to take place by the word on which the cursor is positioned when the user presses ENTER or clicks with the mouse:

```
INIT:
   control enter;
return;
```

```
MAIN:
  word=curword();
  if (word='PROJECT1') then
     submit immediate;
        proc print data=project1;
        run;
     endsubmit;
  else if (word='PROJECT2') then
     submit immediate;
        proc print data=project2;
        run;
     endsubmit;
  else _msg_='Please position the cursor on a valid selection.';
return;

TERM:
return;
```

DATALISTC

Displays a selection list window containing values of selected variables from observations in a SAS data set and returns user selections

See Also:
DATALISTN
LISTC
LISTN
LOCATEC
LOCATEN
SHOWLIST
VARLIST

selections=**DATALISTC**(*data-set-id* ,*var-list*<,*message*<,*autoclose*<,*num-sel*>>>);

Where...	Is type...	And represents...
selections	C	The value of the first character variable from the selected observation, or blank if the selection list window is closed and no selections are made.
data-set-id	N	The identifier assigned when the data set was opened. If *data-set-id* is invalid, the program halts execution.
var-list	C	Up to five variables names, separated by blanks, from the SAS data set to be displayed. The first variable in this list must be character, but the others can be of any type. If the first variable in the list is numeric, the program halts execution. (Use DATALISTN to retrieve the values of numeric variables.)
message	C	Text for a message displayed above the selection list. The default message tells users to make up to the number of selections specified in *num-sel*.
autoclose	C	Whether the selection list window closes automatically after a user makes a selection when only one choice is allowed:
		'Y' for the window to close automatically. (Default)
		'N' for the window to close only when the user explicitly closes it.
		This option is ignored when *num-sel* is not 1. However, use **' '** as a placeholder if you are also specifying a value for *num-sel*.
num-sel	N	The maximum number of items a user can select from the list. To display the list for information purposes only (no selections allowed), specify **0**. To specify unlimited selections, use a value larger than the number of available selections such as 9999.

Details

You can provide a default or initial selected value in the list by providing a value for the *selections* variable prior to calling DATALISTC. If *selections* contains valid entry names when the function is invoked, those names are automatically designated as selected when the selection list is displayed.

If a user closes the selection list window without making a selection, DATALISTC returns a blank value unless there was an initial value for the *selections* variable before DATALISTC was called.

Although a user can position the cursor or mouse pointer anywhere in a row to make a selection from the list, only the value of the first variable is returned. (The other variable values are displayed for information only.)

When multiple selections are allowed, *selections* contains only the value of the first variable in the last selected observation. However, values for displayed variables for all observations that are selected can be returned in the current result list if one is available. The current result list is a special SCL list that is automatically filled with the values selected from a selection list. To create a current result list, use the MAKELIST function to create it and the CURLIST function to designate it as the current result list. The current result list must exist before you call the DATALISTC function.

If the total length of the specified variables in an observation exceeds the width of the zoomed window, the function may not display the rightmost variables. If your host supports scrollbars, users can scroll these variables into view. On other systems, the rightmost variables can be displayed by increasing the size of the selection list window. To increase the size of the window, use CALL WREGION before invoking DATALISTC.

To display a subset of observations matching specific criteria, use the WHERE function before invoking DATALISTC.

By default, a message is displayed asking the user to make one selection and the selection list window closes automatically when the user makes a selection.

When DATALISTC is invoked, the current result list is cleared. After DATALISTC is invoked, the result list contains the following named items:

Element	Type	Description
TAG	C	Identifies the list as one created by the DATALISTC function.
COUNT	N	Number of elements selected. If no selections are made, or if users issue the CANCEL command in the list window, COUNT is 0.
var-name	N or C	Value of variable *var-name* in *var-list* for each selection.

Example 1

Create a selection list containing observations with the values of the variables NAME, STREET, CITY, STATE, and ZIP from the SAS data set identified by the variable CLASSID, which was returned by the OPEN function. NAME contains the value for the row selected. The other variables are displayed for information purposes only.

```
name=datalistc(classid,'name street city state zip');
```

Example 2

Create a selection list containing observations with values of the variables NAME, STREET, CITY, STATE, and ZIP from the open SAS data set identified by the variable CLASSID. Users can make up to three selections from this selection list. The values for NAME, STREET, CITY, STATE, and ZIP for each of the selected observations are then retrieved from the current result list.

```
classid=open('classes');
listid=makelist();
rc=curlist(listid);
name=datalistc(classid,'name street city state zip',' ','',3);
n=getnitemn(listid,'COUNT');
do i=1 to n;
   name=getnitemc(listid,'NAME',i);
   street=getnitemc(listid,'STREET',i);
   city=getnitemc(listid,'CITY',i);
   state=getnitemc(listid,'STATE',i);
   zip=getnitemn(listid,'ZIP',i);
   put name= street= city= state= zip=;
end;
rc=close(classid);
```

DATALISTN

Displays a selection list window containing values of specified variables from observations in a SAS data set and returns user selections

See Also:
DATALISTC
LISTC
LISTN
LOCATEC
LOCATEN
SHOWLIST
VARLIST

selections=**DATALISTN**(*data-set-id,var-list<,message<,autoclose<,num-sel>>>*);

Where...	Is type...	And represents...
selections	N	The value of the first numeric variable from the selected observation, or blank if the selection list window is closed and no selections are made.
data-set-id	N	The identifier assigned when the data set was opened. If *data-set-id* is invalid, the program halts execution.
var-list	C	Up to five variables names, separated by blanks, from the SAS data set to be displayed. The first variable in this list must be numeric, but the others can be of any type. If the first variable in the list is character, the program halts execution. (Use DATALISTC to retrieve the values of character variables.)
message	C	Text for a message displayed above the selection list. The default message tells users to make the number of selections specified in *num-sel*.
autoclose	C	Whether the selection list window closes automatically after a user makes a selection when only one choice is allowed:
		'Y' for the window to close automatically. (Default)
		'N' for the window to close only when the user explicitly closes it.
		This option is ignored when *num-sel* is not 1. However, use **' '** as a placeholder if you are also specifying a value for *num-sel*.

Where...	Is type...	And represents...
num-sel	N	The maximum number of items a user can select from the list. To display the list for information purposes only (no selections allowed), specify **0**. To specify an unlimited number of selections, use a value larger than the number of available selections such as 9999.

Details

You can provide a default or initial selected value in the list by providing a value for the *selections* variable prior to calling DATALISTN. If *selections* contains valid entry names when the function is invoked, those names are automatically designated as selected when the selection list is displayed.

If a user closes the selection list window without making a selection, DATALISTN returns a blank value unless there was an initial value for the *selections* variable before DATALISTN was called.

Although a user can position the cursor or mouse pointer anywhere in a row to make a selection from the list, only the value of the first variable is returned. (The other variable values are displayed for information only.)

When multiple selections are allowed, *selections* contains only the value of the first variable in the last selected observation. However, values for displayed variables for all observations that are selected can be returned in the current result list if one is available. The current result list is a special SCL list that is automatically filled with the values selected from a selection list. To create a current result list, use the MAKELIST function to create it and the CURLIST function to designate it as the current result list. The current result list must exist before you call the DATALISTN function.

If the total length of the specified variables in an observation exceeds the width of the zoomed window, the function may not display the rightmost variables. If your host supports scrollbars, users can scroll these variables into view. On other systems, the rightmost variables can be displayed by increasing the size of the selection list window. To increase the size of the window, use CALL WREGION before invoking DATALISTN.

To display a subset of observations matching specific criteria, use the WHERE function before invoking DATALISTN.

By default, a message is displayed asking the user to make one selection and the selection list window closes automatically when the user makes a selection.

When DATALISTN is invoked, the current result list is cleared. After DATALISTN is invoked, the result list contains the following named items:

Element	Type	Description
TAG	C	Identifies the list as one created by the DATALISTN function.
COUNT	N	Number of elements selected. If no selections are made, or if users issue a CANCEL command in the list window, COUNT is 0.
var-name	N or C	Value of variable *var-name* in *var-list* for each selection.

Example

Create a selection list containing observations with values of the variables ITEMNUM, ITEMAMT, CUSTNAM, and CUSTADR from the SAS data set identified by the variable SALESID. Allow users to make up to three selections from this selection list. The values for each variable for each of the selected observations are then retrieved from the current result list.

```
salesid=open('sales');
   listid=makelist();
   rc=curlist(listid);
   itemnum=datalistn(salesid,'itemnum itemamt custnam custadr','','',3);
   n=getnitemn(listid,'COUNT');
   do i=1 to n;
      itemnum=getnitemn(listid,'ITEMNUM',i);
      itemamt=getnitemn(listid,'ITEMAMT',i);
      custnam=getnitemc(listid,'CUSTNAM',i);
      custadr=getnitemc(listid,'CUSTADR',i);
      put itemnum= itemamt= custnam= custadr=;
   end;
   rc=close(salesid);
```

DCLOSE

Closes a directory

See Also:
DOPEN
FCLOSE
FOPEN
MOPEN

sysrc=**DCLOSE**(*directory-id*);

Where...	Is type...	And represents...

sysrc	N	Whether the operation was successful:
		    0 if successful
		
		    ≠ 0 if not successful.

directory-id	N	The identifier assigned when the directory was opened. If *directory-id* is invalid, the program halts execution.

Details

The DCLOSE function closes a directory previously opened by the DOPEN function. DCLOSE also closes any open members.

Example

Open the directory to which the fileref MYDIR has previously been assigned, return the number of members, and then close the directory:

```
rc=filename('mydir','physical-filename')
did=dopen('mydir');
memcount=dnum(did);
if (dclose(did)) then
   do;
      _msg_=sysmsg();
      SCL statements to handle the error condition
   end;
```

DELETE

Deletes a SAS data set, catalog, catalog entry, view, or access descriptor

See Also:
NEW

sysrc=**DELETE**(*member<,type><,password>*);

Where...	Is type...	And represents...
sysrc	N	Whether the operation was successful: 0 if successful $\neq 0$ if not successful
member	C	The name of the library member or catalog entry.
type	C	The type of member to delete: **'ACCESS'** member is an access descriptor created using SAS/ACCESS software. **'CATALOG'** member is a SAS catalog or catalog entry. If a one- or two-level name is specified, the catalog is deleted. If a four-level name is specified, the entry is deleted. **'DATA'** member is a SAS data file. (Default) **'VIEW'** member is a SAS data view.
password	C	The password assigned to the data set when *type* is **'DATA'**.

Details

DELETE attempts to delete the member specified by the *member* argument and returns a value indicating the success of the operation. If a one-level name is used, the library is assumed to be WORK.

Example

Delete the SAS data set LIB1.MYDATA and the SAS catalog entry LIB2.CAT1.MYPROG.PROGRAM:

```
rc=delete('lib1.mydata');
rc=delete('lib2.cat1.myprog.program','catalog');
```

DELITEM

Deletes an item from an SCL list and optionally deletes all of its sublists

See Also:
DELLIST
DELNITEM
HASATTR
LISTLEN
MAKELIST
MAKENLIST
POPC
POPL
POPN
SETLATTR

list-id=**DELITEM**(*list-id*<,*index*>);

Where...	Is type...	And represents...
list-id	N	The identifier of the list from which the item is to be deleted. The function returns the list identifier that is passed in. An invalid *list-id* produces an error condition.
index	N	The position of the item in the list. The position can be specified as a positive or negative number. By default, *index* is 1 (the first item). If *index* is a positive number, the item is at position *index* from the beginning of the list. If *index* is a negative number, the item is at position ABS(*index*) from the end of the list. An error condition results if the absolute value for *index* is zero or it is greater than the number of items in the list

Details

The item to be deleted is specified by its position in the list that is passed in.

DELITEM does not make a copy of the list before deleting the specified item. The delete operation is performed in place on the list, and the list identifier is returned.

When the item to be deleted is a sublist, DELITEM deletes the item but not the sublist because the sublist may be referenced by other SCL variables or lists.

An error condition results if:

□ the item has the NODELETE attribute.

□ the list has the NOUPDATE or FIXEDLENGTH attribute.

To check the attributes of a list or list item, use HASATTR. To change attributes, use SETLATTR.

DELLIST

Deletes a list and optionally deletes all of its sublists

See Also:
CLEARLIST
COPYLIST
DELITEM
DELNITEM
HASATTR
MAKELIST
MAKENLIST
SETLATTR

rc=**DELLIST**(*list-id*<,*recursively*>);

Where...	Is type...	And represents...
rc	N	Whether the operation was successful: 0 if successful $\neq 0$ if not successful
list-id	N	The identifier of the list to be deleted. An invalid *list-id* produces an error condition.
recursively	C	Whether to recursively delete all the list's sublists and all sublists of its sublists. **'N'** Sublists are not deleted. (Default) **'Y'** Sublists are also deleted.

Details

A list's contents cannot be retrieved after the list is deleted.

If *recursively* is **'Y'**, DELLIST recursively deletes all sublists that do not have the NODELETE attribute. For sublists that have the NODELETE attribute, the sublist identifiers are removed from the deleted list but the sublist is not deleted. Thus, you should store list identifiers for sublists in another list or in an SCL variable so that you can access the lists later. All local lists not explicitly deleted are deleted when the application ends, at the same time when SCL closes open data sets and files.

Recursively deleting a list deletes all of its sublists even if they are referenced in other SCL lists or by other SCL variables. If you do not want a list to be deleted when it is a sublist item in a deleted list, use SETLATTR to assign the NODELETE attribute to the sublist. See the SETLATTR function for a discussion of the NODELETE attribute.

. . . .

Delete lists when they are no longer needed in order to conserve memory. Typically, a DELLIST statement is placed in the termination section (TERM or FSETERM) of the program. Although the program that creates a list is most often responsible for deleting the lists it creates, it does not have to delete them unless that is the appropriate action for the application; it may return the list it created to its caller.

An error condition results if:

□ the list has the NODELETE attribute

□ the list is the local or global environment list (the lists returned by the ENVLIST function)

□ *list-id* is an object or class list identifier.

To check attributes, use HASATTR. To change attributes, use SETLATTR.

If an error condition does result, the list and/or sublists may be partially cleared, and no further items or sublists are deleted.

▶ *Caution: Be careful when deleting lists recursively because you have the potential to delete lists that are needed by other parts of the SCL program.*

DELNITEM

Deletes a named item from an SCL list

See Also:
DELITEM
DELLIST
HASATTR
LISTLEN
MAKELIST
MAKENLIST
NAMEDITEM
NAMEITEM
SETLATTR

list-id=**DELNITEM**(*list-id,name<,occurrence <,start-index<,index>>>*);

Where...	Is type...	And represents...
list-id	N	The identifier of the list from which the item is to be deleted. The function returns the list identifier that is passed in. An invalid *list-id* produces an error condition.
name	C	The name of the item to delete. Item names are converted to uppercase and trailing blanks are ignored when searching the list for a matching name. Thus, the names 'abc' and 'Abc' are converted to 'ABC'.
occurrence	N	The number of the occurrence of the named item to delete. The default is 1 for the first occurrence of the item.
start-index	N	Where in the list to begin searching for the item. By default, *start-index* is 1 (the first item). If *start-index* is positive, the search begins at position *start-index* items from the beginning of the list. If *start-index* is negative, the search begins at the item specified by ABS(*start-index*) items from the end of the list. An error condition results if the absolute value of *start-index* is zero or greater than the number of items in the list.
index	N	The variable to contain the position number of the deleted item. *index* must be initialized to a nonmissing value, or errors result.

Details

DELNITEM searches for a named item and deletes it from the list. The name of the item must match exactly in spelling although trailing blanks and case are ignored.

If *occurrence* and *start-index* are both positive or both negative, the search proceeds forward from the *start-index* item. For forward searches, the search continues only to the end of the list and does not wrap back to the front of the list. If *occurrence* or *start-index* is negative, the search is backwards. For backward searches, the search continues only to the beginning of the list and does not wrap back to the end of the list.

DELNITEM does not make a copy of the list. The delete operation is performed in place on the list. For example, the following statement deletes the first item named 'app' in the list identified by LISTID:

```
listid=delnitem(listid,'app');
```

When the item to be deleted is a sublist, DELNITEM deletes the item but not the sublist because the sublist may be referenced by other SCL variables or lists.

An error condition results if:

□ the item has the NODELETE attribute

□ the list has the NOUPDATE or FIXEDLENGTH attribute

□ the named item is not found in the list.

To check the attributes of a list or list item, use HASATTR. To change these attributes, use SETLATTR.

Example

```
a=makelist();
rc=insertc(a,'a',-1,'var1');
rc=insertc(a,'b',-1,'var2');
rc=insertc(a,'c',-1,'var1');
rc=insertc(a,'d',-1,'var2');
call putlist(a,'Before deleting',0);
pos=0;
rc=delnitem(a,'var1',2,1,pos);
put pos=;
call putlist(a,'After deleting',0);
```

The results of this program are :

```
Before deleting(VAR1='a'
                VAR2='b'
                VAR1='c'
                VAR2='d'
                )[5]
POS=3
After deleting(VAR1='a'
               VAR2='b'
               VAR2='d'
               )[5]
```

Note: [5] is the listid assigned when this example was tested and may be different each time it is run.

DELOBS

Deletes an observation from a SAS data set

See Also:
APPEND
DATALISTC
DATALISTN
FETCH
FETCHOBS
LOCATEC
LOCATEN

sysrc=**DELOBS**(*data-set-id*);

Where...	Is type...	And represents...
sysrc	N	Whether the operation was successful: 0 if successful ≠ 0 if not successful.
data-set-id	N	The identifier assigned when the data set was opened. If *data-set-id* is invalid, the program halts execution.

Details

You must fetch an observation before it can be deleted. Some functions that fetch an observation include FETCH, FETCHOBS, LOCATEC, LOCATEN, APPEND, DATALISTC, and DATALISTN.

Example

Delete the current observation from an open SAS data set. (The example assumes that the data set identifier returned by the OPEN function was stored in the variable MYDATAID.) If the function is unable to delete the observation, a message is displayed on the message line.

```
if (delobs(mydataid)) then _msg_=sysmsg();
```

DESCRIBE

Fills an SCL list with items of descriptive information about a SAS data set, view, or catalog entry

See Also:
ATTRC
ATTRN
ITEMTYPE
MAKENLIST

sysrc=**DESCRIBE**(*source-name,list-id<,type>*);

Where...	Is type...	And represents...

sysrc	N	Whether the operation was successful:
		  0 if successful
		
		  ≠ 0 if not successful

source-name	C	The name of the data set, view, or catalog entry.
list-id	N	The identifier of the list to contain the object's description. An invalid *list-id* produces an error condition.
type	C	The type of object to be described: **'CATALOG'** SAS catalog entry (Default) For three- or four-level names, the default entry type is PROGRAM. **'DATA'** SAS data set (Default for one- or two-level names). **'VIEW'** SAS data view.

Details

The list referenced by *list-id* must be an existing SCL list that was created with one of the SCL list functions. Because DESCRIBE replaces the previous values in the list, the same list can be used repeatedly.

The items of descriptive information are placed into the list as named items, and the names are the attributes described. Only the named attributes that appear in the list are filled in.

The following table shows the attributes that DESCRIBE can place in an SCL list:

If *type* is ...	The items named in the list are ...
DATA or VIEW	any attribute returned by the ATTRN and ATTRC functions.
CATALOG	DESC, for the description of the catalog DATE, for the SAS date value.

For catalog entries, if a numeric or list item named DATE exists in the list, DESCRIBE sets that item's values to a SAS data value. Otherwise, if DATE is character, DESCRIBE assigns a formatted date string using the MMDDYY8. format. Use ITEMTYPE to determine the type of a list item.

Example

Create an SCL list containing the items named DESC and DATE. DESCRIBE fills the DESC and DATE items in the list with information about the catalog entry SASUSER.MYCAT.A.PROGRAM.

```
desc_list=makenlist('L','DESC','DATE');
rc=describe('SASUSER.MYCAT.A.PROGRAM',desc_list,'CATALOG');
```

DEVLIST

Displays a selection list of graphic hardware devices and returns user selections

See Also:
COLORLIST

selections=**DEVLIST**(*catalog-name,device<,message<,autoclose <,num-sel>>>*);

Where...	Is type...	And represents...
selections	C	One or more user selections from the list, or blank if the selection list window is closed and no selections are made.
catalog-name	C	The catalog listing the devices. Usually the catalog SASHELP.DEVICES is used as *catalog-name*.
device	C	The type of device to be listed:
		'CAMERA' lists device catalog entries for film recorders.
		'DEFAULT' returns the current device name, description, and type instead of displaying a list.
		'EXPORT' lists device catalog entries for device drivers that produce a graphics stream file.
		'MONITOR' lists device catalog entries for video displays.
		'PLOTTER' lists device catalog entries for plotters.
		'PRINTER' lists device catalog entries for printers.
message	C	Text for a message displayed above the selection list. The default message tells users to make up to the number of selections specified in *num-sel*.
autoclose	C	Whether the selection list window closes automatically after a user makes a selection when only one choice is allowed:
		'Y' for the window to close automatically. (Default)
		'N' for the window to close only when the user explicitly closes it.
		This option is ignored when *num-sel* is not 1. However, use ' ' as a placeholder if you are also specifying a value for *num-sel*.
num-sel	N	The maximum number of items a user can select from the list. To display the list for information purposes only (no selections allowed), specify **0**. To specify an unlimited number of selections, use a value larger than the number of available selections such as 9999.

Details

The value in *selections* consists of a 40-character description, an 8-character device name, and an 8-character device type. For details on graphic device drivers, see *SAS/GRAPH Software: Reference.*

You can provide a default or initial selected value in the list by providing a value for the *selections* variable prior to calling DEVLIST. If *selections* contains valid entry names when the function is invoked, those names are automatically designated as selected when the selection list is displayed.

If a user closes the selection list window without making a selection, DEVLIST returns a blank value unless there was an initial value for the *selections* variable before DEVLIST was called.

When multiple selections are allowed, *selections* contains the first value selected from the list. However, the values for all selections can be returned in the current result list, if one is available. The current result list is a special SCL list that is automatically filled with the values selected from a selection list. To create a current result list, use the MAKELIST function to create it and the CURLIST function to designate it as the current result list. The current result list must exist before you call DEVLIST.

When DEVLIST is invoked, the current result list is cleared. After DEVLIST is invoked, the result list contains the following named items:

Element	Type	Description
TAG	C	Identifies the list as one created by the DEVLIST function.
COUNT	N	Number of elements selected. If no selections are made, or if users issue a CANCEL command in the selection list window, COUNT is 0.
DESC	C	Device description. There is one DESC element for each selection.
DEVICE	C	Device name. There is one DEVICE element for each selection.
TYPE	C	Device type. There is one TYPE element for each selection.

Examples

Display a list of devices of the type PRINTER available in the catalog SASHELP.DEVICES. After the user selects one device from the list, the program extracts the individual items of information returned by DEVLIST with the substring function.

```
select=devlist('sashelp.devices','printer', 'Select a device.');
descript=substr(select,1,40);
device=substr(select,41,8);
devtype=substr(select,49,8);
```

Use the current result list to process multiple selections:

```
listid=makelist();
rc=curlist(listid);
selection=devlist('sashelp.devices','printer','Select a device',' ',3);
n=getnitemn(listid,'COUNT');
do i=1 to n;
   descript=getnitemc(listid,'DESC',i);
```

```
        device=getnitemc(listid,'DEVICE',i);
        devtype=getnitemc(listid,'TYPE',i);
        put descript= device= devtype=;
    end;
```

DINFO

Returns information about a directory

See Also:
DOPTNAME
DOPTNUM
FINFO
FOPTNAME
FOPTNUM

attribute=**DINFO**(*directory-id,info-item*);

Where...	Is type...	And represents...
attribute	C	The value of the information item (blank if the value of the *info-item* argument is invalid).
directory-id	N	The identifier assigned when the directory was opened. If *directory-id* is invalid, the program halts execution.
info-item	C	The information item to be retrieved.

Details

DINFO returns the value of a system-dependent directory parameter. The information available varies according to the operating system. Refer to the SAS documentation for your host operating system for information about system-dependent directory parameters.

Use DOPTNAME to determine the names of the available system-dependent directory information items. Use DOPTNUM to determine the number of directory information items available.

Example

Open the directory MYDIR, determine the number of directory information items available, and retrieve the value of the last one:

```
rc=filename('mydir','physical-name');
did=dopen('mydir');
numopts=doptnum(did);
foption=doptname(did,numopts);
charval=dinfo(did,foption);
rc=dclose(did);
```

DIRLIST

Opens a selection list window of members of a SAS data library and returns a user's selections

See Also:
CATLIST
FILELIST
LIBLIST

selections=**DIRLIST**(*lib-spec,member-type,num-sel,prefix* <,*data-set-type*<,*sel-excl* <,*message*<,*autoclose*>>>>);

Where...	Is type...	And represents...
selections	C	One or more user selections. Multiple selections are separated by blanks.
lib-spec	C	One or more librefs associated with specific SAS data libraries. To include or exclude SAS data libraries, use one of the name specification styles in Table 20.6. By default, SASHELP is not included in the selection window.
member-type	C	One or more types of SAS data library members. For example, a few common *member-types* are DATA, VIEW, and CATALOG. To include or exclude specific *member-types*, use one of the name specification styles in Table 20.6.
num-sel	N	The maximum number of items a user can select from the list. To display the list for information purposes only (no selections allowed), specify **0**. To specify an unlimited number of selections, use a value larger than the number of available selections such as **9999**.
prefix	C	Whether names displayed in the list contain librefs: **'Y'** Selected names are returned as *libref.name*. **'N'** or **' '** Selected names are returned as *name*.
data-set-type	C	One or more SAS data set types. By default the selection list displays members of all SAS data set types. To include or exclude specific data set types, use one of the name specification styles in Table 20.6. This argument is ignored unless **DATA** is one of the values of *member-type*. For information on data set types, see the description of the TYPE= data set option in *SAS Language: Reference*, page 730, or issue the command HELP DSOPTION.
sel-excl	C	One or more SAS data library members to include or exclude from the list. Specify one form in Table 20.6. If *prefix* is **'N'**, then specify the name here as *member*. If *prefix* is **'Y'**, then specify the name here as *libref.member*.
message	C	Text for a message displayed above the selection list. The default message tells users to make up to the number of selections specified in *num-sel*.
autoclose	C	Whether the selection list window closes automatically after a user makes a selection when only one choice is allowed: **'Y'** for the window to close automatically. (Default)

Where...	Is type...	And represents...
	'**N**'	for the window to close only when the user explicitly closes it.

This option is ignored when *num-sel* is not 1.

Table 20.6
Name Specifications

To specify...	Use...
One or more specific names	names separated with a space.
All names	an asterisk ('*****') or null string ('**'**')
All names *except* those listed after the NOT sign	a NOT sign (¬ **or** ^) followed by one or more names.

Details

You can provide a default or initial selected value in the list by providing a value for the *selections* variable prior to calling DIRLIST. If *selections* contains valid values when DIRLIST is executed, those names are automatically designated as selected when the selection list window opens.

If a user closes the selection list window without making a selection, DIRLIST returns a blank value unless there was an initial value for the *selections* variable before DIRLIST was called.

The values for all selections can be returned in the current result list, if one is available. The current result list is a special SCL list that is automatically filled with the values selected from a selection list. To create a current result list, use the MAKELIST function to create it and the CURLIST function to designate it as the current result list. The current result list must exist before you call the DIRLIST function.

When the function is invoked, the current result list is cleared. After DIRLIST is invoked, the current result list contains the following named elements:

Element	Type	Description
TAG	C	Identifier that the list was created by the DIRLIST function.
COUNT	N	Number of elements selected. If a user does not make any selections or issues a CANCEL command in the selection list window, COUNT is 0.
NAME	C	Name of each selected library member. If *prefix* is '**Y**', the libref is appended to the beginning of each name. There is one NAME element for each selection made.
DESC	C	Description of each selected library member. There is one DESC element for each selection made.
TYPE	C	Type of each selected library member. There is one TYPE element for each selection made.

If the SAS system option DETAILS is set to on, the value for DESC is the data set label.

Example

Display a selection list containing the SAS data sets in the SAS libraries MYLIB1 and MYLIB2 except MYLIB1.ANSWERS and enable users to select up to three data set names. The selections are retrieved from the current environment list using GETNITEMC.

```
listid=makelist();
rc=curlist(listid);
selections=dirlist('mylib1 mylib2','data',3,'Y',' ','^ mylib1.answers');
n=getnitemn(listid,'COUNT');
do i=1 to n;
   member=getnitemc(listid,'NAME',i);
   descript=getnitemc(listid,'DESC',i);
   memtype=getnitemc(listid,'TYPE',i);
   put member= descript= memtype=;
end;
```

DISPLAYED

Reports whether a field or FRAME object is currently visible

See Also:
ERROR
ERROROFF
ERRORON
FIELD
MODIFIED

rc=**DISPLAYED**(*wvar-name*);

Where...	Is type...	And represents...
rc	N	Whether the field or FRAME entry object in the window is visible: 1 if visible 0 if not visible.
wvar-name	C	The field or FRAME entry object in the window. This name cannot be an element of an array or an expression. If *wvar-name* is invalid, the program halts execution.

Details

In SAS/AF applications, DISPLAYED reports that a variable is not visible on the current screen or if the variable has the NONDISPLAY attribute. In FSEDIT, DISPLAYED tells you if a variable is visible on the current screen of a multiscreen application, regardless of whether the variable has the NONDISPLAY attribute.

This function is useful in multiscreen applications in which the application developer wants to be on a specific screen for a variable. DISPLAYED reports if the specified variable is visible on the current screen of a multiscreen application.

If the variable is not currently displayed, your application can use the EXECCMD routine to issue scrolling commands to change the screen position or to issue scrolling commands specific to the procedure (for example, the =*n* command in the FSEDIT procedure).

The field or FRAME entry object cannot be an element of an array. To report this information for an array element, use FIELD instead.

FRAME entry objects can also use the _IS_DISPLAYED_ or _IS_HIDDEN_ method.

Example

Test whether the variable SALARY is displayed on the current screen of an FSEDIT application, and, if not, issue an FSEDIT scrolling command to display the screen containing the variable:

```
if (displayed(salary)=0) then call execcmd('=salary');
```

DISPLAY

Runs an entry created with SAS/AF software

See Also:
CBT
ENTRY
GOTO
NOCHANGE

CALL DISPLAY(*entry<,parameters>*);

Where...	Is type...	And represents...
entry	C	A display entry created using SAS/AF software (FRAME, PROGRAM, SCL, MENU, HELP, or CBT), specified as:
		entry-name
		for a PROGRAM entry in the current catalog.
		entry.type
		for an entry of the specified type in the current catalog.
		libref.catalog.entry
		for a PROGRAM entry in the specified catalog.
		libref.catalog.entry.type
		for an entry of a specified type in a specified catalog.
parameters	N|C	Parameters to pass to the called entry. You can pass parameters to FRAME, PROGRAM, and SCL entries. For the called entry to accept these parameters, it must contain a corresponding ENTRY statement.

Details

DISPLAY can run a FRAME, PROGRAM, SCL, MENU, HELP, or CBT entry and make it the active entry. When the called entry is exited, control returns to the calling program.

You can pass parameters to a FRAME, PROGRAM, or SCL entry. Parameters can be numeric constants, character constants, variables, expressions, and array variables.

Using CALL DISPLAY without any options in the associated ENTRY statement requires a strict correspondence between CALL DISPLAY parameters and ENTRY statement arguments. The arguments and parameters must agree in number, data type, and relative position. If you pass an incorrect number of parameters or a parameter of the incorrect type, SCL halts the execution of the program. The argument-parameter correspondence is less restrictive when you use the options REST=, ARGLIST=, and OPTIONAL= in the ENTRY statement. See ENTRY for examples of these options.

The parameter names in the CALL DISPLAY do not have to match the argument names in the ENTRY statement.

Parameters are passed in one of three ways:

Call-by-reference

passes window variables and local variables and allows values to be returned to the calling program. This method allows the called program to modify values and then return them. If you do not want to return the new values, use the NOCHANGE routine. An example of call-by-reference is

```
array employee{50};
call display('b.program',var1,name,field2,employee{1});
```

Call-by-value

is used for all numeric constants, character constants, and expressions. It does not allow values to be returned to the calling program. An example of call-by-value is

```
call display('b.program',100,'hello',x+y);
```

Note: Use CALL CBT to run CBT applications because it provides more options used by CBT entries. In general, you may want to use CALL GOTO instead of CAL DISPLAY if you do not need control to return to the calling program. This may be helpful for applications with memory constraints.

Example Passing Parameters

Use CALL DISPLAY in program X to pass parameters to program Y. Program Y then declares these arguments with an ENTRY statement. Variables I and S are call-by-reference parameters, and the constant 1 is a call-by-value parameter.

X.SCL contains the program:

```
INIT:
  s = 'abcd';
  i = 2;
  call display('y.frame', i, 1, s);
    /* At this point, after the return from Y, i=7, and s='abcde' */
  put i= s=;
return;


MAIN:
TERM:
 return;
```

Y.SCL contains the program:

```
entry j c 8 str $;
init:
 j = length(str) + c;
 j = j + 2;
 str = str || 'e';
 c = 2;
 return;
```

The following correspondence occurs:

□ The value of variable I passes to variable J.

□ The literal value 1 passes to variable C.

□ The value of variable S passes to variable STR.

After program Y runs, the values of variables J and STR are returned to the variables I and S respectively. The variable C cannot return a value, however, since the corresponding parameter in the CALL DISPLAY is a constant.

Example Passing Array Parameters by Reference

Use CALL DISPLAY to pass array parameters by reference. In this example, the variables S and A are call-by-reference parameters, and the constant 4 is a call-by-value parameter.

Note: Because of the array reference parameter ARR{*}, this example will only work in Release 6.10 and later.

X.SCL contains the program:

```
array a{4} 8;
INIT:

  a{1} = 1; a{2} = 2; a{3} = 3; a{4} = 4;
  s = 0;
  call display('y.frame', s, a, 4);
     /* At this point, after the return from Y,      */
     /* s=10, a{1}=2, a{2}=4, a{3}=6, a{4}=8.  */
  put s= a=;
return;


MAIN:
TERM:
return;
```

Y.SCL contains the program:

```
array arr{*} 8;
entry sum arr len 8;

INIT:
  do i = 1 to len;
     sum = sum + arr{i};
     arr{i} = 2 * arr{i};
  end;
return;
```

The following correspondence occurs:

□ The value of variable S passes to variable SUM..

□ The array variable A is passed to the array variable ARR.

□ The literal value 4 passes to variable LEN.

After program Y runs, the value of the variable SUM is returned to the variable S, and the values in the array ARR are returned to the corresponding values in the array A. The variable LEN cannot return a value, however, since the corresponding parameter in the CALL DISPLAY is a constant.

DMWINDOW

Sets the color and highlighting for lines in the Display Manager OUTPUT and LOG windows

rc=**DMWINDOW**(*window-name,line-type,color,attribute*);

Where...	Is type...	And represents...
rc	N	Whether the operation was successful: 0 if successful ≠ 0 if not successful.
window-name	C	The window to be assigned the colors and display attributes: 'OUTPUT' the OUTPUT window 'LOG' the LOG window
line-type	C	The output area to which the colors and highlighting attributes are to be assigned: 'DATA' Data line 'ERROR' Error line 'NOTES' Notes line (LOG window only) 'SOURCE' Source line (LOG window only) 'WARNING' Warning line (LOG window only) 'BYLINE' Byline line (OUTPUT window only) 'HEADER' Header line (OUTPUT window only) 'TITLE' Title line (OUTPUT window only)
color	C	A color name. SASCOLOR window elements can also be used for *color*. For more information on colors and a list of colors, see *color* in "Common Arguments" on page 222.
attribute	C	A display attribute. If you specify a SASCOLOR window element for *color*, *attribute* is ignored because the SASCOLOR window element contains a display attribute. For more information on display attributes and a list of them, see *attribute* in "Common Arguments" on page 222.

Details

The device must support the color and highlighting attribute in order for SAS to enable it.

Example

Set the highlighting attribute of the title line in the OUTPUT window to blinking and its color to yellow:

```
rc=dmwindow('output','title','yellow','blinking');
```

DNUM

Returns the number of members in a directory

See Also:
DREAD

nval=**DNUM**(*directory-id*);

Where...	Is type...	And represents...
nval	N	The number of members in the directory.
directory-id	N	The identifier assigned when the directory was opened. If *directory-id* is invalid, the program halts execution.

Details

You can use DNUM to determine the highest possible member number that can be passed to DREAD.

Example

Open the directory MYDIR, determine the number of members, and close the directory:

```
rc=filename('mydir','physical-name ');
did=dopen('mydir');
memcount=dnum(did);
rc=dclose(did);
```

DO

Designates a group of statements to be executed as a unit

SAS Statement with limitations in SCL

See also:
CONTINUE
LEAVE

DO
   do-clause;
END;

The forms of the *do-clause* that are supported are:

iterative DO	executes a group of statements repetitively based on the value of an index variable. However, the form DO *i=item-1*, ..., *item-n* is not supported.
DO UNTIL	executes a group of statements repetitively until a condition is true.
DO WHILE	executes a group of statements repetitively as long as a condition is true.

The form DO OVER is not supported.

When you need to force the statements in a DO group to stop executing, you can use the SCL statements CONTINUE or LEAVE.

For details on the DO statement in SAS language, see *SAS Language: Reference.*

DOPEN

Opens a directory

See Also:
DCLOSE
FOPEN
MOPEN

*directory-id=***DOPEN**(*fileref*);

Where...	Is type...	And represents...
directory-id	N	The identifier for the directory: 0 if the directory could not be opened > 0 if identifier assigned. If you try to use an invalid *directory-id* with other functions, the program halts execution.
fileref	C	The fileref assigned to the directory.

Details

DOPEN opens a directory and returns a directory identifier value (a number greater than 0) used to identify the open directory to other SCL functions. The directory to be opened must be identified by a fileref. You must associate a fileref with the directory before calling DOPEN.

You can assign filerefs using the FILENAME statement or the FILENAME function in SCL. Under some operating systems, you can also assign filerefs using system commands.

■ **Host Information** . . . .
The term *directory* used in the description of this function and related SCL functions refers to an aggregate grouping of files managed by the host operating system. Different host operating systems identify such groupings with different names, such as directory, subdirectory, MACLIB, or partitioned data set. Refer to the SAS documentation for your host system for details.

. . . . ■

Example

Assign the fileref **MYDIR** to a directory. (*Physical-name* represents the actual name of the directory in the form required by the host operating system.) Then open the directory, determine the number of system-dependent directory information items available, and close the directory:

```
rc=filename('mydir','physical-name ');
did=dopen('mydir');
infocnt=doptnum(did);
rc=dclose(did);
```

DOPTNAME

Returns directory attribute information

See Also:
DINFO
DOPTNUM

attribute=**DOPTNAME**(*directory-id,nval*);

Where...	Is type...	And represents...
attribute	C	The directory option. If the value of *nval* is out-of-range, the program halts and *attribute* contains the value it held prior to the program halt.
directory-id	N	The identifier assigned when the directory was opened. If *directory-id* is invalid, the program halts execution.
nval	N	The sequence number of the option.

Details

The directory must have been previously opened using DOPEN. The number, names, and nature of the directory information varies between operating systems.

The number of options available for a directory varies depending on the operating system.

Example

Open the directory with the fileref **MYDIR**, retrieve all system-dependent directory information items, write them to the SAS log, and close the directory:

```
rc=filename('mydir','physical-name');
did=dopen('mydir');
infocnt=doptnum(did);
do j=1 to infocnt;
   opt=doptname(did,j);
   put 'Directory information=' opt;
end;
rc=dclose(did);
```

DOPTNUM

Returns the number of information items available for a directory

See Also:
DINFO
DOPTNAME

num-options=**DOPTNUM**(*directory-id*);

Where...	Is type...	And represents...
num-options	N	The number of available directory information items. If an error condition occurs, the program halts and *num-options* contains the value it held prior to the program halt.
directory-id	N	The identifier assigned when the directory was opened. If *directory-id* is invalid, the program halts execution.

Details

The directory must have been previously opened using DOPEN.

Example

Retrieve the number of system-dependent directory information items available for the directory MYDIR and close the directory:

```
rc=filename('mydir','physical-file-name');
did=dopen('mydir');
infocnt=doptnum(did);
rc=dclose(did);
```

DREAD

Returns the name of a directory member

See Also:
DNUM
DOPEN

name=**DREAD**(*directory-id,nval*);

Where...	Is type...	And represents...
name	C	The name of the member, or blank if an error occurs (such as *nval* is out-of-range).
directory-id	N	The identifier assigned when the directory was opened. If *directory-id* is invalid, the program halts execution.
nval	N	The sequence number of the member.

Details

Use DNUM to determine the highest possible member number that can be passed to DREAD. The directory must have been previously opened using DOPEN.

Example

Open the directory identified by the fileref MYDIR, retrieve the number of members and place the number in the variable MEMCOUNT, retrieve the name of the last member and place the name in the variable LSTNAME, and close the directory:

```
rc=filename('mydir','physical-name');
did=dopen('mydir')
lstname='';
memcount=dnum(did);
if (memcount>0) then
    lstname=dread(did,memcount);
rc=dclose(did);
```

DROPNOTE

Deletes a note marker from a SAS data set or an external file

See Also:
FNOTE
FPOINT
NOTE
POINT

rc=**DROPNOTE**(*data-set-id*|*file-id*,*note-id*);

Where...	Is type...	And represents...
rc	N	Whether the operation was successful: 0 if successful ≠ 0 if not successful.
data-set-id|*file-id*	N	The identifier assigned when the data set or external file was opened. If *data-set-id*|*file-id* is invalid, the program halts execution.
note-id	N	The identifier assigned by the NOTE or FNOTE function. If *note-id* is an invalid value, the program halts execution.

Details

DROPNOTE deletes a marker set by NOTE or FNOTE.

Example

Open the SAS data set MYDATA, fetch the first observation, and set a note ID at the beginning of the data set. Return to the first observation by calling POINT, and then delete the note ID by calling DROPNOTE:

```
dsid=open('mydata','i');
rc=fetch(dsid);
noteid=note(dsid);
    more SCL statements
rc=point(dsid,noteid);
rc=fetch(dsid);
rc=dropnote(dsid,noteid);
```

DSID

Searches for a data set name and returns the data set identifier

Release 6.11 Feature

See Also:
OPEN

dsid=**DSID**(<*data-set-name*<,*mode*<,*nth*>>>);

Where...	Is type...	And represents...
dsid	N	The identifier for the data set, or: 0 if the data set is not currently open, is not open in the requested mode, or no *n*th open occurrence exists. < 0 if an error occurs. SYSMSG contains the error text.
data-set-name	C	The SAS data set for which you are looking. The default is _LAST_, which is the last data set created in the current SAS session. A one-level name is assumed to be a data set name in the default SAS data library, WORK. A two-level name is assumed to be *libref.data-set*.
mode	C	Whether to limit the search of SAS data sets to those open in the requested mode: `'I'` INPUT mode, allows random access if the engine supports it; otherwise, defaults to IN mode. `'IN'` INPUT mode, reads sequentially and allows revisiting observations. `'IS'` INPUT mode, reads sequentially but does not allow revisiting observations. `'N'` NEW mode, creates a new data set. `'U'` UPDATE mode, allows random access if the engine supports it; otherwise, defaults to UN mode. `'UN'` UPDATE mode, reads sequentially and allows revisiting observations. `'US'` UPDATE mode, reads sequentially but does not allow revisiting observations. `'V'` UTILITY mode, allows modification of variable attributes and indexes associated with the data set. If *mode* is not specified, DSID returns the *dsid* for the first occurrence of a *data-set-name* open in any mode. For more information on open modes, see OPEN in this chapter.
nth	N	The occurrence of *data-set-name* opened in the specified *mode* to search for. By default, the search returns the first occurrence.

Details

DSID searches all SAS data sets that are currently open. This function is useful for accessing data set identifiers across entries.

Example

Open several data sets and find the first occurrence in various modes:

```
        /* Open several data sets varying the open mode */
dsid1 = open('sasuser.class', 'I');
dsid2 = open('sasuser.class', 'U');
dsid3 = open('sasuser.class', 'U');
dsid4 = open('sasuser.houses', 'U');
dsid5 = open('sasuser.class', 'I');
dsid6 = open('sasuser.houses', 'U');
dsid7 = open('sasuser.houses', 'I');
dsid8 = open('sasuser.class', 'U');

        /* Find the first occurrence open in any mode. */
first = DSID( 'sasuser.houses' );
put first=;

        /* Find the first occurrence open in 'I' */
firstI = DSID( 'sasuser.houses', 'I' );
put firstI=;

        /* Find the second occurrence open in 'I' */
second = DSID( 'sasuser.class', 'I', 2 );
put second=;

        /* Return the fourth occurrence open in 'U' */
secondU = DSID( 'sasuser.class', 'U', 4 );
put secondU=;
```

This example produces the following output:

```
first=4
firstI=7
second=5
secondU=0
```

DSNAME

Returns the data set name associated with a data set identifier

See Also:
OPEN

■ **Release 6.11** . . . .

dataset-name=**DSNAME**(*<dsid>*);

Where...	Is type...	And represents...
dataset-name	C	The data set associated with the specified *dsid* value, or blank if an invalid value is specified for *dsid*.
dsid	C	The identifier assigned when the data set was opened. If called from FSEDIT, FSBROWSE, or FSVIEW, this value is optional. If *dsid* is not specified in an FSEDIT or FSVIEW application, DSNAME returns the name of the current data set. If *dsid* is not specified in a SAS/AF application, DSNAME returns a blank.

Details

With Release 6.11, DSNAME does not require a *dsid*. You can leave the *dsid* out in FSEDIT, FSBROWSE, and FSVIEW, and DSNAME gives information on the data set opened by the procedure.

Example

Determine the name of the SAS data set associated with the variable data-set-id and display this name on the message line:

```
_msg_ = 'The current open data set is ' || dsname( dsid ) || '.';
```

In an FSEDIT or FSVIEW SCL program, display on the command line the name of the data set currently being edited:

```
_msg_ = 'The data set being edited is ' || dsname() || '.';
```

ENDBLOCK

Closes the window created by the BLOCK function

See Also:
BLOCK

CALL ENDBLOCK();

Example

Create a menu with four choices. The first row of blocks contains two blocks with the labels Outline and Index. The second row also has two blocks with the labels Compare Files and Calendar. No third row of blocks is displayed. The memory used in displaying the menu is freed when the ENDBLOCK routine is executed and the window is closed.

```
INIT:
    choice=block('Writers Toolbox','Main Menu',6,
                 'Outline','Index','','',
                 'Compare Files','Calendar','','',
                 '','','','');
    more SCL statements
return;

MAIN:
    more SCL statements
return;

TERM:
    call endblock();
return;
```

ENDLEGEND

Closes the LEGEND window

See Also:
LEGEND
POPLEGEND
PUSHLEGEND
PUTLEGEND

CALL ENDLEGEND();

Details

If the LEGEND window is not currently displayed, the routine has no effect.

For an example using the PUTLEGEND as well as other functions that manipulate a legend window, see LEGEND.

ENDMETHOD

Ends a METHOD statement block

See Also:
METHOD statement

ENDMETHOD;

Details

The ENDMETHOD statement marks the end of a method block in an SCL program. Use ENDMETHOD with a METHOD statement to indicate a block of statements that can be called using the METHOD routine. When the method block is executed, control returns to the calling program when ENDMETHOD is encountered.

Example

End a METHOD block:

```
METHOD;
   SCL statements
endmethod;
```

ENDSUBMIT

Ends statements to be submitted to the SAS System for execution

See Also:
SUBMIT

ENDSUBMIT;

Details

The ENDSUBMIT statement marks the end of a SUBMIT block in an SCL program. Use ENDSUBMIT with SUBMIT to indicate a block of SAS statements to submit to the SAS System for execution.

The ENDSUBMIT statement instructs SCL to stop collecting statements in the PREVIEW buffer and submit the collected statements, based on the options specified for the SUBMIT statement.

Example

Use SUBMIT to invoke the PRINT procedure and ENDSUBMIT to mark the end of the SUBMIT block:

```
submit immediate;
data one;
   do x=1 to 10;
   output;
   end;
run;

proc print;
run;

endsubmit;
```

ENDTABLE

**Establishes the maximum
number of rows for a dynamic
extended table**

SAS/AF software only

See Also:
CURTOP
SETROW
TOPROW

CALL ENDTABLE();

Details

The ENDTABLE routine stops the processing of the GETROW section of a dynamic extended table. A *dynamic extended table* is a table whose maximum number of rows can vary. Call the ENDTABLE routine from the GETROW section of the SCL program when the end of the extended table has been reached.

Because you can define extended tables only in SAS/AF software, you cannot use ENDTABLE in FSEDIT or FSVIEW programs.

The ENDTABLE routine marks only the end of the table for this invocation of the GETROW label. If the user issues a scroll command, the GETROW label is driven again until ENDTABLE is called. This allows the size of the table to change dynamically.

Example

In this example, data for the extended table come from the open SAS data set indicated by the data set identifier value in the variable DSID. The _CURROW_ variable, indicating the current row of the extended table, specifies the observation to fetch. When the value of _CURROW_ exceeds the number of observations in the data set, FETCHOBS returns a nonzero value. This indicates that because the end of the extended table has been reached, ENDTABLE is called to stop processing of the GETROW label.

```
GETROW:
   SCL statements
   if (fetchobs(dsid,_currow_) =-1) then
      call endtable();
   else
      do;
         more SCL statements
      end;
return;
```

ENTRY

Receives parameters from CALL DISPLAY

For use in SAS/AF PROGRAM, SCL, and FRAME entries

See Also:
DISPLAY
NOCHANGE
METHOD

ENTRY *<argument-list><*OPTIONAL*=argument-list>*
    *<*ARGLIST*=arg-list-id* | REST*=rest-list-id>*;

Where...	Is type...	And represents...
argument-list		One or more sets of arguments, with each set specified as *var-list* $	*var-list* $ *length*	*var-list length* where

	var-list		is one or more variables to which the parameter in the corresponding position in the CALL DISPLAY statement is passed. (See the discussion of the DISPLAY routine for details.)
	$		designates the preceding variable or variables as character type.
	length		is a numeric constant that specifies the length of the preceding variable or variables. The length of a character variable does not have to match the length of the corresponding passed parameter. SCL pads or truncates as necessary. The length of a numeric variable is always 8, regardless of the specified length in the ENTRY statement.

Where...	Is type...	And represents...
arg-list-id	N	The identifier for the SCL list that will contain all the arguments passed to the entry. This includes all optional arguments.
rest-list-id	N	The identifier for the SCL list that will contain all arguments passed to the entry, which are not explicitly specified in *argument-list* for either ENTRY or OPTIONAL=.

Details

The ENTRY statement receives parameters from the CALL DISPLAY routine. When there are no options in the ENTRY statement there is a strict correspondence between CALL DISPLAY parameters and ENTRY statement arguments. The arguments and parameters must agree in number, data type, and relative position. If you pass an incorrect number of parameters or a parameter of the incorrect type, SCL halts the execution of the program. The argument-parameter correspondence is less restrictive when you use the options REST=, ARGLIST=, and OPTIONAL= in the ENTRY statement.

    OPTIONAL= specifies one or more optional arguments to be used only if the calling program supplies the corresponding parameters in the CALL DISPLAY parameter list. If they are not supplied, SCL assumes that they are all initialized to missing values.

    OPTIONAL= allows a list of optional arguments to be used only if the calling program supplies the corresponding parameters in the CALL DISPLAY parameter list. If the corresponding parameters in the CALL DISPLAY routine are not supplied, the optional arguments are initialized to missing values.

ARGLIST= and REST= allow a variable number of parameters to be passed to the ENTRY statement. You determine the types and order of the variable arguments. The lists identified by *arg-list-id* and *rest-list-id* are created automatically when the entry is called and deleted automatically when the entry ends. When arrays are passed as parameters, the array is expanded into individual items and these are inserted into the *arg-list-id* and *rest-list-id* lists. ARGLIST= and REST= are mutually exclusive, so you can use only one or the other.

The called program can modify all call-by-reference arguments that it receives. However, it cannot modify any call-by-value arguments. See DISPLAY for a description of call-by-reference and call-by-value.

By default, values for call-by-reference arguments are returned to the calling program. If you want a called program to receive values but not to return values to its calling program, use the NOCHANGE routine.

Examples

The following examples show valid ENTRY statements:

```
entry x y z 8;           /* all parameters are numeric */

entry x y z $ 20;        /* all parameters are character of length 20 */

entry x y 8 z $ 20;      /* parameters X and Y are numeric;
                            parameter X is character of length 20 */

entry x y 8 optional=z $ 20; /* Same as third example, except
                                parameter Z is optional */
```

Assume that A.PROGRAM contains the following CALL DISPLAY:

```
call display('b.program', 1, 2, 3, 4, 5);
```

If B.PROGRAM contained the following:

```
entry x y z u v 8;
INIT:
   put x= y = z= u = v=;
return;
```

the output would be:

```
X=1 Y=2 Z=3 U=4 V=5
```

If B.PROGRAM contained the following:

```
entry x y z 8 optional=u v w 8;
INIT:
   put x= y = z= u = v= w=;
return;
```

the output would be:

```
X=1 Y=2 Z=3 U=4 V=5 W=.
```

If program B contained the following:

```
entry x y z 8 optional=u v 8 arglist=1;
INIT:
   put x= y = z= u = v=;
   call putlist(1);
return;
```

the output would be:

```
X=1 Y=2 Z=3 U=4 V=5
(1 2 3 4 5) [list-id]
```

If program B contained the following:

```
entry arglist=1;
INIT:
   call putlist(1);
return;
```

the output would be:

```
(1 2 3 4 5) [list-id]
```

If program B contained the following:

```
entry x y 8 rest=1;
INIT:
   put x= y=;
   call putlist(1);
return;
```

the output would be:

```
X=1 Y=2
(3 4 5) [list-id]
```

If program B contained the following:

```
entry x y 8 optional=z 8 rest=1;
INIT:
   put x= y= z=;
   call putlist(1);
return;
```

the output would be:

```
X=1 Y=2 Z=3
(4 5) [list-id]
```

ENVLIST

Returns the list identifier of an SCL environment list

See Also:
CURLIST
DELLIST
MAKELIST
MAKENLIST

list-id=**ENVLIST**(<*env-name*>);

Where...	Is type...	And represents...
list-id	N	The identifier of the SCL environment list.
env-name	C	The environment list to return:
		`'G'` the identifier for the global environment list.
		`'L'` the identifier for the local environment list. (Default)

Details

When the SAS session begins, a global environment list is created that persists for the entire session. When a SAS/AF or SAS/FSP application begins (for example, with the AF command or FSEDIT command, respectively) a local environment list is created for that application. This local environment list persists for the duration of that application and is available to each program that runs in that application (for example, an application invoked by the DISPLAY routine).

Environment lists are special lists that can contain numeric, character, and sublist items. These items can be fetched by their names. Environment lists provide a means of creating global variables that can be shared among different SCL programs, much like macro variables. Unlike macro variables, the names in an environment list do not have to be valid SAS names, and the values in an environment list can be other lists, if you want to associate a lot of data with a single name. For example, you can read the contents of a small SAS data set into a list and place the contents in the global environment list so that other SCL programs do not have to read the data set to fetch data.

You can also insert items that do not have names.

The Local Environment List
The local environment list, which is returned by ENVLIST('L'), contains data that are available only to the current application. Each executing application has its own unique local environment list. Both the contents of an application's environment list and the list itself are deleted when the application ends.

The Global Environment List
The global environment list, which is returned by ENVLIST('G'), contains data that all SAS applications can share during the same SAS session. The data remain in the global environment list until an SCL program explicitly removes them. Thus, one application can put data into the global environment list, the application can exit, and another application can fetch the data.

You can only insert global lists into the global environment list. Global lists are those created with MAKELIST or MAKENLIST (using the 'G' visibility value) or new lists copied from other global lists. A fatal error results if you try to insert a local list into the global list.

Recommendations for Modifying Environment Lists

Although it is not required, it is strongly suggested that you only insert named items into the environment lists and that you choose names that are unambiguous. If you add items with simple names, a greater likelihood exists that other applications may unknowingly use the same name and accidentally overwrite your data.

ERROR

Reports whether a field or FRAME entry object contains an invalid value

See Also:
DISPLAYED
ERROROFF
ERRORON
FIELD
MODIFIED

rc=**ERROR**(*wvar-name*);

Where...	Is type...	And represents...
rc	N	Whether the field or FRAME entry object in the window is in error: 1 if in error 0 if not in error.
wvar-name	C	A field or FRAME entry object in the window. This argument cannot be an expression.

Details

Use ERRORON and ERROROFF to set and reset error conditions for the field or FRAME entry object.

The field or FRAME entry object cannot be an element of an array. To report this information for an array element, use FIELD instead.

FRAME entry objects can also use the _IN_ERROR_ method.

Example

Specify the CONTROL statement with the ERROR option in the INIT section of the program. The statements in the MAIN section are submitted only if the FRAME entry object OBJ1 is not in error.

```
INIT:
   control error;
return;

MAIN:
   if (error(obj1)=0) and obj1 NE _blank_ then
      submit continue;
         proc print data=&obj1;
         run;
      endsubmit;
   else
      _msg_='Nothing submitted.  Please correct error.';
return;
```

The following sequence generates a compile error because the variable DS is not a window variable but contains the name of a window variable. ERROR expects to be passed the window variable itself.

```
ds='dsname';
if (error(ds)) then
```

```
    do;
       SCL statements to handle the error condition
    end;
```

ERROROFF

Clears the error flag on one or more fields or FRAME entry objects

See Also:
CONTROL
DISPLAYED
ERROR
ERRORON
FIELD

ERROROFF *wvar-names* |_ALL_;

Where...	Is type...	And represents...
wvar-names	C	One or more fields or FRAME entry objects in the window for which to turn off the error flag, or `'_ALL_'` to turn off the error flag for all fields or FRAME entry objects.

Details

An error flag can be set by attributes assigned to fields or FRAME entry objects or with the ERRORON statement.

Use the following statement to clear the error flag for all fields or all FRAME entry objects in the window:

```
erroroff _all_;
```

Because statements in MAIN do not execute by default if a field is placed in error, use a CONTROL statement that specifies the ERROR option to enable ERROROFF to remove the error flag.

The field or FRAME entry object cannot be an element of an array. To remove the error flag for an array element, use FIELD instead.

FRAME entry objects can also use the _ERROROFF_ method.

Example

If a user enters an invalid value in the field DSNAME, this SAS/AF program resets the value of DSNAME to the default and turns off the error flag. The field DSNAME is assigned type INPUT, so the procedure checks to see whether the SAS data set exists when a user enters a value for DSNAME:

```
INIT:
   control error;
return;

MAIN:
   if (error(dsname)= 1) then
      do;
         dsname='my.default';
         erroroff dsname;
      end;
return;
```

ERRORON

Sets the error flag for one or more fields or FRAME entry objects

See Also:
CONTROL
DISPLAYED
ERROR
ERROROFF
FIELD

ERRORON *wvar-names* |_ALL_;

Where...	Is type...	And represents...
wvar-names	C	One or more fields or FRAME entry objects in the window for which to turn on the error flag, or ' **_ALL_** ' to turn the error flag on for all fields or FRAME entry objects.

Details

To set an error flag for multiple fields, specify the field names following ERRORON, separated by blanks. To set an error flag for all fields in the window, use the following statement:

```
erroron _all_;
```

To clear the error flag for one or more fields, use ERROROFF (see the preceding entry).

ERRORON causes the SCL program to execute when a user presses any key the next time the window is displayed. Any fields for which the error flag is set are marked as modified regardless of whether or not the user has changed the value in the field.

In SAS/FSP applications where a field is placed in error with ERRORON, a user can enter a new value and the error status is removed from the field and reset if the error condition is still met. In SAS/AF applications where a field is placed in error with ERRORON, entering a valid value is not enough to remove the error flag. You must use ERROROFF.

The field or FRAME entry object cannot be an element of an array. To set the error flag for an array element, use FIELD instead.

FRAME entry objects can also use the _ERRORON_ method.

Example

Check for inconsistency in data.

Suppose your application manipulates a SAS data set that contains information on employees and the number of hours they work each week. Because only weekly personnel are allowed overtime, the application should verify that all employees who work overtime hours are weekly employees.

```
if (weekly='N' and overtime>0) then
   do;
      erroron overtime;
      _msg_='Only weekly personnel can have overtime.';
      return;
   end;
```

EVENT

Reports whether a user has pressed a function or ENTER key or mouse button

See Also:
CONTROL ALLCMDS
CONTROL ALWAYS

rc=**EVENT**();

Where...	Is type...	And represents...
rc	N	Whether the operation was successful: 1 a function key, ENTER key or mouse button was pressed since the last event call. 0 a function key, ENTER key or mouse button was not pressed since the last event call.

Details

A mouse click registers as an event only when it occurs in a widget that responds to mouse events (for example, pushbuttons, check boxes, radio boxes, icons, blocks).

EVENT is useful when you want your program to continue a task while waiting for user input. For example, your application can read data from an external source and display the results. When a user presses an appropriate key, you can stop processing and handle the request.

■ **MVS and CMS** . . . . EVENT does not work on MVS and CMS and ASCII DRIVER machines. On these systems you should use the attention handler exit provided in SCL. Refer to the discussion of the BREAK option for the CONTROL statement in this chapter. ■

Example

Display the date and time until a user presses either ENTER or one of the function keys:

```
INIT:
    control allcmds;
return;

MAIN:
    if _status_ in ('C','E') then return;
    if (word(1,'U')='RUN') then
        do while(event()=0);
            datetime=datetime();
            refresh;
        end;
return;

TERM:
return;
```

The variable DATETIME is a numeric window variable with format DATETIME17.2. When a user presses ENTER or a function key, the program exits the loop and returns control to the application. In this example, when a user issues a RUN command, the loop resumes.

EVENT

Contains the type of event that occurred on a FRAME entry object

Character System Instance Variable

SAS/AF Only

See Also:
METHOD
SELF
STATUS
VALUE

Details

EVENT is a System Instance Variable. It is provided automatically by the FRAME entry in SAS/AF, but the SCL compiler does not automatically create a space for it in the SCL data vector. Because of this, you get a warning when you compile your SCL entry if you have a reference to _EVENT_. See _FRAME_ for more details on how to prevent the warning.

To use _EVENT_, you must declare it as a character variable using the LENGTH statement. If it is not declared, the following error will be printed when the _SELECT_ or _OBJECT_LABEL_ method executes.

```
ERROR: Expecting string (P), received SCL number (symbol '_EVENT_').
```

EVENT only has a valid value when a FRAME entry object's _SELECT_ or _OBJECT_LABEL_ method is executing. _EVENT_ can have one of the values shown in the following table.

EVENT Value	Description
' ' (blank)	Modification or selection
'D'	Double click
'C'	Command
'P'	Popmenu request
'S'	Selection or single click

Note that

□ An 'S' select event always precedes a 'D' double click event.

□ On mainframe terminals, a 'D' event can occur only when a user presses the ENTER key on a text entry field that has the **Selection Style** attribute of **Double mouse click**.

Example

The following _SELECT_ method prints the value of _EVENT_ when a FRAME entry object is modified.

```
length _event_ $1;

SELECT:
   method;
   put _event_=;
endmethod;
```

EXECCMD

Executes one or more commands when control returns to the application

See Also:
EXECCMDI

CALL EXECCMD(*cval*);

Where...	Is type...	And represents...
cval	C	One or more commands to execute. To specify multiple commands, place a semicolon between each command.

Details

The commands are collected until another window is displayed or SCL has finished executing and control is returned to the procedure. The commands are then submitted to the command-line processor before the next window is displayed or the current window is redisplayed.

With CONTROL ALWAYS in FSEDIT applications or CONTROL ALLCMDS in SAS/AF applications, statements in MAIN execute before a command issued with CALL EXECCMD. This behavior could introduce an infinite loop. Either execute the EXECCMD routine conditionally or specify the command using EXECCMDI with the NOEXEC parameter.

Example

Open the LIBNAME window and scroll down five items:

```
call execcmd('lib; down 5');
```

EXECCMDI

Executes one or more global commands immediately before processing the next statement, or when NOEXEC is specified, executes one nonglobal command when control returns to the application

See Also:
EXECCMD

CALL EXECCMDI(*command*<,*when*>);

Where...	Is type...	And represents...
command	C	One or more commands to execute. To specify multiple commands, place a semicolon between each command.
when	C	. . . .

Release 6.11

When the commands will be executed:

'EXEC'   executes commands in the command buffer immediately. (Default)

'NOEXEC'   executes the specified non-global command when control returns to the application. Still executes global commands immediately.

. . . .

Details

By default, the EXECCMDI routine immediately executes the specified global command or list of global commands. After executing the command, the program statement immediately following the call to the EXECCMDI routine executes. EXECCMDI is valid only in SCL applications that display a window.

By default, you should issue only display manager global commands and full-screen global commands through this routine. Any procedure-specific commands executed with EXECCMDI are ignored.

An error is displayed on the message line if the string passed to EXECCMDI is not a valid command, but the SCL program is not halted. Any statements following the call to the routine are still executed. If multiple commands are specified and one is invalid, none of the remaining commands are executed.

With the NOEXEC option, EXECCMDI allows execution of only one procedure-specific or custom command. EXECCMDI saves the command in the command buffer and does not execute the command immediately. The program statement immediately following the CALL EXECCMDI routine executes. The command in the command buffer is executed when control returns to the application. If you have multiple EXECCMDI routines that each have the NOEXEC option specified, only the command issued by the last EXECCMDI routine is executed. The previous commands are cleared. The NOEXEC option does not alter the way global commands are handled. Global commands are still executed immediately.

With CONTROL ALWAYS in FSEDIT applications or CONTROL ALLCMDS in SAS/AF applications, EXECCMDI with the NOEXEC option issued from MAIN tells SAS not to go through statements in MAIN again before executing the procedure-specific or custom command specified. This is different from an EXECCMD routine issued from MAIN, which would go through statements in MAIN again before executing the specified command.

We do not recommend combining execution of EXECCMD and EXECCMDI routines because the order of execution may be unexpected.

Example 1

Ensure that the window is the correct size when the application runs:

```
INIT:
    call execcmdi('zoom off');
return;
```

Example 2

From an FSEDIT SCREEN entry, open CONFIRM.FRAME to confirm the delete request before the observation is actually deleted:

```
FSEINIT:
    control always;
    length confirm $ 3;
return;

INIT:
return;

MAIN:
    if word(1, 'U') =: 'DEL' then
        do;
            call display('confirm.frame', confirm);
            if confirm = 'YES' then call execcmdi('delete', 'noexec');
        end;
return;

TERM:
return;
```

CONFIRM.FRAME has two push button objects, YES and NO, and is controlled by the following program:

```
 entry confirm $ 3;

YES:
    confirm = 'YES';
    _status_='H';
return;

NO:
    confirm = 'NO';
    _status_='H';
 return;
```

EXIST

Verifies the existence of a SAS data library member

See Also:
CEXIST
FEXIST
FILEEXIST

rc=**EXIST**(*member-name<,member-type>*);

Where...	Is type...	And represents...
rc	N	Whether the library member exists: 1 if the library member exists 0 if *member-name* does not exist or *member-type* is invalid.
member-name	C	The SAS data library member.
member-type	C	The type of SAS data library member: ACCESS an access descriptor created using SAS/ACCESS software. CATALOG a SAS catalog or catalog entry. DATA a SAS data file. (Default) VIEW a SAS data view.

Details

If *member-name* is blank or a null string, EXIST verifies the existence of the member specified by the system variable _LAST_. If *member-type* contains an invalid value, EXIST returns the value 0. Use CEXIST to verify the existence of an entry in a catalog.

Example

Call the FSEDIT function only if the SAS data set, specified in the variable DSNAME, exists. If the data set does not exist, display a message on the message line:

```
if (exist(dsname)) then call fsedit(dsname);
else _msg_='Data set '||dsname||' does not exist.';
```

Verify the existence of the SAS data view TEST.MYVIEW:

```
rc=exist('test.myview','view');
```

FAPPEND

Appends a record to the end of an external file

See Also:
DOPEN
FGET
FOPEN
FPUT
FWRITE
MOPEN

sysrc=**FAPPEND**(*file-id*<,*cc*>);

Where...	Is type...	And represents...
sysrc	N	Whether the operation was successful: 　0　if successful 　$\neq$ 0　if not successful.
file-id	N	The identifier assigned when the file was opened. If *file-id* is invalid, the program halts execution.
cc	C	A carriage-control character: *blank* indicates that the record starts a new line.

       '0' skips one blank line before this new line.

       '-' skips two blank lines before this new line.

       '1' specifies that the line starts a new page.

       '+' specifies that the line overstrikes a previous line.

       'P' specifies that the line is a terminal prompt.

       '=' specifies that the line contains carriage control information.

       all else
         specifies that the line record starts a new line.

Details

FAPPEND adds the record currently contained in the File Date Buffer (FDB) to the end of an external file.

■ **MVS** . . . .　Records cannot be appended to partitioned data sets.
. . . . ■

Example

Assign the fileref **MYFILE** to an external file and attempt to open the file with the fileref **MYFILE**. If the file is successfully opened, append a record and then close the file:

```
rc=filename('myfile','physical-filename');
fid=fopen('myfile','a');
if (fid>0) then
   do;
      rc=fput(fid,'Data for the new record');
      rc=fappend(fid);
      rc=fclose(fid);
   end;
else
   do;
      SCL statements for the unsuccessful open of the file
   end;
```

FCLOSE

Closes an external file, directory, or directory member

sysrc=**FCLOSE**(*file-id*);

See Also:
DCLOSE
DOPEN
FOPEN
MOPEN

Where...	Is type...	And represents...
sysrc	N	Whether the operation was successful: 0 if successful $\neq 0$ if not successful.
file-id	N	The identifier assigned when the file was opened. If *file-id* is invalid, the program halts execution.

Example

Assign the fileref MYFILE to an external file. (*Physical-filename* represents the actual name of the external file in the form required by the host operating system.) Open the file. If the file is successfully opened, indicated by a positive value in the variable FID, the program reads the first record and then closes the file.

```
rc=filename('myfile', 'physical-filename');
fid=fopen('myfile');
if (fid>0) then
   do;
      rc=fread(fid);
      rc=fclose(fid);
   end;
else
   do;
      _msg_=sysmsg();
      return;
   end;
rc=filename('myfile','');
```

FCOL

Returns the current column position in the File Data Buffer (FDB)

See Also:
FPOS
FPUT
FWRITE

col-num=**FCOL**(*file-id*);

Where...	Is type...	And represents...
col-num	N	The current column position.
file-id	N	The identifier assigned when the file was opened. If *file-id* is invalid, the program halts execution.

Example

Assign the fileref **MYFILE** to an external file. (*Physical-filename* represents the actual name of the external file in the form required by the host operating system.) Attempt to open the file. If the file is successfully opened, indicated by a positive value in the variable FID, put more data into the FDB relative to position POS, write the record, and close the file. Use FCOL combined with FPOS to manipulate data in the FDB.

```
rc=filename('myfile','physical-filename');
fid=fopen('myfile','o');
if (fid>0) then
    do;
        record='This is data for the record.';
        rc=fread(fid);
        rc=fput(fid,record);
        pos=fcol(fid);
        rc=fpos(fid,pos+1);
        rc=fput(fid,'more data');
        rc=fwrite(fid);
        rc=fclose(fid);
    end;
rc=filename('myfile','');
```

The record written to the external file is

```
This is data for the record. more data
```

FDELETE

Deletes an external file

See Also:
FEXIST
FILENAME

sysrc=**FDELETE**(*fileref*);

Where...	Is type...	And represents...

sysrc	N	Whether the operation was successful:
		  0 if successful
		
		  $\neq$ 0 if not successful.

fileref	C	The fileref assigned to the external file to be deleted (up to eight characters).

Details

The file must be identified with a fileref. You must associate a fileref with the external file before calling FDELETE.

■ **MVS** . . . . This function is not supported on the MVS operating system prior to Release 6.07.
. . . . ■

You can assign filerefs using the FILENAME statement or the FILENAME function in SCL. Under some operating systems, you can also assign filerefs using system commands.

Example

Generate a fileref for an external file in the variable FNAME. (*Physical-filename* represents the actual name of the external file in the form required by the host operating system.) Then call FDELETE to delete the file and call the FILENAME function again to deassign the fileref:

```
length fname $ 8;
fname=' ';
rc=filename(fname,'physical-filename');
if (rc=0) and (fexist(fname)) then
   rc=fdelete(fname);
rc=filename(fname,'');
```

FETCH

Reads the next nondeleted observation from a SAS data set into the Data Set Data Vector (DDV)

See Also:
APPEND
FETCHOBS
GETVARC
GETVARN
LOCATEC
LOCATEN
PUTVARC
PUTVARN
SET
UPDATE

sysrc=**FETCH**(*data-set-id* <,'NOSET'>);

Where...	Is type...	And represents...
sysrc	N	Whether the operation was successful: 0 if successful ≠ 0 if not successful − 1 if the end of the data set is reached
data-set-id	N	The identifier assigned when the data set was opened. If *data-set-id* is invalid, the program halts execution.
'NOSET'	C	The instruction to prevent the automatic passing of SAS data set variable values to SCL variables even if the SET routine has been called.

Details

FETCH skips observations marked for deletion. When a WHERE clause is active, the function reads the next observation that meets the WHERE condition.

If the SET routine has previously been called, the values for any data set variables that are also window or SCL variables for the application are automatically passed from the DDV to the SCL Data Vector (SDV). To temporarily override this behavior so that fetched values are not automatically copied to the SDV, use the NOSET option.

Example

Fetch the next observation from the SAS data set MYDATA. If the end of the data set is reached or if an error occurs, SYSMSG retrieves the appropriate message and displays it on the message line.

```
INIT:
   dsid=open('mydata','i');
return;

MAIN:
   rc=fetch(dsid);
   if rc then _msg_=sysmsg();
   else
      do;
         more SCL statements
      end;
return;

TERM:
   rc=close(dsid);
return;
```

FETCHOBS

Reads a specified observation from a SAS data set into the Data Set Data Vector

See Also:
APPEND
FETCH
GETVARC
GETVARN
LOCATEC
LOCATEN
PUTVARC
PUTVARN
SET
UPDATE

sysrc=**FETCHOBS**(*data-set-id,obs-number<,options>*);

Where...	Is type...	And represents...
sysrc	N	Whether the operation was successful: 0 if successful $\neq$ 0 if not successful − 1 if the end of the data set is reached
data-set-id	N	The identifier assigned when the data set was opened. If *data-set-id* is invalid, the program halts execution.
obs-number	N	The number of the observation to read.
options	C	One or more options, separated by blanks:

    'ABS' the value of *obs-number* is absolute; that is, deleted observations are counted.

    'NOSET' The instruction to prevent the automatic passing of SAS data set variable values to SCL variables even if the SET routine has been called.

Details

If SET has previously been called, the values for any data set variables that are also window or SCL variables for the application are automatically passed from the DDV to the SCL Data Vector (SDV) with FETCHOBS. You can use NOSET in the FETCHOBS function to temporarily override this behavior so that fetched values are not automatically copied to the SDV.

FETCHOBS treats the observation value as a relative observation number unless the ABS option is specified. It may or may not coincide with the physical observation number on disk. For example, the function skips observations marked for deletion. When a WHERE clause is active, the function counts only observations that meet the WHERE condition.

If *obs-number* is less than 0, the function returns an error condition. If *obs-number* is greater than the number of observations in the SAS data set, an 'End of file' warning is returned.

Example

Fetch the tenth observation from the SAS data set MYDATA. If the end of the data set is reached, a message to that effect is displayed on the message line. If an error occurs, the SYSMSG function retrieves the error message and displays it on the message line.

```
rc=fetchobs(mydataid,10);
if (rc=-1) then _msg_='End of data set has been reached.';
if (rc ne 0) then _msg_=sysmsg();
```

FEXIST

Verifies the existence of an external file associated with a fileref

See Also:
EXIST
FILEEXIST
FILENAME
FILEREF

rc=**FEXIST**(*fileref*);

Where...	Is type...	And represents...
rc	N	Whether the operation was successful: 1 if successful
		0 if not successful, or there was no logical assignment for the fileref.
fileref	C	The fileref assigned to the external file.

Details

You can assign filerefs using the FILENAME statement or the FILENAME function in SCL. Under some operating systems, you can also assign filerefs using system commands. See FILEEXIST to verify the existence of a file based on its physical name.

Example

Verify the existence of an external file for a fileref that the user enters in the field for the window variable FREF. A message informs the user whether the file exists.

```
if (fexist(fref)) then
   _msg_='The file identified by the fileref '||fref||' exists.';
else
   _msg_=sysmsg();
```

FGET

Copies data from the File Data Buffer (FDB)

See Also:
FPOS
FREAD
FSEP

rc=**FGET**(*file-id,cval<,length>*);

Where...	Is type...	And represents...
rc	N	Whether the operation was successful: 0 if successful − 1 if the end of the FDB was reached or no more tokens were available.
file-id	N	The identifier assigned when the file was opened. If *file-id* is invalid, the program halts execution.
cval	C	A character variable to hold the data.
length	N	The number of characters to retrieve from the FDB.

Details

FGET copies data from the FDB into a character variable. If *length* is specified, only the specified number of characters is retrieved (or the number of characters remaining in the buffer if that number is less). If *length* is omitted, all characters in the FDB from the current column position to the next delimiter are returned. The default delimiter is a blank. The delimiter is not retrieved (see FSEP for more information on delimiters).

After FGET is executed, the column pointer is automatically moved to the next read position in the FDB.

Example

Assign the fileref MYFILE to an external file. (*Physical-filename* represents the actual name of the external file in the form required by the host operating system.) Then attempt to open the file. If the file is successfully opened, read the first record, retrieve the first token of the record and store it in the variable MYSTRING, and then close the file:

```
rc=filename('myfile','physical-filename');
fid=fopen('myfile');
if (fid>0) then
   do;
      rc=fread(fid);
      rc=fget(fid,mystring);
      put mystring;
      rc=fclose(fid);
   end;
rc=filename('myfile','');
```

FIELD

Performs an action on or reports the state of fields or FRAME entry objects

See Also:
ALARM
CURSOR
DISPLAYED
ERROR
ERROROFF
ERRORON
HOME
MODIFIED
PROTECT
UNPROTECT

rc=**FIELD**(*action*<,*wvar-name-1*<,*wvar-name-2*<,*wvar-name-3*>>>);

Where...	Is type...	And represents...
rc	N	Whether the action was successful. The return value is dependent on the action.
action	C	An action, from Table 20.7.
wvar-name-1,. . .,*wvar-name-3*	C	A character variable or expression whose value is one or more fields or FRAME entry objects in the window, separated by spaces. At least one name is required for all actions except ALARM, BLOCKCUROFF, BLOCKCURON, CURSCREEN, HOME, NSCREEN, and SMOOTHSCRL.

Table 20.7 also includes the corresponding methods that can be used in FRAME entries. Methods are documented in *SAS/AF Software: FRAME Entry Usage and Reference.*

Table 20.7   *Actions for the FIELD Function*

Action	Description
ALARM	sounds the bell. This action has a corresponding SCL statement.
BLOCKCUROFF	turns the block cursor off so fields or text entry objects are not highlighted when a user TABS or cursors to them.
BLOCKCURON	turns the block cursor on, which causes input fields to be highlighted when the cursor is on the field or text entry object.
COLOR *color* <*attribute*>	changes the color and display attribute of a field, text entry object, or text label object in the window. SASCOLOR window elements can be used for *color*. If you specify a SASCOLOR window element for *color*, *attribute* is not allowed because the SASCOLOR window element contains a display attribute. For more information on colors and display attributes and a list of them, see *color* in "Common Arguments" on page 222. FRAME entry objects can also use _SET_COLOR_.
COLUMN	returns the column where a field or FRAME entry object is located. This option is valid only in SAS/AF software. FRAME entry objects can also use the _COLUMN_ method.
CUROBS	returns the current observation number for FSEDIT and FSVIEW for the field specified.
CURSOR	positions the cursor in the field or FRAME entry object. If more than one field or object is specified, the cursor is positioned in the last specified. This action has a corresponding SCL statement. FRAME entry objects can also use the _CURSOR_ method.

Action	Description
CURSCREEN	returns the current screen number. For SAS/AF software, this is valid only for multipage PROGRAM entries. For FSEDIT, it reports which screen of a multiscreen application is displayed.
DISPLAYED	returns the total number of fields or FRAME entry objects that are visible or 0 if none of them are currently displayed. For example, if you pass three field names and two are visible, then *rc* is 2. This action has a corresponding SCL function. FRAME entry objects can also use the _IS_DISPLAYED_ and _IS_HIDDEN_ methods.
ERROR	returns the total number of fields or FRAME entry objects that are in error or 0 if none of the specified fields are in error. For example, if you pass two field names and one is in error, then *rc* is 1. This action has a corresponding SCL function. FRAME entry objects can also use the _IN_ERROR_ method.
ERROROFF	removes the error status from one or more fields or FRAME entry objects. This action has a corresponding SCL statement. FRAME entry objects can also use the _ERROROFF_ method.
ERRORON	turns on the error status for one or more fields or FRAME entry objects. Turning on the error status prevents users from ending the SAS/AF application or from leaving the current observation in FSEDIT. The error status also highlights the field or object using the error color and display attributes assigned in the Attribute (or ATTR) window. This action has a corresponding SCL statement. FRAME entry objects can also use the _ERRORON_ method.
GETOBS	indicates that you are in a GET state in FSVIEW. Indicates that the formula is being executed in FSVIEW. Returns 0 in all other applications. If *rc* is 1, the formula is being executed to display the window. If *rc* is 0, the formula is being executed because a variable has been modified. If you are on a new observation, *rc* is always 1.
HOME	moves the cursor to the command line.
ICON *icon-number*	assigns a number for an icon that represents the field if it is a push button in PROGRAM entries. This option is valid only in SAS/AF software. FRAME entry objects can also use the _SET_ICON_ method. For a list of valid icons, see the Appendix.
MODIFIED	returns the total number of fields or FRAME entry objects that were modified, or 0 if none of them are modified. For example, if you pass two field names and both were modified, *rc* is 2. This action has a corresponding SCL function. FRAME entry objects can also use the _IS_MODIFIED_ method.
NSCREEN	returns the number of screens for FSEDIT applications or the number of panes for SAS/AF applications.
PROTECT	protects one or more fields or FRAME entry objects. This prevents a user from modifying the field or FRAME entry object. This action has a corresponding SCL statement. FRAME entry objects can also use the _PROTECT_ method.
PROTECTED	reports whether a field or FRAME entry object is protected. FRAME entry objects can also use the _IS_PROTECTED_ method.
PUTOBS	indicates that the formula is being executed in FSVIEW. If *rc* is 0, the formula is being executed to display the window. If *rc* is 1, the formula is being executed because a variable has been modified. If you are on a new observation, *rc* is always 0. This is the opposite of GETOBS.
ROW	returns the row where a field or FRAME entry object is positioned. This option is valid only in SAS/AF software. FRAME entry objects can also use the _ROW_ method.
SMOOTHSCRL	sets smooth scrolling to **ON**, **OFF**, or **TOGGLE**. Allows smooth scrolling when users drag the thumb in the scroll bar. When smooth scrolling is on, the GETROW sections of AF extended tables are called while the thumb is dragged. In the FSVIEW procedure, the display is refreshed while the thumb is dragged. When smooth scrolling is turned off, the redisplay is deferred until the thumb is released. By default, smooth scrolling is off for SAS/AF and on for FSVIEW.

Action	Description
UNPROTECT	unprotects one or more fields or FRAME entry objects. This enables a user to modify the field or FRAME entry object. This action has a corresponding SCL statement. FRAME entry objects can also use the _UNPROTECT_ method.

Details

The FIELD function combines the functionality of the field statements (CURSOR, DISPLAYED, ERROROFF, ERRORON, PROTECT, and so forth). It also provides additional control over the fields.

The window variable name arguments are not required for the ALARM, BLOCKCUROFF, BLOCKCURON, CURSCREEN, HOME, NSCREEN, and SMOOTHSCRL actions. At least one window variable name is required for the other actions.

The smooth scrolling action enables you to turn on, off, or toggle the scrolling mode. The second parameter is optional and will toggle if not specified.

Examples

Allow smooth scrolling:

```
rc = field( 'smoothscrl', 'on' );
```

Create the array FLDNAMES and pass its elements to the FIELD function to check the error status of the fields. If necessary, move the cursor to the field containing invalid data.

```
array fldnames{*} $ 8 ('dsname','varname','list','x','y');
do i=1 to dim(fldnames);
   if (field('error',fldnames{i})) then
      do;
         _msg_='Field name '||fldnames{i}||' is bad.';
         rc=field('cursor',fldnames{i});
         return;
      end;
end;
```

Turn on the error flag for the fields VAR1 and VAR2:

```
rc=field('erroron','var1','var2');
```

Change a field's color:

```
rc=field('color blue', 'var1');
```

Change a field's color and display attribute:

```
rc=field('color red reverse','var1');
```

Specify a field's color using the name of a SASCOLOR window element:

```
rc=field('color foreground', 'var1');
```

In a DISPLAY window of a PROGRAM entry, create field CHOICE1 with *type* of

PUSHBTNC and `List` attribute of \24\ to use the FSBROWSE icon by default. In the SCL program, use the FIELD function to change the icon to number 28.

```
rc=field('icon 28','choice1');
```

FILEDIALOG

Opens a selection window listing files

Release 6.11 Feature

See also:
FILELIST

rc=**FILEDIALOG**(*dialog-type,file-name<,default-file<,default-dir <,filter-1...<,filter-11>>>>*);

Where...	Is type...	And represents...
rc	N	Whether the operation was successful: 0 if the file does not exist. − 1 if a user cancelled without selecting a file. 1 if *dialog-type* is **'SAVEAS'**, the file exists, and the user wants to replace the file. 2 if *dialog-type* is **'SAVEAS'**, the file exists, and the user wants to append to the file.
dialog-type	C	The type of dialog window to open: **'OPEN'** to list files a user can open **'SAVEAS'** to list files a user can write to
file-name	C	The fully qualified filename, including directory, which the user selected.
default-file	C	The file (without directory information) to be selected by default when the dialog window opens. If you specify a null string (**' '**), the file that was selected last is the default file.
default-dir	C	The default directory to display when the dialog window opens. If you specify a null string (**' '**), the directory that was selected last is be the default directory.
filter	C	One or more filters, which are used to narrow the list of files that are displayed. The number of filter arguments is host specific. If you do not use this argument, all files in the default directory are listed.

Details

Depending on the values of *default-dir* and *filter*, *default-file* may not be in the list of files displayed. Therefore, *default-file* will not be selected.

■ **Operating System** . . . . The formats of the files and filter parameters are all host specific. The Macintosh platform ignores the filter argument. The Windows platform uses all the passed filters. All other platforms use only the first filter passed.

. . . . ■

Example

Allow a user to select a file to open, and see if the user cancelled the window:

```
rc=filedialog('saveas',selfile,'autoexec.sas','/sas','*.sas');
    /* Process the selected file  */
select(rc);
    when(0) put 'New file selected';
    when(1) put 'REPLACE an existing file';
    when(2) put 'APPEND to an existing file';
    when(-1) put 'User pressed cancel';
    otherwise put 'ERROR occurred';
end;
```

FILEEXIST

Verifies the existence of an external file by its physical name

See Also:
EXIST
FEXIST
FILENAME
FILEREF

rc=**FILEEXIST**(*file-name*);

Where...	Is type...	And represents...
rc	N	Whether the external file exists: 1 if the external file exists 0 if the external file does not exist.
file-name	C	The name that identifies the external file to the host operating system.

Details

The specification of the physical name for *file-name* varies according to the operating system.

Although your system utilities may recognize partial physical filenames, you must always use fully qualified physical filenames with FILEEXIST.

Example

Verify the existence of an external file that the user enters in the field for the window variable FNAME. Display a message on the message line informing the user whether the file exists:

```
if (fileexist(fname)) then
    _msg_='The external file '||fname||' exists.';
else
    _msg_=sysmsg();
```

FILELIST

Displays a selection list window showing the currently assigned filerefs and returns user selections

See Also:
CATLIST
DIRLIST
LIBLIST

selections=**FILELIST**(< *sel-excl*<,*message* <,*autoclose* <,*num-sel*>>>>);

Where...	Is type...	And represents...
selections	C	One or more user selections from the list, or blank if no fileref was selected. Multiple selections are separated by blanks.
sel-excl	C	Whether to include or exclude one or more filerefs from the selection list. Specify as:

- One or more filerefs that have been assigned for the current SAS session, separating multiple filerefs by spaces.

- An asterisk ('*') or null string ('') to display all the filerefs defined for the current SAS session.

- A NOT sign (¬ or ^) followed by one or more filerefs, to display all filerefs except those listed after the NOT sign. For example, '^ MYFILE1 MYFILE2' displays all defined filerefs except MYFILE1 and MYFILE2.

message	C	Text for a message displayed above the selection list. The default message tells users to make up to the number of selections specified in *num-sel*.
autoclose	C	Whether the selection list window closes automatically after a user makes a selection when only one choice is allowed:

   'Y' for the window to close automatically. (Default)

   'N' for the window to close only when the user explicitly closes it.

This option is ignored when *num-sel* is not 1. However, use ' ' as a placeholder when you are specifying a value for *num-sel*.

num-sel	N	The maximum number of items a user can select from the list. To display the list for information purposes only (no selections allowed), specify **0**. To specify an unlimited number of selections, use a value larger than the number of available selections such as 9999.

Details

The selection list displays both filerefs and the corresponding physical names of the external files to which the filerefs are assigned, but only the selected fileref is returned.

If you omit all the arguments for FILELIST (for example, **selections= filelist();**), the selection list window has the following characteristics:

□ The list contains all filerefs that have been assigned in the current SAS session.

□ A message asks the user to make one selection.

□ The selection list window closes automatically when the user makes a selection.

You can provide a default or initial selected value in the list by providing a value for the *selections* variable prior to calling FILELIST. If *selections* is assigned a value before FILELIST is invoked, those filerefs are automatically designated as selected when the selection window opens.

If a user closes the selection list window without making a selection, FILELIST returns a blank value unless there was an initial value for the *selections* variable before FILELIST was called.

Selections from the window can be returned in the current result list, if one is available. The current result list is a special SCL list that is automatically filled with the values selected from a selection list. To create a current result list, use the MAKELIST function to create it and the CURLIST function to designate it as the current result list. The current result list must exist before you call the FILELIST function.

When FILELIST is invoked, the current environment list is cleared. After FILELIST is invoked, the current environment list contains the following named items:

Element	Type	Description
TAG	C	Identification of the list as one created by FILELIST.
COUNT	N	Number of filerefs selected. If no selections are made, or if users issue a CANCEL command in the list window, COUNT is 0.
FILEREF	C	Name of each fileref selected. One FILEREF element exists for each selection made.
FILENAME	C	Physical name of the external file for each fileref selected. One FILENAME element exists for each selection made.

Examples

Open a window that displays a list of all defined filerefs except for LISTNUM: The window closes automatically after a user makes a selection.

```
select=filelist('^listnum');
```

Open a window that displays a list of all defined filerefs except LISTNUM. Users can make up to five selections. The selections are retrieved from the current environment list.

```
listid=makelist();
rc=curlist(listid);
select=filelist('^listnum',' ',' ',5);
n=getnitemn(listid,'COUNT');
do i=1 to n;
    fileref=getnitemc(listid,'FILEREF',i);
    physname=getnitemc(listid,'FILENAME',i);
    put fileref= physname=;
end;
```

FILENAME

Assigns or deassigns a fileref for an external file, directory, or output device

See Also:
FEXIST
FILEEXIST
FILEREF

sysrc=**FILENAME**(*fileref*,*file-name*<,*device*<,*host-options*<,*dir-ref*>>>);

Where...	Is type...	And represents...
sysrc	N	Whether the operation was successful: 0 if successful $\neq 0$ if not successful.
fileref	C	The fileref to assign to the external file. A blank *fileref* (**''**) causes an error condition. If the fileref is an SCL character variable with a blank value, a fileref will be generated for you.
file-name	C	The external file. Specifying a blank *filename* deassigns one that was previously assigned.
device	C	The type of device if the fileref points to an output device rather than to a physical file: DUMMY — output to the file discarded GTERM — graphics on the user's terminal NAMEPIPE — a named pipe PIPE — an unnamed pipe **Note:** Some host operating systems do not support pipes. PLOTTER — an unbuffered graphics output device PRINTER — a printer or printer spool file TERMINAL — the user's terminal TAPE — a tape driver.
host-options	C	Host-specific details such as file attributes and processing attributes.
dir-ref	C	Fileref assigned to the directory or partitioned data set in which the external file resides.

Details

The name associated with the file or device is called a *fileref* (file reference name). Other SCL functions that manipulate external files and directories require that the files be identified by fileref rather than by physical filename. A system generated fileref is not displayed in the FILENAME window.

■ **Host Information** . . . .   The term *directory* in this description refers to an aggregate grouping of files managed by the host operating system. Different host operating systems identify such groupings with different names, such as directory, subdirectory, MACLIB, or partitioned data set. Refer to the SAS documentation for your host system for details.

Under some operating systems, you can also assign filerefs using system commands. Depending on the operating system, FILENAME may be unable to change or deassign filerefs assigned outside the SAS System.

Refer to the SAS documentation for your host operating system for information

about the system-dependent options you can specify in the *options* argument.
. . . . ■

The association between a fileref and a physical file lasts only for the duration of
the current SAS session or until you change or discontinue the association using
FILENAME. You can deassign filerefs specifying a null string for the *filename*
argument in FILENAME.

For more information on the arguments that you can use with FILENAME, see
SAS Language: Reference.

Examples

Assign the fileref MYFILE to an external file. *Physical-filename* represents the name
of a file in the appropriate form for your host operating system:

```
rc=filename('myfile','physical-filename');
if (rc ne 0) then
   _msg_=sysmsg();
```

Use a system-generated fileref for the file. The fileref is stored in the variable
FNAME:

```
fname=' ';

rc=filename(fname,'physical-filename ');
if (rc) then
   _msg_=sysmsg();
else
   do;
      more SCL statements
   end;
```

Deassign the fileref MYFILE:

```
rc=filename('myfile','');
```

Assign a fileref for a pipe file with the output from the UNIX command LS, which
lists the files in the directory /u/myid:

```
rc = filename ('myfile','ls /u/myid','pipe');
```

FILEREF

Verifies that a fileref has been assigned for the current SAS session

See Also:
FEXIST
FILEEXIST
FILENAME

sysrc=**FILEREF**(*fileref*);

Where...	Is type...	And represents...

sysrc	N	Whether the operation was successful:
		  0 Fileref and external file both exist.
		
		  < 0 Fileref has been assigned, but the file it points to does not exist.
		
		  > 0 Fileref has not been assigned.

fileref	C	The fileref to be validated (up to eight characters).

Details

A negative return code indicates that the fileref exists but the physical file associated with the fileref does not exist. A positive (nonzero) value indicates the fileref is not assigned.

A fileref can be assigned to an external file using the FILENAME statement or the FILENAME function in SCL. Under some operating systems, filerefs can also be assigned using system commands. See your host companion.

Examples

Test whether the fileref MYFILE is currently assigned to an external file. A system error message is issued if the fileref is not currently assigned.

```
if (fileref('myfile')>0) then _msg_=sysmsg();
```

Test for a zero value to determine if both the fileref and the file exist:

```
if (fileref('myfile') ne 0) then _msg_=sysmsg();
```

FILLIST

Fills an SCL list with text and data

See Also:
MAKELIST
POPMENU
SAVELIST
SEARCH
SEARCHPATH
STRATTR

sysrc=**FILLIST**(*type,source,list-id*<,*attr-list-id* <,*description*>>);

Where...	Is type...	And represents...
sysrc	N	Whether the operation was successful: 0 if successful $\neq$ 0 if not successful.
type	C	The type of file or data source named in *source* and the options to use:

'CATALOG'	a catalog entry named by *source*.
'FILE'	an external file named by *source*.
'FILEREF'	an external file identified by a fileref named in *source*.
'SASICONS'	the numbers for icons provided with SAS software. (*source* is ignored. Specify a null argument **' '** for *source*.)
'SEARCH'	catalog names in the current search path (*source* is ignored). Use the SEARCH function to define the search path or specify **' '** for *source*.

. . . .

Release 6.11

You can specify file options in *type* by enclosing one or more options from Table 20.8 in parentheses and separating them with blanks. For example, to fill a list from an external print file and strip carriage control, use **'FILE(PRINT STRIPCC)'** for *type*.

. . . .

Where...	Is type...	And represents...
source	C	a catalog entry (specified as *libref.catalog.entry.type*), external file, or fileref.
list-id	N	The identifier of the list to fill. An invalid *list-id* produces an error condition.
attr-list-id	N	The identifier of the list to fill with text attribute *source* information when *type* is **'CATALOG'** and the entry type is LOG, OUTPUT, or SOURCE. An invalid *attr-list-id* produces an error condition.
description	C	The catalog entry description text. This argument is ignored if *type* is **'FILE'** or **'FILEREF'**. (The description is displayed in the catalog directory.)

Table 20.8 *Options for type Values*

Option	Action
`'ADDCC'`	adds default carriage control. Used with *type* `'FILE'`, `'FILEREF'`, and `'CATALOG'` and catalog entry types `'LOG'`, `'OUTPUT'`, and `'SOURCE'`.
`'APPEND'`	appends text to an external file. Attempts to open the file in APPEND mode. Used with *type* `'FILE'` or `'FILEREF'`.
`'PRINT'`	designates an external file as a PRINT file (uses host carriage control). Used with *type* `'FILE'` or `'FILEREF'`.
`'STRIPCC'`	removes carriage control. Used with *type* `'FILE'`, `'FILEREF'`, and `'CATALOG'` and catalog entry types `'LOG'`, `'OUTPUT'`, and `'SOURCE'`.
`'TRIM'`	trims trailing blanks. Used with *type* `'FILE'`, `'FILEREF'`, and `'CATALOG'` catalog entry types `'LOG,` `OUTPUT'`, and `'SOURCE'`. `'TRIM'` is useful if you want to use FILLIST to fill a list with items that contain trailing blanks and then remove the blanks so they will not be displayed in a popup-menu produced by POPMENU.

Details

Each line of text in the source file is placed in a separate character item of the list identified by *list-id*. The number of items in the filled list is determined by the number of lines of text. All SCL lists must have been created with MAKELIST before calling FILLIST. FILLIST automatically clears the lists before it fills the lists.

If the data from the external file or catalog entry exceeds 200 characters, it is truncated to 200 character, the maximim length of a character value in an SCL list item.

External Files
If *type* is `'FILE'`, *source* is the name of an external file. If *type* is `'FILEREF'`, *source* is a SAS fileref. FILLIST reads each record of the file into a separate character item.

SLIST Entries
If *type* is `'CATALOG'` and *source* is `'SLIST'`, the types of the items in the filled list are determined by the saved list, and they may be character strings, numbers, and other lists. All item attributes and names are duplicated as are the list attributes. However, the list identifier numbers are different.

LIST Entries
When *type* is 'CATALOG' and the entry type is `'LIST'`, FILLIST reads the contents of a SAS/AF LIST entry into *list-id*. The list contains either all numeric or all character items, depending on the contents of the LIST entry. The attribute list contains the following named values:

Name	Type	Description
INFORMAT	C	The SAS informat for the values
FORMAT	C	The SAS format for the values
MESSAGE	C	The error message assigned to the LIST entry
CAPS	C	Items are capitalized. `'Y'` or `'N'`
SORTED	C	Whether items were automatically sorted. `'Y'` or `'N'`

Name	Type	Description
IGNORECASE	C	Whether item lookup ignores case. **'Y'** or **'N'**
TYPE	C	Type of items. 'N'} for numeric, **'C'** for character
JUST	C	Justification. One of 'L'}, **'R'**, **'C'**, or **'N'** for left, right, center, or none

Note: SAVELIST for LIST entries is not implemented yet.

Catalog Text Entries

When *type* is **'CATALOG'** and the entry type is **'OUTPUT'**, **'LOG'**, or **'SOURCE'**, the first character in each list item contains a FORTRAN carriage control: 1 means a new page starts with this line. See **'STRIPCC'** above. **'ADDCC'** converts all **CC**s to **' '** (blank).

When *type* is **'CATALOG'** and the entry type is **'OUTPUT'**, **'LOG'**, or **'SOURCE'**, any text attributes (such as color and display attributes), are read one element per line into *attr-list-id*, if it is specified. These attributes consist of a character item for each line of text, containing one character for each character in the line plus a prefix descriptor character. The prefix character is **T** for a title line, **H** for a header line, or **D** for a data line. The other characters represent the text display attributes and color, as described in the tables below.

Text Attribute Specifications within Catalog Text Entries

Do not confuse text attributes (color, display, and so on) with list attributes as specified with SETLATTR.

The attribute list filled by FILLIST contains one item for each line of text from the SAS catalog entry. The attribute string for each line has one character for each character of text. Each attribute character represents the SAS Display Manager (DM) color and display attribute. Not all display devices support all DM colors.

Color attributes are represented as:

Color	Value	Color	Value
BLUE	'10'x	WHITE	'70'x
RED	'20'x	ORANGE	'80'x
PINK	'30'x	BLACK	'90'x
GREEN	'40'x	MAGENTA	'A0'x
CYAN	'50'x	GRAY	'B0'x
YELLOW	'60'x	BROWN	'C0'x

Display attributes are represented as:

Attribute	Value
NONE	'00'x
HIGHLIGHT	'01'x
UNDERLINE	'02'x
BLINK	'04'x

Attribute	Value
REVERSE	'08'x

You combine the color and display attribute by adding them together. For example, you can specify GREEN UNDERLINE by adding '40'x to '02'x to yield '42'x. To assign GREEN UNDERLINE to the first 4 characters of a string, you could use a statement like:

```
str = '42424242'x;
```

See also STRATTR, which creates attribute strings.
You can use GETITEMC or POPC to retrieve an item from this list.
An error condition is produced if

□ either list has the NOUPDATE, NUMONLY, or FIXEDLENGTH attribute

□ any item in either list cannot be removed because it has the NODELETE attribute

Example 1

Suppose you have an OUTPUT entry named FINANCE.REPORTS.MONTHLY.OUTPUT that contains the text "Net: ($45,034)" on line 45, where the text **Net:** is white with no highlight attributes while the text **($45,034)** is red reverse. The following statements read the text and attributes and print line 45:

```
INIT:
   text_list=makelist();
   attr_list=makelist();
   rc=fillist('CATALOG','FINANCE.REPORTS.MONTHLY.OUTPUT',text_list,attr_list);
   text=substr(getitemc(text_list,45),2);
   attr=substr(getitemc(attr_list,45),2);
   len = compress(put(2*length(text), 4.));
   attrhex=putc(attr,'$HEX'||len||'.');
   put attr;
   put text;
   put attrhex;
return;
```

Note: SUBSTR removes the carriage control characters.
This example produces the output:

```
ppppp(((((((((
Net: ($45,034)
70707070702828282828282828
```

The line of text consists of five white characters with no attributes, represented by the attribute '70'x, followed by nine red reverse characters, represented by '28'x.

Example 2

The following statements perform an operation similar to a recursive list copy:

```
 rc=savelist('CATALOG','WORK.TEMP.MYLIST.SLIST',mylist);
new_list=makelist();
rc=fillist('CATALOG','WORK.TEMP.MYLIST.SLIST',new_list);
rc=delete('WORK.TEMP.TEMP.SLIST','CATALOG');
```

Lists saved in a permanent catalog with SAVELIST can persist across SAS sessions.

Example 3

Consider two list entries SASUSER.DATA.A.LIST which contains some character data and SASUSER.DATA.DATES.LIST which contains formatted numeric data. The following program reads the data and attributes from these entries and prints the results with PUTLIST:

```
INIT:
   items=makelist();
   attrs = makelist();
   rc=fillist('catalog','sasuser.data.a.list',items,attrs);
   call putlist(items,'A.LIST contents:',0);
   call putlist(attrs,'A.LIST attributes:',0);
   rc=fillist('catalog','sasuser.data.dates.list',items,attrs);
   call putlist(items,'DATES.LIST contents:',0);
   call putlist(attrs,'DATES.LIST attributes:',0);
   rc = dellist(items);
   rc = dellist(attrs);
return;
```

The output for these entries may look like:

```
A.LIST contents:('THIS     '
                 'IS       '
                 'A        '
                 'LIST     '
                 'ENTRY    '
                 'WITH     '
                 'EIGHT    '
                 'ITEMS    '
                 )[5]
A.LIST attributes:(INFORMAT=''
                   FORMAT=''
                   MESSAGE=''
                   CAPS='Y'
                   SORTED='N'
                   IGNORECASE='Y'
                   TYPE='C'
                   JUST='L'
                   )[7]
DATES.LIST contents:(1765
                     11162
                     11813
                     12072
                     )[5]
```

```
DATES.LIST attributes:(INFORMAT='DATE.'
                       FORMAT='DATE.'
                       MESSAGE=''
                       CAPS='Y'
                       SORTED='Y'
                       IGNORECASE='N'
                       TYPE='N'
                       JUST='L'
                       )[7]
```

Note: [5] and [7] are the list identifiers assigned when this example was run and may be different each time the example is run.

FINFO

Returns a file information item

See Also:

DINFO
FOPEN
FOPTNAME
FOPTNUM

item-value=**FINFO**(*file-id,info-item*);

Where...	Is type...	And represents...
item-value	C	The value of the file parameter, or blank if the value given for *info-item* is invalid.
file-id	N	The identifier assigned when the file was opened. If *file-id* is invalid, the program halts execution.
info-item	C	The file information item to be retrieved.

Details

FINFO returns the value of a system-dependent information item for an external file. The information available on files depends on the operating system.

FOPTNUM determines the number of system-dependent information items available. FOPTNAME determines the names of the available items.

Example

Assign the fileref MYFILE to an external file. (*Physical-filename* represents the actual name of the file in the form required by the host operating system.) Then open the file and determine whether LRECL is one of the available information items. If the value of the variable CHARVAL is nonblank, a value is returned for LRECL (logical record length), an attribute used on some host systems.

```
rc=filename('myfile','physical-filename ');
fid=fopen('myfile');
charval=finfo(fid,'lrecl');
if (charval=' ') then
   _msg_='The LRECL attribute is not available for the file.';
else
   _msg_='The LRECL for the file is '||charval||'.';
rc=fclose(fid);
rc=filename('myfile','');
```

See also the example in FOPTNAME.

FKEYNAME

Returns the name of the specified function key

See Also:
GETFKEY
NUMFKEYS
SETFKEY

key-name=**FKEYNAME**(*key-number*);

Where...	Is type...	And represents...
key-name	C	A function key name as listed in the KEYS window. Function key names vary according to device.
key-number	N	The number that corresponds to the order in which the keys are displayed in the KEYS window.

Details

The *key-number* argument identifies a key by its ordinal position in the KEYS window, not by its label. For example, if the first key in the KEYS window is named PF1, use a 1 rather than PF1 for the *key-number* argument to identify that key. To retrieve the corresponding key definitions, use GETFKEY.

You can use this function only in entries that have a DISPLAY window.

Example

Return the name of function key 12:

```
keyname=fkeyname(12);
```

FLDATTR

Changes the color and display attribute of a field, text entry object, or text label object to those stored in an attribute string

See Also:
FLDCOLOR
STRATTR

rc=**FLDATTR**(*wvar-name,string*);

Where...	Is type...	And represents...
rc	N	Whether the operation was successful: 0 if successful ≠ 0 if not successful.
wvar-name	C	The field, text entry object, or text label object to be changed.
string	C	The color and display attributes to apply and the starting and ending character positions within the field.

Details

You can use STRATTR or FILLIST to generate the attribute string. You can also generate the attribute string by assigning hex characters directly to the string.

Color attributes are represented as:

Color	Value	Color	Value
BLUE	'10'x	WHITE	'70'x
RED	'20'x	ORANGE	'80'x
PINK	'30'x	BLACK	'90'x
GREEN	'40'x	MAGENTA	'A0'x
CYAN	'50'x	GRAY	'B0'x
YELLOW	'60'x	BROWN	'C0'x

Display attributes are represented as:

Attribute	Value
NONE	'00'x
HIGHLIGHT	'01'x
UNDERLINE	'02'x
BLINK	'04'x
REVERSE	'08'x

To preserve a color, use the special hex character 'F0'x. To preserve a display attribute, use '0F'x. To preserve both the color and display attribute, add the two special characters together, 'FF'x.

For programs with extended tables you must call this function in the GETROW section of your SCL program.

FRAME entry objects can also use the _SET_COLOR_STR_ method.

Example

Change the first half of the field, ABC, to red reverse.

```
str = strattr( 'red', 'reverse', 1, mlength(abc)/2 );
rc = fldattr( 'abc', str );
```

Suppose the FRAME text entry object, OBJ1, is BLUE REVERSE. To change the third through the seventh character positions of OBJ1 to yellow, you must initialize the first two characters of the attribute string to 'FF'x, then assign YELLOW in the third through seventh characters. Assigning YELLOW to the attribute string can be accomplished either by using STRATTR or by assigning the hex characters directly to the string.

```
str = 'FFFF6060606060'x;
rc = fldattr( 'obj1', str );
```

The previous example could have been written as follows:

```
str = 'FFFF'x;
str = strattr('yellow', '', 3, 5 );
rc = fldattr( 'obj1', str );
```

You can also use the REPEAT function to initialize a string.

```
str = repeat( 'FF', 2 );
str = strattr('yellow', '', 3, 5 );
rc = fldattr( 'obj1', str );
```

FLDCOLOR

Changes the color and display attribute of a field, text entry object, or text label object to those stored in an attribute string

See Also:
FIELD
FLDATTR
STRATTR

rc=**FLDCOLOR**(*wvar-name,color,attribute,start,length*);

Where...	Is type...	And represents...

rc	N	Whether the operation was successful:
		    0 if successful
		
		    ≠ 0 if not successful.

wvar-name	C	The field, text entry object, or text label object to be changed.
color	C	A color name or ' ' to retain the current color. SASCOLOR window elements can also be used for *color*. For more information on colors and a list of colors, see *color* in "Common Arguments" on page 222.
attribute	C	A display attribute or ' ' to retain the current attribute. If you specify a SASCOLOR window element for *color*, *attribute* is ignored because the SASCOLOR window element contains a display attribute. However, you must specify a placeholder (' ') for *attribute* when you specify arguments after it. For more information on display attributes and a list of them, see *attribute* in "Common Arguments" on page 222.
start	N	The position in the field at which to begin applying the specified color and display attributes.
length	N	The number of positions to which the specified color and display attributes are to be applied.

Details

FRAME entry objects can also use the _SET_COLOR_ method.

To change the color for the entire field or FRAME entry object, you can use the FIELD function.

Example

Change the color of the third through seventh character positions in field ABC to red and the display attribute of those positions to high intensity:

```
rc=fldcolor('abc','red','highlight',3,5);
```

Change the color of a field, but leave the attributes alone:

```
rc=fldcolor('abc','red','',3,7);
```

Change the color of a field using a SASCOLOR window element:

```
rc=fldcolor('abc','foreground','',3,7);
```

FNOTE

Identifies the last record that was read

See Also:
DROPNOTE
FPOINT
FREAD
FREWIND

note-id=**FNOTE**(*file-id*);

Where...	Is type...	And represents...
note-id	N	The identifier assigned to the last record that was read. SCL programs should not modify the value of the *note-id* variable. The *note-id* value is required by the FPOINT function to reposition the file pointer on a specific record.
file-id	N	The identifier assigned when the file was opened. If *file-id* is invalid, the program halts execution.

Details

You can use FNOTE like a bookmark, marking the position in the file so that your application can later return to that position using FPOINT.

FNOTE is limited to noting 1,000 records. When that limit is reached, the program halts execution. To free the memory associated with each NOTE identifier, use DROPNOTE.

Example

Assign the fileref MYFILE to an external file. (*Physical-filename* represents the actual name of the file in the form required by the host operating system.) Then attempt to open the file. If the file is successfully opened, indicated by a positive value in the variable FID, read the records, note in the variable NOTE3 the position of the third record read, and then later use FPOINT to point back to NOTE3 to update the file. After the record is updated, the file is closed.

```
rc=filename('myfile','physical-filename');
fid=fopen('myfile','u');
if (fid>0) then
    do;
        rc=fread(fid);              /* Read first record. */
        rc=fread(fid);              /* Read second record. */
        rc=fread(fid);              /* Read third record. */
        note3=fnote(fid);          /* Note position of third record. */
        rc=fread(fid);              /* Read fourth record. */
        rc=fread(fid);              /* Read fifth record. */
        rc=fpoint(fid,note3);      /* Point to third record. */
        rc=fread(fid);              /* Read third record. */
        rc=fput(fid,'New text');   /* Copy new text to FDB. */
        rc=fwrite(fid);            /* Update third record with data in FDB. */
        rc=fclose(fid);            /* Close file. */
    end;
rc=filename('myfile','');
```

FONTSEL

Opens the selector window for host or for portable fonts

Release 6.11 Feature

See Also:
MAKELIST

newfontlist-id=**FONTSEL**(*oldfontlist-id, font-selector*);

Where...	Is type...	And represents...
newfontlist-id	N	The identifier of the list containing the font family, size, weight, and style that is selected.
oldfontlist-id	N	The identifier of the list containing the font information for the selection list. An invalid *oldfontlist-id* produces an error condition. This list can be empty.
font-selector	C	Which font selector to open:
		'Y' to open the host font selector
		'N' to open the portable font selector
		' ' to open the default font selector.

Description

If *oldfontlist-id* is not empty, the selector window opens with the family, size, weight, and style selections specified in the list. If *oldfontlist-id* is empty, the selector opens with the default selections for family, size, weight, and style. The *newfontlist-id* identifier contains information on the family, size, weight, and style that the user selected. The host font selector window enables a user to select fonts available on the host in an environment-specific way. The portable font selector enables a user to select a portable font specification, which is used to find the closest match among fonts available on a host. The host font selector can also be opened from the portable font selector using the System button.

For more information on how to use the font information that is returned, see the documentation for the extended text entry class in release 6.11 of SAS/AF software and its _SET_FONT_ method.

To change the default font selector, use the SAS System option MULTENVAPPL, which is described in *SAS Software: Changes and Enhancements, Release 6.10.*

Example

Make a FRAME entry with a push button named PUSHBTN and an extended text entry widget named ETE. Clicking on the push button executes the code to display the portable font selector. Change the font selector value from **'N'** to **'Y'** to use the host font selector.

```
INIT:
    fontid=makelist();
return;
PUSHBTN:
    fontid=fontsel(fontid,'n');
    rc=putlist(fontid,'FONT',1);
    call notify('ETE','_SET_FONT_',fontid);
    call notify('ETE','_SNUG_FIT_');
return;
TERM:
    rc=dellist(fontid);
```

```
        return;
```

FOPEN

Opens an external file

See Also:
DOPEN
FCLOSE
FILENAME
FILEREF
MOPEN

file-id=**FOPEN**(*fileref*<,*open-mode*<,*record-length*<,*record-format*>>>);

Where...	Is type...	And represents...
file-id	N	The identifier for the file, or 0 if the file could not be opened.
fileref	C	The fileref (up to eight characters) assigned to the external file.
open-mode	C	The type of access to the file:
		'A' APPEND mode, which allows writing new records after the current end of the file.
		'I' INPUT mode, which allows reading only. (Default)
		'O' OUTPUT mode, which defaults to the OPEN mode specified in the host option in the FILENAME statement or function. If no host option is specified, it allows writing new records at the beginning of the file.
		'S' Sequential input mode, which is used for pipes and other sequential devices such as hardware ports.
		'U' UPDATE mode, which allows both reading and writing.
		'W' Sequential update mode, which is used for pipes and other sequential devices such as ports.
record-length	N	The logical record length of the file. To use the existing record length for the file, specify a length of 0 or do not provide a value here.
record-format	C	The record format of the file:
		'B' Data are to be interpreted as binary data.
		'D' Use default record format.
		'E' Use editable record format.
		'F' File contains fixed length records.
		'P' File contains printer carriage control in host-dependent record format.
		'V' File contains variable length records.
		To use the existing record format, do not specify a value here.

Details

▶ *Caution: Use OUTPUT mode with care.*

Opening an existing file for output overwrites the current contents of the file without warning.

. . . .

The FOPEN function opens an external file for reading or updating and returns a file identifier value used to identify the open file to other functions. The external file must be identified with a fileref. You must associate a fileref with the external file before calling the FOPEN function.

You can assign filerefs using the FILENAME statement or the FILENAME function in SCL. Under some operating systems, you can also assign filerefs using system commands.

■ **MVS** . . . .

For MVS data sets with VBA record format, specify 'P' for the *record-format* argument.

. . . . ■

Example

Assign the fileref MYFILE to an external file. Then attempt to open the file for input using all defaults:

```
rc=filename('myfile','physical-filename ');
fid=fopen('myfile');
```

Attempt to open the file for input not using defaults:

```
fid=fopen('file2','o',132,'e');
```

FOPTNAME

Returns the name of an item of information about a file

See Also:
DINFO
DOPTNAME
DOPTNUM
FINFO
FOPEN
FOPTNUM
MOPEN

cval=**FOPTNAME**(*file-id*,*nval*);

Where...	Is type...	And represents...
cval	C	The name of the information item or blank if an error occurred.
file-id	N	The identifier assigned when the file was opened. If *file-id* is invalid, the program halts execution.
nval	N	The number of the information item.

Details

The number, value, and type of information items available vary from operating system to operating system.

Example

Retrieve the system-dependent file information items available and write them to the log:

```
length name $ 8;
rc=filename('myfile','physical-filename ');
fid=fopen('myfile');
infonum=foptnum(fid);
do j=1 to infonum;
   name=foptname(fid,j);
   value=finfo(fid,name);
   put 'File attribute' name 'has a value of' value;
end;
rc=fclose(fid);
rc=filename('myfile','');
```

This example could produce the output:

```
File attribute LRECL has a value of 256.
```

FOPTNUM

Returns the number of information items available about an external file

See Also:
DINFO
DOPTNAME
DOPTNUM
FINFO
FOPTNAME

rc=**FOPTNUM**(*file-id*);

Where...	Is type...	And represents...
rc	N	The number of information items available.
file-id	N	The identifier assigned when the file was opened. If *file-id* is invalid, the program halts execution.

Details

The number, value, and type of information items available depend on the operating system.

Use FOPTNAME to determine the names of the items available for a particular operating system. Use FINFO to retrieve the value of a particular information item.

Example

Open the external file with the fileref MYFILE and determine the number of system-dependent file information items available:

```
fid=fopen('myfile');
infonum=foptnum(fid);
```

For more information, see the example in FOPTNAME.

FORMAT

Verifies that the specified format is valid

See Also:
INFORMAT

rc=**FORMAT**(*format,type*);

Where...	Is type...	And represents...
rc	N	Whether the operation was successful: 1 if successful 0 if not successful.
format	C	A format that is supplied by SAS or created using the FORMAT procedure.
type	C	The type of the format: **'C'** character **'N'** numeric.

Details

The specified format must be known to the SAS session or the operation returns an unsuccessful return code. The function does check that valid widths are specified for formats.

Note: A period at the end of the format name is required.

Examples

Assume that you want to use the $CHAR12. format. Verify that **$CHAR12.** is a valid character format. (The value returned to the variable RC is 1.)

```
rc=format('$char12.','c');
```

Verify that **5.6** is not a valid format for numeric values. (The value returned to the variable RC is 0.)

```
rc=format('5.6','n');
```

FPOINT

Positions the read pointer on the next record to be read

See Also:
DROPNOTE
FNOTE
FREAD
FREWIND

sysrc=**FPOINT**(*file-id*,*note-id*);

Where...	Is type...	And represents...

sysrc	N	Whether the operation was successful:
		    0 if successful
		
		    $\neq$ 0 if not successful.

file-id	N	The identifier assigned when the file was opened. If *file-id* is invalid, the program halts execution.
note-id	N	The identifier assigned by the FNOTE function.

Details

Use FNOTE to provide the *note-id* value that identifies the record. FPOINT determines only the record to read next. It has no impact on which record is written next. When you open the file for update, FWRITE writes to the most recently read record.

Example

Assign the fileref MYFILE to an external file. (*Physical-filename* represents the name of the file in the form required by the host operating system.) Then attempt to open the file. If the file is successfully opened, read the records, use NOTE3 to store the position of the third record read. Later, point back to NOTE3 to update the file, closing the file afterward:

```
rc=filename('myfile','physical-filename ');
fid=fopen('myfile','u');
if (fid>0) then
   do;
       rc=fread(fid);              /* Read first record. */
       rc=fread(fid);              /* Read second record. */
       rc=fread(fid);              /* Read third record. */
       note3=fnote(fid);           /* Note position of third record. */
       rc=fread(fid);              /* Read fourth record. */
       rc=fread(fid);              /* Read fifth record. */
       rc=fpoint(fid,note3);       /* Point to third record. */
       rc=fread(fid);              /* Read third record. */
       rc=fput(fid,'new text');    /* Copy new text to FDB. */
       rc=fwrite(fid);             /* Write data in FDB to third record. */
       rc=fclose(fid);             /* Close file. */
   end;
rc=filename('myfile','');
```

FPOS

Sets the position of the column pointer in the File Data Buffer

See Also:
FCOL
FPUT

*sysrc=***FPOS**(*file-id,nval*);

Where...	Is type...	And represents...

sysrc	N	Whether the operation was successful:
		  0 if successful
		
		  ≠ 0 if not successful.

file-id	N	The identifier assigned when the file was opened. If *file-id* is invalid, the program halts execution.
nval	N	The column at which to set the pointer.

Details

If the specified position is past the end of the current record, the size of the record is increased appropriately. However, in a fixed block or VBA file, if you specify a column position beyond the end of the record, the record size does not change and the text string is not written to the file.

Example

Assign the fileref MYFILE to an external file. (*Physical-filename* represents the name of the file in the form required by the host operating system.) Then attempt to open the file. If the file is successfully opened, indicated by a positive value in the variable FID, place data into the file's buffer at column 12, write the record, and close the file:

```
rc=filename('myfile','physical-filename ');
fid=fopen('myfile','o');
if (fid>0) then
   do;
      rc=fread(fid);
      dataline='This is some data.';
      rc=fpos(fid,12);        /* Position at column 12 in the FDB. */
      rc=fput(fid,dataline);  /* Put the data in the FDB. */
      rc=fwrite(fid);         /* Write the record. */
      rc=fclose(fid);         /* Close the file. */
   end;
rc=filename('myfile','');
```

FPUT

Moves data to the File Data Buffer (FDB) of an external file starting at the FDB's current column position

See Also:
FNOTE
FPOINT
FPOS
FWRITE

rc=**FPUT**(*file-id,cval*);

Where...	Is type...	And represents...
rc	N	Whether the operation was successful: 0 if successful ≠ 0 if not successful.
file-id	N	The identifier assigned when the file was opened. If *file-id* is invalid, the program halts execution.
cval	C	The variable containing the data.

Details

The number of bytes moved to the FDB is determined by the length of the variable. The value of the column pointer is then incremented to one position past the end of the new text.

Example

Assign the fileref MYFILE to an external file. (*Physical-filename* represents the name of the file in the form required by the host operating system.) Then attempt to open the file in APPEND mode. If the file is successfully opened, indicated by a positive value in the variable FID, move data to the FDB using FPUT, append a record using FWRITE, and then close the file:

```
rc=filename('myfile','physical-filename ');
fid=fopen('myfile','a');
if (fid>0) then
   do;
      mystring='This is some data.';
      rc=fput(fid,mystring);
      rc=fwrite(fid);
      rc=fclose(fid);
   end;
else
   _msg_=sysmsg();
rc=filename('myfile','');
```

FRAME

Contains the identifier of the FRAME entry that contains the widget, or it contains the identifier of the FRAME entry if the FRAME entry is being used as a method

Numeric System Instance Variable

See Also:
CFRAME

Details

FRAME is a System Instance Variable. It is provided automatically by the FRAME entry in SAS/AF, but the SCL compiler does not automatically create a space for it in the SCL data vector. Because of this, you get a warning when you compile your FRAME or SCL entry if you have a reference to _FRAME_.

For example, the following program for a FRAME entry,

```
INIT:
    call send( _frame_, '_set_msg_', 'in init section' );
return;
```

generates the following warning when compiled:

```
WARNING: [Line 2]  Variable _FRAME_ is uninitialized
```

The warning is generated because _FRAME_ is being referenced (in the CALL SEND) but the compiler does not think that _FRAME_ has been assigned a value yet. This is expected behavior because _FRAME_ does not have a value until the FRAME executes.

This warning can be ignored. To prevent the warning from being generated, you can use a dummy assignment statement before the INIT section of your program.

```
_frame_=_frame_;

INIT:
    call send( _frame_, '_set_msg_', 'in init section' );
return;
```

FRAME only has a valid value when the FRAME entry's SCL code is running or when a FRAME or FRAME entry object method is running.

Example

Suppose the entry FIRST.FRAME contains an icon. The icon's _SELECT_ method is defined to run the SAS/AF FRAME entry SECOND.FRAME, which contains the program:

```
INIT:
    /* send a method to the current FRAME */
    call send(_CFRAME_, '_set_msg_', 'Running the _SELECT_ method');
return;

TERM:
    /* send a method to the FRAME that contains the icon */
    call send(_FRAME_, '_set_msg_', '_SELECT_ has finished.');
return;
```

When FIRST.FRAME displays and a user selects the icon, SECOND.FRAME displays with the message 'Running the _SELECT_ method'. After the user ends from SECOND.FRAME, FIRST.FRAME displays the message '_SELECT_ has finished.' This is accomplished by sending the _SET_MSG_ method to _CFRAME_ (the FRAME entry that's currently running) in the INIT section and sending _SET_MSG_ to _FRAME_ (the FRAME entry that contains the icon) in the TERM section.

FREAD

Reads a record from an external file into the File Data Buffer (FDB)

See Also:
FGET
FNOTE
FPOINT
FREWIND

sysrc=**FREAD**(*file-id*);

Where...	Is type...	And represents...

sysrc	N	Whether the operation was successful:
		  0 if successful
		
		  $\neq$ 0 if not successful.

file-id	N	The identifier assigned when the file was opened. If *file-id* is invalid, the program halts execution.

Details

The position of the file pointer is automatically updated after the read operation so that successive FREAD functions read successive file records.

Use FNOTE, FPOINT, and FREWIND to position the file pointer explicitly.

Example

Assign the fileref MYFILE to an external file. (*Physical-filename* represents the name of the file in the form required by the host operating system.) Then attempt to open the file. If the file opens successfully, list all of the file's records in the LOG or MESSAGE window.

```
rc=filename('myfile','physical-filename ');
fid=fopen('myfile');
if (fid>0) then
   do while(fread(fid)=0);
      rc=fget(fid,c,200);
      put c;
   end;
rc=fclose(fid);
rc=filename('myfile','');
```

FREWIND

Positions the file pointer to the start of the file

See Also:
FGET

sysrc=**FREWIND**(*file-id*);

Where...	Is type...	And represents...
sysrc	N	Whether the operation was successful: 0 if successful ≠ 0 if not successful.
file-id	N	The identifier assigned when the file was opened. If *file-id* is invalid, the program halts execution.

Details

FREWIND has no effect on a file opened with sequential access.

Example

Assign the fileref MYFILE to an external file. (*Physical-filename* represents the name of the external file in the form required by the host operating system.) Then open the file and read the records until the end of the file is reached. The FREWIND function then repositions the pointer to the beginning of the file. The first record is read again and stored in the File Data Buffer (FDB). The first token is retrieved and stored in the variable VAL.

```
rc=filename('myfile','physical-filename ');
fid=fopen('myfile');
do while (rc ne -1);
   rc=fread(fid);          /* Read a record. */
end;

   /* Reposition pointer at beginning of file. */
if rc= -1  then rc=frewind(fid);
rc=fread(fid);             /* Read first record. */
rc=fget(fid,val);          /* Read first token into VAL. */
put val= ;
rc=fclose(fid);
rc=filename('myfile','');
```

FRLEN

Returns the size of the last record read, or, if the file is opened for output, returns the current record size

See Also:
FCLOSE
FOPEN
FREAD

length=**FRLEN**(*file-id*);

Where...	Is type...	And represents...
length	N	The length of the current record if the file is opened for output, otherwise, the length of the last record read.
file-id	N	The identifier assigned when the file was opened. If *file-id* is invalid, the program halts execution.

Example

Open the file identified by the fileref MYFILE. Determine the minimum and maximum length of records in the external file, and write the results to the log or the MESSAGE window:

```
fid=fopen('myfile');
min=0;
max=0;
if (fread(fid)=0) then
   do;
      min=frlen(fid);
      max=min;
      do while(fread(fid)=0);
         reclen=frlen(fid);
         if (reclen>max) then max=reclen;
         if (reclen<min) then min=reclen;
      end;
      rc=fclose(fid);
   end;
put min= max=;
```

FSEDIT

Displays a SAS data set by observation

SAS/FSP software required

See Also:
FSVIEW
LETTER
NEW

CALL FSEDIT(*data-set-name*<,*screen-name*<,*open-mode*<,*obs-number*>>>);

Where...	Is type...	And represents...
data-set-name	C	The SAS data set to be displayed. Use the syntax <*libref.*>*member-name*<(*data-set-options*)>. If you omit the libref, the default WORK library is used.
		You can add a list of SAS data set options in parentheses following the data set name. All data set options are valid except FIRSTOBS= and OBS=. Refer to Chapter 15 in *SAS Language: Reference* for a listing and descriptions of data set options.
screen-name	C	A screen entry for the FSEDIT session. Use the syntax <*libref.*>*catalog-name*<.*entry-name*<.SCREEN>>. Screen entries are SAS catalog entries of type SCREEN that define custom features for the FSEDIT session.
		A one- or two-level name is interpreted as a catalog name and the default screen entry name, FSEDIT.SCREEN. (A one-level name is interpreted as a catalog in the default SAS data library, WORK.) If the specified catalog does not already exist, it is created.
		If the screen entry does not already exist, a new screen entry is not created unless the user issues a MODIFY command during the FSEDIT session.
		If you want to use predefined data set labels, use an equal sign (=) for *screen-name*. (A modifed SCREEN entry is not saved.) Variable names are used for any fields without labels.
open-mode	C	The type of access to the SAS data set:
		'ADD' adds a new blank observation to the data set, and then opens the FSEDIT window with the new observation displayed for editing.
		'BROWSE' opens the FSBROWSE window for reading observations.
		'EDIT' opens the FSEDIT window for editing observations. (Default)
		'NEW' opens the FSEDIT NEW window for creating the specified SAS data set as a new one before opening the FSEDIT window to enter values in the new data set.
obs-number	N	The first observation to be displayed when the FSEDIT or FSBROWSE window is opened. This argument is ignored unless the value of *open-mode* is 'EDIT' or 'BROWSE'.

Details

The FSEDIT routine calls the FSEDIT procedure, which opens the FSEDIT window to display the specified SAS data set. You can specify BROWSE for *open-mode* to open the FSBROWSE window for browsing the data set instead. You can optionally specify the name of a screen entry to provide a custom display and the number of the observation to be displayed when the window is opened.

If you want to specify *open-mode* or *obs-number* but do not want to specify a screen entry, use a null string (' ') for *screen-name*.

For more information on the commands available in the FSEDIT procedure, see *SAS/FSP Software: Usage and Reference*.

Examples

Open a SAS data set named PERSONAL (in the default SAS data library WORK) for editing:

```
call fsedit('personal');
```

Open the SAS data set PERSONAL, in the library MASTER, for editing using a custom SCREEN entry named PER1 in the catalog MASTER.DISPLAY:

```
call fsedit('master.personal','master.display.per1');
```

Open a SAS data set named MASTER.PERSONAL for browsing using the default FSBROWSE window display:

```
call fsedit('master.personal',' ','browse');
```

To display the predefined labels associated with the SAS data set variables instead of the variable names, specify an equal sign (=) for the *screen-name* argument, as in the following example:

```
call fsedit('master.personal','=','browse');
```

Specify SAS data set options by enclosing them within parentheses immediately following the SAS data set name in the *data-set-name* argument, as in the following examples.

Open a SAS data set named MASTER.PERSONAL, and subset the observations based on the value entered for the numeric variable SCRNUM:

```
call fsedit('master.personal(where=(num='||put(scrnum,5.)||'))');
```

Open a SAS data set named MASTER.PERSONAL, and subset the observations based on the value entered for the character variable SCRNAME:

```
call fsedit('master.personal(where=(name='||quote(scrname)||'))');
```

FSEP

Sets the token delimiters for the FGET function

See Also:
FGET
FREAD

rc=**FSEP**(*file-id,cval*);

Where...	Is type...	And represents...
rc	N	Whether the operation was successful: 0 if successful $\neq$ 0 if not successful.
file-id	N	The identifier assigned when the file was opened. If *file-id* is invalid, the program halts execution.
cval	C	The token delimiter used to separate items in the File Data Buffer (FDB). Each character in the string is considered a delimiter. The default delimiter is a blank.

Example

Suppose the external file has data in this form:

```
John J. Doe,Male,25,Weight Lifter
```

Note that each field is separated by a comma.

Read the file identified by the fileref MYFILE, using the comma as a separator, and write the values for NAME, SEX, AGE, and WORK to the log or the MESSAGE window:

```
fid=fopen('myfile');
rc=fsep(fid,',');
do while(fread(fid)=0);
   rc=fget(fid,name);
   rc=fget(fid,sex);
   rc=fget(fid,agec);
   age=input(agec,best.);
   rc=fget(fid,work);
   put name= sex= age= work=;
end;
rc=fclose(fid);
```

FSLIST

Displays an external file for browsing

SAS/FSP software required

See Also:
FSEDIT
FSVIEW
LETTER

CALL FSLIST(*file* <,*options*>);

Where...	Is type...	And represents...
file	C	The fileref or physical filename of the external file. A physical name must be enclosed in quotation marks.
options	C	One or more carriage-control options for formatting the display, with multiple options separated by blanks and enclosed in one set of quote marks:

CC   use the host operating system's native carriage-control characters.

FORTCC   use FORTRAN-style carriage control.

NOCC   treat carriage-control characters as regular text. (Default)

For CC or FORTCC, you can also specify an overprinting control option:

OVP   print the current line over the previous line when the overprint code is encountered. The OVP option is valid only if the CC or FORTCC option is also specified. The default is NOOVP.

NOOVP   ignore the overprint code and print each line from the file on a separate line of the display.

If you use the FORTCC option, the first column of each line in the external file is not displayed. The character in this column is interpreted as a carriage-control code. Under some operating systems, FORTRAN-style carriage control is the native carriage control. For these systems, the FORTCC and CC options produce the same behavior.

Under some operating systems, the CC option is the default for print files.

Details

The FSLIST routine calls the FSLIST procedure, which opens the FSLIST window to display an external file for interactive browsing. This routine provides a convenient method for examining the information stored in an external file.

For more information on the commands available in the FSLIST procedure, see *SAS/FSP Software: Usage and Reference*.

External files (files maintained by the host operating system rather than by the SAS System) can contain various types of information:

□ data records

□ output from previous SAS sessions

□ SAS source statements

□ carriage-control information.

Examples

Browse an external file to which the fileref MYFILE has previously been assigned. The file contains FORTRAN-style carriage control, and any overprinting is honored.

```
call fslist('myfile','fortcc ovp');
```

Browse the external file named FSLIST.PUB. The filename string has embedded quotes to indicate that a physical filename, not a fileref, is being passed to the FSLIST routine.

```
call fslist('"fslist.pub"');
```

Note: The form of the physical filename depends on the host operating system.

FSVIEW

Displays a SAS data set as a table of observations

SAS/FSP software required

See Also:
FSEDIT
NEW

CALL FSVIEW(*data-set-name*<,*open-mode*<,*formula-entry*<,*options*>>>);

Where...	Is type...	And represents...
data-set-name	C	The SAS data set to be displayed. Use the format <*libref.*>*member-name*<(*data-set-options*)>. If the libref is omitted, the default SAS data library, WORK, is assumed.
		You can add a list of SAS data set options in parentheses following the data set name. All data set options are valid except FIRSTOBS= and OBS=. Refer to Chapter 15 in *SAS Language: Reference* for a listing and descriptions of data set options.
open-mode	C	The type of access to the SAS data set:
		'ADD' add a new blank observation to the data set, and then open the FSVIEW window with the new observation displayed for editing.
		'BROWSE' open the FSVIEW window for reading observations. (Default)
		'EDIT' open the FSVIEW window for editing observations.
		'NEW' open the FSVIEW NEW window for creating the specified SAS data set as a new one before opening the FSVIEW window to enter values in the new data set.
formula-entry	C	The formula entry for the FSVIEW session. Formula entries are SAS catalog entries of type FORMULA that define custom features for the FSVIEW session or that control the display and behavior of the session. Specify as <*libref.*>*catalog-name*<.*entry-name*<.FORMULA>>.

Where...	Is type...	And represents...
		If a one- or two-level name is specified for this argument, the name is interpreted as a catalog name and the default formula entry name is assumed. The default formula entry name is the same as the member name of the data set specified in the *data-set-name* argument. (A one-level name is assumed to refer to a catalog in the default SAS data library, WORK.) If the specified catalog does not already exist, it is created. If the specified formula entry does not already exist, a new formula entry is created.
options	C	Disabling certain FSVIEW window commands for the duration of the FSVIEW session. Separate multiple options with blanks.

BRONLY   disable the MODIFY command so only browsing is allowed. **'EDIT'** and **'ADD'** modes are ignored when **BRONLY** is specified.

NOADD   disable the ADD command so new observations cannot be added to the data set.

NODELETE   disable the DELETE command so observations cannot be deleted.

Details

The FSVIEW routine calls the FSVIEW procedure, which opens the FSVIEW window to display the specified SAS data set. By default, the SAS data set is opened for browsing. You can use the *open-mode* argument to specify that the data set should instead be opened for editing. You can also specify a formula entry and other options for the FSVIEW session.

If you specify NEW for the *open-mode* argument, the FSVIEW NEW window is opened for the user to define a new SAS data set before the FSVIEW window is opened to enter values for that data set.

You can specify SAS data set options by enclosing them within parentheses immediately following the SAS data set name in the *data-set-name* argument, as in the second example in the "Examples" section.

If you want to specify the *options* argument but do not want to specify a formula entry, use a null string (' ') for the *formula-name* argument.

You can specify multiple values for the *options* argument by separating the values with blanks.

For more information on the commands available in the FSVIEW procedure, see *SAS/FSP Software: Usage and Reference.*

Examples

Browse a SAS data set named PERSONAL (in the default SAS data library WORK):

```
call fsview('personal');
```

Edit a SAS data set named PERSONAL in the library MASTER. Only those observations where the SITE variable has the value 5 are displayed.

```
call fsview('master.personal(where=(site=5))','edit');
```

Edit a SAS data set named PERSONAL in the MASTER library. Observations cannot be added or deleted during the FSVIEW session.

```
call fsview('master.personal','edit','','noadd nodelete');
```

FWRITE

Writes a record to an external file

See Also:
FAPPEND
FGET
FPUT

---

*sysrc=***FWRITE**(*file-id<,cc>*);

Where...	Is type...	And represents...

sysrc	N	Whether the operation was successful:
		  0 if successful
		  $\neq 0$ if not successful.

file-id	N	The identifier assigned when the file was opened. If *file-id* is invalid, the program halts execution.
cc	C	A carriage-control character: *blank* starts the record on a new line.
		'0' skips one blank line before a new line.
		'-' skips two blank lines before a new line.
		'1' starts the line on a new page.
		'+' overstrikes the line on a previous line.
		'P' interprets the line as a terminal prompt.
		'=' interprets the line as carriage control information.
		all else starts the line record on a new line.

Details

FWRITE moves text from the File Data Buffer (FDB) to the external file. In order to use the carriage control characters, you must open the file with a RECORD format of **'P'** (PRINT format) in FOPEN.

Example

If the file to which the fileref MYFILE is assigned is successfully opened, write the numbers 1 to 50 to the external file, skipping two blank lines. Then call FSLIST to display the newly created file.

```
rc=filename('myfile','physical-filename');
fid=fopen('myfile','o',0,'P');

do i=1 to 50;
   rc=fput(fid,put(i,2.));

   if (fwrite(fid,'-') ne 0) then do;
      _msg_=sysmsg();
```

```
        put msg;
        return;
    end;
end;

rc=fclose(fid);
call fslist('myfile','cc');
```

GETFKEY

Returns the command assigned to a function key

See Also:
FKEYNAME
NUMFKEYS
SETFKEY

key-command=**GETFKEY**(*key-name*);

Where...	Is type...	And represents...
key-command	C	The command currently assigned to the function key.
key-name	C	The name of the function key as listed in the KEYS window. Function key names vary according to the device. Use FKEYNAME to retrieve the name of a function key.

Details

GETFKEY returns the commands assigned to a function key for the current window. This is the same as the text displayed for the key in the KEYS window.

You can use this function only in entries that have a DISPLAY window.

Example

Return the command assigned to the first function key if the name of the function key is not known:

```
command=getfkey(fkeyname(1));
```

If the value of the first function key is F1, return the command assigned to the first function key:

```
command=getfkey('F1');
```

GETFOOT

Returns the text of a footnote definition

See Also:
GETTITLE
SETFOOT
SETTITLE

foot-text=**GETFOOT**(*foot-num*);

Where...	Is type...	And represents...
foot-text	C	The text of the footnote definition, or blank if the footnote is not defined.
foot-num	N	The number (1 to 10) of the footnote definition.

Details

Use GETFOOT to retrieve any footnote text previously defined in the SAS session through either the FOOTNOTE statement or the SCL SETFOOT routine. Only the footnote text is retrieved. Graphic options such as color or font are not returned.

You can view footnotes in the FOOTNOTES window by using the FOOTNOTE command. Changing any text in the FOOTNOTES window, however, resets all graphically defined FOOTNOTE options such as color, font, and position.

For more information on footnotes, see *SAS Language: Reference*. For more information on graphical footnotes, see *SAS/GRAPH Software: Reference*.

Example

Store the text of FOOTNOTE2 in the variable FNOTE2:

```
fnote2=getfoot(2);
```

GETITEMC

Returns a character value that is identified by its position in an SCL list

See

Also:
GETITEML
GETITEMN
GETNITEMC
GETNITEML
GETNITEMN
ITEMTYPE
LISTLEN
MAKELIST
MAKENLIST
POPC
POPL
POPN
SETITEMC
SETITEML
SETITEMN

cval=**GETITEMC**(*list-id*<,*index*>);

Where...	Is type...	And represents...
cval	C	The character value stored at the specified position in the list.
list-id	N	The identifier of the list containing the value that GETITEMC returns. An invalid *list-id* produces an error condition.
index	N	The position of the item in the list. The position can be specified as a positive or negative number. By default, *index* is 1 (the first item). If *index* is a positive number, the item is at position *index* from the beginning of the list. If *index* is a negative number, the item is at position ABS(*index*) from the end of the list. An error condition results if the absolute value for *index* is zero or it is greater than the number of items in the list.

Details

The value to return is specified by its position in the list. An error results if you attempt to get a character item when the indexed item is numeric or a list identifier. To determine the type of an item in a list before using GETITEMC, use ITEMTYPE.

Example

Return the third and first character items from the list identified by the LISTID variable:

```
citem=getitemc(listid,3);
citem=getitemc(listid);
```

GETITEML

Returns a sublist identifier that is identified by its position in an SCL list

See Also:
GETITEMC
GETITEMN
GETNITEMC
GETNITEML
GETNITEMN
ITEMTYPE
LISTLEN
MAKELIST
MAKENLIST
POPC
POPL
POPN
SETITEMC
SETITEML
SETITEMN

sublist-id=**GETITEML**(*list-id* <,*index*>);

Where...	Is type...	And represents...
sublist-id	N	The identifier of the sublist stored at the specified position in the list.
list-id	N	The identifier of the list containing the value that GETITEML returns. An invalid *list-id* produces an error condition.
index	N	The position of the item in the list. The position can be specified as a positive or negative number. By default, *index* is 1 (the first item). If *index* is a positive number, the item is at position *index* from the beginning of the list. If *index* is a negative number, the item is at position ABS(*index*) from the end of the list. An error condition results if the absolute value for *index* is zero or it is greater than the number of items in the list.

Details

The value to be returned is specified by its position in the list. An error results if you attempt to get a list value when the indexed item is character or numeric. To determine the type of an item in a list before using GETITEML, use ITEMTYPE.

Example

Return the third and first sublist items from the list identified by the LISTID variable:

```
sublist=getiteml(listid,3);
sublist=getiteml(listid);
```

GETITEMN

Returns a numeric value that is identified by its position in an SCL list

See Also:
GETITEMC
GETITEML
GETNITEMC
GETNITEML
GETNITEMN
ITEMTYPE
LISTLEN
MAKELIST
MAKENLIST
POPC
POPL
POPN
SETITEMC
SETITEML
SETITEMN

nval=**GETITEMN**(*list-id*<,*index*>);

Where...	Is type...	And represents...
nval	N	The numeric value stored at the specified position in the list.
list-id	N	The identifier of the list containing the value that GETITEMN returns. An invalid *list-id* produces an error condition.
index	N	The position of the item in the list. The position can be specified as a positive or negative number. By default, *index* is 1 (the first item). If *index* is a positive number, the item is at position *index* from the beginning of the list. If *index* is a negative number, the item is at position ABS(*index*) from the end of the list. An error condition results if the absolute value for *index* is zero or it is greater than the number of items in the list.

Details

The value to be returned is specified by its position in the list. An error results if you attempt to get a numeric value when the indexed value is character or a list identifier. To determine the type of an item in a list before using GETITEMN, use ITEMTYPE.

Example

Return the third and first numeric items from the list identified by the LISTID variable:

```
nitem=getitemn(listid,3);
nitem=getitemn(listid);
```

GETLATTR

Returns the attributes of an SCL list or an item in the list

See Also:
HASATTR
MAKELIST
MAKENLIST
SETLATTR

attributes=**GETLATTR**(*list-id*<,*index*>);

Where...	Is type...	And represents...
attributes	C	A string of words separated by blanks. Each word is a separate attribute for a list or item.
list-id	N	The identifier of the list that GETLATTR processes. An invalid *list-id* produces an error condition.
index	N	The position of the item in the list. The position can be specified as a positive or negative number. By default, *index* is 1 (the first item). If *index* is a positive number, the item is at position *index* from the beginning of the list. If *index* is a negative number, the item is at position ABS(*index*) from the end of the list. An error condition results if the absolute value for *index* is zero or it is greater than the number of items in the list
		If *index* is 0 or is omitted, the attributes returned by GETLATTR are list attributes. If *index* is nonzero, GETLATTR returns the attributes associated with the indexed item instead of the entire list.

Details

The items in *attributes* can be used to assign attributes to another list or item. The string returned as *attributes* contains a blank before and after each attribute, which makes it easy to determine if an attribute is set by searching *attributes* for an attribute name. Use the INDEX function to search the string for a specified attribute. If *index* is omitted, *attributes* contains the combination of one attribute from each row of the following table:

Default Setting	Alternate Setting
DELETE	NODELETE
UPDATE	NOUPDATE
NOFIXEDTYPE	FIXEDTYPE
NOFIXEDLENGTH	FIXEDLENGTH
ANYNAMES	SASNAMES
DUPNAMES	NODUPNAMES
NOCHARONLY	CHARONLY
NONUMONLY	NUMONLY
COPY	NOCOPY

If *index* is supplied, *attributes* is the set of item attributes consisting of the combination of one attribute from each row of the following table:

Default Setting	Alternate Setting
ACTIVE	INACTIVE
WRITE	NOWRITE
DELETE	NODELETE
UPDATE	NOUPDATE
NOFIXEDTYPE	FIXEDTYPE

For detailed information on these attributes, see SETLATTR.

Example

Create a list LISTID with one item and print the sets of list attributes for LISTID and item attributes associated with the first item of LISTID. Note the leading and trailing blanks in the attribute strings, which are evident by embedding the attribute strings in double quote characters.

```
INIT:
  listid = makelist(1);
  listattrs = '"' || getlattr(listid) || '"';
  put listattrs=;
  found = index(listattrs,'UPDATE');
  put found=;
  itemattrs = '"' || getlattr(listid,1) || '"';
  put itemattrs=;
  rc = dellist(listid);
return;
```

The output of this example is:

```
LISTATTRS=" DELETE UPDATE NOFIXEDTYPE NOFIXEDLENGTH ANYNAMES
DUPNAMES NOCHARONLY NONUMONLY COPY "
FOUND=10;
ITEMATTRS=" ACTIVE WRITE NOAUTO NOEDIT DELETE UPDATE NOFIXEDTYPE "
```

FOUND returns the starting position of the word "UPDATE" in the string of list attributes.

GETNITEMC

Returns a character value identified by its name in an SCL list

See Also:
DELNITEM
GETITEMC
GETITEML
GETITEMN
GETNITEML
GETNITEMN
MAKELIST
MAKENLIST
NAMEDITEM
NAMEITEM
SEARCHC
SEARCHL
SEARCHN
SETNITEMC
SETNITEML
SETNITEMN

cval=**GETNITEMC**(*list-id,name<,occurrence <,start-index<,default>>>*);

Where...	Is type...	And represents...
cval	C	The character value found at the named position in the list.
list-id	N	The identifier of the list that GETNITEMC searches. An invalid *list-id* produces an error condition.
name	C	The name of the item to fetch from the list. Item names are converted to uppercase, and trailing blanks are ignored when searching the list for a matching name. Thus, the names 'abc' and 'Abc' are converted to 'ABC'.
occurrence	N	The number of the occurrence of the named item to be returned. The default is 1 for the first occurrence of the item.
start-index	N	Where in the list to begin searching for the item. By default, *start-index* is 1 (the first item). If *start-index* is positive, the search begins at position *start-index* items from the beginning of the list. If *start-index* is negative, the search begins at the item specified by ABS(*start-index*) items from the end of the list. An error condition results if the absolute value of *start-index* is zero or greater than the number of items in the list.
default	C	A default character value to return from GETNITEMC if the named character value is not found.

Details

By default, GETNITEMC starts searching at the beginning of the list and returns the first item found with the specified name. However, you can specify that the search start at a different place in the list by specifying an *start-index* other than 1. You can also specify a different occurrence of the item (for example, the second, tenth, or twentieth) by specifying an *occurrence* other than 1. If the search does not succeed and you have specified a default character value as the fifth parameter, that default value is returned instead of an error condition.

If *occurrence* and *start-index* are both positive or both negative, the search proceeds forward from the *start-index* item. For forward searches, the search continues only to the end of the list and does not wrap back to the front of the list. If *occurrence* or *start-index* is negative, the search is backwards. For backward searches, the search continues only to the beginning of the list and does not wrap back to the end of the list.

GETNITEMC combines the actions of NAMEDITEM and GETITEMC.
An error condition results if:

□ the named item is not a character value.

□ the named item does not exist and *default* is not specified.

Examples

Halt the program if there are fewer than two items named **'Software Sales'** in the list identified by DIRECTORY. Omitting the default value from GETNITEMC designates that the character item must exist in the list. The statement

```
s=getnitemc(directory,'Software Sales',2,-1);
```

is equivalent to the following statements:

```
ssi=nameditem(directory,'Software Sales',2,-1);
s=getitemc(directory,ssi);
```

The second occurrence of **'Software Sales'** starting from the end of the list is returned.

If your application is more general and the named item may not be in the list, you can supply a character value for *default* in the GETNITEMC function:

```
s=getnitemc(directory,'Software Sales',2,-1,defaultc);
```

In situations where your application manipulates an SCL list and cannot guarantee that the named item is character, you should not use GETNITEMC. For example, the call

```
c = getnitemc(listid, 'A', occurrence, startIndex);
```

will generate an error if the named item's type is not character. Instead, when manipulating SCL lists which may contain other types, you should use NAMEDITEM, ITEMTYPE and GETITEMC. The following code is suitable for this use:

```
index = nameditem(listid, 'A', occurrence, startIndex);
if index then
   select (itemtype(listid, index));
     when ('C') c = getitemc(listid, index);
     when ('L') l = getiteml(listid, index);
     when ('N') n = getitemn(listid, index);
   end;
```

GETNITEML

Returns a list identifier value identified by its name in an SCL list

See Also:
DELNITEM
GETITEMC
GETITEML
GETITEMN
GETNITEMC
GETNITEMN
MAKELIST
MAKENLIST
NAMEDITEM
NAMEITEM
SEARCHC
SEARCHL
SEARCHN
SETNITEMC
SETNITEML
SETNITEMN

sublist-id=**GETNITEML**(*list-id,name<,occurrence <,start-index<,default-list-id>>>*);

Where...	Is type...	And represents...
sublist-id	N	The identifier of the sublist item found at the named position in the list.
list-id	N	The identifier of the list that GETNITEML searches. An invalid *list-id* produces an error condition.
name	C	The name of the item to fetch from the list. Item names are converted to uppercase and trailing blanks are ignored when searching the list for a matching name. Thus, the names 'abc' and 'Abc ' are converted to 'ABC'.
occurrence	N	The number of the occurrence of the named item to be returned. The default is 1 for the first occurrence of the item.
start-index	N	Where in the list to begin searching for the item. By default, *start-index* is 1 (the first item). If *start-index* is positive, the search begins at position *start-index* items from the beginning of the list. If *start-index* is negative, the search begins at the item specified by ABS(*start-index*) items from the end of the list. An error condition results if the absolute value of *start-index* is zero or greater than the number of items in the list.
default-list-id	N	The default list identifier to return from GETNITEML if the named sublist is not found.

Details

By default, GETNITEML starts searching at the beginning of the list and returns the first item found with the specified name. However, you can specify that the search start at a different place in the list by specifying an *start-index* other than 1. You can also specify a different occurrence of the item (for example, the second, tenth, or twentieth) by specifying an *occurrence* other than 1. If the search does not succeed and you have specified a default character value as the fifth parameter, that default value is returned instead of an error condition.

If *occurrence* and *start-index* are both positive or both negative, the search proceeds forward from the *start-index* item. For forward searches, the search continues only to the end of the list and does not wrap back to the front of the list. If *occurrence* or *start-index* is negative, the search is backwards. For backward searches, the search continues only to the beginning of the list and does not wrap back to the end of the list.

GETNITEML combines the actions of NAMEDITEM and GETITEML.

An error condition results if:

□ the named item is not a list identifier.

□ the named item does not exist and *default* is not specified.

Examples

Halt the program if there are fewer than two items named 'Marketing' in the list identified by EMP_LIST. Omitting the default value from GETNITEML designates that the sublist item must exist in the list. The statement:

```
listid=getniteml(emp_list,'Marketing',2,-10);
```

is equivalent to the statements:

```
mpos=nameditem(emp_list,'Marketing',2,-10);
listid=getiteml(emp_list,mpos);
```

To list the contents of a list to the MESSAGE or LOG window, use the PUTLIST routine, for example:

```
call putlist(listid,'LISTID=',0);
```

If your application is more general and the named item may not be in the list, supply a list identifier value for *default* in GETNITEML:

```
sslistid=getniteml(emp_list,'Marketing',2,-10,-1);
```

The above call to GETNITEML is equivalent to the following:

```
mpos=nameditem(emp_list,'Marketing',2,-10);
if mpos ne 0 then
    sslistid=getiteml(emp_list,mpos);
else
    sslistid=-1;
```

In situations where your application manipulates an SCL list and cannot guarantee that the named item is a list identifier, you should not use GETNITEML. For example, the call

```
l = getniteml(listid, 'A', occurrence, startIndex);
```

will generate an error if the named item's type is not a list. Instead, when manipulating SCL lists which may contain other types, you should use NAMEDITEM, ITEMTYPE and GETITEML. The following code is suitable for this use:

```
index = nameditem(listid, 'A', occurrence, startIndex);
if index then
    select (itemtype(listid, index));
        when ('C') c = getitemc(listid, index);
        when ('L') l = getiteml(listid, index);
        when ('N') n = getitemn(listid, index);
    end;
```

GETNITEMN

Returns a numeric value identified by its name in the SCL list

See Also:
DELITEM
GETITEMC
GETITEML
GETNITEMC
GETNITEML
LISTLEN
MAKELIST
MAKENLIST
SEARCHC
SEARCHL
SEARCHN
SETNITEMC
SETNITEML
SETNITEMN

nval=**GETNITEMN**(*list-id*,*name*<*occurrence* <,*start-index*<,*default*>>>);

Where...	Is type...	And represents...
nval	N	The numeric value found at the named position in the list.
list-id	N	The identifier of the list that GETNITEMN searches. An invalid *list-id* produces an error condition.
name	C	The name of the item to fetch from the list. Item names are converted to uppercase and trailing blanks are ignored when searching the list for a matching name. Thus, the names 'abc' and 'Abc' are converted to 'ABC'.
occurrence	N	The number of the occurrence of the named item to be returned. The default is 1 for the first occurrence of the item.
start-index	N	Where in the list to begin searching for the item. By default, *start-index* is 1 (the first item). If *start-index* is positive, the search begins at position *start-index* items from the beginning of the list. If *start-index* is negative, the search begins at the item specified by ABS(*start-index*) items from the end of the list. An error condition results if the absolute value of *start-index* is zero or greater than the number of items in the list.
default	N	The default numeric value to return from GETNITEMN if the named numeric value is not found.

Details

By default, GETNITEMN starts searching at the beginning of the list and returns the first item found with the specified name. However, you can specify that the search start at a different place in the list by specifying a *start-index* other than 1. You can also specify a different occurrence of the item (for example, the second, tenth, or twentieth) by specifying an *occurrence* other than 1. If the search does not succeed and you have specified a default character value as the fifth parameter, that default value is returned instead of an error condition.

If *occurrence* and *start-index* are both positive or both negative, the search proceeds forward from the *start-index* item. For forward searches, the search continues only to the end of the list and does not wrap back to the front of the list. If *occurrence* or *start-index* is negative, the search is backwards. For backward searches, the search continues only to the beginning of the list and does not wrap back to the end of the list.

GETNITEMN combines the actions of NAMEDITEM and GETITEMN.

An error condition results if:

□ the named item specified is not a numeric value.

□ the named item does not exist and *default* is not specified.

Examples

The statement:

```
numval=getnitemn(revenue,'Eastern Region');
```

is equivalent to the statements:

```
eastpos=nameditem(revenue,'Eastern Region',2,-1);
numval=getitemn(revenue, eastpos);
```

The preceding statements halt the program if there are fewer than two items named 'Eastern Region' in the list identified by REVENUE. Omitting the default value from GETNITEMN specifies that the numeric item must exist in the list.

If your application is more general and the named item may not be in the list, supply a numeric value for *default* in GETNITEMN:

```
defaultnum=_blank_;
ssval=getnitemn(revenue,'Eastern Region',1,1,defaultnum);
```

The above call to GETNITEML is equivalent to the following:

```
defaultnum=_blank_;
eastpos=nameditem(revenue,'Eastern Region');
if eastpos ne 0 then
    ssval=getitemn(revenue,eastpos);
else
    ssval=defaultnum;
```

In situations where your application manipulates an SCL list and cannot guarantee that the named item is numeric, you should not use GETNITEMN. For example, the call

```
n = getnitemn(listid, 'A', occurrence, startIndex);
```

will generate an error if the named item's type is not numeric. Instead, when manipulating SCL lists which may contain other types, you should use NAMEDITEM, ITEMTYPE and GETITEMN. The following code is suitable for this use:

```
index = nameditem(listid, 'A', occurrence, startIndex);
if index then
    select (itemtype(listid, index));
        when ('C') c = getitemc(listid, index);
        when ('L') l = getiteml(listid, index);
        when ('N') n = getitemn(listid, index);
    end;
```

GETPARMID

Returns the numeric value stored by the SETPARMID routine

See Also:
DISPLAY
ENTRY
SETPARMID

nval=**GETPARMID**();

Where...	Is type...	And represents...
nval	N	The numeric value stored by a previous call to the SETPARMID routine.

Details

SETPARMID stores a value, and GETPARMID retrieves the stored value. SETPARMID and GETPARMID allow only one value to be passed. To pass multiple values between entries, use the ENTRY statement. Additional ways of making values available to other SCL programs include using macro variables and SCL lists.

Example

Retrieve the data set identifier value stored in another program by SETPARMID:

```
dsid=getparmid();
```

GETTITLE

Returns the text of a title definition

See Also:
GETFOOT
SETFOOT
SETTITLE

title-text=**GETTITLE**(*title-num*);

Where...	Is type...	And represents...
title-text	C	The text of the title definition, or a blank if the title is not defined.
title-num	N	The number (1 to 10) of the title definition.

Details

Use GETTITLE to retrieve any title text previously defined in the SAS session through either the TITLE statement or SCL SETTITLE routine. Only the title text is retrieved. Graphic options, such as color or font, are not returned.

You can view titles in the TITLES window by using the TITLE command. Changing any text in the TITLES window, however, resets all graphically defined title options, such as color, font, and position.

For more information on titles, see *SAS Language: Reference*, and for more information on graphical titles, see *SAS/GRAPH Software: Reference*.

Example

Put the text of TITLE2 into the variable TITLE2:

```
title2=gettitle(2);
```

GETVARC

Assigns the value of a SAS data set variable to a character SCL variable

See Also:
FETCH
FETCHOBS
GETVARN
LOCATEC
LOCATEN
PUTVARC
PUTVARN
UPDATE
VARNUM

cval=**GETVARC**(*data-set-id,var-num*);

Where...	Is type...	And represents...
cval	C	The value of the character variable identified by the *var-num* argument.
data-set-id	N	The identifier assigned when the data set was opened. If *data-set-id* is invalid, the program halts execution.
var-num	N	The number of the variable in the Data Set Data Vector (DDV). This value can be obtained using the VARNUM function. In addition, this value is listed next to the variable when you use the CONTENTS procedure or the CONTENTS function in SCL. If the variable specified in *var-num* is invalid, the program halts execution.

Details

Use VARNUM to obtain the number of a variable in a SAS data set. VARNUM can be nested or it can be assigned to a variable that can then be passed as the second argument, as shown in the examples. GETVARC reads the value of a character variable from the current observation in the Data Set Data Vector (DDV) into an SCL variable in the SCL data vector (SDV).

Examples

Nest VARNUM. Read in the value of the character variable NAME from the tenth observation of an open SAS data set. You must have previously opened the data set using OPEN. The data set identifier value for the open data set is stored in the variable MYDATAID.

```
rc=fetchobs(mydataid,10);
user=getvarc(mydataid,varnum(mydataid,'name'));
```

   Assign VARNUM to a variable that can then be passed as the second argument. You must have previously opened the data set using OPEN. You are fetching from observation 10.

```
namenum=varnum(mydataid,'name');
rc=fetchobs(mydataid,10);
user=getvarc(mydataid,namenum);
```

GETVARN

Assigns the value of a SAS data set variable to a numeric SCL variable

See Also:
FETCH
FETCHOBS
GETVARC
LOCATEC
LOCATEN
PUTVARC
PUTVARN
UPDATE
VARNUM

nval=**GETVARN**(*data-set-id,var-num*);

Where...	Is type...	And represents...
nval	N	The value of the numeric variable identified by the *var-num* argument.
data-set-id	N	The identifier assigned when the data set was opened. If *data-set-id* is invalid, the program halts execution.
var-num	N	The number of the variable in the Data Set Data Vector (DDV). You can obtain this value using VARNUM. In addition, this value is listed next to the variable when you use the CONTENTS procedure or the CONTENTS function in SCL. If the variable specified in *var-num* is invalid, the program halts execution.

Details

Use VARNUM to obtain the number of a variable in a SAS data set. You can nest VARNUM or you can assign it to a variable that can then be passed as the second argument, as shown in the "Examples" section. GETVARN reads the value of a numeric variable from the current observation in the Data Set Data Vector (DDV) into an SCL variable in the SCL data vector (SDV).

Examples

Nest VARNUM. Read in the value of the numeric variable PRICE from the tenth observation of an open SAS data set. The data set must have previously been opened using OPEN. The data set identifier value for the open data set is stored in the variable MYDATAID.

```
rc=fetchobs(mydataid,10);
price=getvarn(mydataid,varnum(mydataid,'price'));
```

Assign VARNUM to a variable that can then be passed as the second argument. You must have previously opened the data set using OPEN. You are fetching from observation 10.

```
pricenum=varnum(mydataid,'price');
rc=fetchobs(mydataid,10);
price=getvarn(mydataid,pricenum);
```

GGLOBAL

Returns the text of a SYMBOL, PATTERN, LEGEND, or AXIS statement definition

See Also:
GGLOBALE
GGLOBALN

stmt-text=**GGLOBAL**(*stmt-type,stmt-num*);

Where...	Is type...	And represents...
stmt-text	C	The text of the retrieved SYMBOL, PATTERN, LEGEND, or AXIS statement definition.
stmt-type	C	The type of statement to retrieve: `'SYMBOL'` `'PATTERN'` `'LEGEND'` `'AXIS'` If *stmt-type* is invalid, a missing value is returned.
stmt-num	N	The number of the SYMBOL, PATTERN, LEGEND, or AXIS statement to retrieve. Valid values are from 1 to the value returned by GGLOBALN.

Details

Because a user can change SYMBOL, PATTERN, LEGEND, or AXIS statements during the execution of an application, GGLOBALN must be executed before the GGLOBAL function to set up an internal table used by GGLOBAL.

Note: SYMBOL and PATTERN can generate more than one definition per statement. For more information on SYMBOL, PATTERN, LEGEND, and AXIS statements, see *SAS/GRAPH Software: Reference*.

Example

Assume that the following SYMBOL statements have been defined for the current SAS session:

```
symbol1 c=red;
symbol30 c=blue;
```

Check to see that at least two SYMBOL statements are available. If this condition is true, the text of the second SYMBOL statement is returned to the variable SYMBOL2.

```
numsymb=gglobaln('symbol');
if (numsymb >= 2) then symbol2=gglobal('symbol',2);
```

The value returned to NUMSYMB is 2. The following value is returned to SYMBOL2:

```
SYMBOL30 CV=BLUE CO=BLUE CI=BLUE;
```

■ Release 6.11 . . . .

The value of HEIGHT is also returned:

```
SYMBOL30 CV=BLUE CO=BLUE CI=BLUE HEIGHT=1 ;
```

. . . . ■

GGLOBALE

Deletes an internal table of SYMBOL, PATTERN, LEGEND, or AXIS definitions

See Also:
GGLOBAL
GGLOBALN

sysrc=**GGLOBALE**(*stmt-type*);

Where...	Is type...	And represents...
sysrc	N	Whether the operation was successful: 0 if successful ≠ 0 if not successful
stmt-type	C	The type of statement to delete: **'SYMBOL'** **'PATTERN'** **'LEGEND'** **'AXIS'**

Details

When you have completed processing information concerning the SYMBOL, PATTERN, LEGEND, or AXIS statements, use GGLOBALE to free the memory used for storing the internal table that was created with GGLOBALN.

For more information on SYMBOL, PATTERN, LEGEND, and AXIS statements, see *SAS/GRAPH Software: Reference.*

Example

Free the internal table created by GGLOBALN for the SYMBOL statements, and check the return code to determine if a message needs to be issued:

```
rc=gglobale('symbol');
if rc then _msg_=sysmsg();
```

GGLOBALN

Returns the number of SYMBOL, PATTERN, LEGEND, or AXIS statements that are currently defined

See Also:
GGLOBAL
GGLOBALE

num-stmts=**GGLOBALN**(*stmt-type*);

Where...	Is type...	And represents...
num-stmts	N	The number of SYMBOL, PATTERN, LEGEND, or AXIS definitions currently defined.
stmt-type	C	The type of statement to process: `'SYMBOL'` `'PATTERN'` `'LEGEND'` `'AXIS'`

Details

Information about SYMBOL, PATTERN, LEGEND, or AXIS statements is stored in an internal table and can be retrieved with GGLOBAL. To delete the internal table created by GGLOBALN, use GGLOBALE.

Note: SYMBOL and PATTERN can generate more than one definition per statement. For more information on SYMBOL, PATTERN, LEGEND, and AXIS statements, see *SAS/GRAPH Software: Reference.*

Example

Assume only the following SYMBOL statements have been defined for the current SAS session:

```
symbol1 c=red;
symbol30 c=blue;
```

Return the number of SYMBOL statements currently available in the variable NUMSYMB. The value returned for NUMSYMB is 2, not 30.

```
numsymb=gglobaln('symbol');
```

GOTO

Branches immediately to another entry

SAS/AF software only

See Also:
DISPLAY

CALL GOTO(*entry*<,*action*<,*frame*>>);

Where...	Is type...	And represents...
entry	C	Name of the entry to which to branch. The entry can be any of the SAS/AF display entry types (FRAME, PROGRAM, MENU, CBT, or HELP). The *entry* argument can be
		entry to specify a PROGRAM entry in the current catalog.
		entry.type to specify an entry in the current catalog.
		libref.catalog.entry to specify a PROGRAM entry in a different catalog.
		libref.cat-name.entry.type to specify an entry in a different catalog.
action	C	How the execution stack is to be handled and where control transfers when the specified entry ends:

    'A'   adds *entry* to the top of the execution stack. The specified entry is displayed immediately. When the entry ends, the user returns to the window displayed before the program with the CALL GOTO was executed.

    'C'   clears the current execution stack. The specified entry is displayed immediately, and the stack is cleared. When the entry ends, the user returns to the parent entry, if one was specified in the entry, or exits the AF window. This option may be useful if you have memory constraints. (Default)

    'R'   removes the top entry from the execution stack and places the entry specified in the GOTO routine on the top of the execution stack. The specified entry is displayed immediately. When the entry ends, the user returns to the next entry on the stack rather than to the program containing the GOTO call.

frame	N	The number of the CBT frame if branching to a CBT entry.

Details

The GOTO routine branches immediately to a CBT, HELP, MENU, FRAME, or PROGRAM entry and transfers control to it. Statements that appear after GOTO are not executed because control is transferred to the new entry specified in the GOTO routine.

    GOTO, which always starts a new stream, cannot be used in FSEDIT or FSVIEW programs.

Example

Pass control to MYEND.PROGRAM, and end the SAS/AF session if the user issues the END command. Assume there is no parent entry specified.

```
if _status_='E' then call goto('myend.program','C');
```

GRAY

Grays a single station of a choice group, an entire choice group, a radio box, or a check box

SAS/AF software only

See Also:
ACTIVATE
ISACTIVE
ISGRAY
UNGRAY

rc=**GRAY**(*var-name*<,*station*<,*row*>>);

Where...	Is type...	And represents...
rc	N	Whether the operation was successful: 0 if successful $\neq$ 0 if not successful.
var-name	C	The choice group or FRAME entry object to be grayed.
station	N	The number of the field within the choice group or button within a radio box. This value must be greater than 0 and no larger than the total number of stations defined for the choice group. For PROGRAM entries, use the value 0 as a placeholder if the entire choice group at a specified row is to be grayed.
row	N	The number of the row when the choice group is in the scrollable section of an extended table. The *row* parameter is valid for PROGRAM entries but not for FRAME entries. Specify *row* only when you want to gray a station from outside the extended table's GETROW or PUTROW section. Do not specify *row* if you want to gray a station from GETROW or PUTROW.

Details

Users cannot select a station, choice group, or FRAME entry object that is grayed.

Because choice groups can be defined only in SAS/AF software, you cannot use GRAY in FSEDIT or FSVIEW programs.

For linked action fields in choice groups, the ACTION-type pair is considered one station. For example, the following line in a PROGRAM entry window defines three linked action fields:

```
& &A_____    & &B_____    & &C_____
```

To gray the linked action pair for field B, pass in 2 for the value of *station*, not 4.

FRAME entry objects can also use the _GRAY_ method.

Example

Don't allow users to make a selection from the choice group WINE when the value of AGE is less than 21:

```
if (age<21) then
    rc=gray('wine')
else
```

```
rc=ungray('wine');
```

HASATTR

Reports whether an SCL list or list item has a specified attribute

See Also:
GETLATTR
MAKELIST
MAKENLIST
SETLATTR

rc=**HASATTR**(*list-id,attribute<,index>*);

Where...	Is type...	And represents...
rc	N	Whether the list or item has the specified attribute.
		1 The list or item has the specified attribute.
		0 The list or item does not have the specified attribute.
list-id	N	The identifier of the list that HASATTR searches. An invalid *list-id* produces an error condition.
attribute	C	An attribute for a list or list item, as described in SETLATTR. In addition, you can test for the following special attributes:
		'G' returns 1 if the list is a global list.
		'L' returns 1 if the list is a local list.

. . . .

Release 6.11

'C'   returns 1 if the list identifier is also a class identifier.

'O'   returns 1 if the list identifier is also an object identifier.

. . . .

index	N	The position of the item in the list. The position can be specified as a positive or negative number. By default, *index* is 1 (the first item). If *index* is omitted, HASATTR checks if the specified list has the named *attribute*. If *index* is specified, HASATTR checks if the specified item has the named *attribute*. If *index* is a positive number, the item is at position *index* from the beginning of the list. If *index* is a negative number, the item is at position ABS(*index*) from the end of the list. An error condition results if the absolute value for *index* is zero or it is greater than the number of items in the list.

Details

If no value is specified for *index*, HASATTR queries the attribute of the list. If a nonzero value is specified for *index*, HASATTR queries the attribute of an item in the list.

For a list of attributes for lists and list items, see SETLATTR.

Examples

Clear the list identified by MYLIST only if it has the UPDATE attribute:

```
if hasattr(mylist,'UPDATE') then rc=clearlist(mylist);
```

Determine if the third item in a list has the FIXEDTYPE attribute:

```
isfixed=hasattr(mylist,'FIXEDTYPE',3);
```

HOME

Positions the cursor on a window's command area

See Also:
CURSOR
FIELD

HOME;

Details

In SAS/AF applications, the HOME statement moves the cursor immediately. In FSEDIT and FSVIEW applications, the cursor is moved when control is returned to the application.

See the entry for CURSOR earlier in this chapter for more information on how to position the cursor in a field.

If the PMENU facility is active, the command area for a dialog window is at the bottom of the window.

Some systems do not position the cursor on the pull-down menu for standard windows or the command area for dialog windows.

ICON

Associates an icon with the window

rc=**ICON**(*icon-number*);

Where...	Is type...	And represents...

rc	N	Whether the operation was successful:
		  0 if successful
		
		  $\neq 0$ if not successful.

icon-number	N	The number of the icon to represent the window when it is minimized. If you specify a number for which no icon is defined, the SAS icon is used.

Details

When a user reduces the window into an icon, display manager uses the specified icon to represent the window.

Only systems that display icons support this function. Nongraphical devices ignore the icon setting.

The ICON function is ignored if you are running with the SAS System's Application Work Space (AWS). To run an application without the AWS, use the AWS=NO option on the AF command.

The appendix shows the icons provided with SAS software, along with their identifying numbers.

Example

Associate icon number 107 with the current window. Icon 107 is the icon for SAS/EIS software in the Institute-supplied set of icon definitions.

```
rc=icon(107);
```

ICREATE

Creates an index for a SAS data set

See Also:
ACCESS
CONTENTS
IDELETE
IOPTION
ISINDEX
IVARLIST
OPEN

sysrc=**ICREATE**(*data-set-id,key-name<,var-list<,options>>*);

Where...	Is type...	And represents...
sysrc	N	Whether the operation was successful: 0 if successful ≠ 0 if not successful
data-set-id	N	The identifier assigned when the data set was opened. If *data-set-id* is invalid or if the data set is not opened in UTILITY mode, the index is not created and the function returns a nonzero value.
key-name	C	The name for the index key to be created.
var-list	C	One or more variables from the SAS data set to be indexed. Separated multiple names with blanks.
options	C	Index attributes, with multiple values separated by blanks within a single set of parentheses:

NONUNIQUE|UNIQUE to determine whether the value of the key variables must be unique. The default is NONUNIQUE.

MISSING|NOMISS to determine whether the index can point to missing values. The default is MISSING.

Details

An *index* is an auxiliary data structure used to speed up searches for records specified by the value of a variable, for example, "all the records with AGE greater than 65." To create an index for a SAS data set, you must open the data set in UTILITY mode (see OPEN in this chapter for details).

An index on a single variable is called a *simple index*. If *var-list* contains only one variable name, then a simple index is created.

Note: In this case, *key-name* and *var-list* must both contain the same value. If *var-list* is omitted, *key-name* specifies the index variable.

An index on more than one variable is called a *composite index*. If *var-list* contains more than one variable name, a composite index is created. In this case, *key-name* can be any valid SAS name that is not already used as a variable name in the data set. A composite index is based on the values of these variables concatenated to form a single value.

UNIQUE specifies that the index contains only unique values of the key variables. The creation of such an index prohibits duplicate values for its variables from being stored in the SAS data set. For variables that must be uniquely specified in an observation, such as social security numbers, this option is useful for preventing duplicate values from incorrectly getting into a data set. The function returns an error condition if nonunique values are present and UNIQUE is specified. By default, duplicate values are permitted in an index and thus in its data set.

NOMISS prevents missing values from being pointed to by an index. Unlike UNIQUE, NOMISS does not prevent missing values from being stored in the SAS data set. This feature is useful if the key variables contain many missing values that would make the index large and thus slower to access than if they were excluded. By default, missing values are stored in the index.

Indexes can also be created using

□ the DATASETS and SQL procedures in base SAS software

□ SAS/IML software

□ the CONTENTS window opened by the CONTENTS function in SCL or through the ACCESS procedure or the ACCESS function in SCL.

Example

Create a simple index for the SAS data set WORK.INVOICE. The key variable for the index is the data set variable ITEMTYPE.

```
dsid=open('work.invoice','v');   /* open in UTILITY mode */
rc=icreate(dsid,'itemtype',' ','unique nomiss');
```

In this example, because the value of the *var-list* argument is blank, the key variable for the index is the variable named in the *key-name* argument.

IDELETE

Deletes an index from a SAS data set

*sysrc=***IDELETE***(data-set-id,key-name);*

See Also:
ACCESS
CONTENTS
ICREATE
IOPTION
ISINDEX
IVARLIST

Where...	Is type...	And represents...

sysrc	N	Whether the operation was successful:
		  0 if successful
		
		  $\neq 0$ if not successful.

data-set-id	N	The identifier assigned when the data set was opened. If *data-set-id* is invalid, the program halts execution.
key-name	C	The name of the index key to be deleted.

Details

In order to delete an index for a SAS data set, you must open the data set in UTILITY mode (see the OPEN function in this chapter for details).

You can also delete indexes using

□ the DATASETS and SQL procedures in base SAS software

□ the CONTENTS window opened by the CONTENTS function in SCL or through the ACCESS procedure or the ACCESS function in SCL.

Example

Delete an index for the SAS data set WORK.INVOICE. The name of the index key is ITEMTYPE.

```
dsid=open('work.invoice','v');
rc=idelete(dsid,'itemtype');
```

IMPORT

Creates a SAS data set from an external file

name=**IMPORT**(*data-set-name,file*<,'DEFINE'>);

Where...	Is type...	And represents...
name	C	The last SAS data set that was created.
data-set-name	C	The new SAS data set to create. If the data set already exists, a warning message is displayed when the IMPORT window opens.
file	C	The fileref or physical filename of the external file from which data are to be imported. A physical filename must be enclosed within quotation marks. (See example)
DEFINE	C	To open the DEFINE window before opening the IMPORT window.

Details

▶ *Caution:* *Blank lines in files can cause problems.*

Under some host operating systems, blank lines in the external file may adversely affect the ability of the IMPORT function to extract data from the external file.

. . . .

The IMPORT function returns the name of the last SAS data set that it created from an external data file. This function enables users to easily import raw data from an external file into a SAS data set.

Two auxiliary windows are associated with IMPORT, the DEFINE window and the IMPORT window.

The IMPORT Window

The IMPORT window is the primary window for the IMPORT function. This window is used to define the variables for the SAS data set. The first two lines of the external file are displayed below a ruler in order to help the user identify the columns for the variables.

If you do not specify start and end columns, list input is used, and items must be separated by at least one blank. Users can specify the following fields in the IMPORT window:

Name   names the variable. This can be any valid SAS name.

Start Column   indicates the starting column of the variable in the external file. This is optional.

End Column   indicates the ending column of the variable in the external file. This is optional.

Note: You can specify a starting column without specifying an ending column but not vice versa. If you omit the ending column, it is calculated to be one less than the next starting column.

Type   indicates the type of the variable. Choose the type by pressing ENTER or clicking with the mouse on the appropriate type.

Format   can be any valid SAS format. This is optional. Enter a '?' to get a list of some common formats.

Informat   can be any valid SAS informat. This is optional. Enter a '?' to get a list of some common informats.

Label   specifies a label for the variable. This is optional.

IMPORT Window Commands

Users can issue the following commands in the IMPORT window:

BROWSE
opens an FSBROWSE window in which the newly created SAS data set is displayed for browsing. See *SAS/FSP Software: Usage and Reference* for details of the commands that can be used in an FSBROWSE window.
Note: This command is only valid if SAS/FSP software is licensed at the user's site.

DATASET *data-set-name*
changes the name of the SAS data set being created. This command is useful if you want to create another data set without leaving the IMPORT function. *Data-set-name* is the name of the new SAS data set to create. If the data set already exists, you receive a warning message and the new data set replaces the old one.

DEFINE
opens the DEFINE window.

EDIT
opens an FSEDIT window in which the newly created SAS data set is displayed for editing. See *SAS/FSP Software: Usage and Reference* for details of the commands that can be used in an FSEDIT window.
Note: This command is only valid if SAS/FSP software is licensed at the user's site.

FILE
saves the contents of the IMPORT window as a DATA step to an external file.

HEX <ON|OFF>
displays a record in hexadecimal. Only the first record is displayed in hexadecimal while the next two lines are used for the hexadecimal representation.

INFILE *filespec*
changes the name of the external file to use for input. The *filespec* argument can be either a previously defined fileref or a physical filename. If a physical filename is specified, it must be enclosed in quotes (for example, 'external.file').

LEFT <*n*>
scrolls the two lines of the external file and the ruler to the left *n* spaces. By default, HSCROLL is set to HALF.

LENGTH
displays the length of the longest record that has been read.

LIST

opens an FSLIST window in which the external file is displayed for browsing. See *SAS/FSP Software: Usage and Reference* for details of the commands that can be used in an FSLIST window.

Note: This command is valid only if SAS/FSP software is licensed at the user's site.

RIGHT <*n*>

scrolls the two lines of the external file and the ruler to the right *n* spaces. By default, HSCROLL is set to HALF.

RUN <VERIFY><REPORT>

reads in the raw data and creates the SAS data set. Specifying the VERIFY option allows interactive error correction of the data while they are being read in. The REPORT option writes a detailed error report to the log while the SAS data set is being created. Valid commands for the Verify window are:

PROCEED   the value was corrected and continuous error checking is desired.

GO   the value may or may not have been corrected and no continuous error checking is desired. This also causes the statistics window not to be updated anymore.

CANCEL   cancel the RUN command.

SAVE

saves the contents of the IMPORT window as a DATA step to a catalog entry. The value for *entry* must be a four-level name, and the fourth level must be SOURCE.

SORT <NAME|STARTCOL|ENDCOL>

sorts the variable list in the IMPORT window and deletes variables with blank names.

SORT   sorts the variable information by variable name.
SORT NAME

SORT STARTCOL   sorts the variable information by starting column.

SORT ENDCOL   sorts the variable information by ending column.

The SORT command sorts the Import window display only; the original SAS data set is not affected unless you issue the command RUN. For example, if you define variables C, B, and A, and issue the RUN command, you create a SAS data set with the variables C, B, and A. Then, if you issue the SORT command, the variables are displayed as A, B, and C, but the data set previously created is not affected. However, if you issue another RUN command, the new SAS data set has variables in the order A, B, C.

TEST <*n*>

performs the equivalent of a RUN REPORT command on the first *n* records from the external file. A SAS data set is created. If you do not specify a value for *n*, 1 is assumed.

The DEFINE Window

The DEFINE window is displayed when you issue the DEFINE command. The DEFINE window displays the first line from the external file along with a ruler and delimiter lines. On the delimiter lines, you can use < and > to mark the beginning and end, respectively, of a variable. If the variable is only one character wide, use a vertical bar (|).

To use the DEFINE window, you must align the data values in columns in the data records.

When you issue the END command to exit from this window, the fields are given default variable names and types (numeric or character). The IMPORT window is then opened so that you can change the variable names to suit your application and optionally add formats and informats.

Examples

Create a new SAS data set named MYLIB.NEW using data in the file to which the fileref EXTERN has previously been assigned:

```
name=import('mylib.new','extern');
```

Create a new SAS data set named MYLIB.NEW using data in the file with the physical name SAMPLE1.DATA. The filename string has embedded quotes to indicate that a physical filename, not a fileref, is being passed to the IMPORT function.

```
name=import('mylib.new',"'sample1.data'");
```

Note: The form of the physical filename depends on the host operating system.

INFORMAT

Verifies that the specified informat is valid

See Also:
FORMAT

rc=**INFORMAT**(*informat,type*);

Where...	Is type...	And represents...
rc	N	Whether the operation was successful: 1 if successful 0 if not successful.
informat	C	An informat that is supplied by SAS or created using the FORMAT procedure.
type	C	The type of the informat: **'C'** character **'N'** numeric.

Details

The specified informat must be known to the SAS session or the operation returns an unsuccessful return code. The function does check that valid widths are specified for informats.
Note: A period at the end of the informat name is required.

Examples

Verify that $MYFMT. is a valid character informat defined for the current SAS session: (The value returned to the variable RC is 1.)

```
rc=informat('$myfmt.','c');
```

Verify that **5.6** is not a valid informat for numeric values. (The value returned to the variable RC is 0.)

```
rc=informat('5.6','n');
```

INPUTC

Reads a character string using a character informat

See Also:
INPUTN
PUTC
PUTN

*char-val=***INPUTC**(*char-string,informat*);

Where...	Is type...	And represents...
char-val	C	The character value with the informat applied.
char-string	C	The character string to be read.
informat	C	The character informat.

Details

INPUTC returns the character value with the informat applied. This function is similar to the INPUT function in the DATA step.

For more information on reading a value using an informat, see the INPUT function for the DATA step in *SAS Language: Reference*.

Example

Read the character variable NAME using the $HEX8. informat:

```
informat='$hex8.';
customer=inputc(name,informat);
```

Read the character variable NAME using the $UPCASE3. informat:

```
name='sas';
cval=inputc(name,'$upcase3.');
put cval=;
```

This program produces the output:

```
CVAL=SAS
```

INPUTN

Reads a character string using a numeric informat

See Also:
INPUTC
PUTC
PUTN

num-val=**INPUTN**(*char-string,informat*);

Where...	Is type...	And represents...
num-val	N	The numeric value with the informat applied.
char-string	C	The character string to be read.
informat	C	The numeric informat.

Details

INPUTN returns a numeric value with the informat applied. This function is similar to the INPUT function in the DATA step.

For more information on reading a value using an informat, see the INPUT function for the DATA step in *SAS Language: Reference*.

Example

Read a character variable AMOUNT, containing the value $20,000.00, into the numeric variable SALARY using the COMMA10.2 informat:

```
amount='$20,000.00';
informat='comma10.2';
salary=inputn(amount,informat);
```

Read the value in the variable DATE and apply the JULIAN8. informat.

```
date='90091';
ndate=inputn(date,'julian8.');
put ndate=;
```

This program produces the output:

```
NDATE=11048
```

INSERTC

Inserts a character value into an SCL list

See Also:
DELITEM
DELNITEM
GETITEMC
GETITEML
GETITEMN
GETNITEMC
GETNITEML
GETNITEMN
HASATTR
INSERTL
INSERTN
MAKELIST
MAKENLIST
POPC
POPL
POPN
SETITEMC
SETITEML
SETITEMN
SETLATTR
SETNITEMC
SETNITEML
SETNITEMN

rc=**INSERTC**(*list-id,cval*<,*index*<,*name*>>);

Where...	Is type...	And represents...
rc	N	The modified list, or an error number. The value passed as *list-id* is returned unless there is an error. The value 0 means out of memory.
list-id	N	The identifier of the list into which *cval* is inserted. An invalid *list-id* produces an error condition.
cval	C	The character value to insert into the list.
index	N	The position where *cval* is inserted into the list. The position can be specified as a positive or negative number. By default, *index* is 1 (the first item). If *index* is a positive number, the item is at position *index* from the beginning of the list. If *index* is a negative number, the item is at position ABS(*index*) from the end of the list. *index* must be in the range [− (*n*+1), − 1] or [1,*n*+1] where *n* is the length of the list. An error condition results if the absolute value for *index* is zero or it is greater than the number of items in the list.
name	C	The item name for the inserted character item. *name* is converted to uppercase and trailing blanks are removed. If omitted, the item is not given a name.

Details

The character item is inserted such that after you insert a character item at position *index*, you can retrieve it from position *index* with GETITEMC.

INSERTC does not make a copy of the list. The insertion is performed in place. You can append an item to an SCL list of length *n* by inserting at *index*=n+1 or at *index*= − 1.

An error condition results if:

□ the list has any of the following attributes:

    □ NOUPDATE

    □ FIXEDLENGTH

    □ NUMONLY

    □ SASNAMES, and *name* is omitted or it is not a valid SAS name.

    □ NODUPNAMES, and *name* duplicates the name of a list item.

□ the absolute value for *index* is greater than 1 plus the number of items in the list. or is 0.

To check the attributes of a list or list item, use HASATTR. To change attributes, use SETLATTR.

Examples

Assume that LISTID already exists and contains all character values.
Insert **'Australia'** at the beginning of the list:

```
listid=insertc(listid,'Australia');
```

Insert **'U.S.A.'** at the end of the list:

```
listid=insertc(listid,'U.S.A.',-1);
```

Insert **'CANADA'** as the third item in the list:

```
listid=insertc(listid,'CANADA',3);
```

After this insertion, return the value that was third in the list before inserting
'CANADA' shifted the value from the third to the fourth position:

```
cval=getitemc(listid,4);
```

INSERTL

Inserts a list identifier into an SCL list

rc=**INSERTL**(*list-id,sublist-id<,index<,name>>*);

See Also:
DELITEM
DELNITEM
GETITEMC
GETITEML
GETITEMN
GETNITEMC
GETNITEML
GETNITEMN
HASATTR
INSERTC
INSERTN
MAKELIST
MAKENLIST
POPC
POPL
POPN
SETITEMC
SETITEML
SETITEMN
SETLATTR
SETNITEMC
SETNITEML
SETNITEMN

Where...	Is type...	And represents...
rc	N	The modified list, or an error number. The value passed as *list-id* is returned unless there is an error. The value 0 means out of memory.
list-id	N	The identifier of the list into which *sublist-id* is inserted. An invalid *list-id* produces an error condition.
sublist-id	N	The identifier of the sublist to insert into the list. An error condition results if *sublist-id* is not a valid list identifier.
index	N	The position where *sublist-id* is inserted into the list. The position can be specified as a positive or negative number. By default, *index* is 1 (the first item). If *index* is a positive number, the item is at position *index* from the beginning of the list. If *index* is a negative number, the item is at position ABS(*index*) from the end of the list. *index* must be in the range $[-(n+1), -1]$ or $[1,n+1]$ where *n* is the length of the list. An error condition results if the absolute value for *index* is zero or it is greater than the number of items in the list.
name	C	The item name for inserted sublist item. *name* is converted to uppercase and trailing blanks are removed. If omitted, the item is not given a name.

Details

The sublist identifier item is inserted such that after you insert a sublist item at position *index*, you can retrieve it from position *index* with GETITEML.

INSERTL does not make a copy of the list. The insertion is performed in place. You can append an item to an SCL list of length *n* by inserting at *index*=*n*+1 or at *index*= − 1.

An error condition results if:

□ the list has any of the following attributes:

  □ NOUPDATE

  □ FIXEDLENGTH

  □ NUMONLY

  □ CHARONLY

  □ SASNAMES, and *name* is omitted or it is not a valid SAS name

  □ NODUPNAMES, and *name* duplicates the name of a list item

□ the absolute value for *index* is greater than 1+ the number of items in the list or is 0.

□ you attempt to insert a local list into a global list.

To check the attributes of a list or list item, use HASATTR. To change attributes, use SETLATTR.

Examples

Assume that LISTID already exists and contains all list identifier values.
Insert a sublist at the beginning of the list:

```
listid=insertl(listid,newlist);
```

Insert a sublist at the end of the list:

```
listid=insertl(listid,newlist,-1);
```

Insert the sublist NEWLIST so that it becomes the third item from the end of the list:

```
listid=insertl(listid,newlist,-3);
```

INSERTN

Inserts a numeric value into an SCL list

rc=**INSERTN**(*list-id,nval<,index<,name>>*);

See Also:
DELITEM
DELNITEM
GETITEMC
GETITEML
GETITEMN
GETNITEMC
GETNITEML
GETNITEMN
HASATTR
INSERTC
INSERTL
MAKELIST
MAKENLIST
POPC
POPL
POPN
SETITEMC
SETITEML
SETITEMN
SETLATTR
SETNITEMC
SETNITEML
SETNITEMN

Where...	Is type...	And represents...
rc	N	The modified list, or an error number. The value passed as *list-id* is returned unless there is an error. The value 0 means out of memory.
list-id	N	The identifier of the list into which *nval* is inserted. An invalid *list-id* produces an error condition.
nval	N	The numeric value to insert into the list.
index	N	The position where *nval* is inserted into the list. The position can be specified as a positive or negative number. By default, *index* is 1 (the first item). If *index* is a positive number, the item is at position *index* from the beginning of the list. If *index* is a negative number, the item is at position ABS(*index*) from the end of the list. *index* must be in the range $[-(n+1), -1]$ or $[1,n+1]$ where *n* is the length of the list. An error condition results if the absolute value for *index* is zero or it is greater than the number of items in the list.
name	C	The item name for the inserted numeric item. *name* is converted to uppercase and trailing blanks are removed. If omitted, the item is not given a name.

Details

The numeric value is inserted such that after you insert a numeric item at position *index*, you can retrieve it from position *index* with GETITEMN.

INSERTN does not make a copy of the list. The insertion is performed in place. You can append an item to an SCL list of length *n* by inserting at *index=n+1* or at *index= − 1*.

An error condition results if:

□ the list has any of the following attributes:

  □ NOUPDATE

  □ FIXEDLENGTH

  □ CHARONLY

  □ SASNAMES, and *name* is omitted or it is not a valid SAS name.

  □ NODUPNAMES, and *name* duplicates the name of a list item.

□ the absolute value of *index* is greater than 1 plus the number of items in the list, or is 0.

To check the attributes of a list or list item, use HASATTRR. To change attributes, use SETLATTR.

Example

Assume the list MYLIST contains four items, named **'A'**, **'B'**, **'C'**, and **'D'**, with the values 1, 4, 9, and 16, respectively. Insert two new items: a string at the default position 1 (the beginning of the list), and a number at position − 1 (the end of the list). The new number is given the name **'E'**.

```
call putlist(mylist,'Before: ',0);
mylist=insertc(mylist,'Squares');
mylist=insertn(mylist,25, -1,'E');
call putlist(mylist,'After: ',0);
```

Produce the following output:

```
Before: (A=1
         B=4
         C=9
         D=16
         )[3]
After: ('Squares'
        A=1
        B=4
        C=9
        D=16
        E=25
        )[3]
```

Note: [3] is the listid assigned when this example was run. This value may be different if you run this example.

INSTANCE

Creates an instance of a class and returns its identifier

See Also:
APPLY
ENTRY
LOADCLASS
LOADRES
METHOD statement
NOTIFY
SEND
SUPAPPLY
SUPER

object-id=INSTANCE(*class-id*<,*arg*>);

Where...	Is type...	And represents...
object-id	N	The identifier assigned to the new object.
class-id	N	The identifier for the class, which is returned by the LOADCLASS function.
arg	N	An argument to pass to the _INIT_ method.

Details

When creating an instance, INSTANCE copies the list of instance variables from the specified class to the new instance, sends the specified class' _INIT_ method to the new instance, and passes *arg* as an argument to the _INIT_ method. If *arg* is not specified, no argument is passed to the _INIT_ method. To indicate that the numeric parameter is optional, the _INIT_ method of all classes should use the OPTIONAL= option in their METHOD statement or ENTRY statement.

A common practice is to use an SCL list as *arg*. You can then pass an arbitrary list of data which will be accessible in the _INIT_ method.

To delete an object created with INSTANCE, use its _TERM_ method, for example:

```
objectid=instance(classid);
call send (objectid,'_TERM_');
```

You cannot use the INSTANCE function to create instances of the Frame class.

For more information on classes and methods, see *SAS/AF Software: FRAME Usage and Reference.*

Example

Load a class named Queue, a subclass of the Object class, and create two instances of the Queue class. The Inqueue class is instantiated with a maximum number of items. The Outque class does not have a maximum. Assume that the _INIT_ method declares an OPTIONAL= parameter.

```
queue=loadclass('applib.classes.queue');
inqueue=instance(queue, max_items);
outqueue=instance(queue);
```

Assume the _INIT_ method of the Queue class is declared as:

```
_init_: method optional= maxItems 8;
    more SCL statements
endmethod;
```

IOPTION

Returns options for index and key variables

See Also:
ACCESS
CONTENTS
ICREATE
IDELETE
ISINDEX
IVARLIST

options=**IOPTION**(*data-set-id,key-name*);

Where...	Is type...	And represents...	
options	C	Index key options separated by a blank:	
		MISSING	The index can contain missing values.
		NOMISS	The index does not contain missing values.
		NONUNIQUE	The index can contain nonunique values.
		UNIQUE	The index contains only unique values.
data-set-id	N	The identifier assigned when the data set was opened. If *data-set-id* is invalid, the program halts execution.	
key-name	C	An index key.	

Details

An *index* is an auxiliary data structure used to speed up the selection of records specified by the value of a variable.

You can create indexes using

□ the DATASETS and SQL procedures in base SAS software

□ SAS/IML software

□ the CONTENTS window opened by the CONTENTS function in SCL or through the ACCESS procedure or the ACCESS function in SCL.

IOPTION returns a blank string when an error occurs.

Example

Return the options of the defined key index ITEMTYPE for the SAS data set WORK.DATAONE. If the value returned to the OPTIONS variable is blank, the message returned by the SYSMSG function is displayed on the message line.

```
dsid=open('work.dataone','i');
options=ioption(dsid,'itemtype');
if (options=' ') then _msg_=sysmsg();
```

ISACTIVE

Returns the number of the active button in a radio box or check box or the active station in a choice group

SAS/AF software only

See Also:
ACTIVATE
GRAY
ISGRAY
UNGRAY

station=**ISACTIVE**(*var-name*<,*row*>);

Where...	Is type...	And represents...
station	N	Information on the selected status of the choice group, radio box, or check box:
		> 0 when the station is active
		0 when no station is active in a choice group
		− 1 when no station is active
var-name	C	The choice group or FRAME entry object to be tested.
row	N	The row number when the choice group is in the scrollable section of an extended table in a PROGRAM entry. *row* is valid for PROGRAM entries but not for FRAME entries. Specify *row* only when you want to check the active station from outside the extended table's GETROW or PUTROW section. Do not specify *row* if you want to check the active station from GETROW or PUTROW.

Details

Because choice groups, radio boxes, and check boxes can be defined only in SAS/AF software, you cannot use ISACTIVE in FSEDIT or FSVIEW programs.

FRAME entry objects can also use the _IS_ACTIVE_ method.

Example

Suppose your application has a choice group named HOBBY in which the third station displays the value **'TENNIS'**. Branch to an appropriate program when a user selects the **TENNIS** station (either by pressing ENTER or by clicking the mouse button):

```
if (isactive('hobby')=3) then call display('tennis.program');
```

ISGRAY

Reports whether a choice group, check box, or radio box is grayed

SAS/AF software only

See Also:
ACTIVATE
GRAY
ISACTIVE
UNGRAY

rc=**ISGRAY**(*var-name*<,*station*<,*row*>>);

Where...	Is type...	And represents...

rc	N	Whether the station is grayed if you pass a value for *station*:
		
		1 the station is grayed
		
		0 the station is not grayed.
		    If *station* is omitted, a return code of 0 indicates that no station in the choice group is grayed:
		
		— *n* the total number of stations if the entire choice group is grayed.
		
		   m the number of stations that are grayed if the entire choice group is not grayed.

var-name	C	The choice group or FRAME entry object to be tested.
station	N	The number of the field within the choice group or the button within a radio box. A valid station has to be greater than 0 and no larger than the total stations defined for the choice group.
row	N	The number of the row when the choice group is in the scrollable section of an extended table. The *row* parameter is valid for PROGRAM entries but not for FRAME entries. Specify *row* only when you want to check if the station is gray from outside the extended table's GETROW or PUTROW section. Do not specify *row* if you want to check if the station is gray from GETROW or PUTROW. For FRAME entry objects, you can also use the _ISGRAY_ method.

Details

FRAME entry objects can also use the _IS_GRAY_ method.

Because choice groups can be defined only in SAS/AF software, you cannot use ISGRAY in FSEDIT or FSVIEW programs.

Examples

Test whether the choice group WINE at the third row of an extended table is grayed:

```
if (isgray('wine',0,3)) then
    do;
        /* SCL program statements */
    end;
```

Find out how many stations are defined for a choice group:

```
rc=gray('wine');
total=abs(isgray('wine'));
```

ISINDEX

Returns the type of index for a SAS data set variable

See Also:
ACCESS
CONTENTS
ICREATE
IDELETE
IOPTION
IVARLIST

index=**ISINDEX**(*data-set-id,var-name*);

Where...	Is type...	And represents...
index	C	The type of the index: (blank) No index has been created for the specified variable. BOTH The variable is a member of both simple and composite indexes. COMP The variable is a member of a composite index. REG The variable is a regular (simple) index.
data-set-id	N	The identifier assigned when the data set was opened. If *data-set-id* is invalid, the program halts execution.
var-name	C	The name of a variable in the SAS data set. If *var-name* is not a variable in the data set, the function returns a blank value.

Details

An *index* is an auxiliary data structure used to assist in the location (that is, selection) of records specified by the value of a variable. An index is called a *simple index* if it contains the value of only one variable. A *composite index* is based on the values for more than one variable merged to form a single value. A given SAS data set can have multiple simple indexes, composite indexes, or any combination of these.

You can create indexes using

□ the DATASETS and SQL procedures in base SAS software

□ SAS/IML software

□ the CONTENTS window opened by the CONTENTS function in SCL or through the ACCESS procedure or the ACCESS function in SCL.

Example

Return the type of index for the variable FNAME in the SAS data set WORK.DATAONE:

```
dsid=open('work.dataone','i');
ixtype=isindex(dsid,'fname');
```

ISSEL

Returns the selection number for a specified row of a selection list

SAS/AF software only

See Also:
NSELECT
SELECT
SELECTED
UNSELECT

selection=**ISSEL**(*row*);

Where...	Is type...	And represents...
selection	N	The row's selection number or 0 if the row is not selected.
row	N	The number of the row being queried.

Details

You can use the ISSEL function in two ways:

□ to determine in what order a certain row was selected

□ to determine if a row is being selected or deselected.

Because you can define extended tables only with SAS/AF software, you cannot use ISSEL in FSEDIT or FSVIEW programs. ISSEL is valid only for PROGRAM entries. FRAME entry objects must use the _ISSEL_ method.

In order for an extended table to be considered a selection list, you must specify a number of selections in the SETROW routine.

Example

Suppose that your application has a selection list with ten rows and that the user has just selected row 3 and then row 5. If ISSEL is called with the *row* argument equal to 5, then the value 2 is returned for *selection* because row 5 was the second selection.

You can also use ISSEL in the PUTROW section of an extended table application to test whether a row is selected. Call the function for the desired row and check the *selection* value to see if its value is positive (the row has been selected) or zero (the row has been deselected):

```
PUTROW:
   if (issel(_CURROW_)) then
      do;
         process the selected row
      end;
   else
      do;
         process the deselected row
      end;
return;
```

ITEMTYPE

Reports the type of an item in an SCL list

type=**ITEMTYPE**(*list-id*<,*index*>);

See Also:
GETITEMC
GETITEML
GETITEMN
GETNITEMC
GETNITEML
GETNITEMN
INSERTC
INSERTL
INSERTN
MAKELIST
MAKENLIST
POPC
POPL
POPN
SETITEMC
SETITEML
SETITEMN
SETNITEMC
SETNITEML
SETNITEMN

Where...	Is type...	And represents...
type	C	The type of the specified item: **'C'** The item is a character item. **'N'** The item is a numeric item. **'L'** The item is a sublist item.
list-id	N	The identifier of the list containing the item whose type is returned by ITEMTYPE. An invalid *list-id* produces an error condition.
index	N	The position of the item in the list. The position can be specified as a positive or negative number. By default, *index* is 1 (the first item). If *index* is a positive number, the item is at position *index* from the beginning of the list. If *index* is a negative number, the item is at position ABS(*index*) from the end of the list. An error condition results if the absolute value for *index* is zero or it is greater than the number of items in the list

Details

An item's type is determined by the function that creates the item.

The item type...	Is created by the functions...
C (character)	SETITEMC, SETNITEMC, INSERTC
N (numeric)	SETITEMN, SETNITEMN, INSERTL, MAKELIST, MAKENLIST
L (sublist)	SETITEML, SETNITEML, INSERTN

IVARLIST

Returns the variable names for an index key

See Also:
ICREATE
IDELETE
IOPTION
ISINDEX

varlist=**IVARLIST**(*data-set-id,key-name*);

Where...	Is type...	And represents...
varlist	C	One or more index variables (separated by a blank) for the specified key, or a blank if *key-name* is invalid.
data-set-id	N	The identifier assigned when the data set was opened. If *data-set-id* is invalid, the program halts execution.
key-name	C	The name for an index key.

Details

An *index* is an auxiliary data structure used to speed up the selection of records specified by the value of a variable.

An index is called a *simple index* if it contains the value of only one variable. A *composite index* contains the values for more than one variable merged to form a single value. A given SAS data set can have multiple simple indexes, composite indexes, or a combination of these.

You can create indexes using

□ the DATASETS and SQL procedures in base SAS software

□ SAS/IML software

□ the CONTENTS window opened by the CONTENTS function in SCL or through the ACCESS procedure or the ACCESS function in SCL.

Example

Return the variable list indexed for the key ITEMTYPE in the SAS data set WORK.DATAONE. Assume ITEMTYPE is a simple index (that is, it contains the values of only one variable). The returned VARLIST contains the string ITEMTYPE.

```
dsid=open('work.dataone','i');
varlist=ivarlist(dsid,'itemtype');
```

KEYCOUNT

Returns the number of observations that meet the criteria specified by an index key

Release 6.11 Feature

See Also:
SETKEY

▶ *Caution:* *Using KEYCOUNT with composite keys may show a larger number of observations matching the search criteria than you expect.*

nobs=**KEYCOUNT**(*data-set-id*);

Where...	Is type...	And represents...
nobs	N	The number of observations that meet the criteria, or < 0 if an error occurred. The error message is stored in *sysmsg*.
data-set-id	N	The identifier assigned when the data set was opened. If *data-set-id* is invalid, the program halts execution.

Details

KEYCOUNT returns the number of observations that meet the criteria specified by the index key variable. The index key variable was specified with the last SETKEY function used on the data set. After KEYCOUNT executes, the data set points to the first observation that meets the criteria defined by the last SETKEY function. Use FETCH or FETCHOBS to read the observation.

Using a composite key with SETKEY operates the same way as the WHERE function only when the condition is EQ. The value returned when the condition is EQ is the same as if the variables specified in the composite key are connected by WHERE conditions using AND or ALSO. (See Example 2.)

For all other conditions (GT, GE, LT, or LE) specified with SETKEY for a composite key, the composite key variables are concatenated together to form the index key. The number returned by the KEYCOUNT function is the number of observations in the data set that satisfy the composite key. For example, if the composite index consists of variables SEX and AGE and the condition is GT (greater than), the values to search for are concatenated such that key values of **F** for SEX and 13 for AGE yield an index key of **F13**. Because the search is performed on the concatenated values, some values may meet the search condition that you did not expect such as SEX of **M** and AGE of 11, since the string **M11** is considered greater than the string **F13**. (See Example 3.)

Example Data

The examples use observations from the SASUSER.CLASS data set. Create a simple index for data set SASUSER.CLASS using ICREATE or the DATASETS procedure with AGE as the index variable. Also, create a composite index for SASUSER.CLASS called COMP made up of variables SEX and AGE.

Example 1 - Using a Simple Index Key

Set up a search criteria of age=13. SETKEY specifies that the key variable is AGE and the condition is equality.

```
   /*  Locate observations where 'age = 13'  */
dsid = open( 'sasuser.class', 'v' );

   /* Create the simple index */
rc = icreate(dsid,'age');
name = ''; sex = '';
age = 13;
```

```
call set( dsid);
rc = setkey(dsid,'age','eq');
nobs = keycount(dsid);

if (nobs < 0) then _msg_ = sysmsg();
else
   do;
       put 'Number of observations found:' nobs;
       do while (fetch(dsid) ne -1);
          put name= sex= age=;
       end;
   end;
```

This program produces:

```
Number of observations found: 3
name=Alice sex=F age=13
name=Becka sex=F age=13
name=Jeffery sex=M age=13
```

Example 2 - Using Composite Index Key with Condition 'EQ'

Set up search criteria of SEX=F and AGE=13. SETKEY specifies that the key is named COMP and the condition for the search is equality.

```
    /*  Locate observation where 'sex="F"' and 'age=13'  */
dsid = open( 'sasuser.class', 'v' );

    /*  Create index */
rc = icreate(dsid, 'comp','sex age');
name = ''; sex = 'F'; age = 13;
call set(dsid);
rc = setkey(dsid,'comp','eq');
nobs = keycount(dsid);

if (nobs < 0) then _msg_ = sysmsg();
else
do;
   put 'Number of observations found:' nobs;
   do while (fetch(dsid) ne -1);
      put name= sex= age=;
   end;
end;
```

This program produces:

```
Number of observations found: 2
name=Alice sex=F age=13
name=Becka sex=F age=13
```

Example 3 - Using Composite Index Key with Condition 'GT'

Set up search criteria of SEX=F and AGE greater than 13. SETKEY specifies that the key is named COMP and the condition for the search is greater-than. This example illustrates the unexpected results returned by KEYCOUNT when you use composite index keys and SETKEY using a 'GT' argument.

```
  /*  Locate observations where 'sexage' > 'F13'  */
dsid = open( 'sasuser.class', 'v' );

  /* Create index */
rc=icreate(dsid,'comp','sex age');
name = ''; sex = 'F'; age = 13;
call set( dsid );
rc = setkey(dsid,'comp','gt');
nobs = keycount( dsid);

if (nobs < 0) then _msg_ = sysmsg();
else
do;
   put 'Number of observations found:' nobs;
   do while (fetch(dsid) ne -1);
      put name= sex= age=;
   end;
end;
```

This program lists 14 observations, composed of observations in the indexed data set that met the search criteria of SEX||AGE>=F13.

```
Number of observations found: 14
name=Gail sex=F age=14
name=Tammy sex=F age=14
name=Mary sex=F age=15
name=Sharon sex=F age=15
name=Thomas sex=M age=11
name=James sex=M age=12
name=John sex=M age=12
name=Robert sex=M age=12
name=Jeffrey sex=M age=13
name=Alfred sex=M age=14
name=Duke sex=M age=14
name=Guido sex=M age=15
name=William sex=M age=15
name=Philip sex=M age=16
```

You can see that James at AGE=12 does not meet the SETKEY requirement of AGE > 13 and SEX > 'F'. However, his observation was selected because the values were concatenated before the comparison was made.

LASTCMD

Returns the text of the last command issued from the application window

See Also:
WORD

cmdtext=**LASTCMD**();

Where...	Is type...	And represents...
cmdtext	C	Text of the last command issued from application window.

Details

If the command contains multiple words, only the first word is returned.

   LASTCMD is usually used in conjunction with CONTROL ENTER, ALWAYS, or ALLCMDS.

Example

Retrieve the last command issued in the window and execute a subroutine based on that command name:

```
INIT:
   control always;
return;

MAIN:
   cmd=lastcmd();
   if cmd='GO' then
      _msg_='Last command was '||cmd;
return;
```

LASTKEY

Returns the number of the last function key pressed from the window

See Also:
FKEYNAME
GETFKEY
SETFKEY
CONTROL

keynum=**LASTKEY**();

Where...	Is type...	And represents...
keynum	N	The number of the function key, which was pressed in the application window, or 0 if ENTER is pressed.

Details

The value returned is the ordinal position of the key definition in the KEYS window. You must have a window variable or text in the DISPLAY window for this function to work.

To retrieve the name of the last function key pressed by a user, use FKEYNAME.

LASTKEY is used in conjunction with CONTROL ENTER, ALWAYS, and ALLCMDS. LASTKEY does not retrieve the number of a function key that has a global command assigned to it.

Example

Return the number of the last function key a user pressed. (This example requires a window with at least one window variable.)

```
INIT:
   control allcmds;
return;

MAIN:
   keynum=lastkey();
   if (keynum ne 0) then
      put 'Last function key is ' keynum;
   else
      put 'Last function key is not defined or the ENTER key was pressed';
return;
```

LEAVE

Stops processing the current DO group and resumes with the next statement in sequence

SAS Statement with limitations in SCL

See also:
DO

LEAVE *<label>*;

Where...	Is type...	And represents...
label	C	the name of a program label associated with the DO group.

Details

The LEAVE statement is provided in SCL to control the execution of DO groups. When you need to force the statements in a DO group to stop executing, you can use the LEAVE statement to stop executing statements in a DO group and start executing a statement that is outside of that DO group.

For details on the LEAVE statement in SAS language, see SAS Technical Report P-222 *Changes and Enhancements to Base SAS Software.*

Example of LEAVE Statements Without Label Names

If a LEAVE statement does not contain the name of a program label, the program stops executing the statements in the DO group and starts executing the first statement after the DO group's END statement.

For example, when the condition in the IF statement in the following program is true (that is, when the value of SUM > 10), the program jumps immediately to the statement following the END statement, in this case, the PUT statement.

```
INIT:
return;

MAIN:
 do while(i<5);
   sum+i;
   i=i+2;
   if (sum>10) then
     do;
        leave;
     end;
   put sum=;
   end;
totalsum=sum;
return;
TERM:
return;
```

Example of LEAVE Statements With Label Names

For example, when the condition sum > 50 is true, the program leaves the LAB1 DO group and returns to the next statement following the DO group, in this case the PUT statement.

```
INIT:
 sum=45;
return;
MAIN:
  link LAB1;
return;
LAB1:
 do i=1 to 10;
    if (sum>10) then
        do;
         k=0;
         do until (k>=20);
             sum+k;
             if (sum>50) then
                 leave LAB1;
             k+2;
         end;
        end;
  end;
put 'LEAVE LAB1, sum >50 ' sum=;
return;
TERM:
return;
```

LEFT

Returns a left-aligned character string

See Also:
RIGHT
CENTER

lstring=**LEFT**(*string*<*,length*>);

Where...	Is type...	And represents...
lstring	C	The left-aligned character string. If the destination variable *lstring* already exists, then specifying a length in the LEFT function affects the current length of *lstring* only if the specified length is less than the trimmed length of the string.
string	C	The character string to be left-justified.
length	N	The length in which the character string is to be left-justified. The default is the maximum length of *lstring*.

Details

Any leading blanks in the string are removed so that the first character in the string is nonblank. The default length of the returned value is the trimmed length of the left-aligned string. Use *length* to specify a different maximum length for the returned string.

To right-justify a character string, use RIGHT. To center a character string, use CENTER.

For LEFT to work properly when *lstring* is a window variable, set the justification field (**JUST**) in the field attribute window for *lstring* to **'NONE'**.

LEGEND

Displays a LEGEND window or refreshes the current LEGEND window

See Also:
ENDLEGEND
POPLEGEND
PUSHLEGEND
PUTLEGEND

CALL LEGEND(<*window-name*<,*back-color*<,*border-color*<,*border-attr*>>>>);

Where...	Is type...	And represents...
window-name	C	The name displayed in the window border. Once assigned, a window name displays on succeeding legend windows until it is changed by another LEGEND routine that assigns a different name or a null string (*' '*) to delete the name from the current legend window.
back-color	C	A background color name or '' for the default color. SASCOLOR window elements can also be used for *back-color*. For more information on colors and a list of colors, see *color* in "Common Arguments" on page 222.
		The default background color is the SASCOLOR window element "Secondary Background."
border-color	C	A border color name or '' for the default color. SASCOLOR window elements can also be used for *border-color*. For more information on colors and a list of colors, see *color* in "Common Arguments" on page 222.
		The default border color is the SASCOLOR window element "Secondary Border."
border-attr	C	A border attribute or '' for the default attribute. If you specify a SASCOLOR window element for *border-color*, *border-attr* is ignored because the SASCOLOR window element contains a display attribute. For more information on display attributes and a list of them, see *attribute* in "Common Arguments" on page 222.
		The default border attribute is the SASCOLOR window element "Secondary Border."

Details

The LEGEND routine displays legend text that has been previously specified with the PUTLEGEND routine. You can specify any combination of optional arguments for LEGEND.

By default, the LEGEND window has the following characteristics:

□ The window occupies rows 1 through 6 and columns 1 through the width of the display device.

□ The window name is the name specified by the last LEGEND routine or the name of the current LEGEND window.

Before invoking the LEGEND routine, you may need to resize the associated application window so it does not obscure the LEGEND window. You can accomplish this by using the WDEF routine or by assigning a new window size in the General Attributes window for SAS/AF entries or in the Parameters window for SAS/FSP entries. For information on assigning attributes for SAS/AF and SAS/FSP windows, see *SAS/AF Software: Usage and Reference* and *SAS/FSP Software: Usage and Reference*, respectively.

Additionally, you can specify a size for a legend window by using the WREGION routine prior to calling the legend.

Example

Suppose you have two FRAME entries, X and Y. Assume X.FRAME contains two pushbuttons named PUSHPOP and ENDLGND, and X.SCL contains the corresponding object labels. When the PUSHPOP button is activated, the PUSHLEGEND call will save X's legend, and the Y.FRAME will be displayed. Y will then set up and display its own legend. After the return from Y, the POPLEGEND call will restore X's legend.

If the ENDLGND button is activated, ENDLEGEND will close the LEGEND window, and the application window will be restored to its original size.

X.SCL contains the following program:

```
INIT:
      /* Get number of rows and columns for later use */
   nr = winfo('numrows');
   nc = winfo('numcols');

      /* Resize application window to start at row 10 */
   call wdef(10, 1, nr-9, nc);

      /* Set size on legend window - row 1 through row 9.  Pass a null */
      /* string as the fifth parameter to indicate that the legend     */
      /* window has no command area.                                   */
   call wregion(1, 1, 9, nc, '');

      /* Set up legend text and display it */
   call putlegend(1, 'This is line one of legend for X', 'yellow', 'none');
   call putlegend(2, 'This is line two of legend for X', 'yellow', 'none');
   call legend('Sample LEGEND Window for X', 'gray', 'blue');
return;

MAIN:
return;

   /* PUSHPOP label.  If this is executed, we'll save the current */
   /* legend, and call y, which will display it's own legend.     */
PUSHPOP:

      /* Push and call */
   call pushlegend();
   call display('y.frame');

      /* Restore original legend */
   call poplegend();
return;


        /* ENDLGND label. If this is executed, the legend window will be  */
        /* closed, and the application window will be restored to its     */
```

```
             /* original size.                                        */
   ENDLGND:
      call endlegend();
      call wdef(1, 1, nr, nc);
   return;


   TERM:
   return;
```

Y.SCL contains the following program:

```
   INIT:

         /* Set up and display Y's own legend window */
      nr = winfo('numrows');
      nc = winfo('numcols');
      call wdef(10, 1, nr-9, nc);
      call wregion(1, 1, 9, nc, '');
      call putlegend(1, 'This is line one of legend for Y', 'yellow', 'none');
      call putlegend(2, 'This is line two of legend for Y', 'yellow', 'none');
      call legend('Sample LEGEND Window for Y', 'gray', 'blue');
   return;
   MAIN:
   TERM:
   return;
```

LENGTH

Returns the length of a trimmed character string

See Also:
MLENGTH

length=**LENGTH**(cval, < *'NOTRIM'* >);

Where...	Is type...	And represents...
length	N	The length of the trimmed character string.
cval	C	The character value whose length is to be determined.

. . . .

Release 6.10

'NOTRIM'	C	That trailing blanks should be counted as part of the string length.

. . . .

Details

The resulting value is the position of the rightmost nonblank character in the specified string *cval*.

LENGTH returns the nontrimmed length of a string if NOTRIM is specified.

The $CHAR format and informat must be assigned to a variable for leading blanks to be considered in determining the length of a variable. By default, variables automatically remove leading blanks when the value is assigned to them.

Examples

Return the length of the character variable S:

```
length s $ 5;
s='ab ';
l=length(s);
put 'L='l;
```

This program produces the output:

```
L=2
```

Return the length of the character variable S, using the NOTRIM option:

```
s = 'xy ';
l = length(s, 'notrim');
put 'L='l;
```

This program produces the output:

```
L=4
```

LENGTH

Specifies the length of variables

SAS Statement with limitations in SCL

LENGTH *<variable-list>* *<DEFAULT=n>*;

Where...	Is type...	And represents...
variable-list	C	One or more variables specified as *variable-1*<. . . *variable-n*><$>*length*, where
		variable — names a variable to be assigned a length.
		$ — designates that the preceding variable or variables are character type.
		length is a numeric constant that specifies the length of the preceding variable or variables. *length* can range from 1 to 200 for character variables. All numeric variables have a length of 8. If you specify a different length for a numeric variable, SCL still reserves 8 bytes for it.
DEFAULT=*n*	N	The maximum length of character variables not defined using a LENGTH statement.

Details

In SCL, LENGTH is a declarative statement and can be used only to set the lengths of nonwindow variables. If you attempt to specify a length for a window variable, a compile error will occur.

You typically place LENGTH statements at the beginning of your program, before the first labeled section. A compiler error occurs if you attempt to place a LENGTH statement within a DO group or within a conditional clause.

You can use the LENGTH statement to reduce the amount of memory required to store character-type nonwindow variables. For example, if your program assigns only single-character values to the variable CODE, you can save 199 bytes of storage space by defining the length of the variable explicitly in the SCL program. To do so, use a statement like the following:

```
length code $ 1;
```

For details on the LENGTH statement in SAS language, see *SAS Language: Reference*.

Example

Set the maximum length of all character variables not defined by a LENGTH statement to 150:

```
length default=150;
length a $ 8;

INIT:
  b='';
  max_a=mlength(a);
  max_b=mlength(b);
```

```
        put max_a= max_b=;
    return;
```

The output is:

```
    MAX_A=8 MAX_B=150
```

LETTER

Displays the FSLETTER window or sends a letter created with the FSLETTER procedure

SAS/FSP software required

See Also:
FSEDIT

CALL LETTER(*entry<,open-mode<,data-set-name>>*);

Where...	Is type...	And represents...
entry	C	A catalog containing LETTER, FORM, or EDPARMS entries or a specific LETTER, FORM, or EDPARMS entry. A one- or two-level name is assumed to be *catalog* or *libref.catalog*. The catalog is created if it does not already exist.
open-mode	C	The type of access to the FSLETTER window: **'BROWSE'** opens the catalog or entry for browsing.
		'EDIT' opens the catalog or entry for editing. (Default)
		'PRINT' prints a letter for each observation in the SAS data set specified using *data-set-name*. The SEND window is not displayed for the items that are printed. **PRINT** mode is valid only when the entry specified is a letter.
		'SEND' displays the FSLETTER SEND window for one observation or letter, enabling a user to customize it. To use this option, you do not have to specify a value for *data-set-name*. If a data set name is provided, the letter is displayed in the SEND window with the fields filled with values from the first observation in the data set. This mode is valid only when the entry specified is a letter.
data-set-name	C	The SAS data set containing values for the fill-in fields. Use the syntax *<libref.>member-name<(data-set-options)>*. If you omit *libref*, the default SAS data library, WORK, is used.
		Specify `' '` to use the _LAST_ data set. If no _LAST_ data set exists, the program halts execution.
		You can add a list of SAS data set options following the data set name. The list must be enclosed in parentheses. Valid data set options include DROP, KEEP, RENAME, WHERE, and CNTLLEV. Refer to Chapter 15 in *SAS Language: Reference* for a listing and descriptions of these data set options.

Details

The LETTER routine displays the FSLETTER window or sends a letter.

Note:　The FSLETTER window is not displayed if a PRINT argument is used.

If the value supplied for *letter-entry* is a three- or four-level name, the user is returned to the calling application when the FSLETTER window is closed. If a one- or two-level name is supplied, the user is returned directly to the calling application when the FSLETTER Directory window is closed.

SAS data set options can be specified by enclosing them within parentheses immediately following the *data-set-name* argument, as in the following example:

```
call letter('my.letters.subscrib','print',
            'personal(where=(name="John"))');
```

Examples

Open the FSLETTER window to edit a document named SUBSCRIB:

```
call letter('my.letters.subscrib');
```

Send a copy of the SUBSCRIB letter for each observation in the SAS data set SUBSCRIB.DATA. Direct FSLETTER output to a print file when you use CALL LETTER:

```
rc=filename ('myfile','physical-file-name');
call execcmdi('prtfile myfile');
call letter('my.letters.subscrib','print','subscrib.data');
```

SEND mode for the letter SUBSCRIB accepts user input.

Send a copy of the SUBSCRIB letter for the first observation in the SAS data set SUBSCRIB.DATA:

```
call letter('my.letters.subscrib','send','subscrib.data');
```

LIBLIST

Displays a selection list window of libref names and returns the user's selection

See Also:
CATLIST
DIRLIST
FILELIST

selections=**LIBLIST**(< *sel-excl*<,*engine*<,*message*<,*autoclose* <,*num-sel*>>>>>);

Where...	Is type...	And represents...
selections	C	One or more librefs from the list, or blank if no selection is made. Multiple selections are separated by blanks.
sel-excl	C	One or more librefs to include or exclude from the selection list window. Specify names using a style in Table 20.9.
engine	C	One or more engines to be used as criteria for determining which librefs are displayed. Specify names using a style in Table 20.9.
message	C	Text for a message displayed above the selection list. The default message tells users to make up to the number of selections in *num-sel*.
autoclose	C	Whether the selection list window closes automatically after a user makes a selection when only one choice is allowed: **'Y'** for the window to close automatically. (Default) **'N'** for the window to close only when the user explicitly closes it. This option is ignored when *num-sel* is not 1. However, use **' '** as a placeholder for this argument.
num-sel	N	The maximum number of items a user can select from the list. To display the list for information purposes only (no selections allowed), specify **0**. To specify unlimited selections, use a value larger than the number of available selections such as **9999**.

Table 20.9
Name Specifications

To specify...	Use...
One or more specific names	names separated with a space, for example **'MYLIB'** or **'MYLIB1 MYLIB2'**.
All names	an asterisk (**'*'**) or null string (**' '**).
All names *except* those listed after the NOT sign	a NOT sign (¬ or ^) followed by one or more names. For example, **'^MYLIB1'** displays all defined librefs except **'MYLIB1'**.

Details

The selection list contains both librefs and the physical names of the operating system files, but only the selected libref is returned.

If you omit all the arguments for LIBLIST (for example, *selections*=**liblist();**), the selection list window has the following characteristics:

□ The list contains all librefs that have been assigned in the current SAS session.

□ A message asks the user to make one selection.

□ The selection list window closes automatically when users make a selection.

You can provide a default or initial selected value in the list by providing a value for the *selections* variable prior to calling [whatever]. If *selections* contains valid names when LIBLIST is invoked, those values are automatically designated as selected when the selection list window is displayed.

If a user closes the selection list window without making a selection, LIBLIST returns a blank value unless there was an initial value for the *selections* variable before LIBLIST was called.

Selections from the window can be returned in the current result list, if one is available. The current result list is a special SCL list that is automatically filled with the values selected from a selection list. To create a current result list, use the MAKELIST function to create it and the CURLIST function to designate it as the current result list. The current result list must exist before you call the LISTLIST function.

When LIBLIST is invoked, the current result list is cleared. After LIBLIST is invoked, the result list contains the following named items:

Element	Type	Description
TAG	C	Identifies the list as one created by the LIBLIST function.
COUNT	N	Number of librefs selected. If no selections are made, or if users issue a CANCEL command in the list window, COUNT is 0.
LIBREF	C	Name of each libref selected. There is one LIBREF element for each selection made.
LIBNAME	C	Physical name of the operating system file for each libref selected. There is one LIBNAME element for each selection made.

Example

Create a selection list that displays all librefs except MYLIB1 and MYLIB2, and display the message **'Choose a libref'**. By default, the window closes automatically after the user makes a selection.

```
select=liblist('^mylib1 mylib2','*',Choose a libref');
```

Create a selection list that displays all librefs associated with the V609 engine, and exclude the librefs SASHELP and MAPS. Allow users to make up to three selections.

```
select=liblist('^sashelp maps','v609', 'Choose up to 3 librefs','',3);
```

Create a current result list to receive user selections. Use MAKELIST to create the list and CURLIST to define it as the current result list. Display all librefs except MYLIB1 and MYLIB2, and allow users to make up to five selections. Use a DO loop to retrieve the selections from the current result list.

```
listid=makelist();
rc=curlist(listid);
select=liblist('^ mylib1 mylib2',' ','Choose up to 5 librefs','', 5);
n=getnitemn(listid,'COUNT');
do i=1 to n;
   libref=getnitemc(listid,'LIBREF',i);
   physname=getnitemc(listid,'LIBNAME',i);
   put libref= physname=;
end;
```

LIBNAME

Assigns or deassigns a libref for a SAS data library

See Also:
LIBREF

sysrc=**LIBNAME**(*libref*<,*SAS-data-library*<,*engine*<,*options*>>>);

Where...	Is type...	And represents...
sysrc	N	Whether the operation was successful: 0 if successful $\neq 0$ if not successful
libref	C	The libref to assign.
SAS-data-library	C	The physical name of the SAS data library to be associated with the libref. Specify this name as required by the host operating system.
engine	C	The engine that will be used to access SAS files opened in the data library. If you are specifying a SAS/SHARE server, then the engine should be REMOTE.
options	C	Options honored by the specified engine.

Details

■ **Host Information** . . . .   Some systems allow a *SAS-data-library* value of ' ' (with a space) to assign a libref to the current directory. The behavior of LIBNAME when a single space is specified for *SAS-data-library* is host dependent.

If no value is provided for *SAS-data-library* or if *SAS-data-library* has a value of '' (with no space), LIBNAME disassociates the libref from the associated data library.

Under some operating systems, the user can assign librefs using system commands outside the SAS session.

On UNIX systems, you can use '.' to specify the current directory.

. . . . ■

Examples

Assign the libref NEW to the SAS data library V606.DATA. If an error or warning occurs, the message is displayed on the message line.

```
if (libname('new','v606.data')) then _msg_=sysmsg();
```

Deassign the libref NEW that has been previously associated with the data library V606.DATA in the preceding example. If an error or warning occurs, the message is displayed on the message line.

```
if (libname('new')) then _msg_=sysmsg();
```

LIBREF

Verifies that a libref has been assigned

See Also:
LIBNAME

sysrc=**LIBREF**(*libref*);

Where...	Is type...	And represents...
sysrc	N	Whether the operation was successful: 0 if successful
		$\neq$ 0 if not successful.
libref	C	The libref to be verified.

Example

Verify a libref. If an error or warning occurs, the message is displayed on the application window's message line.

```
if (libref('sashelp')) then _msg_=sysmsg();
```

LISTC

Displays a selection list window containing character values and returns the user's selection

See Also:
DATALISTC
DATALISTN
LISTN

selections=**LISTC**(*entry*<,*message*<,*autoclose*<,*num-sel*>>>);

Where...	Is type...	And represents...
selections	C	One or more character values selected by a user, or blank if no selection is made. Multiple selections are separated by blanks.
entry	C	A HELP, LIST, or MENU entry, specified as *entry.type* for an entry in the current catalog or *libref.catalog.entry.type* for an entry in a different catalog.
message	C	Text for a message displayed above the selection list. The default message tells users to make up to the number of selections in *num-sel*. The default is 1.
autoclose	C	Whether the selection list window closes automatically after a user makes a selection when only one choice is allowed:
		'Y' for the window to close automatically. (Default)
		'N' for the window to close only when the user explicitly closes it.
		This option is ignored when *num-sel* is not 1. However, use **' '** as a placeholder when you are specifying a value for *num-sel*.
num-sel	N	The maximum number of items a user can select from the list. To display the list for information purposes only (no selections allowed), specify **0**. To specify an unlimited number of selections, use a value larger than the number of available selections. The default is one selection.

Details

LISTC automatically displays a selection list containing character values that are stored in a LIST, HELP, or MENU entry. If a LIST entry is used, the type of the list must be character. Typically, a LIST entry is used if the selections in the LIST entry are self-explanatory. A HELP or MENU entry is used if a definition is needed next to the selection.

For a selection list produced from a LIST entry, you can provide a default or initial selected value by specifying a value for *selections* prior to calling LISTC. If *selections* contains valid values when the function is invoked, those values are automatically designated as selected when the selection list is displayed.

When multiple selections are allowed, *selections* contains the first value selected from the list. However, the values for all selections can be returned in the current result list, if one is available. The current result list is a special SCL list that is automatically filled with the values selected from a selection list. To create a current result list, use the MAKELIST function to create it and the CURLIST function to designate it as the current result list. The current result list must exist before you call LISTC. Values can be retrieved from the list using GETITEMC.

Examples

Create LIST_C and make it the current list. Use LISTC to display a selection list containing the values ABC, DEF, GHI, and JLK, which are stored in MYCHAR.LIST and allow a user to make up to 4 selections.

```
list_c=makelist();
cur_list=curlist(list_c);
   /* Display and list and put the user selections in  */
   /* SELECTIONS, then print that number.               */
selections=listc('mychar.list',' ',' ',4);
put 'User selected' selections;
   /* Find out the number of items in LIST_C and print the number.  */
num_selected=listlen(list_c);
put 'Total number selected is' num_selected;
   /* Get the selections from the current list  */
   /* and print each one.                        */
do i=1 to num_selected;
   item=getitemc(list_c,i);
   put 'Item' i 'is ' item;
end;
```

Testing the program and selecting GHI, DEF, JKL, and then ABC produces the following output:

```
User selected GHI DEF JKL ABC
Total number selected is 4
Item 1 is GHI
Item 2 is DEF
Item 3 is JKL
Item 4 is ABC
```

LISTLEN

Reports the length of an SCL list

See Also:
MAKELIST
MAKENLIST

n=**LISTLEN**(*list-id*);

Where...	Is type...	And represents...
n	N	The length of the SCL list, or status information: > 0 The length of a nonempty list. 0 The list is empty. − 1 The list identifier is invalid.
list-id	N	The identifier of the list whose length is being queried, or any other number.

Details

The length of a list is the number of items in the list, excluding the contents of sublists. Because LISTLEN returns -1 if *list-id* is an invalid list identifier, you can use LISTLEN to check that a list exists. For example,

```
listid=getniteml(envlist('G'),'MYLIST');
invalid=(listlen(listid)=-1);
if invalid then
   do;
      put 'MYLIST in the global environment has been deleted.';
      stop;
   end;
```

Example

Create the empty list LISTA, and then insert LISTA into a copy of itself, LISTB. The lengths of the two lists are then computed and stored in the variables LEN_A and LEN_B.

```
lista=makelist();
listb=copylist(lista);
listb=insertl(listb,lista);
len_a=listlen(lista);
len_b=listlen(listb);
_msg_='The length of LISTA is '||len_a||' and the length of LISTB is '||len_b;
```

This example shows that the length of LISTA is 0 while the length of LISTB is 1.

LISTN

Displays a selection list window containing numeric values and returns the user's selection

See Also:
DATALISTC
DATALISTN
LISTC

first-selection=**LISTN**(*entry*<,*message*<,*autoclose*<,*num-sel*>>>);

Where...	Is type...	And represents...
first-selection	N	The first value selected by a user.
entry	C	A LIST entry. *entry*.LIST specifies a LIST entry in the current catalog. To specify a LIST entry in a different catalog, use *libref.catalog.entry*.LIST.
message	C	Text for a message displayed above the selection list. The default message tells users to make the number of selections in *num-sel* or 1 if no *num-sel* is specified.
autoclose	C	Whether the selection list window closes automatically after a user makes a selection when only one choice is allowed: **'Y'** for the window to close automatically. (Default) **'N'** for the window to close only when the user explicitly closes it. This option is ignored when *num-sel* is not 1. However, use **' '** as a placeholder when you are specifying a value for *num-sel*.
num-sel	N	The maximum number of items a user can select from the list. To display the list for information purposes only (no selections allowed), specify **0**. To specify an unlimited number of selections, use a value larger than the number of available selections. The default is one selection.

Details

LISTN automatically displays a selection list containing numeric values stored in a LIST entry. The type of the list must be numeric. The numeric values are displayed using the specified format. If no format is specified, the values are displayed using the BEST. format.

When multiple selections are allowed, *first-selection* contains the first value selected from the list. However, the values for all selections can be returned in the current result list, if one is available. The current result list is a special SCL list that is automatically filled with the values selected from a selection list. To create a current result list, use the MAKELIST function to create it and the CURLIST function to designate it as the current result list. The current result list must exist before you call the LISTN function. Values can be retrieved from the list using GETITEMN.

Example

Create LIST_N and make it the current list. Use LISTN to display a selection list containing the numbers 1, 2, 3, and 4, which are stored in MYLIST.LIST and allow a user to make up to 4 selections.

```
list_n=makelist();
cur_list=curlist(list_n);
    /*  Display and list and put the first user selection in  */
    /*  SELECTED_FIRST, then print that number.               */
selected_first=listn('mylist.list',' ',' ',4);
put 'First selection is ' selected_first;
    /*  Find out the number of items in LIST-N and print the number.  */
num_selected=listlen(list_n);
put 'Total number selected is ' num_selected;
    /*  Get any other selections from the current list  */
    /*  and print each number.                          */
do i=1 to num_selected;
   item=getitemn(list_n,i);
   put 'Item ' i 'is ' item;
end;
```

Testing the program and selecting 3, 2, 4, and 1, produces the following output:

```
First selection is 3
Total number selected is 4
Item 1 is 3
Item 2 is 2
Item 3 is 4
Item 4 is 1
```

LOADCLASS

Loads a class for later instantiation and returns its identifier number

See also:
APPLY
INSTANCE
LOADRES
NOTIFY
SEND
SUPAPPLY
SUPER

class-id=LOADCLASS(*class-name*);

Where...	Is type...	And represents...
class-id	N	The identifier assigned to the class object.
class-name	C	The CLASS catalog entry to load.

Details

LOADCLASS loads a class object from a CLASS catalog entry. The identifier number returned by LOADCLASS can be used to create an instance of the class with the INSTANCE function.

If *class-name* is a one- or two-level name, the current search path is used to find the CLASS entry. If the class was previously loaded, the same class identifier is returned. Otherwise, the class is loaded from the catalog into the application class list, and the class identifier is returned in *class-id*.

For more information on classes, see *SAS/AF Software: FRAME Entry Usage and Reference.*

Example

Load an OBJECT subclass called SASUSER.CLASSES.TIMER and use the INSTANCE function to create an instance of the TIMER class.

```
timerclass = loadclass('sasuser.classes.timer');
timer=instance(timerclass);
```

LOADRES

Loads a RESOURCE entry

See also:
APPLY
INSTANCE
LOADCLASS
NOTIFY
SEND
SUPAPPLY
SUPER

Syntax

resource-id=**LOADRES**(*resource-name*);

Where...	Is type...	And represents...
resource-id	N	The identifier assigned to the resource list.
resource-name	C	The RESOURCE catalog entry to load. If *resource-name* is a one- or two-level name, the current search path is used to find the RESOURCE entry.

Details

LOADRES loads a list of classes from a RESOURCE entry. This list is called a resource list. RESOURCE entries are primarily used by FRAME entries, although you can create RESOURCE entries for nonwidget classes as well. This function is useful for loading several classes or even entire class hierarchies at one time without having to load several CLASS entries. For more information on classes and class hierarchies, see *SAS/AF Software: FRAME Entry Usage and Reference.*

If a class contained in the resource list has already been loaded, the existing class replaces the class in the resource list (although the RESOURCE entry is not modified). This prevents duplicate class lists for the same class name.

Example

Load a resource list stored in APPQR.HIER1.GROUPS.RESOURCE, then load several classes contained in the RESOURCE entry. After the LOADRES call, the LOADCLASS calls do not have to read the classes from the catalog.

```
groups = loadres('appqr.hier1.groups.resource');
c1=loadclass('appqr.hier1.c1.class');
c2=loadclass('appqr.hier1.c2.class');
c3=loadclass('appqr.hier1.c3.class');
```

LOCATEC

Searches a SAS data set for an observation that contains a specified character value

See Also:
FETCH
FETCHOBS
GETVARC
GETVARN
LOCATEN
SET

rc=**LOCATEC**(*data-set-id*,*var-num*,*cval*<,*sort*<,*direction* >>);

Where...	Is type...	And represents...
rc	N	Whether the operation was successful: >0 if successful 0 if not successful.
data-set-id	N	The identifier assigned when the data set was opened. If *data-set-id* is invalid, the program halts execution.
var-num	N	The number of the variable to search for. This number can be returned by VARNUM. If *var-num* is invalid, the program halts execution and sends a message to the log.
cval	C	The character value to search for. Preceding blanks are part of the argument. Trailing blanks are not. Left-justify character values to facilitate searching. If *cval* is not a character value, the program halts execution and sends a message to the log.
sort	C	Whether the SAS data set is sorted: **'A'** data set is sorted in ascending order. **'D'** data set is sorted in descending order. **'U'** data set is not sorted. (Default)
direction	C	The direction in which to search the SAS data set: **'A'** search all observations, starting with the first observation. (Default) **'B'** search from the previous observation backward. **'F'** search from the next observation forward.

Details

LOCATEC searches all observations, starting with the first observation by default, skipping observations marked for deletion. When a WHERE clause is active, the function searches the observations that meet the WHERE condition for a match. If a matching observation is found, it is loaded into the Data Set Data Vector (DDV). Otherwise the current observation remains in the DDV.

LOCATEC returns the number of observations read before a match is found. This number may not correspond to the observation number where the match is found because LOCATEC skips deleted observations and, if there is a WHERE clause active, only reads those observations meeting the WHERE condition. Also, if a direction is specified for the search, the number returned is the number of observations read from the previous observation where the search began. By default, the search direction is forward, starting with the first observation in the data set. Use *direction* to set the search direction.

If the data set is sorted, specifying **'A'** or **'D'** for *sort* uses the more efficient binary search algorithm. Perform a binary search only when you have member-level access so that no one else can be editing the data set concurrently. With a binary search, LOCATEC makes assumptions about how the data are sorted and that it can identify the first and last observations. If others are editing the data set concurrently, they could append an observation so the data set is no longer in sorted order. Then, the binary search may not find the correct values. LOCATEC does not search for partial values.

Example

Locate a customer whose name is SMITH in the PAYROLL data set, opened with a DSID of PAYID, which is sorted by NAME. The customer's name is specified in the window variable CUSTOMER.

```
customer='SMITH';
rc=locatec(payid,varnum(payid,'name'),customer,'a');
if (rc=0) then
    _msg_='There is no customer named '||customer||'.';
else
    do;
        more SCL statements
    end;
return;
```

LOCATEN

Searches a SAS data set for an observation that contains a specified numeric value

See Also:
FETCH
FETCHOBS
GETVARC
GETVARN
LOCATEC
SET

rc=**LOCATEN**(*data-set-id,var-num,nval<,sort<,direction>>*);

Where...	Is type...	And represents...
rc	N	Whether the operation was successful: > 0 if successful 0 if not successful
data-set-id	N	The identifier assigned when the data set was opened. If *data-set-id* is invalid, the program halts execution.
var-num	N	The number of the variable to search for. This number can be obtained by VARNUM. If *var-num* is invalid, the program halts execution and sends a message to the log.
nval	N	The numeric value to search for. If *nval* is not a numeric value, the program halts execution and sends a message to the log.
sort	C	Whether the SAS data set is sorted: 'A' data set is sorted in ascending order. 'D' data set is sorted in descending order. 'U' data set is not sorted. (Default)
direction	C	The direction in which to search the SAS data set: 'A' search all observations, starting with the first observation. (Default) 'B' search from the previous observation backward. 'F' search from the next observation forward.

Details

LOCATEN searches all observations, starting with the first observation by default, skipping observations marked for deletion. When a WHERE clause is active, the function searches the observations that meet the WHERE condition for a match. If a matching observation is found, it is loaded into the Data Set Data Vector (DDV). Otherwise the current observation remains in the DDV.

LOCATEN returns the number of observations read before a match is found. This number may not correspond to the observation number where the match is found because LOCATEN skips deleted observations and, if there is a WHERE clause active, only reads the observations meeting the WHERE condition. Also, if a direction is specified for the search, the number returned is the number of observations read from the previous observation where the search began. By default, the search direction is forward, starting with the first observation in the data set. Use *direction* to set the search direction.

If the data set is sorted, specifying **'A'** or **'D'** for *sort* uses the more efficient binary search algorithm. Perform a binary search only when you have member-level access so that no one else can be editing the data set concurrently. With a binary search, LOCATEN makes assumptions about how the data are sorted and that it can identify the first and last observations. If others are editing the data set concurrently, they could append an observation so the data set is no longer in sorted order. Then, the binary search may not find the correct values.

Example

Locate a house whose price is $64,000 in the SASUSER.HOUSES data set, which is opened with a *data-set-id* of INVID. The price is specified in the window variable PRICE.

```
invid=open('sasuser.houses');
price=64000;
rc=locaten(invid,varnum(invid,'price'),price,'a');
if (rc=0) then
    _msg_='There is no house priced at '||putn(price,'dollar9.2')||'.';
else
    do;
        obs=curobs(invid);
        _msg_='The specified price was found in observation '||obs;
    end;
return;
```

LOCK

Locks or unlocks a SAS file or SAS catalog entry

SAS/SHARE software required

*sysrc=***LOCK**(*member<,action>*);

Where...	Is type...	And represents...
sysrc	N	Whether the operation was successful: 0 if successful ≠ 0 if not successful
member	C	A SAS data library member or SAS catalog entry. The value you specify can be a one-, two-, three-, or four-level name. A one-level name is presumed to be a libref, while a two-level name defaults to the SAS file type DATA.
action	C	An action to be performed on the SAS file or catalog entry: **'CLEAR'** unlocks the specified SAS file(s) or SAS catalog entry. **'LOCK'** locks the specified SAS file(s) or SAS catalog entry. (Default) **'QUERY'** queries the lock status of a SAS file or a SAS catalog entry. _SWNOLKH not currently locked. RC of -60099. _SWLKUSR locked by another user. RC of -630097. _SWLKYOU locked by the caller. RC of -630098.

Details

If *action* is not provided, the action defaults to LOCK. You must access the file identified in *member* using the SHARE engine. Otherwise, you get an error message when the statement executes. For further information, see *SAS/SHARE Software: Usage and Reference, Volume 6, First Edition.*

LOCK is not related to UNLOCK, which unlocks individual observations and does not necessarily require SAS/SHARE software.

Examples

Lock the data library associated with a libref of A, unlock data view LIB.A, and lock LIB.A.B.PROGRAM. Then, query the lock state of the FOO.ONE data set:

```
rc=lock('a');
rc=lock('lib.a.view','clear');
rc=lock('lib.a.b.program');
rc=lock('foo.one.data','query');
if (rc=%sysrc(_SWLKUSR)) then
    _msg_='Data set foo.one is currently locked.';
```

LOOKUPC

Searches for a string among a list of valid tokens

rc=**LOOKUPC**(*string,token-1*<, . . .,*token-12* >);

Where...	Is type...	And represents...
rc	N	Whether the operation was successful: 0 no match is found > 0 position in token list if a unique match was found < 0 negative of position in the token list if a duplicate token was found.
string	C	The character value to search for.
token	C	Up to 12 character values, separated by commas.

Details

A *token* can be a name, literal, digits, or special characters. This function is useful for looking up valid commands.

The function accepts abbreviations as valid commands. That is, the function reports a match if the search string matches the starting characters of a token.

LOOKUPC does not search the token list for embedded strings. For example, the search string LIST would not be found in the token NEWLIST.

Example

Get the command (SURVEY, NEWLIST, or ADDNAME) the user issued from the command line, and check to see if the command is valid:

```
array cmds{*} $8 ('SURVEY','NEWLIST','ADDNAME');
INIT:
   control always;
return;
MAIN:
   cmdword=WORD(1,'u');
   cmdnum=lookupc(cmdword,cmds{1},cmds{2},cmds{3});
        select;
            when (cmdnum=1)
               SCL statements to process the SURVEY command
            when (cmdnum=2)
               SCL statements to process the NEWLIST command
            when (cmdnum=3)
               ACL statements to process the ADDNAME command
            otherwise _msg_='Command conflict';
        end;
```

In this example, SUR, NEWL, and ADDN are considered valid commands.

LVARLEVEL

Fills an SCL list with the unique values of a variable from a SAS data set

See also:
CURLIST
MAKELIST
OPEN
VARLEVEL
VARSTAT

rc=**LVARLEVEL**(*dsid,varname,n-level*<,*list-id*>);

Where...	Is type...	And represents...
rc	N	Whether the operation was successful: 0 if successful ≠ 0 if not successful
dsid	N	The identifier assigned when the data set was opened. An invalid *dsid* produces an error condition occurs.
varname	C	The variable whose unique formatted values are to be reported.
n-level	N	The name of the variable in which the function stores the number of unique values, or levels. This variable must be initialized to a nonmissing value before its value is set by LVARLEVEL.
list-id	N	The identifier of the list to fill with the unique formatted values. If *list-id* is not provided, the values are placed in the current result list. An invalid *list-id* produces an error condition.

Details

The values are placed in the list identified by *list-id* or in the current result list identified by CURLIST, if *list-id* is not specified. The values placed in the list are always character values. It is an error if *list-id* is omitted and you have not created a current result list with the CURLIST function.

n-level must be a variable because LVARLEVEL uses it to store the number of unique values it finds. *n-level* must be initialized to any value except missing prior to executing LVARLEVEL.

Examples

Placing Values in the Current List
Get the unique formatted values for the data set variable NAME from SASUSER.CLASS, place the values in the current list, and print them:

```
dsid=open('sasuser.class');
nlevels=0;
rc=curlist(makelist());
rc=lvarlevel(dsid,'name',nlevels);
put nlevels=;
call putlist(curlist(),'levels',0);
rc=close(dsid);
```

Placing Values in a Specified List

Get the unique formatted values for the data set variable NAME from SASUSER.CLASS, place the values in the list specified, and print them:

```
dsid=open('sasuser.class');
nlevels=0;
listid=makelist();
rc=lvarlevel(dsid,'name',nlevels,listid);
put nlevels=;
call putlist(listid,'levels',0);
rc=close(dsid);
rc=dellist(listid);
```

MAKELIST

Creates an SCL list

See Also:
COPYLIST
CURLIST
DELITEM
DELLIST
DELNITEM
ENVLIST
FILLIST
GETITEMC
GETITEML
GETITEMN
GETLATTR
HASATTR
GETNITEMC
GETNITEML
GETNITEMN
INSERTC
INSERTL
INSERTN
ITEMTYPE
LISTLEN
MAKENLIST
NAMEDITEM
NAMEITEM
POPC
POPL
POPN
POPMENU
PUTLIST
REVLIST
ROTLIST
SAVELIST
SEARCHC
SEARCHL
SEARCHN
SETITEMC
SETITEML
SETITEMN
SETLATTR
SETNITEMC
SETNITEML
SETNITEMN
SORTLIST

list-id=**MAKELIST**(< *n*<,*visibility*>>);

Where...	Is type...	And represents...
list-id	N	The identifier of the new list, or 0 if the list could not be created.
n	N	The number of items to place in the list initially. By default, *n* is 0.
visibility	C	Whether the list is global or local: **'G'** The list is global and can be shared by all applications executing in the same SAS session. A global list is deleted when the SAS session ends. **'L'** The list is local to the current SAS application. A local list is deleted when the application ends. (Default)

Details

MAKELIST creates an empty list or a list with the number of items specified in *n*. Each item contains a missing value. Use the list identifier returned by MAKELIST with all other SCL list functions that use the list.

SCL lists can contain numeric, character, or other list items. Each item can have a name. This list also has attributes, as do the items. See Chapter 4, "Defining SCL Lists for Creating Data Dynamically" for a complete description of using SCL lists.

Example

Create lists in the local and global environments:

```
n = 12;
   /*  Make an empty local list.  */
list1=makelist();
   /*  Make a local list with 24 items.  */
list2=makelist(2*n);
   /*  Make an empty global list.  */
list3=makelist(0,'G');
```

MAKENLIST

Creates an SCL list with named items

See Also:
DELNITEM
GETNITEMC
GETNITEML
GETNITEMN
MAKELIST
NAMEDITEM
NAMEITEM
SETNITEMC
SETNITEML
SETNITEMN

list-id=**MAKENLIST**(*visibility,name-1<, . . .,name-n>*);

Where...	Is type...	And represents...
list-id	N	The identifier of the new list, or 0 if the list could not be created.
visibility	C	Whether the list is global or local: **'G'** The list is global and can be shared by all applications executing in the same SAS session. A global list is deleted when the SAS session ends. **'L'** The list is local to the current SAS application. A local list is deleted when the application ends. (Default)
name	C	One or more list item names separated by commas. Item names are converted to uppercase and trailing blanks are removed. Each name can be any SCL string. The same name can be used more than once.

Details

MAKENLIST creates a list with a number of items equal to the number of names specified. Each item contains a missing value. Use the list identifier returned by MAKENLIST with all remaining functions that manipulate the list. When you create a list with named items, you can assign or access list values by their names as well as their positions. However, it is more efficient to access items by position rather than name.

You can use MAKENLIST to create structures that group related information into one list. For example, an observation in a SAS data set can be placed in a named list where each named item corresponds to the data set variable of the same name.

Note that the *visibility* argument (**'L'** or **'G'**) is required and is the first argument, unlike the MAKELIST function. Note also that this function does not use an *n* argument.

Using MAKENLIST is a shortcut for using MAKELIST and naming each item independently.

Example

The following statement:

```
mylist=makenlist('L','A','B','C');
```

is equivalent to these four statements:

```
mylist=makelist(3,'L');
rc=nameitem(mylist,1,'A');
rc=nameitem(mylist,2,'B');
rc=nameitem(mylist,3,'C');
```

METHOD

**Executes a method block
defined in an SCL entry**

See Also:
DISPLAY
LINK
NOCHANGE
METHOD statement

CALL METHOD(*entry,label*<*,parameters*>);

Where...	Is type...	And represents...
entry	C	A catalog entry of type SCL. To specify an entry in the current catalog, use *entry* or *entry.type*. To specify an entry in a different catalog, use *libref.catalog.entry.type.* If *type* is not specified, it defaults to SCL.
label	C	The name of the method block in the SCL entry.
parameters	C	Arguments to pass to the method block. The SCL entry that receives these parameters must declare each of them within a METHOD statement.

Details

The name of the SCL entry must be specified in the first parameter of the CALL METHOD routine. The method block label must be specified in the second parameter of CALL METHOD. These two parameters are required for CALL METHOD. The remaining parameters are optional parameters passed to the method block. These optional parameters should agree with the number of arguments, relative positions, and data types in the corresponding method block unless the REST= or ARGLIST= options are used in the method block. The parameter names in CALL METHOD do not have to match the argument names in the method block.

The method block containing a sequence of SCL statements can be defined in the current SCL entry or another external SCL entry. If the method block is defined in the current entry, it is more efficient to use a LINK statement instead of a METHOD routine.

Parameters are passed in one of the following ways:

Call by reference

passes variables and enables values to be returned to CALL METHOD. This approach enables the called method block to modify values and then return them.

An example of a call by reference is

```
call method('b.scl','abc',var1,name,field2);
```

If you do not want to return the values, use the NOCHANGE() routine in the method block.

Call by value

is used for all numeric constants, character constants, and expressions. It does not return values to the calling METHOD routine.

An example of a call by value is:

```
call method('b.scl','abc',100,'hello',x+y);
```

Example

Call the method block labeled ABC in the SCL entry CODE. The following three parameters are passed: the contents of the variable A, the literal value 3, and the contents of the variable C:

```
call method('CODE.SCL','abc',a,3,c);
```

The method block can return modified values to the variables A and C if the NOCHANGE routine is not specified in the method block.

METHOD

Begins a statement block that can be called by the METHOD routine

See Also:
APPLY
ENDMETHOD
METHOD routine
NOCHANGE
SEND
SUPAPPLY
SUPER

METHOD *<argument-list>* *<OPTIONAL=argument-list>*
  <ARGLIST=arg-list-id | REST=*rest-list-id>< / RESIDENT>*;

Where...	Is type...	And represents...
argument-list		One or more sets of arguments, with each set specified as *var-list* $	*var-list* $ *length*	*var-list length* where
		var-list — is one or more variables to which the parameter in the corresponding position in the CALL METHOD, CALL SEND, CALL SUPER, CALL APPLY or CALL SUPAPPLY routine is passed. (See the discussion of these calling routines for details.)
		$ — designates the preceding variable or variables as character type.
		length — is a numeric constant that specifies the length of the preceding variable or variables. The length of a character variable does not have to match the length of the corresponding passed parameter. SCL pads or truncates as necessary. The length of a numeric variable is always 8, regardless of the specified length in the METHOD statement.
arg-list-id	N	The identifier for the SCL list that will contain all the arguments passed to the method. This includes all optional arguments.
rest-list-id	N	The identifier for the SCL list that will contain all arguments passed to the method, which are not explicitly specified in *argument-list* for either METHOD or OPTIONAL=.
RESIDENT	C	The entire SCL entry will be saved in resident memory. If you use this function frequently, specify the RESIDENT option to improve performance.

Details

The METHOD statement begins a method block, which is a labeled block of SCL statements. The block begins with a METHOD statement and ends with an ENDMETHOD statement. This block contains one or more additional SCL statements. A method block is a way to make a frequently-used routine available to many different programs. Methods are a primary component of object-oriented programming.

The METHOD statement receives parameters from the calling routine. When there are no options in the METHOD statement there is a strict correspondence between calling routine parameters and METHOD statement arguments. The arguments and parameters must agree in number, data type, and relative position. If you pass an incorrect number of parameters or a parameter of the incorrect type, SCL halts the execution of the program. The argument-parameter correspondence is less restrictive when you use the options REST=, ARGLIST=, and OPTIONAL= in the METHOD statement.

OPTIONAL= specifies one or more optional arguments to be used only if the calling program supplies the corresponding parameters in the calling routine parameter list. If they are not supplied, SCL assumes that they are all initialized to missing values.

OPTIONAL= allows a list of optional arguments to be used only if the calling program supplies the corresponding parameters in the calling routine parameter list. If the corresponding parameters in the calling routine are not supplied, the optional arguments are initialized to missing values.

ARGLIST= and REST= allow a variable number of parameters to be passed to the METHOD statement. You determine the types and order of the variable arguments. The lists identified by *arg-list-id* and *restlid-id* are created automatically when the entry is called and deleted automatically when the entry ends. When arrays are passed as parameters, the array is expanded into individual items and these are inserted into the *arg-list-id* and *rest-list-id* lists. ARGLIST= and REST= are mutually exclusive, so you can use only one or the other.

The /RESIDENT option of the METHOD statement instructs SCL to keep a copy of the methods resident in memory after they are first executed. The entire SCL entry is maintained, not just those METHOD blocks that have the /RESIDENT option. If an SCL entry is not resident, CALL METHOD reads the entry from the catalog each time. If the entry is resident, the entry is not re-read from the catalog on subsequent calls.

Executing Method Blocks

Execution of the method block starts at the METHOD statement and ends with the ENDMETHOD statement. After executing a method block, control returns to the calling routine or the command line.

Calling Method Blocks

Other SCL programs call a method block by specifying its label in a CALL METHOD, CALL APPLY, CALL SUPER, CALL SUPAPPLY, and CALL SEND routine. Only SCL entries can contain method blocks.

Testing Method Blocks

A method block can be tested individually by invoking a TESTAF command with the label=*method-name* option with the SCL debugger, for example:

```
testaf label=method-name
```

Scope of Method Block Variables

All the variables defined in a method block are global to that entry. There is no variable scoping implied within a method block. You cannot use a GOTO or a LINK statement to jump into the method block in the current entry. The label for the method block is the only entry point to a METHOD block.

Passing Parameters to Method Blocks

The parameter-receiving mechanism for the METHOD statement is very similar to that mechanism for the ENTRY statement. The METHOD statement receives parameters from the third argument of the calling METHOD routine. The calling METHOD routine must agree with the corresponding METHOD statement in the following ways unless ARGLIST=, REST=, or OPTIONAL= are specified, or SCL halts the execution of the calling METHOD routine:

□ The number of arguments received must be the same as the number of parameters passed.

□ The relative positions of the arguments passed must match the parameters in the corresponding METHOD statement.

□ The data types of both sets of variables must agree.

The argument names in the calling routine do not have to match the parameter names in the METHOD statement.

Returning Values to the Calling Routine

A called method block can modify any argument it receives. However, it cannot return new values to calling routine parameters that are numeric literals, character literals, or expressions. By default, values for variables are returned to the calling routine. If you want a called method block to receive values but not return values to its calling routine, use the NOCHANGE routine.

Example Containing Two Method Blocks

```
array narr(*) 8; /* Reference array. Dimensions determined at run time*/
array carr(*) $; /* Reference array. Dimensions determined at run time*/
length temp size 8 tempc $ 200;

/* Generic sort routine for any size of 1-dimension numeric array */
nsort: method narr 8;
     /* find dimensions from the calling program */
  size = dim(narr);
   /* -- Bubble Sort -- */
  do i = 1 to size - 1;
     do j = i+1 to size;
        if narr(i) > narr(j) then
           do;
             temp = narr(i);
             narr(i) = narr(j);
             narr(j) = temp;
           end;
     end;
  end;
  /* Array narr is now sorted with ascending order */
endmethod;

     /* Generic sort routine for any size of 1-dimension char array */
csort: method carr $;
```

```
size = dim(carr);   /* find dimensions from the calling program */
    /* -- Bubble Sort -- */
size = dim(carr);
do i = 1 to size - 1;
    do j = i+1 to size;
        if carr(i) > carr(j) then
            do;
                tempc = carr(i);
                carr(i) = carr(j);
                carr(j) = tempc;
            end;
    end;
end;
    /* Array carr is now sorted with ascending order */
endmethod;
```

Example of Calling a Method

Assume that the method block CSORT is defined in SCL entry ABC. To call
CSORT, use the following statement in any SCL entry or FSEDIT application to call
the method block CSORT, which is equivalent to an external called routine:

```
array carr(3) $ 20('c','b','a');
call method('abc.scl','csort',arrdim,msg,carr);
put carr=;
```

The output is

```
CARR=
CARR[1]='a'
CARR[2]='b'
CARR[3]='c'
```

If the preceding method blocks are defined in an SCL entry, the block NSORT is
equivalent to an internal called routine when it is invoked by the following LINK
statement:

```
MAIN:
    link nsort;
    other SCL statements
return;
```

Example of Using the REST= Argument

Sum a variable number of numbers, and print out the sum. The method ignores any
character types passed in.

```
length totsum 8;

SUMPRINT: method msg $ REST=rest_list;
    if rest_list = . then
        do;
            put 'No numbers to sum were passed in!';
            return;
        end;
    totsum = 0;
```

```
do i = 1 to listlen( rest_list );
   type = itemtype( rest_list, i );
   if ( type = 'N' ) then
      do;
         valn = getitemn( rest_list, i );
         totsum = totsum + valn;
      end;
end;

put msg totsum;
endmethod;
```

Use the following CALL METHOD routine to invoke the SUMPRINT method:

```
call method('test.scl','sumprint', 'The total is: ',15,30,1);
```

The output of this example is:

```
The total is: 46
```

Example Using the /RESIDENT Option

Use RESIDENT in a program:

```
PRNTERR: method errno 8 REST=parms /RESIDENT
```

METHOD

Contains the name of the method that is currently executing

Character System Instance Variable

See Also:
SELF
SUPER
VALUE

Details

METHOD is a System Instance Variable. It is provided automatically by the FRAME entry in SAS/AF, but the SCL compiler does not automatically create a space for it in the SCL data vector. Because of this, you get a warning when you compile your SCL entry if you have a reference to _METHOD_. See _FRAME_ for more details on how to prevent the warning.

METHOD is useful when you have one or more methods that share the same section of code but which require a CALL SUPER.

To use _METHOD_, you must declare it as a character variable using the LENGTH statement.

METHOD only has a valid value when a method is running.

Example Using _METHOD_

For a FRAME entry object, you may define the _UPDATE_ and the _BUPDATE_ method to execute the same section of code if they perform similar functions:

```
length _method_ $40;
BUPDATE:
UPDATE:
   method;
    ... code for _UPDATE_ and _BUPDATE_ methods here ...

   call super(_self_, _method_);
endmethod;
```

Without _METHOD_, you would not know which method to do a CALL SUPER on, so you would have to code the above as:

```
BUPDATE:
   method;
   methodName = '_BUPDATE_';
   link update1;
endmethod;

UPDATE:
   method;
   methodName = '_UPDATE_';
   link update1;
endmethod;

UPDATE1:
    ... code for _UPDATE_ and _BUPDATE_ goes here ...

   call super(_self_, methodName);
return;
```

MLENGTH

Returns the maximum length of a variable

See Also:
LENGTH

length=**MLENGTH**(*var*);

Where...	Is type...	And represents...
length	N	The maximum length of a variable.
var	C	The variable.

Details

MLENGTH is different from LENGTH, which returns the trimmed length. For window variables, MLENGTH returns the length of the variable in the display.

If a numeric variable is passed to the MLENGTH function, the function always returns a length of 8 for the variable.

Example

LENGTH returns the value 2 because the value of S is **ab**. MLENGTH returns the value 5 because the maximum size of the variable M, determined by the LENGTH statement in this example, is 5.

```
length s $ 5;
s='ab';
l=length(s);
m=mlength(s);
```

MODIFIED

Reports whether a field or FRAME entry object has been modified

See Also:
DISPLAYED
ERROR
ERROROFF
ERRORON
FIELD
OBSINFO

rc=**MODIFIED**(*wvar-name*);

Where...	Is type...	And represents...
rc	N	Whether the field has been modified: 1 if modified. 0 if not modified.
wvar-name	C	The field or FRAME entry object in the window. This name cannot be an element of an array or an expression. If *wvar-name* is invalid, the program halts execution.

Details

A variable's state changes to modified when a user types any character in the field and presses ENTER or a function key or selects a FRAME entry object.

The field or FRAME entry object cannot be an element of an array. To report this information for an array element, use FIELD instead.

The ERRORON statement causes MODIFIED to return a value of 1.

FRAME entry objects can also use _IS_MODIFIED_.

Example

Open an FSEDIT window for the SAS data set specified in the DSNAME variable if the window variable DSNAME is modified with the name of an existing SAS data set. The FSEDIT function displays the data set for interactive editing.

```
if (modified(dsname) and dsname ne ' ' ) then
   call fsedit(dsname);
else
   _msg_='Please enter a valid data set name.';
```

The following are examples of invalid syntax that will not compile:

```
rc=modified('xyz');  /* A literal string is used. */
rc=modified(a||b); /* Concatenation of two variables. */
rc=modified(a{i}); /* An array element is used. */
```

MODVAR

Changes the name, label, format, or informat of a variable in a SAS data set

See Also:
OPEN
VARFMT
VARINFMT
VARLABEL
VARLEN
VARNAME
VARNUM
VARTYPE

sysrc=**MODVAR**(*data-set-id,var-name,new-name<,label<,format<,informat>>>*);

Where...	Is type...	And represents...
sysrc	N	Whether the operation was successful: 0 if successful ≠ 0 if not successful.
data-set-id	N	The identifier assigned when the data set was opened. If *data-set-id* is invalid, the program halts execution.
var-name	C	The variable whose attribute or attributes you want to change. The variable must already exist in the SAS data set.
new-name	C	The new name to assign to the variable. The value must be a valid SAS name and cannot already exist in the SAS data set.
label	C	The label to assign to the variable.
format	C	The format to assign to the variable.
informat	C	The informat to assign to the variable.

Details

The data set must be opened in UTILITY (V) mode, or the function halts execution.

If you do not want to change an argument, insert a null string (*''*) as a placeholder.

Example

Change only the label for the variable PHONENUM in the SAS data set CUSTOMR:

```
dsid=open('customr','v');
if dsid then
    do;
        rc=modvar(dsid,'phonenum','','Office Phone');
        rc=close(dsid);
    end;
```

MOPEN

Opens a directory member file

See Also:
DOPEN
FCLOSE
FOPEN

file-id=(directory-id,member-name <open-mode<,record-length<,record-format>>>);

Where...	Is type...	And represents...
file-id	N	The identifier for the file, or 0 if the file could not be opened. You can use a *file-id* that is returned by the MOPEN function like you would use a *file-id* returned by the FOPEN function.
directory-id	N	The identifier that was returned by DOPEN when the directory was opened. If *directory-id* is invalid, the program halts execution.
member-name	C	The member name in the directory.
open-mode	C	The type of access to the file: **'A'** APPEND mode, which allows writing new records after the current end of the file. **'I'** INPUT mode, which allows reading only. (Default) **'O'** OUTPUT mode, which defaults to the OPEN mode specified in the host option in the FILENAME statement or function. If no host option is specified, it allows writing new records at the beginning of the file. **'S'** Sequential input mode, which is used for pipes and other sequential devices such as hardware ports. **'U'** UPDATE mode, which allows both reading and writing. **'W'** Sequential update mode, which is used for pipes and other sequential devices such as ports.
record-length	N	The logical record length of the file. To use the existing record length for the file, specify a length of 0 or do not provide a value here.
record-format	C	The record format of the file: **'B'** Data are to be interpreted as binary data. **'D'** Use default record format. **'E'** Use editable record format. **'F'** File contains fixed length records. **'P'** File contains printer carriage control in host-dependent record format. **'V'** File contains variable length records. To use the existing record format, do not specify a value here.

Details

▶ *Caution: Use OUTPUT mode with care.*

Opening an existing file for output may overwrite the current contents of the file without warning.

. . . .

The member is identified by *directory-id* and *member-name* instead of by a fileref. You can also open a directory member by using FILENAME to assign a fileref to the member, followed by a call to FOPEN. However, using MOPEN saves you from having to use a separate fileref for each member.

If the file already exists, it defaults to the output mode (APPEND or REPLACE) based on the host option specified with the FILENAME statement. For example,

```
rc=filename('file',physical-name,' ','mod');
fid=fopen('file','o');
rc=fput(fid,'This is a test.');
rc=fwrite(fid);
rc=fclose(fid);
```

If **'file'** already exists, FWRITE appends the new record instead of writing it at the beginning of the file. However, if there is not a host option specified with the FILENAME function, the output mode implies replace.

If the open fails, use SYSMSG to retrieve the message text.

■ **Host Information** . . . .   The term *directory* in this description refers to an aggregate grouping of files managed by the host operating system. Different host operating systems identify such groupings with different names, such as directory, subdirectory, MACLIB, or partitioned data set. Refer to the SAS documentation for your host system for details.

Opening a directory member for output is not possible on some operating systems.

. . . . ■

Example

Assign the fileref MYDIR to a directory. (*Physical-name* represents the actual name of the directory in the form required by the host operating system). Then open the directory, determine the number of members, retrieve the name of the first member, and open that member. The last three arguments to MOPEN are the defaults.

```
rc=filename('mydir','physical-name ');
did=dopen('mydir');
frstname=' ';
memcount=dnum(did);
if (memcount>0) then
   do;
      frstname=dread(did,1);
      fid=mopen(did,frstname,'i',0,'d');
         SCL statements to process the member
      rc=fclose(fid);
   end;
else
   _msg_=sysmsg();
rc=dclose(did);
```

MSG

Contains the text to display on the window's message line the next time the window is refreshed

Character System Variable

See Also:
SYSMSG

Details

MSG is a System Variable that is created for every SCL program you compile. The compiler creates a space for _MSG_ in the SCL data vector.

Typically an application displays error and warning messages on the window's message line. The text for system error and warning messages can be obtained using the SYSMSG or STDMSG functions. You can also assign your own text to the _MSG_ variable. Messages are displayed when the window refreshes.

FRAME entries can also use the _GET_MSG_ and _SET_MSG_ methods to query and update the _MSG_ variable.

MSG is not displayed if the window has BANNER set to NONE.

Example

Display a message if a data set cannot be opened.

```
INIT:
   dsid = open('sasuser.class');
   if dsid eq 0 then
      _msg_ = sysmsg();
return;
```

NAMEDITEM

Returns the index of a named item in a list

See Also:
DELNITEM
GETNITEMC
GETNITEML
GETNITEMN
MAKELIST
MAKENLIST
NAMEITEM
SEARCHC
SEARCHL
SEARCHN
SETNITEMC
SETNITEML
SETNITEMN

index=**NAMEDITEM**(*list-id,name<,occurrence<,start-index>>*);

Where...	Is type...	And represents...
index	N	The position of the item in the list, or 0 if the named item is not found.
list-id	N	The identifier of the list that NAMEDITEM searches. An invalid *list-id* produces an error condition.
name	C	The name of the item to search for. If *name* is specified, it is converted to uppercase and trailing blanks are removed before searching. If *name* is blank, the first unnamed item is returned.
occurrence	N	The number of the occurrence of the named item to search for. The default is 1 for the first occurrence of the item.
start-index	N	Where in the list to begin searching for the item. By default, *start-index* is 1 (the first item). If *start-index* is positive, the search begins at position *start-index* items from the beginning of the list. If *start-index* is negative, the search begins at the item specified by ABS(*start-index*) items from the end of the list. An error condition results if the absolute value of *start-index* is zero or greater than the number of items in the list.

Details

NAMEDITEM searches only the top level of the list specified by *list-id*. That is, it does not search sublists. Several functions that access items in a list by position have counterparts that access items by their names such as GETITEMC versus GETNITEMC. Because it is more efficient to retrieve an item by its position rather than by its name, you can use NAMEDITEM to find the position and then use the functions that access items by position rather than by name.

If *occurrence* and *start-index* are both positive or both negative, the search proceeds forward from the *start-index* item. For forward searches, the search continues only to the end of the list and does not wrap back to the front of the list. If *occurrence* or *start-index* is negative, the search is backwards. For backward searches, the search continues only to the beginning of the list and does not wrap back to the end of the list.

Examples

Swap the numeric values associated with the first and last occurrence of the item named **'X'**:

```
    /*  Return first occurence of X.  */
 first=getnitemn(listid,'X');
    /*  Return last occurence of X.   */
 last=getnitemn(listid,'X',1,-1);
 list=setnitemn(listid,last,'X');
 list=setnitemn(listid,first,'X',1 -1);
```

The following example shows a slightly more efficient way to perform the swap operation. This method does not require a second search for the item, and it can also detect when item **'X'** does not exist in the list.

```
    /*  Return the position number of the first item X. */
 ifirst=nameditem(listid,'X');
 if (ifirst>0) then
    do;
       first=getitemn(listid,ifirst);
         / * Return the position of the last item X.  */
       ilast=nameditem(listid,'X',1,-1);
       list=setitemn(listid,getitemn(listid,ilast),ifirst);
       list=setitemn(listid,first,ilast);
    end;
```

Note: This example checks to see if there is at least one item named **'X'** but never checks to see if there is another item named **'X'**. It assumes that there is at least one more item named **'X'**.

NAMEITEM

Returns and optionally replaces the name of an item in an SCL list

See Also:
DELNITEM
GETNITEMC
GETNITEML
GETNITEMN
HASATTR
MAKELIST
MAKENLIST
NAMEDITEM
SETLATTR
SETNITEMC
SETNITEML
SETNITEMN

item-name=**NAMEITEM**(*list-id*<,*index*<,*new-name*>>);

Where...	Is type...	And represents...
item-name	C	The name of the specified list item, or blank if the item does not have a name.
list-id	N	The identifier of the list containing the indexed item. An invalid *list-id* produces an error condition.
index	N	The position of the item in the list. The position can be specified as a positive or negative number. By default, *index* is 1 (the first item). If *index* is a positive number, the item is at position *index* from the beginning of the list. If *index* is a negative number, the item is at position ABS(*index*) from the end of the list. An error condition results if the absolute value for *index* is zero or it is greater than the number of items in the list
new-name	C	The new name to assign to the list item.

Details

NAMEITEM returns the name of the item at the list position specified by the value for *index*. If a value for *new-name* is also provided, the function assigns that name to the item, replacing the old name.

An error condition results if

□ the value for *new-name* is provided and the list has any of the following attributes:

  □ NOUPDATE

  □ SASNAMES and *new-name* is not a valid SAS name

  □ NODUPNAMES and *new-name* duplicates the name of another item in the list.

To check the attributes of a list or list item, use HASATTR. To change attributes, use SETLATTR.

NEW

Defines a new SAS data set interactively

See Also:
FSEDIT
FSVIEW
NEWVAR

CALL NEW(*data-set-name,model-data-set,num-obs,display-window*);

Where...	Is type...	And represents...
data-set-name	C	The SAS data set to be created. The syntax of the *data-set-name* argument is *<libref.>member*. The default library, WORK, is used if the libref is omitted. If a null string ' ' is specified for *data-set-name*, the DATA*n* naming convention is used to create a data set in the WORK.library.
model-data-set	C	An existing SAS data set after which the new SAS data set is to be modeled. Use a null string (' ') as a placeholder if you do not want to specify a model data set.
num-obs	N	The number of initial observations for the new SAS data set. This value must be equal to or greater than 0. All variables in all observations initially contain missing values. The value for *num-obs* cannot be a missing value.
display-window	C	Whether the NEW window is displayed so that variable definitions for the new SAS data set can be edited before the data set is created: '**Y**' displays the NEW window to allow editing of the variable names and attributes before the new data set is created. (Default) '**N**' does not display the NEW window. The variable definitions in the new SAS data set will be an exact replica of those in the model data set. A value must also be supplied for *model-data-set*.

Details

NEW creates a new blank data set. However, it does not replace an existing data set.

If *data-set-name* is an existing data set, the program halts execution. To prevent the program halt, use EXIST to determine if the data set already exists, DELETE to delete the data set, and CALL NEW to create a new data set with the same name.

. . . .

By default, the routine opens the NEW window to enable a user to define interactively the names and attributes of the variables in the new data set. The NEW window opened by this routine is the same as the one displayed when the NEW= option is used with the PROC FSEDIT or PROC FSVIEW statements in SAS/FSP software.

You can specify a model data set so that all the names and attributes of the model are automatically copied to the new data set. (Only the variable names and variable attributes of the model data set are copied, not the values it contains.) When a model data set is specified, you can use *display-window* to bypass the NEW window and create the new data set with the same variable names and attributes as the model data

▶ *Caution: Using an existing data set causes a program halt.*

set. Open the NEW window only if you want to enable users to alter the variable names and attributes before the new data set is created.

Use *num-obs* to specify the number of blank observations initially generated for the new data set. All variables in all observations of the new data set initially contain missing values.

Examples

Create a new SAS data set with a name that the user supplies in the field for the window variable DATASET. Before attempting to create the data set, check whether a SAS data set with the specified name already exists. If so, issue a message on the application window's message line. The new data set is modeled after the existing data set MODEL.A, and the user is not given the opportunity to modify the variable definitions (the NEW window is not opened). The new data set is created with ten blank observations.

```
if (exist(dataset)) then
   _msg_='Data set '||dataset||' already exists.';
else
   do;
      call new(dataset,'model.a',10,'n');
      _msg_='Data set '||dataset||' has been created.';
   end;
```

Create a new SAS data set with a name that the user supplies in the field for the window variable DATASET. These statements display the NEW window for the user to define the variables in the data set. No model data set is used.

```
if (exist(dataset)) then
   _msg_='Data set '||dataset||' already exists.';
else
   do;
      call new(dataset,' ',1,'y');
      _msg_='Data set '||dataset||' has been created.';
   end;
```

NEWVAR

Adds a variable to a new SAS data set

See Also:
OPEN

*sysrc=***NEWVAR**(*data-set-id,var-name,type<,length<,label <,format<,informat>>>>*);

Where...	Is type...	And represents...
sysrc	N	Whether the operation was successful: 0 if successful $\neq$ 0 if not successful.
data-set-id	N	The identifier assigned when the data set was opened. If *data-set-id* is invalid, the program halts execution. The SAS data set must be opened with an open mode of NEW.
var-name	C	The name to be assigned to the new variable. The name must be a valid SAS name.
type	C	The data type of the new variable: **'C'** for a character variable **'N'** for a numeric variable.
length	N	The length of the new variable. For a character variable, this value can be between 1 and 200. For a numeric variable, it can be between 3 and 8. On some systems, the minimum length can be 2.
label	C	The label for the new variable. This is a character string from 1 to 40 characters. If the label contains single quotes, use two single quotes for each of these internal single quotes, or surround the label with double quotes. Each set of two single quotes counts as one character.
format	C	The format for the new variable. This must be a valid SAS format name. Formats can be either defined by the user or supplied by the SAS System. If not specified, a default format is assigned. If *type* is **'C'**, a character format should be specified. Otherwise a numeric format should be specified.
informat	C	The informat for the new variable. This must be a valid SAS informat name. Informats can be either defined by the user or supplied by the SAS System. If not specified, SAS assigns a default informat. If *type* is **'C'**, a character informat should be specified. Otherwise a numeric informat should be specified.

Details

▶ *Caution: The data set must be opened in NEW mode, or SCL halts program execution.*

Opening an existing SAS data set in NEW mode creates a new data set that overwrites the old data set. When the data set is closed after using NEWVAR, the SAS data set is created with zero observations. If the variable name matches a variable name already defined for the data set with a previous NEWVAR function, the new definition overrides the previous definition.

Example

Open a new SAS data set, MYDATA, in NEW mode, and then add two variables to it: the numeric variable NUM, and the character variable CHAR. The variable NUM has a length of 8, and the variable CHAR has a length of 20. The label of the variable CHAR is set to **STRING**.

```
dsid=open('mydata','n');
rc=newvar(dsid,'num','n',8);
rc=newvar(dsid,'char','c',20,'string');
rc=close(dsid);
```

NEXTCMD

Discards the current command on the command line

See Also:
NEXTWORD
WORD

CALL NEXTCMD();

Details

NEXTCMD deletes the words up to the next semicolon or the end of the command. If a semicolon is not found, the entire contents of the command line are deleted.

Ordinarily, you clear the command line after reading a command or a series of commands. NEXTCMD is usually used in conjunction with CONTROL ENTER, ALWAYS, or ALLCMDS.

If the command line contains two or more commands separated by semicolons, only the first command on the command line is executed during the current execution of the MAIN section. The next command is executed when control is returned to the program or when another entry is displayed, as in the use of the DISPLAY routine.

Example

Suppose you have an FSEDIT application and you want to prevent everyone but one user from deleting observations. You can use NEXTCMD to remove the DELETE command.

```
FSEINIT:
    control always;
return;

INIT:
return;

MAIN:
    if word(1,'u') =: 'DEL' and
        symget('sysjobid') ne 'SASXXX' then
            do;
                call nextcmd();
                _msg_='You are not authorized to delete observations';
            end;
return;

TERM:
return;
```

NEXTWORD

Deletes the current word and advances to the next word in the current command

See Also:
NEXTCMD
WORD

CALL NEXTWORD();

Details

A *word* is the text at the current position up to the next blank or semicolon. A semicolon denotes the end of a command in addition to the end of a word. NEXTWORD is used with WORD and is usually used in conjunction with CONTROL ENTER, CONTROL ALWAYS, or CONTROL ALLCMDS.

If the command line contains two or more commands separated by semicolons, only the first command on the command line is executed during the current execution of the MAIN section. The next command is executed when control is returned to the program or when another entry is displayed as in the use of the DISPLAY routine.

Examples

If a user issues the command **AXX BXX CXX DXX**, the succession of words is as follows:

	Initial	After 1st NEXTWORD	After 2nd NEXTWORD
word(1)	AXX	BXX	CXX
word(2)	BXX	CXX	DXX
word(3)	CXX	DXX	*blank*

If a user issues the command **XYZ;**, the succession of words is as follows:

	Initial	After 1st NEXTWORD	After 2nd NEXTWORD
word(1)	XYZ	*blank*	*blank*
word(2)	;	;	;
word(3)	;	;	;

NOCHANGE

Causes the called program to return the same values for the variables it received as parameters in an ENTRY statement

SAS/AF software only

See Also:
APPLY
DISPLAY
ENTRY
METHOD Statement
NOTIFY
SEND
SUPAPPLY
SUPER

CALL NOCHANGE();

Details

The NOCHANGE routine causes the called program to return the same values for the variables it received as parameters in an ENTRY statement. This routine is used in the called program that contains the ENTRY statement.

NOCHANGE has no effect on reference arrays. See the ARRAY statement in this chapter for more information on reference arrays.

Example

Have program A call program B and pass to it the parameters X, Y, and Z. Have program B test the system _STATUS_ variable for the value C (indicating that a CANCEL command has been issued). If the user exits program B with a CANCEL command, then no updated values are returned to program A.

Program A

```
INIT:
return;

MAIN:
    call display('mylib.test.b.program',x,y,z);
return;

TERM:
return;
```

Program B

```
 entry a b c 8;

INIT:
return;

MAIN:
    SCL statements
return;


TERM:
    if _STATUS_='C' then call nochange();
return;
```

NOTE

Returns an observation ID for the current observation of a SAS data set

See Also:
DROPNOTE
POINT
REWIND

note-id=**NOTE**(*data-set-id*);

Where...	Is type...	And represents...
note-id	N	The identifier assigned to the observation.
data-set-id	N	The identifier assigned when the data set was opened. If *data-set-id* is invalid, the program halts execution.

Details

You can use the observation ID value to return to the current observation using POINT. Observations can be marked using NOTE and then returned to later using POINT. Each *note-id* is a unique numeric value. There can be up to 1,000 *note-id*s per open data set.

To free the memory associated with an observation ID, use DROPNOTE.

Examples

CALL CUROBS to display the observation number. Call NOTE to mark the observation. Call POINT to point to the observation that corresponds to NOTEID.

```
INIT:
   dsid=open('sasuser.fitness','i');
return;

MAIN:
      /* Go to observation 10 in data set */
   rc=fetchobs(dsid,10);
   if (abs(rc) ne 0) then
      do;
         put "FETCHOBS FAILED";
         return;
      end;
      /* Display observation number in MSG window */
   cur=curobs(dsid);
   put "CUROBS=" cur;
      /* Mark observation 10 using NOTE */
   noteid=note(dsid);
      /* Rewind pointer to beginning of data set using REWIND */
   rc=rewind(dsid);
      /* FETCH first observation into DDV */
   rc=fetch(dsid);
      /* Display first observation number */
   cur=curobs(dsid);
   put "CUROBS=" cur;
      /* POINT to observation 10 marked earlier by NOTE */
   rc=point(dsid,noteid);
      /* FETCH observation into DDV */
   rc=fetch(dsid);
      /* Display observation number 10 marked by NOTE */
   cur=curobs(dsid);
   put "CUROBS=" cur;
```

```
    return;

    TERM:
       if (dsid >0) then rc=close(dsid);
    return;
```

The output produced by this program is:

```
    CUROBS=10
    CUROBS=1
    CUROBS=10
```

NOTIFY

Sends a method to a widget that is identified by its name

FRAME entries only

See Also:
APPLY
INSTANCE
LOADCLASS
LOADRES
SEND
SUPAPPLY
SUPER

CALL NOTIFY(*widget-name,method-name<,parameters>*);

Where...	Is type...	And represents...
widget-name	C	The widget to which to send the method, or ' . ' (a string containing a period) to send the method to the FRAME entry object.
method-name	C	The method to invoke.
parameters	N, C	Additional numeric or character arguments, separated by commas, that are required by the method.

Details

CALL NOTIFY sends a method to a widget in a FRAME entry by specifying the widget name. CALL NOTIFY, a special interface to CALL SEND, may be called only from the SCL program for the FRAME entry to which the widget belongs because that is the only code in which the widget's name is not ambiguous.

For more information on FRAME entries, see *SAS/AF Software: FRAME Entry Usage and Reference.*

Note: As with CALL DISPLAY, the SCL compiler cannot determine what data types are expected for each of the parameters passed to a method. When the application executes, SAS/AF software verifies that each parameter is correct. If there is a type error, the SCL program halts.

In most cases, quote the widget name so that the value of the widget is not passed to CALL NOTIFY. For example, the following code hides the widget OBJ1:

```
    call notify('obj1','_hide_');
```

However, if OBJ1 has a value of **OK**, the following code hides the widget named OK:

```
    call notify(obj1,'_hide_');
```

If the value of OBJ1 is not the name of a widget, the program halts.
Similarly, be sure to quote *method-name* unless *method-name* is an expression.

Examples

Suppose you have a FRAME entry with two pushbuttons, **OK** and **NOT_OK**. The following code causes **OK** to be grayed when a user clicks on **NOT_OK**.

```
NOT_OK:
    call notify('ok','_gray_');
return;
```

The following example fills a list with the set of widgets in the FRAME entry.

```
widgets=makelist();
call notify('.','_get_widgets_',widgets);
```

NSELECT

Returns the number of rows that have been selected in a selection list

SAS/AF software only

See Also:
ISSEL
SELECT
SELECTED
UNSELECT

num-rows=**NSELECT**();

Where...	Is type...	And represents...
num-rows	N	The number of rows selected.

Details

Because you can define extended tables only in SAS/AF software, you cannot use NSELECT in FSEDIT or FSVIEW programs. NSELECT is valid only for PROGRAM entries. FRAME entry objects must use the _GET_NSELECT_ method.

In order for an extended table to be considered a selection list, you must specify a number of selections in the SETROW routine.

Example

Return the number of rows selected:

```
nsel = nselect();
_msg_ = 'You have selected ' || nsel || ' rows.';
```

NUMFKEYS

Returns the number of function keys available for the device

See Also:
FKEYNAME
GETFKEY
SETFKEY

fkeynum=**NUMFKEYS**();

Where...	Is type...	And represents...
fkeynum	N	The number of function keys available for the device.

Details

You can use this function only in entries that have a window variable or text in the DISPLAY window.

You can use NUMFKEYS when you want to use SCL to return the number of function keys, then disable procedure-specific commands and Display Manager commands and redefine the function keys while a window is open. When you redefine the function keys, you can limit the commands that can be used in an application window. (If you do this, you may want to restore the settings with SETFKEY before the application window closes.)

Example

Assign a custom PMENU. Then use NUMFKEYS to find out how many function keys a user's device has. Use SETFKEY to disable them and again to restore the settings when the window closes.

```
array command (100) _temporary_;

INIT:
     /* Assign the PMENU entry to the window.  */
   rc=pmenu('editdata.pmenu');
     /* Turn the PMENU facility on.  */
   call execcmd('pmenu on');
     /* Execute the MAIN section even if a user makes  */
     /* an error or issues an unknown command.         */
   control enter;
     /* Determine the number of function keys on a user's keyboard.  */
   numkeys=numfkeys();
   do n=1 to numkeys;
      command{n}=getfkey (fkeyname(n));
        /* Disable function key assignments.  */
      call setfkey(fkeyname(n),'');
   end;
   return;
MAIN:
     Statements to process custom commands
   return;
TERM:
     /* Restore command assignments to function keys.  */
   do n=1 to numkeys;
      call setfkey(fkeyname(n),command{n});
   end;
     /* Turn the PMENU facility off.  */
   call execcmd('pmenu off');
   return;
```

OBSINFO

Returns information on the current observation in an FSEDIT application

FSEDIT applications only

See Also:
CUROBS

rc=**OBSINFO**(*info-item*);

Where...	Is type...	And represents...
rc	N	A value that depends on the information requested. See the descriptions of individual *info-type* values for details.
info-item	C	One information item from Table 20.10.

Table 20.10 *Information Items for the OBSINFO Function*

Option	Description

Release 6.11

`'ALTER'`	Reports whether the currently-displayed observation can be edited: 0 The observation cannot be edited. If ALTER=0 and LOCKED=0, the observation is open in FSBROWSE. If ALTER=0 and LOCKED=1, the observation is open in FSEDIT, but the observation is locked. 1 The observation can be edited. If ALTER=1 and LOCKED=0, then the observation is open in FSEDIT.

`'CUROBS'`	Reports the number of the current observation.
	  n The number of the observation.
	
	  −1 The data set is accessed using an engine that does not support observation numbers.
	
	CUROBS returns a missing value (.) when
	• there are no observations in the data set.
	• no observations meet the specified WHERE condition.
	• you are on a deleted observation.

`'DELETED'`	Reports whether the currently displayed observation is marked for deletion. 1 The observation is marked for deletion. 0 The observation is not marked for deletion.
`'LOCKED'`	Reports whether the currently displayed observation is locked by another user. 1 The observation is locked. 0 The observation is not locked.
`'MODIFIED'`	Reports whether a value has been changed in any data set variable in the currently displayed observation or the observation is new. 1 A variable has been changed or the observation is new. 0 No data set variables have been changed.
`'NEW'`	Reports whether the currently-displayed observation is a new observation. 1 The observation is new.

Option	Description

0   The observation already exists in the data set.

Example

Obtain information about the observation currently displayed in the FSEDIT window:

```
rc=obsinfo('curobs');
rc=obsinfo('deleted');
rc=obsinfo('locked');
rc=obsinfo('new');
rc=obsinfo('modified');
```

OPEN

Opens a SAS data file

See Also:
CLOSE
MODVAR
NEWVAR

data-file-id=**OPEN**(<*data-file-name*<,*mode*>>);

Where...	Is type...	And represents...
data-file-id	N	The data file identifier or 0 if the data file could not be opened.
data-file-name	C	The SAS data file to be opened. Use the syntax <*libref.*>*member-name*<(*data-set-options*)>.
		The default value for *data-file-name* is _LAST_, which is the last data file created in the current SAS session. If the libref is omitted, WORK is assumed.
		You can add a list of SAS data set options following the data file name. The list must be enclosed in parentheses. The FIRSTOBS= and OBS= options are ignored. All other data set options are valid.
mode	C	The type of access to the data file:

 'I' opens the data file in INPUT mode. Values can be read but not modified. (Default). Observations are read in random order.

 'IN' opens the data file in INPUT mode. Observations are read sequentially, and you are allowed to revisit an observation.

 'IS' opens the data file in INPUT mode. Observations are read sequentially, but you are not allowed to revisit an observation.

 'N' opens the data file in NEW mode and creates a new data file. If *data-file-name* already exists, the data file is replaced without warning.

 'U' opens the data file in UPDATE mode and allows modifications to values in the data file. Observations are read in random order.

Where...	Is type...	And represents...
	'UN'	opens the data file in UPDATE mode to allow modifications. Observations are read sequentially, and you are allowed to revisit an observation.
	'US'	opens the data file in UPDATE mode to allow modifications. Observations are read sequentially, but you are not allowed to revisit an observation.
	'V'	opens the data file in UTILITY mode. This mode must be used to change any variable attributes or to manipulate any associated data file indexes.

Details

OPEN opens a SAS data file (a SAS data set or a SAS/ACCESS view descriptor) and returns a unique numeric data set identifier, which is used in most other SCL functions that manipulate data sets.

If *mode* is **'I'** or **'U'**, OPEN defaults to the strongest access mode available in the engine. That is, if the engine supports random access, OPEN defaults to random access. Otherwise, the file is opened in **'IN'** or **'UN'** mode automatically. Files are opened with sequential access and a system level warning is set.

Note that both **'IS'** and **'IN'** (as well as **'US'** and **'UN'**) refer to sequential access. However **'IN'** allows revisiting an observation while **'IS'** does not.

By default, a SAS data file is opened with a control level of RECORD. Refer to Chapter 15 in *SAS Language: Reference* for details on the CNTLLEV data set option.

A data file that is already opened can be opened again with the following restrictions:

□ If the data file is already opened in UPDATE or INPUT mode, it cannot be opened again in UTILITY mode.

□ If the data file is already opened in UTILITY mode (so that variables can be dropped, inserted, or changed), it can only be opened again in NEW mode.

A data file that is already open in any mode can be opened again in NEW mode because that replaces everything in the old data file.

An open SAS data file should be closed when it is no longer needed.

Examples

Open the data file PRICES in the library MASTER using INPUT mode:

```
dsid=open('master.prices','i');
if (dsid=0) then _msg_=sysmsg();
else _msg_='PRICES data file has been opened';
```

You can pass values from SCL variables to be used on data set options. Open the data set MYDATA, and use the WHERE= data set option to apply a permanent WHERE clause using the value from the numeric variable SCRNUM:

```
dsid=open('mydata(where=(num='|| put(scrnum,5.)||'))');
```

Open the data set MYDATA, and use the WHERE= data set option to apply a permanent WHERE clause using the value from the characater variable SCRNAME:

```
dsid=open('mydata(where=(name='|| quote(scrname)||'))');
```

OPTGETC

Returns the current setting of a SAS system option having a character value

See Also:
OPTGETN
OPTSETC
OPTSETN

cval=**OPTGETC**(*option-name*);

Where...	Is type...	And represents...
cval	C	The setting of the SAS system option, or a blank if *option-name* is invalid.
option-name	C	The name of the character SAS system option to retrieve.

Details

If you attempt to use OPTGETC to get information about a numeric option, an error message is generated. To determine whether a SAS system option has a numeric or character setting, refer to the SAS Companion for your host or to *SAS Language: Reference.*

You can view current option settings by using the OPTIONS procedure in the SAS session or by using the OPTIONS command to open the display manager OPTIONS window.

For options that have ON/OFF settings (for example, DATE/NODATE) use OPTGETN.

Example

Check to see if new SAS data sets will be compressed.

```
if optgetc('compress')='YES'
   then _msg_='Observations are compressed.';
else _msg_='Observations are not compressed.';
```

OPTGETN

Returns the current setting of a SAS system option having a numeric or binary value

See Also:
OPTGETC
OPTSETC
OPTSETN

nval=**OPTGETN**(*option-name*);

Where...	Is type...	And represents...
nval	N	The setting of the SAS system option, or a blank if *option-name* is invalid. For options with binary settings of ON or OFF, the function returns 1 if the setting is on, and 0 if it is off.
option-name	C	The name of the numeric SAS system option to retrieve.

Details

If you attempt to use OPTGETN to get information about a character option, an error message is generated. To determine whether a SAS system option has a numeric or character setting, refer to the SAS Companion for your host or to *SAS Language: Reference.* In addition to options with numeric settings, use OPTGETN for options with binary settings of ON and OFF because these options have the numeric value 1 for ON and 0 for OFF.

You can view current option settings by using the OPTIONS procedure in the SAS session or by using the OPTIONS command to open the display manager OPTIONS window.

Examples

Return the current line size, and place it in the variable LINESIZE:

```
linesize=optgetn('linesize');
```

Return the setting of the CAPS option and place it in the variable CAPS. The value returned is 0 if NOCAPS option is in effect or 1 if CAPS is in effect.

```
caps=optgetn('caps');
```

OPTSETC

Assigns a value to a SAS system option with a character setting

See Also:
OPTGETC
OPTGETN
OPTSETN

rc=**OPTSETC**(*option-name,cval*);

Where...	Is type...	And represents...
rc	N	Whether the operation was successful: 0 if successful ≠ 0 if not successful.
option-name	C	The name of the character SAS system option to set.
cval	C	The new character setting for the option.

Details

If you attempt to use OPTSETC to assign a value to a numeric option, an error message is generated. To determine whether a SAS system option has a numeric or character setting, refer to the SAS Companion for your host operating system or *SAS Language: Reference.*

You can view current option settings by using the OPTIONS procedure in the SAS session or by using the OPTIONS command to open the display manager OPTIONS window.

For options that have ON/OFF settings (for example, DATE/NODATE), use OPTSETN.

Example

Set the COMPRESS option to allow compression of new SAS data sets.

```
rc=optsetc('compress','yes');
```

OPTSETN

Assigns a value to a SAS system option with a numeric or binary setting

See Also:
OPTGETC
OPTGETN
OPTSETC

rc=**OPTSETN**(*option-name,nval*);

Where...	Is type...	And represents...
rc	N	Whether the operation was successful: 0 if successful $\neq 0$ if not successful.
option-name	C	The name of the numeric SAS system option to set.
nval	N	The new numeric setting for the option. For options with binary settings of ON and OFF, specify *nval* of 1 to turn the option on and 0 to turn it off.

Details

If you attempt to use OPTSETN to assign a value to a character option, an error message is generated. To determine whether a SAS system option has a numeric or character setting, refer to the SAS Companion for your host operating system or *SAS Language: Reference.*

In addition to options with numeric settings, use OPTSETN for options with the binary settings of ON and OFF because the options have the numeric value 1 for ON and 0 for OFF.

You can view current option settings by using the OPTIONS procedure in the SAS session or by using the OPTIONS command to open the display manager OPTIONS window.

Examples

Set the LINESIZE option and then check to see if the return code is nonzero. If it is, the error message is displayed on the message line.

```
rc=optsetn('linesize',78);
if (rc) then _msg_=sysmsg();
```

Turn on the CAPS option:

```
rc=optsetn('caps',1);
```

PATHNAME

Returns the physical name of a SAS data library or an external file

See also:
FILENAME
FILEREF
FEXIST
FILEEXIST

file-name=**PATHNAME**(*fileref*);

Where...	Is type...	And represents...
file-name	C	The physical name of an external file or library, or blank if *fileref* is invalid.
fileref	C	The fileref assigned to an external file or a library.

Example

Verify that the fileref **MYFILE** is associated with an external file using the FILEREF function, and then use PATHNAME to retrieve the actual name of the external file:

```
rc=fileref('myfile');
if (rc=0) then do;
     fname=pathname('myfile');
     put "Path = " fname;
end;
```

PMENU

Changes the PMENU for an application

rc=**PMENU**(*pmenu*);

Where...	Is type...	And represents...
rc	N	Whether the operation was successful: 0 if the PMENU entry was assigned successfully. However, the PMENU function does not verify that *pmenu* exists. ≠ 0 if not successful
pmenu	C	The PMENU entry to assign. If the PMENU entry resides in a different catalog, specify a value of the form *libref.catalog.pmenu*. If a one-level name is specified, the PMENU entry is searched for in the current catalog, then in SASUSER.PROFILE, then in SASHELP.FSP.

Details

The PMENU function only changes the pull-down menu associated with the window. It does not turn on the pull-down menus. If the pull-down menus are on, the new pull-down menu is displayed immediately.

See Chapter 26, "The PMENU Procedure," in *SAS Procedures Guide, Version 6, Third Edition* for more information on creating custom PMENU entries. FRAME entries can also use the _SET_PMENU_ method.

Example

Change the default PMENU associated with an application to MYPMENU in the catalog NEWLIB.TESTS:

```
rc=pmenu('newlib.tests.mypmenu');
```

POINT

Locates an observation identified by the NOTE function

See Also:
DROPNOTE
NOTE

sysrc=**POINT**(*data-set-id,note-id*);

Where...	Is type...	And represents...
sysrc	N	Whether the operation was successful: 0 if successful ≠ 0 if not successful.
data-set-id	N	The identifier assigned when the data set was opened. If *data-set-id* is invalid, the program halts execution.
note-id	N	The identifier assigned to the observation by the NOTE function or −1 to go to the previous nondeleted observation in the data set. If *note-id* is invalid, the program halts execution and sends a message to the log.

Details

POINT locates the observation identified by the *note-id* argument, which is a value returned from NOTE. POINT sets up to read from the SAS data set. The Data Set Data Vector is not updated until a read is done using FETCH or FETCHOBS.

If *note-id* is a missing or invalid value, the program halts execution and sends a message to the log.

Example

Call NOTE to obtain an observation ID for the last read observation of the SAS data set MYDATA. Call POINT to point to the observation that corresponds to *note-id*. Call FETCH to return the observation marked by the pointer.

```
dsid=open('mydata','i');
rc=fetch(dsid);
noteid=note(dsid);
   more SCL statements
rc=point(dsid,noteid);
rc=fetch(dsid);
   more SCL statements
rc=close(dsid);
```

POPC

Removes and returns a character value from an SCL list

See Also:
DELITEM
GETITEMC
GETITEML
GETITEMN
HASATTR
INSERTC
INSERTL
INSERTN
ITEMTYPE
MAKELIST
POPL
POPN
SETLATTR

cval=**POPC**(*list-id*<,*index*>);

Where...	Is type...	And represents...
cval	C	The character value removed from the list.
list-id	N	The identifier of the list from which *cval* is removed. An invalid *list-id* produces an error condition.
index	N	The position of the item in the list. The position can be specified as a positive or negative number. By default, *index* is 1 (the first item). If *index* is a positive number, the item is at position *index* from the beginning of the list. If *index* is a negative number, the item is at position ABS(*index*) from the end of the list. An error condition results if the absolute value for *index* is zero or it is greater than the number of items in the list.

Details

POPC, along with INSERTC, is useful for implementing stacks and queues of character values.

An error condition results if:

□ the item has the NODELETE attribute

□ the list has the FIXEDLENGTH or NOUPDATE attribute

□ the list is empty

□ the specified item is not a character item.

To check the attributes of a list or list item, use HASATTR. To change attributes, use SETLATTR. Use ITEMTYPE to test if an item is character, when the list contains non-character items.

Examples

The examples assume all list items are character. A and B are equivalent. Both remove the first item in an SCL list.

```
A:   cval1=popc(listid);
     put cval1=;
```

```
B:   cval2=getitemc(listid);
     put cval2=;
     listid=delitem(listid);
```

Remove the last character value from a list:

```
cval=popc(listid,-1);
```

This example creates an SCL list called TODOQ which represents a queue of tasks to do. A SAS/AF FRAME entry has a field named NEWTASK for entering a new task into the TODOQ queue. A second field TODO displays the first task in the to-do queue. A DONE button removes the top task in the TODOQ queue.

```
INIT:
   todoq = makelist();
   call notify('done', '_gray_');
return;

NEWTASK:
   todoq = insertc(todoq, newtask, -1); /* Enqueue */
   newtask = '';
   cursor newtask;
return;

DONE:
   done = popc(todoq);    /* Dequeue */
return;

MAIN:
   if listlen(todoq) then
      do;
        call notify('done', '_ungray_');
        todo = getitemc(todoq);
      end;
   else
      do;
        call notify('done', '_gray_');
        todo = '';
      end;
return;

TERM:
   rc = dellist(todoq);
return;
```

POPL

Removes and returns a list identifier from an SCL list

See Also:
DELITEM
GETITEMC
GETITEML
GETITEMN
HASATTR
INSERTC
INSERTL
INSERTN
ITEMTYPE
LISTLEN
MAKELIST
POPC
POPN
SETLATTR

sublist-id=**POPL**(*list-id*<,*index*>);

Where...	Is type...	And represents...
sublist-id	N	The identifier of the sublist removed from the list.
list-id	N	The identifier of the list from which *sublist-id* is removed. An invalid *list-id* produces an error condition.
index	N	The position of the item in the list. The position can be specified as a positive or negative number. By default, *index* is 1 (the first item). If *index* is a positive number, the item is at position *index* from the beginning of the list. If *index* is a negative number, the item is at position ABS(*index*) from the end of the list. An error condition results if the absolute value for *index* is zero or it is greater than the number of items in the list.

Details

POPL, along with INSERTL, is useful for implementing stacks and queues of list identifiers.

An error condition results if:

□ the item has the NODELETE attribute

□ the list has the FIXEDLENGTH or NOUPDATE attribute

□ the list is empty

□ the specified item is not a sublist item

To check the attributes of a list or list item, use HASATTR. To change attributes, use SETLATTR. Use ITEMTYPE to test if an item is a list identifier when the list contains non-list items.

Examples

The examples assume all list items are sublist identifiers.

A and B are equivalent. Both remove the first item from the list.

```
A:  list=popl(listid);


B:  list=getiteml(listid);
    listid=delitem(listid);
```

Remove and return the last sublist identifier in the list:

```
list=popl(listid,-1);
```

The program searches, retrieves, and deletes the first sublist item from the list LISTID.

```
LOOP:
do i=1 to listlen(listid);
   if itemtype(listid,i)='L' then
      do;
```

```
                              list=popl(listid,i);
                              leave loop;
                         end;
                    end;
                      other SCL statements
```

POPLEGEND

Restores to the LEGEND window the last contents saved with the PUSHLEGEND routine

See Also:
ENDLEGEND
LEGEND
PUSHLEGEND
PUTLEGEND

CALL POPLEGEND();

Details

POPLEGEND is useful if several entries in a CALL DISPLAY nested sequence have their own legends and you want to restore the original legend of each calling entry when a called entry ends.

If no legend contents have been saved, this function is ignored.

To save the contents of the LEGEND window, use PUSHLEGEND>

For an example using the PUTLEGEND as well as other functions that manipulate a legend window, see LEGEND.

POPMENU

Displays a pop-up menu containing character items in an SCL list

See Also:
FILLIST
GETITEMC
GETLATTR
HASATTR
INSERTC
LISTLEN
MAKELIST
SETLATTR

index=**POPMENU**(*list-id*<,*max-popup*<,*row*,*column*>>);

Where...	Is type...	And represents...
index	N	The index of the list item selected from the menu, or 0.
list-id	N	The identifier of the list containing the character items to display in the pop-up menu. An invalid *list-id* produces an error condition.
max-popup	N	If the list is longer than *max_popup*, the menu is displayed in a window with a scrollable listbox.
row	N	The starting row of the pop-up menu.
column	N	The starting column of the pop-up menu.

Details

If the list contains too many items to fit in a pop-up menu, POPMENU displays the choices in a list box with scrollbars. If no display window is available, POPMENU always puts the menu in a list box.

An item in the list that has the INACTIVE attribute cannot be selected and is grayed on devices that support graying, but it is still displayed in the menu. You can use SETLATTR to assign an item the INACTIVE attribute or restore the item to an ACTIVE state.

If the pop-up menu is displayed in a list box, inactive items are marked with a dash ('-'), indicating that they may not be selected.

POPMENU returns 0 if:

□ the user cancelled the pop-up menu or closed it without making a selection.

□ the list is empty.

□ the list contains numeric or sublist items.

□ there is insufficient memory to create the pop-up.

For the last three cases above, the pop-up menu is not displayed.

If *row* and *column* are specified and either is outside the boundaries of the current window, the pop-up menu is positioned elsewhere on the window.

Note: Some window systems do not allow row and column positioning of pop-up menus. They may appear at location of the cursor of the last click with the pointing device.

POPN

Removes and returns a numeric value from an SCL list

See Also:
DELITEM
GETITEMC
GETITEML
GETITEMN
HASATTR
INSERTC
INSERTL
INSERTN
ITEMTYPE
MAKELIST
POPC
POPL
SETLATTR

nval=**POPN**(*list-id*<,*index*>);

Where...	Is type...	And represents...
nval	N	The numeric value removed from the list.
list-id	N	The identifier of the list from which *nval* is removed. An invalid *list-id* produces an error condition.
index	N	The position of the item in the list. The position can be specified as a positive or negative number. By default, *index* is 1 (the first item). If *index* is a positive number, the item is at position *index* from the beginning of the list. If *index* is a negative number, the item is at position ABS(*index*) from the end of the list. An error condition results if the absolute value for *index* is zero or it is greater than the number of items in the list

Details

POPN, along with INSERTN, is useful for implementing stacks and queues of numeric values.

An error condition results if:

□ the specified item in the list has the NODELETE attribute

□ the list has the FIXEDLENGTH or NOUPDATE attribute

□ the list is empty

□ the specified item is not a numeric item.

To check the attributes of a list or list item, use HASATTR. To change attributes, use SETLATTR. Use ITEMTYPE to test if an item is numeric, when the list cotnains nonnumeric items.

Examples

The examples assume all list items are numeric.

A and B are equivalent. Both remove the first item from the list.

```
A:   nval=popn(listid);


B:   nval=getitemn(listid);
     listid=delitem(listid);
```

Remove and return the last numeric value from a list.

```
nval=popn(listid,-1);
```

This example shows the SCL for a SAS/AF FRAME entry that creates a new list called DATETIMES and treats it as a stack. The entry has displays SAS datetime values when the button PUSH is pressed and pops and displays SAS datetime values from the DATETIMES stack when the button POP is pressed.

```
INIT:
   datetimes = makelist();
   call notify('pop', '_gray_');
return;

PUSH:
   datetime = datetime();
   datetimes = insertn(datetimes, datetime);
   call notify('pop', '_ungray_');
return;

POP::
   datetime = popn(datetimes);
   if listlen(datetimes) = 0 then
      call notify('pop', '_gray_');
return;

TERM:
   rc = dellist(datetimes);
return;
```

PREVIEW

Manipulates an application's preview buffer

SAS/AF software only

See Also:
ENDSUBMIT
SUBMIT
WREGION

rc=**PREVIEW**(*action*<,*argument-1*<,*argument-2*<,*argument-3*>>>);

Where...	Is type...	And represents...
rc	N	Whether the operation was successful: 　0　if successful. − 1　For actions that open the PREVIEW window, the CANCEL command was used to exit the PREVIEW window. For other actions, the requested operation was not performed successfully.
action	C	An action from Table 20.11.
argument	C	Up to three arguments for the specified action from Table 20.11.

Table 20.11　*Actions for the PREVIEW Function*

Action	Description
'BROWSE'	opens the PREVIEW window for browsing only. You can optionally specify a window title as *argument-1*.
'CLEAR'	clears the preview buffer. Any statements that were generated previously using SUBMIT statements or that were included using the COPY and INCLUDE actions are lost. No optional arguments are used with this action.
'CLOSE'	closes the PREVIEW window. No optional arguments are used with this action.
'COPY'	copies a catalog entry of type SOURCE, OUTPUT, or LOG into the preview buffer. You must specify the name of the entry to be copied as *argument-1*. See the description of the SAVE action for the syntax for *argument-1*.
'DISPLAY' | **'EDIT'**	opens the PREVIEW window to display the contents of the preview buffer for editing. All standard text editor commands are valid in this window. Control stays with the PREVIEW window until the PREVIEW window is exited. Issue the END command to exit the window and return to the SAS/AF program. Changes the user makes to the statements in the window are not reversed by issuing a CANCEL command. The SCL program, however, can check for the return code of −1 from the PREVIEW function, indicating that a CANCEL command was issued in the PREVIEW window, and then choose not to save the contents of the PREVIEW window. You can optionally specify a window title as *argument-1*.
'FILE'	saves the current contents of the PREVIEW window to an external file. With this action, you must specify the fileref for the external file as *argument-1*. You must specify a fileref. Physical filenames are not allowed. You can specify 'APPEND' for *argument-2* to append the contents of the preview buffer to the contents of the external file.
'HISTORY'	Saves or appends the statements submitted from SCL programs to a catalog member. You must specify the name of an entry as *argument-1*, in one of the following forms: *entry*　　　saves the submitted statements in SASUSER.PROFILE.*entry*.SOURCE.

Action	Description

	entry.SOURCE — saves the submitted statements in SASUSER.PROFILE.*entry*.SOURCE.
	libref.catalog.entry — saves the submitted statements in *libref.catalog.entry*.SOURCE.
	libref.catalog.entry.SOURCE — saves the submitted statements in *libref.catalog.entry*.SOURCE.

Once a history destination is set, it stays through the application until a reset is performed. To clear the destination, invoke PREVIEW again by passing the HISTORY action without any succeeding argument. The application stops appending the submitted statements to the previously specified SOURCE entry.

You can also optionally specify a description of up to 40 characters for the entry as *argument-2*.

Action	Description
'INCLUDE'	copies into the PREVIEW window the contents of an external file. With this action, you must specify the fileref for the external file as *argument-1*. A physical filename is not allowed.
'LINES'	returns the number of the last non-blank line in the PREVIEW window.
'MODIFIED'	returns 1 if the PREVIEW window was modified and 0 if it was not modified.
'OPEN'	displays the PREVIEW window and returns control immediately to the SCL program. New SAS statements are displayed continually as they are generated.

This window is displayed until the application closes or until you use the PREVIEW function and specify the CLOSE action. Thus, specifying OPEN enables you to keep the window open throughout an application by allowing control to return to the procedure while the window is open. With OPEN, you can optionally specify a window title as *argument-1*.

'PRINT' — prints the contents of the PREVIEW window. This action allows three arguments:

You can optionally use *argument-1* to name a form to control printing. Use *name* or *name*.FORM to specify a form in the current catalog. Use *libref.catalog.name* or *libref.catalog.name*.FORM to specify a form in a different catalog. If you do not specify a form, SASHELP.FSP.DEFAULT.FORM is used. For more information on forms, see *SAS Language: Reference*.

You can optionally use *argument-2* to specify a fileref for a print file. If this argument is blank or missing, the printout is sent to the default system printer.

You can optionally use *argument-3* to specify append mode. Use 'A' to append the output to the print file. If this argument is blank or missing, each new PRINT option replaces the contents of the print file.

'SAVE' — copies the contents of the PREVIEW window to a catalog member. With this action, you must specify the name of an entry as *argument-1*:

entry	saves the contents in SASUSER.PROFILE.*entry*.SOURCE.
entry.type	saves the contents in SASUSER.PROFILE.*entry.type*. Entry types can be SOURCE, LOG, and OUTPUT.
libref.catalog.entry	saves the contents in *libref.catalog.entry*.SOURCE.
libref.catalog.entry.type	saves the contents in *libref.catalog.entry.type*.

You can also optionally specify a description for the entry as *argument-2*. Only the first 40 characters of the description are saved.

You can also optionally specify 'APPEND' as *argument-3* to append the contents of the PREVIEW window to the specified catalog entry.

Details

The PREVIEW buffer is where statements generated by SUBMIT blocks are stored before they are submitted for execution.

Example

Manipulate the PREVIEW window. The user enters values in text entry widgets DSNAME (the name of a SAS data set to be created), MIMIC (the name of an existing SAS data set after which the new data set is modeled), and FNAME (the fileref of a file in which submitted SAS statements will be stored). If the user does not issue a CANCEL command from the application window, PREVIEW displays the statements in the PREVIEW window. If the user does not issue a CANCEL command from the PREVIEW window, the statements are submitted for execution. If a user issues a CANCEL command from the application or from the PREVIEW window, the PREVIEW window is cleared of all statements. When a user presses the RUN button, the statements are submitted.

```
INIT:
   control label;
return;

RUN:
   submit;
      data &dsname;
         set &mimic;
      run;
   endsubmit;
   if (_status_ ne 'C') then
      do;
         if (preview('EDIT') = -1) then
            rc=preview('clear');
         else
            do;
               rc=preview('FILE',FNAME);
               submit continue;
               endsubmit;
            end;
      end;
   else
      rc=preview('clear');
return;
```

PROTECT

Assigns protection to a field or FRAME entry object

See Also:
DISPLAYED
ERROR
ERROROFF
ERRORON
FIELD
MODIFIED
UNPROTECT

PROTECT *wvar-names* | _ALL_;

Where...	Is type...	And represents...
wvar-names	C	One or more fields or FRAME entry objects in the window to protect, or '**_ALL_**' to protect all fields or FRAME entry objects.

Details

To set an error flag for multiple fields, specify the field names following PROTECT, separated by blanks.

Protecting a window variable prevents the cursor from tabbing to the associated field or FRAME entry object. You can use the PROTECT statement to temporarily override the PROTECT attribute specified for a SAS/AF variable or an FSEDIT variable. The variable to be protected cannot be an element of an array. To protect an array element, use the FIELD funtion.

If you protect a window variable with the PROTECT statement in FSEDIT applications and issue the MODIFY command to edit the custom screen, the PROTECT attribute is saved for this variable in the PROTECT window.

FRAME entry objects can also use _PROTECT_. Protecting some FRAME entry objects (block, check box, icon, list box, pushbutton, radio box, scroll bar, and slider) is the same as calling the GRAY function or the _GRAY_ method.

The protection status remains in effect until the UNPROTECT statement is used.

The following statements are incorrect because they do not name window variables:

```
protect a{i};
protect a||b;
```

Example

Prevent the user from changing the value of the window variable DATASET once it has been entered:

```
if (modified(dataset) and ERROR(dataset)=0) then protect dataset;
```

PUSHLEGEND

**Saves the contents of the
LEGEND window**

See Also:
ENDLEGEND
LEGEND
POPLEGEND
PUTLEGEND

CALL PUSHLEGEND();

Details

PUSHLEGEND is useful if several entries in a CALL DISPLAY nested sequence
have their own legends and you want to restore the original legend of each calling
entry when a called entry ends.

To restore a pushed legend to the LEGEND window, use POPLEGEND.

For an example using the PUTLEGEND as well as other functions that manipulate
a legend window, see LEGEND.

PUT

**Writes text to the Message or
Log window**

SAS Statement with limitations in
SCL

PUT'*character-string*' | *variable-name* | *variable-name*=>_ALL_;;

Where...	Is type...	And represents...
character-string	C	Literal text to write to the Message or Log window.
variable-name	C	One or more variables whose name and value are written to the Message or Log window.
ALL	C	That all variables and their values should be written to the Message or Log window.

Differences in PUT Statement Execution

SCL supports only the forms of the PUT statement shown in "Syntax." You can
combine these forms, for example:

```
PUT 'character-string' variable-name=;
```

For details on the PUT statement in SAS language, see *SAS Language: Reference.*

PUTC

Returns the formatted value of a character value using the specified character format

See Also:
INPUTC
INPUTN
PUTN

formatted-val=**PUTC**(*char-val,format*);

Where...	Is type...	And represents...
formatted-val	C	The character value with the specified format applied.
char-val	C	The character value to be formatted.
format	C	A character format.

Details

The *format* can be an SCL variable or a character literal.

See the PUT function in "The DATA Step" in *SAS Language: Reference* for more information on returning a value using the specified format.

Example

Use PUTC to format the value a user enters into the field VALUE.

```
MAIN:
 value=putc(value,'$QUOTE.');
 put value=;
return;
```

Entering SAS into the field, displays "SAS" in the field and produces the output:

```
VALUE="SAS"
```

PUTLEGEND

Specifies the contents of one line in the LEGEND window

See Also:
ENDLEGEND
LEGEND
POPLEGEND
PUSHLEGEND

CALL PUTLEGEND(*line,text<,color<,attribute>>*);

Where...	Is type...	And represents...
line	N	Number for the line on which the text is to display. If this value is larger than the MAXROW returned from the WINFO function, the line number is ignored.
text	C	Text to display on one line of the LEGEND window. Once you specify text for a legend line, that text is redisplayed each time the LEGEND routine is called. To delete the text for a line, you can specify either new text or a null string ('') for that line number.
color	C	A color name or '' for the default color. SASCOLOR window elements can also be used for *color*. For more information on colors and a list of colors, see *color* in "Common Arguments" on page 222.
		The default color is the SASCOLOR window element "Informational Text."
attribute	C	A display attribute or '' for the default attribute. If you specify a SASCOLOR window element for *color*, *attribute* is ignored because the SASCOLOR window element contains a display attribute. For more information on display attributes and a list of them, see *attribute* in "Common Arguments" on page 222.
		The default attribute is the SASCOLOR window element "Informational Text."

Details

Use multiple PUTLEGEND routines to display multiple lines. The default legend window size allows four lines of text. You can change the LEGEND window size by using WREGION. To display the legend window, use LEGEND.

For an example using the PUTLEGEND as well as other functions that manipulate a legend window, see LEGEND.

PUTLIST

Displays the contents of an SCL list in the MESSAGE or LOG window.

See Also:
MAKELIST
MAKENLIST
NAMEITEM

CALL PUTLIST(*list-id*<,*label*<,*indent*>>);

Where...	Is type...	And represents...
list-id	N	The identifier of the list to be printed. This value was returned by the function that created the list.
label	C	Specifies the label for the printed output.
indent	N	Specifies the number of characters to indent list items in the printed list.

Details

After printing the optional label, PUTLIST prints a left parenthesis '(' to mark the beginning of the list, followed by the list of items separated by blanks. Each named item is preceded by its name and an equal sign (=), but nothing is printed before items that do not have names. PUTLIST ends the list with a right parenthesis ')', followed by the list's identifier number within square brackets.

If a value for *indent* is greater than or equal to 0, the list is printed in a vertical format where each list item is printed on its own line. Sublists are indented the number of spaces to the right that is specified by *indent*.

PUTLIST identifies an invalid list identifier with the text **<invalid list id>[*listid*]** if the list contains sublists that have been deleted.

Examples

The following examples are based on an SCL list whose list identifier is stored in the variable A. This list contains the numbers 17 and 328 and the character value "Any Characters."

List in Simplest Form
The statement

```
call putlist(a);
```

produces the following output:

```
(17 328 'Any characters' )[7]
```

List With Values Indented
The following statement

```
call putlist(a,'A=',2);
```

produces:

```
A=(  17
     328
     'Any characters'
   )[7]
```

List with Sublist Item Replacing Numeric Item

Replace the second item in the list A with the list identifier for sublist B, which contains the values -4.75 and 12.875.

```
        /*  Assign the second item to list B.  */
a=setiteml(a,b,2);
name=nameitem(a,1,'MIN');
name=nameitem(a,2,'B');
call putlist(a,'A=',2);
```

These statements produce the following output. Note that the list B has a list identifier of 7.

```
A=(  MIN=17
     B=(  -4.75
          12.875
       )[5]
     'Any characters'
   )[7]
```

List Added to Itself as a Sublist

If a sublist appears more than once in the list being printed, PUTLIST prints only

```
(...) [listid]
```

for the second and subsequent occurrences of the list. To view the full contents of the list, scan the output of PUTLIST for other occurrences of

```
[listid]
```

This prevents infinite loops if a list contains itself.

Create and display a recursive list:

```
r1=makelist();
r1=setnitemn(r1,1,'X');
r1=setniteml(r1,r1,'SELF');
call putlist(r1,'R1=',2);
```

These statements produce the following information in the MESSAGE or LOG window. Note that the full contents of the list with the identifier 7 is printed only once. The other occurrence is represented with (...)[7].

```
R1=(  X=1
      SELF=(...)[7]
   )[7]
```

PUTN

Returns the formatted value of a numeric value using the specified numeric format

See Also:
INPUTC
INPUTN
PUTC

formatted-val=**PUTN**(*num-val*, *format*);

Where...	Is type...	And represents...
formatted-val	C	The character value with the format applied.
num-val	N	The numeric value to be formatted.
format	C	A numeric format.

Details

The *format* can be an SCL variable or a character literal.

For more information on writing a value using a format, see the PUT function for the DATA step in *SAS Language: Reference*.

Example

Use PUTN to format the variable NETPD using the DOLLAR12.2 format and store the value in the variable SALARY.

```
INIT:
 netpd=20000;
 put netpd=;
 fmt='dollar12.2';
 salary=putn(netpd,fmt);
 put salary=;
return;
```

This program produces the output:

```
NETPD=20000
SALARY=  $20,000.00
```

PUTVARC

Writes a character value to the Data Set Data Vector(DDV) for a SAS data set

See Also:
APPEND
FETCH
FETCHOBS
GETVARC
GETVARN
PUTVARN
VARNUM
UPDATE

CALL PUTVARC(*data-set-id,var-num,cval*);

Where...	Is type...	And represents...
data-set-id	N	The identifier assigned when the data set was opened. If *data-set-id* is invalid, the program halts execution.
var-num	N	The number of the variable in the SAS data set. This is the number next to the variable when the CONTENTS procedure lists the variables in the SAS data set. You can use the VARNUM function to obtain this value.
cval	C	The character value to be written to the DDV.

Details

After PUTVARC writes a character value to a data set variable, you can use UPDATE to update the observation in the SAS data set.

If you use CALL SET, do not use the PUTVARN and PUTVARC routines for any variables that would be linked by SET. UPDATE and APPEND automatically move the data from the SCL data vector (SDV) to the Data Set Data Vector (DDV) before writing the observation to the physical file. Therefore, the value of the corresponding data set variable will be updated with the value from the SDV, not the value specified with PUTVARC.

Example

Change an employee's last name from **SMITH** to **UPDIKE** in the variable NAME in the data set referenced by the data set identifier PAYID:

```
vnum=varnum(payid,'name');
rc=locatec(payid,vnum,'SMITH','u');
if (rc>0) then
   do;
       call putvarc(payid,vnum,'UPDIKE');
       rc=update(payid);
   end;
```

PUTVARN

Writes a numeric value to the Data Set Data Vector (DDV) for a SAS data set

See Also:
APPEND
FETCH
FETCHOBS
GETVARC
GETVARN
PUTVARC
UPDATE
VARNUM

CALL PUTVARN(*data-set-id,var-num,nval*);

Where...	Is type...	And represents...
data-set-id	N	The identifier assigned when the data set was opened. If *data-set-id* is invalid, the program halts execution.
var-num	N	The number of the variable in the SAS data set. You can use the VARNUM function to obtain this value.
nval	N	The numeric value to be written to the DDV.

Details

To update the observation in the SAS data set, use UPDATE.

If you use SET, do not use the PUTVARN and PUTVARC routines for any variables that would be linked by SET. The UPDATE and APPEND functions automatically move the data from the SCL Data Vector (SDV) to the Data Set Data Vector (DDV) before writing the observation to the physical file. Therefore, the value of the corresponding data set variable will be updated with the value from the SDV, not the value specified with PUTVARN.

Example

Change an item's price from 1.99 to 2.99 in the data set referenced by the data set identifier PAYID:

```
vnum=varnum(payid,'price');
rc=locaten(payid,vnum,1.99,'u');
if (rc>0) then
   do;
      call putvarn(payid,vnum,2.99);
      rc=update(payid);
   end;
```

REFRESH

Redisplays a window using current field or widget values

REFRESH;

Details

Refreshing a window can result in updating window variable values. FRAME entries can also use the _REFRESH_ method.

Example

Suppose the field NAME is displayed on the left side of PROGRAM entry and that NEW.PROGRAM is sized so that it displays on the right side of the window. When the following code runs, NAME changes to red and then NEW.PROGRAM displays. If the REFRESH statement were not present, NAME would not appear red until control returned to the application.

```
rc=field('color red','name');
refresh;
call display('new.program');
```

RENAME

Renames a SAS data set, view, catalog, or catalog entry

See Also:
DELETE

*sysrc=***RENAME**(*old-name,new-name<,type<,description>>*);

Where...	Is type...	And represents...

sysrc	N	Whether the operation was successful:
		    0 if successful
		
		    ≠ 0 if not successful

old-name	C	The current name of member. This can be a one-, two-, or four-level name.
new-name	C	The new one-level name of member.

type	C	The type of member to rename:
		    'ACCESS' access descriptor created using SAS/ACCESS software.
		
		    'CATALOG' SAS catalog or catalog entry.
		
		    'DATA' SAS data file. (Default)
		
		    'VIEW' SAS data view.

description	C	The description of the catalog entry. Only valid when the value of *type* is CATALOG.

Details

To rename an entry in a catalog, specify the four-level name for *old-name* and a one-level name for *new-name*. You must specify CATALOG for *type* when renaming an entry in a catalog.

Example

Rename a SAS data set from DATA1 to DATA2. Also rename a catalog entry from A.PROGRAM to B.PROGRAM:

```
rc1=rename('sasuser.data1','data2');
rc2=rename('sasuser.profile.a.program','b','catalog');
```

REPLACE

Substitutes a replacement string for a reference to an SCL variable in the SUBMIT block

REPLACE *variable, replacement-string;*

Where...	Is type...	And represents...
variable	C	The variable whose value the replacement value is substituted for.
replacement-string	C	The value to substitute for the variable's value.

Details

The REPLACE statement enables you to substitute additional text, conditional on the variable being nonblank in an SCL program. REPLACE substitutes a replacement string for a reference to an SCL variable in the SUBMIT block only if the variable is not blank. It also functions as an implicit IF statement determining when to substitute the string in the SUBMIT block. Using the REPLACE statement reduces the amount of code needed to generate statements to be submitted.

The REPLACE statement is evaluated when the program is compiled. Different replacement strings cannot be generated based on conditions at execution time. For example, the following statements cause errors when you compile the program:

```
if (x) then
    replace y '&y';
else
    replace y '&z';
```

If you use multiple REPLACE statements for the same variable, the last REPLACE statement is used and a warning is generated by the compiler to that effect.

A good programming practice is to collect all the REPLACE statements in one place in your SCL program.

You can also use the REPLACE option in the ATTR window of a PROGRAM entry to specify the replacement string. However, this can be overridden by REPLACE statements in the SCL program.

SCL performs substitution according to the following rules:

□ The replacement string cannot exceed 200 characters since quoted character literals cannot exceed 200 characters. However, the generated code can exceed 200 characters.

□ If the value of the SCL variable is blank (or _BLANK_), then no substitution is performed.

□ If the value of the SCL variable is not equal to blank, then SCL performs substitution into the replacement string for the variable and substitutes the resulting string into the SUBMIT block.

The replacement string can reference other SCL variables.

Note: Replacement strings are not recursive. When you refer to another variable in the replacement string, the program uses the current value of the variable, not its value based on its replacement string.

Example

```
replace dsname 'data=&dsname';
   . . .
submit continue;
   proc print &dsname;
   run;
endsubmit;
```

If DSNAME contains ' ' (or _BLANK_), the submitted statements are:

```
submit continue;
   proc print;
   run;
endsubmit;
```

However, if DSNAME contains `work.sample`, the submitted statements are:

```
submit continue;
   proc print data=work.sample;
   run;
endsubmit;
```

RETURN

Stops executing statements in the program section that is currently executing

SAS Statement with limitations in SCL

See also:
RUN
STOP

RETURN;

Details

The RETURN statement stops executing statements in the current section of the SCL program. Control passes to the next section in the program execution cycle.

For details on the RETURN statement in SAS language, see *SAS Language: Reference, Version 6, First Edition.*

REVLIST

Reverses the order of the items in an SCL list

See Also:
HASATTR
MAKELIST
MAKENLIST
ROTLIST
SETLATTR
SORTLIST

list-id=**REVLIST**(*list-id*);

Where...	Is type...	And represents...
list-id	N	The identifier of the list to reverse. The function returns the list identifier that is passed in. An invalid *list-id* produces an error condition.

Details

Any names and attributes that are assigned to list items remain with the items when they are reversed.

REVLIST does not make a copy of the list before reversing the order of the list items. The list is modified in place. To keep a copy of the original list, use COPYLIST before REVLIST.

An error condition results if the list has the NOUPDATE attribute.

To check attributes, use HASATTR. To change attributes, use SETLATTR.

Example

Make a nonrecursive copy of the list identified by MYLISTID, reverse the items in the copied list, and assign the new list identifier to the variable REVLISTID:

```
revlistid = revlist(copylist(mylistid));
```

REWIND

Positions the data set pointer to the beginning of a SAS data set

See Also:
FETCH
FETCHOBS
FREWIND
NOTE
POINT

sysrc=**REWIND**(*data-set-id*);

Where...	Is type...	And represents...

sysrc	N	Whether the operation was successful:
		  0 if successful
		
		  ≠ 0 if not successful.

data-set-id	N	The identifier assigned when the data set was opened. If *data-set-id* is invalid, the program halts execution. The data set cannot be opened in IS, US, or N mode.

Details

After a call to REWIND, a call to FETCH reads the first observation in the data set.
    If there is an active WHERE clause, REWIND moves the data set pointer to the first observation that satisfies the WHERE condition.

Example

Call FETCHOBS to fetch the tenth observation in the data set MYDATA. Then call REWIND to return to the first observation and fetch the first observation:

```
dsid=open('mydata','i');
rc=fetchobs(dsid,10);
rc=rewind(dsid);
rc=fetch(dsid);
```

RGBDM

Returns the name supported by Display Manager (DM) for a color.

Release 6.11 Feature

DM-color-name=**RGBDM**(*color-name*<,*RGB-color*>});

Where...	Is type...	And represents...
DM-color-name	C	The name of the DM-supported color that is closest to *color-name*.
color-name	C	A color name to look up. Any SAS/GRAPH color name is allowed as well as SASCOLOR window elements. Arbitrary RGB colors can be specified using the CXrrggbb convention. For more information on colors, see *color* in "Common Arguments" on page 222.
RGB-color	C	If specified, this returns *color-name* in the CXrrggbb format.

Description

The RGBDM function provides a way to determine both the closest DM-supported color for a specified color and the RGB values for a color name. If *color-name* is a variable and the color specified is a valid color abreviation, the variable is updated with the complete color name. For instance, the color "R" would be translated to "RED" and the *RGB-color* would be "CXFF0000" (depending on the host operating system). The value for *RGB-color* may be different depending on the host operating system.

For more information on the CXrrggbb format, see *SAS/GRAPH Software: Reference*.

Example

Display the color components of several different colors.

```
length rgbclr $ 8;
INIT:
    /* this will display txtclr=RED rgbclr=CXFF0000 */
  txtclr = RGBDM("RED", rgbclr);
  put txtclr= rgbclr=;

    /* this will display txtclr=RED */
  txtclr = RGBDM("CXF00000");
  put txtclr=;

    /* this will display txtclr=RED clr=RED */
  clr='R';
  txtclr = RGBDM(clr);
  put txtclr= clr= ;

    /* this will display the foreground color in RGB values */
  txtclr = RGBDM("FOREGROUND", rgbclr);
  put txtclr= rgbclr=;
return;
```

RIGHT

Returns a right-aligned character value

See Also:
CENTER
LEFT

rstring=**RIGHT**(*string*<,*length*>);

Where...	Is type...	And represents...
rstring	C	The right-aligned character string. If an *rstring* already exists, then specifying a length in the RIGHT function changes the current length of *rstring* to the specified length.
string	C	The character string to be right-justified.
length	N	The length in which the character string is to be right-justified. The default is the maximum length of *rstring*.

Details

The string is justified by padding with leading spaces. The default length is the maximum length of *rstring*. If the length has not been defined with a LENGTH statement and if the variable is not a window variable, then the default SCL variable length is 200 characters.

To left-justify a character string, use LEFT. To center a character string, use CENTER.

For **RIGHT** to work properly when *rstring* is a window variable, set the justification attribute (**JUST**) for *rstring* to **'NONE'**.

RLINK

Reports whether a link exists between the current SAS session and a remote SAS session

SAS/CONNECT software required

See Also:
RSESSION
RSTITLE

rc=**RLINK**(*remote-session-id*);

Where...	Is type...	And represents...
rc	N	Whether the operation was successful: 1 Link exists. 0 Link does not exist.
remote-session-id	C	The name of the remote session (REMOTE= value) that is being tested.

Details

See *SAS/CONNECT Software: Usage and Reference, Version 6, First Edition* for details on accessing remote hosts from the SAS System.

To get the name of the last remote host linked to during the current SAS session, use OPTGETC with the 'REMOTE' option.

Example

Check to see if the link is active:

```
REMSESS=optgetc('remote');
msg=sysmsg();
put msg REMSESS;

rc=rlink(REMSESS);
   if (rc=0) then
      msg='No link exists.';
   else
      msg='A link exists.';
put msg;
```

ROTLIST

Rotates the items in an SCL list

See Also:
HASATTR
MAKELIST
MAKENLIST
REVLIST
SETLATTR
SORTLIST

list-id=**ROTLIST**(*list-id*<,*n*>);

Where...	Is type...	And represents...
list-id	N	The identifier of the list to rotate. The function returns the list identifier that is passed in. An invalid *list-id* produces an error condition.
n	N	The number of times to rotate the list. The default is 1.

Details

The items are rotated the number of times specified by *n*. If the value for *n* is positive, the items are rotated from right to left. This means that each rotation moves the item at the front of the list to the end of the list (that is, from position 1 to position -1). If the value for *n* is negative, the items are rotated from left to right. This moves the item at the end of the list to the front of the list (that is, from position -1 to position 1).

When a list is rotated, item names and attributes are moved with the elements.

Fetching a named item from a list that has more than one item with that same name may return a different item from the list after rotating than was returned before rotating.

ROTLIST does not make a copy of the list before rotating the order of items in the list. The list is modified in place. To keep a copy of the original list, use COPYLIST before ROTLIST.

An error condition results if the list has the NOUPDATE attribute.

To check a list's attributes, use HASATTR. To change these attributes, use SETLATTR.

Examples

Manipulate the list identified by LISTID, which contains the five character values A, B, C, D, and E. Display the list, rotate it right to left one time and display that list, and then rotate it left to right twice and display that list:

```
call putlist(listid,'Input list=');
listid = rotlist(listid); /* Rotate 1 time */
call putlist(listid,'Rotated  1=');
listid = rotlist(listid,-2);
call putlist(listid,'Rotated -2=');
```

The preceding statements produce the following changes. The net result is that the list is rotated backwards one time.

```
Input list=('A' 'B' 'C' 'D' 'E')[3]
Rotated  1=('B' 'C' 'D' 'E' 'A')[3]
Rotated -2=('E' 'A' 'B' 'C' 'D')[3]
```

Note: [3] is the listid assigned when this example was run. This value may be different if you run this example.

RSESSION

Returns the name, description, and SAS System version of a remote session

SAS/CONNECT software required

See Also:
RLINK
RSTITLE

cval=**RSESSION**(*n*);

Where...	Is type...	And represents...
cval	C	Up to 48 characters of information identifying a remote session: Characters 1 through 8 contain the session identifier (REMOTE= value)
		Characters 9 through 48 contain the description
n	N	The number of the remote session to identify.

Details

RSESSION returns the session identifier and corresponding description for a remote session established with SAS/CONNECT software. You must have previously defined the description using RSTITLE.

If no remote link exists, the returned value is blank. If a link exists but no description has been specified, characters 9 through 48 in the returned value are blanks.

Release 6.07 or later of the SAS System must be running on both the local and remote host systems in order to use this function.

See *SAS/CONNECT Software: Usage and Reference, Version 6, First Edition* for more information about establishing a link between local and remote hosts.

Example

Retrieve the name and description of remote session number 1:

```
value=rsession(1);
```

RSTITLE

Defines a description for an existing connection to a remote session

SAS/CONNECT software required

See Also:
RLINK
RSESSION

*sysrc=***RSTITLE**(*session-id,description*);

Where...	Is type...	And represents...

sysrc	N	Whether the operation was successful:
		   0 if successful
		   $\neq 0$ if not successful.

session-id	C	Up to eight characters identifying the remote session (REMOTE= value).
description	C	Up to 40 characters to associate with the remote session. The string can be long.

Details

You can retrieve the information saved by RSTITLE by using RSESSION to build a list of connections. You can then use the list to select a connection when submitting statements to a remote host.

Release 6.07 or later of the SAS System must be running on both the local and remote host systems in order to use this function.

See *SAS/CONNECT Software: Usage and Reference* for more information about establishing a link between local and remote hosts.

Example

Define the description "MVS Payroll Data" for the remote session with the identifier A:

```
session='A';
descrip='MVS Payroll Data';
rc=rstitle(session,descrip);
```

RUN

Stops executing statements in the program section that is currently executing

Alias for RETURN

SAS Statement with limitations in SCL

See also:
RETURN
STOP

RUN;

Details

In SCL, RUN is treated as an alias for RETURN.

For details on the RUN statement in SAS language, see *SAS Language: Reference, Version 6, First Edition.*

SASNAME

Verifies that a name is a valid SAS name

rc=**SASNAME**(*name*);

Where...	Is type...	And represents...
rc	N	Whether the operation was successful: 1 the name is a valid SAS name 0 the name is not a valid SAS name.
name	C	The name to be verified as a valid SAS name.

Details

SASNAME verifies that a specified name is a valid SAS name. SAS names can be up to eight characters long. The first character must be a letter (A, B, C, . . . , Z) or underscore (_). Other characters can be letters, numbers (0, 1, . . . 9), or underscores. Blanks cannot appear in SAS names, and special characters (for example, $, @, #), except underscores, are not allowed.

Example

Examine the window variable DSNAME to see if it contains a valid SAS name. If the name is not valid, the window variable DSNAME is defined to be in error, and a message is displayed on the message line.

```
erroroff dsname;
rc=sasname(dsname);
if (rc=0) then
   do;
      erroron dsname;
      _msg_='An invalid data set name has been specified.';
   end;
```

Note: In this example, the value for DSNAME must be a one-level SAS name. SASNAME considers a two-level name of the form *libref.data-set-name* invalid because it contains the dot (.) character.

SASTASK

Determines whether a SAS procedure is running

rc=**SASTASK**();

Where...	Is type...	And represents...
rc	N	Whether the operation was successful:
		1 a SAS procedure is active
		0 no SAS procedure is active.

Example

Check whether a SAS procedure is currently running before attempting to submit code to the SAS System. If so, display a message informing the user why the code cannot be submitted.

```
if (sastask()) then
   _msg_='Cannot submit because a procedure is currently active.';
else
   do;
      submit continue;
         data a;
            x=1;
         run;
      endsubmit;
   end;
```

SAVELIST

Stores SCL list items in a SAS catalog entry or an external file

See Also:
FILLIST
LISTLEN
MAKELIST
STRATTR

sysrc=**SAVELIST**(*type,target,list-id* <,*attr-list-id*<,*description*>>);

Where...	Is type...	And represents...

sysrc	N	Whether the operation was successful:
		  0 if successful
		  $\neq 0$ if not successful.

type	C	The type of file in which the list items are stored: **'CATALOG'** saves text in a SAS catalog entry. **'FILE'** saves text in an external file named in *source*. **'FILEREF'** saves text in an external file identified by a fileref named in *source*.

. . . .
Release 6.11

You can specify file options in *type* by enclosing one or more options from Table 20.12 within a set of parentheses and separating them with blanks. For example, to save a list to an external print file, stripping carriage control, use **'FILE(PRINT STRIPCC)'** for *type*.
. . . .

target	C	The name of the catalog entry, external file, or fileref into which the list items are stored. For catalog entries, this must be a four-level name (*libref.catalog.entry-name.entry-type*).
list-id	N	The identifier of the list containing the items to be stored in a SAS file or external file. An invalid *list-id* produces an error condition. For text catalog entries, the first character in each item in the list contains the FORTRAN carriage control: 1 means a new page starts with this line.
attr-list-id	N	The identifier of the list to fill with text attribute information when *type* is **'CATALOG'**. An error condition results if *attr-list-id* is not a valid list identifier.
description	C	The catalog entry description text. This argument is ignored if the value for *type* is **'FILE'** or **'FILEREF'**. (The description is displayed in the catalog directory.)

Table 20.12 *Options for type Values*

Option	Action
`'ADDCC'`	adds default carriage control. Used with *type* `'FILE'`, `'FILEREF'`, and `'CATALOG'` and catalog entry types `'LOG'`, `'OUTPUT'`, and `'SOURCE'`.
`'APPEND'`	appends text to an external file. Attempts to open the file in APPEND mode. Used with *type* `'FILE'` or `'FILEREF'`.
`'PRINT'`	designates an external file as a PRINT file (uses host carriage control). Used with *type* `'FILE'` or `'FILEREF'`.
`'STRIPCC'`	removes carriage control. Used with *type* `'FILE'`, `'FILEREF'`, and `'CATALOG'` and catalog entry types `'LOG'`, `'OUTPUT'`, and `'SOURCE'`.
`'TRIM'`	trims trailing blanks. Used with *type* `'FILE'`, `'FILEREF'`, and `'CATALOG'` and catalog entry types `'LOG`, `'OUTPUT'`, and `'SOURCE'`. `'TRIM'` is useful if you want to use FILLIST to fill a list with items that contain trailing blanks and then remove the blanks so they will not be displayed in a popup-menu produced by POPMENU.

Details

SAVELIST stores the items from an SCL list into a SAS catalog entry or an external file.

When *type* is `'CATALOG'` and the *entry-type* element of *target* is SLIST, the list can be re-created, including names and list and item attributes, with the FILLIST function although the list identifiers will be different. The lists you save with SAVELIST can persist across SAS sessions if you save them in a permanent catalog.

When a list is stored into any file type other than an SLIST catalog entry, each item in the list identified by *list-id* must be a character string. Each string is stored as a separate line of text. When *type* is `'CATALOG'` and the entry type of *target* is LOG, OUTPUT, or SOURCE and a value is specified for *attr-list-id*, the attribute list items must also contain text. See the description of FILLIST for a description of the attribute specifications. If the value for *attr-list-id* is omitted or is 0, then no attributes are stored with the catalog entry. Any value specified for *attr-list-id* is ignored when a list is stored in an external file or an SLIST catalog entry.

When SAVELIST writes a list, each item that has the NOWRITE attribute is not written to the file. This is useful for placing temporary run time values on a list that should not be written to the file because of its transient nature. For example, if you place data set identifiers in lists to be saved with SAVELIST and restored with FILLIST in another task or another SAS session, the data set identifiers become invalid. Thus, use SETLATTR to set the NOWRITE attribute on that list item.

(Do not confuse text attributes, like color and highlight, with list attributes as specified with SETLATTR.) To check the attributes of a list or list item, use HASATTR. To change attributes, use SETLATTR.

Example

Perform operations similar to copying a list recursively with COPYLIST(mylistid,'Y'):

```
/* Assume the catalog WORK.TEMP exists: */
rc=savelist('catalog','work.temp.mylist.slist',mylistid);
newlistid=makelist();
rc=fillist('catalog','work.temp.mylist.slist',newlistid);
rc=delete('work.temp.mylist.slist','catalog');
```

SAVESCREEN

Saves the values of data entry fields without exiting from the window

SAS/AF software only

CALL SAVESCREEN();

Details

SAVESCREEN copies the current values of all window variables into the user's profile for later restoration. The values are stored for recall across invocations of the SAS System in a catalog entry named SASUSER.PROFILE*entry*.AFPGM, where *entry* is the name of the SAS/AF entry whose values are saved. This is similar to the SAS/AF program window SAVE command.

The saved values can be reloaded with the RECALL command in the application window, or with the AUTORECALL=YES option on the AF command that invokes the application.

Example

Save the final contents of the fields in an application window:

```
TERM:
    call savescreen();
return;
```

SCREENNAME

Returns the name of the current window

name=SCREENNAME();

Where...	Is type...	And represents...
name	C	The four-level name of the current window.

Details

The SCREENNAME function returns the name of the current window. For example, assume there are two PROGRAM entries named SURVEY and NEWMAP in a catalog named MYLIB.TESTS. When SURVEY is executing, SCREENNAME returns MYLIB.TESTS.SURVEY.PROGRAM. When NEWMAP is executing, SCREENNAME returns MYLIB.TESTS.NEWMAP.PROGRAM.

In the FSEDIT and FSVIEW procedures, SCREENNAME returns the name of the SCREEN or FORMULA entry currently in use by the application.

Example

Display the window name on the message line

```
_msg_=screenname();
```

SEARCH

Creates or manipulates the current catalog search path

See Also:
CEXIST
DISPLAY
SEARCHNAME

rc=**SEARCH**(*cat-name*);

Where...	Is type...	And represents...
rc	N	Whether the operation was successful: 　0　if successful − 1　if not successful.
cat-name	C	The catalog to push to the front of the current search list. Instead of a specific catalog name, you can specify:

`'-DISABLE'`		to disable the current search list.
`'-ENABLE'`		to enable the current search list. If there is no disabled list, the current search list remains empty.
`'-POP'`		to remove the first name in the current search list.
`'-POPALL'`		to clear the current search list.

Note: You must include the hyphen (-) as the first character in each of these argument values. Otherwise, the value will be treated as a catalog name in the WORK library.

Details

You do not need to know the exact location of a catalog member, only that it is in one of the catalogs in the current search path.

When a function that uses the current search path is called, the catalogs in the search path are searched from first to last until the specified entry is found or until the end of the search path is reached.

If there is no current search path or if the current search path has been disabled or overridden, the search is limited to the current catalog.

Example

Set up a search list with MYLIB1.CAT1, MYLIB1.CAT2 and MYLIB1.CAT3. Because each time SEARCH is called the new value of the argument is pushed to the front of the list, MYLIB1.CAT3 is searched first. If MYPROG.PROGRAM only exists in MYLIB1.CAT1, it still executes correctly because MYLIB1.CAT1 also is in the search path.

```
rc=search('mylib1.cat1');
rc=search('mylib1.cat2');
rc=search('mylib1.cat3');
call display('myprog.program');
```

SEARCHC

Searches for a character value in an SCL list and returns its position number

See Also:
MAKELIST
MAKENLIST
NAMEDITEM
SEARCHL
SEARCHN

index=**SEARCHC**(*list-id,cval<,occurrence<,start-index <,ignore-case<,prefix>>>>*);

Where...	Is type...	And represents...
index	N	The index in the SCL list of the item with the specified character value, or 0 if the value was not found.
list-id	N	The identifier of the list to search for *cval*. An invalid *list-id* produces an error condition.
cval	C	The character value to search for.
occurrence	N	The occurrence of the value to search for. The default is 1 for the first occurrence of the item.
start-index	N	Where in the list to begin searching for the item. By default, *start-index* is 1 (the first item). If *start-index* is positive, the search begins at position *start-index* items from the beginning of the list. If *start-index* is negative, the search begins at the item specified by ABS(*start-index*) items from the end of the list. An error condition results if the absolute value of *start-index* is zero or greater than the number of items in the list.
ignore-case	C	How to compare string values: '**Y**' ignores the case of the character strings. '**N**' uses the case when comparing character strings. (Default)
prefix	C	Whether to treat the value as a prefix: '**Y**' does a prefix comparison and searches for any items that have *cval* as a prefix. SEARCHC compares only the first *m* characters where *m* is the length of *cval*. '**N**' does not do a prefix search but compares all characters to *cval*. (Default)

Details

SEARCHC does not search any sublists of the list identified by *list-id* for the character value. The value for *cval* is compared only to the character values in the list identified by *list-id*.

If *occurrence* and *start-index* are both positive or both negative, the search proceeds forward from the *start-index* item. For forward searches, the search continues only to the end of the list and does not wrap back to the front of the list. If *occurrence* or *start-index* is negative, the search is backwards. For backward searches, the search continues only to the beginning of the list and does not wrap back to the end of the list.

To search for items by their name rather than by their value, use NAMEDITEM instead.

Examples

Search for the third occurrence of the string **'ABC'** in the list identified by MYLISTID:

```
third=searchc(mylistid,'ABC',3);
```

Find the position of the next-to-last occurrence of a string that begins with **'SAS'**, ignoring case:

```
last2=searchc(mylistid,'sas',2,-1,'Y','Y');
```

SEARCHL

Searches for a list identifier in an SCL list and returns its position number

See Also:
MAKELIST
MAKENLIST
NAMEDITEM
SEARCHC
SEARCHN

index=**SEARCHL**(*list-id,sublist-id<,occurrence<,start-index>>*);

Where...	Is type...	And represents...
index	N	The index in the SCL list of the sublist identifier, or 0 if the value was not found.
list-id	N	The identifier of the list to search for *sublist-id*. An invalid *list-id* produces an error condition.
sublist-id	N	The identifier of the sublist to search for.
occurrence	N	The occurrence of the list identifier to search for. The default is 1 for the first occurrence of the item.
start-index	N	Where in the list to begin searching for the item. By default, *start-index* is 1 (the first item). If *start-index* is positive, the search begins at position *start-index* items from the beginning of the list. If *start-index* is negative, the search begins at the item specified by ABS(*start-index*) items from the end of the list. An error condition results if the absolute value of *start-index* is zero or greater than the number of items in the list.

Details

SEARCHL does not search any sublists of the list identified by *list-id* for the sublist identifier. The value for *sublist-id* is compared only with the list values in the list identified by *list-id*.

If *occurrence* and *start-index* are both positive or both negative, the search proceeds forward from the *start-index* item. For forward searches, the search continues only to the end of the list and does not wrap back to the front of the list. If *occurrence* or *start-index* is negative, the search is backwards. For backward searches, the search continues only to the beginning of the list and does not wrap back to the end of the list.

To search for items by their name rather than by their value, use NAMEDITEM instead.

Example

Search the list identified by MYLISTID for the third occurrence of the identifier for the sublist item identified by the value of NAMELISTID:

```
third=searchl(mylistid,namelistid,3);
```

SEARCHN

Searches for a numeric value in an SCL list and returns its position number

See Also:
MAKELIST
MAKENLIST
NAMEDITEM
SEARCHC
SEARCHL

index=**SEARCHN**(*list-id*,*nval*<,*occurrence*<,*start-index*>>);

Where...	Is type...	And represents...
index	N	The index in the SCL list of the item with the specified numeric value, or 0 if the value was not found.
list-id	N	The identifier of the list to search for *nval*. An invalid *list-id* produces an error condition.
nval	N	The numeric value to search for.
occurrence	N	The occurrence of the value to search for. The default is 1 for the first occurrence of the item.
start-index	N	Where in the list to begin searching for the item. By default, *start-index* is 1 (the first item). If *start-index* is positive, the search begins at position *start-index* items from the beginning of the list. If *start-index* is negative, the search begins at the item specified by ABS(*start-index*) items from the end of the list. An error condition results if the absolute value of *start-index* is zero or greater than the number of items in the list.

Details

SEARCHN does not search any sublists of the list identified by *list-id* for the numeric value. The value for *nval* is compared only to the numeric values in the list identified by *list-id*.

If *occurrence* and *start-index* are both positive or both negative, the search proceeds forward from the *start-index* item. For forward searches, the search continues only to the end of the list and does not wrap back to the front of the list. If *occurrence* or *start-index* is negative, the search is backwards. For backward searches, the search continues only to the beginning of the list and does not wrap back to the end of the list.

To search for items by their name rather than by their value, use NAMEDITEM instead.

Example

Search for the third occurrence of the number 46 in the list identified by MYLISTID:

```
third=searchn(mylistid,46,3);
```

SEARCHPATH

Reports the complete pathname of a SAS catalog entry

Release 6.11 Feature

See Also:
SEARCH

path-name=**SEARCHPATH**(*entry-name<.entry-type>*);

Where...	Is type...	And represents...
path-name	C	The path (four-level name) for the specified entry if it was found in the current catalog or in the search path. If the entry was not found, the value is blank.
entry-name	C	The SAS catalog entry to search for.
entry-type	C	The type of catalog entry to search for. If you do not specify an entry type, the default is PROGRAM.

Details

SEARCHPATH returns the full four-level SAS library member name for a catalog entry if the entry is found in one of the catalogs in the current search path. If an entry with the specified name appears in more than one catalog in the search path, only the path to the first entry found is returned. If no search path is defined, the search is limited to the current catalog (the catalog in which the executing entry is stored).

Use SEARCH to define the search path for your application.

Example

Load a stored list from a catalog entry if the entry is found in the current search path.

```
    /* search path established for three catalogs */
rc=search('mylib.cat1');
rc=search('mylib.cat2');
rc=search('mylib.cat3');

    /* Search all three catalogs for this entry.  */
entryname=searchpath('amortize.program');
put entryname=;
```

This program produces the output:

```
'mylib.cat2.amortize.program'
```

SELECTED

Returns the number of the row that corresponds to a user's choice in a selection list

SAS/AF software only

See Also:
ISSEL
NSELECT
SELECT
UNSELECT

row=**SELECTED**(*nval*);

Where...	Is type...	And represents...
row	N	The number of the selected row or -1 if the value specified for *nval* is greater than the total number of selections.
nval	N	The number of the selection.

Details

You can use SELECTED only for selection lists built with extended tables in PROGRAM entries. FRAME entry objects must use the _SELECTED_ method. Because you can define extended tables only in SAS/AF software, you cannot use SELECTED in FSEDIT or FSVIEW programs.

In order for an extended table to be considered a selection list, you must specify a number of selections in the SETROW routine.

Example

Suppose the application displays a selection list with ten rows and the user selects row 3 and then selects row 5. If SELECTED is called with the value 2 specified for *nval* (as in the following statement), then the value returned in the variable ROW is 5 because row 5 was the second selection.

```
row=selected(2);
```

SELECT

Selects a specified row of a selection list

SAS/AF software only

See Also:
ISSEL
NSELECT
SELECTED
UNSELECT

rc=**SELECT**(*row*);

Where...	Is type...	And represents...
rc	N	Whether the operation was successful: 0 if successful ≠ 0 if not successful.
row	N	The number of the row to select.

Details

The selection highlights the specified row. SELECT is useful to force the selection of a row. For example, you can use this function to set initial values or defaults. Ordinarily, a user selects a row by pressing ENTER or clicking with the mouse on the row.

You can use SELECT only for selection lists built with extended tables in PROGRAM entries. FRAME entry objects must use the _SELECT_ROW_ method. Because you can define extended tables only in SAS/AF software, you cannot use SELECT in FSEDIT or FSVIEW programs.

In order for an extended table to be considered a selection list, you must specify a number of selections in the SETROW routine.

Example

Select row 5 of the selection list:

```
INIT:
    call setrow(10,2);
    rc=select(5);
return;
```

SELECT

Executes one of several statements or groups of statements

SAS Statement with limitations in SCL

SELECT <*(select-expression)*>;
  WHEN-*1* <*(when-expression)*> *statement(s)*;
  <*. . .* **WHEN**-*n* <*(when-expression)*> *statement(s)*;>
  <**OTHERWISE** <*statement(s)*>;>
END;

Where...	Is type...	And represents...
select-expression	C	An expression that evaluates a single value. This argument is optional. If used, *select-expression* must be in parantheses.
when-expression	C	A constant or an expression that evaluates a single value.
statement(s)	C	One or more executable SAS statements, including DO, SELECT, and null statements. A null statement used in a WHEN statement causes SAS to recognize a condition as true without taking further action. Null statements in OTHERWISE statements prevent SAS from issuing an error message when all WHEN conditions are false.

Differences in SELECT Statement Execution

For SELECT groups in SCL, WHEN statements of the form WHEN(*a1, a2, a3*) are not supported. However, the following forms are supported:

□ WHEN(*constant*)

□ WHEN(*expression*).

OTHERWISE is an optional statement. If OTHERWISE is omitted, and no WHEN conditions are met, the program halts.

Each WHEN statement implies a DO group of all statements until the next WHEN or OTHERWISE statement. Therefore the following program is valid:

```
select(x);
   when(1)  call display('a');
            optionally, more SCL statements
   when(2)  call display('b');
            optionally, more SCL statements
   otherwise call display('bad');
            optionally, more SCL statements
end;
```

For details on the SELECT statement in SAS language, see *SAS Language: Reference.*

Example

Show how to use expressions with the SELECT statement.

```
select;
    when(x=1)        put 'one';
    when(2<x<5)      put 'between two and five';
    when(x>5 or x<0) put 'other';
end;
```

SELF

Contains the identifier of the object for the currently executing method, or the identifier of the FRAME entry if the FRAME entry is not running as a method

Numeric System Instance Variable

See Also:
METHOD
SEND
SUPER
VALUE

Details

SELF is a System Instance Variable. It is provided automatically by the FRAME entry in SAS/AF. For SCL entries, the SCL compiler does not automatically create a space for _SELF_ in the SCL data vector. Because of this, you get a warning when you compile your SCL entry if you have a reference to _SELF_. See _FRAME_ for more details on how to prevent the warning.

SELF only has a valid value when the FRAME entry's SCL code is running or when a method is running.

Example

Suppose a FRAME entry contains an icon. The icon's _SELECT_ method is defined as follows:

```
length _method_ $40;
SELECT:
   method;
      call send( _self_, '_set_icon_', 2 );
      call super( _self_, _method_ );
   endmethod;
```

When a user selects the icon, the _SELECT_ method executes and _SELF_ contains the identifier of the icon.

In a FRAME entry, _SELF_ contains the identifier of the FRAME entry if the FRAME entry is not running as a method. For example, you can send a method to the FRAME entry from the INIT section using _SELF_.

```
INIT:
   call send( _self_, '_set_msg_', 'in init section' );
return;
```

SEND

Sends a method to an object that is identified by its number

See Also:
APPLY
ENTRY
INSTANCE
LOADCLASS
LOADRES
METHOD
NOTIFY
SUPAPPLY
SUPER

CALL SEND(*object-id,method-name<,parameters>*);

Where...	Is type...	And represents...
object-id	N	The identifier associated with the object for which the method is invoked.
method-name	C	The name of the method to send. The method must be defined for the object's class or one of the classes from which the object inherits methods. Case and trailing blanks are ignored in method names.
parameters	N, C	One or more numeric or character arguments that are required by the method. Separate multiple arguments with commas.

Details

The SEND routine passes one or more arguments to a method in the form of parameters to the routine. The method may modify any of these parameters and pass values back to the calling program via the parameters, or the method may modify the object's instance variables. You can use the _GET_WIDGET_ method to return the *object-id* for a widget. For information on classes, objects, widgets, and methods, see *SAS/AF Software: FRAME Entry Usage and Reference.*

The classes provided with SAS/AF software include a set of predefined methods. Subclasses you define from these classes inherit those methods. You can also define your own methods. Methods are defined with the METHOD statement in an SCL entry, or they may be entire SAS/AF entries (SCL, PROGRAM, FRAME, HELP, and MENU entries are allowed). A METHOD statement uses the syntax of an ENTRY statement to declare the types and names of the parameters the method expects.

The parameters passed to CALL SEND must match the parameter definitions of the METHOD or ENTRY statement of the method. You may specify optional parameters using the OPTIONAL= option for the METHOD or ENTRY statement of the method. You may specify variable lengths and types for parameters using the ARGLIST= and REST= options in the METHOD or ENTRY statement of the called method.

The same method may be defined for one or more classes; each class has its own definition of the method. Therefore, when a method is invoked, the appropriate method definition is determined based on the object's class. If the object's class does not define the specified method, SAS/AF searches the hierarchy of parent classes until it finds the method definition.

When a method executes, the SCL variable _SELF_ is automatically initialized to the object identifier *object-id*, allowing the method to invoke other methods on the same object. Also, any of the object's automatic instance variables are initialized if the SCL program uses a variable of the same name and type as the automatic instance variable. If a character variable named _METHOD_ is declared, it will be initialized with the method name.

If an SCL method executes a CALL SEND routine or otherwise invokes a method, the values of all automatic SCL variables in the calling method are copied into the object. After the called method executes, the automatic SCL variables are reinitialized with the values of the caller's instance variables. Other routines that execute methods are APPLY, NOTIFY, SUPAPPLY, and SUPER.

Note: If an object is a widget in an extended table, you may invoke methods only during the GETROW and PUTROW sequences or for _INIT_ and _TERM_ methods. Also, in a FRAME SCL entry, to send methods to widgets in an extended table, you may use CALL NOTIFY rather than CALL SEND.

Example 1

Send a _TERM_ method to an icon widget whose name is ICON1 and whose identifier is stored in the variable ICON1ID:

```
call notify('.','_get_widget_','icon1',icon1id);
call send(icon1id,'_TERM_');
```

Example 2

The following example sets the message displayed in a FRAME entry window. The system instance variable _FRAME_ contains the object identifier for the FRAME entry object.

```
call send (_FRAME_,'_set_msg_',
          'ERROR: The data set '||dsname||'does not exist.');
```

SET

Links SAS data set variables to SCL variables of the same name and data type

See Also:
APPEND
FETCH
FETCHOBS
GETVARC
GETVARN
LOCATEC
LOCATEN
PUTVARC
PUTVARN
UPDATE

CALL SET(*data-set-id*);

Where...	Is type...	And represents...
data-set-id	N	The identifier assigned when the data set was opened. If *data-set-id* is invalid, the program halts execution.

Details

Using SET can significantly reduce the coding required for accessing variable values for modification or verification. After a CALL SET, whenever a read is performed from the SAS data set, the values of the corresponding SCL variables are set to the values of the matching SAS data set variables. If the variable lengths do not match, the values are truncated or padded according to need. When UPDATE or APPEND is called, the values written to the SAS data set are the values of the SCL variables. If you do not use SET, then you must use GETVARC, GETVARN, PUTVARC, and PUTVARN to explicitly move values between data set variables and SCL variables.

As a general rule, call SET immediately following OPEN if you want to link the data set and SCL variables.

If you use SET, do not use PUTVARN and PUTVARC for any variables that would be linked by SET. UPDATE and APPEND automatically move the data from the SCL data vector to the data set data vector before writing the observation to the physical file.

Example

Automatically set the values of the SCL variables NAME and SALARY when an observation is fetched for a window with fields NAME and SALARY. The SAS data set PERSONEL has three variables: NAME, SALARY and DEPT.

```
dsid=open('personel','i');
call set(dsid);
rc=fetchobs(dsid,10);
```

SETCR

Controls the cursor's response to the carriage return key

See Also:
CONTROL

CALL SETCR(*advance,return<,modify>*);

Where...	Is type...	And represents...
advance	C	How the cursor moves when a user presses the carriage return key
		'STAY' The cursor does not move.
		'HTAB' The cursor moves to the next field in the same row. This option makes the carriage return key work like a horizontal tab key. When the last field in the current row is reached, the cursor moves to the first field in the next row.
		'NEWL' The cursor moves to the first field in the next line. This option makes the carriage return key work like a new-line key. When the last line is reached, the cursor moves to the first field in the first line.
		'VTAB' The cursor moves to the first field in the next line in the current column. This option makes the carriage return key work like a vertical tab key. When the last field in the current column is reached, the cursor moves to the top of the next column.
		'HOME' The cursor moves to the command line or to the first field in the window if the window has no command line.
return	C	Whether a carriage return passes control back to the application:
		'RETURN' passes control to the application, whether or not a field is modified. That is, the MAIN section of an SCL program is executed. If *modify* is omitted, the default system behavior for *return* is used.
		'NORETURN' does not pass control to the application unless a field is modified.
modify	C	Whether the field should be marked as modified:
		'MODIFY' A carriage return on a field is considered a modification of the field if the field is not protected.

Where...	Is type...	And represents...
	`'NOMODIFY'`	A carriage return on a field is not considered a modification of the field.

Details

SETCR works like a more powerful version of CONTROL ENTER for defining the behavior of the carriage return key. This routine overrides the CONTROL ENTER/NOENTER statement.

FRAME entries ignore SETCR.

Example

Move the cursor vertically to the first field in the next line in the current column when the user presses the carriage return key. Control does not pass to the application and the field is not modified by a carriage return.

```
call setcr('vtab','noreturn','nomodify');
```

SETFKEY

Assigns a command to a function key

See Also:
FKEYNAME
GETFKEY
NUMFKEYS

CALL SETFKEY(*key-name,command*);

Where...	Is type...	And represents...
key-name	C	The function key name as listed in the KEYS window. Function key names vary according to device used.
command	C	The command to assign to the key.

Details

You can use SETFKEY only in entries that have a DISPLAY window containing fields or text. You cannot use it to assign function key settings in windows that use BLOCK to display block menus.

Example

Use FKEYNAME to return the name of a particular function key and GETFKEY to return the command stored in the function key. If the command is not CANCEL, SETFKEY sets the function key definition to CANCEL.

```
INIT:
    keyname=fkeyname(1);
    command=getfkey(keyname);
    if (command ne 'CANCEL') then
        call setfkey(keyname,'CANCEL');
    end;
return;
```

SETFLD

Assigns a value to up to ten blank variables

See Also:
CLRFLD

CALL SETFLD(*value,variable-1<, . . . ,variable-10>*);

Where...	Is type...	And represents...
value	C	The character value to assign.
variable-1,. . ., variable-10	C	Up to ten character variables whose value you want changed to *value* from blank.

Details

If the variable is blank, *value* is assigned to the variable. No values are changed for variables that are not blank.

This function is useful in setting the default values for a series of fields.

Example

Set each of the variables SYM1 through SYM5 to the value **-REQUIRED-** for each variable that is blank:

```
call setfld('-REQUIRED-',sym1,sym2,sym3,sym4,sym5);
```

The statement above is the equivalent to the following statements:

```
if (sym1=' ') then sym1='-REQUIRED-';
if (sym2=' ') then sym2='-REQUIRED-';
if (sym3=' ') then sym3='-REQUIRED-';
if (sym4=' ') then sym4='-REQUIRED-';
if (sym5=' ') then sym5='-REQUIRED-';
```

SETFOOT

Sets the text of a footnote definition

See Also:
GETFOOT
GETTITLE
SETTITLE

CALL SETFOOT(*foot-num,foot-text*);

Where...	Is type...	And represents...
foot-num	N	The number (1 to 10) of the footnote definition to create or modify.
foot-text	C	Text for the footnote definition.

Details

SETFOOT works just like the FOOTNOTE statement and clears all footnote definitions numbered higher than the one created. You cannot use SETFOOT to set graphic options such as color, tint, and position.

You can view footnote definitions in the FOOTNOTES window by using the FOOTNOTE command. Changing any text in the FOOTNOTES window, however, resets all graphically defined footnote options such as color, font, and position.

For more information on footnotes, see *SAS Language: Reference*. For more information on graphical footnotes, see *SAS/GRAPH Software: Reference*.

Example

Create a footnote numbered 5. The statement deletes all footnotes with numbers greater than 5.

```
call setfoot(5,'This is the Fifth Footnote');
```

SETITEMC

Stores a character value at an indexed position in an SCL list

See Also:
DELITEM
GETITEMC
GETITEML
GETITEMN
HASATTR
INSERTC
INSERTL
INSERTN
ITEMTYPE
LISTLEN
MAKELIST
MAKENLIST
SETITEML
SETITEMN
SETLATTR
SETNITEMC
SETNITEML
SETNITEMN

rc=**SETITEMC**(*list-id,cval<,index<,autogrow>>*);

Where...	Is type...	And represents...
rc	N	The identifier of the modified list, or an error number. The value passed as *list-id* is returned unless there is an error. The value 0 means out of memory.
list-id	N	The identifier of the list into which *cval* is stored. An invalid *list-id* produces an error condition.
cval	C	The character value to store in the list.
index	N	The position of the item in the list. The position can be specified as a positive or negative number. By default, *index* is 1 (the first item). If *index* is a positive number, the item is at position *index* from the beginning of the list. If *index* is a negative number, the item is at position ABS(*index*) from the end of the list. An error condition results if the absolute value for *index* is zero or it is greater than the number of items in the list
autogrow	C	Whether the list can expand to accommodate a new item:

'N' the list's size cannot change. (Default)

'Y' the list's size can increase to accommodate a new item that is being added to the list. The list expands only if *index* is greater than the current number of items in the list and the list does not have the FIXEDLENGTH attribute.

Details

Using SETITEMC is analogous to assigning a character value to an indexed item in an array. SETITEMC assigns a specified character value to an item in the list identified by *list-id*.

index specifies the list position of the item whose value is assigned. If *autogrow* is **'Y'**, *index* can be greater than the length of the list. SETITEMC then expands the list to a total of *index* items, sets all other new items to missing values, and places the new character value *cval* into the list. SETITEMC can add items only to the end of the list. Use INSERTC to insert character values elsewhere in the list.

SETITEMC replaces an existing item in a list and even changes its type unless the item or the list has the FIXEDTYPE attribute.

SETITEMC does not make a copy of the list before assigning the new character item. The list is modified in place.

An error condition results if:

□ the absolute value of *index* is zero or it is greater than the number of items in the list and *autogrow* is **'N'**.

□ the absolute value of *index* is greater than the length of the list and the list has the FIXEDLENGTH attribute (even if *autogrow* is **'Y'**).

□ the list or item has the NOUPDATE attribute.

□ the list has the NUMONLY attribute.

□ the list or item has the FIXEDTYPE attribute and the function attempts to set the item to a different type. For example, if item 4 is numeric and has the FIXEDTYPE attribute, the following statement fails:

```
list=setitemc(list,'abc',4);
```

To check the attributes of a list or list item, use HASATTR. To change attributes, use SETLATTR.

SETITEML

Stores a list identifier at an indexed position in an SCL list

See Also:
DELITEM
GETITEMC
GETITEML
GETITEMN
GETLATTR
HASATTR
INSERTC
INSERTL
INSERTN
ITEMTYPE
LISTLEN
MAKELIST
MAKENLIST
SETITEMC
SETITEMN
SETLATTR
SETNITEMC
SETNITEML
SETNITEMN

rc=**SETITEML**(*list-id,sublist-id<,index<,autogrow>>*);

Where...	Is type...	And represents...
rc	N	The identifier of the modified list, or an error number. The value passed as *list-id* is returned unless there is an error. The value 0 means out of memory.
list-id	N	The identifier of the list into which *sublist-id* is stored. An invalid *list-id* produces an error condition.
sublist-id	N	The identifier of the list identifier to store in the list. An invalid *sublist-id* produces an error condition.
index	N	The position of the item in the list. The position can be specified as a positive or negative number. By default, *index* is 1 (the first item). If *index* is a positive number, the item is at position *index* from the beginning of the list. If *index* is a negative number, the item is at position ABS(*index*) from the end of the list. An error condition results if the absolute value for *index* is zero or it is greater than the number of items in the list
autogrow	C	Whether the list can expand to accommodate a new item: **'N'** the list's size cannot change. (Default)
		'Y' the list's size can increase to accommodate a new item that is being added to the list. The list expands only if *index* is greater than the current number of items in the list and the list does not have the FIXEDLENGTH attribute.

Details

Using SETITEML is analogous to assigning a list identifier value to an indexed item in an array. SETITEML assigns a sublist to an item in the list identified by *list-id*.

index specifies the list position to which the sublist item is assigned. If *autogrow* is **'Y'**, *index* can be greater than the length of the list. SETITEML then expands the list to a total of *index* items, sets all other new items to missing values, and places the new list identifier into the list. SETITEML can add sublists only to the end of the list. Use INSERTL to insert list identifiers elsewhere in the list.

SETITEML replaces an existing item in a list and even changes its type unless the item or the list has the FIXEDTYPE attribute.

SETITEML does not make a copy of the list before assigning the new sublist item. The list is modified in place.

An error condition results if:

□ the absolute value for *index* is zero or it is greater than the number of items in the list when *autogrow* is `'N'`.

□ the absolute value of *index* is greater than the length of the list and the list has the FIXEDLENGTH attribute (even if *autogrow* is `'Y'`).

□ the list or item has the NOUPDATE attribute.

□ the list has the CHARONLY or NUMONLY attribute.

□ the list or item has the FIXEDTYPE attribute and the function attempts to set the item to a different type. For example, if item 4 is numeric and has the FIXEDTYPE attribute, the following statement fails:

```
list=setiteml(listid,mylist-id,4);
```

□ *sublist-id* identifies a local list and *list-id* identifies a global list (you cannot place local lists into global lists).

SETITEMN

Stores a numeric value at an indexed position in an SCL list

See Also:
DELITEM
GETITEMC
GETITEML
GETITEMN
GETLATTR
HASATTR
INSERTC
INSERTL
INSERTN
ITEMTYPE
LISTLEN
MAKELIST
MAKENLIST
SETITEMC
SETITEML
SETLATTR
SETNITEMC
SETNITEML
SETNITEMN

rc=**SETITEMN**(*list-id,nval<,index<,autogrow>>*);

Where...	Is type...	And represents...
rc	N	The identifier of the modified list, or an error number. The value passed as *list-id* is returned unless there is an error. The value 0 means out of memory.
list-id	N	The identifier of the list into which *nval* is stored. An invalid *list-id* produces an error condition.
nval	N	The numeric value to store in the list.
index	N	The position of the item in the list. The position can be specified as a positive or negative number. By default, *index* is 1 (the first item). If *index* is a positive number, the item is at position *index* from the beginning of the list. If *index* is a negative number, the item is at position ABS(*index*) from the end of the list. An error condition results if the absolute value for *index* is zero or it is greater than the number of items in the list
autogrow	C	Whether the list can expand to accommodate a new item: `'N'` the the list's size cannot change. (Default) `'Y'` the list's size can increase to accommodate a new item that is being added to the list. The list expands only if *index* is greater than the current number of items in the list and the list does not have the FIXEDLENGTH attribute.

Details

Using SETITEMN is analogous to assigning a numeric value to an indexed item in an array. SETITEMN assigns a numeric value to an item in the list identified by *list-id*.

    index specifies the list position of the item whose value is assigned. If *autogrow* is **'Y'**, *index* can be greater than the length of the list. SETITEMN then expands the list to a total of *index* items, sets all other new items to missing values, and places the new numeric value *nval* into the list. SETITEMN can only add values to the end of the list. Use INSERTN to insert numeric values elsewhere in the list.

    SETITEMN replaces an existing item in a list and even changes its type unless the item or the list has the FIXEDTYPE attribute.

    SETITEMN does not make a copy of the list before assigning the new numeric item. The list is modified in place.

    An error condition results if:

□ the absolute value of *index* is zero or it is greater than the number of items in the list and *autogrow* is **'N'**.

□ the absolute value of *index* is greater than the length of the list and the list has the FIXEDLENGTH attribute (even if *autogrow* is **'Y'**).

□ the list or item has the NOUPDATE attribute.

□ the list has the CHARONLY attribute.

□ the list or item has the FIXEDTYPE attribute and the function attempts to set the item to a different type. For example, if item 4 is character and has the FIXEDTYPE attribute, the following statement fails:

```
list=setitemn(list,5000,4);
```

SETKEY

Defines an index key for retrieving observations from a SAS data set

See also:
ICREATE
IDELETE
IOPTIONS
IVARLIST
KEYCOUNT
SET
WHERE

nval=**SETKEY**(*data-set-id*<,*key-name*<,*condition*<,*scroll-option* <,*list-id*>>>>);

Where...	Is type...	And represents...

nval	N	Whether the operation was successful:
		  0 if an active key was successfully set or cleared
		  $\neq 0$ if an error or warning condition occurred.

data-set-id	N	The identifier assigned when the data set was opened. If *data-set-id* is invalid, the program halts execution.
key-name	C	The index key to be used for retrieval.

condition	C	Comparison criteria for the key value:
		  'EQ' equal to the key value (Default)
		  'GE' greater than or equal to the key value
		  'GT' greater than the key value
		  'LE' less than or equal to the key value
		  'LT' less than the key value.

scroll-option	C	Whether observations can be randomly retrieved:
		  'SCROLL' observations can be retrieved in random order. (Default)
		  'NOSCROLL' observations can only be retrieved sequentially. This option improves performance when the data set is accessed via the REMOTE engine and the IS mode is specified for the second argument of the OPEN function. Those options reduce the number of data transfer operations that are required to read the data set.

Release 6.11

list-id	N	The list that contains the values of the index key variables. You have to use SETNITEMC and SETNITEMN to assign the values to the corresponding key variables in the list. An invalid *list-id* produces an error condition.

Details

SETKEY enables you to set an active key in an open data set to a simple or composite key. It establishes a set of criteria for reading SAS data set observations by evaluating the value of the variables from the SDV against the key value in the observations.

Using a composite key with SETKEY operates the same way as the WHERE function only when the condition is 'EQ'. The value returned when the condition is 'EQ' is the same as if the variables specified in the composite key are connected by WHERE conditions using AND or ALSO.

For all other conditions (GT, GE, LT, or LE) specified with SETKEY for a composite key, the composite key variables are concatenated together forming the index key. The number returned by the KEYCOUNT function is the number of observations in the data set that satisfies the composite key. For example, if the composite index consists of variables SEX and AGE and the condition is greater than, the values to search for are concatenated such as F13 for SEX of F and AGE of 13. Because the search is performed on the concatenated values, some values may meet a search condition that you did not expect such as SEX of M and AGE of 11.

SETKEY works only after SET is called in the SCL program or when a list identifier is passed. The list identifier must point to a list that contains the values of the index key variables. Once an active key is set through SETKEY, it remains active until

□ the data set is closed

□ another key is set

□ the current setting is cleared by passing the data set identifier alone to SETKEY.

The data set is automatically positioned at the first observation that meets the specified criteria. Use FETCH or FETCHOBS to read the observation.

SETKEY returns an error code if a WHERE clause is in effect. Index keys cannot be used in conjunction with WHERE clauses.

Example 1

Apply a key retrieval to the data set MYDATA, which subsets the data set into only those observations where the variable AGE has a value greater than or equal to 20:

```
    /* assuming a simple key AGE has been defined */
age=20;
dsid=open('MYDATA','I');
call set(dsid);
rc=setkey(dsid,'age','ge');
do while(fetch(dsid) ne -1);
   name=getvarc(dsid,1);
   put name=;
end;
```

Example 2

Search the data set CHILDREN for all boys who are 5 years old or older. The composite key ATTR created by ICREATE is used for retrieval. The values of the composite key variables are concatenated and the search is performed on the combined value. In this example, the key selects observations where AGE||SEX $\geq$ 5M. The FETCH function within the DO-loop returns all observations with variable AGE>=5. Because some of the observations may not have a matched concatenated key part, you need an additional check on the value of variable SEX to skip unmatched observations.

```
dsid=open('children','v');

    /* create a composite key ATTR with AGE as primary key variable */
rc=icreate(dsid,'attr','age sex');
call set(dsid);
age=5;
sex='M';
rc=setkey(dsid,'attr','ge');
do while(rc=0);
        /* FETCH function applies the retrieval criteria and */
        /* retrieves all observations for which AGE >=5       */
    rc=fetch(dsid);
    if (rc) then leave;
        /* filter out observations for which SEX is not 'M' */
    if (upcase (sex) ne 'M') then
        continue;
    child=getvarc(dsid,varnum(dsid,'name'));
    put child=;
end;
rc = close (dsid);
```

Example 3

Rewrite the program in example 2 to use the *list-id* argument instead of CALL SET. Using an SCL list avoids possible name collisions. Also, it allows you to set the retrieval criteria for observations at runtime instead of compile time.

```
dsid = open ( 'children','v');
rc = icreate( dsid, 'attr','age sex');
list = makelist();
list = setnitemc (list,cval,'sex');  /* cval contains the value of 'M' */
list = setnitemn (list,nval,'age');  /* nval contains the value of 5 */
rc = setkey (dsid,'attr','ge','',list);

    /* Print out all names with age >= 5 and sex= 'M' */
do while ( rc= 0 );
  rc = fetch (dsid);
  if (rc) then leave;
  sex1 = getvarc (dsid, varnum(dsid, 'sex'));
  if (upcase (sex) ne 'M') then
      continue;
  child = getvarc (dsid, varnum(dsid, 'name'));
  put child=;
  end;
rc = close (dsid);
```

SETLATTR

**Sets the attributes of an SCL
list or an item in a list**

See Also:
GETLATTR
HASATTR
MAKELIST
MAKENLIST

rc=**SETLATTR**(*list-id,attributes<,index>*);

Where...	Is type...	And represents...
rc	N	The success of the operation: 　0　if successful 　$\neq$ 0　if not successful.
list-id	N	The identifier of the list whose attributes or item attributes are set. An invalid *list-id* produces an error condition.
attributes	C	One or more attributes of the list or list item, shown in the tables below, separated by blanks. Attributes for lists are ignored when you are setting list item attributes, and attributes for list items are ignored when you are setting list attributes. This enables you to create a single attribute string that you can apply to lists or list items.
index	N	The position of the list item whose attributes are being modified. The position can be specified as a positive or negative number. By default, *index* is 1 (the first item). If *index* is a positive number, the item is at position *index* from the beginning of the list. If *index* is a negative number, the item is at position ABS(*index*) from the end of the list. If *index* is zero or omitted, SETLATTR sets list attributes. An error condition results if the absolute value for *index* is zero or it is greater than the number of items in the list

Table 20.13　*Attribute Values for Lists and List Items*

Attribute	Description
'DEFAULT'	combines all the default attributes.
'DELETE'	allows the list or item to be deleted. (Default)
'FIXEDTYPE'	prevents changes in the type of the item. See also NUMONLY and CHARONLY. For a list, prevents changes in the type of all individual items.
'NODELETE'	prevents a list or list item from being deleted. List items that do not have the NODELETE attribute can be deleted from a list with this attribute. A list without this attribute can be deleted even though it contains items with the NODELETE attribute.
'NOFIXEDTYPE'	allows the type of an item to change. For a list, allows the type of each item to change as long as the list does not have the CHARONLY or NUMONLY attribute and the item does not have the FIXEDTYPE attribute. (Default)
'NOUPDATE'	prevents updates to the value for a list item. For a list, updates are not allowed to any item, even those with the UPDATE attribute. This enables you to make a list read-only in one step without having to make each individual item read-only.

Attribute	Description
`'UPDATE'`	allows updates to the value of a list item. For a list, UPDATE allows updates to all items that do not have the NOUPDATE attribute. (Default)

Table 20.14 *Attribute Values for Lists Only*

Attribute	Description
`'ANYNAMES'`	allows item names to be any character string although names are always converted to uppercase and trailing blanks are removed. (Default)
`'CHARONLY'`	requires all items to have character values.
`'COPY'`	copies the list during a recursive copy operation if it is a sublist. (Default)
`'DUPNAMES'`	allows duplicate names in the list. (Default)
`'FIXEDLENGTH'`	prevents the list length from changing.
`'NOCHARONLY'`	allows items to have numeric and list identifier values. (Default)
`'NOCOPY'`	prevents the list from being copied during a recursive copy operation if it is a sublist. Instead, only the list identifier is copied to the target list. No recursion takes place for the list.
`'NODUPNAMES'`	requires all item names to be unique.
`'NOFIXEDLENGTH'`	allows the list length to change. (Default)
`'NONUMONLY'`	allows the list to contain character and list identifier values. (Default)
`'NUMONLY'`	requires all items to have numeric values.
`'SASNAMES'`	requires all items in the list to be named, and requires all names to be valid SAS names with no leading or trailing blanks.

Table 20.15 *Attribute Values for List Items Only*

Attribute	Description
`'ACTIVE'`	makes the item active in a pop-up menu opened by POPMENU. (Default)
`'INACTIVE'`	prevents the item from being active in a pop-up menu opened by the POPMENU function (users cannot select it).
`'NOWRITE'`	prevents the item from being written by the SAVELIST function.
`'WRITE'`	allows the item to be written when the list is stored via SAVELIST. (Default)

Details

If *index* is omitted or zero, the attributes are assigned to the list. Otherwise the attributes are assigned to the item at the position specified by *index*. Item attributes are attached to the items in the list, not the position in the list, so that an item keeps its attributes after rotating or reversing the list or after inserting and deleting other items. That is, if you assign the NODELETE attribute to the fourth item in the list and then delete the item at position 2, the item still has the NODELETE attribute even though it is now at position 3.

If a list has the NOCOPY attribute, it is not copied if it is a sublist in a recursive call of COPYLIST. Instead, only the list identifier is copied to the target list and no recursion takes place on the list. You can still copy a list with NOCOPY if it is the source (top-level) list.

Attribute Pairs

The attributes for lists and list items come in mutually exclusive pairs. For example, NOUPDATE designates that UPDATE is off. Setting one attribute of a mutually exclusive pair automatically turns off the other. The attribute pairs are shown in the following table.

Attribute	Complement Attribute	Applies To
ACTIVE	INACTIVE	Items
ANYNAMES	SASNAMES	Lists
COPY	NOCOPY	Lists
DELETE	NODELETE	Items and Lists
DUPNAMES	NODUPNAMES	Lists
NOCHARONLY	CHARONLY	Lists
NOFIXEDLENGTH	FIXEDLENGTH	Lists
NOFIXEDTYPE	FIXEDTYPE	Items and Lists
NONUMONLY	NUMONLY	Lists
UPDATE	NOUPDATE	Items and Lists
WRITE	NOWRITE	Items and Lists

The attributes of a list (such as CHARONLY, NUMONLY, FIXEDTYPE, and NOUPDATE) do not apply to sublists contained within them. You must set these attributes on the sublists if you wish them to have these attributes.

Both list and item attributes are copied by COPYLIST, but not the password.

Most of the list functions that alter lists or their contents are affected in some way by list and item attributes. See the documentation for the individual functions to see how they are affected.

Using Passwords to Protect List Attributes from Modification

You can assign a password to list attributes, which enables you to protect them. The password is stored with the list and must be supplied in subsequent SETLATTR statements in order to modify either list or item attributes. The password is specified as **PASSWORD=*password*** in the attribute string. The password may not contain any blanks, but case is significant (the passwords frobble and FROBBLE are different).

The following statements illustrate assigning a password:

```
pwd='password=grombaq';
myattr='nodelete noupdate';
rc=setlattr(mylist,myattr||' '||pwd);
```

If an SCL program attempts to modify the value of one of the items in MYLIST, the program halts because the list has the NOUPDATE attribute. If you want to permit updates of the list again, you can execute

```
rc=setlattr(mylist,pwd ||'update');
```

Note: An error condition results if you attempt to alter list attributes without specifying the PASSWORD= option and password.

You can remove the password from a list with NOPASSWORD=, allowing any SCL program to change attributes or to set the password. Either of the following statements removes the previously set password from the list identified by MYLIST:

```
rc=setlattr(mylist,'no'||pwd);
```

```
rc=setlattr(mylist,'nopassword=grombaq');
```

You must supply the correct password in order to remove it.

Examples

Distinction between NODELETE list and NODELETE item attributes
The NODELETE list attribute means the list itself cannot be deleted with DELLIST. The NODELETE item attribute indicates an item cannot be deleted from the list regardless of the item's type.

The following statements show this distinction:

```
a=makelist(3);
b=makelist();
a=setiteml(a,b,3);   /*  Set 3rd item in A to B.  */
   /* Give the list B the NODELETE attribute.      */
   /* DELLIST(b) will be an error.                 */
rc=setlattr(b,'NODELETE');
   /* give the 3rd item in A the NODELETE attribute */
   /* DELITEM(a, 3) will be an error               */
rc=setlattr(a,'NODELETE',3);
   /* Move B to second item in list and set        */
   /* third item with 0.                           */
a=setiteml(a,b,2);
a=setitemn(a,0,3);
   /* Remove B from the list A, but B still exists  */
a=delitem(a,2);
   /* DELITEM(a,2) will be an error now            */
```

Refer to CLEARLIST and DELLIST for more information on the DELETE and NODELETE attributes.

SETNITEMC

Assigns a character value to a named item in an SCL list

See Also:
DELNITEM
GETNITEMC
GETNITEML
GETNITEMN
HASATTR
INSERTC
INSERTL
INSERTN
MAKELIST
MAKENLIST
NAMEDITEM
NAMEITEM
SETITEMC
SETITEML
SETITEMN
SETLATTR
SETNITEML
SETNITEMN

rc=**SETNITEMC**(*list-id,cval,name*<*,occurrence*<*,start-index* <*,index*>>>);

Where...	Is type...	And represents...
rc	N	The identifier of the modified list, or an error number. The value passed as *list-id* is returned unless there is an error. The value 0 means out of memory. You may use the same variable as *list-id* since this value is the same as *list-id*.
list-id	N	The identifier of the list containing the named item. An invalid *list-id* produces an error condition.
cval	C	The character value to assign to the named item.
name	C	The name of the item. If the named item is not found in the list, it is inserted into the list. Item names are converted to uppercase and trailing blanks are ignored when searching the list for a matching name. Thus, the names 'abc' and 'Abc' are converted to 'ABC'.
occurrence	N	The occurrence of the named item to assign the specified value, starting from the position specified in *start-index*. The default is 1 for the first occurrence of the item.
start-index	N	Where in the list to begin searching for the item. By default, *start-index* is 1 (the first item). If *start-index* is positive, the search begins at position *start-index* items from the beginning of the list. If *start-index* is negative, the search begins at the item specified by ABS(*start-index*) items from the end of the list. An error condition results if the absolute value of *start-index* is zero or greater than the number of items in the list.
index	N	A variable to contain the index of the modified or inserted item.

Details

SETNITEMC does not make a copy of the list before the item is modified or inserted. The list is modified in place. If the named item is not found in the list (and the list does not have the FIXEDLENGTH attribute), the item is inserted into the list.

If you specify a variable for *index*, SETNITEMC returns the index of the modified or inserted item. You can reference this index to access the same item with SETITEMC and other SCL list functions as long as the items do not change positions (for example, as a result of an insert or delete operation). If the position of items in a list is stable, using the *index* argument and subsequent index-based functions such as SETITEMC rather than name-based functions improves performance because the list does not have to be searched multiple times to find a name match.

If *occurrence* and *start-index* are both positive or both negative, the search proceeds forward from the *start-index* item. For forward searches, the search continues only to the end of the list and does not wrap back to the front of the list. If the named item is not found, it is inserted at the end of the list. If *occurrence* or *start-index* is negative, the search is backwards. For backward searches, the search continues only to the beginning of the list and does not wrap back to the end of the list. If the named item is not found, it is inserted at the beginning of the list.

The result of using SETNITEMC is similar to combining NAMEDITEM and SETITEMC. For example, the statement

```
mylist=setnitemc(mylist,'Jones','NAMES',1,1,i);
```

performs the same operations as the following statements:

```
i=nameditem(mylist,'NAMES');
   /* If NAMES isn't found, insert it at the end of the list. */
if i=0 then mylist=insertc(mylist,'Jones',-1,'NAMES');
else mylist=setitemc(mylist,'Jones',i);
```

An error condition results if:

□ either the item or the list has the NOUPDATE attribute.

□ either the item or the list has the FIXEDTYPE attribute and the new value is being assigned to a numeric or sublist item.

□ the list has the NUMONLY attribute.

□ the named item was not found and the list has the FIXEDLENGTH attribute.

To check the attributes of a list or list item, use HASATTR. To change attributes, use SETLATTR.

SETNITEML

Assigns a list identifier to a named item in an SCL list

See Also:
DELNITEM
GETNITEMC
GETNITEML
GETNITEMN
HASATTR
INSERTC
INSERTL
INSERTN
MAKELIST
MAKENLIST
NAMEDITEM
NAMEITEM
SETITEMC
SETITEML
SETITEMN
SETLATTR
SETNITEMC
SETNITEMN

rc=**SETNITEML**(*list-id,sublist-id,name <,occurrence<,start-index<,index>>>*);

Where...	Is type...	And represents...
rc	N	The modified list, or an error number. The value passed as *list-id* is returned unless there is an error. The value 0 means out of memory. You may use the same variable as *list-id* since this value is the same as *list-id*.
list-id	N	The identifier of the list containing the named item. An invalid *list-id* produces an error condition.
sublist-id	N	The identifier of the sublist identifier to assign to the named item. An error condition results if *sublist-id* is not a valid identifier.
name	C	The name of the item. If the named item is not found in the list, it is inserted into the list. Item names are converted to uppercase and trailing blanks are ignored when searching the list for a matching name. Thus, the names 'abc' and 'Abc' are converted to 'ABC'.
occurrence	N	The occurrence of the named item to assign the specified value, starting from the position specified in *start-index*. The default is 1 for the first occurrence of the item.

Where...	Is type...	And represents...
start-index	N	Where in the list to begin searching for the item. By default, *start-index* is 1 (the first item). If *start-index* is positive, the search begins at position *start-index* items from the beginning of the list. If *start-index* is negative, the search begins at the item specified by ABS(*start-index*) items from the end of the list. An error condition results if the absolute value of *start-index* is zero or greater than the number of items in the list.
index	N	A variable to contain the index of the modified or inserted item.

Details

SETNITEML does not make a copy of the list before the item is modified or inserted. The list is modified in place. If the named item is not found in the list (and the list does not have the FIXEDLENGTH attribute), the item is inserted into the list.

If you specify a variable for *index*, SETNITEML returns the index of the modified or inserted item. You can reference this index to access the same item with SETITEML and other SCL list functions as long as the items do not change positions (for example, as a result of an insert or delete operation). If the position of items in a list is stable, using the *index* argument and subsequent index-based functions such as SETITEML rather than name-based functions improves performance because the list does not have to be searched multiple times to find a name match.

If *occurrence* and *start-index* are both positive or both negative, the search proceeds forward from the *start-index* item. For forward searches, the search continues only to the end of the list and does not wrap back to the front of the list. If the named item is not found, it is inserted at the end of the list. If *occurrence* or *start-index* is negative, the search is backwards. For backward searches, the search continues only to the beginning of the list and does not wrap back to the end of the list. If the named item is not found, it is inserted at the beginning of the list.

The result of using SETNITEML is similar to combining NAMEDITEM and SETITEML. For example, the statement

```
mylist=setniteml(mylist,employeelistid,'NAMES',1,1,i);
```

performs the same operations as the following statements:

```
i=nameditem(mylist,'NAMES');
   /* If NAMES isn't found, insert it at the end of the list. */
if i=0 then mylist=insertl(mylist,employeelistid,-1,'NAMES');
else mylist=setiteml(mylist,employeelistid,i);
```

An error condition results if:

□ *list-id* identifies a global list and *sublist-id* identifies a local list. Local lists cannot be placed into global lists.

□ the list has the NOUPDATE, NUMONLY, or CHARONLY attribute.

□ either the item or the list has the FIXEDTYPE attribute, and the new value is being assigned to a character or numeric item.

□ the item has the NOUPDATE attribute.

□ the named item was not found and the list has the FIXEDLENGTH attribute.

To check the attributes of a list or list item, use HASATTR. To change attributes, use SETLATTR.

SETNITEMN

Assigns a numeric value to a named item in an SCL list

rc=**SETNITEMN**(*list-id,nval,name* <,*occurrence*<,*start-index*<,*index*>>>);

See Also:
DELNITEM
GETNITEMC
GETNITEML
GETNITEMN
HASATTR
INSERTC
INSERTL
INSERTN
MAKELIST
MAKENLIST
NAMEDITEM
NAMEITEM
SETITEMC
SETITEML
SETITEMN
SETLATTR
SETNITEMC
SETNITEML

Where...	Is type...	And represents...
rc	N	The identifier of the modified list, or an error number. The value passed as *list-id* is returned unless there is an error. The value 0 means out of memory. You may use the same variable as *list-id* since this value is the same as *list-id*.
list-id	N	The identifier of the list containing the named item. An invalid *list-id* produces an error condition.
nval	N	The numeric value to assign to the named item.
name	C	The name of the item. If the named item is not found in the list, it is inserted into the list. Item names are converted to uppercase and trailing blanks are ignored when searching the list for a matching name. Thus, the names 'abc' and 'Abc' are converted to 'ABC'.
occurrence	N	The occurrence of the named item to assign the specified value, starting from the position specified in *start-index*. The default is 1 for the first occurrence of the item.
start-index	N	Where in the list to begin searching for the item. By default, *start-index* is 1 (the first item). If *start-index* is positive, the search begins at position *start-index* items from the beginning of the list. If *start-index* is negative, the search begins at the item specified by ABS(*start-index*) items from the end of the list. An error condition results if the absolute value of *start-index* is zero or greater than the number of items in the list.
index	N	A variable to contain the index of the modified or inserted item.

Details

SETNITEMN does not make a copy of the list before the item is modified or inserted. The list is modified in place. If the named item is not found in the list (and the list does not have the FIXEDLENGTH attribute), the item is inserted into the list.

If you specify a variable for *index*, SETNITEMN returns the index of the modified or inserted item. You can reference this index to access the same item with SETITEMN and other SCL list functions as long as the items do not change positions (for example, as a result of an insert or delete operation). If the position of items in a list is stable, using the *index* argument and subsequent index-based functions such as SETITEMN rather than name-based functions improves performance because the list does not have to be searched multiple times to find a name match.

If *occurrence* and *start-index* are both positive or both negative, the search proceeds forward from the *start-index* item. For forward searches, the search continues only to the end of the list and does not wrap back to the front of the list. If the named item is not found, it is inserted at the end of the list. If *occurrence* or *start-index* is negative, the search is backwards. For backward searches, the search continues only to the beginning of the list and does not wrap back to the end of the list. If the named item is not found, it is inserted at the beginning of the list.

The result of using SETNITEMN is similar to combining NAMEDITEM and SETITEMN. For example, the statement

```
mylist=setnitemn(mylist,5000,'AMOUNTS',1,1,i);
```

performs the same operations as the following statements:

```
i=nameditem(mylist,'AMOUNTS');
    /* If AMOUNTS isn't found, insert it at the end of the list. */
if i=0 then mylist=insertn(mylist,5000,-1,'AMOUNTS');
else mylist=setitemn(mylist,5000,i);
```

An error condition results if:

□ either the item or the list has the NOUPDATE attribute.

□ either the item or the list has the FIXEDTYPE attribute, and the new value is being assigned to a character or sublist item.

□ the list has the CHARONLY attribute.

□ the named item was not found and the list has the FIXEDLENGTH attribute.

To check the attributes of a list or list item, use HASATTR. To change attributes, use SETLATTR.

SETPARMID

Makes the value of an SCL numeric variable available between SCL programs

See Also:
DISPLAY
ENTRY
GETPARMID

CALL SETPARMID(*nval*);

Where...	Is type...	And represents...
nval	N	The numeric value to be stored for retrieval by GETPARMID.

Details

SETPARMID stores a number to be retrieved by calling GETPARMID. This enables one program to store a value using SETPARMID and another program to retrieve it using GETPARMID.

SETPARMID and GETPARMID allow only one value to be passed. To pass multiple values between entries, use the ENTRY statement. Additional ways of making values available to other SCL programs include using macro variables and SCL lists.

Example

Open the SAS data set MYDATA and then store the data set identifier value using SETPARMID so that other programs can access the data set using GETPARMID:

```
dsid=open('mydata','i');
call setparmid(dsid);
```

SETROW

Defines extended tables, dynamic tables, and selection lists

SAS/AF software only

See Also:
CURTOP
ENDTABLE
TOPROW

CALL SETROW(*num-rows*<,*num-sel*<,*sel-order*<,*dynamic*>>>);

Where...	Is type...	And represents...
num-rows	N	The maximum number of rows for the table.
num-sel	N	The number of items a user can select from the list. To display the list for information purposes only (no selections allowed), specify **0**. To specify unlimited selections, use a value larger than the number of available selections such as 9999. If *num-sel* is 1, then selecting one row unselects any previously selected row.
sel-order	C	The selection order:
		'Y' selected items are highlighted and moved to the top of the list in the order in which they are selected.
		'N' selected items are highlighted but they are not moved to the top of the list. (Default)
		'A' the selection list window automatically closes when the user makes a selection if only one selection is allowed. This option is valid only if *num-sel* is 1.
		'B' combines Y and A.
dynamic	C	Whether the table is dynamic:
		'Y' specifies that the extended table is a dynamic table. Use the ENDTABLE routine in the GETROW section to specify that no more rows are available. If the table is dynamic, *num-rows* can be 0.

Details

In PROGRAM entries an extended table has a specified number of rows, and a dynamic table has an unspecified number of rows. You cannot use the SETROW statement in the GETROW or PUTROW section of an SCL program. In order to use SETROW, you must have specified the EXTENDED TABLE attribute from the GATTR window.

You can also use extended tables, both regular and dynamic, as selection lists. The second and third arguments, *num-sel* and *sel-order*, define a selection list. Making an extended table a selection list automatically turns on the block cursor. Use FIELD to turn off the block cursor.

To define a dynamic table that is not a selection list, specify 0 for *num-sel* and ' ' for *sel-order*.

You can use SETROW only on extended tables. Because you can define extended tables only in SAS/AF software, you cannot use SETROW in FSEDIT or FSVIEW programs. FRAME entries must use the _SET_MAXROW_ method.

Example 1

Specify an extended table with 20 rows:

```
call setrow(20);
```

Example 2

Specify a selection list with 20 rows. Three selections are allowed, and the selections are moved to the top of the table.

```
call setrow(20,3,'y');
```

Example 3

Specify a dynamic table:

```
call setrow(0,0,'','y');
```

Example 4

Specify a dynamic table used as a selection list. Three selections are allowed, and the selections are not moved to the top of the table.

```
call setrow(0,3,'n','y');
```

SETTITLE

Sets the text of a title definition

See Also:
GETFOOT
GETTITLE
SETFOOT

CALL SETTITLE(*title-num,title-text*);

Where...	Is type...	And represents...
title-num	N	The number (1 to 10) of the title definition to create or modify.
title-text	C	Text for the title definition.

Details

SETTITLE works just like the TITLE statement and clears all title definitions numbered higher than the one created. You cannot use SETTITLE to set graphic options such as color, font, and position.

You can view title definitions in the TITLES window by using the TITLE command. Changing any text in the TITLES window, however, resets all graphically defined title options such as color, font, and position.

For more information on titles, see *SAS Language: Reference*. For more information on graphical titles, see *SAS/GRAPH Software: Reference*.

Example

Create a title numbered 2. The statement deletes all titles with numbers greater than 2.

```
call settitle(2,'This is the Second Title');
```

SHOWLIST

Displays a selection list window containing up to 13 items and returns user selections

See Also:
DATALISTC
DATALISTN
LISTC
LISTN

selection=**SHOWLIST**(*cval-1*<, . . . ,*cval-12*>,*message*);

Where...	Is type...	And represents...
selection	C	The user's selection, or blank if no selection is made.
item	C	Up to 13 items, separated by commas, for the selection list.
message	C	Text for a message displayed above the selection list. Regardless of how many *item* values are supplied, the last argument is assumed to be the message. Use a null string (' ') to specify the default message, which instructs users to make one selection.

Details

SHOWLIST automatically displays a custom selection list and returns the user's selections. Only one user selection is allowed, and the selection list window closes automatically after the user makes a selection.

You can provide a default or initial selected value in the list by providing a value for the *selection* variable prior to the execution of SHOWLIST. If the *selection* variable contains a value that corresponds to one of the *item* arguments when SHOWLIST executes, that selection is designated as selected when the selection list is displayed.

If a user closes the selection list window without making a selection, SHOWLIST returns a blank value unless there was an initial value for the *selection* variable before SHOWLIST was called.

Example

Open a selection list window that displays a list of three colors:

```
color='BLUE';
color=showlist('RED','BLUE','GREEN','Please select a color.');
```

Because the variable COLOR is assigned a value before SHOWLIST executes, and the value **BLUE** is one of the arguments for SHOWLIST, then the item BLUE in the list is highlighted with an asterisk when the list is displayed.

SORT

Sorts a SAS data set by one or more variables

sysrc=**SORT**(*data-set-id,varlist-1<. . .varlist-4>*);

Where...	Is type...	And represents...
sysrc	N	Whether the operation was successful: 0 if successful $\neq 0$ if not successful.
data-set-id	N	The identifier assigned when the data set was opened. If *data-set-id* is invalid, the program halts execution.
varlist	C	One to four lists of variables or options separated by blanks. For a list of options, the first character in the list must be a forward slash (*/*). Variables and options cannot be mixed in the same list.

Details

SORT uses the sorting program that SAS supports on your operating system. If a variable list contains more than one variable, the data set is sorted by those variables in the order in which they are specified.

You can use the following options for *varlist*, depending on your operating system:

```
DIAG
EQUALS
FORCE
LEAVE
LIST
MESSAGE
NODUPKEY
NODUPLICATES
NOEQUALS
OUTPUT
REVERSE
SORTSEQ=ASCII | EBCDIC | DANISH | FINNISH | NATIONAL | NORWEGIAN | SWEDISH
SORTSIZE
SORTWKNO
TAGSORT
TRANTAB
```

SAS views cannot be sorted in place. To sort views, you must specify an output SAS data set.

Example

Use the SORT function with the options NODUPKEY, NODUPLICATES, and TAGSORT to sort the SAS data set MYDATA by the variables A in ascending order and B in descending order:

```
rc=sort(mydataid,'a descending b','/ nodupkey noduplicates tagsort');
```

SORTLIST

Sorts the items in an SCL list by value or by name

See Also:
HASATTR
MAKELIST
REVLIST
ROTLIST
SETLATTR

rc=**SORTLIST**(*list-id*<,*options*<,*start-index*<,*n-items*>>>);

Where...	Is type...	And represents...
rc	N	The identifier of the sorted list. The value passed as *list-id* is returned unless there is an error. The value 0 means out of memory.
list-id	N	The identifier of the list to sort. An invalid *list-id* produces an error condition.
options	C	How the sort operation is performed. Multiple options can be specified, separated by blanks. Each option can be abbreviated to a unique substring. The substring can be as short as the first character for all options except `'NAME'` and `'NODUP'`, which may be abbreviated to two characters, `'NA'` or `'NO'`, respectively. Later keywords override previous keywords

`'ASCENDING'` Sort the list in ascending order. (Default)

`'DESCENDING'` Sort the list in descending order.

`'IGNORECASE'` Ignore case when comparing string values. Case is always ignored when sorting by name because names are always converted to uppercase.

`'NAME'` Sort the list by item name. Unnamed items appear before named items in an ascending sort.

`'NODUP'` Delete duplicate items when sorting. All but the first item in the sort range that have the same value (or the same name if sorting by name) are deleted. The default is not to delete duplicates.

`'OBEYCASE'` Obey case when comparing string values. This is the default when sorting by value.

`'VALUE'` Sort the list by item value. In an ascending sort, character items precede list identifiers, which precede numeric missing values, followed by non-missing numeric values. (Default)

start-index	N	The starting position for sorting a range of items in the list. By default, *start-index* is 1 (the first item). If *start-index* is positive, the range begins *start-index* items from the beginning of the list. If *start-index* is negative, the range begins at the item specified by ABS(*start-index*) items from the end of the list. An error condition results if the absolute value of *start-index* is zero or greater than the number of items in the list.

Where...	Is type...	And represents...
n-items	N	The number of items in the list to sort. The default is all items between *start-index* and the opposite end of the list. To explicitly specify all items, specify −1.

Details

SORTLIST does not make a copy of the list before it is sorted. The list is modified in place.

Sublists contained in the sorted list are not sorted recursively.

When you specify the **'NODUP'** and **'IGNORECASE'** options, the character list items or names that are spelled the same but differ only in case are considered duplicates and all but the first occurrence are removed from the sorted list.

An error occurs if the list has the NOUPDATE attribute or an item to be removed has the NODELETE attribute, if NODUP is specified. Use HASATTR to check the attributes of a list or item. To change attributes, use SETLATTR.

Example 1

Sort the first 10 items in a list in descending order:

```
list=sortlist(list,'D',1,10);
```

Example 2

Sort the last 16 items in a list in ascending order:

```
list=sortlist(list,'',-1,16);
```

Example 3

Sort the second ten items in a list in ascending name order, deleting items with duplicate names:

```
list=sortlist(list,'NODUP ASCENDING NAME',11,10);
```

STATUS

Contains the status of program execution or overrides the normal flow of control

Character System Variable

See Also:
EVENT

Details

STATUS is a System Variable that is created for every SCL program you compile. The compiler creates a space for _STATUS_ in the SCL data vector. _STATUS_ is maintained as a single character string variable.

When an SCL program executes, _STATUS_ can have one of the following values:

STATUS Value	Description
' ' (blank)	A field or FRAME entry object was modified or selected
'E'	An END or equivalent command was issued.
'C'	A CANCEL or equivalent command was issued.
'P'	A pop-up menu event occurred Valid only for FRAME entries. Valid only for FRAME entries.
'G'	The GETROW section was called for the top row of an extended table.
'K'	A command other than an END or CANCEL, or their equivalents, was issued. Valid only for FRAME entries.
'D'	A widget was selected with a double click. Valid only for FRAME entries.

In addition to the execution values, you can assign values to _STATUS_. The values you can assign to _STATUS_ are the following:

Assign _STATUS_...	When you want to...
H	terminate the current window without further input from the user. Control returns to the program or window that invoked the application. Note that the TERM section of the program is not executed in this case. In FSEDIT, if a user modified a data set variable value in the current observation, the modified values are not written to the SAS data set.
R	resume execution of the SCL program without exiting the application in SAS/AF or the current observation in FSEDIT. When you set the value of the _STATUS_ variable to 'R', the procedure ignores the END or CANCEL command the user just issued. This value is useful only when set in the TERM section of your program or the _PRETERM_ method of a FRAME entry object because the specified action (not allowing an exit from the program or the current observation) occurs after the user has issued an END or CANCEL command in SAS/AF or attempted to leave an observation in FSEDIT.

Assigning a value to _STATUS_ does not imply an immediate return. The value of _STATUS_ is queried only after the SCL program returns control to the application. To return control to the application after assigning a value to _STATUS_, use the STOP or RETURN statement.

FRAME entries can also use the _GET_STATUS_ and _SET_STATUS_ methods to query and udpate the _STATUS_ variable.

Example

The following program calls OKTOEND.FRAME to display a confirmation window that allows the user to select 'ok' or 'cancel' in response to the END command. OKTOEND returns a 1 if it's ok to end or 0 if it's not.

```
TERM:
      /* check if the END command was issued */
   if _status_ eq 'E' then
   do;
      call display( 'oktoend.frame', ok );
      /* check if the user wants to cancel the
         END command */
      if ok eq 0 then
         do;
            _status_ = 'R';
            return;
         end;
   end;

   rest of the TERM section
return;
```

STDMSG

Displays the text of the SAS System message generated by an unknown command

See Also:
NEXTCMD
NEXTWORD
SYSMSG
WORD

cval=**STDMSG**();

Where...	Is type...	And represents...
cval	C	The message text. A blank means that no window exists in which to display the message.

Example

Use WORD to read a command from the command line in a PROGRAM entry and check the command for validity. If the command is not valid, the standard message is displayed. Valid commands in this case are PRINTIT and FILEIT. Any other commands produce the standard error message for invalid commands.

```
INIT:
   control always;
return;
MAIN:
   if _status_ in ('C' 'E') then return;
   command=word(1);
   call nextcmd();
   select(upcase(command));
      when('PRINTIT') _msg_='PRINTIT is specified';
      when('FILEIT') _msg_='FILEIT is specified';
      otherwise
         do;
            call execcmdi(command);
            stdmsg=stdmsg();
            if stdmsg ne _blank_ then _msg_=stdmsg;
            return;
         end;
   end;
return;
TERM:
return;
```

STOP

Stops executing statements in the program section that is currently executing

SAS Statement with limitations in SCL

See also:
STATUS

STOP;

Example

The chain of execution is begun by executing OBJ1 and includes LAB1 and LAB2. When the STOP statement is executed the chain of execution ends, and the two PUT statements are never executed. Control is passed to MAIN.

```
INIT:
    control label;
return;

MAIN:
    put 'in MAIN';
return;

OBJ1:
    link LAB1;
    put 'after link to LAB1';
return;

LAB1:
    link LAB2;
    put 'after link to LAB2';
return;

LAB2:
    stop;
return;

TERM:
return;
```

STRATTR

Defines a color and highlighting attribute string

See Also:
FLDATTR
FLDCOLOR

cval=**STRATTR**(*color,attribute,start,length*);

Where...	Is type...	And represents...
cval	C	The string containing color and display attributes.
color	C	A color name or ' ' to retain the current color. SASCOLOR window elements can also be used for *color*. For more information on colors and a list of colors, see *color* in "Common Arguments" on page 222.
		Use a null value (' ') to retain the current color.
attribute	C	A display attribute or ' ' to retain the current attribute. If you specify a SASCOLOR window element for *color*, *attribute* is ignored because the SASCOLOR window element contains a display attribute. However, you must specify a placeholder (' ') for *attribute* when you specify arguments after it. For more information on display attributes and a list of them, see *attribute* in "Common Arguments" on page 222.
start	N	The starting character position to store in the attribute string.
length	N	The number of character positions to store in the attribute string.

Details

STRATTR defines a string that you can use with FLDATTR to change the color and display attributes of fields or portions of fields in the application's window. STRATTR can be called multiple times to create a string with multiple attributes in it.

Characters whose positions are after *start* + *length* - 1 do not change color or attributes. Characters whose positions are before the start position must be initialized to the special hex character 'FF'x in order to maintain their current color and attribute. For more information on using hex characters, see the FLDATTR function.

To change the color for the entire field or FRAME entry object, the FIELD function can be used.

Example

Define an attribute string named STR that contains red reverse in the first half of the string and blue highlight in the second half and apply it to the field ABC.

```
half = mlength(abc)/2;
str = strattr( 'red', 'reverse', 1, half );
str = strattr( 'blue', 'highlight', half+1, half );
rc = fldattr( 'abc', str );
```

SUBMIT

Submits statements to the SAS System for execution

See Also:
ENDSUBMIT
PREVIEW

SUBMIT<*when* <*where*> <*host*>> <STATUS>;

Where...	Is type...	And represents...
when	C	When to submit the generated statements for execution and what action, if any, the procedure must take. If this option is not specified, the statements within the SUBMIT block are collected by SCL in a PREVIEW buffer. Options are listed in Table 20.16.
where	C	Determines where statements are submitted for execution. If this option is omitted, the statements are submitted to the SAS System for execution. EDIT submits the statements to the display manager PROGRAM EDITOR window. SQL submits the statements to SQL for processing from both TESTAF and AF modes.
host	C	Instructions for submitting the code on a specific operating system: LOCAL executes on the current system. (Default) REMOTE executes on a remote host.
STATUS	C	The instruction to display the status window at all times, even if the current application has a display window. Use this option with the CONTINUE option. By default, SCL displays the status window only if the CONTINUE option is used with the SUBMIT statement and the current application has no display window.

Table 20.16   When Options for the SUBMIT Statement

Option	Description
CONTINUE	specifies that at the end of the current SUBMIT block, the procedure submits all statements stored in the PREVIEW window and returns control to the SCL program. Execution of the program continues with the statement following ENDSUBMIT.
IMMEDIATE	specifies that at the end of the current SUBMIT block, the procedure submits all statements stored in the PREVIEW window and returns control to the procedure. You cannot use this option with FRAME entries because its action could prevent the execution of other labeled sections. **Note:** This means that any statements following ENDSUBMIT are not executed on this pass through the SCL program. To execute the statements following ENDSUBMIT, use conditional logic to branch around the SUBMIT IMMEDIATE statement.

Option	Description
PRIMARY	specifies that at the end of the current SUBMIT block, the procedure submits all SAS statements stored in the PREVIEW window and the user is returned to the primary window, that is, the entry specified with the CATALOG= option in the AF command. If the current entry is the primary entry for the application, this option restarts the current entry. **Note:** This means that any statements following ENDSUBMIT are not executed on this pass through the SCL program. To execute the statements following ENDSUBMIT, use conditional logic to branch around the SUBMIT PRIMARY statement.
TERMINATE	specifies that at the end of the current SUBMIT block, the procedure submits all SAS statements stored in the PREVIEW window and closes the AF window.

Details

SUBMIT labels the beginning of a block of SAS statements to be submitted to the SAS System. When SUBMIT is encountered, SCL collects all the statements between SUBMIT and ENDSUBMIT and places them in the PREVIEW buffer. Based on the value of *when*, SCL submits the statements to the SAS System for execution at the appropriate time.

The *where* and *host* options are valid only if the *when* option is specified.

By default, when control returns to SCL the program continues to execute the statements following ENDSUBMIT.

You can use the REMOTE command to override the *host* option of a SUBMIT statement. That is, in the SUBMIT statement, you can choose not to use the *host* option **REMOTE** and instead use the REMOTE command to control whether the generated code is executed on the local or remote host. For more information on the REMOTE command, see Chapter 11, "Submitting SAS and SQL Statements and Issuing Host Commands."

The ASIS option in the CONTROL statement allows a SUBMIT block to be submitted without formatting.

When an AF application that is invoked from an autoexec file uses both SUBMIT CONTINUE REMOTE and LOCAL blocks, the order of execution may not be correct. In this situation, you can avoid problems by using the following in place of the SUBMIT CONTINUE REMOTE blocks:

```
submit continue;
   rsubmit;
      SCL statements
   endrsubmit;
endsubmit;
```

Note: If CONTROL LABEL is specified, a window variable section must not contain a SUBMIT IMMEDIATE block.

Example 1

Submit a simple SAS program that invokes the PRINT procedure for a previously referenced SAS data set:

```
submit continue;
   proc print;
   run;
endsubmit;
```

SUPAPPLY

Invokes the inherited definition of a method and passes the method's arguments in an SCL list

Release 6.11 Feature

See Also:
APPLY
INSTANCE
METHOD
NOTIFY
SEND
SUPER

CALL SUPAPPLY(*object-id,method-name,arg-list-id*);

Where...	Is type...	And represents...
object-id	N	The object for which the method is invoked.
method-name	C	The name of the method to invoke.
arg-list-id	N	The list containing the arguments required by the method. An invalid *arg-list-id* produces an error condition.

Details

SUPAPPLY provides the same functionality as SUPER except that you can pass arguments in an SCL list to an inherited method, called a super method. SUPAPPLY provides a way of building a dynamic parameter list at run time instead of coding a fixed parameter list.

A super method is the method found by searching in the parent class of the currently executing method. The method name is typically the current method, which is stored in the variable _METHOD_. However, any other method name can be used. The object identified in *object-id* must be the object whose method is currently executing. The identifier for this object is stored in the system instance variable _SELF_. For more information on System Instance Variables, see Chapter 2, "Using SCL Variables."

For more information on classes, objects, widgets and methods, see *SAS/AF Software: FRAME Entry Usage and Reference.*

Example

Consider an Object class that has a TRANSACTION method that receives a variable length parameter list of transactions to record on a data set. A subclass of this class records the transactions in an audit trail data set that contains two numeric variables DATETIME and TCOUNT, which record the date/time and number of transactions processed. This example shows the TRANSACTION method, which invokes the inherited TRANSACTION method then records the size of the transaction (the number of items in the argument list) on a data set. The object has three automatic instance variables: AUDIT, TC_VNUM, and DT_VNUM. AUDIT is a data set ID for an audit data set. TC_VNUM is the variable number for the TCOUNT variable. DT_VNUM is the variable number for the DATETIME variable.

```
/* TRANSACT.SCL : TRANSACTION method */
MAIN:
   entry arglist= transactions;
   length audit tc_vnum dt_vnum 8; /* auto iv's */
   call supapply(_self_,'transaction',transactions);
   if audit then
      do;
         nTransactions=listlen(transactions);
         rc=putvarn(audit,tc_vnum,nTransactions);
         rc=putvarn(audit,dt_vnum,datetime());
         rc=update(audit);
      end;
```

```
return;
```

This method may be invoked with an arbitrary number of transactions, using either CALL SEND or CALL APPLY where the SCL variable listOftransactions is an SCL list containing one or more transaction objects.

```
call send (obj,'transaction',t1,t2,t3,t4,t5);
call send (obj,'transaction',t1,t2);
call apply(obj,'transaction',listOftransactions);
```

SUPER

Invokes the inherited definition of a method

See Also:
APPLY
INSTANCE
METHOD
NOTIFY
SEND
SUPAPPLY

CALL SUPER(*object-id,method-name*<,*parameters*>);

Where...	Is type...	And represents...
object-id	N	The identifier associated with the object for which the method is invoked.
method-name	C	The name of the method to invoke.
parameters	N, C	Additional numeric or character arguments that are required by the method. Separate multiple options with commas.

Details

The SUPER routine invokes a super method on the object identified by *object-id*. A *super method* is the method inherited from the parent class of the currently executing method. The method name is typically the name of the currently executing method, stored in the System Instance Variable _METHOD_, but any other method name can be used. The object identified by *object-id* must be the same object whose method is currently executing. The identifier for this object is stored in the System Instance Variable _SELF_.

For more information on System Instance Variables, see Chapter 2. For more information on objects and methods, see *SAS/AF Software: FRAME Entry Usage and Reference*.

You use SUPER to execute an inherited method as part of another method that performs additional actions.

Example 1

Override a class's _INIT_ method with a method block called SUBINIT. The SUBINIT method executes the inherited _INIT_ method and in addition creates new SCL list and stores it in the object's instance variable SUBLIST:

```
length _method_ $40;
SUBINIT:
   method optional= arg 8;
      call super(_self_,_method_,arg);
      _self_=setniteml(_self_,makelist(),'sublist');
   endmethod;
```

Example 2

Define a method block called TERM, which overrides the _TERM_ method for a new class. The method does some cleanup processing based on data the object created in the _INIT_ method (or in other methods) and then invokes the inherited _TERM_ method.

```
TERM:
   method;
           /* Do cleanup processing based on the new class */
       l = getniteml(_self_, 'SUBLIST', 1,1, 0);
       if l and listlen(l) >= 0 then
           rc = dellist(l, 'Y');
       call super(_self_, '_TERM_');
   endmethod;
```

SYMGET

Returns the character value stored in a macro variable

See Also:
SYMGETN
SYMPUT
SYMPUTN

cval=**SYMGET**(*macro-var*);

Where...	Is type...	And represents...
cval	C	The character value stored in the macro variable.
macro-var	C	The macro variable.

Details

SYMGET returns the character value of a specified SAS macro variable. SYMGET reflects execution-time settings of macro variables whereas "&*macro-var*" does not.

Examples

Return the value the macro variable SYSJOBID at program compile time:

```
cval="&sysjobid";
```

Return the value of the macro variable SYSJOBID at program execution time:

```
cval=symget('sysjobid');
```

SYMGETN

Returns the numeric value stored in a macro variable

See Also:
SYMGET
SYMPUT
SYMPUTN

nval=**SYMGETN**(*macro-var*);

Where...	Is type...	And represents...
nval	N	The numeric value stored in the macro variable.
macro-var	C	The macro variable.

Details

SYMGETN returns the numeric value of a specified SAS macro variable. SYMGETN reflects execution-time settings of macro variables whereas "&*macro-var*" does not.

Examples

Return the value the macro variable UNIT at program compile time:

```
nval=&unit;
```

Return the value the macro variable UNIT at program execution time:

```
nval=symgetn('unit');
```

SYMPUT

Stores a character value in a SAS macro variable

See Also:
SYMGET
SYMGETN
SYMPUTN

CALL SYMPUT(*macro-var,cval*);

Where...	Is type...	And represents...
macro-var	C	The macro variable.
cval	C	The character value to store in the macro variable.

Details

The SYMPUT routine stores a character value in a SAS macro variable.

Example

Store the character value **newdata** in the macro variable DSN:

```
call symput('dsn','newdata');
```

SYMPUTN

Stores a numeric value in a SAS macro variable

See Also:
SYMGET
SYMGETN
SYMPUT

CALL SYMPUTN(*macro-var,nval*);

Where...	Is type...	And represents...
macro-var	C	The macro variable.
nval	N	The numeric value to be stored in the macro variable.

Details

The SYMPUTN routine stores a numeric value in a SAS macro variable.

Example

Store the numeric value 1000 in the macro variable UNIT:

```
call symputn('unit',1000);
```

SYSMSG

Returns the text of SCL error messages or warning messages

See Also:
SYSRC

cval=**SYSMSG**();

Where...	Is type...	And represents...
cval	C	Text of the error message produced by SCL.

Details

SYSMSG returns the text of error messages or warning messages produced when SCL encounters an error condition. If no error message is available, the returned value is blank. The internally stored error message is reset to blank after a call to SYSMSG, so subsequent calls to SYSMSG before another error condition occurs will return blank values.

Refer to Chapter 2, "Using SCL Variables," for more information on the _MSG_ system variable.

Example

Use SYSMSG to display the system error message generated if FETCH cannot copy the next observation into the Data Set Data Vector for the SAS data set identified by the value stored in DSID. The return code is 0 only when a next record is successfully fetched.

```
rc=fetch(dsid);
if rc ne 0 then _msg_=sysmsg();
```

SYSRC

Returns a system error number or the exit status of the most recently called entry

See Also:
SYSMSG

rc=**SYSRC**(*<display-stat>*);

Where...	Is type...	And represents...

rc	N	The SAS System return code for the most recent error or warning condition if *display-stat* is omitted. Otherwise, the exit status of the most recently called entry:
		  0 if a user used an END command
		  − 1 if the user used a CANCEL command

display-stat	N	Causes the SYSRC function to return the status of the most recent exit status of CALL DISPLAY. The value of the argument does not matter, only whether any value is specified.

Details

If you pass an argument to SYSRC, the function returns the exit status of the most recently called execution of CALL DISPLAY rather than the SAS System return code for the most recent error or warning condition. Thus, you can use SYSRC to determine how a user terminated an entry called with CALL DISPLAY.

To return the SAS System return code, do not specify any value for *display-stat*. Refer to Chapter 18, "SAS System Return Codes," for more information on how to use return code values.

Example

Determine how a user exited from another entry called within the current application.

```
call display('test.program');
if sysrc(1)=-1 then
   _msg_='User exited TEST.PROGRAM with a CANCEL command';
else
   _msg_='User exited TEST.PROGRAM with an END command';
```

SYSTEM

Issues a host system command

rc=**SYSTEM**(*cval*);

Where...	Is type...	And represents...
rc	N	The host system return code. Typically, a value of 0 reports that the command was executed successfully and a nonzero value reports that the command was not successfully executed. However, some operating systems may return nonzero values for successful operations. Refer to the *SAS Companion* for your host for details.
cval	C	The host command to be executed. To enter the host command processor for your system, specify a blank string (' ').

Details

Using SYSTEM is equivalent to using the X command for issuing a system command. The action that takes place depends on the command issued. The window may be temporarily overwritten due to the actions of the command issued. The commands that can be issued are operating-system dependent.

Example

Issue the DIR command to the host operating system:

```
rc=system('dir');
if (rc) then _msg_='Failed to execute DIR system command.';
```

TOPROW

Scrolls a row to the top of an extended table

SAS/AF software only

See Also:
CURTOP
ENDTABLE
SETROW

CALL TOPROW(*row*);

Where...	Is type...	And represents...
row	N	The number of the table row to be scrolled to the top of the table.

Details

The TOPROW routine cannot be called in the GETROW or PUTROW section of an SCL program.

You can use TOPROW only on extended tables in PROGRAM entries. Because you can define extended tables only in SAS/AF software, you cannot use TOPROW in FSEDIT or FSVIEW programs.

Example

Scroll the fifth row to the top of the table:

```
call toprow(5);
```

Suppose you have a PROGRAM entry window with three character fields:

1. VALUE, in the nonscrollable area of the window. Turn the CAPS attribute off for VALUE.

2. NAME, the first field in the extended table's logical row. Turn the CAPS attribute off for NAME.

3. SEX, the second field in the extended table's logical row.

When a user enters a name in **VALUE**, the table scrolls so the corresponding row is at the top of the table.
This program controls the window:

```
INIT:
  dsid=open('sasuser.class');
  call set(dsid);
  call setrow(0,0,'','y');
  vnum=varnum(dsid,'name');
return;

MAIN:
  rc=where(dsid,"name contains '"||value|| "'");
  any=attrn(dsid,'any');
  if any then do;
    rc=fetch(dsid);
    firstmatch=getvarc(dsid,vnum);
    rc=where(dsid);
    recnum=locatec(dsid,vnum, firstmatch);
    call toprow(recnum);
  end;
return;

TERM:
```

```
        if dsid then dsid=close(dsid);
    return;

    getrow:
        if fetchobs(dsid,_currow_)=-1 then call endtable();
    return;
```

TRACEBACK

Displays the traceback of the entire SCL execution stack

Release 6.11 Feature

See Also:
MAKELIST
TRACEBACK debugger
    command

CALL TRACEBACK (<*list-id*>);

Where...	Is type...	And represents...
list-id	N	The identifier of the SCL list to store traceback information. You must create the list before passing it to TRACEBACK. An invalid *list-id* produces an error condition.

Details

The execution stack consists of the current program being executed and all programs that were called to display the current program. TRACEBACK displays the stack as a list of entry names and associated line numbers. The line number for an entry indicates the location where it transferred control to the next entry in the list.

Example

A.SCL calls B.PROGRAM at line 10 and B.PROGRAM calls C.FRAME at line 15. The TRACEBACK routine is executed at line 20 of C.FRAME.

```
call traceback();
```

and produces this output :

```
In routine: WORK.A.C.SCL line 20
Called from WORK.A.B.PROGRAM line 15
Arguments passed to DISPLAY:
  1 (Character Literal) = 'C.FRAME'
Parameters passed to DISPLAY ENTRY:
  1 S = 'SASUSER'
  2 $T0 = 25
Called from WORK.A.A.SCL line 10
Arguments passed to DISPLAY:
  1 (Character Literal) = 'B.PROGRAM'
Parameters passed to DISPLAY ENTRY:
  1 X = 5
  2 (Character Literal) = 'SASUSER'
Traceback:(WORK.A.C.SCL=20
          WORK.A.B.PROGRAM=15
          WORK.A.A.SCL=10
          )[541]
```

Save the current traceback in an SCL list and print the traceback list.

```
tb = makelist();
```

```
call traceback(tb);    /* line 20 */
call putlist(tb, 'Traceback:', 0);
rc = dellist(tb);
```

This program produces the output:

```
Traceback: (WORK.A.C.SCL=20
            WORK.A.B.PROGRAM=15
            WORK.A.A.SCL=10
            )[541]
```

Note: [541] is the list identifier assigned when these examples were run and may be different each time the examples are run.

UNGRAY

Ungrays a single station in a choice group, an entire choice group, a check box, or a radio box

SAS/AF software only

See Also:
ACTIVATE
GRAY
ISACTIVE
ISGRAY

rc=**UNGRAY**(*var-name*<,*station*<,*row*>>);

Where...	Is type...	And represents...
rc	N	Whether the operation was successful: 0 if successful $\neq 0$ if unsuccessful
var-name	C	The choice group or FRAME entry object to be ungrayed.
station	N	The number of the field within the choice group or the button within the radio box.
row	N	The number of the row when the choice group is in the scrollable section of an extended table. The *row* parameter is valid for PROGRAM entries but not for FRAME entries. Specify *row* only when you want to ungray a station from outside the extended table's GETROW or PUTROW section. Do not specify *row* if you want to ungray a station from GETROW or PUTROW.

Details

You can use UNGRAY along with GRAY to control the availability of a choice group, a station, or a FRAME entry object based on the program flow.

When a FRAME entry object is ungrayed, it becomes unprotected and reverts to its normal color. The ungrayed object can once again receive input such as mouse clicks. FRAME entry objects can also use the _UNGRAY_ method.

Example

Make a station available only when the value of variable DEPT is ADMIN.

```
if (dept='ADMIN') then
   rc=ungray('personal',3);
else
   rc=gray('personal',3);
```

UNLOCK

Releases a lock on the current observation

sysrc=**UNLOCK**(*data-set-id*);

See Also:
CLOSE
DATALISTC
DATALISTN
FETCH
FETCHOBS
LOCATEC
LOCATEN
OPEN

Where...	Is type...	And represents...

sysrc	N	Whether the operation was successful:
		    0 if successful
		
		    ≠ 0 if not successful.

data-set-id	N	The identifier assigned when the data set was opened. If *data-set-id* is invalid, the program halts execution.

Details

A data set opened in UPDATE mode receives RECORD-level locking by default. Whenever an application reads an observation from a data set opened in UPDATE mode, it obtains a lock on the observation. Any of the following functions lock an observation when the data set is opened in UPDATE mode:

DATALISTC
DATALISTN
FETCH
FETCHOBS
LOCATEC
LOCATEN

Observation locks are implicitly released when a different observation is read. You can use UNLOCK to explicitly release a lock on the last observation read when the user is finished with the observation but has not read another observation.

This function is useful when observations from a secondary SAS data set are read to lookup values.

Note: UNLOCK is not directly related to the LOCK function, which locks SAS catalogs, catalog members, and data sets, and which requires SAS/SHARE software. However, if the data set in question is accessed through SAS/SHARE using the REMOTE engine, then UNLOCK can be used to allow other applications to access individual observations. See *SAS/SHARE Software: Usage and Reference* for more information.

Example

Call FETCH to read a new observation from the SAS data set MYDATA, which is opened in UPDATE mode. After any data from the observation are processed, call UNLOCK to release the lock on the observation:

```
dsid=open('mydata','u');
rc=fetch(dsid);
   more SCL statements
rc=unlock(dsid);
```

UNPROTECT

**Removes protection from a field
or FRAME entry object**

See Also:
DISPLAYED
ERROR
ERROROFF
ERRORON
FIELD
MODIFIED
PROTECT

UNPROTECT *wvar-names* | _ALL_;

Where...	Is type...	And represents...
wvar-names	C	One or more fields or FRAME entry objects in the window to unprotect, or '**_ALL_**' to unprotect all fields or FRAME entry objects.

Details

To set an error flag for multiple fields, specify the field names following
UNPROTECT, separated by blanks.

Use UNPROTECT to temporarily override the PROTECT attribute specified in
the SAS/AF ATTR window or the FSEDIT Attributes PROTECT window. The
variable to be protected cannot be an element of an array. To protect an array
element, use FIELD.

UNPROTECT, when used with PROTECT, enables you to unprotect and protect
fields selectively and thus force the user to enter values in a predetermined order.

If you unprotect a window variable with the UNPROTECT statement in FSEDIT
applications and issue the MODIFY command to edit the custom screen, the
PROTECT attribute is removed for this variable in the PROTECT window.

FRAME entry objects can also use _UNPROTECT_. Unprotecting some FRAME
entry objects (block, check box, icon, list box, pushbutton, radio box, scroll bar, and
slider) is the same as calling the UNGRAY function or the _UNGRAY_ method.

Example

Enable users to enter values for fields that were previously protected:

```
if (modified(dataset)) then
  do;
     protect dataset;
     unprotect vars;
     cursor vars;
     _msg_='Please type the names of the variables to be printed.';
  end;
```

UNSELECT

Unselects a specified row of a selection list

SAS/AF software only

See Also:
ISSEL
NSELECT
SELECT
SELECTED

rc=**UNSELECT**(*row*);

Where...	Is type...	And represents...

rc	N	Whether the operation was successful:
		  0 if successful
		
		  $\neq 0$ if not successful.

row	N	The row number to unselect. If an invalid row number is specified, no action is taken.

Details

UNSELECT unhighlights the specified row. This function is useful to force the deselection of a row. Normally the user selects and unselects a row by pressing ENTER or clicking with the mouse on the row.

You can use UNSELECT only for selection lists built with extended tables in PROGRAM entries. FRAME entry objects must use the _UNSELECT_ROW_ method. Because you can define extended tables only in SAS/AF software, you cannot use UNSELECT in FSEDIT or FSVIEW programs.

In order for an extended table to be considered a selection list, you must specify a number of selections in the SETROW routine.

Example

Force row 5 to be deselected:

```
rc=unselect(5);
```

UPDATE

Writes values from the Data Set Data Vector (DDV) to the current observation in a SAS data set

See Also:
APPEND
FETCH
FETCHOBS
GETVARC
GETVARN
PUTVARC
PUTVARN
SET

sysrc=**UPDATE**(*data-set-id*);

Where...	Is type...	And represents...

sysrc	N	Whether the operation was successful:
		  0 if successful
		  ≠ 0 if not successful

data-set-id	N	The identifier assigned when the data set was opened. If *data-set-id* is invalid, the program halts execution.

Details

The data set must have been opened in UPDATE mode. The observation to be updated is the current observation. To place values in the DDV, use PUTVARC, PUTVARN, or SET.

Example

Update the current observation in the open SAS data set that has its data set identifier value stored in the variable MYDATAID. If the return code, RC, is nonzero, the system error message is displayed on the message line.

```
rc=update(mydataid);
if rc then _msg_=sysmsg();
```

VALUE

Contains the value of a FRAME entry object

Character or Numeric System Instance Variable

See Also:
SELF
METHOD

Details

VALUE is a System Instance Variable. It is provided automatically by the FRAME entry in SAS/AF, but the SCL compiler does not automatically create a space for it in the SCL data vector. Because of this, you get a warning when you compile your FRAME or SCL entry if you have a reference to _VALUE_. See _FRAME_ for more details on how to prevent the warning.

If the FRAME entry object has a character value, you must declare _VALUE_ as a character variable using the LENGTH statement.

Numeric FRAME entry objects and character FRAME entry objects cannot share the same methods if the methods use _VALUE_ because _VALUE_ cannot be declared as both a numeric and character variable in the same SCL entry. Doing so results in one of the following execution errors:

```
ERROR: Expecting string ($), received SCL number (symbol '_VALUE_').
ERROR: Expecting number (#), received SCL string (symbol '_VALUE_').
```

VALUE only has a valid value when a FRAME or FRAME entry object method is running.

Example

Suppose a FRAME entry contains two text entry objects, OBJ1 and OBJ2. OBJ1 is subclassed and its _SELECT_ method is defined as follows:

```
length _value_ text $20;

SELECT:
   method;
       call send( _frame_, '_get_widget_', 'obj2', obj2 );
       call send( obj2, '_get_text_', text );
       _value_ = text;
endmethod;
```

When OBJ1 is modified, the _SELECT_ method queries the object identifier for OBJ2 and retrieves its value. It then assigns that value to OBJ1 by assigning TEXT to _VALUE_.

VARFMT

Returns the format assigned to a SAS data set variable

See Also:
VARINFMT
VARNUM

format=**VARFMT**(*data-set-id*,*var-num*);

Where...	Is type...	And represents...
format	C	The format assigned to the specified variable.
data-set-id	N	The identifier assigned when the data set was opened. If *data-set-id* is invalid, the program halts execution.
var-num	N	The number of the variable's position in the SAS data set. This number is next to the variable in the list produced by the CONTENTS procedure. The VARNUM function returns this number.

Details

If no format has been assigned to the variable, a blank string is returned.

Example

Obtain the format of the variable NAME in the SAS data set MYDATA:

```
length fmt $ 12;
dsid=open('mydata','i');
if dsid then
   do;
      fmt=varfmt(dsid,varnum(dsid,'name'));
      rc=close(dsid);
   end;
```

VARINFMT

Returns the informat assigned to a SAS data set variable

informat=**VARINFMT**(*data-set-id*,*var-num*);

See Also:
VARFMT
VARNUM

Where...	Is type...	And represents...
informat	C	The informat assigned to the variable.
data-set-id	N	The identifier assigned when the data set was opened. If *data-set-id* is invalid, the program halts execution.
var-num	N	The number of the variable in the SAS data set. This is the number next to the variable when the CONTENTS procedure is used to list the variables in the SAS data set. The VARNUM function returns this number.

Details

If no informat has been assigned to the variable, a blank string is returned.

Example

Obtain the informat of the variable NAME in the SAS data set MYDATA:

```
length infmt $ 12;
dsid=open('mydata','i');
if(dsid) then
   do;
      infmt=varinfmt(dsid,varnum(dsid,'name'));
      rc=close(dsid);
   end;
```

VARLABEL

Returns the label assigned to a SAS data set variable

See Also:
VARNUM

cval=**VARLABEL**(*data-set-id*,*var-num*);

Where...	Is type...	And represents...
cval	C	The label assigned to the specified variable.
data-set-id	N	The identifier assigned when the data set was opened. If *data-set-id* is invalid, the program halts execution.
var-num	N	The number of the variable in the SAS data set. This is the number next to the variable when the CONTENTS procedure is used to list the variables in the SAS data set. The VARNUM function returns this number.

Details

If no label has been assigned to the variable, a blank string is returned.

Example

Obtain the label of the variable NAME in the SAS data set MYDATA:

```
length lab $ 40;
dsid=open('mydata','i');
if dsid then
   do;
      lab=varlabel(dsid,varnum(dsid,'name'));
      rc=close(dsid);
   end;
```

VARLEN

Returns the length of a SAS data set variable

See Also:
VARNUM

length=**VARLEN**(*data-set-id,var-num*);

Where...	Is type...	And represents...
length	N	The length of the variable.
data-set-id	N	The identifier assigned when the data set was opened. If *data-set-id* is invalid, the program halts execution.
var-num	N	The number of the variable in the SAS data set. This is the number next to the variable when the CONTENTS procedure is used to list the variables in the SAS data set. The VARNUM function returns this number.

Example

Obtain the length of the variable ADDRESS in the SAS data set MYDATA:

```
dsid=open('mydata','i');
if dsid then
   do;
      namelen=varlen(dsid,varnum(dsid,'address'));
      rc=close(dsid);
   end;
```

VARLEVEL

Reports the unique values of a SAS data set variable

See Also:
LVARLEVEL
VARNAME
VARSTAT

rc=**VARLEVEL**(*array-name,n-level,data-set-id,var-name*);

Where...	Is type...	And represents...
rc	N	Whether the operation was successful: 0 if successful $\neq 0$ if not successful.
array-name	C	The array that will contain the unique variable values. This should be a character array with element size large enough to hold the longest value. Values are assigned to array items by the function.
n-level	N	The name of the variable in which the function stores the number of unique values, or levels. This variable must be initialized to a nonmissing value before its value is set by the VARLEVEL function.
data-set-id	N	The identifier assigned when the data set was opened. If *data-set-id* is invalid, the program halts execution.
var-name	C	The variable for which unique values are to be returned.

Details

VARLEVEL fills the array *array-name* with the unique values of the SAS data set variable *var-name*.

This function returns values in the specified array. It also returns the total number of unique values in the *n-level* argument. Therefore, the second argument to this function cannot be a literal. If the number of unique values found exceeds the dimension of the array, the function returns only DIM(*array-name*) levels. That is, VARLEVEL requires the static allocation of an array big enough to hold all the unique values.

LVARLEVEL provides the same functionality, but it stores the unique values in an SCL list rather than an array. Because an SCL list can grow dynamically, you should consider using it rather than VARLEVEL.

Example

Get the unique formatted values for the data set variable X. Use ASORT to sort those values in ascending order. If NLEVELS is greater than 25, only the first 25 values are written to the array.

```
array values {25} $ 20;
dsid=open('mylib.data','i');
nlevels=0;
rc=varlevel(values,nlevels,dsid,'x');
rc=asort(values);
do i=1 to dim(values);
   put values(i);
end;
```

VARLIST

Displays a selection list window of the variables in a SAS data set and returns the user's selections

See Also:
DATALISTC
DATALISTN
LISTC
LISTN
SHOWLIST

selections=**VARLIST**(*data-set-id,var-type<,num-sel<,message<,autoclose <,sel-order<,exclude<,select >>>>>>*);

Where...	Is type...	And represents...
selections	C	One or more user selections from the list, or blank if no selection is made. Multiple selections are separated by blanks.
data-set-id	N	The identifier assigned when the data set was opened. If *data-set-id* is invalid, the program halts execution.
var-type	C	The type of the variable: '**C**' lists character variables. '**N**' lists numeric variables. '**A**' lists all variables. (Default)
num-sel	N	The maximum number of items a user can select from the list. To display the list for information purposes only (no selections allowed), specify **0**. To specify an unlimited number of selections, use a value larger than the number of available selections such as 9999. The default is 1.
message	C	Text for a message displayed above the selection list. The default message tells users to make up to the number of selections specified in *num-sel*.
autoclose	C	Whether the selection list window closes automatically after a user makes a selection when only one choice is allowed: '**Y**' for the window to close automatically. (Default) '**N**' for the window to close only when the user explicitly closes it. This option is ignored when *num-sel* is not 1. However, use ' ' as a placeholder for this argument.
sel-order	C	Whether selections are moved in the selection list window: '**Y**' moves selected items to the top of the list. '**N**' does not move selected items to the top of the list. (Default)
exclude	C	The variables to be excluded from the selection list. Separate multiple variables by at least one blank.
select	C	The variables to be selected for the selection list. Separate multiple variables by at least one blank.

Details

VARLIST uses the following steps for each variable in the data set to determine the variables to display:

□ If one or more variable names are specified in the *select* argument, the function includes those variables in the selection list. Variables not in the *select* argument list do not appear in the selection list.

□ If one or more variable names are specified in the *exclude* argument, the function excludes those variables from the selection list.

□ If a value is specified for the *var-type* argument, the function excludes all variables that are not of the specified type.

You can provide a default or initial selected value in the list by providing a value for the *selections* variable prior to calling VARLIST. If *selections* contains valid variable names when the function is invoked, those names are automatically designated as selected when the selection list is displayed.

If a user closes the selection list window without making a selection, VARLIST returns a blank value unless there was an initial value for the *selections* variable before VARLIST was called.

The values for all selections can be returned in the current result list, if one is available. The current result list is a special SCL list that is automatically filled with the values selected from a selection list. To create a current result list, use the MAKELIST function to create it and the CURLIST function to designate it as the current result list. The current result list must exist before you call the VARLIST function. You can use GETITEMC to retrieve these selections.

Examples

Display all variables and allow the user to select only one:

```
select=varlist(dsid,'a',1);
```

This statement displays only character variables, allows two selections, uses a custom message, moves the selections to the top of the list when they are selected, and excludes the variables NAME and ADDRESS:

```
select=varlist(dsid,'c',2,'Choose a variable','','y','name address');
```

Display a selection list window containing the character variables from an open SAS data set, excluding the variables NAME and ADDRESS. Users can make two selections. The selected variable names are retrieved from the current result list. LISTLEN returns the number of selections because there is only one element in the list for each selection made.

```
listid=makelist();
rc=curlist(listid);
select=varlist(dsid,'c',2,'Choose a variable','','y',
               'name address');
n=listlen(listid);
do i=1 to n;
   varname=getitemc(listid,i);
   put varname=;
end;
```

VARNAME

Returns the name of a SAS data set variable

See Also:
VARNUM

var-name=**VARNAME**(*data-set-id,var-num*);

Where...	Is type...	And represents...
var-name	C	The variable's name.
data-set-id	N	The identifier assigned when the data set was opened. If *data-set-id* is invalid, the program halts execution.
var-num	N	The number of the variable in the SAS data set. This is the number next to the variable when the CONTENTS procedure is used to list the variables in the SAS data set. VARNUM returns this number.

Example

Copy the names of the first five variables in the SAS data set CITY into an SCL variable. The variable names are separated by blanks.

```
length varlist $ 80;

dsid=open('city','i');
varlist=' ';
do i=1 to min(5,attrn(dsid,'nvars'));
   j=9*(i-1)+1;
   substr(varlist,j,8)=varname(dsid,i);
end;
put varlist=;
```

VARNUM

Returns the number of a SAS data set variable

See Also:
VARNAME

var-num=**VARNUM**(*data-set-id*,*var-name*);

Where...	Is type...	And represents...
var-num	N	The position number of the variable in the SAS data set variable or 0 if the variable is not in the SAS data set.
data-set-id	N	The identifier assigned when the data set was opened. If *data-set-id* is invalid, the program halts execution.
var-name	C	The variable's name.

Details

VARNUM returns the variable number for a SAS data set variable. This is the same variable number that is next to the variable in the CONTENTS window.

Example

Obtain the number of a variable in the SAS data set CITY given the name of the variable:

```
dsid=open('city','i');
citynum=varnum(dsid,'cityname');
rc=fetch(dsid);
name=getvarc(dsid,citynum);
```

VARSTAT

Calculates simple statistics for SAS data set variables

See also:
LVARLEVEL
VARLEVEL

rc=**VARSTAT**(*data-set-id,varlist-1,statistics,varlist-2*);

Where...	Is type...	And represents...
rc	N	Whether the operation was successful: 0 if successful $\neq$ 0 if not successful.
data-set-id	N	The identifier assigned when the data set was opened. If *data-set-id* is invalid, the program halts execution.
varlist-1	C	One or more numeric variables for which to create the statistics.
statistics	C	One or more statistics, separated by blanks, from Table 20.17. For more information on these statistics, see the *SAS/STAT User's Guide, Version 6, Fourth Edition.*
varlist-2	C	One or more output variables to contain the values produced by the specified statistics. The number of output variables must equal the number of variables in *varlist-1* multiplied by the number of *statistics*.

Table 20.17
Statistics

Statistic	Description
CSS	sum of squares of a variable's values, corrected for the mean
CV	coefficient of variation of a variable's values
KURTOSIS	kurtosis of a variable's values
MAX	largest value for a variable
MEAN	mean of a nonmissing variable's values
MEDIAN	median value for a variable
MIN	smallest value for a variable
MODE	value with the most observations for a variable
N	number of observations on which calculations are based
NMISS	number of observations with missing values
NUNIQUE	number of observations having a unique value for a variable
RANGE	range of values for a variable
SKEWNESS	skewness of a variable's values
STD	standard deviation of a variable's values
STDERR	standard error of the mean
SUM	sum of nonmissing variable values

Statistic	Description
USS	uncorrected sum of squares for a variable
VAR	variance of a variable's values

Details

If more than one input variable is specified with more than one statistic, each statistic is calculated on all variables before the next statistic is calculated.

Example

Calculate the maximum, mean, and minimum values for the variables I and X from the data set MY.NUMBERS:

```
dsname='my.numbers';
length imax xmax imean xmean xmin imin 8;
   /* declare the results as numeric */
varname='i x';
numberid=open(dsname);
if (numberid=0) then
   do;
       _msg_='Cannot open '||dsname;
       return;
   end;
statcode=varstat(numberid,varname,'max mean min',
                    imax,xmax,imean,xmean,imin,xmin);
put 'Variable X';
put xmax= xmean= xmin=;
put 'Variable I';
put imax= imean= imin=;
rc=close(numberid);
return;
```

VARTYPE

Returns the data type of a SAS data set variable

See Also:
MODVAR
VARNUM

type=**VARTYPE**(*data-set-id,var-num*);

Where...	Is type...	And represents...
type	C	The variable's type : C for a character variable N for a numeric variable.
data-set-id	N	The identifier assigned when the data set was opened. If *data-set-id* is invalid, the program halts execution.
var-num	N	The position number of the variable in the SAS data set. This is the number next to the variable when the CONTENTS procedure is used to list the variables in the SAS data set. VARNUM returns this number.

Example

Place the first five numeric variables of the SAS data set MYDATA into an SCL variable:

```
length varlist $ 44;
dsid=open('mydata','i');
varlist=' ';
j=0;
do i=1 to nvar(dsid) while (j<5);
   if (vartype(dsid,i)='N') then
      do;
         varlist=varlist||' '||varname(dsid,i) ;
         j+1 ;
      end;
end;
rc=close(dsid);
```

WAIT

Suspends execution of the next program statement

Release 6.11 Feature

CALL WAIT(*seconds*);

Where...	Is type...	And represents...
seconds	N	The number of seconds before continuing execution.

Details

You can also use WAIT to allow the screen to refresh before performing another task.

Example

Wait for 4.5 seconds between the times stored in TIME1 and TIME2, and then display those values in the Message or Log window:

```
time1 = datatime();
call wait( 4.5 );
time2 = datetime();
put time1= time2=;
```

Take the last three digits before and after the decimal point from the two times: TIME1=872.229 and TIME2=876.749. Subtracting TIME2 from TIME1 results in 4.52 seconds total wait time.

```
time1=1069234872.22999 time2=1069234876.74999
```

WDEF

Resizes the active window

See Also:
WINFO
WREGION

CALL WDEF(*start-row,start-col,num-rows,num-cols*);

Where...	Is type...	And represents...
start-row	N	The starting row for the window.
start-col	N	The starting column for the window.
num-rows	N	The number of rows for the window.
num-cols	N	The number of columns for the window.

Details

The active window is redefined and displayed in the area specified by WDEF. The WDEF routine performs the same function as the WDEF display manager command. See *SAS Language: Reference* for more information on the WDEF display manager command.

For windows that are not of type STANDARD, you must call WDEF before the window is displayed.

WDEF is frequently used to define a smaller size for a window that will display along with a legend window.

Example

Use WDEF to resize the current window to occupy the bottom half of the window before calling another program, which is sized to display in the top half of the window. Then, return the window back to its original size.

```
call wdef(13,1,12,80);
call wregion(1,1,11,80);
call display('tophalf.program');
call wdef(1,1,24,80);
```

WHERE

Applies a WHERE clause to a SAS data set

See Also:
OPEN
FETCH
FETCHOBS
SETKEY

sysrc=**WHERE**(*data-set-id*<,*clause-1*<, . . . ,*clause-5*>>);

Where...	Is type...	And represents...

sysrc	N	Whether the operation was successful:
		   0 if successful
		
		   $\neq$ 0 if not successful.

data-set-id	N	The identifier assigned when the data set was opened. If *data-set-id* is invalid, the program halts execution.
clause-1	C	The condition for the search expressed as a WHERE clause without the keyword WHERE. The arguments *clause-1*, *clause-2*, *clause-3*, *clause-4*, and *clause-5* are treated as multiple lines of the WHERE clause. If the clause starts with the keyword ALSO, the new WHERE clause is considered to be a subclause of the current WHERE clause. Specifying no clauses undoes all current temporary WHERE clauses that have been applied to the SAS data set.
clause-2	C	Continuation of the WHERE clause.
clause-3	C	Continuation of the WHERE clause.
clause-4	C	Continuation of the WHERE clause.
clause-5	C	Continuation of the WHERE clause.

Details

The WHERE function may take advantage of indexing. The syntax of the WHERE clause is the same as for the WHERE statement in base SAS software. Any WHERE clause applied by the WHERE function is only temporary and is considered to be a subclause of any WHERE clause issued at open time. To apply a permanent WHERE clause to a SAS data set, use the WHERE= data set option following the data set name in OPEN.

The WHERE clause subsets the observations to which you have access. You must then issue a function such as FETCH or FETCHOBS to read observations from the subset. When a WHERE clause is active, FETCHOBS fetches the specified observation by counting only observations that meet the WHERE condition.

To create views with more complicated WHERE clauses, use the SQL procedure or the SUBMIT CONTINUE SQL statement.

To remove only the last WHERE condition, use

```
rc=WHERE(dsid,'undo');
```

To remove all WHERE conditions, use

```
rc=WHERE(dsid);
```

or

```
rc=WHERE(dsid,'clear');
```

Examples

Apply a WHERE clause to the SAS data set MYDATA, which subsets the data set into only those observations where the variable X is equal to 1 and the variable Z is less than 0:

```
dsid=open('mydata','i');
rc=where(dsid,'x=1','and z<0');
```

Instead of using one WHERE clause, you can separate the WHERE clause into two statements. The following statements are equivalent to the first example:

```
dsid=open('mydata','i');
rc=where(dsid,'x=1');
   more SCL statements
rc=where(dsid,'also z<0');
```

You can pass values from SCL variables to the WHERE clause. Subset the data set referenced by DSID based on the value entered for the numeric variable SCRNUM:

```
rc=where(dsid,'num= '||put(scrnum,5.));
```

To subset based on a character value, you can use the quote function to return the quoted value. (Otherwise, you must use double quotation marks around the WHERE condition since the quoted value itself must be enclosed in quotation marks.) Subset the data set referenced by DSID based on the value entered for the character variable SCRNAME and use the quote function to return the quoted value:

```
rc=where(dsid,'name= '||quote(scrname));
```

Combine the previous two WHERE conditions into one statement:

```
rc=where(dsid,'num= '||put(scrnum,5.)||' and name= '||quote(scrname));
```

You can use the ATTRN function with the ANY argument to check to see if any observations meet your WHERE condition and then conditionally execute SCL code. Apply a WHERE clause to the SAS data set MYDATA, which subsets the data set into only those observations where the variable X is equal to 1. Use ATTRN with ANY before fetching the first observation of the subset.

```
dsid=open('mydata', 'i');
rc=where(dsid,'x=1');
if attrn(dsid,'any')>0 then
   rc=fetch(dsid);
```

WINFO

Returns information about the current window

See Also:
WDEF
WREGION

$rc=$**WINFO**($info\text{-}item<,aux\text{-}info>$);

Where...	Is type...	And represents...
rc	N	Either the position of a window element or the status of a window characteristic or operation.
info-item	C	A characteristic of the window or an action, listed in Table 20.18.
aux-info	N	An additional argument required by the *info-item* actions listed: *pane-number*, for **'PANECOL'** and **'PANEROW'** The number of the pane to be queried. For example, in an extended table the nonscrollable section is pane 1 and the scrollable portion is pane 2. *item-id*, for **'PMENUGRAY'** The item identifier you specified with the ID= option for the ITEM statement in PROC PMENU when you built the menu. Use the negative of the ID number to gray a selection and the positive ID number to ungray a selection. *item-id*, for **'PMENUSTATE'** The item identifier you specified with the ID= option for the ITEM statement in PROC PMENU when you built the menu. Use the negative of the ID number to turn off the check mark or radio button for the selection and the positive ID number to turn on the check mark or radio button. Whether the menu selection gets a check mark or radio button depends on the STATE= option when the menu was built. *flag*, for **'POPUP'**, which can have the value: 0 to disable pop-up events. 1 to enable pop-up events.

Table 20.18   *Values for info-item*

Value	Returns
'BACKCOLOR'	**1** if the device supports background colors.
'BATCH'	**1** if the application is running in batch mode.
'COMMAND'	**1** if the window has a command line.
'CURSCREEN'	The number of the SCREEN or FRAME entry where the cursor is situated.
'CURSORCOL'	The column number of the cursor position.

Value	Returns
'CURSORROW'	The row number of the cursor position.
'GRAPHICS'	**1** if the user's output device supports graphics.
'ICON'	The number of Institute-supplied icons available under the user's host operating system. Refer to host documentation for information on whether the SAS System supports icons under your host operating system.
'LOGON'	**1** if a logon was specified when the SAS/AF application was invoked.
'MAXCOL'	The maximum number of columns to which the window can grow excluding the command and border areas.
'MAXROW'	The maximum number of rows to which the window can grow excluding the command and border areas.
'MONO'	**1** if the device is monochrome.
'NSCREEN'	The windows currently open in an application:
	FSEDIT applications return the number of screens defined for the current FSEDIT window.
	FSVIEW applications return **4** to indicate the four parts of the FSVIEW window: the column title area, the row number or ID column area, the data area, and the area above the column titles.
	SAS/AF applications return **1** or **2** if you used ∧ ∧ ∧ or ¬ ¬ ¬ to divide the entry's window into two or more frames.
'NUMCOLS'	The current number of columns in the window.
'NUMROWS'	The current number of rows in the window.
'NUMXINCH'	The number of pixels per horizontal inch of the window (valid only for FRAME entries).
'NUMYINCH'	The number of pixels per vertical inch of the window (valid only for FRAME entries).
'NUMXPIXEL'	The window width in pixels (valid only for FRAME entries).
'NUMYPIXEL'	The window height in pixels (valid only for FRAME entries).
'PANECCOL'	The column position of the cursor relative to the pane of the window in which it resides. Use *aux-info* to specify the pane.
'PANECROW'	The row position of the cursor relative to the pane of the window in which it resides. Use *aux-info* to specify the pane.
'PANECOL'	The number of columns in a specified pane. Use *aux-info* to specify the pane.
'PANEROW'	The number of rows in a specified pane. Use *aux-info* to specify the pane.
'PMENU'	**1** if a PMENU entry has been specified for this program regardless of whether the PMENU facility is currently active for the window.
'PMENUGRAY'	**0**, when it grays or ungrays selections in the window's pull-down menus. Use *aux-info* to specify which selection to gray or ungray.

. . . .

Release 6.11

'PMENUSTATE'	**0**, when it enables or disables the state of a selection in the window's pull-down menus. Use *aux-info* to specify the state.

. . . .

'POPUP'	**0**, when it enables or disables pop-up events in the window. Use the *aux-info* argument to specify whether events are to be enabled or disabled.

Value	Returns
`'STARTCOL'`	The current column on which the window starts.
`'STARTROW'`	The current row on which the window starts.
`'UICON'`	The number of user-defined icons available under the user's host operating system.

. . . .

Release 6.11

`'XPIXCELL'`	The width (in pixels) of the DM (display manager) font.

. . . .

`'XPIXEL'`	The horizontal location (in pixels) of the most recent mouse event.

. . . .

Release 6.11

`'YPIXCELL'`	The height (in pixels) of the DM (display manager) font.

. . . .

`'YPIXEL'`	The vertical location (in pixels) of the most recent mouse event.

Example

Store the current size of the window, and then resize it back to its original size:

```
sr=winfo('startrow');
sc=winfo('startcol');
nr=winfo('numrows');
nc=winfo('numcols');
call wdef(13,1,12,80);
call display('tophalf');
call wdef(sr,sc,nr,nc);
```

WNAME

Specifies a name for the active window

See Also:
WDEF
WINFO
WREGION

CALL WNAME(*window-name*);

Where...	Is type...	And represents...
window-name	C	Up to 80 characters for the window's name.

Example

Use WNAME to change the window name to "TimeData Application":

```
call wname('TimeData Application');
```

WORD

Returns a word from the command on the command line

See Also:
CONTROL
NEXTCMD
NEXTWORD

word-text=**WORD**(*word-pos*<,*case*>);

Where...	Is type...	And represents...
word-text	C	The text of the word.
word-pos	N	The position of the word to be retrieved from the command line. Specify either 1, 2, or 3 for the first, second, or third word.
case	C	The type of case conversion to be performed: 'L' converts the word to all lowercase characters 'U' converts the word to all uppercase characters. By default the SAS System leaves all commands in the case in which they are entered.

Details

WORD returns the first, second, or third word of the command issued on the command line. A *word* is the text from the current position up to the end of a leading number, or the next blank or semicolon.

To support custom commands in your application, you must use a CONTROL statement with either the ENTER, ALWAYS, or ALLCMDS option specified. When one of these options is specified on the CONTROL statement and multiple commands are specified on the command line, separated by semicolons, the MAIN section is executed for each command specified on the command line. MAIN is executed only once unless multiple commands separated by semicolons are entered.

With CONTROL ALWAYS specified, words entered on the command line that are not valid SAS commands are not flagged in error. Refer to the discussion in this chapter on the CONTROL statement for specific benefits to each CONTROL statement option before deciding which is best for your application.

WORD cannot capture display manager global commands because the SCL program is not executed when a display manager command is issued.

Example 1

Suppose a user types the command **AXX BXX CXX DXX** on the command line. Use WORD to return the value of the command:

```
word1=word(1);
word2=word(2);
word3=word(3);
```

In this example, the values returned are:

```
word1 is AXX
word2 is BXX
word3 is CXX.
```

To retrieve more than three words, use NEXTWORD.

Example 2

Suppose a user types the command **123ABC** on the command line. Use WORD to return the value of the command:

```
word1=word(1);
word2=word(2);
```

In this example, the values returned are:

```
word1 is 123
word2 is ABC
```

WORDTYPE

Identifies the type for a word on the command line

Release 6.11 Feature

See Also
CONTROL
WORD

type=**WORDTYPE**(*word-pos*);

Where...	Is type...	And represents...
type	C	One of the following word types:
		DATE — when a word is a SAS date constant such as 25AUG94.
		DATETIME — when a word is a SAS datetime constant such as 25AUG94:08:15:39.30.
		EOD — end of command. There are no more words on the command line.
		INTEGER — when a word is an integer such as 6.
		NAME — when a word is a SAS name such as data.
		NUMBER — when a word is a numeric constant that contains a decimal point '.', or a scientific notation 'E', for example, 6.5.
		SEMI — when a word is a semicolon.
		SPECIAL — when a word is a special operator such as '=', ' + ', and so on.
		STRING — when a word is a character string, for example mydata.
		TIME — when a word is a SAS time constant such as 08:16:30.
		UNKNOWN — the word type is unknown to the SAS tokenizer.
word-pos	N	The position of the word to be retrieved from the command line. Specify either 1, 2, or 3 for the first, second, or third word.

Details

WORDTYPE returns the type of the first, second, or third word currently on the command line. A word is the text at the current position and up to the end of a leading number or the next blank or semicolon. You can use this function with WORD.

To support custom commands in your application, you must use a CONTROL statement with either the ENTER, ALWAYS, or ALLCMDS option specified. With CONTROL ALWAYS specified, words entered on the command line that are not valid SAS commands are not flagged in error. Refer to the discussion of the CONTROL statement in this chapter for specific benefits to each CONTROL statement option before deciding which is best for your application.

Example

Return the type of the three words currently on the command line:

```
w1=word(1); w1type=wordtype(1); put w1= w1type=;
w2=word(2); w2type=wordtype(2); put w2= w2type=;
w3=word(3); w3type=wordtype(3); put w3= w3type=;
```

If a user types **ABC = 3** on the command line, this program produces the following output:

```
W1=ABC W1TYPE=NAME
W2== W2TYPE=SPECIAL
W3=3 W3TYPE=INTEGER
```

WOUTPUT

Manipulates the display manager OUTPUT window

*sysrc=***WOUTPUT**(*action<,argument-1<,. . .,argument-3>>*);

Where...	Is type...	And represents...
sysrc	N	Whether the operation was successful: 　0　if successful 　$\neq 0$　if not successful.
action	C	An action to perform, from Table 20.19.
argument-1,. . ., argument-3	C	Additional arguments for the actions listed below.

Table 20.19　*Actions for the WOUTPUT Function*

Action	Description
'CLEAR'	clears the OUTPUT window. There are no additional arguments for this action.
'DROPNOTE'	clears the note and causes it to use its default behavior to write only the last output.
'FILE'	writes the current contents of the OUTPUT window to an external file. This action allows two additional arguments: 　*argument-1*　Fileref for the external file to which the window contents are to be written. This argument is required. 　*argument-2*　Append mode. By default, each new output replaces any current contents of the external file. Specify the value 'A' to append the output to the external file instead.
'NOTE'	marks to get the next created output. The NOTE action has a direct effect on the FILE, PRINT and SAVE actions. When the output is written via WOUTPUT, the pointer is reset to the end of the current output.
'POPOFF'	turns off the AUTOPOP option of the OUTPUT window.
'POPON'	turns on the AUTOPOP option of the OUTPUT window.
'PRINT'	prints the current contents of the OUTPUT window. This action allows three additional arguments, all of which are optional:

Action	Description	
	argument-1	Name of a form to control printing. Use *name*.FORM or simply *name* to specify a form in the current catalog. Use *libref.catalog.name*.FORM or *libref.catalog.name* to specify a form in a different catalog. The default form is the one specified in the FORMNAME option.
	argument-2	Fileref for a print file. If this argument is blank or if it is not specified, the printout is sent to the default system printer.
	argument-3	Append mode. Use the value 'A' to append the output to the current contents of the print file. If this argument is blank or if it is not specified, each new output replaces the previous contents of the print file.
'SAVE'		saves the current contents of the OUTPUT window in a catalog entry of type SOURCE, LOG, or OUTPUT. This action allows three additional arguments:
	argument-1	Name of the entry in which the window contents are saved. The name can be a one- or three-level name. A one-level name saves the entry in SASUSER.PROFILE*name*.OUTPUT. A three-level name saves the entry in *libref.catalog.name*.OUTPUT. You can also use the four-level name of the form *libref.catalog.entry.type*, where *type* is SOURCE, LOG, or OUTPUT. This argument is required.
	argument-2	Description of up to 40 characters.
	argument-3	Append mode. Specify the value 'A' to append the output to the current contents of the entry. By default, each new output replaces the previous contents of the entry.

Details

The list of options varies by the action specified.

Example

Print the OUTPUT window and append it to the file to which the fileref EXTERN has previously been assigned. Use the form specified in a previous FORMNAME option:

```
rc=woutput('print','','extern','a');
```

WREGION

Defines the boundaries for the next window that displays

See Also:
WDEF
WINFO

CALL WREGION(*start-row,start-col,num-rows,num-cols,options*);

Where...	Is type...	And represents...
start-row	N	The starting row for the next window.
start-col	N	The starting column for the next window.
num-rows	N	The number of rows for the next window.
num-cols	N	The number of columns for the next window.
options	C	One or more window attributes that the window's size needs to accommodate:

	`' '`	no command line, command menu, or scroll bars
	`'CMDLINE'`	a command area
	`'HSBAR'`	a horizontal scroll bar
	`'INNERSIZE'`	interior size is determined by the values of *num-rows* and *num-cols*
	`'PMENU'`	a command menu
	`'VSBAR'`	a vertical scroll bar

Details

The size of the next window depends on whether it has a command area, a pmenu, and scroll bars. (The command area includes the message line.) By default, WREGION assumes that the next window will have all of these attributes. You can use *options* to change this assumption. Note that *options* does not cause the next window to have these attributes but rather it helps WREGION determine the correct size.

'INNERSIZE' specifies that the values of *num-rows* and *num-cols* will control the interior size of the window. Normally, the *num-rows* and *num-cols* control the exterior size of the window (including the borders).

WREGION does not affect the size of subsequent FSEDIT windows opened using CALL FSEDIT. The function cannot resize windows when a SAS/AF or FSEDIT application is called with the NOBORDER option.

Examples

Specify a WREGION for the LEGEND window. Notice the *options* argument to WREGION is a null string designating that none of the display options are used in the LEGEND window. The window size is four rows long: two lines of text and the top and bottom borders.

```
call wregion(1,1,4,80,'');
call putlegend(1,'This is line 1 of the legend','yellow','none');
call putlegend(2,'This is line 2 of the legend','yellow','none');
call legend('mylegend window name','','white','reverse');
```

Execute a WREGION function and invoke a PROGRAM entry. The application window for the entry has a command line. However, because scrolling is not necessary, the HBAR and VBAR options are not specified. Only the CMDLINE option is specified.

```
call wregion(1,1,20,80,'cmdline');
call display('another.program',a,b,c);
```

APPENDIX **Icon Appendix**

This appendix shows the icons that are provided with release 6.10 of SAS software.
A star (*) denotes icons that are available in releases 6.09 and later.

1 KEYS	2 HELP	3 LOG	4 OUTPUT	5 PROGEDIT	6 LIBNAME
7 DIR	8 VARIABLE	9 FILENAME	10 NOTEPAD	11 TITLES	12 FOOTNOTE
13 OPTION	14 SETINIT	16 GRAPH	17 AF	18 CATALOG	23 FSEDIT
24 FSBROWSE	25 FSVIEW	26 FSLIST	27 FSLETTER	28 APPTMNT	29 SYMBOL
30 PATTERN	31 INFOASST	32 ACCESS	33 DCALC	34 SQL	35 AXIS
36 LEGEND	37 QUERY	39 SITEINFO	40 FSFORM	46 GRAPH1	47 GRAPH2

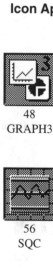

48
GRAPH3

49
GRAPH4

50
LABWIN

52
TRADRECV

54
INSIGHT

55
DESIGNOF

56
SQC

57
PRJMGM

58
FORECAS

59
EIS

60
SASLOGO

62
MANAGER

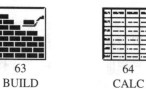
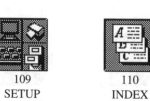

63
BUILD

64
CALC

* 73
IMAGE

* 74
IMAGEDIT

101
BROWSE

102
TUTOR1

103
DATAMGMT

104
WRITING

105
DATAANAL

106
PLANTOOL

107
EIS

108
RESULTS

109
SETUP

110
INDEX

111
EXIT

112
OVERVIEW

113
PRINCIPL

114
DIRECTIO

115
CUSTOMIZ

116
GOBACK

117
ACTIVE

118
EDIT

119
CREATE

120
DBMSACCS

121
COMBINE

122
SORT

123
UTILITY

124
LISTING

125
TABLES

126
COUNTS

127
DESNRPRT

128
BARCHRTS

129
PIECHRTS

130
PLOTS

131
MAPS

132
ELEMTRY

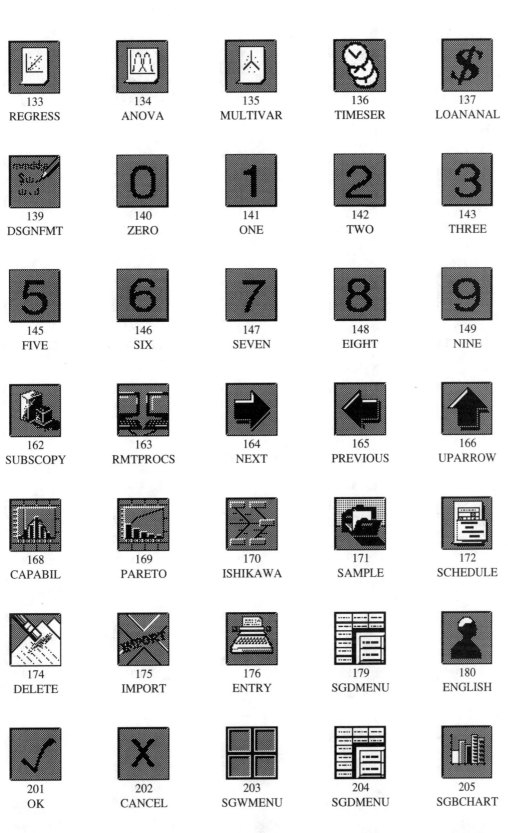

133 REGRESS	134 ANOVA	135 MULTIVAR	136 TIMESER	137 LOANANAL	138 TRANSPOS
139 DSGNFMT	140 ZERO	141 ONE	142 TWO	143 THREE	144 FOUR
145 FIVE	146 SIX	147 SEVEN	148 EIGHT	149 NINE	* 161 GAMES
162 SUBSCOPY	163 RMTPROCS	164 NEXT	165 PREVIOUS	166 UPARROW	167 DNARROW
168 CAPABIL	169 PARETO	170 ISHIKAWA	171 SAMPLE	172 SCHEDULE	173 COPY
174 DELETE	175 IMPORT	176 ENTRY	179 SGDMENU	180 ENGLISH	181 DEFINE
201 OK	202 CANCEL	203 SGWMENU	204 SGDMENU	205 SGBCHART	206 SGSPLOT
207 SGRPLOT	208 SGDISTRB	209 SGFIT	210 SGSUMRY	211 SGTABLE	260 TPTEXT

262 TPSELECT	264 TPFOCUS	266 TPCOPY	267 TPLINE	268 TPMOVE	269 TPRECTAN
270 TPHELP	271 TPNOJOIN	272 TPLNJOIN	273 TPSPJOIN	274 TPLNREGR	275 TPVBAR
276 TPSTBAR	277 TPCIRCLE	278 TPINCR	279 TPDECR	280 TPPOLYGN	281 TPPOLYLN
301 DESKTOP	302 SAMPSYS	303 DEVELOP	304 CRTLABEL	305 APPS	306 BUILDEIS
307 ADDOBJ	308 METABASE	309 PUBAPPS	310 PRVAPPS	311 CRTAPPS	312 RUNAPPS
313 REGSTR	314 ATTRIB	401 CUSTMENU	402 PERCENT	403 SASPGM	404 DEVSETUP
405 BATSETUP	406 BASICINF	407 ADEVENTS	408 PATGRP	409 XPATGRP	410 USERS
411 STUDY	412 ADTABLES	441 REPORTS	442 RATEFUNC	443 START	444 STOP

445
PROCESS

446
SHOW

447
DISKLIST

448
FILELIST

449
VIEWREPT

450
SERVCMD

451
SHOWSERV

452
OPTCHNG

453
OPTSHOW

454
OPTRSET

455
OPTSAVE

456
SPAWN

457
TRACE

458
CONVERT1

459
CONVERT2

460
PDB

998
SASICON

999
SPELL

1001
MACROWIN

1002
PROC

1003
RMTPROCS

1004
PHCLINIC

1010
SASLOGO

1011
SASBUSY

1012
INSTALL

1013
POINTER1

1014
POINTER2

Glossary

argument list
in Screen Control Language, the values that are passed to a routine for processing. These values can be any SCL expressions, such as variable names, numeric or character literals, or computed values.

array
in the SAS language, a group of variables of the same type available for processing under a single name.

array name
a name selected to identify a group of variables or temporary data elements. It must be a valid SAS name that is not the name of a variable in the same DATA step or SCL program. See also array.

array reference
a reference to the element to be processed in an array. See also array.

assignment statement
a DATA step statement that evaluates an expression and stores the result in a variable. An assignment statement has the following form:
variable = expression;

attention handler
in Screen Control Language, a block of code that executes when a user interrupts the application with the system's BREAK, INTERRUPT, or ATTENTION key. A CONTROL BREAK statement installs an attention handler by specifying a user-defined statement label. The block of code following the statement label is executed when a user interrupts the program.

autoexec file
a file containing SAS statements that are executed automatically when the SAS System is invoked. The autoexec file can be used to specify some SAS system options, as well as librefs and filerefs that are commonly used.

block menu
a menu containing choices represented by blocks generated by the BLOCK statement in Screen Control Language or by block objects in FRAME entries.

branching
in Screen Control Language, the process of altering program execution to an executable statement that does not follow the currently executing executable statement.

breaking
in the Screen Control Language debugger, the process of suspending program execution.

breakpoint
in the Screen Control Language debugger, an executable program statement at which the debugger suspends program execution.

button

in SAS/AF software, a field that is programmed to display as a highlighted button. These fields can be programmed in SAS Screen Control Language (SCL) to execute a command or call another catalog entry, for example. See also Screen Control Language (SCL).

call-by-reference

in Screen Control Language, a type of parameter passing in which the parameters are variable names or array references. Call-by-reference parameter passing allows values to be returned to the calling program. See also call-by-value and parameter passing.

call-by-value

in Screen Control Language, a type of parameter passing in which the parameters are numeric constants, character constants, or expressions. Call-by-value parameter passing does not allow values to be returned to the calling program. See also call-by-reference and parameter passing.

class

in object-oriented methodology, the template or model for an object, which includes data describing the object's characteristics (instance variables) and the operations (methods) that it can perform. See also subclassing.

command list

in Screen Control Language, a sublist (named _CMDLIST_) of the local environment list. The command list contains the components of the DM command used to invoke the current SAS/AF application. See also environment list.

data set

under MVS, a collection of information that the operating system can identify and manage as a unit. Data sets under MVS correspond to files under other systems.

data set data vector (DDV)

in Screen Control Language, a temporary storage area for the variable values from one observation of a data set that was opened by the program. The DDV is empty until an observation is read from the associated data set.

data set identifier (DSID)

in Screen Control Language, a unique, positive number that is returned by the OPEN function to identify a newly opened data set each time the program runs. This number is cleared either by the CLOSE function or when the program terminates.

DATA step

a group of statements in a SAS program that begins with a DATA statement and ends with either a RUN statement, another DATA statement, a PROC statement, the end of the job, or the semicolon that immediately follows instream data lines. The DATA step enables you to read raw data or other SAS data sets and use programming logic to create a SAS data set, write a report, or write to an external file.

declarative statement

a statement that supplies information to the SAS System and that takes effect when the system compiles program statements.

directory

under host operating systems, a unit of storage for files or a unit that catalogs information about files. See the appropriate SAS companion for a technical description of directories on your host operating system.

directory pathname

a pathname that identifies a directory but not a specific file. A directory pathname does not include a filename or a filename extension.

DO group

a sequence of statements headed by a simple DO statement and ended by a corresponding END statement.

environment list

in Screen Control Language, a special SCL list that contains local or global values. Values that are placed in local environment lists are available only in the same SCL application invocation. Values that are placed in global environment lists can be accessed in any SCL application. The lists can contain numeric, character, and sublist items, all of which can be retrieved by specifying their names. Names in environment lists do not have to be valid SAS names. See also global environment list and local environment list.

executable statement

an SCL statement that performs an action at run time. All SCL statements are executable except ARRAY, ENTRY, LENGTH, REPLACE, comments, and statements inside SUBMIT blocks.

execution phase

in Screen Control Language, the stage at which the SCL program is executed, from initialization through termination. During this phase, the program typically validates field values, calculates values for computed variables based on user input, invokes secondary windows, queries and executes user-issued commands, and retrieves values from SAS data sets or from external files.

execution stack

a stack that keeps run-time information of SCL programs being executed with the current program at the top of the stack.

expression

in Screen Control Language, any valid SCL expression. Debugger expressions are the same as SCL expressions except that function calls and the IN operator are not supported. An expression can be simple or compound. A compound expression uses AND or OR (for example, x+y, a>b & b<c, str1=str2).

extended table

a window (in a PROGRAM entry) or a window element (in a FRAME entry) that displays values in a tabular format by repeating a set of fields (or other objects, in a FRAME entry). The number of rows that are displayed is determined by the Screen Control Language program or by an attribute of the extended table object in the FRAME entry. Extended tables are either static or dynamic:

static extended tables   tables whose number of rows is fixed.

dynamic extended tables   tables whose number of rows can vary.

external file

a file maintained by the host operating system that the SAS System can read data from and route output to. External files can contain raw data, SAS programming statements, procedure output, or output created by the PUT statement.

field

a window area in which users enter information and in which your application displays information that changes in response to users' input or as a result of program calculations.

field validation

the process of checking user-entered values either against attributes that have been specified for that field or against conditions that have been specified in the Screen Control Language program.

file data buffer (FDB)

in Screen Control Language, a temporary storage area for one record value of an external file that has been opened by the program. The FDB is empty until a record is read from the associated file. Record values remain in the FDB until another record is read in, until the record is written back to the file, or until the file is closed.

fileref

a name temporarily assigned to an external file or to an aggregate storage location that identifies it to the SAS System. Do not confuse filerefs with librefs. Filerefs are used for external files; librefs are used for SAS data libraries. See also libref.

flow of control

in Screen Control Language, the order in which statements are executed. The flow of control can be altered by conditional statements such as IF/THEN-ELSE, LINK, and RETURN.

function

a routine that can accept arguments, perform an operation, and return a value. For example, the ABS function returns the absolute value of a numeric argument. Functions can return either numeric or character results. Some functions are included with the SAS System; users can write others using SAS/TOOLKIT software.

global environment list

in Screen Control Language, an environment list containing data that all SCL applications can share during the same SAS session. The data remain in the global environment list until SCL execution explicity removes the data or until the SAS session ends. See also environment list and local environment list.

icon

a graphical window element that displays a pictorial representation, often of another window or an action such as printing a file.

index

in SAS software, a component of a SAS data set that enables the SAS System to access observations in the SAS data set quickly and efficiently. The purpose of SAS indexes is to optimize WHERE-clause processing and facilitate BY-group processing.

initialization phase
in Screen Control Language, the stage at which initialization steps are performed before a window is displayed in SAS/AF software or before an observation is displayed in SAS/FSP software. In SAS/FSP software, the initialization phase begins with the FSEINIT label and includes the INIT label, which is executed before each observation is displayed. In SAS/AF software, the initialization phase begins with the INIT label and usually ends with a RETURN statement. During this phase, the program typically initializes variables and computed fields, imports values through macro variables, displays an initial message on the message line, and opens SAS data sets that are used or referenced in the application.

inner sublist
in a nested SCL list, the innermost list. See also nested list and outer list.

instance variable
in object-oriented methodology, the characteristics or data associated with an object via a name. Instance variables for widget objects are called attributes and are defined through attribute windows. All objects created from the same class have the same set of instance variables. New instance variables are specified by name, type, and initial value, and whether they are automatically initialized when an SCL method executes.

jumping
in the Screen Control Language debugger, the process of altering the flow of control by restarting program execution at a specified line and bypassing intervening statements.

key variable
a variable that is used to index SAS data sets.

legend window
in Screen Control Language, a display-only, dynamic window for presenting information to users. By default, the legend window has four lines of text and is positioned at the top of the display.

libref
the name temporarily associated with a SAS data library.

list box
a rectangular window element that contains a scrollable list of items. Selected items are stored in special SCL lists.

list identifier
in Screen Control Language, a unique number that is assigned to each SCL list that is created in an application.

loaded program
in Screen Control Language, a program that resides in the execution stack. See also execution stack.

local environment list
in Screen Control Language, an environment list containing data that are available only to entries invoked in the same SCL application. This list is deleted when the application ends. See also environment list and global environment list.

locking

a technique for detecting conflicts among the requests from different SAS tasks. A task obtains a lock on a member (for example, a SAS data set) or record (observation) based on the open mode and control level for that SAS data set. In SAS/SHARE software, you can lock a SAS data library, data set, catalog, or catalog entry using the LOCK statement or LOCK command.

logical row

in SAS/AF software, the row of fields or objects that is repeated in an extended table. See also extended table.

message area

the area immediately below a window's command line or action bar that displays messages from the SAS System or from the Screen Control Language reserved variable _MSG_.

method

in object-oriented methodology, an operation that is defined for a class and can be executed by any object created from that class. Methods can be defined in Screen Control Language (SCL) and implemented with SCL routines.

method block

in Screen Control Language, a labeled statement block in SCL entries that begins with a METHOD statement, ends with an ENDMETHOD statement and contains one or more SCL statements. A method block can be called by different SAS/AF entries.

named list

in Screen Control Language, a list structure that contains one or more items with assigned names.

nested list

in Screen Control Language, a data structure in which a list contains sublists. These sublists, called nested lists, are especially useful for creating collections of records or other data structures.

nonwindow variable

in Screen Control Language, a variable used in a program but not associated with an object in a window. Values for nonwindow variables are stored in the SCL data vector (SDV) until the SCL program terminates and closes the SDV.

object

in object-oriented methodology, a specific representation of a class. An object inherits all the characteristics (instance variables) of its class as well as the operations (methods) that class can execute. For example, a push button object is an instance of the Push Button class. The terms object and instance are often used interchangeably.

outer list

in Screen Control Language, the first list in a nested-list structure. An outer list contains one or more sublists.

parameter

in Screen Control Language, a value passed from one entry in an application to another. For example, in SAS/AF applications, parameters are passed between entries using the CALL DISPLAY and ENTRY statements.

parameter list

in Screen Control Language, the values that a program receives from a calling program through the ENTRY statement. These values can be any SCL expression, such as variables, numeric or character literals, or computed values. See also parameter passing.

parameter passing

in Screen Control Language, the process of communicating values from a calling program to a receiving program. Parameters are declared in receiving programs with the ENTRY statement. See also call-by-reference and call-by-value.

program data vector

the temporary area of memory, or storage area, where the SAS System builds a SAS data set, one observation at a time. Note that the program data vector is a logical concept that is independent of physical implementation.

program variable

a variable used in a Screen Control Language program. See also nonwindow variable and window variable.

record

a logical unit of information consisting of fields of related data. A collection of records makes up a file.

recursive list

in Screen Control Language, a data structure in which a list can contain itself or other sublists that contain it either directly or indirectly.

remote host

a computer physically removed from yours that you can log in to.

remote session

a SAS session running in a special mode on the remote host. No output or log messages are displayed on the remote host; instead, the results of a remote SAS session are transmitted back to the log and output files on the local host.

reserved label

in Screen Control Language, a special label that designates when the corresponding section of an SCL program executes. Examples include INIT, MAIN, TERM, FSEINIT, FSETERM, GETROW, and PUTROW.

return code

in Screen Control Language (SCL), a value returned by an SCL function indicating whether the function successfully accomplished the specified task.

RGB

a color-coding scheme that specifies a color in terms of percentages of red, green, and blue components.

SAS data library

a collection of one or more SAS files that are recognized by the SAS System and that are referenced and stored as a unit. Each file is a member of the library.

SAS/ACCESS software
a software interface that makes data from an external database management system (DBMS) directly available to the SAS System and SAS System data directly available to a DBMS.

SASUSER library
a default permanent SAS data library that is created at the beginning of your first SAS session. It contains a PROFILE catalog that stores the tailoring features you specify for the SAS System. You can also store other SAS files in this library. See also SAS data library.

SCL data vector (SDV)
in Screen Control Language, a temporary storage area for the values of all SCL variables for the current program. The SDV is deleted when the program terminates.

SCL statement
in Screen Control Language, a string of keywords, names, special characters, and operators that instructs the SCL compiler to perform an operation, gives information to the compiler, or controls the behavior of certain aspects of an application's window. There are two types of SCL statements: declarative statements, which provide information to the SCL compiler but do not result in executable code, and executable statements, which are compiled into intermediate code and result in some action when the SCL program is executed. All SCL statements must end with a semicolon.

SCL variable
in Screen Control Language, a named storage location to which values can be written and from which values can be retrieved. A value is referenced through the use of the variable's name in the SCL program. Some SCL variables are automatically linked to fields and objects in an application's window. See also window variable.

Screen Control Language (SCL)
a programming language provided in SAS/AF and SAS/FSP software to development interactive applications that manipulate SAS data sets and external files; display tables, menus, and selection lists; generate SAS source code and submit it to the SAS System for execution; and generate code for execution by the host command processor.

selection list
in SAS/AF software, a list of items in a window from which users can make one or more selections. Sources for selection lists are LIST entries, special SCL functions, and extended tables.

shared data environment
See environment list.

stepping over
in Screen Control Language, a debugging process that treats a DISPLAY, FSEDIT, or FSVIEW routine as a single statement that the debugger does not step through. Debugging continues at the next executable statement of the current SCL program. See also stepping through.

stepping through
in Screen Control Language, a debugging process that allows a program called by a DISPLAY, FSEDIT, or FSVIEW routine to be debugged as a series of single

statements, suspending execution at each statement. This process is also known as stepping into.

subclassing
in object-oriented methodology, the process of deriving a new class from an existing class. A new class inherits the characteristics (instance variables) and operations (methods) of its parent, and it can contain custom instance variables and methods. See also class.

SUBMIT block
in Screen Control Language, a group of SAS statements that are submitted together to the SAS System for processing. A SUBMIT block consists of a SUBMIT statement, one or more SAS language statements, and an ENDSUBMIT statement.

system variable
in Screen Control Language, an automatically defined reserved variable. Examples include _MSG_ and _STATUS_.

table lookup
a processing technique used to retrieve additional information from an auxiliary source based on the values of variables in the primary source.

temporary breakpoint
in Screen Control Language, a breakpoint that is removed as soon as the execution is suspended. A temporary breakpoint is ignored if another permanent breakpoint is encountered before the execution reaches it.

termination phase
in Screen Control Language, the stage at which a program performs any termination steps that are required after a user issues the END or CANCEL command (in SAS/AF software) or performs any processing steps that are required before the current observation is written to the data set and another observation is read (in FSEDIT and FSBROWSE applications). The termination phase usually begins with the TERM label and usually ends with a RETURN statement. During this phase in SAS/AF applications, the program typically updates and closes SAS data sets and external files that have been opened by the application; it also exports values through macro variables and submits statements to the SAS System for execution. During this phase in FSEDIT and FSBROWSE applications, the program typically manipulates SAS data set values before the observation is updated and updates additional SAS data sets. In FSEDIT and FSBROWSE applications, the statements in the FSETERM block perform the steps that end the program.

tracepoint
in Screen Control Language, a designated statement at which the debugger temporarily suspends execution, displays a notification message, and resumes program execution.

variable
in data vectors, a location in the SCL data vector or the program data vector to which values can be written and from which values can be read. Variables can be permanent or temporary.

warning
a message in the SAS log or Message window that indicates that the SAS system took corrective action to continue processing the program.

watched variable

in Screen Control Language, a variable that the debugger monitors during program execution. If the value of a watched variable changes, the debugger suspends execution and displays the old and new values of the variable. A watched variable is monitored continuously until the watch is canceled.

WHERE clause

one or more WHERE expressions used in a WHERE statement, WHERE function, or WHERE= data set option.

WHERE expression

a type of SAS expression used to specify a condition for selecting observations for processing.

widget

a component of a graphical user interface that displays information or accepts user input. For example, a text entry field is a widget used to display and enter text.

window variable

in Screen Control Language, a variable that passes values back and forth between an SCL program and an application window. Each window variable is linked to a particular field in a window.

WORK data library

the SAS data library automatically defined by the SAS System at the beginning of each SAS session or SAS job. It contains SAS files that are temporary by default. When the libref USER is not defined, the SAS System uses WORK as the default library for SAS files created with one-level names.

Index

L

O

X

Y

Z

Special Characters

Your Turn

If you have comments or suggestions about *SAS® Screen Control Language: Reference, Version 6, Second Edition*, please send them to us on a photocopy of this page or send us electronic mail.

For comments about this book, please return the photocopy to

> SAS Institute Inc.
> Publications Division
> SAS Campus Drive
> Cary, NC 27513
> **email:** yourturn@unx.sas.com

For suggestions about the software, please return the photocopy to

> SAS Institute Inc.
> Technical Support Division
> SAS Campus Drive
> Cary, NC 27513
> **email:** suggest@unx.sas.com